170 MCM
McMahon, Darrin M.
    Happiness : : a history /

WITHDRAWN

38235000260446

06-1062

W9-BNJ-915

HAPPINESS:
A HISTORY

Also by Darrin M. McMahon

*Enemies of the Enlightenment: The French Counter-Enlightenment
and the Making of Modernity*

Darrin M. McMahon

HAPPINESS: A HISTORY

Atlantic Monthly Press
New York

BISHOP IRETON H.S. LIBRARY
ALEXANDRIA, VIRGINIA

Copyright © 2006 by Darrin M. McMahon

All rights reserved. No part of this book may be reproduced in any form or by any electronic or mechanical means, or the facilitation thereof, including information storage and retrieval systems, without permission in writing from the publisher, except by a reviewer, who may quote brief passages in a review. Any members of educational institutions wishing to photocopy part or all of the work for classroom use, or publishers who would like to obtain permission to include the work in an anthology, should send their inquiries to Grove/Atlantic, Inc., 841 Broadway, New York, NY 10003.

Every effort was made to secure permissions for photographs and text. Any omissions brought to the publishers' attention will be corrected in future printings.

Published simultaneously in Canada
Printed in the United States of America

Library of Congress Cataloging-in-Publication Data

McMahon, Darrin M.
Happiness : a history / Darrin M. McMahon.
p. cm.
Includes bibliographical references and index.
ISBN-10: 0-87113-886-7
ISBN-13: 978-0-87113-886-6
1. Happiness—History. 2. Happiness—Social aspects. I. Title.
BJ1481.M46 2005
170—dc22 2005048009

Atlantic Monthly Press
an imprint of Grove/Atlantic, Inc.
841 Broadway
New York, NY 10003

Distributed by Publishers Group West

www.groveatlantic.com

06 07 08 09 10   10 9 8 7 6 5 4 3

*For Courtney, partner in pursuit,
who has endured all the moods
that writing a book on happiness entails,
and invented some of her own*

CONTENTS

My steps have held fast to your paths; my feet have not slipped.
—Psalm 17:5

The struggle itself toward the heights is enough to fill a man's heart. One must imagine Sisyphus happy.
—Camus, *The Myth of Sisyphus*

PREFACE

"One may contemplate history from the point of view of happiness," observed the German philosopher Georg Wilhelm Friedrich Hegel, "but history is not the soil in which happiness grows. The periods of happiness in it are the blank pages of history."[1]

There have been times in cultivating this project—in which hours of drudgery yielded only barren pages and arid drafts—when I was forced to confront the irony that writing a book on happiness might make me miserable. Usually I did so with a smile, laughing faintly at myself. But I was also tempted on occasion to concede Hegel's dictum and be done with it. *My* history of happiness, it seemed at such times, would prove an empty book.

For how to write a history of something so elusive, so intangible—of this "thing" that is not a thing, this hope, this yearning, this dream? As another German philosopher, Immanuel Kant, rightly observed, "the concept of happiness is such an indeterminate one that even though everyone wishes to attain happiness, yet he can never say definitely and consistently what it is that he really wishes and wills."[2] It is disconcerting for any author to be forced to admit the difficulty—perhaps impossibility—of even defining the subject of his inquiry. And it is more daunting still to know that countless men and women have spent their entire lives searching for this very "thing," only to have it elude their grasp. Was happiness like Eurydice of Greek myth, I wondered, who slips from our arms when we turn to behold her, disappearing as soon as we catch a glimpse?

That thought has given me pause. So, too, has the peculiar nature of the subject itself. As Sigmund Freud recognized nearly a century ago, "happiness . . . is something essentially subjective." He went on to assert that "no matter how much we may shrink with horror from certain situations—of a galley-slave in antiquity, of a peasant during the Thirty Years' War, of a victim of the Holy Inquisition, of a Jew awaiting a pogrom—it is nevertheless impossible for us to feel our way into such people," to gauge their pleasure and pain. If even such sad cases could harbor happy thoughts, I wondered, how could anyone hope to write the history of the term? "It seems to me unprofitable," Freud concluded, "to pursue this aspect of the problem any further."[3]

And yet, living in the West at the turn of the twenty-first century, I found it impossible to leave the problem at that. For happiness—its promise, its expectation, its allure—was everywhere around me. In New York City, where I made my home in the roaring 1990s, people splashed themselves, both literally and figuratively, with a cologne whose very name—Happy—captured the ethos of the time. In London, illicit pleasure seekers offered the drug of the decade—ecstasy—stamped with a smiling face. In Vienna, every morning I drank orange juice whose label proclaimed, "[Have a] happy day," while on the television, Bavarian automakers promised that "happiness is the curve." In Paris, like so many other places, a trip to the local bookstore revealed a contemporary obsession. Entire walls of popular psychology and new age religion beckoned in the direction of everlasting content. They beckon still. "Don't worry, be happy," intones the popular song. When one contemplates that great modern icon, the smiling yellow happy face, it becomes possible to think of this suggestion, rather sadly, as a command.

We can be happy, we will be happy, we should be happy. We have a right to happiness. Surely this is our modern creed. But have human beings always felt this way? Is it correct to assume, with Freud's contemporary the American philosopher William James, that "how to gain, how to keep, how to recover happiness, is in fact for most men at all times the secret motive of all they do, and of all they are willing to endure"?[4] Is happiness eternal—universal—or does it have a history, a specific record of time and place?

The title of this book alone, of course, reveals my conviction that, Hegel and Freud notwithstanding, happiness can be treated historically. But let me draw attention to the indefinite article from the start. This is *a* history of happiness, not *the* history of happiness; it makes no such grandiose claims. On the contrary, writing this book has made me painfully aware of how much I have had to leave out. There are infinite histories of happiness to be written—histories not only of the struggles and pursuits of the peasants, slaves, and apostates mentioned by Freud—but of early-modern women and late-modern aristocrats, nineteenth-century bourgeois and twentieth-century workers, conservatives and radicals, consumers and crusaders, immigrants and natives, gentiles and Jews. There are fascinating national and regional variations of this history to consider, a fact that social scientists in recent years have begun to explore, devoting considerable effort to attempts to measure the comparative happiness or "subjective well-being" of peoples. Are Swedes happier than Danes? Americans than Japanese? Russians than Turks? Are some cultures happier than others?[5]

Such questions highlight the fact that, although for reasons of personal interest and professional expertise I have concentrated my history on the experience of "the West" (an imperfect term that I use broadly for lack of a better, without celebration or geographical precision), it is undoubtedly the case that happiness might be studied fruitfully from a variety of different cultural and historical perspectives.[6] As the recent international success of the Dalai Lama's *The Art of Happiness: A Handbook for Living* makes clear, the search for happiness is now a global concern, one with roots, however shallow or deep, in many different cultural and religious traditions. In the end, William James may well have been right. Perhaps happiness is, was, and ever shall be the ultimate human end in every time and place.

Yet it is also perfectly clear that the manner in which men and women understand happiness—how they propose, and whether they expect, to achieve it—varies dramatically across cultures and over time. And as I hope this book will demonstrate, happiness has occupied a particularly prominent place in the Western intellectual tradition, exerting its influence on many aspects of Western culture and thought. As the late Harvard historian Howard Mumford Jones once pointed out in contemplating both the challenge and the hubris of any such undertaking, a history of happiness would be "not merely a history of mankind, but also a history of ethical, philosophic, and religious thought."[7]

Although I have no intention of attempting anything so rash as a "history of mankind," I do believe that a history of happiness, at least initially, should be an intellectual history, a history of conceptions of this perennial human end and the strategies devised to attain it, as these have evolved in different ethical, philosophical, religious, and, I would add, political contexts. For whatever else it might be (and it is, assuredly, many things), happiness in the West has functioned above all as an idea—an idea and aspiration that for particular reasons has exercised a powerful hold on the Western imagination. Given, as Freud recognized, the immense difficulty, even impossibility, of ever judging another's state of happiness with precision (indeed, of judging our own), I have chosen instead to focus on representations of the term and concept as these have developed over time. The changes, we shall see, have been dramatic—so much so that the "happiness" of yesterday bears only a scarce resemblance to the "happiness" of today. But by charting the history of this development, and tracing the genealogy of what is now an overarching aspiration, I hope to show that there are important connections nonetheless.

Born in the ancient world of classical Greece, shaped profoundly by the Judeo-Christian tradition, only to emerge as a radical new force during the Age of Enlightenment, happiness and its pursuit have fascinated ever since, fundamentally influencing our modern expectations and experience. No contemporary effort to achieve happiness, it is clear, can properly be understood without consideration of this past—a past, as we shall see, that has not always been a happy affair. Replete with struggles and disappointments, disillusion and despair, the pursuit of happiness has a dark side. It is, observed the nineteenth-century critic Thomas Carlyle, a "shadow of ourselves."[8]

In following the outlines of this shadow in light and dark, I have drawn on many sources, including art and architecture, poetry and scripture, music and theology, literature, myth, and the testimony of ordinary men and women. But by and large, I rely on what were once called, without irony or inverted commas, the great books of Western civilization. In teaching these books in Europe and America over the past several years, it has been my experience that debate regarding their continued relevance disappears the moment one bothers to read them. I continue to subscribe to this opinion, and it is clearly reflected here.

But by defending what is, in effect, a return in this instance to a quite traditional form of intellectual history, I do not mean to suggest that the history of happiness (or the history of any subject, for that matter) should be approached only in this way. My own past scholarship is deeply indebted to the work of a wide variety of social and cultural historians, and I have little doubt that future endeavors will draw heavily (and gratefully) on their labors. Moreover, as I point out in several places in my notes, much of the material examined in this book deserves to be studied in further detail and treated in other ways: In the rich, contextualized approach developed by the so-called Cambridge School of textual analysis; from the perspective of the growing subdiscipline known as the History of Emotions; or finally, as several young scholars are doing right now, from the standpoint of literary criticism.[9] In the study of happiness, as in the study of most things, methodological pluralism is only to be encouraged.

Having said this, I do feel strongly that the approach adopted in this book is a necessary beginning, and also a revelatory one, if for no other reason than it allows me to take a view of the *longue durée*, following changes and continuities that might otherwise be missed. What I hope will become clear as a result is not only the centrality of the issue of happiness to the Western tradition, but the centrality of that same tradition and legacy to contemporary concerns. Whether we choose to recognize the fact or not, our present preoccupation with happiness has been shaped fundamentally by the deep and abiding influence of the classical and Judeo-Christian experience. We moderns—so ready to countenance our cultural liberation from the past, so ready in our technological prowess and global sophistication to view with condescension much that has come before—ignore this experience at a cost. For though some would bemoan the fact, it remains with us, influencing our actions and desires, forming who we are.

One last editorial remark. Anthony Ashley Cooper, the third Earl of Shaftesbury and an important eighteenth-century moralist, once asked, "If Philosophy be, as we take it, the Study of Happiness, must not everyone, in some manner or other, either skillfully or unskillfully philosophize?"[10] In my experience, the answer to this question is a resounding yes. And so I have tried here to reach out to that perhaps mythic, certainly endangered, species, "the ordinary reader," writing without condescension, I hope, but at the same time with a self-conscious effort to enliven as well as to analyze and explain. I have even attempted (God forbid) to have fun, recklessly ignoring the warning of the Oxford don and Anglican archbishop of Dublin, Richard Whately, who cautioned in the nineteenth century that happiness is no laughing matter. The humanities are simply too important to be left to dour scholarly eyes alone. And we humanists need to recall more often that the rightful owner of our subject—the humanities—is humanity itself, of which we form only a tiny fraction.

Some of these goals are undoubtedly ambitious. But it is my hope that, as in the pursuit of happiness itself, there may be value in striving to attain them nevertheless, even when I fall short of my ultimate end.

New York City
October 2004

INTRODUCTION:
THE TRAGEDY
OF HAPPINESS

The search for happiness is as old as history itself, one might venture, and in a certain sense that claim would be true. For in the opening pages of Book One of what is widely regarded as the first work of history in the West—*The History* of Herodotus—we find the quest for happiness bound up in this inaugural record of the "great and wonderful deeds" of human affairs. Croesus, the fabulously wealthy king of Lydia, has summoned before him the itinerant sage Solon, lawgiver of Athens and a man who has traveled over much of the world in search of knowledge. The Lydian king lacks nothing, or so he believes, and attempts to convince Solon of the fact, dispatching servants to lead the wise Athenian around his stores of treasures so that he might marvel at "their greatness and richness." Needing nothing, Croesus nonetheless reveals that he is in need, for he is overcome by a "longing" to know who is the happiest man in the world. Foolishly, he believes that this man is himself.[1]

Solon's answer, however, threatens to dispel this illusion. The happiest man, he claims, is not Croesus but Tellus, a father from Athens who was killed in battle in the prime of life. And the second happiest men—two young brothers named Cleobis and Biton—are also dead, having passed away in their sleep after pulling their mother to a village festival, yoked to her cart like a pair of oxen.

Not surprisingly, Croesus is perplexed by these answers, perplexed and then enraged, eventually sending Solon away, "thinking him assuredly a stupid man."[2] The Lydian's proud refusal to hear the wisdom in Solon's words sets in motion a series of events that eventually bring down Croesus and his kingdom, embroiling the peoples of Greece and Persia in nearly one hundred years of war. The great clash of civilizations that would draw to a close only with the Greek victories at Thermopylae, Salamis, and Plataea in 480–479 BCE might thus be read as the awful outcome of the search for human happiness.

In truth, it is unlikely that the historical figures Solon and Croesus ever met, though the real Solon probably did have something to say on the subject of happiness.[3] Still, the central place of this episode in Herodotus's *History* reminds us that this chronicle of human conflict is also a chronicle of human striving. Painting with a broad brush, Herodotus vows famously in the work's opening paragraph to capture all so "that time may not draw the color from what man has brought into being." The pursuit of human happiness, it would seem, has been with us from the start.

But what are we to make of Solon's response? Two well-built brothers, who shut their eyes for a well-earned rest, never to wake again. A young family man cut down in the prime of his life, leaving his wife and sons behind. On what terms might such people—such *dead* people—possibly be considered "happy"? What could Herodotus have meant, and how might he have been understood by those who gathered to hear his tales at the agora, the marketplace of the fifth-century Mediterranean world? To know this, we must listen with more care than Croesus to Solon's response. And we must do so while suspending our own beliefs about what happiness is, or what happiness should be. For nothing could be further from this early Greek ideal than our modern conceptions of the term.

In the first place, Herodotus employs not any single word to describe the object of Croesus's desire, but several, drawing on a number of closely related terms that had come down to him from the great epic period of Homer and Hesiod in the eight and ninth centuries BCE.[4] Herodotus makes use, for example, of the term *olbios*, which, along with its close cousin *makarios*, may be rendered (imperfectly) as "blessed." In the Homeric hymns and the Hesiodic poems, these complex terms are used frequently in reference to the heroes, to the gods, and to those who enjoy their favor, indicating divine sanction, freedom from suffering, and general prosperity, both material and moral. Thus, in the Homeric *Hymn to Apollo*, the master of the Cretans addresses a god disguised as an ordinary man with some confusion: "Stranger—though you are nothing like mortal men in shape or stature, but are as the immortal gods—hail and all happiness to you," employing here a variant of *olbios*.[5] But in the *Hymn to Hermes*, the poet uses a form of *makarios* to describe the cave dwelling of the god Hermes and his mother, which is full of "nectar and lovely ambrosia," with "much silver and gold," fine clothing, and other things "such as are kept in the sacred houses of the blessed." Like the Olympians who know no hardship and are beautifully clad, richly fed, and secure in their possessions and persons, those who are *olbios* or *makarios* are similarly favored.[6] They are, one might say, "fortunate." And so we find Herodotus, and through him, Solon, speaking of those who possess what Croesus claims to enjoy as having *eutychia*, or "luck." To live in the favor of the gods, to be blessed, is to live with fortune on one's side.

Finally, Herodotus uses one other adjective to capture all these subtleties—*eudaimon* (and the noun, *eudaimonia*)—indicating a flourishing, favored life. The word was first employed in extant Greek literature by Hesiod. "Happy and lucky the man" (*eudaimôn te kai olbios*), he declares in the *Work and Days*, who knows and keeps the holy days, who understands omens, who avoids transgression, and "who does his work without offending the deathless gods."[7] But the word was emerging in Herodotus's own time as the preferred—and absolutely central—term to designate the elusive quality for which Croesus yearned. Comprising the Greek *eu* (good) and *daimon* (god, spirit, demon), *eudaimonia* thus contains within it a notion of fortune—for to have a good daimon on your side, a guiding spirit, is to be lucky—and a notion of divinity, for a *daimon* is an emissary of the gods who watches over each of us, acting invisibly on the Olympians' behalf. As a leading classicist has observed, "*Daimon* is occult power, a force that drives men forward where no agent can be named," and it is this aspect of the term that helps to account for the unpredictable force that leads Croesus, like all men, impelling him forward in pursuit of he knows not what.[8] For if to have a good *daimon* means to be carried in the direction of the divine, to have a bad *daimon*, a *dysdaimon* (or *kakadaimon*) is to be turned aside, led astray, or countered by another. The gods, alas, are as capricious as mortals, as that unhappy wife of Shakespeare's Othello, Desdemona, learns to her dismay. Her name is simply a variation on the Greek word for unhappy, *dysdaimon*, as Shakespeare certainly knew. He was probably also aware that *daimon* is the Greek root of the modern word "demon," a fiend or an evil spirit who haunts. Something of that vaguely sinister connotation is embedded in *eudaimonia* itself.

Thus, when Croesus asks Solon after hearing of the blessedness of Tellus, Cleobis, and Biton, "Is the happiness [*eudaimonia*] that is mine so entirely set at naught by you that you do not make me the equal of even private men?" Solon's response makes clear that in matters of chance, one can never be too sure:

> Croesus, you asked me, you who know that the Divine is altogether jealous and prone to trouble us, you asked me about human matters. In the whole length of time there is much to see that one would rather not see—and much to suffer likewise. I put the boundary of human life at seventy years. These seventy years have twenty-five thousand two hundred days, not counting [leap years] . . . so that all the days of a man's life are twenty-six thousand two hundred and fifty; of all those days not one brings to him anything exactly the same as another. So, Croesus, man is entirely what befalls him. To me it is clear that you are very rich, and it is clear that you are the king of many men; but the thing that you asked me I cannot say of you yet, until I hear that you have brought your life to an end well.[9]

This is the wisdom of a world in which inscrutable forces constantly threaten to subvert human aims, a world ruled by fate or by the gods, in which suffering is all pervasive and uncertainty is woven into the fabric of daily experience. Today it is sometimes tempting to think of early Greek life in the manner by which it has largely come down to us—as myth—imagining it, deliciously, as a sunny, sensual affair, flowing with the unflinching purpose of Attic oarsmen, clean as classical marble, sweet as ambrosia. But such reveries hide the less pleasant facts: that thunder or an eclipse could induce terror, that pestilence and hunger periodically wiped out entire communities, that horribly disfigured men and women were a presence in every town, that children were as apt to die before their fifth birthday as to live longer, that bloody warfare was a constant reminder of the fragility of existence. In a world such as that, life was less something to be made than something to be endured. Only those who did so successfully could be deemed fortunate, blessed, happy.

It is in part for this reason that Solon judges Tellus, Cleobis, and Biton worthy of the epithet of "happy." All three successfully negotiated life's perils while they lived, and then died with honor at the moment of their greatest glory. Of Tellus, we are told:

> In the first place, [his] city was in a good state when he had sons—good and beautiful they were—and he saw children in turn born to all of them, and all surviving. Secondly, when he himself had come prosperously to a moment of his life—that is, prosperously as it counts with us—he had, besides, an ending for it that was most glorious: in a battle between the Athenians and their neighbors in Eleusis he made a sally, routed the enemy, and died splendidly, and the Athenians gave him a public funeral where he fell and so honored him greatly.[10]

Living in a city ravaged neither by plague nor by marauding armies, the father and grandfather of beautiful children who survived childbirth unscarred and unmarked, himself healthy and of sufficient means, honored in life as in death, Tellus managed to run the gaunt-let of life without falling and to leave it with honor and grace.

Cleobis and Biton also performed this most perilous of feats. Blessed with "sufficiency of livelihood and besides, a strength of body," these two prizewinning athletes from the Argive were late in taking their mother to a temple for the feast of Hera. Unharnessing the oxen that pulled their cart, they drew it themselves at a much faster pace for many miles, and when they arrived, they were seen by all who had gathered for the feast:

> The Argive men came and stood around the young men, congratulating them on their strength, and the women con-gratulated the mother on the fine sons she had; and the mother, in her great joy at what was said and done, stood right in front of the statue and there prayed for Cleobis and Biton, her own sons, who had honored her so signally, that the goddess should give them whatsoever is best for a man to win. After that prayer the young men sacrificed and banqueted and laid them down to sleep in the temple where they were; they never rose more, but that was the end in which they were held.[11]

It is the last line that prevents us from yielding to the temptation to pull these tales into our own time, to see the "happiness" of Tellus, Cleobis, and Biton in recognizable terms as a function simply of their robust health, their relative prosperity, their familial harmony, their noble achievements, and their public esteem. All these factors, to be sure, figure in Solon's reckoning, but it is the end—death—that gives them meaning, ensuring in its finality that one's good fortune, one's blessedness, can no longer be taken away. It is a good death that the goddess deems "best for a man to win," so that is the reward she bestows. Where life is governed by uncertainty, one can count no man happy until he is dead, for as Solon warns, "to many the god has shown a glimpse of blessedness only to extirpate them in the end."[12]

And this, of course, is precisely the destiny of Croesus, whose downfall is presented as a cautionary tale of the hubris of deeming oneself happy in a world where it is impossible to control one's fate. Men and women, Solon says, are what "befall" them, a certainty that applies equally to rich and poor. Although wealth may help to satisfy our desires and even shield us from certain pains, it can do nothing, ultimately, to withstand ill fortune or the wrath of the gods, for "no single person is self-sufficient." Shortly after Solon's departure, Croesus learns the awful truth of those words, receiving "a great visitation of evil." His son is killed in a freak accident, Croesus himself misinterprets an oracle at Delphi and is lured into a disastrous war as a consequence, and his kingdom is destroyed by invading Persian armies. Only as a captive, facing imminent destruction atop a funeral pyre whose flames lick at his feet, does Croesus realize the wisdom of Solon's words and the folly of his own pride. "No one who lives is happy," he exclaims, calling out three times the name of the Athenian sage and recounting his own fate for the benefit of all who "are in their own eyes blessed."[13] Only when Croesus has fully repented is the god moved. "Suddenly, out of a clear sky, with no wind in it, there gathered clouds, and a storm burst and a violent rain with it; and the fire was quenched." Croesus is saved at the final hour, but only after he has renounced the belief that he was, or ever can be, happy while still alive.

In the understanding of Herodotus and his contemporaries, then, happiness is not a feeling, nor any subjective state, a point highlighted by the irony that Croesus originally *thinks* that he is happy, only to be shown otherwise. Happiness, rather, is a characterization of an entire life that can be reckoned only at death. To believe oneself happy in the meantime is premature, and probably an illusion, for the world is cruel and unpredictable, governed by forces beyond our control. A whim of the gods, the gift of good fortune, the determination of fate: Happiness at the dawn of Western history was largely a matter of chance.

We tend to think of this general conception of the world, in which suffering is endemic and happiness largely beyond our control, as in a broad sense "tragic." And in the context of the Athenian world known to Herodotus, that word is not at all misplaced. For it was precisely there, in precisely that period, the fifth century BCE, that "tragedy" (*tragoidia*) took the stage as a new word and a new form of art. Performed annually in honor of the god Dionysus at the spring-time festival known as the City Dionysia, *tragoidia* initially referred only to a general type of theatrical performance. Roughly equivalent to our modern word "play," it implied neither content nor emotional tone. But that *tragoidia* should come to take on associations with what we now think of as tragedy, more generally speaking, is hardly surprising. As any reader of the great playwrights of the period—Aeschylus, Sophocles, and Euripides—will know, fifth-century BCE Athenian "tragedies" seldom have happy endings. On the contrary, they return again and again to situations in which seemingly inno-cent figures are overwhelmed by circumstances they cannot control. Forced to make impossible choices between irreconcilable alterna-tives, the likes of Agamemnon and Antigone, Orestes and Oedipus, Electra and Medea are hunted down by gods and pursued by famil-ial curses, overwhelmed by fate and defeated by the very nature of things. And although those figures inevitably contribute to their own undoing through hubris and folly, the crux of the tragic dilemma is that there can be no easy resolution of conflict, no decision without grave costs, no simple, happy ending. Agamemnon, in Aeschylus's *Oresteia*, is in this respect an altogether typical figure. He must *either* sacrifice his own daughter at the behest of the gods, *or* relinquish his honor by abandoning the Greek campaign against Troy. The trag-edy of his dilemma is that he cannot have it both ways. Torn between duty and love, justice and self-sacrifice, family and city, and any number of other irreconcilable ends, the protagonists of the Greek tragic stage are caught up in circumstances and trapped by them-selves. Inhabiting a world in which conflict is inevitable and struggle preordained, they cannot *make* themselves happy, for among mortals in this tragic universe, "no man is happy," as the Messenger in Euripides's *Medea* darkly proclaims. The Chorus in Sophocles's *Philoctetes* is bleaker still, bemoaning the "unhappy race":

Of mortal man doomed to an endless round
Of sorrow, and immeasurable woe!

In this play, as in so many others of the genre, the only salvation for
the titular hero is through the unlikely intervention of a god. Just as
the heavens opened to shower rain on Croesus atop his pyre, Hercules arrives at the final moment of Sophocles's play to extricate
Philoctetes from his plight. Hercules is a deus ex machina (*theos ek
mēchanēs*)—literally a "god from the machine"—a reference to the
Greek convention in *tragoidia* of lowering an actor in the guise of a
deity onto the stage by a crane or some other such contraption as a
way to bring the drama to a close. It may be argued, as Aristotle would
do in the *Poetics,* that this is a clumsy way to end a play. But the deus
ex machina serves perfectly to dramatize a much more important
point: In the tragic tradition, happiness is almost always a miracle,
requiring the direct intervention of the divine.

Herodotus was a contemporary of Sophocles, who probably knew
him personally and almost certainly knew his work. Not surprisingly,
the tale of Croesus shares many features of the same tragic outlook.
Croesus, too, is caught up in circumstances beyond his control, the
victim, Herodotus tells us, of a family curse visited upon the offspring
of one of Croesus's distant ancestors, who by slaying his master invoked the wrath of the gods. And though Croesus surely contributes
to his own demise through his misinterpretation of the oracle, his
misreading of events, and his presumptuous certainty that he is the
happiest of all men, it is clear that the destruction of his kingdom and
the death of his son are an inordinate price to pay for any actual faults
he has committed. In the end, we must conclude, Croesus suffers not
so much for what he has done as for the kind of world he inhabits, a
world in which "fate that is decreed, no-one can escape," a world in
which "no one who lives is happy."[14] Where human agency is frustrated, human choice contradictory, and human suffering inevitable,
happiness, if it comes at all, is largely what befalls us. That is the tragic
predicament.

This tragic vision was by no means original to Herodotus or even to the formal classical tragedies performed on the fifth-century Athenian stage. Without question, each of these new genres—*historia* and *tragoidia*—laid out this vision with an unprecedented sharpness and self-conscious clarity. But the general understanding of happiness on which they rely is much older. When the poet Semónides of Amórgos, a small island in the Cyclades archipelago of the Aegean, observed in the seventh century BCE that "We who are human have no minds, / but live, from day to day, like beasts and know nothing / of what God plans to make happen to each of us," he was merely articulating the long-standing wisdom of his ancestors. A surviving fragment of another of Semónides's pearls of wisdom—"A women thick around the ankles is no good"—may give us pause in accepting his general authority without reservation.[15] But with respect to his account of the human condition, at least, we can be confident that his judgment was widely shared. Harking back to a perennial, prehistoric view of the world in which the rhythms of time were understood through myth and the universe through the play of the gods, this fatalistic mind-set animates the epic poetry of Homer, for whom the gods alone are the "blessed ones," and human beings "of all creatures that breathe and crawl across the earth" the most dismal, the most agonized.[16] A similar outlook is central to the stories of classical Greek mythology, of ancient Egypt, and of a great many other traditional cultures.

This fact helps account for the longevity of the link connecting happiness to luck and fate.* That link held fast long after the fifth century BCE, and in certain respects it endures today. It is striking that in virtually every Indo-European language, the modern word for happiness is cognate with luck, fortune, or fate. The root of "happiness,"

---

*Strictly speaking, luck and fate are opposed, in that one implies randomness and the other preestablished order. When considered from the standpoint of human happiness, however, the two are closely related, in that each denies the role of human agency in determining the course of human events. Whether the universe is predetermined or unfolds chaotically, what *happens* to us—our happiness—is out of our hands.

for example, is the Middle English and Old Norse *happ*, meaning chance, fortune, what *happens* in the world, giving us such words as "happenstance," "haphazard," "hapless," and "perhaps." The French *bonheur*, similarly, derives from *bon* (good) and the Old French *heur* (fortune or luck), an etymology that is perfectly consistent with the Middle High German *Glück*, still the German word for happiness *and* luck. In Italian, Spanish, and Portuguese, *felicità, felicidad*, and *felicidade* all stem from the Latin *felix* (luck, sometimes fate), and the Greek *eudaimonia* brings together good fortune and good god. One could multiply these examples at much greater length, but the point would be the same: In the Indo-European language families, happiness has deep roots in the soil of chance.

That so many of these modern words for happiness emerged only in the late Middle Ages and the early Renaissance, while the wheel of lady fortune (Fortuna) continued to turn, is itself testimony to the strength of this enduring connection. For as we shall see, by this stage the tragic understanding of happiness had been challenged by a number of competing conceptions—above all, post-Socratic philosophy and the Christian religion. For all his indebtedness to both those traditions, however, Chaucer did not hesitate in the fourteenth century to have his monk observe in *The Canterbury Tales:*

> And thus does Fortune's wheel turn treacherously
> And out of happiness bring men to sorrow

Nor did Shakespeare, several centuries later, allow his Renaissance humanism to obscure the hap of hap. One might hope for "happy hap" but could rest assured that "hap what hap may."[17] Down to the present day, what the historian Jackson Lears has called the "culture of chance" has played an important role in configuring our fortunes.[18]

Yet despite the stubborn persistence of horoscopes in our newspapers, palm readers on our street corners, and casinos as our places of recreation, most Westerners tend to resist, like Einstein, the notion that life or the universe is a dice player's game. Happiness might be thwarted by a random act of violence, we concede, a terrorist strike, or a freak

accident. And most of us are probably willing to allow, rather more pro-
saically, that "shit happens," in the contemporary phrase, for better or
for worse. But when it comes to the ultimate trajectory of our lives, we
are generally loath to leave happiness to chance. To be happy is a right,
we believe, a natural human entitlement, perhaps even a "moral obligation," to cite a chapter title of a recent best-selling book.[19] Arguably,
there is no greater modern assumption than that it lies within our power
to find happiness. And arguably there is no greater proof of that than
our feeling that we have failed when we are unable to do so.

This book tells the story—the history—of how people in the West
came to harbor that belief. It is a long story, and in telling it, I hope to
make what is today an unexamined assumption appear strange—less
a certainty of the universe than a species of faith. The product of
Greek and Roman philosophy and centuries of Judeo-Christian reflection, modern conceptions of happiness, we will see, were born in the
seventeenth and eighteenth centuries, in an age we now call the Enlightenment. It was in that period that considerable numbers of men
and women were first introduced to the novel prospect that they could
be happy—that they *should* be happy—in this life.

Granted, the idea was not entirely without precedent. Just as some
human beings had long imagined happiness to lie in a remote, a
otherworldly place—in the fields of Elysium, say, or the islands of the
blessed, in the Hyperborean regions, in Heaven, Paradise, or a vanished Golden Age—others had been prepared to speculate on the prospects of happiness on earth. Yet in both classical philosophy and
Christian practice, happiness of this immanent variety was exceed-
ingly rare—the preserve of a "happy few," whose outstanding virtue
or exceptional favor made them more than mere men. As Aristotle
observed, a life of happiness "would be superior to the human level,"
tantamount to the divine.[20] His happy few were a "godlike" few—a
description that applies equally well to the Socratic sage or the Platonic philosopher, the Stoic ascetic or the Epicurean wise man, the
Catholic saint or Calvin's predestined elect. In all of those incarna-
tions, the happy man—and less frequently, the happy woman—was
thought of as one who approached the gods, who had gone beyond the

merely human, who had achieved a form of transcendence. For much of Western history, happiness served as a marker of human perfection, an imagined ideal of a creature complete, without further wants, desires, or needs.

The Enlightenment fundamentally altered this long-standing conception, presenting happiness as something to which all human beings could aspire *in this life.* The basic default position of humanity, happiness was not a gift from God or a trick of fate, a reward for exceptional behavior, but a natural human endowment attainable in theory by every man, woman, and child. Indeed, where human beings were unhappy, Enlightenment thinkers argued, something must be wrong: with their beliefs, with their form of government, with their living conditions, with their customs. Change these things—change ourselves—and we could become in practice what all were intended by nature to be. Happiness, in the Enlightenment view, was less an ideal of godlike perfection than a self-evident truth, to be pursued and obtained in the here and now.

Such a dramatic shift in the nature of human expectations did not occur overnight. Initially the preserve of a social and intellectual elite, the Enlightenment's promise of human happiness on earth spread gradually outward. By the end of the eighteenth century, with the outbreak of the American and French revolutions, happiness could claim widespread recognition as a motivating ideal. Thomas Jefferson took it for granted that enlightened citizens of the world would agree with him when he judged in the Declaration of Independence that the right to the pursuit of happiness was a "self-evident truth." And the French, in proclaiming their own Declaration of Rights of Man and the Citizen in 1789, understood that few would find fault with the lofty goal articulated in the last line of the document's preamble securing the "happiness of all." A great human pursuit had begun. It continues still.

The first half of this book examines the ways in which a classical and Christian concept was transformed into an earthly end. The second half investigates the ambiguities of this coming to earth. For what did it really mean to demand, and to expect, a lifetime of happiness in a still-imperfect world? Perpetual pleasure? Endless euphoria? Purely material gain? And if human beings had a right to happiness, then did not others have a duty to provide it? To what extent were happiness and freedom commensurate—or happiness and virtue, happiness and reason, happiness and truth? Was happiness simply a state of feeling, the calculus of pleasure and pain? Or did it continue to be a reward, a precious prize to be earned at the cost of sometimes painful sacrifice?

These are but a few of the many vexing questions raised by this curious Enlightenment pursuit. Their persistence, long after the eighteenth century, highlights the fact that try as it might, the Enlightenment did not wholly succeed in separating happiness from its religious and metaphysical past. Enchanted still, happiness retained the allure of transcendence, the intimation of the divine. And it was in large part for this reason that it continued to command such power. In the name of happiness, human beings continued to search for the strength of the gods of old, tempted by the prospect that our dominion over nature and control of fortune might make gods of us all, that the happy many might replace the happy few.

But even though the close observer could detect traces of the transcendent in the happiness of the post-Enlightened world, the nature of the pursuit was undoubtedly changing. Slowly, the goal became less to make more of man—to ask him to rise above—than to feed him the ambrosia that had been taken from heaven, to deliver him his due. And over time, this would create a sense of entitlement and expectation that was fraught with danger. Even in a post-Enlightened world, the attempt by mortals to walk on hallowed ground—to become gods themselves or to banish them altogether—was a perilous affair. The Greeks had called it hubris, excessive pride, the refusal to accept the natural limits that separated the sacred from the profane. And they raised the specter of divine retribution for those who dared to cross that line, the suffering and sadness visited upon the tragic heroes who reached (overreached) for what was fit only for the gods. "Many are the forms of the daimon-ly, many things unhoped-for the gods bring to pass" was the stereotyped conclusion to Euripidean tragedies.[21] There were good *daimones* and bad *daimones,* good demons and bad demons: To be under the spell of either was to be haunted and possessed.

To think of the search for happiness in this sense as a form of possession—possession by an alien force that moves through us, like the force that carried Croesus to his doom—may help account in mythic terms for a phenomenon that commentators long after the Greeks have described in different ways: the frustrating tendency of the search for happiness to lead human beings astray. It is this tendency to which Aeschylus gave voice when he complained of the "deceitful deception" of the gods, asking, "What mortal man shall avoid it?"

> Benign and coaxing at first
> It leads us astray into nets which
> No mortal is able to slip,
> Whose doom we can never flee.[22]

Many since have been moved to similar reflections, and together they raise a disturbing prospect for all who live in a post-Enlightened age. Might not the search for happiness entail its own undoing? Does not our modern commandment to be happy produce its own forms of discontent?

PART I

The Making of a Modern Faith

The mere search for higher happiness, not merely its actual attainment, is a prize beyond all human wealth or honor or physical pleasure.

—Cicero, fragment from the lost manuscript *Hortensius*

For the gate is narrow and the way is hard that leads to life, and there are few who find it.

—Matthew 7:14

1

THE HIGHEST GOOD

Happiness is what happens to us, and over that we have no control. That, in a line, is the received understanding of the ancient Greeks and of much of the world of antiquity. From the Mediterranean basin, extending deep into the lands traveled by Herodotus and beyond, this venerable wisdom was widely shared, a common feature of ancient civilizations in Asia Minor, Egypt and the Levant, Persia and Mesopotamia. The legions who quaked under the pharaoh, or the multitudes who scratched out a living from the soil of Persian kings, also experienced the world as a precarious place, served up by their social betters and delivered from on high. Most were constrained to accept what came to them, scarcely daring to think that they might alter their circumstances or significantly influence the many happenings of a lifetime. It was easier and far more prudent to assume the worst and hope for the best, leaving happiness to the gods.

Such a fatalistic view had held sway from time immemorial, helping untold millions comprehend the mysteries of existence as it still does in many pockets of the world. Sharpened and refined in the fifth century BCE by Herodotus and the tragic playwrights of Athens, this view received its consummate expression in their work. Yet ironically, in that same time and place, a new perspective on happiness was taking shape. At its most basic level, this view held that human beings might hope to influence their fate through actions of their own.

Perhaps we should not be surprised by the coincidence. For do we not see already in the striving of Herodotus's Croesus, or in the heroic efforts of the protagonists of the tragic stage, evidence of a yearning to break free of the confines of a fatalistic world, to challenge the caprice of fortune, to resist the final verdict of the gods? "Fate that is decreed, no man can escape" is the summary judgment of Herodotus. But the crime of Croesus, like that of the heroes of Sophocles, Aeschylus, and Euripides, is to defy this unchanging law of the universe. They fail, and we are asked to seek counsel in their failure. But we are also meant to sympathize with their attempt.

Certainly, those who heard Herodotus or traveled to the City Dionysia in Athens for the festival of *tragoidia* had ample reason to be sympathetic to human agency. Herodotus's *History,* after all, is a heroic account of the Greeks' victory over the armies of the Persian empire in the early fifth century BCE, a feat that was due in no small measure to their courage, savvy, and will. Herodotus himself took pains to emphasize the point, extolling the Greeks for their love of freedom. And if the defeat of an enemy that had threatened to enslave them did not attest sufficiently to the powers of collective agency, then life in fifth-century Athens probably did. For it was here, in the Athenian *polis* or city-state, that the world witnessed the invention of a new type of government—*demokratia,* from *demos* (people) + *kratos* (power).

Democracy was only one of the many varieties of authority exercised in the hundreds of city-states of ancient Greece. They ranged in form from hereditary kingship to aristocracy to oligarchy to a type of one-man rule by a strongman or boss, whom the Greeks revealingly described with a non-Greek word, *tyrannos.* With the exception of the latter, however, rarely were these forms truly distinct. For example, the Spartan constitution, conceived by the seventh-century lawgiver Lycurgus, comprised hereditary kingship (monarchy), an aristocratic council of prominent elders (oligarchy), and a general assembly consisting of male citizens over thirty (democracy) all rolled into one.

Other of the city-states arranged matters differently, in innovative ways. But almost all made some provision for citizens to participate directly in the affairs of the *polis*, whether through approval of the decisions of military leaders, participation in the law-courts, voting on measures of public importance, or institutionalized debate. As one leading historian observes, "politics," in the sense of "direct participation in the making of rational choices after discussion," was "central to all Greek cities."[1] By the beginning of the fifth century, some measure of self-government was a distinctive feature of Greek political life.

It is important to appreciate what a radical departure this was from previous norms. As another eminent scholar rightly enjoins, "If we are to understand the Greeks' experience we must recognize that it was a freakish exception to that of the overwhelming number of human beings and societies that came before and after."[2] Whereas earlier civilizations—such as those of Egypt or Mesopotamia, India or China —were ruled hierarchically, with mighty monarchs holding sway over extensive empires, administered by large bureaucracies, standing armies, and powerful priestly castes, the Greeks tended to rule themselves. In their small, autonomous *poleis*, where citizens staffed the army and collected public funds, a premium was placed on self-reliance and self-control.

This was a shared feature of classical Greek culture. But it was above all in the *polis* of Athens that the common process of self-government and self-rule was furthest advanced. Building on a system of law that had been laid down first by the chief magistrate Solon at the beginning of the sixth century (the same Solon who figures centrally, if imaginatively, in Herodotus's *History*), then broadened considerably by the reformer Cleisthenes in 508 BCE, Athens gradually overcame the usurpations of tyrants and the resistance of oligarchs to extend the basis of its rule. By the end of the fifth century, this extension was considerable, encompassing some forty thousand adult male citizens who had the right to participate directly in the voting and debates of the sovereign general assembly, the *ecclesia*. An extraordinary body, which for critical votes might require a quorum as large as six thousand to get under way, the *ecclesia* was in many respects the closest thing to direct democracy the world has ever known. Persons of rank and fortune inevitably exercised considerable influence there, as they did in the much smaller Council of Five Hundred (the *boulē*), which reviewed and referred business to the larger body. But on the whole, the citizens of Athens governed themselves with remarkable equality.[3]

It is thus with reason that the general Pericles, a democratic reformer in his own right and the greatest of the Athenian statesmen of the fifth century, took such pride in his homeland. As he boasted to his fellow citizens in a famous oration of 431 BCE, while Athens was mired in the long Peloponnesian War with Sparta:

> Our constitution does not copy the laws of neighboring states; we are rather a pattern to others than imitators ourselves. Its administration favors the many instead of the few; this is why it is called a democracy. If we look to the laws, they afford equal justice to all in their private differences; if to social standing, advancement in public life falls to reputation for capacity, class considerations not being allowed to interfere with merit; nor again does poverty bar the way, if a man is able to serve the state he is not hindered by the obscurity of his condition. The freedom which we enjoy in our government extends also to our ordinary life. There, far from exercising a jealous surveillance over each other, we do not feel called upon to be angry with our neighbor for doing what he likes, or even to indulge in those injurious looks which cannot fail to be offensive. . . .[4]

Having praised Athen's freedom and tolerance, Pericles proceeded to laud its material and cultural wealth. A mercantile nation with an extensive network of colonies and trading posts spread throughout the Mediterranean, Athens was rich, and it put that wealth to good use, constructing the Parthenon and many of the other architectural treasures that stand to this day. "We provide plenty of means for the mind to refresh itself from business," Pericles continued. "We celebrate games and sacrifices all the year round, and the elegance of our private establishments forms a daily source of pleasure and helps to banish spleen, while the magnitude of our city draws the produce of the world into our harbor, so that to the Athenian the fruits of other countries are as familiar a luxury as those of his own."[5] Rich, cosmopolitan, pleasure-loving, Athens could also afford to indulge the life of the mind, producing not only great works of tragedy and history but also poetry, art, and philosophy as well. Periclean Athens, truly, was a golden age.

Of course, Pericles's portrait was hardly disinterested. Self-flattering and selective, it left a good deal unsaid. The general made no mention of the fact that the same Athenian empire that brought such riches to the metropole could rule over its colonies with an iron fist. Nor did he dwell on the unsettling truth that his "free" city was built on the backs of slaves, who numbered as many as a hundred thousand by the end of the fourth century BCE; or that women and resident foreigners enjoyed none of the benefits of male citizenship.[6] Nonetheless, and judging by the standards of the time, Athens's accomplishments were undeniably great. Even the grudging observer will be inclined to forgive Pericles his overstatement and grant that he had a point when he declared at the end of his oration: "In short, I say that as a city we are the school of Hellas; while I doubt if the world can produce a man, who where he has only himself to depend upon, is equal to so many emergencies, and graced by so fortunate a versatility as the Athenian."[7]

Which brings us back to happiness. Although it would be reductive to say that Athenian democracy was the *cause* of the emergence of happiness as a new and apparently realizable human end, it was nevertheless in Athens, democratic Athens, that individuals first put forth that great, seductive goal, daring to dream that they might pursue—and capture—happiness for themselves. Surely we may admit some connection between context and concept, between a society in which free men had grown accustomed, through rational inquiry and open deliberation, to decide matters for themselves, and the effort to extend the sway of self-rule ever further, even to the long-standing domain of the gods. Freed by Athenian prosperity from the need to direct life solely to the pursuit of survival, a fortunate few could afford to turn their attention to the pursuit of other things.

Many drew on the versatility and self-dependence so lauded by Pericles. But one man stands out with respect to happiness as an innovator and founder. As another great student of happiness, Saint Augustine, would later attest, it was Socrates who was the first to consider in detail what would draw the "sleepless and laborious efforts" of all subsequent philosophers: the "question of the necessary conditions for happiness."[8] Socrates, admittedly, was not much of a democrat himself; he tended to spurn politics for matters of the soul. But he shared wholeheartedly in a belief that was central to the democratic ethos of his times: that human beings, through their own rational conduct, can exercise control over their lives. Socrates's achievement was to apply this same spirit to the pursuit of happiness. In doing so, he created a longing that would fascinate classical minds for centuries, and that has haunted human beings ever since.

The Birth of Ultimate Desire

In the history of happiness, as in the history of philosophy, Socrates is a pivotal figure. But, like the object of his inquiry, he is elusive, leaving us with neither a coherent body of thought nor any written testimony of his teachings. He lived, we know, from 470 to 399 BCE, when he was put to death by the democratic rulers of Athens for allegedly denying the city's gods and corrupting its youth. A citizen, he served bravely as a soldier. He had a wife, but he seems to have preferred the company of younger men, who flocked to him as a teacher and guide. He was not rich, and was apparently quite ugly, though charismatic and seductive; and he cultivated the art of asking questions—difficult questions—with consummate skill.

Beyond these bare details, our knowledge is sketchy, and the little more that we do know comes secondhand, primarily from Socrates's most brilliant student, Plato. In a series of some twenty-four dialogues, Plato used the figure of his master as a character in order to preserve the form and content of his teachings.[9] Plato was a much younger man, who lived from c. 427 to c. 347 BCE. Inevitably, he altered a great deal, infusing Socrates's observations with his own to such an extent you can't separate the lessons of the master from those of the student. But the fluid blend of Socratic-Platonic teaching evident in the dialogues nonetheless conveys a sense of Socrates's radical departure from all previous Greek thought. Whereas earlier philosophers had focused largely on questions of natural science, logic, and the grounds of knowledge (epistemology), asking how the world is made and how we know it, Socrates insisted dramatically on the importance of human conduct (ethics), asking how we should best live our lives. And while the epic poets and tragic playwrights had accepted that human happiness was beyond human agency—controlled by luck, fate, or the gods—Socrates adopted as his point of departure the proposition that happiness is within the human grasp. "What being is there who does not desire happiness?," he asks his companions in Plato's early dialogue, the *Euthydemus*. "Well, then," he answers, "since we all of us desire happiness, how can we be happy?—that is the next question."[10] Transforming Croesus's quest from an outrageous act of hubris to the highest form of inquiry, Socrates grounds the search for happiness in natural human longing. "Nor is there any need to ask why a man desires happiness," he reiterates elsewhere; "the answer is already final."[11] That desire, says Socrates, is self-evident.

At first reckoning, this assertion—repeated in a number of Plato's other dialogues—seems perfectly straightforward. It may, in fact, be true.[12] Certainly, the desire for pleasure must be counted a universal trait, in animals and human beings alike. But by "happiness," Socrates has something else in mind—something loftier, grander—a higher goal that lies beyond mere enjoyment or satisfaction of the senses. And whether human beings instinctively long for that is far less clear. Only when we realize that Socrates declares happiness a natural human longing at the very moment that he invents it as a new, and apparently realizable, form of desire do we begin to suspect that the elusive something for which we naturally yearn may be less inherent to our nature than originally thought.

Evidence for this suspicion can be found throughout Plato's work. But nowhere is it more apparent than in his middle dialogue, the *Symposium*. Written sometime around the year 385 BCE, but set much earlier, less than a decade after the death of Herodotus, in roughly 416, the work is an imaginative reconstruction of an actual banquet held at the house of the Athenian poet Agathon, not far from the Theater of Dionysus. The tragedies of Sophocles were still being performed there, but the guests have gathered on this occasion to pay homage to another playwright—Agathon himself—who has been awarded a prize for *tragoidia* in the City Dionysia. The guests, who include Socrates, the comic dramatist Aristophanes, and a small group of Athenian notables, are distinguished, and the mood is festive, befitting a party.

We may wonder initially at this juxtaposition of tragedy and celebration. And yet in ancient Greek life, the two were frequently linked. Happiness might be hard to come by, but fleeting pleasures were less difficult to find. For all their talk of suffering, the Greeks knew how to enjoy themselves. It is noteworthy that some of the earliest Greek sculpture—the celebrated *kouroi*, large statues of adolescent males in the bloom of youth—frequently depict their subjects smiling, as if to convey that a tragic outlook on life need not spoil a brave or cheerful face. The wrath of the gods could show itself at any moment. But this was all the more reason to make the most of their indulgence, to relish the times of our reprieve.

The City Dionysia is a case in point. Although the springtime festival culminated in the presentation of *tragoidia*, it was a festival nonetheless, a raucous celebration devoted to none other than Dionysus, the god of wine. In the Greek conception, Dionysus was *polygethes*, the bringer of many joys, who delivers sleep and respite from earthly cares, forgetfulness and periods of sweet abandon.[13] The Greeks drank deeply in his honor at the festival in Athens, as well as at the numerous other celebrations held regionally in his name. Wine consumption—in vast quantities—was a central feature of these festivals, and in the words of one distinguished scholar, an "intoxicated time of license seems common to all."[14] Drinking, dancing, the sacrifice of goats, often the parading through town of a giant phallus to raise the mood: All this

The Greek Smile. An Attic kouros
from Anavysos, c. 525 BCE. National
Archaeological Museum, Athens.
Photo Credit: Nimatallah/Art
Resource, NY.

induced an atmosphere of gaiety, rejoicing, and "ectasy," the standing (*stasy*) outside (*ec*) of one's normal self.[15] Even the unhappiness of
an unhappy ending gave way to mirth. In Athens, the final performance
of the cycle of three plays that constituted a complete *tragoidia* was
regularly followed by a "satyr play," a lighthearted romp featuring a
chorus of satyrs—those mythological half-men/half-goats, who think
like the one and rut like the other.

Unfortunately, we possess only a single complete satyr play, the
Cyclops of Euripides. But this, together with the fragments of numerous others, is enough to give us a good sense of what they were about:
in a word, fun. Bawdy, humorous, amoral, the plays reflect the same
carefree spirit that animates their central figures, who frolic and gorge
themselves while displaying a relentless devotion to the activity most
pleasing to their master Dionysus: drinking themselves silly. If the
tragoidia proper invariably ended on a sober note, the satyr plays were
lubricated throughout.

"The man who does not enjoy drinking is mad," declares Silenus,
father of the satyrs and a central character in the *Cyclops*. He adds that

"in drink one can raise *this* [his prick] to a stand, catch a handful of breast and look forward to stroking [a woman's] boscage"—finding, as it were, a little shrubbery in the shrubbery.[16] Such coarseness is by no means uncommon to these plays. The satyrs themselves were frequently represented onstage with enormous, exaggerated erections, and such strap-on accoutrements inevitably invited lewd asides. When a young boy marvels at the size of one such appendage in an extant fragment from Aeschylus's *Net-Fishers,* the satyr responds by noting, "What a cocklover the little fellow is."[17] Presumably, the line drew a laugh. The catharsis of tragedy gives way to comic relief.

The transition was apparently natural enough, reminding us that the tragic spirit was never solely doom and gloom. "There is vengeance from the gods," an early poet, Alcman of Sparta, observes, "but blessed is he who blithely winds out all his days of life without tears."[18] If happiness, in the tragic understanding, was ultimately out of our hands, then it made sense to amuse ourselves when we could. The chorus of the *Cyclops* is clear on the matter: "Happy the man who shouts the Bacchic cry, off to the revel, the well-beloved juice of the vine putting the wind in his sails. His arm is around his trusty friend, and he has waiting for him the fresh, young body of his voluptuous mistress upon her bed, and his locks all gleaming with myrrh he says, 'Who will open the door for me?'"[19] Friendship, love, a bellyful of wine—perhaps, as the satyr suggests, "dancing and forgetfulness of cares"—were ever at hand to take the sting from the pain of existence. The Greeks made full use of all these palliatives when they could.

The opportunities were abundant. In addition to the City Dionysia, there were countless religious festivals and processions, like the pilgrimage from Athens to Eleusis or the fetching of the great fire at Delos on the island of Lemnos, in which days of fasting and abstinence were followed by public rejoicing and ritual intercourse, drinking, dancing, and song. There were the great athletic contests, culminating in the panhellenic games at Olympia, but held also at Delphi, Corinth, Nemea, and scores of lesser locations. The spirit of competition was pursued with deadly seriousness by the participants, but the spectators could afford to treat themselves and their bodies with more

indulgence. There were public feasts and civic celebrations, replete
with music and munificence. There were comedies, which, like the
satyr plays, tended to end on a high note, usually with a celebration.
There were parties, public feasts or impromptu drinking nights in one
of Athens' many taverns. And for those of greater means, there were
private banquets—symposia—held in the privacy of one's own home.

It is the last of these institutions, of course, that gave Plato the title
of his dialogue. The word remains familiar today, although it is far more
likely to summon images of sober gatherings, plastic name tags, and
daylong retreats than riotous evenings during which drunkenness and
debauchery often played a central role. But riotous is what the symposia could easily be: privileged male dinner parties that began with
feasting and ended with fucking, fueled by binge drinking and sometimes fighting along the way.[20] The comic playwright Eubulus describes the degeneration of the symposium as the wine flowed in ever
greater draughts, leading in stages from shouting to loud revelry to
black eyes to court summonses to bile and tossing the furniture
about.[21] The latter was apparently a favorite pastime, and it was not
at all rare to conclude festivities by spilling out of the *andrōn*, the spe-
cially designed men's room where the symposium itself was held, to
go smash something up or wreak havoc in the town. The Greeks even
possessed a special word for the practice—the *komos*—a ritualized al-
coholic riot.

Where violence was lacking, other passions might play. The mirth
of a great many symposia was enhanced by the presence of *hetaera*, a
sort of elegant Greek geisha or call girl whose many services included
(but were not limited to) music making and scintillating conversation.
For those so inclined, the pretty wine pourer or flute boy might be
open to seduction, and if nothing else, he was usually good to look at.
Infinite gradations of cheaper fare—prostitutes both male and female—could be readily summoned for a price, to ensure that no guest
was deprived if the lubricious desires of Dionysus moved him.[22]

To be sure, more refined satisfactions were also on hand; excess was
not always the norm. Ever mindful of balance, the Greeks, as one
scholar has recently argued, evinced caution even in their keenest

pleasures, concerned lest they be consumed by them.[23] Xenóphanes of Cólophon leaves us with a comparatively chaste picture in his poem "The Well-Tempered Symposium." The floor has been cleared of stray crumbs and shells and bones; the wine is mixed with water; the rhythms of the lyre animate the music of close friendship. One can readily imagine noble Greeks reclining on their couches after the meal, joining in exalted conversation and song:

> Now the floor is swept clean, and the hands of all who are
> present are washed, and the cups are clean. One puts the
> garlands on, another passes the fragrant myrrh on a dish. The
> mixing bowl is set up and stands by, full of the spirit of cheer,
> and more wine still stands ready and promises no disappoint-
> ment; sweet wine, in earthen jars, preserving its bouquet. In
> the middle of all, frankincense gives out its holy fragrance,
> and we have water there too, cold and crystal and sweet. . . .
> Merriment and singing fill all the corners of the house.[24]

The copious supplies of wine—habitually blended with water in a bowl so large that it was referred to as a *krater*—should give us pause. For even Xenóphanes admits that as long as the men have made their li- bation to the god, "and prayed to be able to conduct themselves like gentlemen as occasion demands," it will not be "drunk-and-disorderly to drink as much as one can and still get home without help."[25] Inde- pendent locomotion was hardly an exacting standard of sobriety. It is safe to assume that, at least in many cases, one added set of shoul- ders was required to complete the journey.

Such ritualized debauchery may well call to mind the image of the stag night or the fraternity party, replete with call girls and vomit and the breaking of things. That image tends to clash with a received sense of the symposium as a refined and rarified occasion. And though part of the reason for this disjuncture is likely our own failure of imagina- tion—a tendency to idealize the Greeks, rendering them more lofty than they actually were—it also probably owes something to the en- during legacy of the *Symposium* itself. For Plato's account of the drink-

Winged Eros and a seated
personification of Eudaimonia, Red-
figure squat lekythos, late 5th century
BCE, © copyright the Trustees of
the British Museum.

ing party creates a very different impression of this central Greek institution.

In the first place, Plato tells us, Agathon's guests agree shortly after
the meal to forgo any hard or forced drinking. A number of the company admit to suffering hangovers from the night before, but the
choice is nonetheless portentous, as much an effort to set the party's
mood in advance as a concession to weak constitutions. Next, the
guests voluntarily dispatch with the flute girl, ensuring that their
glances will not be distracted by fetching limbs. Music, at this gathering, will be made by words alone. Finally, the philosopher Socrates is
an attendance, and according to Plato, he was a man who generally
avoided symposia as a low form of fun.[26] He arrives late (and only after
a second invitation), clad in sandals, which is itself a rare occurrence.
In normal circumstances, the philosopher prided himself on being an
anypodetos, a man who went without shoes.

Plato's symposium, then, is intended from the outset to be a special gathering, a party of a rarified sort. Not coincidentally, it subscribes

closely to the model that Plato had already suggested in his early dialogue, the *Protagoras*. There, Socrates disparages common drinking
parties for their slurred speech and sensual distractions, observing that
a proper symposium ideally should be a more sober affair. "Where the
party consists of thorough gentlemen who have had a proper education, you will see neither flute-girls nor dancing girls nor harp-girls,
but only the company contenting themselves with their own conversation, and none of these fooleries and frolics—each speaking and listening decently in turn."[27] Proper education necessarily entails for
Socrates the education of desire. So, fittingly, having renounced the
quotidian pleasures of the drinking feast, the guests of the *Symposium*
vow to consecrate their energy to conversation alone. They choose as
their subject the nature of Eros, the great god of desire.

Each of the guests delivers a speech in honor of Eros, from which it
quickly emerges that this is an immensely powerful god whose force
is intimately bound up with the yearning for human happiness. He is
"the oldest of the gods, the most deserving of our respect, and the
most useful for those men . . . who want to attain virtue and happiness," observes Phaedrus, the first speaker of the evening.[28] Somewhat
later, the doctor Eryximachus adds that the influence of the "great
and awe-inspiring" Eros is "unbounded" and "absolute," capable of
bringing us "complete happiness," while Aristophanes, after recovering from a bout of hiccups, notes that "Eros is the most friendly toward men . . . our helper, [who] cures those evils whose cure brings
the greatest happiness to the human race."[29] Agathon, in a grand rhetorical flourish befitting a poet, concludes that though all the gods are
happy, Eros is "the most happy, since he is the most beautiful and the
best."[30]

To this much, all the participants save the still-silent Socrates agree.
But beyond Eros's power and proximity to happiness, there is little
else on which the guests can establish common ground. One speaker,
Pausanias, refuses to see Eros as a single entity, claiming that he
must be divided in two as Common Eros and Heavenly Eros—the
one, a seedy creature drawn by sexual appetite and so depraved that
he will even sleep with women; the other, a more transcendent being

Detail of Eudaimonia in the retinue
of Aphrodite, Red-figure squat
lekythos, 410–400 BCE,
© copyright the Trustees of
the British Museum.

attracted by mind as well as beauty, who finds his consummate
expression in the higher love between boys and older men. Eryximachus, on the other hand, views Eros as a pantheistic force found
not only in the hearts of gods and humans but "also in nature—in the
physical life of all animals, in plants that grow in the ground, and in
virtually all living organisms."[31] Finally, Aristophanes maintains in a
celebrated fable that human beings were originally joined two at a time
to form complete wholes. Overly powerful, these four-legged creatures
provoked the suspicion of the gods, who had them sundered to reduce
their strength; now each half walks the earth in search of its other.
The fable explains our sexual orientation, for men originally joined to
men will seek their complement in the same sex, while those originally joined to women will seek their other half accordingly. It also
explains our sense of longing and loss, as we wander the earth in search
of the one who will make us whole. "[W]here happiness for the human
races lies," Aristophanes concludes, is "in the successful pursuit of love."
Eros is the great benefactor who will "[return] us to our original condition, healing us, and making us blessed and perfectly happy."[32]

   A pantheistic force animating the world; a schizophrenic deity both
plebeian and patrician; a guide who leads us only to ourselves: Eros,

BISHOP IRETON H.S. LIBRARY
ALEXANDRIA, VIRGINIA

clearly, is no simple god. He is, Socrates contends, no god at all. Drawing together the strands of these various reflections, Socrates maintains that Eros is, rather, a "great spirit" who is "midway between what
is divine and what is human," his ambiguous nature owing to the
strange circumstances of his conception.[33] Sired at the birthday party
of Aphrodite, the goddess of beauty and love, Eros is the child of Poverty, who came to the festivities uninvited as a beggar, and the god
Plenty, a welcome guest who passed out there drunk. How Plenty is
able to perform in such a state, we are not told (presumably, a feat of
the gods), but perform he does, producing a son who is neither "mortal nor immortal." Now fully grown, Eros takes after his mother. Constantly in need, he is "hard, unkempt, barefoot, homeless." But, like
his father, he is "brave, enterprising, and determined." Having inherited "an eye for beauty and the good," Eros continually searches for
these two qualities through love, as befits one conceived in the presence of Aphrodite.[34]

Straddling the human and the divine, Eros is an emissary, conducting "all association and communication, waking or sleeping,"
between the gods and men.[35] His twofold nature explains his defining characteristic—desire itself. For what is desire but the human
acknowledgment that one is in need, that one is lacking? As Socrates
explains, "the man who desires something desires what is not available to him, and what he doesn't already have in his possession."[36] And
what is it that Eros lacks? Precisely those qualities that surrounded
him at the moment of his divine conception, the qualities held by the
self-sufficient gods: goodness and beauty, or, in a word, happiness, for
to be "happy means possessing what is good and beautiful."[37] Part
human, Eros is incomplete—he yearns; part god, he yearns for what is
godlike, happiness.

Unfortunately, like all who know his power, Eros is easily misled,
prone to seek the good in places it cannot be found: in the pursuit of
money, for example; in purely carnal sex, in fame, in people who do us
harm. Midway between the gods and men, Eros is also "midway between wisdom and folly," rendering desire a volatile force. Elsewhere,
in his greatest dialogue, the *Republic,* Plato dwells at length on the

potential hazards of this force, noting in the voice of Socrates that "there is a dangerous, wild, and lawless form of desire in everyone." Even those who appear entirely moderate and measured on the surface can catch sight of the dark potential of Eros in their dreams, where uninhibited desire will shrink from nothing, including murder or "trying to have sex with a mother . . . or with anyone else at all, whether man, god, or beast."[38] It is not difficult to see why Sigmund Freud would later find in the "*Eros* of the divine Plato" an important precedent for his own work.[39]

For Plato, Eros's potential for wickedness and folly demanded that desire be carefully disciplined. We can never hope to subdue Eros (nor would we want to), but we can direct his power toward the genuinely good and the genuinely beautiful, learning to love the right things in the right way. In the *Symposium*, Socrates begins to sketch the outlines of this education of desire, suggesting that the ascent to happiness will be a long and arduous process. Beginning in youth, the potential lover of the good is led gradually from the love of the physical beauty of individuals to the love of physical beauty in general. From there the apprentice is trained to put a higher value on beauty of the mind, gradually learning as a lover of wisdom, a philosopher, to look beyond what he once desired. "Whereas before, in servile and contemptible fashion, he was dominated by the individual case, loving the beauty of a boy, or a man, or a single human activity, now he directs his eyes to what is beautiful in general, as he turns to gaze upon the limitless ocean of beauty." Onward and upward, the lover of wisdom ascends in search of the pure form of beauty, beauty itself:

> Such is the experience of the man who approaches, or is
> guided towards, love in the right way, beginning with the
> particular examples of beauty, but always returning from them
> to the search for that one beauty. He uses them like a ladder,
> climbing from the love of one person to love of two; from two
> to love of all physical beauty; from physical beauty to beauty
> in human behavior; thence to beauty in subjects of study;
> from them he arrives finally at that branch of knowledge

which studies nothing but ultimate beauty. Then at last he understands what true beauty is.[40]

This final consummation—likened in the even more eroticized accounts given in the dialogues *Phaedrus* and the *Republic* to "intercourse" between the lover of wisdom and truth—can be described only as a sort of intellectual orgasm in which desire is sated and happiness flows forth. "That, if ever," Socrates recounts in the *Symposium*, "is the moment . . . when . . . life is worth living."[41]

This vision of the rapturous contemplation of beauty would have tremendous impact on the Western mystical tradition. Here, however, it is important to appreciate that for Plato, the happiness induced by the intimate encounter with beauty need not be fleeting. If the great orgasmic moment itself was necessarily ephemeral, the discipline of desire, and the proper ordering of the soul required to induce it, were not. Through self-control, the lover of wisdom could ensure that the "better elements of the mind" prevailed; that one passed life here, in this world, "in happiness and harmony."[42]

The quest of Croesus—to achieve happiness through one's own volition—Socrates affirms, is a realizable dream, albeit one carried out on terms vastly different than those imagined by the Lydian king. Indeed, Socrates's vision entails a thoroughgoing rejection of *all* previous conceptions of what it might mean to be happy. Just as he purges the symposium of wine, women, and song, he sets aside the sensual pleasures that had long consoled the Greeks in their tragic world. Happiness is not hedonism. Nor is it ultimately to be found in those pathways of misdirected desire that have long deceived men and women in pursuit: good fortune, pleasure, power, riches, fame, even health or familial love. In place of all these things, Socrates preaches philosophy with unflinching ardor, insisting that the right ordering of the soul and the elevation of Eros will alone ensure our most coveted end. But to attain this pinnacle of desire, all others must be controlled and even renounced. As Socrates never tires of insisting, the true lover of wisdom will be as impervious to physical hardship as to the haphazardness of chance. To follow in his footsteps is to leave behind a world in which one's happiness is controlled by the chaos of fortune or the predeterminations of fate. Happiness, Socrates insists, lies within our power.

Requiring a radical reappraisal of the standards of the world, Socrates's vision is necessarily disruptive, even revolutionary, a point that Plato takes pains to remind us toward the end of the *Symposium*. For just as Socrates has completed his paean to Eros, the party is interrupted by shouting, music, and a loud hammering on the front door. A group of drunken revelers stand outside, led by Alcibiades, a young man of physical beauty, whom Socrates once befriended and may have loved. Boisterous and impassioned, the revelers have come to congratulate Agathon on his success in the manner of a more traditional symposium. With a flute girl on his arm, and already terribly drunk, Alcibiades seeks to crown Agathon with a garland of laurels. But as he does so, he notices Socrates in the room and flies into the jealous rage of a lover spurned. Chugging down a large bowl of unmixed wine and bidding the others to do the same, he explains how he was once "seduced" by the "wild passion for philosophy" preached by Socrates. His words turned all of Alcibiades's former beliefs "upside down," convincing him that he was living the life of a slave, in thrall to his lowest passions. Unable to direct Eros in the appropriate manner of a lover of wisdom, Alcibiades attempted to take Socrates as his (physical) lover and was rebuked. He now likens Socrates to Silenus and the satyrs, the only difference being that the seductive philosopher beguiles with his words rather than his flute. The comparison notwithstanding, it is clear from Alcibiades's behavior that he is the more satyr-like of the two. With a soul prone to violent passions and governed by an "insane" sexual frenzy, the figure of Alcibiades is intended as testimony to the dangers of misplaced desire.[43]

A man of great gifts and charisma who studied with Socrates in his youth but later left him estranged, Alcibiades is a complicated historical figure. A wily politician and a brilliant military commander, he was also a demagogue and a schemer who seduced other men's wives, betrayed Athens during the Peloponnesian War, and was eventually murdered. Plato, like Socrates, was fascinated by him, and used his

figure in a number of dialogues, including the eponymous *Alcibiades*,
to represent positions he strongly opposed. In the *Symposium*, Alcibiades
serves a similar function. An embodiment of lawlessness who is ruled
not by reason but by the lowest passions, he is a fitting representative
of the older sympotic culture that Plato deplored. In crashing Agathon's
party, he quickly brings the rarified discussion of happiness crashing
down to earth. And that is where the party ends—on the floor, with
the guests passed out drunk. Only Socrates is still upright at daybreak,
carrying on about the proper relationship between comedy and tragedy. In a sense, the two have come together at his feet. After tucking
in his hosts, he takes his leave, headed for the baths.

The ease with which Alcibiades is able to upset this special celebration —redirecting desire from higher happiness to the lower realms
of pleasure—is altogether instructive. For in the same way that Plato
was inclined to associate the sympotic lifestyle with the vulgar hedonism of democratic Athens, he likewise associated symposia with politics.[44] Socrates—or at least the Socrates of Plato's dialogues—tended
scrupulously to avoid both. And thus Alcibiades's intervention is doubly symbolic, representing not only the elusiveness and fragility of
Socrates's new form of happiness, but also what Plato regarded as the
fragility and shortcomings of democracy. When Alcibiades appeals to
the "jury" of guests in an attempt to warn them of the dangers of
Socratic philosophy, his action is meant to call to mind the very real
charges brought against Socrates by the rulers of democratic Athens
some seventeen years after this great feast. Accused of failing to honor
the old gods and of leading the city's youth astray, Socrates was condemned to death in sad recompense for having offered to the people
of Athens what he described in his own trial defense as the "reality of
happiness."[45] If the figure of Alcibiades is something of a classical
Judas—able to recognize that Socrates is nobler and better than anyone "in the past or present," but unable to follow his call—he is also
an executioner, a symbol of the turbulent democratic man who appeals
to the basest parts of our soul.[46]

Plato's hatred of democracy is notorious. An aristocrat himself, he
never forgave Athens for having condemned the man he considered

the most just who ever lived. It is not surprising that he heaps scorn on democratic institutions throughout his work. In book eight of the *Republic*, Plato infamously describes democratic man as a slave to unnecessary desires, ruled by "useless and unnecessary pleasures," and he likens democratic leaders to evil wine-pourers who slate the people's thirst for license and illusory freedom.[47] Turbulent and unstable, the soul of democratic man is fickle and changing, led by the lowest appetites and prone, like an unruly symposium, to devolve into chaos. Democratic man, Plato concludes, is not free but a slave, only one step removed from tyranny. The same culture that produced Socrates, with its manifold pleasures and its penchant for self-rule, allegedly militates against the possibility of human happiness that Socrates dared to dream.

We may find this judgment ironic, perverse, or ill conceived. It is unquestionably bleak. For as the ease with which Alcibiades brings down Socrates's rarified symposium attests, Plato believed that human desire was all too quickly diverted. Only in special circumstances can our unruly appetites be properly disciplined to seek the truth, and only in special circumstances can we educate our desire so that it will successfully seek the good for which it yearns. In the *Republic*, Plato goes so far as to suggest that the one way this goal can be widely achieved is coercively, in a state—a political state—where philosophers rule as kings and kings rule as philosophers, devoting themselves to inculcating true justice, true wisdom, and true happiness in the city and its citizens alike. Prior to that time, Plato believed, only Socrates can be said to have claimed the elusive prize to which his philosophy pointed the way. He alone approached the goal of "becoming like a god," of being truly happy.[48]

Whether Socrates was in fact a corrupter of youth will likely remain a contested question. What is far more certain is that his new view of happiness entailed a radical rejection of all previous norms. In this respect, if in no other, his accusers were right to fear him, and their readiness to do so is instructive, highlighting the Socratic sleight of hand that drew our attention at the beginning of this section. How, we must ask again, can our *desire* for happiness be considered *natural* at the moment of its birth? Clearly, we all feel desires, but as both Socrates and Plato hasten to emphasize, the vast majority of us follow Eros, not back to the ethereal realm of goodness and beauty from whence he purportedly came, but down to the earthly material world where he is so often lost and confused amid the pleasures of the senses. There—here—far away from the transcendent forms—happiness proper can hardly be conceived. How can it be that we naturally desire what we have never even known?[49]

Plato himself would seem to admit as much, prescribing a radical program to reorient our desires—to change our natural human nature. And yet perhaps we should also grant that he had hit upon something profound. For who among us has never felt that our own freedoms and fleeting satisfactions are not enough to give us what we want? Even in the extraordinary luxury of our modern democracies, so far removed from Plato's own, something like an instinct is apt to suggest that we yearn for more than our wealth and precious freedoms can provide. Do the pleasures we know now suffice to quell our longings, or do they incite us, embolden us, to long for more?

Human desire is ubiquitous, spilling out from all places and into all things. By giving it a comprehensive new goal, and insisting that it lies within our grasp, Socrates and Plato create a longing of tremendous power. Their happiness is the sum of all desires, the final resting place of Eros, the highest good. As such, says Socrates, happiness is a "powerful and unpredictable force."[50] Even he would likely be surprised by the strange directions in which it has led posterity—so far that we can almost imagine, like him, that our natural desire for happiness is completely natural, owing nothing to these early imaginings.

The End of Existence

Anyone who has ever walked the gilded halls of the Vatican, or taken a survey course in European art history, will know Raphael's filial fresco *The School of Athens,* in which this devoted son of the Renaissance pays homage to the movement's philosophical forefathers. A sumptuous

symbol of the endurance of Greek thought and of its central place in
the church—literally embedded in the walls—the work also captures
a received contrast between its two principal figures, Plato and Aristotle.
Framed in an archway that leads to the heavens, surrounded by the
greatest minds of the classical world, the two men dominate the work,
creating harmonious tension at its heart. Whereas the long-bearded
Plato gestures upward beyond the vast space of the enclosure, Aristotle
checks him horizontally, his hand steady in the plane of the earth.
The tome on his arm is exposed, also facing down, while Plato clutches
his great black book tightly to his side, accentuating the vertical
movement of his gesture. And though Plato is precipitously balanced
in midstep, as if straining to leave the earth, Aristotle has both feet
planted firmly on the ground. A study in contrasts, Raphael's masterpiece presents these two giants as philosophical and temperamental

Raphael, *The School of Athens*, 1510–11, Stanza della Segnatura,
Vatican Palace, Vatican State.

opposites: one striving for wisdom in the world beyond; the other searching to find it here in the world below.

There is a good deal of truth to this simple opposition, and it is often repeated. As the nineteenth-century English poet Samuel Taylor Coleridge summarized famously, Plato and Aristotle placed "two opposite systems . . . before the mind of the world." "Every man is born an Aristotelian, or a Platonist," he continued. "They are the two classes of men, beside which it is next to impossible to conceive a third."[51]

On the surface, this characterization applies equally well to the two men's conceptions of happiness. And Aristotle does approach the subject from a new, and overwhelmingly immanent, perspective. If Socrates and Plato are skeptical of the given world, inclined to cast their gazes on high, Aristotle looks far more indulgently on the things of this earth, prepared to pay heed to the limits of the empirical and to work within its bounds.

Yet Aristotle was also an admirer of Socrates—he was said to have taught with a bust of the martyred philosopher in his classroom—and a longtime student of Plato, in whose Academy at Athens he

Raphael, detail of *The School of Athens*, Stanza della Segnatura, Vatican Palace, Vatican State.

spent nearly twenty years, from 367 to 347 BCE. After serving as a tutor in Macedonia to the young Alexander the Great, Aristotle returned to Athens behind his pupil's armies and established his own school, the Lyceum. Athen's democracy was drawing to a close, and what was left of the city's fragile independence would soon be completely destroyed as its dominions were forcibly incorporated into the Macedonian empire following Alexander's death in 323 BCE. But the dream of happiness born in the previous century was preserved in Aristotle's school. Despite his different methods and approach, he shared many of Socrates and Plato's larger aspirations. Serving to further reinforce one of their central objectives—that of making happiness the goal of all human activity—his work saddled this ultimate end with contradictions as daunting as those he had been bequeathed.

Aristotle's reflections on happiness can be found throughout his writings, but he engages the subject most rigorously in what has come to be known as the *Nichomachean Ethics,* named after Aristotle's son, Nichomachus, who helped collate the text following his father's death. Like so much of Aristotle's work, the *Ethics* was never intended as a finished project. It comprises, rather, a set of notes from which he probably lectured at the Lyceum. Necessarily fragmentary, they nonetheless provide our most complete picture of Aristotle's conception of happiness.

"Every craft and every investigation, and likewise every action and decision," the work famously begins, "seems to aim at some good."[52] The sentence is revealing both of the *Ethics'* chief intention and of the overriding assumption of Aristotle's thought: that nature does not act in vain. In the Aristotelian universe, all things, whether natural or created, man-made or divine, are *intended* to fulfill a purpose. Just as the acorn is intended to become an oak, a knife is intended to cut, and a ship captain is intended to pilot ships, man, Aristotle believes (and, as we shall see, he emphatically means *man*), is intended for some end, some purpose, some telos. The goal of his investigation—its good—will be to discern the nature of this final destination.

Aristotle proceeds by way of analogy. We say that the function of a flautist is to play the flute, and that the function of a sculptor is to sculpt. Every way of life, every profession—what the Greeks called a "craft" (*technē*)—would seem to have a distinct purpose. Can we say that there is a distinct purpose to living in general, a craft of life? Aristotle believes we can, and he tries to identify this purpose by isolating our most distinctly human activity. Some creatures—plants—vegetate and grow; they live. Other creatures—animals—move according to their senses. Only human beings are capable of reason. Our unique human activity is thus to live and act in accordance with reason.

But there is obviously a tremendous difference between mere life and the good life, between a human being who reasons well and one who doesn't reason at all. In order to account for these differences, Aristotle pushes his analogy with craftsmanship even further:

> Let us return once again to the good we are looking for, and consider just what it could be, since it is apparently one thing in one action or craft, and another thing in another; for it is one thing in medicine, another in generalship, and so on for the rest.
>
> What, then, is the good in each of these cases? Surely, it is that for the sake of which the other things are done; and in medicine this is health, in generalship victory; in house-building a house, in another case something else, but in every action and decision it is the end, since it is for the sake of the end that everyone does the other things.
>
> And so, if there is some end of everything that is pursued in action, this will be the [highest] good. . . .[53]

What, then, is the highest good of the craft of life, the good for which all others are simply means, the end that is complete in and of itself? In Aristotle's view, this final end is happiness. Just as the good doctor procures health through medicine, and the good general procures victory through war, the good human being will procure happiness through life. It is our natural telos—the end we ought to reach if we live well—and our highest attainment to be won by cultivating the

faculty that sets us apart from all other creatures and acting accordingly. To be a good human being, Aristotle affirms, is to live according to our special human virtue, reason. And to be a good human being
is to be a happy human being. Happiness, Aristotle concludes, is an
"activity of the soul expressing virtue."[54]

In its apparent coherence and seeming simplicity, Aristotle's formulation is monumental. Adopting what is, in effect, the central and
revolutionary contention of Socrates and Plato before him, Aristotle
takes their assertion that human happiness is a function of virtue and
states it far more directly. His point of departure—that human beings, like all things in the world, are *intended* to fulfill a purpose—
involves a major teleological assumption, one whose truth is far less
apparent in our own time than it has been for much of Western history. The ancient Greeks, however, believed that human beings and
the world they inhabit participate in a larger order that gives them
meaning. Like Socrates and Plato, Aristotle assumes this to be the
case. And also like them, he is confident that human reason can give
us insight into our specific human function. Unlike them, he believes
that we should look to the world around us—the world of phenomena
—for guidance in forming our judgments on these matters.

It is therefore of particular interest not only that Aristotle dismisses
Plato's quasi-mystical idea of the form of pure good as vague, unsub-
stantiated, and impractical—for "clearly it is not the sort of good a
human being can pursue in action or possess [which is] just the sort
we are looking for in our present inquiry"—but also that he turns to
popular conceptions of happiness to begin his investigation into what
this end might practically entail. Aristotle readily acknowledges that
most people form some idea of the nature of *eudaimonia*, even if they
don't believe it lies within their power to attain. And so he thinks that
we should consider what they have to say on the matter. True, he is
often condescending; he dismisses, for example, the view that he attributes to "the many, the most vulgar"—that happiness consists in
pleasure—as "completely slavish," befitting the lives of "grazing animals" more than human beings. But he considers it all the same, de-
liberating on a number of others as well, a move that draws attention

to the fact that debate over the proper meaning of happiness was already taking shape in the classical world. Weighing heavily into that debate himself, Aristotle is more than prepared to draw on much of what he hears. As he summarizes these views in another work, the *Rhetoric:*

> We may define happiness as prosperity combined with virtue; or as independence of life; or as the secure enjoyment of the maximum of pleasure; or as a good condition of property and body, together with the power of guarding one's property and body and making use of them. That happiness is one or more of these things pretty well everybody agrees.
>
> From this definition of happiness it follows that its constituent parts are:—good birth, plenty of friends, good friends, wealth, good children, plenty of children, a happy old age, also such bodily excellences as health, beauty, strength, large stature, athletic powers, together with fame, honour, good luck, and virtue. A man cannot fail to be completely independent if he possesses these internal and these external goods; for besides these there are no others to have. (Goods of the soul and of the body are internal. Good birth, friends, money, and honour are external.) Further, we think that he should possess resources and luck, in order to make his life really secure.[55]

This, to Aristotle, is "happiness in general," a compilation of "all the features," as he says in the *Ethics,* "that people look for in happiness" when they consider it in everyday terms.[56] In stark contrast to the views of Socrates and Plato, this general understanding of happiness is in keeping with the reflections dispensed by Solon to Croesus, entailing health and security, pleasure and prosperity, honor and virtue, good friends and good fortune to the end of one's days. Nor is this similarity coincidental, for Aristotle believes that any theoretical account of happiness must "harmonize" with the "facts"—it must be at least partially consistent, that is, with "common beliefs." By taking into account views that are "traditional, held by many," with others entertained by a more reflective minority, "a few reputable men," Aristotle hopes to guard against theoretical abstruseness.[57] He also reveals a bias that is rare in the philosopher: a predilection for the status quo.

Thus, he is quick to acknowledge that although pleasure is by no means the sole constituent of happiness, it is certainly a contributing element. External goods, likewise—money, friends, children, good birth, and physical beauty—are all frankly accepted as necessary components of happiness, for we "cannot, or cannot easily, do fine actions if we lack the resources," and "we do not altogether have the character of happiness if we look utterly repulsive or are ill-born, solitary or childless. . . ."[58] Similarly, Aristotle concurs with the widely held Greek belief that happiness must be judged over a lifetime, for even "the most prosperous person may fall into a terrible disaster in old age." Granting virtue a central place in the attainment of happiness, Aristotle nonetheless rejects the view, held by Socrates and Plato, that virtue on its own is enough to secure our highest end. "Someone might possess virtue," he counters, but still "suffer the worst evils and misfortunes." To call this person happy would be "to defend a philosopher's paradox."[59]

Fortune is forever fickle, a proposition that Aristotle cannot bring himself to deny. It guarantees that factors over which we have relatively little or no control (birth, beauty, luck) play some role in determining happiness. Yet at the same time, he is engaged in the task of showing how happiness is brought about through virtuous activity in accordance with reason. This is his overall emphasis, and, initially, he seems quite sanguine about the prospect of its realization, observing that "anyone who is not deformed [in his capacity] for virtue will be able to achieve happiness through some sort of learning and attention." Happiness, apparently, "will be widely shared."[60]

But when we consider that Aristotle, like many (though not all) of his contemporaries, believed that women and those he deemed "natural slaves" were inherently deformed in just this way—deficient in reason, and so deficient in the capacity for virtue—our sense of the scope of his intended allotment narrows considerably. Children, too, are debarred, given that their faculty of deliberative reason is not yet fully developed; and so are all those without sufficient resources to assure leisure, education, and independence. Restricted from the outset to free men, men of means, the pool of candidates for happiness only grows smaller as we work through Aristotle's account.

What of those who do satisfy the fundamental criteria; who are, as it were, potentially fit? Aristotle prescribes a lifelong regime of habituation to virtue, the most stable and controlling element in governing happiness. He understands that the study of virtue can never be an exact science in which unfailing rules of behavior are decreed from above. He urges, rather, that virtue be cultivated through practice, so that it gradually becomes second nature, with individuals developing an inherent sense of the right response with which to approach life's many vagaries. The principal rule of thumb is Aristotle's famous doctrine of the mean, which advises us to calibrate our behavior between extremes. Through reason, practice, and example, the virtuous man will come to know the appropriate middle way between cowardice and rashness, or stinginess and prodigality, or boastfulness and self-deprecation. He will cultivate the appropriate virtues of character —courage, liberality, and self-respect—and gauge his behavior accordingly. Discussing in detail a number of such virtues—magnificence, moderation, gentleness, modesty, friendliness, and righteous indignation, among others—Aristotle puts forth an ideal of harmony and balance in which desire is tempered through rational restraint, and life lived in keeping with our highest human faculty.

The habituation to virtue counseled by Aristotle is thus a practical education in the craft of life, to be carried out from youth and conducted, ideally, within the shepherding structure of a virtuous society. It is an elite education and an education for elites, designed to produce men not unlike those who ruled in many contemporary Greek city-states. In fact, the *Nichomachean Ethics* is really a prelude to Aristotle's *Politics*, which aims to identify the best regimes for promoting the virtuous behavior—the happiness—of its citizens. In such optimal environments, the greatest number of human beings would be able to realize their full potential, becoming what they are intended to be, while adopting, in turn, positions of responsibility and authority within the polis. In these, what might be called "eudaimono-cracies," the happy would lead.[61]

Even in such ideal circumstances, we are left to wonder about the attainability of happiness as described in the *Ethics*. For toward the end of the work, Aristotle concedes that the virtues of character he has so assiduously expounded are, at best, capable of conferring only "secondary" happiness.[62] Above them lies the highest expression of our highest faculty, the pure exercise of reason: what Aristotle terms "contemplation" or "study." While all other forms of activity are merely "human," contemplation is divine. Aristotle dwells at length on how the gods, traditionally assumed to be more "blessed and happy" than other beings, are also popularly supposed to pass their time in pure contemplation. "Hence," Aristotle concludes, "the gods' activity that is superior in blessedness will be an activity of study. And so the human activity that is most akin to the gods' will, more than any other, have the character of happiness." In the end, the life of pure contemplation is the most godlike life. It is "superior to the human level."[63]

What are we to make of this surprising turn? Having advocated a philosophy designed to realize human happiness on earth, the apparently worldly Aristotle turns his gaze upward in a manner reminiscent of Plato. Unable to conceive of perfect happiness without reference to the gods, he unwittingly casts a shadow on the life that the bulk of his *Ethics* recommends. As the contemporary philosopher Jonathan Lear has observed, Aristotle suggests that "those who know most about human life know that what is best is to organize life so as to escape its ordinary conditions—even the conditions of excellence within it. What is best about being human is the opportunity to break out of being human."[64] As a consequence, the prospects for earthly happiness would seem rather bleak. Not only will most men and women be denied true happiness from the outset—barred for reasons of birth and circumstance—but even the relative elite who manage to live in keeping with the ethical virtues will fall short. Theirs is but a

"secondary happiness" that pales before the godlike activity of contemplation. Open to an even smaller number, this summit will be
experienced only in comparatively brief intervals, for not all of life may
be spent in study.

The natural telos of man, we are led to conclude, is unnaturally
difficult to fulfill. In Aristotle's world, there may be such a thing as
the "happy few," but perhaps more telling is the unhappy majority that
this ideal creates. For the majority of humanity, Aristotle's happiness
is not only unattainable; it casts a shadow on the rest of life that must
remain, by definition, imperfect.

Yet for all its intangibility, Aristotle's teaching on happiness
only enhanced the allure of this enigmatic end. Drawing acolytes from
across the ancient world—his fame bolstered by his early association
with Alexander—Aristotle affirmed the central place of *eudaimonia* in
classical ethics and thought. Henceforth, happiness would serve as the
overriding philosophical concern, the ultimate end of existence. And
as more people came to focus on this elusive end, new teachers would
present themselves to help guide others on their way.

Surgery for the Soul

In the lower left quadrant of Raphael's masterpiece, two figures sit
as if in quiet rebuke of the work's title. A garlanded man, consoled by
the arm of a friend, writes intently in an open book, captured in ambiguous union with a second sage—solitary, distant, bearded, and
grave—who sits, gazing, behind him. By rights these men should be
closer to the two giants of the center, for their lasting influence was
almost as great. Epicurus, in garlands, founded a school that would
shape a current of thought powerful well into the nineteenth century, while the bearded Zeno, the father of Stoicism, did much the
same.

In the context of the ancient world, their importance was respect-
fully acknowledged—so much so that within several decades of Aristotle's death, the literate traveler to Athens would not have failed to

Raphael, detail of *The School of Athens*, Stanza della Segnatura,
Vatican Palace, Vatican State.

pass "the Garden" of Epicurus, the home where his adherents gathered daily just minutes from the Dipylon Gate. Nor would the traveler have missed the public lectures and discussions of Zeno, held at
the Stoa Poikile, a colonnade closer to the city center from which his
followers derived their name. Alongside Aristotle's own center of learning, the Lyceum, and that of his teacher, the Academy, these and
numerous other philosophic schools openly competed for adherents,
offering the possibility of earthly happiness in return. By the close of
the fourth century BCE, happiness—*eudaimonia*—was the undisputed
goal of them all.[65]

This unanimity is testimony to the power of the philosophical tri-
umvirate of Socrates, Plato, and Aristotle, whose work would continue
to define the terms of ethical debate in the West for centuries to come.
Happiness as ultimate desire, happiness as final end—this is their
legacy, as it is of classical Greek philosophy as a whole. Yet the number
of schools offering different means to that end is also testimony to the

fact that by the close of the fourth century BCE, their legacy was disputed or, more precisely, regarded as incomplete. All three raised expectations they could not entirely fulfill. To many, their goal of earthly happiness was enticing, but happiness for the godlike few was unacceptably grim. Was there no other way of satisfying this nagging desire?

Zeno and Epicurus address precisely this question, aiming far more explicitly than their predecessors to alleviate human pain. "Empty is that philosopher's argument by which no human suffering is therapeutically treated," Epicurus maintains, adding that "just as there is no use in a medical art that does not cast out the sicknesses of bodies, so too there is no use in philosophy, if it does not throw out suffering from the soul."[66] Speaking of the tradition of Zeno, the Roman Stoic Cicero observes similarly, "There is, I assure you, a medical art for the soul. It is philosophy. . . ."[67] If the significant contribution of Socrates, Plato, and Aristotle was the identification of happiness as the ultimate state of human health, then the task of their successors was to help diagnose and manage our ills. Both Epicurus and Zeno do this by managing desire itself.

Unfortunately, we know comparatively little about them. Of Zeno, born in roughly 335 BCE, we are told by the third-century historian Diogenes Laertius in his *Lives of the Eminent Philosophers* that the Stoic founder "was sour and of a frowning countenance," had thick legs and was flabby and fond of green figs.[68] Originally of Citium, on the island of Cyprus, Zeno traveled to Athens in his mid-twenties, apparently drawn by an interest in the teachings of Socrates. After studying for a number of years with various teachers, he branched out on his own, courting students around the Stoa in regular meetings that took on the character of a religious cult. He wrote profusely, and died around 263 BCE, but not a single scrap of his work survives, leaving us heavily dependent on the accounts of men like Diogenes, and the writings of later Stoics like the Greek-speaking Epictetus, and the Romans Seneca, Cicero, and Marcus Aurelius. Though imperfect, these sources are all we have.

Knowledge of Epicurus is only slightly less spotty. An Athenian citizen born on the island of Samos in 341 BCE, Epicurus lived an itinerant life as a soldier, student, and schoolteacher before settling in Athens in 306 BCE. He purchased a large house there, "the Garden," where he gathered adherents and launched his own philosophical school. He wrote prolifically until his death in 270 BCE, producing perhaps as many as three hundred papyrus rolls, more than any previous Greek philosopher. But of this tremendous output, just a few fragments remain. As with Zeno, the accounts of later followers—notably the Roman Epicurean Lucretius—are central sources for understanding his influence and his thought.

Despite these lacunae, it is possible to speak with some assurance of the general teachings of Zeno and Epicurus, and of the schools they founded. Both retain the Platonic and Aristotelian emphasis on human beings' responsibility for happiness. Unlike the chastened Croesus and the chastised heroes of the tragic stage, Zeno and Epicurus believe that fate and fortune are ours to control. "I have anticipated you, Fortune," Epicurus affirms, "and have barred your means of entry. Neither to you nor to any other circumstance shall we hand ourselves over as captives."[69] The Stoics, similarly, refuse to cede themselves to the centurions of fate. Happiness is our own possession, they argue, even when we have nothing else.

This message resonated in the changing social and political context of the late fourth and early third centuries BCE. The rise of the empire of Alexander the Great, and its rapid fragmentation following his death, had shattered the comparative order and cohesion of the Greek polis. The ensuing Hellenistic period, which dates roughly from Alexander's death until the consolidation of Rome, witnessed the decline of the intimate, self-governing city-state and its gradual replacement by sprawling, multicultural empires and vast, anonymous urban centers. In this setting of disruption and dislocation, scholars have long argued, men and women were apt to experience a heightened sense of powerlessness and cultural anomie, which rendered them particularly receptive to the agency and control preached by Stoics and Epicureans alike. Each offered their followers the comforting belief that they could retain power over their lives in increasingly complex and impersonal worlds. Though democracy was no longer—

banished from the world for the following two thousand years—its early emphasis on self-sufficiency lived on in the hope that men and women could make happiness for themselves.

In this respect, Epicureans and Stoics remained true to, and even accentuated, the Socratic stress on the immunity of happiness to luck. But both schools also broke sharply with their classical predecessors. In the case of Epicurus, this is most apparent in his unapologetic insistence that "pleasure is the beginning and goal of a happy life."[70] We are drawn to pleasure naturally, he believes, just as we naturally flee pain and disturbance. Rather than fight against nature in the search for happiness on high, we should accede to its power; nature will lead us to our destination.

Epicurus's insistence on the centrality of pleasure—an insistence with roots in other Greek traditions but at odds with the Socratic, Platonic, and Aristotelian precedents—is based upon his radically materialist understanding of physics. In Epicurus's view, the universe is composed entirely of combinations of matter and void, atoms and emptiness. Although he grants that there are gods, immortal and blessed, he believes that they never concern themselves with the functioning of the world or of those who live within it. It makes no sense, consequently, to speak of Providence or Platonic forms, divine intention or an immaterial soul. Like everything else in the universe, human beings are merely assemblages of matter, and consciousness is but complex atomic motion. For Epicurus, it follows directly that sensations are not only the source of all experience but also the source of all good and evil. What causes pleasure is good, and what causes pain is bad. That is nature's way.

Zeno also urges his followers to order their lives "in agreement with nature," but he conceives differently of this slippery concept.[71] For him, the universe is not a random chaos of matter in motion but an orchestrated, harmonious whole, ordained by Providence and permeated by an underlying reason that the Stoics call *logos*. Appearances to the contrary notwithstanding, the world is ever as it should be, guided by a purposeful creator who gives the universe meaning, even when we cannot discern that meaning directly. Seeing that the universe is rational, and that human beings are part of this ordered realm, Zeno enjoins his followers to bring their individual natures into harmony with nature as a whole.

The way to this end is virtue. By living virtuously, we order our lives in keeping with the order of the world, and it is from this rational correspondence that happiness is born. Deeply indebted to Socrates in this respect, Zeno goes well beyond Aristotle to make virtue the sole constituent of happiness. All "secondary" goods—riches, honor, birth, beauty—are irrelevant, indifferent to the highest good. In direct contrast to the Epicureans, the Stoics reject even the importance of pleasure and pain. "The happy man is content with his present lot, no matter what it is," Seneca maintains.[72] Cicero goes so far as to argue that the man of perfect virtue will be happy even under torture, even on the rack.[73] The well-being of the happy man is completely impervious to the cruelest twists of fate.

On the surface, these two schools could not be more at odds, apparently justifying our current use of the terms "stoic" and "epicurean" to refer to, respectively, one who is "indifferent to pleasure or pain," and one who is "devoted to sensual pleasure."[74] Such contemporary definitions are misleading, for they hide the essential similarities of the schools. When we look beyond the surface, we begin to take note of a crucial convergence.

Most important, both Epicureanism and Stoicism are ascetic doctrines, demanding the strict regulation of desire. Despite our modern definitions, Epicurus never taught hedonism. As he says explicitly in one of his extant fragments:

When we say that pleasure is the goal, we are not talking about the pleasure of profligates or that which lies in sensuality, as some ignorant persons think . . . ; rather, it is freedom from bodily pain and mental anguish. For it is not continuous drinking and revels, nor the enjoyment of women and young boys, nor of fish and other viands that a luxurious table holds, which make for a pleasant life, but sober reasoning, which examines the motives for every choice and avoidance, and which drives away those opinions resulting in the greatest disturbance to the soul.[75]

Pleasure, in other words, is defined negatively as the absence of bodily pain (what Epicurus called the state of *aponia*) and the absence of mental anguish or anxiety (the state of *ataraxia*). These are the true goals, and to reach them, he counsels "sober reasoning," or what he refers to elsewhere as "prudence," the cultivation of knowledge of the world and knowledge of oneself. We must understand, for example, the physical laws of the universe so as to rid ourselves of unnecessary fears caused by false beliefs: the vengeance of the gods, the horrors of the afterlife, and other spurious notions that exist only in our minds. It is not surprising that thinkers in the eighteenth century would later seize on this Epicurean theme—stressed to great effect by Lucretius —to help justify their own view that "superstition" was antithetical to happiness.

From Epicurus's perspective, prudence also involved knowledge of self or, more properly, the knowledge of desire. Why do we long for this or that? Will short-term satisfaction be offset by long-term pain? How is it that we choose to refrain from a certain opportunity but follow another? What draws us forward, and why? If we are honest with ourselves, Epicurus believes, probing and unsparing in our answers, we will see that the vast majority of our desires are idle or empty, irrelevant to the health of the body or the peace of the mind, the final goals of a happy life. The singular task of the Epicurean acolyte is to learn how to winnow and sort, separating the necessary desires from those that will lead us astray. Self-knowledge, like knowledge of the world, enables us to free ourselves from the sources of pain.

Although this is a complicated process, the essential point is that Epicurus believes our necessary desires to be extremely limited: The requirements for happiness are few. "The voice of the flesh cries, 'Keep me from hunger, thirst, and cold!'" Epicurus writes. "The man who has these sureties and who expects he always will would rival even Zeus for happiness."[76] Food and drink—*frugal* food and drink, for "plain dishes offer the same pleasure as a luxurious table"—shelter, and a modicum of security should be enough to satisfy anyone whose desires are properly in order. By contrast, "He who is not satisfied with a little, is satisfied with nothing."[77] Here and elsewhere, Epicurus sounds surprisingly Stoic, even observing in one instance that "all physical pain is negligible: that which is intense lasts but a brief time, while chronic physical discomfort has no great intensity."[78] It is not without reason that Seneca later concluded the "teachings of Epicurus are upright and holy and, if you consider them closely, austere." His "pleasure" was, in truth, "sober" and "abstemious," wholly in keeping with virtue.[79]

Seneca was admittedly an indulgent Stoic—he devotes much of his own essay on happiness, "De Vita Beata," to defending his wealth and luxurious lifestyle. But his ruminations on Epicurus's austerity and the suggestion of similarity with the tradition of Zeno are worth considering, for they cut to the heart of what was originally most innovative about both schools of belief. Epicurus, no less than his Stoic counterpart, taught that happiness is a function of the ratio of satisfied desires to desire. By radically restricting the number of our total wants, we help ensure our ability to satisfy them in full, decreasing as much as possible our dependence on all that is not within our power. The same ascetic move is what lies behind the Stoic injunction to restrict our passions and emotions, conceived by Zeno as "irrational and unnatural movement in the soul," or "impulse in excess."[80] If we are angry at our inability to achieve fame, frightened by the prospect of disease, frustrated by the failure to fulfill our sexual appetites, or annoyed by the actions of others, it is probably because we have put our confidence in places it should not be. At this juncture, we can do one of two things: either expand our means to attain our desires or reduce our desires to suit our means. "That which is happy," Epictetus affirms, "must possess in full all that it wants, must resemble a person who has achieved his fill—neither hunger nor thirst can come near it."[81] And as he and Epicurus emphasize, the surest way to protect oneself from hunger is to stifle all cravings, to give up one's appetite.

It is this effort above all—the attempt to make happiness completely independent of external goods—that lends insight into why these two philosophies were conceived, and subsequently flourished, in complex social and political environments in which little beyond one's own reaction to circumstances could be completely controlled or counted upon. In this respect, the teachings of Zeno and Epicurus are a fitting response to the heightened anonymity, uncertainty, and complexity of the sprawling empires that succeeded the polis in the Hellenistic age. But just as importantly, they are a response to the impossible demands raised by the teachings of their predecessors. Socrates, Plato, and Aristotle may have taught that happiness was no longer the preserve of the gods, to be bestowed or withheld at will; yet in practice, they were remarkably pessimistic about the attainability of this end, for all save the godlike few. Having implanted an ambiguous desire in the human breast, they failed to entirely appease it, leaving us perpetually wanting, yearning, unfulfilled.

Epicurus and Zeno respond to this new form of human malady with drastic medicine, aiming to cure us of unfulfilled longing. If the "school of a philosopher is a surgery," as Epictetus observes, then theirs is one of invasive procedure in which festering needs are cut out to make us fit for our final end.[82] This is a radical treatment, for in essence it seeks to fulfill the desire for happiness by eradicating desire itself. What sort of medicine is this, we are forced to ask, that aims to make us happy by stripping us down to our barest needs, rendering us impervious even to torture? We are left to decide what is more severe, the sickness or the cure. Does such therapy ask of us too much or too little?

It may be wondered how many were successful in achieving this dramatic state of renunciation. In the case of Epicureanism, the rigorous demands of the master were frequently neglected in favor of a much cruder hedonism that Epicurus would have abhorred. Stoicism posed even further problems of fulfillment. Cicero can say that "heaven willing, philosophy will ensure that he who has obeyed its laws . . . will always be a happy man," but he adds immediately that the question of "how far philosophy actually *keeps* this promise" is another affair. In his view, "the mere fact that the promise has been *given* is already a matter of the very first importance."[83]

Large numbers of men and women living in the ancient world undoubtedly agreed, a fact that underscores what is perhaps the most significant contribution of these two schools. From the beginning,

Epicureans and Stoics offered their medicine to any who would take it. Whereas Plato and Aristotle restricted happiness to the privileged few, Epicurus and Zeno proposed to make gods of many, the former accepting women and slaves into his garden, and the latter preaching the natural kinship of all humankind. As either matter in motion or emanations of *logos,* all were potential candidates for the salvation of happiness, and many presented themselves as aspirants. By the time of Jesus, there were Epicurean communities throughout the Mediterranean world, and 450 years after Epicurus's death, the Garden was still functioning. Stoicism, too, spread to become virtually a Roman state religion, enlisting peasants and artisans, politicians like Cicero and Seneca, emperors like Marcus Aurelius, and slaves like Epictetus. With reason are Epicurus and Zeno regarded as founders of two of the greatest schools of Athens, surpassed only by Plato and Aristotle.

The Parting of Ways

Sometime in the late fifth century BCE, Prodicus wrote a tale. A contemporary of Socrates, possibly his early teacher and assuredly his later rival, Prodicus belonged to a loose school of philosophers known as the Sophists. In the opinion of their detractors, the Sophists argued less for the sake of truth than for the fees they received to argue, a practice that Socrates abhorred. And so, although Prodicus figures in a number of Plato's dialogues, he is generally presented in a somewhat disparaging light.

The *Symposium* is no exception. When, at the beginning of the dialogue, Eryximachus proposes that every guest make a speech in praise of Eros, he compares the task to the sort of eulogies once conducted in praise of the legendary heroes and gods. "Prodicus," he says, "does that sort of thing beautifully," referring to the type of tale that he was known to write, of which the most famous was the tale in question, *The Choice of Hercules.*[84] The compliment is barbed, for Eryximachus adds that he has also read eulogies of salt and other "such trifles," implying that Prodicus's choice of subject—the mythological heroes and gods of old—is not only outdated but fundamentally misconceived. The urgent matter of the day, the speaker believes, like Socrates and Plato, is neither the nature of trifling matter, nor the matter of mythical beings, but the real forces that shape our lives, leading us to happiness.

Plato had other reasons to dislike Prodicus beyond his choice of subjects for praise. Ranging from his Sophism to his rivalry with Socrates, the list might possibly bear another. For it is perhaps not altogether fanciful to suppose that the barbed allusion in the *Symposium* extends beyond Prodicus's person and the subject of his praise to *The Choice of Hercules*, a work whose defining episode involved an opposition that Plato and Socrates were intent on destroying.

Consider the nature of the tale. At a critical moment in his life, the young Hercules comes upon two women at a crossroads, both of extreme stature. One is Virtue (*aretē*), chaste and pure, dressed in white; the other is voluptuous, dressed like a whore. As Hercules approaches, the latter rushes to meet him, crying, "I see that you are in doubt about which path to take in life. Make me your friend; follow me, and I will lead you along the pleasantest and easiest road. You shall taste all the sweets of life; and hardship you shall never know." When asked her name, she replies, "my friends call me Happiness [*eudaimonia*], but among those who hate me, I am nicknamed vice" (*kakia*).[85] After hearing her plea, Hercules turns away, choosing the more difficult road, the well-worn tragic path that leads to unavoidable suffering and pain. This, truly, is a hero's task. Virtue may well be Hercules's reward, but in keeping with the ancient wisdom of the tragic tradition, this hero will not be happy. He cannot make himself so.

This is today the road less traveled. And though it is tempting to add that Hercules's choice made all the difference, in reality nothing could be further from the truth. The mythical tale is noteworthy primarily as an illustration of a parting of ways, a last deviation from the dominant path followed in the centuries to come. It may not be until the end of the eighteenth century, with the philosophy of Immanuel Kant, that a thinker would again so radically oppose happiness to virtue. Already in Prodicus's time, Socrates and his followers undertook to unite them, to make them coincide. Few since have dared to call

Albrecht Dürer, *Hercules at the Crossroads*, ("Der Hercules"), c. 1498–99.
Fine Arts Museum of San Francisco, Gift of Col. David McC. McKell.

happiness a whore. And fewer still have believed that in pursuing it, they would lead themselves astray.

Far more characteristic of the road taken is a slightly later tale, the so-called *Pinax* or *Tabula*. Often attributed to another contemporary of Socrates who figures in Plato's dialogues, Cebes of Thebes, the work was in fact written centuries later, by an unknown author influenced by the Stoics. The tale chronicles a moment on a journey in which a group of pilgrims arrives at the temple of Saturn and engages with its wise old keeper about the meaning of a picture on the wall. The vast tablet, they learn, is an allegory of human life, depicting the route of those who aspire to live it well. Full of false paths and guarded enclosures, the painting is organized in walled concentric circles, in each of which dwell men and women who have been led off track by one of life's many deviations: fortune or avarice, luxury or grief, ignorance or intemperance, false learning or opinion, to name only a few. In the innermost circle, at the height of all virtues, sits a "sedate, comely woman, upon a lofty seat, in a liberal but plain and unaffected dress, crowned with a flourishing crown, in a very beautiful manner."[86] She is happiness herself, the queen of virtue, attended by fortitude, justice, integrity, modesty, decency, freedom, abstinence, and those intrepid travelers who have chosen to enjoy her reign. The contrast with Prodicus's work could not be more striking. Here, happiness *is* virtue. All who fail to serve her, in a manner of speaking, are whores.

It seems somehow appropriate, or at least in keeping with the dominant history of the West, that *The Choice of Hercules* was lost. It survives only in pieces and in name. The *Pinax*, by contrast, weathered time in at least thirteen Greek manuscripts that, although scattered in the chaos of late antiquity, resurfaced in the hunt for ancient texts carried out during the Renaissance. Convinced that the work's author had learned happiness and virtue directly from Socrates, fifteenth- and sixteenth-century scholars translated the tale into countless European languages, cultivating and Christianizing it in the process. Often used as a model for elaborate engravings and an illustration of the correspondence between image and word, the work remained popular well into the eighteenth century.[87]

The triumph and endurance of this anonymous text symbolizes perfectly the triumph and endurance of a classical ideal. By the time of its authorship, and for many centuries thereafter, men and women chose the way to happiness as a matter of course. That they were prepared to do so—to set out in the conviction that they might reach this end largely of their own volition—is one of the highest achievements of

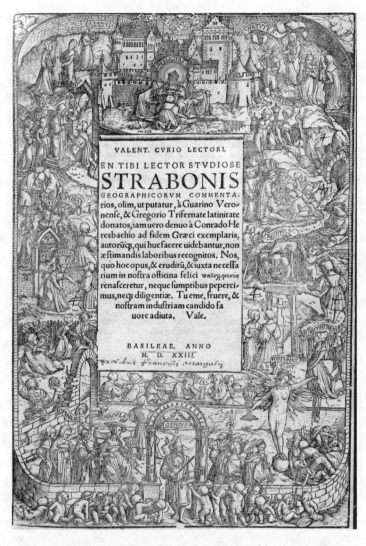

The title page to a 1523 edition of the works of Strabo, the first-
century Greek geographer, with commentary. The border is an
engraving by Hans Holbein the Younger of Cebes's Tablet, with
Happiness (Felicitas) reigning supreme at the top. [Beinecke Rare
Book and Manuscript Library, Yale University.]

the classical world. The fork in the road had been abolished. The task of the hero, the man of virtue, was no longer to turn aside, conceding tragically like Croesus that "no one who lives is happy." The task was rather to carry on, becoming godlike, blessed and happy of one's own accord. Happiness was not in conflict with virtue. Happiness was virtue's reward.

This departure, this change in direction, is profound. But though its importance is difficult to overstate, it should be qualified, for few figures in the ancient world ever discounted entirely the daimon in *eudaimonia*—that chance or divine element in human affairs that defies even our most careful calculation and planning. Enough of the older tragic sentiment remained to console men and women in their pain. If happiness was now a possibility, it was still rare.

As we shall see, it was only in the eighteenth century that human beings took upon themselves exclusive responsibility for happiness, casting aside both God and fortune, severing the ties that had long held happiness to forces over which we have no control. Perhaps it was this refusal (perhaps an inability) to bear the total burden of happiness that sustained the ancients in their vaunted fortitude, protecting them against what is a peculiarly modern onus: the weight we pile upon those who not only suffer but suffer for their *failure* to be happy. It is doubtful whether the ancients ever cultivated this form of guilt, although as early Christian missionaries would discover in the first centuries after the death of Jesus, guilt in its more general forms was a temptation to which the ancient world was by no means immune.

We will return to this story. What should be stressed here is that in the space of roughly two hundred years—from the middle of the fifth century to the middle of the third century BCE—ancient Greek thinkers elevated the idea of human happiness to a privileged place in the hierarchy of ends. Picked up in turn by their Roman successors, it would remain there, virtually unchallenged in the West, until the time of Christ. To be sure, Greeks and Romans alike disputed the means to happiness. But as we have seen, the most powerful currents in ancient thought—the four great schools of Athens—shared fundamental assumptions. All could agree that happiness was an objective rather than a subjective state, to be measured in lifetimes, not in moments. Less a function of feeling than of rational development, happiness was virtue's compensation, the harmony of a well-balanced soul. Pleasure might accompany it, surely, but on the whole, sensual enjoyment was viewed even by Epicurus with a certain skepticism and even outright disdain. The product of perpetual craft, happiness required discipline and hard work, conducted always under the hand of reason. For the ancients, the achievement of happiness was an immensely difficult task, yet one regarded as the natural telos of human life.

Looking back on these classical conceptions from the distance of over two millennia, we see them imperfectly, through the glass of our own assumptions. Viewed in this way, the schools' suspicion of pleasure— their efforts to discipline the passions in the pursuit of a higher end than evanescent emotion—may strike many as odd. More inclined to think of happiness as *feeling* good than *being* good, the modern observer is apt to wonder whether there is not something distant, something intangible and even cold about this rational happiness that scarcely dares to crack a smile.

The inability to see clearly may be a mirror in its own right, a reflection of the limits of our own assumptions. And yet it is fair to ask whether this lack of lucidity is merely a result of the remove of time. Did not the ancients themselves struggle to see their highest end? It is revealing in this connection that for all their emphasis on the happiness of mortals, the ancients resorted time and again to analogies with the divine, likening the happy state to the transcendent. "You shall live as a god among men," Epicurus promises, ensuring that the happy man "is not like a mortal being."[88] A life of happiness for Aristotle, as for Socrates and Plato before him, was "a god-like life," "superior to the human level," and as such, difficult for mere mortals to conceive, let alone attain. Ever on the horizon, just beyond the sight line, blurry and indistinct, happiness continued to entice. But in the rarefied air of the classical schools, many lost sight or lost their way, while many others were never admitted at all. Left to wander on life's devious paths beyond the confines of these inner sancta, they searched for happiness where they could, until it was found—refound—in the face of God.

2

PERPETUAL FELICITY

Hic Habitat Felicitas. Here dwells happiness. The words, like the image they annotate, are well preserved. Carved in red-painted travertine, carefully suspended on the wall of a bakery in Pompeii, they remained there for centuries, packed in ash by the eruption of Mount Vesuvius that buried the city in 79 CE.[1] They are a vivid reminder that although higher happiness may be elusive, many people at many times have sought felicity much closer to home.

Rome. The very name suggests power and prosperity, glory and grandeur, earthly majesty and might. There are strong connotations of discipline, too, of course—the fortitude and sacrifice of the legions as they manned the frontiers, extending the borders of a tiny central-Italian republic at the end of the sixth century BCE outward into a dominion that, by the time of Christ, held sway over much of the world. And there are suggestions of decadence, the fabled fiddling of Nero as his city burned, the jeering excess of the Circus, the outrages of Caligula, the vomitoriums of the patrician class. But lying somewhere between these two extremes, and running somehow throughout, is the *via media* of simple satisfaction, a delight in life's comforts and the basic pleasures of existence that is evoked so candidly, so unabashedly, by the crude lines of this proud Pompeian penis.

Hic Habitat Felicitas, "Here dwells happiness," National Archaeological Museum, Naples. Photo: Alinari/Art Resource, NY.

The *fascinum*, as the Romans called the phallus, was a symbol of prosperity, fertility, power, and luck. Much like the horseshoe in later times, it graced the entryways of a good many Roman buildings from at least the second century BCE, serving as an offering, an invitation, and a charm to ward off bad fortune, while summoning the simple but essential fruits of existence: security, bounty, fecundity. The connection with *felicitas* was straightforward. For though this word derived immediately from *felix*—meaning lucky, fortunate, or successful—the radical sense of the term was "fertility."[2] Closely associated with fruitfulness, *felicitas* implied the presence of a life-giving force, a *dynamis* peculiar to plants, persons, or objects that radiated outward and could be absorbed by others, or taken in. *Arbores felices* ("happy trees," trees of good fortune) were commonly incorporated into fecundity rituals as a way to promote abundance and growth. And at Roman weddings, witnesses frequently expressed their good intentions to the newlyweds with cries of "Feliciter" or "Felicia"—good fortune and fecundity, happiness and success!

In a similar connection, Plutarch recounts the tale of Valeria, the beautiful temptress who, in passing the Roman general Sylla Felix at the theater, placed her hand directly on him and explained, "I too wish to partake a little in your felicity (*felicitas*)."[3] Like animal magnetism, Sylla's felicitas—his sexuality, good fortune, and prowess in battle—was seen as a vital, communicable force. Valeria later attempts to get closer to the source itself by sleeping with the famed general, a scene that calls to mind Marlon Brando's infamous remark in Bernardo Bertolluci's film *The Last Tango in Paris*. "Your happiness is my happenis," Sylla might also have said in good conscience. The connection would not have been incongruous.

Playing on the direct association between felicity and fecundity, the penis of Pompeii was thus perfectly placed in a Roman bakery of the first century CE, bidding bread, and other living things, to rise and fill with life. Despite what to modern eyes may seem its somewhat shocking manner of presentation, the fascinums' associations with happiness—abundance and good fortune, procreation and power—were hardly without precedent in the ancient world. The Greeks of the epic age had described those who were *olbios* or *makarios* as not only rich in *eutychia* (good luck, the direct Greek translation of the Latin *felicitas*), but also rich in the things of this earth. That same precedent prompted Aristotle to include a number of these attributes—wealth, security, ample offspring, luck—in his list of "the features that people look for in happiness" when they considered it in everyday terms. Even the comparatively otherworldly Plato understood the powerful bonds that connected *eros* to *eudaimonia,* and in many other religious and philosophical traditions such associations were common.

Still, the Roman concept of *felicitas* is noteworthy for its particularly candid expression, its frank avowal that worldly pleasures and powers were signs of the beneficence of the gods. In the late Republic and early Empire—as Rome attained the commanding heights of its prosperity and dominion—this expression grew even bolder still: Felicitas was worshipped directly as a goddess.[4] In the years 151 and 150 BCE, the wealthy official C. Licinius Lucullus established a temple in her honor in the Velabrum, the valley in Rome between the Capitoline and the Palatine Hills. His grandson, the Roman consul L. Licinius Lucullus, expanded it considerably, and then in 44 BCE Julius Caesar authorized construction of another near the Curia Hostilia, the meeting place of the Roman Senate, so accentuating Felicitas's proximity to power.[5] Official feast days and sacrifices—Festivals of Felicitas— were regularly held in the goddess's honor.[6] And during the reign of Galba in the first century CE, Felicitas began to appear on the back of Roman coins in complement to the image of the emperor, often as Felicitas Temporum ("The Felicity of the Times") or Felicitas Publica ("Public Prosperity"). Generally depicted with her trademark caduceus, a wand coiled by a serpent that symbolized peace, and a cornucopia bursting with fruits of the harvest that symbolized bounty, the goddess circulated through the realm. Diffusing wealth and good fortune, peace and security, fecundity of the womb and of the field, Felicity united public power and private prosperity under the aegis of the Roman state.

Yet if the cult of Felicitas suggests something of the Romans' ease in their earthly city—an untroubled satisfaction with the things of this world—we should not suppose that their comfort went unchallenged or was ever entirely undisturbed. Well before the Romans conquered

Felicitas Temporum on a coin bearing the image of the
Emperor Vespasian (69–79 CE), © copyright the
Trustees of the British Museum.

A Seated Felicitas Publica on a coin bearing the image
of the Emperor Hadrian (117–138 CE), © copyright the
Trustees of the British Museum

Greece in the second century BCE, they had looked upon their classical brethren with high regard, absorbing the teachings of the Platonic,
Aristotelian, Epicurean, and Stoic schools. Cultivated by Roman acolytes and innovative successors such as Cicero, Seneca, and Lucretius,
these teachings ensured that the higher happiness of the Greeks endured to raise doubts about the felicity of pleasure and the efficacy of
daily enjoyments to take us to our end. The same impulse that had
led Socrates to suspect that true happiness lay beyond the vulgar hedonism of the symposium persisted, prompting Romans, too, to question whether all they had in Rome was enough to give them what they
desired.

The legacy of the Greeks was undoubtedly important in this regard,
feeding a stubborn human refusal to rest content in what we have. But
equally important was the spectacle of excess—of having too much
—and in the first century BCE, that spectacle was already apparent
to some, generating deep misgivings about the sanctity of Roman
felicitas.

"The more the money grows the more the greed / Grows too; also
the anxiety of greed," Horace observed.[7] He was, with Virgil, the greatest of the Roman poets, and it is no coincidence that he made his name
in that same remarkable century before Christ, when regret, and a
longing for simpler times, were very much of the mood. Amid unprecedented material splendor, the fall of the Republic, and the civil wars

that followed the death of Caesar in 44 BCE, Horace looked back from his own Augustan age to what he called "the virtues of plain living," the simple traits that he believed had once made Romans strong.[8] Even now they might be cultivated away from the metropolis and its decadent delights:

> Happy the man who, free from cares,
> like men of old still works
> his father's fields with his own oxen,
> encumbered by no debt.[9]

Honest, hardworking, self-reliant, robust, this was the happy husband-man, the Horacian *beatus vir*, a solitary farmer content to work his fields and cultivate his garden with quiet dignity and honor. He draws simple, honest pleasures from simple, honest things: close friendship and warm conversation, wholesome labor and sweat, the soothing delights of nature, a drop of wine. Never taking his life for granted, he understands that what is here today may be gone tomorrow: "Always expect reversals: be hopeful in trouble, / Be worried when things go well."[10] He avoids excess: "That man does best who chooses the middle way."[11] And he is ever satisfied with what he has: "That man alone is happy / And wears his crown secure who can gaze untempted / At all the heaped-up treasure of the world."[12] Above all, he lives each day with fullness, as if it were his last: "So my dear chap, while there's still time, enjoy the good things of life, and never forget your days are numbered."[13] In the celebrated translation of John Dryden:

> Happy the man, and happy he alone,
> Who can call today his own;
> He who secure within can say:
> Tomorrow do thy worst, for I have lived today.[14]

Carpe diem. Seize the day. Press the juice from the grapes of life.

Blending Stoic virtue and self-sufficiency with republican chastity, Epicurean discretion, and a general preference for the Aristotelian middle way, Horace's recommendations for living draw on a loose set of received classical ideals. They reflect a broader Roman eclecticism and willingness to draw freely from the teachings of the classical schools. But they also reflect the concern that the basic values of the Roman character were being lost. Thus does Horace hark back again and again to the oasis of his Sabine farm on the outskirts of the city, dramatizing what he deemed a necessary return to the natural and the Roman's natural return.

> This is what I prayed for. A piece of land—not so very big,
> with a garden and, near the house, a spring that never fails,
> and a bit of wood to round it off. All this and more
> the gods have granted. So be it. I ask for nothing else,
> O son of Maia, except that you make these blessings last.[15]

Here, the happy man is in his element. He feels good in his skin. His needs are few, his nobility complete. Forming nature as he is formed by it, he exudes innocence, well-being, and humble gravitas.

> But as for me, my simple meal consists
>
> Of chicory and mallow from the garden
> And olives from the little olive tree.
>
> Apollo grant that I be satisfied
> With what I have as what I ought to have
>
> And that I live my old age out with honor,
> In health of mind and body, doing my work.[16]

Like the noble Cincinnatus, immortalized by Livy, plowing and spading out a ditch, Horace's happy husbandman embodies a widely shared Roman ideal, conjuring pastoral pleasures and rural retreats, the independence, innocence, and peace of a meditative country life. Much the same can be glimpsed on the horizon of Cicero's musings at Tusculum, his country seat, or seen ambling over the landscape of Marcus Cato's or Marcus Varro's reflections on the pastoral life in *De*

Agri Cultura or *Rerum Rusticarum,* respectively. It is an attractive ideal, and as such, it would provide the backdrop to centuries of Western pastoral poetry, setting the scene as well for the Jeffersonian planter, the English country squire, and countless other embodiments of earthly content.

Yet this same idyll could quickly degenerate into escapist fantasy or an idle dream of a vanished (or expectant) golden age. In Horace's less guarded moments, he is capable of crossing that line:

> So let us seek the Blessed Fields and Wealthy Isles,
> Where every year the land unploughed gives grain,
> And vines unpruned are never out of flower,
> And olive shoots unfailing bud, and set their fruit,
> And dusky fig ungrafted graces its own tree. . . .[17]

Virgil is even less restrained, indulging in the *Georgics* and other works pastoral fancies of rural retirement and boundless fertility:

> O farmers, happy beyond measure, could they but know
> their blessings! For them, far from the clash of arms, most
> righteous Earth, unbidden, pours forth from her soil an easy
> sustenance. . . . The peace of broad domains, caverns, and
> natural lakes, and cool vales, the lowing of oxen, and soft
> slumbers beneath the trees—all are theirs. They have
> woodland glades and the haunts of game; a youth hardened
> to toil and inured to scanty faire; worship of gods and rever-
> ence for age; among them, as she departed from the earth,
> Justice left the last imprint of her feet. . . . Happy is he
> who has succeeded in learning the laws of nature's
> working. . . .[18]

Innocent in and of themselves, these romanticized accounts of an imaginary golden age nonetheless reveal a deep dissatisfaction with the present, a period that was certainly gilded but manifestly less than golden. Horace and Virgil might benefit from the munificence of their wealthy patron, Maecenas, and bask in the accolades of the emperor Augustus. But when they turned their critical faculties from rural retreats to the earthly city around them, they saw much to regret. "As a result of envious greed few people can say that they've had a happy life," Horace observes.[19] Gluttony, licentiousness, concupiscence, and envy. "So it is that we can rarely find a man who says he has lived a happy life and who, when his time is up, contentedly leaves the world like a guest who has had his fill."[20] The image of an age ruled by passions without restraint is the inverse of the idyll of bucolic perfection. If the countryside was an oasis, the city was depraved. This, at any rate, was the image that many would take away: from classical republicans and their imitators down through the eighteenth century, to Christian contemporaries and chroniclers of pagan perversions. Together they read in Roman records of moral decay a self-indictment of the city of man.

But if Romans themselves recognized their divergence from a happy *via media*, it was Christian commentators who did the most to decry the pagan departure from the true road to happiness. Whereas Horace confronted his age with an image of simple country joy and a reminder of what real Roman *felicitas* could be, Christians savaged the idol of earthly satisfaction and content. As Saint Augustine would later demand to know, in mocking classical pretensions to happiness and the Roman cult of Felicitas, "If the pagan books and rites are true, and Felicity is a goddess, why is it not established that she alone should be worshipped, since she could confer all blessings and, in this economical fashion, bring a man to happiness? . . . Does anyone desire anything for any other reason than to secure happiness?"[21]

The rhetorical flourish is instructive: As we shall see, Christian polemicists conceded the end; they disputed only the means. In the Romans' refusal to abandon their false gods, they saw a sign not just of their willful blindness but of the patent insufficiency of Felicitas to deliver what they, like all men, truly desired. "How can a man escape unhappiness, if he worships Felicity as divine and deserts God, the giver of felicity?" Augustine insisted. "Could a man escape starvation by licking the painted picture of a loaf, instead of begging real bread from someone who had it to give?"[22] False bread was what the pagans had to offer, bread that, notwithstanding the promise of a proud Pompeian penis, would never rise and fill with life but could only weigh down with the force of death, leaving the spirit to starve. Christianity alone could satisfy real human hunger in the knowledge that man did not live simply by bread. For those who sought to replace fleeting *felicitas temporum* with a perpetual felicity for all time, the body of Christ was the one true manna of those who would live like gods.

Walking in the Way of the Lord

In the springtime of the year 203, a young North African woman was taken into custody by Roman soldiers in the city of Carthage, in what is now contemporary Tunisia. Twenty-two, of good family, well educated, married, and nursing a child, Vibia Perpetua was charged with violating a decree issued the previous year by the Roman emperor Septimus Severus outlawing conversion to Christianity. Still only a catechumen, as yet unbaptized, she and a small group of companions, including her personal slave, Felicitas, hastened to have themselves ritually cleansed in custody, entering the church in full and so courting the violent death with which they were promptly rewarded. On what is now remembered as March 7, and what was then the birthday feast of Severus's son, Geta, the group was fed to wild animals, mauled, and slain by the sword before jeering spectators in a small Carthage arena. In this way did their flesh become food for pagan pleasure at the very moment that they themselves were taken into the mystical body of Christ.[23]

The persecution of Christians, as of Jews, was by no means an unprecedented phenomenon in the Roman Empire of the early third century. Since the death of Jesus in approximately 30 CE, the extraordinary rise of the new faith bearing his name had drawn suspicion throughout the empire, precipitating a number of persecutory campaigns in places as far afield as Lyon, Rome, and Asia Minor. But those initiated by

Severus were among the first to be carried out on an empire-wide basis and among the first to strike with particular force in Roman North Africa, where budding Christian communities had developed largely in peace.[24] In this respect, the festivities of Carthage set something of an ominous precedent, initiating a wave of orchestrated violence that would continue sporadically for the next century, culminating in the Great Persecution of the emperor Diocletian in the year 303.

At the same time, they introduced pagans, firsthand, to the surprising fortitude of a revolutionary creed. For though the majority of the spectators who gathered on this particular day in March had undoubtedly beheld blood sports before, it is unlikely that any had witnessed a spectacle like that which unfolded on the feast day of Geta. As we are told by a direct witness, Perpetua and her companions "marched from the prison to the amphitheater joyfully, as though they were going to be in heaven, with calm faces, trembling, if at all, with joy rather than fear." When they were scourged and taunted, "they rejoiced at this that they had obtained a share in the Lord's suffering."[25] And when they were persecuted and reviled, they were manifestly glad. Embracing their ordeal with an eagerness that seemed to delight in pain, they greeted death with open arms. By all accounts, the onlooking crowd was uncomprehending. They did not know it, but their response was fitting. For what these men and women were witnessing in the blood and dust of an African spring was nothing less than a radical new vision of human happiness.

Steeped as it is in the primary narrative of suffering, the Christian religion may fail to call happiness immediately to mind. It is, after all, a tradition that has been described appreciatively as the "worship of sorrow," a tradition whose foremost symbol is an instrument of torture.[26] And yet these same facts notwithstanding, the promise of happiness was absolutely central to the early development and reception of the faith. "We are treated as impostors, and yet are true; . . . as sorrowful, yet always rejoicing," the apostle Paul writes to his brethren in Corinth sometime in the early 50s CE.[27] In effect, this was the central paradox of the early Christian experience: The "good news" of Christ's message was precisely his promise of redemption *through* suffering—and through suffering the passage to an eternal felicity different from anything ever known. We need only think of Christ's frequent injunction to "rejoice and be glad" to appreciate that the appeal of this new faith lay in more than just its invitation to participate in the sacrifice of its founder.

Consider the nature of Christ's promise as recorded in the Gospels, particularly in the Sermon on the Mount and the Sermon on the Plain in Matthew and Luke. Set down, many scholars argue, in roughly the years 80–90 CE, each sermon begins with a series of "beatitudes" or blessings, a venerable form so named because of the Vulgate translation of the Greek term with which they begin. *Beati* in Latin, *makarios* in Greek, the terms are often rendered in English as "blessed," although "happy" would serve equally well, as indeed it does in translations such as the French, where "heureux" from the Old French *heur* is used in the canon. More revealing, though, is the original Greek term itself, a word that, as we have seen, was employed by classical authors, including Plato and Aristotle, to signify "happy" or "blessed." Virtually interchangeable with *eudaimon*, *makarios* was frequently used as a direct synonym, although it gradually acquired a slightly more exalted sense.[28] The classically educated reader of the first century, in any case, would not have failed to associate the word with the tradition of Greek philosophy.

Even more immediately pertinent, however, is the fact that *makarios* was also the word chosen by Hellenized Jews in the second century BCE when they looked for an appropriate term to replace the classical Hebrew *asher* or *'ashrê* (אשר) in the Septuagint, the Greek translation of the Jewish Bible (Old Testament). Meaning "happy" or "blessed," *asher* is the term used in the so-called Ashrel, the Hebrew beatitudes that one finds scattered throughout the various books of the Jewish Bible.* "Happy are those who do not follow the advice of the wicked," we read, "or take the path that sinners tread . . . but their delight is in the law of the Lord" (Psalms 1:1–2). Or "Happy are those whose way

---

*"Asher" (Happy) is also the name of the founder of one of the twelve tribes of Israel, the son of Jacob and the maid Zilpah, upon whose birth his mother declares, "Happy am I!" (Genesis 30:12–13). It is probably further relevant in this connection that Asherah was a Canaanite goddess of fertility.

is blameless, who walk in the law of the Lord" (Psalms 119:1). In these cases, the first step to happiness is the step itself.

That connection may be more than just a coincidence or a bad pun. Many lexicographers believe that *asher* is derived from the root *'sr* (in Ugaritic and Arabic, *'tr*), meaning "to go," "to go straight," or "to advance." Others suggest a slightly different root, *ysr*, "to be upright."[29] And though, given the age and evolution of all Semitic languages, etymologies of this sort are inevitably perilous, it is certainly the case that *asher* and its many inflected forms gradually took on meanings close in sense, if not in structure, to both of these roots. Variants of the term are used in the Hebrew Bible synonymously with the noun "step," as when the psalmist writes, "My steps have held fast to your path; my feet have not slipped" (Psalms 17:5), thus rendering the beatitude "Happy are those . . . who walk in the law of the Lord" of special interest.[30] The one who walks here—who advances—is also upright, steadfast in pursuit of the commandments of God.

For all save the crippled and lame, however, there is probably nothing inherently happy about putting one foot in front of the other. So why this close connection? Any answer can only be speculative, but some have suggested that the link with the verb *'sr* points to an act in which believers went in search of happiness. "It was probably the pilgrimage to the temple," one scholar writes. Quite literally, "this act makes believers 'happy.'"[31] Whether or not one is willing in this way to trace the steps of the happy directly to the feet of the Western Wall, it is certainly the case that the nomadic tribes of Israel held movement in particularly high regard. Movement through time, movement through space, movement as a model for the unfolding of humanity—this was the central metaphor of the Exodus narrative, in which a people was formed by marching to its collective deliverance along the route marked out by Moses and the law of the Lord. Behind them lay the bondage of Egypt, and on the horizon lay the happiness of the promised land, a place of peace and rest and abundance, where milk and honey flowed.

Of course, the children of Israel never really get there. No sooner have they begun their journey than they begin to stray, wandering in the desert from the straight path of God. And not long after setting foot in Canaan, they commit "evil in the sight of the Lord," resorting to enmity, unkindness to strangers, the worship of idols, and other sins (Judges 3:7). Milk and honey, as a consequence, do not flow. Spatially, God's people have arrived in the promised land, but morally and temporally, their destination must remain on the horizon. With good reason does the Seder of Passover, the Jewish feast held in remembrance of the Exodus from Egypt, conclude to this day with the saying "Next year in Jerusalem." Even for those already there, deliverance lies in the future, in another place, bidding us to set our course in its direction, to walk in its way.

The term *asher* thus signified happiness in several different senses. At once journey and arrival, it implied the blessedness of living in line with God's commandments, garnering his favor and keeping his ways, *and* the bounty of the final destination, the time when the Lord would once again collect his chosen people in the promised land, ushering in a period of everlasting justice and peace. This ultimate arrival in Jerusalem would bring with it the total salvation and deliverance presaged in Exodus. But in the meantime, the children of Israel must seek to appreciate the journey, observing God's law with fidelity, while rejoicing in the goodness of his creation:

> Happy is everyone who fears the Lord, who walks in his ways.
> You shall eat the fruit of the labor of your hands; you shall be
>   happy, and it shall go well with you.
> Your wife will be like a fruitful vine within your house; your
>   children will be like olive shoots around your table.
> Thus shall the man be blessed who fears the Lord.
> The Lord bless you from Zion. May you see the prosperity of
>   Jerusalem all the days of your life.
> May you see your children's children. Peace be upon Israel!
> (Psalm 128)

This is the happiness of nomads, shepherds, and farmers, the blessings of a people long enslaved and continually at war with hostile enemies and hostile terrain. Not surprisingly, the early tribes of Israel held aloft what the world only grudgingly offered up. A verdant oasis flowing with milk and honey and a plentiful supply of rain were fitting rewards for a parched people who had long wandered in the desert. Like the early Greeks and virtually all traditional cultures, the peoples of ancient Israel conceived of happiness in some measure in material terms. To be happy or blessed was not only to know God's favor, but also to safely enjoy the things that an uncertain world was so quick to deny: prosperity, family, fertility, peace, security, longevity, a good name. In this respect the descriptive epithet of the Hebrew beatitudes was close in meaning to the Greek *makarios* and could even stand comparison with the Romans' more earthly *felicitas*.

Yet there were also crucial differences, and in many respects these are the more important. The Jewish stress on deliverance—the collective deliverance of God's chosen people—presaged a fundamental innovation in the conception of human happiness. When God intervened decisively in human history to deliver his children, the world would be forever changed, transformed out of all recognition, permanently altered. Human beings played an important role in this process, for they would be delivered only when they had arrived. Their ability to "step" forward on the path of God's law was crucial. But it was God's shepherding grace that guided them forward and his decisive intervention that would ultimately transform their lives. The envisioned future reward would be unprecedented in character and kind. Listen as the prophet Isaiah describes this future, in the voice of the Lord:

> For I am about to create new heavens and a new earth; the
>   former things shall not be remembered or come to mind.
> But be glad and rejoice forever in what I am creating; for I am
>   about to create Jerusalem as a joy, and its people as a delight.
> I will rejoice in Jerusalem, and delight in my people; no more
>   shall the sound of weeping be heard in it, or the cry of
>   distress. (Isaiah 65:17–19)

Rather than simply return, that is, to some previously known state, the inhabitants of the new Jerusalem would experience happiness of another metaphysical kind. Many, to be sure, insisted on comparing this happiness to that of already extant idylls—to the joy of a lost golden age, say, or the perfect contentment known in paradise by Adam and Eve. They could hardly do otherwise. But the distinguishing characteristic of the New Jerusalem was that it was just that, new. Always steps ahead on time's horizon, its happiness could only ever be imagined until it was known.

A strange law of perspective operates in such circumstances. "As the promise is postponed," one scholar observes, "so it is also elaborated, heightened, and ultimately transformed. It loses its precise historical and geographical dimensions, but it shines all the more brightly in mental space. The promise becomes utopian."[32] As the prospect of the actual realization of the New Jerusalem receded in time, its importance loomed ever larger. Already in the general period in which Isaiah was writing—probably some two centuries before the Babylonian captivity of the sixth century BCE, when the defeated Jewish people were scattered from the promised land—prophetic voices began to call for, and to predict, the coming of a new leader, a new savior, a Messiah to point the way back to the kingdom of God. In the centuries that followed, other voices joined those of Isaiah and Jeremiah, Ezekiel and Zechariah, Joel and Daniel, hoping to usher in not only the end of the Jewish journey but the end of history itself. For those who heeded such apocalyptic predictions, the culmination of arrival would be the culmination of time, the advent not only of milk and honey but of the free-flowing eternal paradise in which suffering would be abolished forever. Here is one such voice from the first century CE:

And then healing shall descend in dew
And disease shall withdraw,
And anxiety and anguish and lamentation pass from among
    men,
And gladness proceed through the whole earth;
And no one shall again die untimely,
Nor shall any adversity suddenly befall.[33]

It was into this context of prolonged and lavish expectation that Jesus of Nazareth stepped. And though this was only one context of many, its influence was powerful and profound. Whether or not Jesus actually uttered the words that are recorded, long after the fact, in John 14:6, "I am the way," we can be fairly certain that he was greeted by many of his earliest disciples as if he had. Christ (*Christus*), "the anointed one," seemed to these men and women to be the long-awaited savior who would lead in a direction whose path was familiar but whose destination was uncharted. In doing so, he revealed a new truth, a new kingdom, and not least, a new happiness. In form, content, and many of its words, the beatific promise was recognizable. But it was also unmistakably new. Here are the beatitudes as recorded in Matthew:

> Happy/Blessed [*makarios*] are the poor in spirit, for theirs is
> the kingdom of heaven.
> Happy are those who mourn, for they will be comforted.
> Happy are the meek, for they will inherit the earth.
> Happy are those who hunger and thirst for righteousness, for
> they will be filled.
> Happy are the merciful, for they will receive mercy.
> Happy are the pure in heart, for they will see God.
> Happy are the peacemakers, for they will be called children of
> God.
> Happy are those who are persecuted for righteousness's sake,
> for theirs is the kingdom of heaven. (Matthew 5:3–11)

And here they are recorded in Luke:

> Happy/Blessed are you who are poor, for yours is the kingdom
> of God.
> Happy are you who are hungry now, for you will be filled.
> Happy are you who weep now, for you will laugh.
> Happy are you when people hate you, and when they exclude
> you, revile you, and defame you on account of the Son of
> Man.

Rejoice in that day and leap for joy, for surely your reward is
   great in heaven. . . . (Luke 6:20–23)

Access to heaven and dominion over the earth, justice, mercy, the direct experience of God, laughter and rejoicing, the plenitude of a full
belly—this was a lavish promise by any measure, yet one partially recognizable to all who had searched for the promised land on the horizon
of the holy. Those who pursued justice and the way of the Lord would
be given their due, granted mercy and intimacy in the family of God,
allowed to share in the rich legacy of his kingdom. The hungry would
be filled, the mournful would laugh, their gifts would be great.

   This much—the end—was partly familiar to readers of Jewish scripture. But what were the followers of Jesus to make of the means, the
steps that he traced for all who would go happily in the way that led
through him? Whereas earlier sages, both Israelite and Greek, had
counseled the avoidance of suffering as a condition of happiness—
urging their followers to flee, scorn, or simply bear it like Job—Christ
recommends suffering's active embrace. The emphasis is on the promise of future reward: Those who endure pain now will be granted pleasure in a time to come. But the beatitudes, like Christ's ministry as a
whole, also present a baffling injunction. Are we not asked to seek
happiness directly in poverty, in hunger, in tears—exalting even as we
are hated and reviled? And is not suffering itself—with its awful culmination in death—to be treated as the very height of passion? "I
want to know Christ and the power of his resurrection and the sharing of his sufferings by becoming like him in his death," yearns the
apostle Paul, who understands that to suffer for Christ is a privilege
(Philippians 3:10). To seek happiness in sadness, pleasure in pain,
joy in sorrow, ecstasy in death—this was a strange route indeed.

   It was certainly a significant deviation from the main thoroughfare
of the Jewish faith. If the children of Abraham had always been sensi-
tive to the prevalence of suffering, they rarely recommended it as such.
On the contrary, to take innocent enjoyment in the good things of
life—to find pleasure in family, food, love, and wine, community,
music, or dance—remains, to this day, a means of honoring God and

his creation in the Jewish tradition. This is the central message of the Book of Ecclesiastes, composed probably in the third century BCE. Searching for satisfaction in knowledge, pleasure, labor, and toil, the author of the text concludes that all human striving is pointless, despairing in the well-known refrain "Vanity of vanities! All is vanity." "So I hated life," the author writes initially, "because what is done under the sun was grievous to me; for all is vanity and a chasing after wind" (Eccl. 2:17). Crucially, however, this realization leads to a higher wisdom, a greater acceptance of human limitations and God's will. There is a time for everything: to weep and laugh, to mourn and dance, to love and hate. God attends to all.

> I have seen the business that God has given to everyone to be
>   busy with.
> He has made everything suitable for its time; moreover he has put
>   a sense of past and future into their minds, yet they cannot
>   find out what God has done from the beginning to the end.
> I know that there is nothing better for them than to be happy
>   and enjoy themselves as long as they live;
> Moreover, it is God's gift that they all should eat and drink
>   and take pleasure in all their toil.
> I know that whatever God does endures forever; nothing can be
>   added to it, nor anything taken from it. . . . (Eccl. 3:10–14)

God alone is eternal. And so we must fear him and keep his commandments, "for that is the whole duty of everyone" (Eccl. 12:13). But this does not preclude savoring the wholesome pleasures of existence:

> Go, eat your bread with enjoyment, and drink your wine with
>   a merry heart; for God has long ago approved what you do.
> Let your garments always be white; do not let oil be lacking
>   on your head.
> Enjoy life with the wife whom you love, all the days of your
>   vain life that are given you under sun, because that is your
>   portion in life. . . . (Eccl. 9:7–9)

We are urged to appreciate what we have and what we do while we can.

How different, by contrast, is the way marked out by Christ, which seems to lead in the opposite direction. For if the disaffected, the "poor in spirit," are really *makarios,* and if those who mourn are really blessed, are not the men and women who in the common view are "sad" actually happy, and those who are treated as "happy" actually sad? How difficult it is for moderns to fully comprehend those who chose willingly this alternate route, embracing Christ's calling in deadly earnest in the earliest days, seeking beatitude in martyrdom, happiness in torment and grief.

It is in large part for this reason that the account of Perpetua and Felicitas is so compelling. Based on a diary kept in prison by Perpetua

Saints Perpetua and Felicitas, 6th century,
Archbishop's Palace, Ravenna.
Photo: Alinari/Art Resource, NY.

herself, it is an archetype of the genre of personal passion (the *passio*)—
preserved, narrated, and embellished by an anonymous associate who
likely visited the condemned in prison and probably witnessed the
events in the arena firsthand. For no other previous martyrs do we
possess this type of evidentiary window. A chronicle of the willful assumption of Christ's suffering, it is a precious source for anyone seeking to understand the transformative power of this nascent faith.

Peering into Perpetua's world through this tiny crack of a document, we catch sight immediately of the proximity and presence of
God. The anonymous narrator who introduces the tale calls attention
to this from the start, forbidding the reader to think that "supernatural grace was present only among men of former times." On the contrary, God works continually in the world, and he has reserved his most
"extraordinary graces" for the "last stages of time." Citing from the
Acts of the Apostles a passage that in turn is taken from the apocalyptic prophet Joel, the narrator invokes the beginning of the end. "In
the last days, God declares, I will pour out my Spirit upon all flesh and
their sons and daughters shall prophesy and on my manservants and
my maidservants I will pour my Spirit, and the young men shall see
visions and the old men shall dream dreams."[34] The extraordinary
events surrounding the martyrdom of Perpetua and her companions,
the narrator implies, are signs that God is now pouring out his Spirit
in abundance, suggesting that the last stages of time are at hand.

Whether Perpetua herself believed this is not entirely clear. Certainly, in the first generations after Jesus's death, many of his disciples accepted the approaching end of time without question.
Having renewed God's covenant, Christ had died for our sins, but
he would soon come again—apparently in marvelous circumstances.
In the so-called Little Apocalypse of the Gospel of Mark (13:3–37)—
a book generally regarded as the earliest of the four Gospels, written
between 65 and 75 CE—Jesus speaks of an imminent upheaval, sig-
naled by tremendous wars and famines and followed by the return
of the "Son of Man coming in clouds with great power and glory" to
gather the elect (13:26–27). Similarly, the Book of Revelation, likely
written around either the year 69 or 95 CE on the island of Patmos,

weaves together apocalyptic themes circulating in the early Christian community to paint a collective portrait of the *parousia*, the second coming of Christ. Following the great battle at Armageddon, in which the forces of the Lord will do battle with those of the Beast, Jesus will descend to rule on earth for one thousand years (the millennium) before defeating Satan in a final confrontation. At that stage, time will come to an end, heaven will reign on earth, and the elect will be gathered with God in the New Jerusalem, where Eden's tree of life will again bear fruit.

Drawing extensively on the imagery of the Hebrew prophets, writings of this kind grounded the ministry of Christ in centuries of Jewish messianic and apocalyptic expectation, while taking literally the promise recorded in Matthew that "the kingdom of God is at hand" (4:17). Christ, it is true, had also cautioned that no one would know the "day or hour" of his final return, a warning that, as the years passed, seemed to argue against the belief that the *parousia* would occur anytime soon. But the belief was kept alive by religious enthusiasts well into the fifth century, to be revived periodically thereafter.

It is likely that Perpetua's Christian community was of their number. Not only were they well acquainted with various apocalyptic texts (the Book of Revelations, as well as such noncanonical writings of the second century as the Apocalypse of Saint Peter), but they were also probably influenced by a millennial sect, the Montanists, who flourished in Asia Minor from roughly 165 CE.[35] Preaching a cultlike asceticism in preparation for the final judgment, the Montanists believed in the imminent end of the world, crediting the Holy Spirit with imparting new revelations to visionaries in the final days to complement Christ's original teaching. For the Montanists, as for many other early Christians, the Holy Spirit was a living force, manifesting itself in the dreams of the chosen, speaking through Christ's followers in tongues, giving voice to continued prophecy and prediction, suffusing the bodies of its favored recipients. The shaking, quaking presence of which we read today in the Acts of the Apostles was more for these men and women than just the rustling of pages. It was a vivid description of the powerful force moving through their lives.

Regardless of whether Perpetua had direct contact with Montanist teaching, she undoubtedly believed in the immanent presence of Christ. Jesus of Nazareth may have died over a century and a half previously, but he continued to live, bringing men and women to birth daily in the baptismal font, reviving them with his living flesh in holy communion, and breathing new life into their spirits with his own. In miraculous healings and glossolalia (speaking in tongues), in the apparition of visions and wondrous signs, in the revelation of new prophecy in trances and dreams, the Holy Spirit was present to Perpetua in immediate, vivid ways.

This helps explain the eagerness with which Perpetua and her fellows set out willingly on their road to death. For simply by paying token obeisance to the emperor, it bears emphasizing—by denying their identities as Christians—any one of these men and women could have spared themselves their horrible fate.[36] Yet to do so was unthinkable precisely because they viewed the call to martyrdom as a direct solicitation from God, a precious invitation from the ever present Christ to participate directly in his passion, to suffer and die, as did he. This was what Paul had described as the greatest privilege. Neither punishment nor condemnation, the call to martyrdom was, on the contrary, the ultimate mark of divine favor. In the communities of early Christianity, there was no clearer sign that the Holy Spirit had settled on one in the fullness of grace.

But what an immense burden this was to bear. Could one support the weight of the divine presence? Could one shoulder the cross? If martyrdom was a privilege, it was also a trial, the ultimate test of one's worthiness before God. At heart, Perpetua's diary is thus a record of spiritual struggle, a tortured account of her painful effort to pull herself free from the clutches of life.

The hands that would hold her grasped firmly. "While we were still under arrest," Perpetua observes in the very first line of the account written in her own voice, "my father out of love for me was trying to persuade me and shake my resolution."[37] So, too, is she shaken by the visits of her mother, brother, and child. "I was in pain because I saw them suffering out of pity for me. These were the trials I had to endure for many days."[38] Consumed by worry for her infant, whom she is still nursing, Perpetua obtains permission to have the child stay with her in prison while she awaits sentencing. But it is clear that this can be only a temporary expedient. Soon, her father returns to try to bend her again to his will:

> Daughter, he said, have pity on my grey head—have pity on me your father. . . . Do not abandon me to be the reproach of men. Think of your brothers, think of your mother and aunt, think of your child, who will not be able to live once you are gone. Give up your pride! You will destroy all of us!
>
> . . . This was the way my father spoke out of love for me, kissing my hands and throwing himself down before me. With tears in his eyes he no longer addressed me as his daughter but as a woman. I was sorry for my father's sake, because he alone of all my kin would be unhappy to see me suffer.
>
> I tried to comfort him by saying: "It will all happen in the prisoner's dock as God wills; for you may be sure that we are not left to ourselves but are all in his power."
>
> And he left me in great sorrow.[39]

Intriguingly, Perpetua makes no mention of her husband here, or anywhere else, causing us to wonder whether she considers him of those kin who would not be "unhappy to see [her] suffer." Was Perpetua fleeing more than just this world when she chose to go with God? Was her withdrawal from her family tinged with resentment and even anger at their failure to understand her, at their refusal to accept her identity as a follower of Christ?

We should not, though, allow such speculation to distract our attention from the more salient issue: Perpetua's own conviction that what moved her was the will of God. For it was ultimately this deep and abiding sense that fed her courage, that allowed her to break with what, for a young Roman woman, would have been the immensely powerful hold of the paterfamilias. When, at the final sentencing of the prisoners, her father tries to dissuade her one last time, begging, "Have pity on your father's grey head; have pity on your infant son. Offer the sacrifice for the welfare of the emperors," Perpetua stands firm, answering simply, "I will not." And when asked by the Roman official if she is indeed a Christian, she is unflinching: "Yes, I am." In that simple affirmation, uttered in the full knowledge of its final consequences, Perpetua pulls free. Though her protesting father is beaten by the presiding guards, moving her to pity, she is not shaken as before, but departs with the other prisoners "in high spirits," joyfully (*et hilares descendimus*). When later she learns that her child will not join her again, having been successfully weaned, she accepts this calmly as God's will. "So I was relieved of any anxiety for my child and of any discomfort in my breasts."[40] It is difficult to imagine a clearer, more poignant, illustration of Christ's awesome injunction in Matthew 10:37: that whoever loves father or mother, daughter or son "more than me is not worthy of me"; and that "whoever loses his life for my sake will find it" (10:39).[41]

But just what exactly did she and her companions hope to find? Most immediately, they could expect the embrace of a new type of family—a new community—based on radically different premises than any they would have known. Broadly speaking, egalitarian and, broadly speaking, communal, the early charismatic sects of Mediterranean Christendom demanded renunciation—of money, of social ties, of one's past—in return for deep solidarity and intimate support.[42] Undoubtedly, the apostle Paul's claim that in the community of Christ there "was neither Jew nor Greek, slave nor free, male nor female" (Galatians 3:28) was always more complicated in practice than in theory. But in the several generations following Jesus's death, it was a powerful ideal nonetheless. The fact that the well-bred Perpetua could address her newfound companions—including the former slaves Revocatus and Felicitas—as "brothers and sisters" is testimony to this truth. In giving up her old family, Perpetua gained a new one.

Perpetua, moreover, clearly enjoyed a special place in this new community. Very early in the diary, she relates how one of her fellow prisoners approached her with a request: "Dear sister, you are greatly

privileged; surely you might ask for a vision to discover whether you
are condemned or freed." The prisoner asks for nothing less than a
vision from God, and Perpetua is confident that she can provide it.
"Faithfully I promised that I would, for I knew that I could speak with
the Lord, whose great blessings I had come to experience."[43] In direct dialogue with the divine, Perpetua is singled out by the Holy
Spirit, and so is singled out within the community of which she formed
a part. For a young Roman woman, raised in traditions of deference to
men, this opportunity for leadership may well have proved attractive,
as it did for other Christian women of the early church.

Yet ultimately it was something more than just community—and
position within that community—that moved all of these men and
women to join this new, Christian family, to rip themselves free from
their former lives at the price of life itself. In Perpetua's richly evocative dreams, we gain much clearer insight into why.

The diary records four of Perpetua's visions, and a fifth by her companion Saturus. Not surprisingly, all negotiate in one way or another
the tension of their upcoming trial in the arena. Perpetua dreams of
climbing "a ladder of tremendous height made of bronze, reaching all
the way to the heavens." To the sides are attached weapons of various
sorts: "There were swords, spears, hooks, daggers, and spikes; so that
if anyone tried to climb up carelessly or without paying attention, he
would be mangled and his flesh would adhere to the weapons." And at
the foot of the ladder "lay a dragon of enormous size, [who] would
attack those who tried to climb up and try to terrify them from doing
so." With the help of Saturus and "in the name of Jesus Christ,"
Perpetua treds on the dragon's head and is able to make the ascent.[44]

Replete with images drawn, most likely, from scriptural passages
with which she was familiar—the reference to Jacob's ladder in Genesis 28:12, for example, or to the dragon described in Revelations 12—
this lush vision plays out Perpetua's spiritual struggle, enacting and
resolving the anxiety of her approaching ordeal, her quest to go up to
God. In a later vision, this becomes even clearer, with Perpetua dreaming intriguingly that she is a man, naked and rubbed in oil, engaged
in combat with a gladiator of marvelous size. After defeating the

opponent in the arena, she awakes to realize "that it was not with wild animals that I would fight but with the Devil," and that ultimately she would prevail. "I knew I would win the victory."[45]

Such premonitions most likely gave comfort to Perpetua and her companions, easing their worry about their upcoming trial in the ring. Far more concretely, they offered palpable images of what they could expect from a blessed death. The reign of paradise on earth might or might not be at hand, but in the meantime, God would gather his fold in the fields of heaven. At the end of her ascent up the ladder, Perpetua envisions a resplendent resting place for those able to endure the climb:

> Then I saw an immense garden, and in it a grey-haired man sat in shepherd's garb; tall he was, and milking sheep. And standing around him were many thousands of people clad in white garments. He raised his head, looked at me, and said: "I am glad you have come, my child."
>
> He called me over to him and gave me, as it were, a mouthful of the milk he was drawing; and I took it into my cupped hands and consumed it. And all those who stood around said: "Amen!" At the sound of this word I came to, with the taste of something sweet still in my mouth.[46]

Perhaps a reference to the mixture of milk and honey that North African catechumens were given at the time of baptism—their first entry into new life—this "sweet something" is literally a foretaste of what Perpetua hoped to find in the "immense garden" of eternal life. Her companion Saturus is even more explicit, recording in the diary his vision of how he and Perpetua are "carried towards the east by four angels." "Free of the world," they see "an intense light" and know that this is what the "Lord promised us." A "great open space" opens up before them, a garden "with rose bushes and all manner of flowers" and trees as tall as cypresses, "their leaves constantly falling." Fellow martyrs greet them; others play in peace and serenity, shepherded by the Lord:

Then we came to a place whose walls seemed to be constructed of light. And in front of the gate stood four angels, who entered in and put on white robes. We also entered and we heard the sound of voices in unison chanting endlessly: "Holy, holy, holy!" In the same place we seemed to see an aged man with white hair and a youthful face, though we did not see his feet. On his right and left were four elders, and behind them stood other aged men. Surprised, we entered and stood before a throne: four angels lifted us up and we kissed the aged man and he touched our faces with his hand. And the elders said to us "Let us rise." And we rose and gave the kiss of peace. Then the elders said to us: "Go and play."

To Perpetua I said "Your wish is granted."

She said to me: "Thanks be to God that I am happier here now than I was in the flesh."[47]

When Saturus awakes from his vision, he, too, can taste his future. "And then," he writes, "I woke up happy."[48]

Formed from the fertile stock of late Jewish reflection on the afterlife, pagan imaginings of the pastoral bliss of Elysium, and the rich imagery of Gentile scripture, these remarkable visions reveal the extent to which the Christian heaven was assuming vivid shape. Even more basically, they reveal the extent to which the promise of happiness lay at the heart of the early Christian message. *Deo gratias, ut quomodo in carne hilaris fui, hilarior sim et hic modo,* Perpetua observes in Saturus's vision of eternal life. Literally, "Thanks be to God that I am now *more joyful* [my emphasis] than I was in the flesh." Was it not precisely this prospect—the hope of achieving an end to suffering through suffering itself—that steeled the courage of these martyrs, that prompted them to the extraordinary sacrifices they so willingly assumed? Paul, for his part, had known how to draw conviction from his convictions. "If with merely human hopes I fought with wild animals at Ephesus," he writes in his first letter to the Corinthians, "what would I have gained by it if the dead are not raised, 'Let us eat and drink, for tomorrow we die'" (1 Corinthians 15:32). Like Perpetua and her companions, Paul understood that the fleeting pleasures of the world—mortal life itself—was but a small sacrifice to make in return for life eternal. "Now is your time of grief," Christ tells his disciples in the Gospel of John, "but I will see you again and you will rejoice, and no one will take away your joy" (16:22).

This same promise is repeated throughout the New Testament, and its effect is powerful. For to an even greater extent than with the promised kingdom of the children of Israel, the happiness outlined in the beatific vision was at once specific in its suggestion of rich rewards and extremely, luxuriantly vague. Here the imagination could be set free to revel in the delights of the kingdom of God, to fantasize the total fulfillment that would justify one's earthly pains. The ecstatic consummation of divine love, the release, the rapture, the bliss—the happiness of the newly promised arrival would be entire, eternal, endless, and complete. For now it could only be imagined. "What no eye has seen, nor ear heard, nor the human heart conceived," Paul writes in 1 Corinthians, is "what God has prepared for those who love him." Now we see this only imperfectly, "through a glass, darkly, but then face to face."[49] Even the perpetual felicity imagined by Perpetua and Felicitas would be as nothing compared to the real thing.

But this was not only, to borrow a later phrase from Augustine, a "happiness of hope," a compelling promise of future joy, but also an injunction to rejoice *now* in the expectation of that promise's fulfillment—even, or perhaps especially, in the face of great suffering. When Perpetua awakes from her dream, she already tastes the sweetness of new life; when Saturus comes to, he is happy already. "Rejoice and be glad"—today—Christ says in the Sermon on the Mount, "for great is your reward in heaven. . . ." (Matthew 5:12). It is telling that this commandment follows immediately upon the last of the beatitudes in Matthew: "Happy are you when people revile you and persecute you and utter all kinds of evils against you falsely on my account" (5:11).[50] The ecstasy of the imagined reward was commensurate with the intensity of the suffering expended to achieve it.

The beatific vision, then, entailed a decisive turn away from the main paths of both classical and Jewish experience, as well as a frank rejection of the carpe diem hedonism of late Roman *felicitas*. Whereas in the classical account, happiness encompassed the span of a lifetime, Christian beatitude was without end. And whereas classical happiness remained a comparatively cerebral affair—cool, deliberative, rational—Christian happiness was unabashedly sensual in its imagined ecstasies. Feeling, intense feeling, was what flowed forth with Christ's blood, transformed in the miracle of the crucifixion from the fruit of intense pain to the sweet nectar of bliss. The Stoics had suggested that the happy man could be happy *even* on the rack, happy *in spite of* suffering. Christianity took this a step further, proposing that happiness was not just impervious to pain, but its direct outcome and consequence. The rack, the instrument of torture—the cross—becomes the site and symbol of a more general process of conversion, a place of spiritual alchemy where the base metal of human pain is converted into the gold of divine rapture. With good reason is Christ's suffering and death termed the "passion." His infinite capacity to experience anguish is directly proportionate to his infinite capacity to convey the experience of joy.

Thus, the crucifixion—"a stumbling-block to Jews and foolishness to Gentiles," as Paul openly acknowledged (1 Corinthians 1:23)—was treated by Christians as a triumph and cause for exaltation. The momentous site of victory over suffering, death, and despair, the cross was an invitation to participate directly in the passion of Christ. "For to this you have been called," Peter observes to the righteous, "because Christ also suffered for you, leaving you an example, so that you should follow in his steps" (1 Peter 2:21). In doing so, Perpetua and her companions demonstrated their total confidence that Christ had shown the way, and their complete faith in the prize that would complete their journey.

And so happiness—or, in the Latin, *felicitas*—was an intimate, if unlikely, partner in this early tale of Christian suffering, as was Perpetua's servant herself. Of the latter we are told only toward the end of the text that, being eight months pregnant, Felicitas worried that she would be prevented from joining her companions in the arena, for Roman law forbade the execution of expectant mothers. Sharing her fears, her "comrades in martyrdom" prayed for an early birth, hurrying life so that Felicitas herself might die. Evidently, their prayers were answered. Before their encounter in the ring, Felicitas delivered a baby girl, freeing herself to set out with her friends on what they described as "the road to hope." Both literally and figuratively, felicity walked with them, as these *beatissimi martyres,* these "most happy martyrs," walked to their final end.[51]

The Happiness of Hope

Some two centuries later, on the very day of the year that Perpetua and Felicitas had walked to their end, a congregation gathered in the bustling Mediterranean port city of Hippo (now Annaba, Algeria) to spiritually retrace their steps. Throughout North Africa and the greater Roman world, others did the same, retelling the *passio* of the two young women in a rite of remembrance that continues to this day. Still others traveled on Roman roads to the tombs of the martyrs themselves, commemorating Perpetua and Felicitas directly as penitents had done since shortly after their death. Great feasts they held there (*agape*), joyous festivities flowing with food and wine, ardor and exuberance of such earthly intensity that in 397 the Council of Carthage sought to curtail them. The pilgrims continued to come, regardless, taking part in a wider cult of martyrs then exploding across the dying Roman Empire. Drawn by talk of miracles and healings performed at the martyrs' tombs, the pilgrims were moved by a desire to make contact with the divine. For here one stood at the gateway to another life, a place where the pious could catch sight of Paradise itself.

   Those who participated directly in this cult of martyrs considered themselves a lucky few. But the men and women attending feast day services in Hippo possessed a luck of their own. For their bishop in the first three decades of the fifth century was Aurelius Augustinus— Saint Augustine. A gifted orator, he spoke with particular rapture on these days of remembrance. And so, after reading with tenderness from the passio of Perpetua and Felicitas, he reminded his flock of why they had died:

Today we are celebrating the feast of two holy martyrs, who were not only outstanding for their surpassing courage when they suffered, but who also, in return for such a great labor of piety, signified by their own names the reward awaiting them and the rest of their companions. Perpetua, of course, and Felicity are the names of two of them, but the reward of them all. The only reason, I mean, why all the martyrs toiled bravely for a time by suffering and confessing the faith in the struggle, was in order to enjoy perpetual felicity.[52]

Augustine was preaching to a largely illiterate congregation and so spoke more plainly than he otherwise might have done. But his assertion that through their names, Perpetua and Felicitas bore witness to the "gift we are going to receive" was a commonplace of his thought, repeated on successive feast days, and underlined in many of his writings.[53] No other church father, in fact, spoke with such consistency, rigor, and passion of the pursuit of happiness in Christian life.

Born and raised in the North African city of Thagaste, in what is today inland Algeria, in 354, Augustine grew up only several hundred miles from the Carthage of Perpetua and Felicitas, and in fact studied in that city as a young man. The Carthage that Augustine experienced, however, like the Roman Empire as a whole, was a vastly different place from that the two martyrs had known. The conversion of Emperor Constantine around the year 313 had begun the process of transforming Christianity from a persecuted sect into the official religion of the realm, though the steady erosion of imperial power—culminating in the sacking of Rome in 410 by invading German tribes—ensured that no creed ruled with the same force that had once fed martyrs to the lions. The late Roman world of Saint Augustine was a place in which ideas and creeds competed openly for takers like shouted wares in a marketplace bazaar.

Augustine entered this marketplace with no clear idea of what goods he might find. His mother, Monica, was a Christian, and perhaps also a Donatist, a member of an intensely devout, and ultimately schismatic, sect that flourished in North Africa in the late fourth century.

But Augustine's father was a poor, unlettered pagan who nonetheless understood that classical learning was the ticket that carried bright boys to better places. Enlisting the patronage of a local grandee, he managed to send Augustine to school, first in Thagaste and then in Carthage. He died while his son was still a young man, leaving Augustine to seek spiritual guidance where he could. For already Augustine had adopted the prejudice of educated pagans, looking down on the faith of his mother as the fodder of the simpleminded.

Viewed from without, Augustine's intellectual journey in the following years holds to a straight line, leading from his student days to his time as a teacher in Carthage to his march on Rome as an ambitious young man to his seizure of the prestigious professorship of rhetoric in the court city of Milan, at the extraordinary age of thirty. Internally, however, Augustine wandered, zigzagging in search of meaning and of what his classical education led him to believe was his ultimate end. From the moment he read Cicero's encomium to wisdom, the now lost *Hortensius*, in his teens, he made the search for higher happiness his final goal. And he believed, with great faith, that philosophy was the staff that would guide him there.[54]

Augustine covered more ground than most. In fact, his early life is a veritable tour through the schools of late classical learning. He sought happiness in the pages of Cicero and the Stoics. He inquired into the secrets of Epicurus. He wrestled with the legacy of Aristotle, and he engaged the tradition of Plato and his more modern (Neoplatonist) interpreters. He also journeyed further afield, gazing at the stars in the hope of divining his fate in the secrets of astrology. He became a convert to the teachings of Mani, the third-century founder of Manicheanism, an ascetic religion that portrayed the world as a struggle between Matter and Spirit, Dark and Light. And he pushed on with his professional pursuits in the hope that fame, honor, and fortune would bring him what he desired. If Augustine later came to understand the twists and turns of the pursuit of happiness—its psychological highways and emotional cul-de-sacs—it was in large part because he had traveled down so many of those roads himself.

With good reason does much of Augustine's writing—the largest extant corpus of any single author of the ancient world—abound in metaphors of movement. He describes himself as a sailor on a "stormy sea" in search of a quiet port, a wayfarer on "crooked paths" hungry and thirsty for shelter. Augustine was a seeker, and only when he had lost himself on what seemed every available route did he fully appreciate the depths of his misery. As he recounts in a poignant scene in his autobiography, the *Confessions*, it was at the height of his worldly success, on the eve of delivering a major speech in praise of the emperor, that Augustine realized how far from his goal he had strayed:

> As I walked along one of the streets in Milan I noticed a poor beggar who must, I suppose, have had his fill of food and drink, since he was laughing and joking. Sadly I turned to my companions and spoke to them of all the pain and trouble which is caused by our own folly. My ambitions had placed a load of misery on my shoulders and the further I carried it the heavier it became, but the only purpose of all the efforts we make was to reach the goal of peaceful happiness. This beggar had already reached it ahead of us, and perhaps we should never reach it at all. For by all my laborious contriving and intricate maneuvers I was hoping to win the joy of worldly happiness, the very thing which this man had already secured at the cost of the few pence which he had begged.[55]

Augustine understood, of course, that the drunken man's state was illusory, or at best short-lived. Yet he still regarded him "the happier man." Whereas the beggar was flushed with cheerfulness, Augustine was "eaten away with anxiety." And whereas the beggar earned his money for wine by wishing a good day to passersby, Augustine fed his pride by "telling lies" in praise of the emperor's worth. All his learning had proved futile—it was "no source of happiness to me." He wandered in circles. His misery was complete.[56]

Augustine broke free from this labyrinth of despair with his dramatic conversion to Christianity in 386. In the *Confessions,* he goes over in painstaking detail the ground that led him to the garden in Milan where he took his final step. As a consequence, that journey has remained a subject of intense scrutiny ever since. But what is most apparent is how Augustine's conversion responded to the failure of his classical quest. In the future bishop of Hippo's monumental interpretation, Christianity became not only "the way" to happiness but also the way to account for the futility of all other earthly pursuits.

Augustine developed this interpretation slowly, over the course of his entire Christian career. But it is significant that he was already plotting its principal outlines within weeks of his conversion, giving testimony to this fact in his first completed work, the revealingly entitled *De beata vita,* The Happy (or Blessed) Life.[57] Written while he awaited his formal reception into the church in the rite of baptism, the work recounts a series of discussions with his mother and a small group of friends who have joined him at a country house outside of Milan for his birthday. In form, the work is a classical dialogue, likely indebted to Cicero's *Hortensius,* in which Augustine himself assumes the Socratic role and his mother and friends serve as interlocutors. Each morning the small symposium gathers after breakfast, advancing in stages and through dialectical argument toward the final goal of ascertaining the meaning of a happy life. "Neither dependent upon fate nor subject to any mishap," happiness, the group learns, in good classical fashion, must "always endure" and so cannot be "snatched away through any severe misfortune." Intimately linked to the cultivation of the soul and to the attainment of wisdom, happiness is "fullness" or plenitude flowing in such a way that the one who experiences it lacks nothing, knows no want. Those who are happy are "not in need" but are filled with the "supreme measure" of wisdom. To be happy is thus to be suffused with truth, to "have God within the soul," to "enjoy God."[58]

In the final pages of the dialogue, Augustine illustrates this description with two metaphors that reveal his enormous debt to Plato, and to the latter's third-century interpreters, Porphyry and Plotinus. Likening God to both a "fountain of truth" whose waters we crave and a "hidden sun" that pours forth a light detectable only by the eye of the soul, Augustine presents our yearning for happiness as the desire to see without obstruction, a longing to completely satisfy our thirst. He recognizes, however—and this is the catch—that neither of these identical goals is attainable in life. Just as we "hesitate to turn with courage toward [the] light and to behold it in its entirety," unable to stand the intensity of its brightness, so are we unable to drink our fill. In Augustine's view, we cannot receive our "supreme measure" on earth:

> As long as we are still seeking, and not yet satiated by the fountain itself, satisfied, to use our word, by fullness [*plenitudo*], we must confess that we have not yet reached our measure; therefore, notwithstanding the help of God, we are not yet wise and happy.[59]

Destined to continue seeking until the end of our days, we may draw closer to God, see him more clearly. But on the road of life, we will always suffer thirst. Happiness, here, is not our measure.

Conceived in the Christianized language of Neoplatonic philosophy, Augustine's early account of the search for happiness had not yet acquired the theological rigor of his later works. Yet it expresses vividly the truth of his own experience, providing an early account of his discovery that the turn toward God is not an end but a beginning. Pointing Augustine in the direction he would follow for the rest of his life, *De beata vita* paved the way for his greatest work, *The City of God Against the Pagans*. Begun in 413 when he was fifty-nine and completed when he was seventy-two, just five years before his death, *The City of God* consists of well over one thousand pages in modern editions and is without question Augustine's magnum opus. On one level an attempt to explain the unthinkable invasion of Rome in 410—the first violation of the "eternal city" by a foreign army in nearly eight hundred years—the work is at the same time a *summa*, a summary of Augustine's thought. The same reason that explained how the Christian God could allow a calamity on the order of the taking of Rome—and why the false gods of the pagans were helpless to stop it— explained why men and women suffer in this world. *The City of God* is an explanation of evil, and of why the earthly quest for happiness is doomed.

Augustine undertook this sweeping exposition in a number of ways. He provided, for example, a theory of history that accounted for human events in terms of providential logic, showing how God's hand was forever at work in the world, frustrating the pretensions of empires and individuals to independence. Rome had grown mighty not through its own initiative but because it served God's plan. And now God was realizing his larger purpose through Rome's fall, hastening time toward its final end in the day of judgment. When that day would come, Augustine emphasized (like others before), no one could know, and his insistence on the point helped put an end to formal millennial speculation within the church. Still, one could be sure that behind the apparent chaos of human events lay a divine logic, not always discernible to the naked eye but giving order and meaning to the whole nonetheless.

This was the grand explanation. There was another, closer to home. For if the fall of Rome revealed the fragility of all human things, it also exposed what Augustine called the "lust to domination" so long central to Roman rule and now turned back on itself.[60] In the awful specter of the rape and pillage of the eternal city, one witnessed directly the savagery and cruelty that surround us at all times. "Men are plundered by their fellow-men and taken captive, they are chained and imprisoned, exiled and tortured, limbs are cut off and organs of sense destroyed, bodies are brutally misused to gratify the obscene lust of the oppressor, and many such horrors are of a frequent occurrence."[61] This was only the beginning of a list of the "vast mass of evils" that covered the earth, and which had done so continually since the first man and woman fell in the Garden of Eden.[62] In heeding the Devil's temptation, "You will be like gods," Adam and Eve had abandoned the Creator of their own free will, foolishly succumbing to the belief that they could live of their own light, without the light of the Lord. The rest of human history—filled with suffering, loneliness, and despair— served as a rebuke to this primordial presumption and pride.

This was the doctrine of original sin, a doctrine hardly original to Augustine. Virtually all early Christians agreed that something fatal had happened in the Garden of Eden, and that it was through our parents' fault that imperfection had entered the world. Yet they disagreed extensively over the ultimate consequences of this transgression and regarding its final effect on the human race. In one influential view—articulated by Augustine's theological contemporary and rival, the Roman Briton Pelagius—the Fall was not irrevocable but had been undone by Christ. Men and women did not carry sin in their bones, were not irreparably, congenitally marred. On the contrary, they were fully capable of perfection, and it was their duty to realize this end, heeding Christ's call to "be perfect, even as your father in Heaven is perfect" (Matthew 5:48). In the Pelagian view, this was an obligation that could be fulfilled.

Augustine objected deeply to this view, and it was largely as a result of his protracted battle against it that the church condemned "Pelagianism" as a heresy, with monumental consequences for the future of the West. According to Augustine, original sin was no minor transgression but a totally transformative act. Banished from the "unalloyed felicity" of Paradise, Adam and Eve had bequeathed to posterity the just punishment for their crime of pride, setting off a "chain of disasters" that had permanently altered human beings for the worse. "The effect of that sin was to subject human nature to all the process of decay which we see and feel, and consequently to death also. And man was distracted and tossed about by violent and conflicting emotions, a very different being from what he was in paradise before his sin. . . ."[63] Nowhere were human beings now self-sufficient, free of need; nowhere did they live as they wished. When they tried to love with purity, they felt jealousy and contempt. When they struggled for peace, hate reared in their breasts. Everywhere, we were at odds with ourselves. Even our bodies eluded our control. Augustine the young man and Augustine the wizened priest knew that lust "moves or fails to move" our members "by its own right." And though he paused with amusing deadpan to consider the case of those who can produce at will "musical sounds from their behind (and without any stink)," he understood that such impressive bodily control could do nothing to arrest the onset of disease, or to halt our sickness unto death.[64] We were not masters of our selves.

Here was the cause of why Augustine and all others had failed—and would continue to fail—in their quest for happiness on earth. God had condemned humanity to suffer the same punishment as our ancestors who had turned away from him. Vainly, we sought to live by our own light, but in our awkward stumbling in the dark, we were forced to confront the impossibility of that task. Amid the death and suffering of the world, our very yearning for happiness was a bitter reminder of our original sin, a bitter reminder of our own inability to satisfy ourselves. With good reason did Augustine entitle a chapter of his work "True happiness, which is unattainable in our present life."

And so it was in vain that "all these philosophers have wished, with amazing folly, to be happy here on earth and to achieve bliss by their own efforts."[65] Augustine took aim at the "effrontery of the Stoics," who with "stupefying arrogance" maintained that even a man "enfeebled in limb and tormented in pain" would not blush to call this life a "life of happiness."[66] To Augustine, such claims were patently absurd. The heirs of Aristotle and Epicurus, at least, were more honest in recognizing suffering for what it was. But they, too, were preposterous in their efforts to escape it. Like those Romans who worshipped directly before the goddess Felicity, their protestations were pointless.

Augustine reserved words of praise only for the Platonists, reiterating the respect he had shown in *De beata vita,* and which he maintained throughout his life. They alone had directed man's gaze upward. They alone had understood that a transcendent God was the "author of the universe, the source of the light of truth, and the bestower of happiness." And they alone had begun to chart the course toward that "spring which offers the drink of felicity." Such were the similarities between their thought and Christianity, Augustine believed, that he was willing to speculate that Plato himself might have received knowledge of the Old Testament while on a purported trip to Egypt. We know that this was not the case. But Augustine's readiness to entertain the idea is informative, highlighting how difficult it was for this great adversary of the pagans to abandon completely his pagan past. In the Platonic, and Neoplatonic, understanding of the journey of the soul as a return to God—a journey back to the One from which we are separated at birth—Augustine found a compelling model to describe his own struggle to regain a vanished wholeness. He also found a vocabulary readily adaptable to Christian ends. As no shortage of commentators have observed, it was not the least of Augustine's many contributions to the long-term development of Christianity that he infused a strong element of Platonic thought into the faith. In doing so, he helped ensure that the pagan goal of happiness as the rest or completion of the soul remained very much a part of the Christian promise.

Yet if Platonism was the "philosophy that approximates most nearly to Christianity," Augustine fully understood that in the end it, too, fell short of the mark. Like the other schools of the pagan world, the Platonists flirted with the conceit that we could achieve happiness in this world of our own free will. For human beings vitiated by original sin, this was simply not possible; happiness was beyond our control. God alone, through his grace, could transform and heal us. As Augustine emphasized again and again, true happiness was "the gift of God," to be imparted only at death and only to the chosen few.[67]

The disturbing implication of this judgment was that God in his wisdom had "predestined" those who would be saved. And indeed the rudiments of a theory of predestination can certainly be found scattered throughout his works, as Martin Luther and John Calvin, among others, would later observe. But unlike these men, Augustine refused to dwell at length on the mysteries of the dispensation of grace. He spoke rather with passion of what he called "the happiness of hope." Beyond this world and its veil of tears, all Christians could take solace in the thought that they were being led to the Lord, where our journey would be brought to its happy resolution and end. Here the blessed would see God "face to face," see him eternally through the spirit, and all desires would be fulfilled. Absolved of doubts, of fears, of longings, we would be made right again, as our ancestors were in the beginning, when "true joy flowed perpetually from God." There we could drink our fill, perpetually, in the kingdom without end. But until that time we would always suffer thirst.

This vision of life was essentially "tragic" in the sense that it downplayed the role of human agency in determining human fate, and tragic, too, in that it presented earthly existence as invariably steeped in suffering and pain. And yet by transforming the end of existence from a boundary into a gateway opening up onto eternal life, Augustine's account offered a very different take on the tragic adage of old, "Call no man happy until he is dead." In the Christian conception, happiness *was* death, a proposition that dealt a severe blow to the impact of earthly fortune and the vagaries of chance. If, as in the classical reckoning, death completed happiness, as it did for Cleobis and Biton, marking the end of a favored life, in the Christian conception, death was both a culmination and a beginning—the culmination of earthly pain and the onset of infinite beatitude, the beginning of happiness without end. And whereas the classical hero was thus wise to confront existence with continual foreboding—envisioning a happy ending only in hubris or as the unlikely intervention of a god from the machine—the Christian pilgrim could travel with the comfort of hope that he was moving in the direction of a better place. The struggle of the journey was itself a constant reminder that struggle was not in vain, for to suffer was to suffer in righteous punishment, in expiation, in forward movement and progress along the way. The trail of the journey becomes a trial, but also a continual reminder that the pain of each step has a purpose. This is the pilgrim's promise.

When viewed in this manner, the passing landscape of the world need not beckon us to stay. For what a fleeting thing must be the happiness of life when measured against happiness without end. And yet there is another perspective to this same Christian glance, an ambiguity in the tragic regard of Augustine that should give us pause. The same author who speaks in the *City of God* of our mortal lives as a "kind of hell on earth" recounts with reverence the "innumerable blessings" and many "good things of which this life is full." He speaks of man as "a work of such wonder and grandeur as to astound the mind," praising the "remarkable powers" of our reason and the "astounding achievements of human industry." And he reflects with incredible tenderness on the "beauty and utility of the natural creation."

> The manifold diversity of beauty in sky and earth and sea; the abundance of light, and its miraculous loveliness, in sun and moon and stars; the dark shades of woods, the color and fragrance of flowers; the multitudinous varieties of birds, with their songs and their bright plumage; the countless different variety of living creatures of all shapes and sizes. . . . Then there is the mighty spectacle of the sea itself, putting on its different colors like changing garments, now green, with all the many varied shades, now purple, now blue. . . . Who could give a complete list of all these natural blessings?[68]

This is the voice of a man who loved life immensely, who would be sorry to see it go; the voice of a man who felt deeply the loveliness of the universe, who savored at every moment the precious wonder of existence, who delighted in the simple fact of being in the world. True, the world's very beauty and fragility, its transitory passing, and our inability to hold it in our eyes, becomes a further cause of pain. But this is the sweet sorrow of continual parting, the infusion of all experience with the intensity of knowing that one may never come this way again. Despite its inherent sadness, life is a precious gift, and our knowledge of its transience only renders it more so. That, too, is the voice of one who knows that the world is a passing landscape, who knows that "as long as [man] is in this mortal body, he is a pilgrim in a foreign land, away from God. . . ."[69]

Mystical Return

In hoc paradiso, intelligibili incessu deus deambulat. "In this intelligible Paradise, God goes walking." And he asks, *Adam, ubi es?*

Adam, where are you? This is the voice of the creator rebuk-
ing human nature. It is as if He said: Where are you now after
your transgression? For I do not find you there where I know
that I created you, nor in that dignity in which I made you in
My image and likeness, but I rebuke you as a deserter from
happiness [*beatitudinis*], a fugitive from the true light, hiding
yourself in the secret places of your bad conscience, and I
enquire into the cause of your disobedience. Do you suppose
that I do not know what you have done or whither you have
fled or how . . . ?[70]

Though called by contemporaries "John, the Scot," the author of this
ninth-century gloss on the book of Genesis was Irish. Hence the epithet later added to his name, "*Eriugena*," a native of the island of saints.
He was an heir to the treasures of learning that had been amassed in
the monasteries of this island refuge in the sixth, seventh, and eighth
centuries while so much in Europe was either lost or destroyed,
crumbled into pieces like the Roman Empire itself, crushed by the
force of invading Vandals, Huns, Saxons, and Goths. Yet by Eriugena's
time, the ramparts of this scholarly redoubt were themselves exposed, threatened not by the forces that had decimated Rome but
by Northmen, Vikings, and Danes, who began to raid the Celtic fringe
in the late eighth century. Men like Eriugena went where they could,
living like Adam, in hiding, or fleeing abroad as refugees. They brought
with them bits of their precious trove: knowledge of scripture, knowledge of the Latin fathers, and, what was most rare in ninth-century
Europe, knowledge of Greek. As the monk and scholar Heiric of
Auxerre marveled with some jealousy, "Ireland, despising the dangers
of the sea, is migrating almost *en masse* with her crowd of philosophers
to our shores, and all the most learned doom themselves to voluntary
exile to attend the bidding of Solomon the Wise."[71]

The Solomon in question was Charles the Bald, grandson of
Charlemagne and king of the newly consolidated empire of the West
Franks. A patron of the arts, he converted his court into an asylum for
scholars, which emerged in the ninth century as the seat of a substan-

tial revival of letters, the seat of what is now called the Carolingian Renaissance. When Eriugena arrived there sometime around the year 847, he quickly proved himself to be a renaissance man, at once poet, theologian, philosopher, and wit. What separates "a Scot from a sot?" King Charles is said to have inquired of the hard-drinking sage. "Only the table," Eriugena replied.[72] The line is probably apocryphal, but it reflects the indulgence with which Eriugena was received. Appointed by Charles to head his palace school, John the Scot was given leave to ponder the perplexities of Paradise and the revealed word of God.

It was in this role that Eriugena reflected at length on the passage from Genesis referred to above: "They heard the sound of the Lord God walking in the garden at the time of the evening breeze, and the man and his wife hid themselves from the presence of the Lord God among the trees of the garden" (Genesis 3:8). "What is meant by the walking of Him Who is always everywhere?" Eriugena wondered, citing the question of St. Ambrose, who in the fourth century had wondered the very same thing.[73] Was this not a way of indicating the general presence of God? And if so, then was it not also right to say that "there is a kind of walking of God through the sequence of the Holy Scriptures . . . so that when we recall these passages, we recognize the voice of the Lord as he is walking"? God, it would seem, is forever "walking in the minds of men," but we, in our bad conscience and sin, hide in shame, refusing to detect his presence, to return his loving gaze.[74] The question that had haunted Augustine—how to go to God?—gnawed also at this Irish sage, intensified perhaps by the exile's natural longing for return. As Eriugena reflected in a long poem dedicated to his patron, when listening to the scriptures he could hear the voice of the almighty walking, calling us home:

For the God-Word proceeded from the womb of the Virgin—
     in an increase of the light that the darkness of night had
     over-come—
for us unhappy men [*nos homines miseros*], banished from the light of
     paradise,
buried in the darkness of sin formerly committed,

leaving of our own free-will the shining seats of light,
bound down in justice with the chains of unending death.
Thus the mortal race would pay and expiate its debts
and feel the pains deserved by its inflated pride.
The God-Word willed to restore to us and give us back our former
    home.[75]

How human beings, willful "deserters of happiness," could return to
the home they had forsaken of their own free will became for Eriugena,
like all spiritual exiles born of Adam and banished into the world, a
question of the utmost importance.

The question was not new. Central to the early church, it had been
posed in various ways ever since, occupying Augustine, among others,
as we have seen. Augustine's theology of sin was an explicit attempt
to account for our inability to return to the wholeness of our pristine
state—the state of paradise that human beings now recalled imperfectly in their yearning for a felicity that they could no longer realize
or see. Well suited to an increasingly institutionalized church forced
to come to terms with the fact that the kingdom of God was not immediately at hand, Augustine's theology of sin sought to free us from
what he regarded as a dangerous illusion: the "Pelagian" belief, akin
to pagan arrogance, that we could achieve salvation—secure happiness—on our own.

In countering this view, Augustine tried to strike a careful balance
between free will and grace, human agency and the dynamic power of
God. But it was a delicate balance, and in some minds it tipped dangerously close to a tragic fatalism with respect to our position in the
world. As a consequence, long before Luther and Calvin weighed in, at
the time of the Reformation, with their attempt to propel Augustine's
authority further in this direction, figures in the church were devoting critical energy to putting weight on the other side.

Eriugena was one of those figures, and the mid-ninth-century court
of Charles the Bald was a particularly important place for struggle
around the fulcrum. As an interested party observed in a letter to
Hincmar, the archbishop of Reims and a leading figure at Charles's

court: "New superstitions and a damaging doctrine on predestination" had emerged, with voices spreading dubious judgments. Claiming the authority of Augustine, these voices, the letter claimed, argued that "God's predestination applies both to good and bad."[76] Not only, that is, had God in his infinite wisdom prepared the elect for happiness and salvation, but he had allegedly predestined the damned for destruction as well, bringing their souls into existence solely so that they could then be destroyed. *Praedestinatio gemina,* contemporaries called it, "twin predestination." By this view, either we were born to eternal happiness or we were not. The unlucky, no matter how hard they might try, "*cannot correct themselves from error and sin.*"[77]

Whether Augustine himself actually taught this doctrine remains a contested question. But what is most immediately relevant is that already in the ninth century there were people in the church who worried about the dangers that such a doctrine could pose. Double predestination, they argued, not only presented a terrible picture of the true, loving God but also threatened to subvert all efforts at moral and spiritual reform. Undermining free will, it would undermine the church's position as the sole mediator of God's grace, unleashing havoc on the world.

Eriugena weighed into this debate at the urging of Charles, producing in 850 or 851 *De praedestinatione (On Predestination),* a vigorous defense of free will. A complex treatise, the work sought to deny that the authority of Augustine could be used in defense of the doctrine of double predestination, and in that aim it was not altogether successful. The reasoning behind the attempt was tortuous. But Eriugena's conclusions were perfectly clear: "And so with all the orthodox faithful I anathematize those who say that there are two predestinations or a twin predestination or one divided into two parts or a double," Eriugena observed. Just as God's eternal and unchangeable law had "predestined no one to evil, since it is good, so has it predestined no one to death, since it is life."[78]

In making his case, Eriugena had swung to the other extreme—so much so that *De praedestinatione* was suspected of tending too close to the Pelagian heresy, overestimating the power of human agency while

making light of the power of sin. As if to confirm the fact, a number of
Eriugena's other writings were later condemned. But though John the
Scot himself endangered a delicate balance, his general momentum
was consistent with the broader thrust of Catholic doctrine and practice as it was developing in the ninth century, and as it would continue to evolve for the next several hundred years. We had forsaken
happiness, Eriugena argued, of our own free will, but because of this
fact, we could be moved to return to it by similar means. By taking
proper steps to court God's gaze and to accept his grace, we could help
ensure that when he walked among us, his presence would be known.

Eriugena developed this belief throughout his writings, but it was
in a work that was not his own that he did the most to influence the
thinking of those who came after. Again at the bidding of Charles
the Bald, he translated into Latin from the original Greek the whole
of the extant corpus of the writings of a then obscure author by the
name of Dionysius, falsely believed to have been the Athenian disciple of Paul mentioned in the Acts of the Apostles 17:34: "But some
of them joined him and became believers, including Dionysius the
Areopagite. . . ." We now know that the Dionysius in question was in
fact no one of the sort (despite his own claims to the contrary). A prodigious author, he lived much later, perhaps in Syria, and probably in
the sixth century, although that cannot be established for sure. What
is clear is that this so-called Pseudo-Dionysius had read deeply in Platonic and Neoplatonic philosophy, which he blended skillfully with
Christian doctrine to create what he called, in the title of one of his
major works, "mystical theology."

Disparaging the body and all things material, Pseudo-Dionysius
presented the whole of reality—and God himself—as pure, unchanging mind (*nous*), a super essence that encompassed all things but was
not perceptible by conventional means. Only by a process of radical
self-emptying and denial, mental discipline and ascetic purification,
could we train "the eye of the mind" to open to the presence of God.
All who failed to engage in this process—what Plato likened in his
famous metaphor of the cave as an ascent from darkness to light—

would remain utterly blind to God's true radiance. As Pseudo-Dionysius counsels at the beginning of *The Mystical Theology*:

> My advice to you as you look for a sight of the mysterious things, is to leave behind you everything perceived and understood, everything perceptible and understandable, all that is not and all that is, and, with your understanding laid aside, to strive upward as much as you can toward union with him who is beyond all being and knowledge. By an undivided and absolute abandonment of yourself and everything, shedding all and freed from all, you will be uplifted to the ray of the divine shadow which is above everything that is.[79]

To abandon oneself and everything besides may not seem a particularly uplifting message, its central metaphor notwithstanding. But the lure of renunciation and transcendence—the temptation to leave one's sorrows behind and soar above all earthly cares—is rooted deep in the human psyche. Plato himself had put forth a compelling vision of the erotic longing of the soul to merge in ecstatic union with what lay beyond the limits of perceived reality. And when this vision was integrated with an evolving Christian tendency to disparage the body as the host of earthly sin, the result was a powerful impulse to spiritual uplift. Like a thermal wind, it promised to bear aloft all who would raise their minds to higher things, bearing us, as the medieval mystic Hildegard of Bingen would observe, like "a feather on the breath of God."

Already in the fourth century, the desert fathers had known such powerful currents, straining and striving upward to see God through great feats of earthly denial. These men were prepared to leave everything behind, and in the person of Saint Simeon Stylites, their ascetic daring achieved new heights. The fifth-century hermit erected a pillar (*stylos*) in the sand that soared some sixty feet into the sky. Cut off from the world, Simeon lived atop his perch for thirty-six years, having his meager food and water sent up at the end of a string. This was a literal effort to bring oneself closer to God, and it was mimicked throughout the Eastern church. As a much later recluse was moved to observe, "A man that Studies Happiness must sit alone like a Sparrow upon the House Top, and like a Pelican in the Wilderness."[80] By severing all contact with the world to focus only on happiness on high, these solitary souls attempted to soar to private communion with God.

And then there were those emaciated ones who conceived of fasting and dietary rigor as a way to a similar end—a means to cleanse the body of the putrid flesh of the apple that weighed it down, so that the soul could ascend upward to a more spiritual feast. Isidore of Seville recommended the practice heartily in the seventh century, observing that to fast "is a holy thing, a heavenly work, the doorway to the kingdom, the form of the future, for he who carries it out in a holy way is united to God, exiled from the world, and made spiritual."[81] At roughly the same time, an Irish hymn, perhaps known to Eriugena, invited the holy to partake in the great feast of the eucharist. The word itself means "gratitude" or "giving thanks" (from *eu* + *charis,* thanks, grace, or joy). But it is also akin to the Greek verb *chairein,* meaning "to rejoice." Whether the monks who chanted the following lines were familiar with this root (probably not), they surely soared in song as if they were:

> Come. Holy people, eat the body of Christ, drinking the holy
> blood by which you are redeemed. We have been saved by
> Christ's body and blood; having feasted on it, let us give
> thanks to God. All have been rescued from the jaws of hell by
> this sacrament of body and blood. . . . The Lord, offered as
> sacrifice for us all, was both priest and victim. . . . He gives
> the celestial bread to the hungry and offers drink from the
> living fountain to the thirsty.[82]

"Happy are those called to his supper."[83] Christ as tender lamb, Christ as unleavened bread, Christ as sweet wine became for the most discriminating palate the only form of food, blessed morsels to sustain the soul while the flesh wasted away into the mystical body of Jesus.

Those who practiced such penitential rigors probably did not require theological pronouncements on predestination to know that they could bring themselves to a higher state through effort of their own. Nor were the musings of a Dionysius necessary to move their minds. Yet the co-incidence of both these currents gave lift to a movement of Christian mysticism in the ninth century that was just beginning its ascent. In light of the received belief that Pseudo-Dionysius's writings were a voice from the early church—a direct message from a disciple of Paul—they proved tremendously influential. Few other writers, one commentator observes, are "likely to have exercised a greater influence upon Christian mysticism," while another calls Pseudo-Dionysius "the father of scientific mystical theology."[84] Scientific or not, his work as translated and made known by Eriugena would have great impact for centuries, influencing the likes of Saint Thomas Aquinas and Saint Bonaventure, Meister Eckhart, John of the Cross, Theresa of Ávila, and perhaps Hildegard of Bingen, to name only a few of the more important voices in the Western mystical tradition affected by his work.

Mystical bliss. Gian Lorenzo Bernini, *The Ecstasy of Saint Theresa*, 1645–52, Cappella Cornaro, Santa Maria della Vittoria, Rome. Photo: Scala/Art Resource, NY.

There is one possible exception to this pride of place—Anicius Manlius Severinus Boethius, also a sixth-century author whose most influential work was discovered and made widely known only in the Carolingian age. Seeing that Boethius was likewise a Neoplatonist and also deeply concerned with questions of free will and fate, it is not surprising that Eriugena took a deep interest in his thought as well. Eriugena wrote glosses on several of Boethius's works and also composed a short account of his life, explaining how Boethius was born into an aristocratic family at the end of the Roman Empire, then imprisoned, and put to death as a Catholic martyr c. 524 by the Ostrogothic king at Ravenna, Theodoric. But while awaiting execution, Boethius managed, like Perpetua, to compose a short tract, *The Consolation of Philosophy*, which earned him the perpetual devotion of Eriugena and the broader educated public of the ninth century. It would prove, along with those of Dionysius, to be one of the most important writings of the Middle Ages.

In part autobiographical, the work describes the intellectual journey of a condemned prisoner, the movement of his mind to God, as he is guided by the faithful hand of Lady Philosophy, who appears to him in the midst of his despair. When the prisoner inveighs with the "white heat" of resentment against the bad luck of his incarceration, Philosophy points out that those who trust in Fortune are always destined to be deceived. "You must have heard how Croesus, king of the Lydians, after being only recently an object of fear to Cyrus, became thereafter a pitiable figure when consigned to the flames of the pyre," Philosophy observes.[85] The "groans of tragedy" would ever be heard when men placed their hopes for happiness in the ephemeral goods of the world. Riches, high position, fame, pleasure, good feeling, and power—"All these paths to happiness turn out to be byways, and cannot guide a man to the goal that they promise."[86] Like the body, "that most tawdry and frail of things," they yielded only fleeting pleasures and certain pains. Mere "appearances of the true good," these earthly ends were in fact illusions, for there was just one such highest end. "We must acknowledge," Philosophy enjoins, "that God is happiness itself."[87]

Having reached this familiar conclusion, Philosophy then draws another, considerably more bold:

> Since men become happy by achieving happiness, and happiness is itself divinity, clearly they become happy by attaining divinity. Now just as men become just by acquiring justice, and wise by acquiring wisdom, so by the same argument they must become gods once they have acquired divinity. Hence every happy person is God; God is by nature one only, but nothing prevents the greatest possible number from sharing in that divinity.[88]

Here was a radical claim, built, to be sure, upon the classical commonplace that the happy man lived a "godlike life," but going well beyond it to suggest that those who are happy literally become God, sharing directly in his essential essence and participating in his spirit and power. And though there were some scriptural precedents for this suggestion—Saint Peter's claim, for example, that Christ has given us everything we need for "godliness," so that we may become "participants of the divine nature" (2 Peter 1:4)—Boethius did not allude to them here. Rather, like Dionysius, he placed his trust in another guide to lead us back from whence we came. "Under my guidance, along my path, and in my conveyance you can return safely to your native land," Lady Philosophy explains to the prisoner, before gesturing in the direction that he must go. The steps that the prisoner will take to God involve not walking but mystical, spiritual flight:

> For I have wings equipped to fly
> Up to the high vault of the sky.
> Once these are harnessed, your swift mind
> Views earth with loathing, far behind:
> Climbs through the sphere of boundless air,
> Surveys the clouds below it there;
> Up through the sphere of fire can go,
> Ablaze with aether's supple flow;

> Then to the starry halls can run,
> Merge with the pathways to the sun. . . .[89]

As in many of the writings of Pseudo-Dionysius, the imagery here is Platonic, probably borrowed directly from the account of the winged souls in Plato's dialogue the *Phaedrus*. But the metaphor of ascent toward light, with its attendant counsel to leave behind the darkness of worldly things, was readily adaptable to more explicitly Christian ends.

It is in this way that Eriugena conceives of Saint John the Evangelist as the perfect illustration of his own theory of "deification," the psychic and bodily transformation of the blessed into God, and the incorporation—through him, with him, in him—into the unity of the Holy Spirit.[90] John in Eriugena's conception is the apostle who achieved the greatest heights of contemplation, the apostle whose fitting symbol is the soaring eagle. He is "the mystical bird, who flies fast and looks upon the face of God," who in contemplating the word, "rises above every visible and invisible creature, soars over all understanding, and, deified, enters into God who deifies him":

> The voice of the mystical eagle sounds in the ears of the
> Church. Let our exterior sense catch the sound that passes;
> let our mind penetrate the meaning that abides. This voice is
> the voice of the high-flying bird, not he that flies above the
> material air and aether and the limits of the whole sensible
> world, but he that transcends all contemplation, beyond all
> the things that are and all the things that are not. He does
> this with the swift-flying wings of profound theology, the
> glances of clear and lofty contemplation.[91]

And lest there be any doubt regarding his "Boethian" blessedness, Eriugena is perfectly clear: "John was, therefore, not just a man, but more than a man, when he rose above himself and all things that are. . . . For he could not otherwise ascend to God, without first becoming God."[92]

Saint John with Eagle, early
9th century, The Metropolitan
Museum of Art, The Cloisters
Collection, (1977.421).

John's mystical ascension, then, is preceded by a radical breaking out of his human condition, an escape from the body and an abandonment of the self in which the saint goes beyond the strictly human confines of reason and understanding to achieve a state of divine illumination and ecstatic union with God. This was bliss, divine rapture, the convulsive flowing forth and coalescence with the love of God that later mystics would not fail to describe in frankly erotic terms: as the cleaving to the breast of Mary and the taking in of her warm milk, as the consummation of the soul as "bride of Christ" in marriage with the bridegroom Jesus, or any number of other highly charged images that emanated from the minds of men and women who offered their chastity to God. And though Eriugena conceived of an endless variety of levels of mystical attainment—with each soul striving, in life as in death, to "know" with greater "knowledge," to experience ever closer intimacy with the ultimately unknowable God—he conceived of the mystical flight of John as the living standard by which others should be measured. Those mortals who would emulate this saint in the pursuit of our highest good must strive also to "transmute into God," to become God, to participate directly in his truth, to know if only in the flash of a moment the intense spiritual happiness that would be ours eternally in death. This was the exile's ultimate return.

If a number of Eriugena's more creative pronouncements "led him into error," drawing him away from the strict orthodoxy of the church, his general appeal to strive upward to God in an effort to become him reflected the beginnings of a much broader current in the accepted teaching and practice of medieval Christianity. Like the writings of Boethius and Pseudo-Dionysius that Eriugena so admired and imitated, his *Homily* would become a familiar text in medieval libraries, bidding the faithful to follow the evangelist's example, combining philosophical reflection, intense meditation, and ascetic denial in the attempt to return to, and then enter, our true home.[93]

It need hardly be said that this was a privileged journey—a journey to be carried out primarily in the sacred space of the monastery, convent, or hermitage, where one could wrestle more effectively with the many temptations of the world. No less than the philosophy practiced in the schools of Greece and Rome, the perfection of Christian godliness required education, training, and time—precious resources in the Middle Ages that meant effectively that the higher happiness of the theologians was a monopoly of those who could afford to devote their lives to higher things. As a later writer, the Franciscan saint Bonaventure would emphasize in his thirteenth-century *Journey of the Mind to God*, "Since happiness is nothing else than the enjoyment of the Supreme Good, and the Supreme Good is above us, no one can enjoy happiness unless he rise above himself. . . ."[94]

However true these words, Bonaventure's stress on lofty transcendence should not allow us to overlook the far greater number who were forced to cling much closer to earth, eking out an existence on the land or huddling together in Europe's crowded cities and towns. Even one

Giotto di Biandolini, *The Ecstasy of St. Francis*, 1297–1300,
Upper church, San Francesco, Assisi. Note the
penumbra or halo around Saint Francis and
Christ indicating their beatitude.
Photo: Scala/Art Resource, NY.

as high-minded as Bonaventure, after all, could not be expected to keep the advice of his order's founder, Saint Francis, "to glory in the cross of tribulation and afflictions," with unerring devotion. Nor could he expect to strive without fail "ever to be joyful" in living a life of denial. "It is not right for the servant of God to show sadness and a dismal face," Saint Francis added, but clearly the saints themselves were sometimes wrong. Mere mortals, struggling to survive, could only hope to steal a smile as best they could.[95]

But we should not suppose that they never did. The ordinary people of the long Middle Ages knew their moments of merriment. If they managed to survive the perils of infancy—and probably close to a quarter

of all babies died within a year of birth—they stood a decent chance
of living at least into their thirties, and so of weathering the climactic
shifts that killed their crops, and the pestilence, disease, and war that
killed their neighbors and friends. These were necessarily resilient
people, accustomed to pain but all the more receptive to pleasure
when they could find it: folklore and stories to entertain them at night,
a harvest festival or a religious feast, music, drinking, dance.[96] For
most, food was seldom abundant, and meat was rare, but a snared par-
tridge tasted the better for it, to say nothing of a fatted pig. And
though few could afford the luxury of (let alone read) an early recipe
book like the English *Pleyn delit,* many probably felt those words as they
sat by the fire with their bellies full. When their bellies were empty,
they could dream fantasies of the island of Cockaigne, where turkeys
flew ready-roasted and rivers ran with wine, or invoke one of the many
popular tales of other such mythical places, where human beings knew
no want.[97] A juggler, a magician, or a mendicant friar who understood
the art of spinning a yarn could just as easily distract the mind with
pleasing illusions, in the same way that a joust or a hunt or a game of
chess might divert the lord of the manor. Monks in their monasteries
prayed for the salvation of souls; theologians scaled the heights of ecstasy; and the world labored to get by. Its gravity was strangely compelling—so much so that even from the top of their candlelit towers,
theologians deigned to look down now and then, away from their
books, and some were drawn by what they saw.

Between Heaven and Earth

Rapid ascent to glory by imitation of Christ's passion—this was the
way to happiness chosen by Perpetua, Felicitas, and the other martyrs of the early church. More conscious of the waning of apocalyptic
power, Augustine counseled the acceptance of a difficult journey
through life—inevitably painful but sustained by elevating hope.
Boethius, Pseudo-Dionysius, Saint Simeon, and Eriugena imagined a
new path to God, envisioning the flight of the soul upward in mysti-

cal bliss. Otherworldly all, none of these visions was strictly incompatible, and their paths often crossed, with martyrs and mystics, sinners and saints coexisting in the common space of the church, imagining together the possibility of perfect happiness in God. But despite this apparent harmony, each new path opened up to God's glory altered both the cumulative journey and the final place of arrival, subtly transforming the image of happiness professed by a church that was ever changing while striving always to stay the same.

The thirteenth century was a period of such subtle transformation, in which Christians in Western Europe began to conceive of yet another way to perfect happiness—a means, a path that combined locomotion with lift. To travel along this new way was not to race forward with the rapid steps that had delivered Perpetua and Felicitas to their passion. Nor was it to endure the tragic pilgrimage of Augustine, or the world-renouncing takeoff and flight of mystical ascent. It was rather to proceed deliberately, progressively, in a manner that combined elements of all these routes, stepping and rising simultaneously along what Saint Thomas Aquinas likened in the fourth book of his *Summa Against the Gentiles* to a great "ladder of being."[98]

The metaphor of the ladder had long figured in both pagan and Jewish thought, extending as far back as the Book of Genesis, in which Jacob dreams his memorable dream "that there was a ladder set up on the earth, the top of it reaching to heaven; and the angels of God were ascending and descending on it" (Genesis 28:12). The cult of Mithras in the late Roman Empire made similar use of this symbol of spiritual approach, and the same device was often used in place of the metaphor of flight to illustrate the Platonic and Neoplatonic ascent of the soul. Ladders, not surprisingly, featured in depictions of Christian contemplation from early on, appearing, as we have seen, in one of the most vivid of Perpetua's dreams. Likewise, a ladder accompanies the figure of Philosophy, who visits Boethius in his cell. She is described as wearing a robe embroidered with two symbols, the Greek letters Π and Θ, that stand, respectively, for practical and theoretical philosophy. In between can be seen "the depiction of a ladder, whose rungs allowed ascent from the lower letter to the higher letter."[99]

The Deposition with Ladder (left), St. Peter's Church, Naevsted, Denmark (c. 1375). Mills-Kronborg Collection, Courtesy of the Index of Christian Art, Princeton University; and *The Ladder of Divine Ascent* (Jacob's Ladder), Lambeth Bible, mid-twelfth century, Lambeth Palace Library, London.

Although a venerable symbol, the ladder by the thirteenth century was being used in new ways and with considerably greater frequency.[100] It appears in paintings alongside the mangled body of the crucified Christ, an inspiration and a tool for those who would raise themselves to him. It features prominently in Canto 21 of "Paradise" in Dante's *Divine Comedy,* in which Dante ascends to the seventh heaven to behold "a ladder rising up so far above me that it soared beyond the reaches of my sight," a ladder with "so many splendors descending along its bright rungs that I thought every lamp in heaven was pouring forth its rays."[101] And it is the central symbol around which Aquinas constructs his vision of the ordered hierarchy of the universe. "The lowest level of all is that of non-living bodies," Aquinas explains,

Diptych with Coronation of the Virgin and the Last Judgement, French,
ca. 1260–70. Note the ladder with ascending angel in the lower left corner.
The Metropolitan Museum of Art, The Cloisters Collection, 1970. (1970.324.7ab).

in which production, emanation, or movement is possible only "when
one body acts on another." The living things closest to these are the
plants, "in which there is already some interior production," the movement of juices and the creation of seed. Then there is the level of
"animals endowed with sense-awareness," which have a "form of production peculiar to themselves," and following the animals are human
beings, distinguished by intellect or mind, the "highest, most perfect
level of life." Intellect itself is also divided into further levels, proceeding from that of human beings to the mind of angels, "in which intel-
lects know themselves . . . by knowing themselves in themselves."
Finally, there is the "acme of perfection," pure intellect above the
highest rung, which belongs to God, "in whom to exist is to understand . . . so that in God the idea in his mind is what God himself is."[102]

An ordered universe, in which all creation has a purpose and place; a hierarchy of existence proceeding from matter to mind; God as pure intellect, thought thinking itself—the picture would have been familiar to those acquainted with the theme of the "great chain of being." Implicit already in Plato but given its clearest formulation by Aristotle, the great chain of being is an understanding of the universe as an interlocked chain composed, in the words of its foremost historian, "of an immense, or . . . infinite number of links ranging in hierarchical order from the meagerest kinds of existents . . . through 'every possible' grade up to the *ens perfectissimum*," the perfect being, God.[103] Aquinas, in this instance, substitutes the metaphor of the ladder, but the picture he paints is recognizably Aristotelian, a fact that is not at all coincidental.

It would be an exaggeration to say that Aristotle had been completely forgotten in the West, for even in the darkest days since the breakup of Rome, a smattering of his writings was familiar to scholars and theologians. Yet his great works on ethics, metaphysics, and natural science were largely unknown even by Augustine's time, preserved only, in Greek original and Arabic translations, in the more civilized empires of Byzantium and Islam. When, in the late twelfth and thirteenth centuries, these works began to trickle back to Christian Europe—often accompanied by the sophisticated commentaries of Muslim and Jewish commentators like Averroës and Maimonides—they presented Catholic theologians with a major dilemma. For here was an entire intellectual system, forceful, coherent, and self-contained, that made no mention whatsoever of the Christian God. In the simplest of terms, Aristotle must either be converted or disproved. And though this task fell on many shoulders, one man bore the greatest burden. Thomas Aquinas assumed the responsibility of converting Aristotle to Christ.

Born to minor gentry in a castle outside of Aquino, north of Naples, in 1224 or 1225, Aquinas was intended early on for a career in the church. His parents packed him off to monastery school at the age of five, and in his teens he was transferred to the freewheeling University of Naples, where, like students throughout the ages, he experimented with the new and unknown. He read fresh and innovative writings, most importantly the expanded corpus of Aristotle, which the Neapolitans had brought together earlier than most. In time he joined the Dominicans, a recently formed order that sustained itself by begging in the service of poverty, preaching, piety, and instruction. For a young man of good family, this was a radical move. But Aquinas fit well in his new habit of white wool. As a Dominican friar he was able to see the world, traveling to Paris, to Cologne, and back to Paris, where he taught at the Sorbonne. And with the Dominicans he was able to satisfy his voracious appetite for learning.

Aquinas's contemporaries were duly impressed. The story is told that he regularly dictated to multiple scribes—simultaneously—on different subjects. Another legend credits him with the ability to compose in his sleep.[104] But whatever the extent of his powers, it is clear that Aquinas possessed an astonishing capacity for synthetic production.

Both the *Summa contra Gentiles* (1259–1264), the "summary against the gentiles," and the *Summa Theologiae* (1266–1268), the "summary of theology," provide ample illustration of this capacity. The works are vast compilations of Catholic theology, written to guide students and teachers through the complexities of the faith. In the case of the *Summa contra Gentiles*, the goal was to arm Dominican missionaries in the field with rapid responses to the queries of unbelievers. The *Summa Theologiae*, by contrast, composed in the high Scholastic style of public disputation, aimed to answer any, and every, question the world's most inventive minds might put to defenders of the faith. From the basic—"Does God exist?"—to the bizarre—"Why do fat men produce little semen?" (1a. 119.2)—Aquinas is nothing if not thorough, bringing the full force of the tradition to bear in his responses, drawing amply on the fathers of the church. At the same time, he makes extensive use of the West's great intellectual rediscovery, placing Aristotle, whom he refers to simply as "the philosopher," alongside Augustine as twin defenders of the faith and twin authorities on what rapidly emerges as a central Thomistic concern: happiness.

In many basic respects, Aquinas is content to confirm Augustine's teachings on the matter. A theologian of the church, he is not in a position to seriously question established tradition, nor is that his intention. Book 3 of the *Summa contra Gentiles*, for example, contains a chapter entitled "Man's Ultimate Happiness Is Not in This Life," while the *Summa Theologiae* asks, with apparent candor, whether there are any who are perfectly happy on earth. After considering the question with direct reference to Augustine's *City of God*, Aquinas concludes, unsurprisingly, that there are not. "True happiness" (*beatitudo perfecta*) is "impossible" in life.[105] Only in heaven will the soul know the ecstasy of its final place of rest. Much like Augustine and the Christian Neoplatonists, Aquinas interprets Saint Paul's assurance in 1 Corinthians 13:12 ("For now we see through a glass darkly; but then face to face") as a promise of the beatific vision that awaits us in heaven.[106] Gazing upon God unmediated by any obstruction—seeing perfectly with our souls, not imperfectly with our eyes—we will partake of pure and everlasting bliss, "perfect pleasure—a more perfect delight of the senses than that which animals enjoy, since the intellect is higher than the senses." Nothing, nothing at all, will be lacking, for "in that final happiness every human desire will be fulfilled," and our joy shall be untainted by "sadness or worry that it may be disturbed."[107] In heaven, Aquinas affirms, the saints "shall be inebriated by the plenty of thy house, and thou wilt make them drink of the torrent of thy pleasure."[108] The saved will literally be drunk on God.

Aquinas is every bit as thirsty as Augustine, ready to conceive of man as a parched pilgrim, a wayfarer, *homo viator*. In these respects, he walked comfortably in the footsteps of church doctrine, unwilling, and unable, to stray too far from the beaten path. Yet Aristotle also forced him to alter the inclination of his step. If complete happiness came only in death, might there not still be a perfection of the journey, a blessedness of the route? Perhaps, Aquinas proposed, we could hope to find an "imperfect happiness" here on earth while traveling to the "perfect happiness" of heaven.

The theological distinction between perfect and imperfect happiness—what Aquinas is inclined to call *beatitudo* and *felicitas*, or *beatitudo* and *beatitudo imperfecta*, though he sometimes mixes the terms—had been put forth slightly earlier in the thirteenth century by William of

Auxerre, a professor at the University of Paris. But it was Aquinas who developed the distinction most fully, and he did so by explicit appeal to Aristotle.[109]

In the Aristotelian world, recall, all things have a purpose—a final end or *telos* that they are intended to fulfill in accordance with their natures. When the circumstances are right, an acorn will become an oak—a flourishing oak—and a man will become a good man, a happy man. It is the virtue of each—the unique form of excellence distinct to every aspect of creation—to reach its highest stage of development, and perfectly to realize itself. In human beings, Aristotle believes, the virtue that sets us apart, our highest faculty, is reason. And the *telos* for which we are intended is to cultivate reason to its ultimate perfection, a process that will culminate in the final end—the end without end—happiness.

Taking care to stress the role of God in this process of intention and development, Aquinas nonetheless agrees with Aristotle's assessment. In both the *Summa contra Gentiles* and the *Summa Theologiae*, he leads the reader steadily down the Aristotelian path, reaching very similar conclusions:

> Man's ultimate happiness consists in the contemplation of truth, for this operation is specific to man and is shared with no other animals. Also it is not directed to any other end since the contemplation of truth is sought for its own sake. In addition, in this operation man is united to higher beings (substances) since this is the only human operation that is carried out both by God and by the separate substances (*angels*).[110]

Aristotle observes in the final book of the *Nichomachean Ethics* that contemplation is the most "god-like" human activity, and Aquinas agrees that reflection is what brings us closest to God. He is quick to emphasize that the purest form of this reflection will come only in heaven. But he recognizes that the activity has counterparts, however imperfect, here on earth. "In this life there is nothing so like

this ultimate and perfect happiness as the life of those who contemplate the truth," Aquinas affirms.[111] Aristotle was not wrong to
consider reflection the highest form of earthly happiness. His understanding was simply incomplete, for he had not yet been exposed to
divine revelation. Now that human beings possessed access to the
truth of Christ, the prospect of "double happiness" (*duplex felicitas*)
opened up before them:

> The ultimate perfection of rational or intellectual beings is
> twofold. In the first place, the perfection they can reach is
> through natural capacities [in this world], for this can be
> called bliss [*beatitudo*] or happiness [*felicitas*] in a sense: thus
> Aristotle identified our ultimate joy with his highest contem-
> plative activity, that is to say with such knowledge as is
> possible to the human mind in this life. . . . But beyond this
> happiness there is yet another, to which we look forward in
> the future, the happiness of seeing God "as he is."[112]

We not only can be happy in a sense in this life, but can be happy
again in the next.

It must be emphasized that these two forms of happiness stand in
a clear relationship of hierarchy—as the imperfect to the perfect.
Aquinas leaves no doubt that there are many evils in life that cannot
be avoided, and that human beings will always be plagued by unfulfilled desire. Given that "full and sufficient happiness excludes every
evil and fulfills every desire," it follows that perfect happiness on earth
will forever elude us.[113]

Nevertheless, Aquinas's opening up of a space in which "some partial happiness can be achieved in this life" continued a process of
restoring agency to the individual that had received impetus from the
work of Eriugena and others during the Carolingian Renaissance. It
also restored independent dignity to the world. For by arguing that
there are certain "natural capacities" that permit men and women to
reach purely earthly goals, Aquinas put forth a less sweeping interpretation of the effects of the Fall. "Human nature," he observed in the

Summa Theologiae, "is not so completely corrupted by sin as to be totally lacking in natural goodness." Like a sick man who can still perform certain movements on his own, we are able to do some good things on earth even in our natural (sickly) state. But in order to "move with the full motion of a man who is healthy," we need to be cured.[114]

Aquinas views life as a long process of healing, or to return to the metaphor of the ladder, as a steady process of ascent in which we raise ourselves ever closer to God. It is critical that he believes that we participate in this process ourselves. The natural virtues staked out by Aristotle—justice, fortitude, gentleness, and temperance—give testimony to the power of the unaided human intellect to survey life's terrain and to blaze trails to a better end. In Aquinas's optimistic view, men and women are fully capable of discerning the natural laws that give direction to their lives.

Yet in order to travel further in the direction of perfect happiness, further toward recovery and health, we need assistance. To rely solely on natural knowledge and the natural strength of the will is to ensure that we will come up short, for natural virtue only ever leads to imperfect ends. In order to continue forward and upward in the direction of the perfect happiness that is our final goal, we must follow Christ. Here, too, we begin on our own, attempting to follow the rules revealed in scripture under the guidance of the church, to live in keeping with the beatitudes, to keep the living law. But for all mortals, our natural abilities will ultimately hold us back. It is only when we have received what Aquinas calls the "theological virtues" of charity, hope, and faith that we will have the full strength to pull ourselves to our final end. Infused by grace and granted by God, the theological virtues are gifts freely given, bestowed on those whom the Lord, in his wisdom, deems worthy. They make us better than ourselves. And though Aquinas maintains that we can never know who might receive them, or at what point, he does observe that "When a person begins to make progress in the acts of the virtues and gifts, one can hope that he will attain both the perfection which belongs to the journey and that of the destination."[115] As we move closer to our own perfection, we move closer to perfection itself.

Thus, for Aquinas, happiness is a process, a continual becoming, in which we rise to our full potential by fully realizing ourselves. Preeminently a man of theory, a theologian and philosopher, Aquinas envisioned our greatest realization and highest earthly happiness as a life of pure contemplation—the life, in effect, of a monk. But if in this respect Aquinas joined Aristotle in envisioning abstract reflection as the most godlike way to live, he also shared with the author of the *Nichomachean Ethics* a belief in the secondary human happiness of practical ethical achievement, the happiness, that is, of virtue in the world. And also like Aristotle, Aquinas recognized the necessity of means to cultivate higher ends. It was difficult to do good in the world when one was starving or sick, difficult to give alms without alms to give, difficult to live a life of contemplation without the basic necessities of life fulfilled. None of these things—health, a satisfied belly, power, wealth—were ends in themselves, and to treat them as such would be fatal. But they could legitimately serve as means.[116]

In more than just abstract ways, then, Aquinas, and the wider current of which he formed a part, served to rehabilitate the standing of life in this world, as well as to consolidate, on firm theological ground, the role of human effort in contributing to our ascent up the ladder of being. The fact that we could pull ourselves higher, partly on our own, had the effect of narrowing the conceptual distance between man and God, rendering human life potentially more heavenly.

There were some willing to go even further than this. The thirteenth-century rage for Aristotelian philosophy spread with such intensity in certain quarters that the church grew alarmed, fearing (and not without reason) a revival of the Pelagian heresy of old. In Paris, in particular, students at the Sorbonne pursued the study of Aristotle with enthusiasm, daring even to affirm his superiority to Christ. The bishop of the city, Stephen Tempier, was forced to put an end to this blasphemy. In 1277 he condemned some 210 propositions culled from the manifestos of contemporary Aristotelians, including the claim that "Happiness is to be had in this life and not another."[117] This was a radical proposition, by no means the norm. But it was put forth regardless, and there were others like it. With justice has the eminent medievalist Georges Duby traced what he calls the "mold" of earthly happiness precisely to these radical Aristotelian circles. "Happiness made by man alone, happiness which could be won by intelligence"—this was the incipient dream that wafted out from the schools of Paris, allowing its scent to settle on the courtly love of knights and their ladies, and on the pages of such works as Dante's *Divine Comedy* and the *Roman de la rose*.[118]

Of course, many continued to look suspiciously on the more earthly of these productions, even for a time casting doubt on Aquinas himself. But these doubts were quickly dispelled, and in 1323, less than fifty years after his death, Thomas Aquinas was made a saint. Ironically, his feast day was set for March 7, forcing the church to push that of Perpetua and Felicitas back to the eighth.[119] By bringing Aristotle into the Christian fold, the theologian from Aquino had cleared a new path—a middle way—between heaven and earth, bidding us to linger a little longer and savor the journey, pushing back perpetual felicity by a day.

Journey to the End

Still they can be seen. Roadside markers. Indentations in stone. Walkways smoothed by rough feet and the press of knees. Silent echoes of passage. Traces of the movement of souls.

Europe remains covered in paths, and some are still well traveled. Yet the sound of footsteps is only a patter now compared to the great march of pilgrims who shuffled across the continent at the height of the Middle Ages. Lumbering like armies, they were, in some cases, precisely that—holy warriors who fell on Jerusalem or crossed the Pyrenees in the tragic illusion that crucifying heretics or slaughtering Jews was the way to their Lord. Santiago de Compostela, a city that from the ninth century had served as the reputed resting place of the remains of Saint James, grew to become the spiritual staging ground for the reconquest of Muslim Spain. Amid the tens of thousands of penitents who arrived each year were knights who prayed to Santiago Matamoros, Saint James the Moor Slayer, to guide their swords home.

Missteps, mistaken routes, fatal deviations, trails of blood: Medieval pilgrims took countless wrong turns. More often, they struggled innocently to find their way, walking alone and in groups, in long, coarse tunics, a plain satchel at the side, a hat against the sun, a sturdy wooden staff—braving wolves and thieves and the demons of night. They traveled to Rome to gaze on the tombs of Peter and Paul; to Canterbury or Walsingham; to Cologne for the relics of the three wise kings; to Monte Gargano to pay homage to the memorial of the archangel Michael; to Chartres for the Marian shrine. They set out for Einsiedeln to see the Black Madonna, or Loreto to see the house of the Virgin. They wandered to the edge of town to pray: at a grotto, at the tomb of a local martyr, at the roadside image of a saint.

Pilgrims, Trinity Chapel, Canterbury Cathedral.

These could be simple outings—a day's hike, a stolen hour before sunrise—or great voyages, over sea and land from Dublin to Rome, journeys measured in months. As the anonymous author of the twelfth-century *Pilgrim's Guide* makes clear, a traveler might wander for weeks on any of the four great routes that led through France to Santiago de Compostela.[120] There was much to see. Formal stations connected the way—basilicas, reliquaries, crypts to which the pilgrim could pay homage. There were local curiosities, like the tomb of Léonard of Limousin, the patron saint of prisoners, at Limoges. The author of the *Pilgrim's Guide* doubted the authenticity of the relics there. But he acknowledged that the thousands of chains that hung above them— the grateful offerings of former prisoners—were real indeed. There was amusement as well—fellowship, stories, and song; adventure; and the strange ways of distant lands. Probably French, and probably a priest, the author of the *Guide* warned in coarse Latin of the barbarous customs of Navarre. "Ugly, debauched, and perverse," the men of those parts would kill a Frenchman for a pittance. And they "shame-lessly fornicate[d] with animals." How the author knew that, he did not say.[121]

Why did they come, these sacred travelers? And why did they go? Their reasons naturally varied—to do penance for a crime, to ask for charity or forgiveness, to rid themselves of guilt. Some came to exorcise a sin, to fulfill an obligation, to give thanks. Others were drawn by the promise of miraculous healings, the prospect of adventure, or a simple change of routine.

But there was another, more basic reason that impelled these travelers—a reason at once profound and prosaic: They desired to reach the end. To set foot on the sacred ground of a pilgrimage site was to stand at the point of entry to another world. *Ad limina*, medieval authors called it, "on the threshold," a new beginning, a place of joy. Here the dark curtains of the world opened, ever so slightly, to let in the light of the eternal beyond. Here pilgrims could bathe in that light, wash away the filth that gathered on life's way. Here they could drink, give themselves the strength to carry on. And here they could catch a glimpse, if only through stained glass, of the perpetual felicity that drew so many to this place. "Numerous, in effect, are the bodies of the saintly martyrs and confessors who lie here—bodies whose souls reside amidst the joys of Paradise," the author of the *Pilgrim's Guide* observed in reference to the cemetery at Aliscamps, just outside of Arles.[122] To set foot on sacred ground was to stand as close to the happiness of heaven as most mere mortals could.

Ad limina was a privileged place. But though a threshold, it was also a barrier that cordoned off the end of the earth, separating the sacred from the profane. Through the broken bones of a martyr, one could see the light of heaven, but while doing so, one stared directly at death. The way to perpetual felicity lay across that great divide.

While waiting to take their final step, all men and all women were forced to endure the trials of the journey. As the knight declares in that classic account of late-medieval pilgrimage, Chaucer's *Canterbury Tales,* "The world is but a thoroughfare of woe, and we are pilgrims passing to and fro. . . ." The merry band of travelers encounters its share of mirth along the way. But they understand that these moments are fleeting,

> For ever the latter end of joy is woe
> God knows that worldly joy is soon ago.[123]

The line might almost have been uttered by the chorus in an ancient tragedy. Just as Augustine had conceived of life's pilgrimage in an essentially tragic mode, many others continued to use the language of fate and fortune to describe the daily happenings that befall us all.

Strictly speaking, of course, there was no room for fortune or chance in the Christian conception of the world: God's providence governed all. But from at least the time of Boethius, commentators, if not always in the strictest orthodoxy, had continued to use this pagan language to emphasize the essential transience of all earthly things.[124] They, too, called no man happy until he was dead, and they knew that even the most fortunate in this life would fall like Croesus in the end, or meet their downfall in death like the Greek heroes of old. Well into the Renaissance, fortune's wheel continued to turn, and it is a measure of that revolution—a conception come full circle—that the word "happiness," like *bonheur, Glück,* and the other terms that rolled from European tongues in the Middle Ages and early Renaissance, retained its linguistic connection to *hap.* If, and when, one knew *lasting* happiness, it would be only by the grace of a God who intervened from beyond the stage of the world.

This is where the link to the tragic past ended, and another began. To be sure, there were other important similarities between Christian happiness and the happiness of the ancient world, particularly of the post-Socratic kind. Christians, too, conceived of happiness as an objective state at the end of a well-marked path. A *summum bonum,* a highest good, happiness remained a *telos,* an end, and virtue the principal means to guide the way. But whereas the ancients had conceived of virtue as almost entirely the result of human striving, won only by the efforts of a happy few, Christians understood virtue as a divine gift, obtainable, in theory, by all. There was disagreement over the role human effort played in cultivating this gift—disagreement that would explode in violence at the time of the Reformation. But few Christians denied that perfect happiness could be had only by grace. And no Christian denied that although the identity of the elect was hidden from human view, all might receive it—whether male or female,

A fifteenth-century representation of Philosophy consoling Boethius
(left) and Fortune turning her wheel. Coëtivy Master, Paris,
c. 1460–70, The J. Paul Getty Museum, Los Angeles, © The J. Paul Getty Museum.

noble or slave, commoner or king. Popes as well as peasants set out on pilgrimage and whirled in the dance of death. And popes as well as peasants were entitled to the happiness of hope, and the hope of happiness—ecstasy everlasting, eternal bliss that would make amends for all our earthly pains.

Thus, despite its deep debt to the ancients, Christianity had blazed new trails, removing happiness from the midst of the world, while spreading its universal promise to the four corners of the earth. Transforming the Jewish narrative of a people's deliverance in life into an ethic of universal deliverance in death, Christianity profoundly altered the Western gaze. Backward, men and women now looked, to a vanished period of happiness, a paradise lost. And forward, they yearned for the moment when God would remake his kingdom in a paradise regained. In the meantime, all must bear their burden as best they could, taking heart in Christ's pledge of redemption, courage in the example of the saints, and delight in the promise of perpetual felicity to come.

A counsel to patience, the happiness of hope was a powerful force, giving men and women the strength to carry on. At the same time, it armed them with an explanation for their pain. In the medieval Christian conception, unhappiness was not an aberration, an individual failing or fault, but the natural condition of every human being since the Fall. Continually renewed in Sunday sermons and the extraordinary number of holidays that ordered Christian time—from the joyous celebrations of Christ's birth and resurrection (merry Christmas and happy Easter) to the countless festivities in honor of the saints—the happiness of hope provided men and women with a means to endure.

But it also could easily be used as a justification for suffering that might otherwise be avoided, an excuse for needless inequality, oppression, and pain. Forever close at hand, Christian happiness was also, always, just beyond reach. Did not the faithful ever feel that they were being led along? Perhaps an element of suspicion was always right beneath the surface, for in a sense it was called into being by Christianity itself. In its rejection of Roman *felicitas*, Christianity had denied the things of this earth, casting aspersions on sex and sensuality, wealth and well-being, power and pride. Yet notwithstanding its continual reminder that our reward in heaven was ultimately inconceivable—"What no eye has seen, nor ear heard"—the church could scarcely fail to present this reward in terms that appealed directly to the senses. Beatitude would satisfy our hunger, quench our thirst, gratify all our longings. "In that final happiness every human desire will be fulfilled," Aquinas assured, and his assurance begs a question. Was not Christianity promising the very thing it denied, "a torrent of perpetual pleasure," a lifeless lifetime of eternal bliss? If human desire was to be rewarded then, why must it be denied so completely in the here and now? Aquinas had already taken steps toward narrowing the gap between the imperfect happiness of earth and the perfect happiness of heaven. In the coming centuries, men and women would bring the two closer still.

3

FROM HEAVEN
TO EARTH

Early in the thirteenth century, Lotario dei Segni completed a short
manuscript to which he appended the name *De Miseria Condicionis
Humane, The Misery of the Human Condition*. A cardinal and a deacon who
would later be ordained Christ's vicar on earth as Pope Innocent III,
Lotario was arguably less miserable than most. But that did little to
prevent him from doing full justice to the title of his work.

From birth to death, Lotario explains, men and women are simply
"vile." Conceived in the "stench of lust" and formed of the "filthiest
sperm," we spend our earthly days in misery, toil, and degradation.[1]
Racked by envy and greed, tortured by vanity and rage, depleted by
gluttony, sloth, and lust, we are forever trapped in the webs of our
seven deadly sins, ensnared by our own iniquity. The effort to escape
is futile. "Who indeed has ever spent even a single delightful day in
his own pleasure?" Lotario asks. Guilt, anger, or concupiscence is ever
at hand to spoil the moment. "Sudden woe always follows worldly joy,
and what begins with gladness ends in sorry."[2] As with gluttony, so with
the product of all our desires: "What goes in vilely, comes out vilely,
expelling a horrible wind above and below, and emitting an abominable
sound."[3] The outcome of human appetite, in a word, is filth.

These are the by-products of man. "Alive, he brings forth lice and tapeworms; dead, he begets worms and flies; alive, he produces dung and vomit; dead, he produces rottenness and stench."[4] A seething, stinking mass of sin, we suffer in this world. And all those who are not saved will suffer in the next, rotting in the infernal darkness of hell, knowing there "an unfailing supply of torments." With reason, it seems, does Lotario offer a new beatitude: "Happy are those who die before they are born, experiencing death before knowing life." With reason do babies cry at birth.[5]

Such kicking, screaming shrieks of despair were certainly audible in the European Middle Ages. Partly as a consequence, it was once commonly assumed that they typified the tenor of this so-called dark age. A long black night that descended on Europe from the fall of the Roman Empire until the awakening of the fifteenth-century Renaissance, this was a period, it seemed, when humanity wandered blindly in ignorance and despair, fumbling like man in Lotario's dark vision, "a sojourner on the earth, and a wayfarer," enduring the world as a place of exile, "confined in the body as in a prison."[6]

Few informed observers share this view today. On the contrary, they tend to emphasize the technological and intellectual vitality of the Middle Ages, drawing particular attention to the "renaissance" of the Carolingian ninth century, and the "renaissance" that began in the twelfth, leading to the establishment of the great European universities, the building of the High Gothic cathedrals, and the revival of interest in Aristotle that reached its apogee in the work of Thomas Aquinas. They might also point to the fact that contemplation of the misery of the human condition was hardly unique to the Middle Ages. Arguably, only after Europeans had endured the terrible carnage of the Black Plague, which wiped out roughly one quarter to one third of the total population in the second half of the fourteenth century, were they fully prepared to take up *De Miseria Condicionis Humane*. Works bearing that same title continued to appear throughout the great Renaissance of the fifteenth and sixteenth centuries, while many others spread the theme of *contemptus mundi*. To take only one example, Thomas à Kempis's fifteenth-century masterpiece, the *Imitation of*

Christ, went to great length to remind its readers, "Life on earth is truly wretched." It was among the most widely read works of the fifteenth and sixteenth centuries.[7]

It is misleading, then, to conceive of the transition to the European Renaissance as a stark passage from dark to light. Rather, change occurred as it more often does, in subtle modulations and tones. Those critics, commentators, artists, and theologians who attempted to depict happiness during this time drew their colors from the palette of their predecessors, even as they combined and built them up in new ways. They extended their interest in ancient authors, pushing on the boundaries of Christian doctrine and testing the limits of original sin. And they took upon themselves the unfinished projects of the Middle Ages. *The Misery of the Human Condition* is a case in point. Lotario had promised to follow that work with another that he believed would serve as its perfect complement, a work to glorify the "dignity of human nature." "Just as in this book the haughty man is humbled," Lotario wrote in the preface to *De Miseria Condicionis Humane*, "so in the next the humble man [will] be exalted."[8] Lotario died before he was able to compose his sequel. But authors in the fifteenth and sixteenth centuries did so for him. Reviving interest in what the Romans had termed the *studia humanitis*—grammar, rhetoric, poetry, ethics, and history—the "humanists" of the Renaissance aimed to cultivate learning that would, in the words of Leonardo Bruni, one of their leading proponents, "perfect man." In doing so, they carried the pursuit of happiness in new and unexpected directions.

The Dignity of Man

If there were ever such a thing as "Renaissance Man," Giovanni Pico della Mirandola was he.[9] Born to a local prince in the northern Italian duchy of Ferrara (Emilia Romagna) in 1463, Pico availed himself of his noble circumstances to devote his life entirely to learning. He enrolled at the University of Bologna when still a child, studying canon law there before moving to the University of Ferrara, and then to the University of Padua, a leading center of Aristotelian scholarship. He traveled the European continent, spending time at the University of Paris, and gaining entrance into Lorenzo de Medici's Platonic Academy in Florence, where he befriended Marsilio Ficino, the greatest Platonist of the age. He knew not only Latin and Greek but Hebrew, Aramaic, Arabic, and Syriac and used these languages in a quest to show the underlying unity of all knowledge. For Pico, the newly rediscovered riches of classical Greece and Rome, the mythology of ancient Egypt, the secrets of the Talmud and Cabala, the mysteries of Zoroaster, and the wonders of the natural world alike complemented the truths of Christianity. He made it his short life's work to demonstrate this correspondence, offering to do so, publicly, at the impressive age of twenty-three.

Vowing to pay the travel costs of anyone in Europe who would come to Rome to debate him, Pico put forth nine hundred "theses" or conclusions on an astonishing array of subjects. They would, he claimed, "show not that I know many things, but that I know things which many people do not know."[10] Undoubtedly this was true. But Pico never had the opportunity to prove the point. A Vatican commission deemed a number of his theses of dubious orthodoxy, canceling the public dis-

Anonymous, 16th century, Pico della Mirandola (1463–94). Galleria Palatina, Palazzo Piti, Florence. Photo: Scala/ Art Resource, NY.

putation and forcing Pico to write a formal apology before quietly with-
drawing, first to France, and finally to Florence, where he spent the
last years of his life writing in a villa provided by Lorenzo de Medici at
Fiesole. He died at the age of thirty-one and is buried in the great
church of San Marco.

Although Pico produced a great many other works—including an Italian imitation of Plato's *Symposium* and a critique of astrology that later
influenced the mathematician and astronomer Johannes Kepler—he is
invariably remembered for his nine hundred theses, or more precisely,
for their introductory oration, "De Dignitate Hominis," "On the Dignity of Man" (1486). Often invoked as *the* manifesto of the Renaissance,
this brief essay, more than any single work of the period, has seemed to
generations of commentators to capture the spirit of the times.[11] Jacob
Burckhardt, the greatest nineteenth-century scholar of the Renaissance,
wrote that it was in fifteenth-century Italy that "men and mankind were
. . . first thoroughly and profoundly understood," and that it was Pico
who plumbed their depths. "The loftiest conceptions on this subject,"
Burckhardt believed, were uttered in this brief oration, "which may
justly be called one of the noblest of that great age."[12]

Burckhardt saw much that was noble in Pico. But it was above all
the Italian's apparent sense of the freedom and majesty of man that
captivated the Swiss historian, seeming to him to mark an abrupt departure from all previous conceptions. Citing a long passage from "De
Dignitate Hominis," Burckhardt marveled at the liberality of Pico's
vision. "In conformity with thy free judgment," God tells Adam toward the beginning of Pico's work,

> thou art confined by no bounds; and thou wilt fix limits of
> nature for thyself. I have placed thee at the center of the
> world, that from there thou mayest more conveniently look
> around and see whatsoever is in the world. Neither heavenly
> nor earthly, neither mortal nor immortal have We made thee.
> Thou, like a judge appointed for being honorable, art the
> molder and maker of thyself. Thou mayest sculpt thyself into
> whatever shape thou dost prefer.[13]

Here, in Burckhardt's view, was the very epitome of the Renaissance achievement, what he called famously—borrowing a phrase—the "discovery of the world and of man." Human beings could now be works of art. After the long sleep of the Middle Ages, in which men and women "lay dreaming or half awake beneath a common veil . . . woven of faith, illusion, and childish prepossession," they now, Burckhardt contended, awoke to see themselves, and the world around them, with open eyes.[14] Genuine "individuals," Renaissance men were "modern," brimming with possibility and potential, able to chart the course of their lives for themselves without stumbling under the accumulated weight of Christian superstition. In these respects, "De Dignitate Hominis" seemed the perfect counterpart to Innocent III's *De Miseria Condicionis Humane*. Slowly, man was moving from misery to dignity, and from there, to happiness on earth.[15]

Burckhardt's vision of the Renaissance was, and remains, powerful. In television documentaries and newspaper articles, in museum exhibitions and travel brochures, one can still find many of its central features offered up as received wisdom. Professional historians, however, have come to think of this view largely as "myth."[16] By looking more closely at Pico's work itself, one can see why.

Without question, the image of humanity presented in "De Dignitate Hominis" is inspiring. Repeatedly Pico urges us to marvel at ourselves. Nothing is "more wonderful than man," he begins, quoting a variety of sources to emphasize the point. Unlike all other elements of creation, we have no fixed rung on the ladder of being, what Pico calls "the ladder of the Lord," no decided place within the structure of the universe. Instead, we are "chameleons," able to "grow downward" to become like beasts, or to climb upward, cultivating our reason to join "the higher natures, which are divine." With justice are we "thought to be a great marvel," the animal most genuinely "worthy of wonder."[17]

But if human mutability—the capacity to "fashion," "fabricate," and "transform" ourselves—draws Pico's awe, it is not there that he places the dignity of man.[18] Dignity lies in God, in whose image we are made. And so it is how we choose to exercise our freedom to fashion ourselves that determines our greatness or our depravity, our dignity or our contempt. In this respect, Pico shows himself to be wholly conventional. "Let us spurn earthly things," he enjoins, "let us struggle toward the heavenly. Let us put in last place whatever is of the world; and let us fly beyond the chambers of the world to the chamber nearest the most lofty divinity."[19] By ascending toward God up the great ladder of being, we become worthy of ourselves.

We are, to put it mildly, a long way from Burckhardtian modernity. And this is to speak only of man's dignity. Like virtually every one of his contemporaries who took up the subject, Pico was also prepared to chronicle human shortcomings. Just as Innocent III had conceived a paean to man's majesty as a necessary counterpart to his record of human depravity, writers of the Renaissance frequently tempered their wonder with dismay. When Hamlet declares that man was both "the paragon of animals" *and* a "quintessence of dust," he was merely repeating common wisdom. In the Renaissance, no less than in the Middle Ages, dignity and depravity were two sides of a coin.[20]

Granted, Pico himself rarely wallows in filth. But in a work completed several years after "On the Dignity of Man"—the *Heptaplus,* or the *Seven-fold Narration of the Six Days of Genesis* (1489)—he makes it clear that human freedom was curtailed by the fatal events in the Garden. "Through the first Adam, who obeyed Satan rather than God and whose sons we all are according to the flesh," Pico writes, "we degenerated into beasts, disgracing the form of man." And now, in the aftermath of our fatal free choice, it is only through the "newest Adam," through Jesus Christ, that we "are reformed by grace and regenerated." Without him, we are liable to succumb to our animal selves, for when "the image of God has been blotted out by the stain of sin, we begin to serve the beasts in us, wretchedly and unhappily . . . sinking to the ground, eager for earthly things, forgetting . . . our Father, His kingdom, and the original dignity given to us."[21] Mindful always of our own weakness, we must say, with the apostle, "Our sufficiency is from God."[22]

A significant corrective to the view that Pico was somehow an apologist for an early modern Prometheus unbound, the *Heptaplus* places man in the only spot its Renaissance author could have conceived: the center of the Christian cosmos. Created in God's image, man is indeed noble. The earth, the elements, and the beasts wait upon him, the heavens labor on his behalf, the angels watch over his salvation and beatitude. Composed of matter and spirit, reason and substance, human beings are microcosms of the universe, "which we encompass within us." But like the planets of the solar system, we are moved in our orbits by God:

> The heavenly bodies, although adapted to circular motion, are not in themselves sufficient to perform this motion, but need the divine mover to turn and revolve them. They are suited to perpetual revolution only insofar as they can receive, not produce it.
>
> It is no different for us and the angels. Our nature is such that we cannot go in a circle and come back upon ourselves, but we can be moved in a circle and brought back to God by the motive power of grace. Hence comes that saying, "Whosoever are led by the Spirit of God, they are the sons of God" [Romans 8:14]. "Who are led," it says, not "who move." We differ from the heavens in that they are moved by the necessity of their nature and we in proportion to our freedom. The moving spirit knocks unremittingly at the door of your soul. If you fail to hear, you will be left wretched and unhappy in your own torpor and weakness. If you let it in, you will be carried back at once, full of God, along the orbit of religion to the Father, to the Lord, to possess life forever in him. . . . This is the true felicity. . . .[23]

In Pico's pre-Newtonian, geocentric universe, gravity is grace, and the human orbit, a Neoplatonic journey back to the Creator. It is in this return to "the beginning from which we sprang," a return that culminates in the "contemplation of the face of God" at death, that "true and perfect felicity" lies. It is a journey, Pico makes clear, that we cannot complete ourselves. "To this level man cannot go" but must be "drawn"—by Christ, "who is felicity itself."[24] For this quintessential Renaissance figure, true felicity, perfect happiness, is not of this earth. Nor is it within our power alone to achieve, "since nothing can rise above itself by relying on its own strength."[25]

Pico does, it is true, speak also of a second, or "natural" felicity (*felicitas naturalis*), which is independent of the motive power of grace. This is the potential that lies within all created things to realize themselves in the way that God has intended. Whereas circular motion, "through which a body is carried around to the point from which it started," serves Pico as the metaphor for perfect felicity, "linear motion, by which the elements are carried to their proper places, stands for the felicity through which things are established in the perfection of their own nature." In Pico's physics, based overwhelmingly on Aristotle, only immortal and incorruptible bodies (the planets and the soul) move in circles. And they must be moved. But elements of a less exalted sort "need no other force than the impulse of levity or gravity imposed on them at creation, just as individual things are brought to their natural felicity by their own proper impetus and force." All things in the created world, that is, can propel themselves to a relative felicity in keeping with the best workings of their own natures.[26]

Thus, Pico can refer, rather strangely, to the "felicity" of fire, which, when it has attained its natural perfection, "is happy to the extent that it is capable of happiness." "More happy are the plants, which also have life; and happier still are the animals, which have been allotted consciousness, so that the more perfection they have, the more divinity they find within themselves." At the top of this ladder is majestic man, who exceeds all save the angels in his potential for natural happiness. "Being possessed of those extraordinary endowments greatly conducive to felicity, intelligence and the freedom of choice," man can cultivate his innate gifts through philosophy.[27] Whereas religion "urges, directs, and impels" us to perfect felicity, philosophy serves as the "guide to natural felicity."[28]

It is tempting to see here the "Renaissance spirit" that generations of commentators have claimed to find: the carving out, in this world, of an autonomous realm, where natural felicity might be pursued through reason. Unquestionably, Pico makes room for such a realm, doing so, moreover, by explicit appeal to the ancients. If his model of the circular journey of the soul to perfect happiness is Neoplatonic, his linear metaphor of the movement of the individual to the end of natural felicity is Aristotelian. As in Raphael's *School of Athens,* the two thinkers are harmonized in Pico's thought. Together they counsel the discipline of the passions, the cultivation of virtue, the development of reason, and the quest for harmony and balance in this world, as in the next.

All of this is without question. It is not, however, without precedent. In fact, although Pico does not say so directly, his distinction between natural and supernatural happiness is largely a gloss on Saint Thomas Aquinas's perfect and imperfect beatitude. In fundamental respects, Pico merely develops this notion, reiterating Thomas's emphasis on the gulf between the two types of beatitude.[29] Natural felicity, Pico insists, is but "the shadow of [true] felicity."[30] And "whoever does not put his faith in Christ . . . is rightly deprived not only of the first felicity, but also of the second, the natural, since it is only a corrupt and fallen nature that does not desire grace." In short, there can be "no philosophy which separates man from religion."[31]

It would, consequently, be a mistake to see the author of this leading Renaissance manifesto—and to see the Renaissance itself—as carrying out a dramatic break with the "otherworldly" Middle Ages and the patristic past of old. Pico was in truth a representative figure, but not for the reasons frequently assumed. The humanism that he typified, like the period in which he lived, developed naturally, often indistinguishably, out of the concerns of preceding centuries. With good reason does one leading scholar observe, "There was nothing particularly new or original about Renaissance views of man."[32]

But though the humanists of the fifteenth and sixteenth centuries did not discover man or his happy world, they did intensify interest in both. If not altogether in substance, at least in tone the movement can be taken at its word. It *did* mark a "rebirth": in hunger, in enthusiasm, in the curiosity to know. More for his appetite than for his answers, Pico was a symbol of his age. Hunting down lost manuscripts, rummaging about in forgotten corners of monasteries, sifting through the rubble of the ancient world, he and his fellow humanists pulled treasures from the past, and above all from classical antiquity, to which they accorded a status, prestige, and sanctity greater than ever before. They learned Greek and perfected their Latin on Roman models, attempting to "purify" a language that humanists believed had been debased during the Middle Ages. And armed with these tools, they returned, reexamined, and revivified the sources themselves. Leonardo Bruni undertook a new translation of Aristotle's *Nichomachaen Ethics* (from Greek into Latin) so that contemporaries could be sure of what the sage had said. It was one of some thirty-two new translations of the philosopher's work carried out during the quattrocento.[33] Others gathered, edited, and republished the works of the Roman Stoics—above all, Cicero, Seneca, and Epictetus—and they reacquainted Europeans with the basic doctrines of Epicurus, principally through the study of his Roman imitator and successor, Lucretius. Finally, the Renaissance witnessed a massive revival of interest in Plato, whose collected works, in Greek, had been brought to Florence from Constantinople in 1420 by the scholar Jean Aurispa. By 1440, more than twenty-one translations were completed, with Bruni, Ficino, and others issuing Latin and vernacular editions of the *Symposium, Phaedrus, Phaedo, Crito, Republic,* and the other dialogues, along with extensive commentaries on Plato's work. Some even went so far as to argue, echoing Augustine's judgment (though even more strongly) that Plato's writings represented a pagan "theology," a science of the study of the true God. It was partly Pico's acceptance of this claim—that God could speak just as relevantly, if less directly, through the words of the pagan authors as he did through the biblical prophets—that drew to him the suspicion of the Vatican.

Pico took greater care in the future to contain his enthusiasm, but the slip pointed to a potential tension. Just as the incorporation of Aristotle into the teachings of the church by Aquinas had worked to mitigate the impact of original sin, creating a space for the cultivation of a natural felicity on earth, so did the Renaissance's extended engagement with classical thought make room for further reflection on the potential for happiness in life. Accelerating a process that had begun the moment Jesus of Nazareth set foot on Roman roads, the humanists pounded classicism into Judeo-Christianity and Judeo-

Christianity into classicism. As Christian Stoics, Christian Platonists, Christian Aristotelians, and even, warily, Christian admirers of Epicurus, Renaissance scholars grappled again and again with the overriding classical end.[34] Not surprisingly, they produced, as one scholar has observed, "an extraordinarily large number of treatises on such subjects as human happiness, misery [and] the greatest good."[35]

With titles like *De Christiana felicitate, De Viri felicitate,* and *De Vitae felicitate,* these works ranged to a considerable extent along the axis connecting the pure felicity of death to the imperfect happiness of life. A Neoplatonist like Ficino, for instance, could observe in a long letter on happiness written to Lorenzo de Medici that felicity is to be found only in the mystical pleasures of the soul wrought by the beatific vision and the contemplation of truth. "Because the happiest thing of all is to possess the object of one's love," he writes, with direct reference to Plato; "whoever lives in the possession of what he loves, lives content and satisfied." And since the love of God was the highest love, "the happiness of man therefore consists in God alone."[36] A man of Stoic leanings, like the humanist Coluccio Salutati, by contrast, could draw on his deep readings in Cicero and Seneca to extend the sway of happy activity on earth, emphasizing the importance of practical virtue, based on the cultivation of reason, as a means to quell the passions that upset us in life. Then again, Leonardo Bruni, profoundly indebted to Aristotle, emphasizes the role played by fortune and circumstance in shaping the happiness of even the most virtuous life.

> For it is possible for a wise and good man, learned and accomplished though he be in all the virtues, to be reduced to a state of poverty, bereavement, or exile; he could lose his country, have his patrimony taken from him, his children and relatives killed. He might even be cast into a tyrant's prison, be put upon the rack and subjected to horrible, pitiable tortures. Who could still call him happy amid so many evils, even though he were overflowing with virtues?[37]

Not, certainly, the humanists Lorenzo Valla or Gianozzo Manetti, the latter of whom displays considerable indulgence toward earthly pleasures and delights in his treatise *De Dignate et Excellentia Hominis* on the "dignity and excellence of man." Both scholars defended the consonance of a chastened Epicureanism with Christianity.

Notwithstanding this considerable range of opinion, virtually no humanist was prepared to doubt Pico's central assumption that true or perfect happiness was not of this world. Many in fact continued to dismiss the possibility of earthly happiness altogether, concurring with the late-fifteenth-century Bolognese scholar Filippo Beroaldo, who observed simply that "no one is happy." Neither the author nor his audience seemed to see any contradiction between that conclusion and the title of the work in which it was drawn, an *Oration on Felicity*.[38]

And yet, as Salutati was quick to point out, "We humans, stupid and mad, strive to be happy nevertheless in the world, and, what is more inane, we believe and boast that we are blessed and happy among these false and mundane things."[39] Whether foolishly misguided or not, more than a few Renaissance men and women did strive for a measure of worldly happiness, and their momentum carried them up against the limits of received assumptions. In calling to account an author who shared Beroaldo's views on the inherent misery of life, the Bolognese notary and student of Aristotle Benedetto Morandi demanded to know how one could write treatises on human happiness while denying the prospect altogether. If human beings were incapable of felicity on earth, he argued in his own "On Human Happiness," then "nature would have conceded the faculty for acquiring [it] in vain." Vowing to concentrate solely on the happiness of which "man is capable"—assisted by neither God nor the angels—Morandi went so far as to doubt how one who had never known happiness in life could be expected to enjoy it in death. Following Aristotle, and like Pico and Thomas Aquinas before him, Morandi was prepared to carve out a realm, however imperfect, in this world for the pursuit of human ends.[40]

It was precisely this impulse—an impulse born of the sustained reengagement with classical thought, thought that took as its point of departure the cultivation of earthly ends—that motivated men and women in the fifteenth and sixteenth centuries to begin to reconceive, slowly, haltingly, happiness here below. The same spirit that could lead Raphael to imbed the schools of Athens in the walls of the Vatican could lead a painter as religiously inclined as Agnolo Bronzino to imagine felicity clothed only in classical garb. His *Allegory of Happiness* (*Allegoria della felicità*) is a modern rendering of the Romans' Felicitas Publica, whose image and allegory had become widely known to the humanists through their passion for collecting antique coins.[41]

But whereas antiquarians and nusmismatists like Andrea Fulvio, Enea Vico, and Sebastiano Erizzo lavished attention in long treatises on "the almost infinite number of coin images" that graced Roman specie, Bronzino focused exclusively on Felicitas Publica herself, lavishing praise on the different goods of this earth that she conferred.[42] A pert-breasted young woman drawn in the elongatedly pudgy Mannerist style, Happiness herself commands the canvas as she commands our gaze, set in grandeur on a regal throne. In one hand, she clutches her trademark caduceus, and in the other, a cornucopia bursting with fruit, symbols, respectively, of public peace and prosperity. To Happiness's left stands Justice, dangling her scales. Coldly erotic, she

Felicitas Publica from Cesare Ripa's *Iconologia* (1593), a widely reproduced Renaissance manual providing descriptions of hundreds of allegorical images. Here Felicitas is seated on a throne with her caduceus and horn of plenty. Beinecke Rare Book and Manuscript Library, Yale University.

Orazio Gentieschi, *Public Felicity Surmounting Perils,* or
Triumph of Fortune, 1624, Musée de Louvre, Paris.
Photo: Scala/Art Resource, NY.

Public Felicity in an eighteenth-
century English translation
of Ripa's *Iconologia* (London,
1729). Yale Center for British
Art, Paul Mellon Fund.
Photo: Richard Caspole.

strikes a pose as if for the catwalk, draping a free hand seductively over the base of her sword. Cupid/Eros, for his part, is more eager. Spilling into Happiness's lap, this naughty nymph prepares to pierce her with his golden shaft. But lest he transgress, fawning Prudence—Janus-faced to look forward and backward, to the future and to the past—keeps watch over her delicate charge, guarding Happiness from violation. Glory and trumpeting Fame hover overhead, while Time, in possession of the celestial sphere, and Fortune, with her wheel of fate, genuflect at Happiness's feet. At the extreme left, blind Envy flees from view. Folly, in a fool's cap, is trod under Prudence's step, and Justice subdues both Fury (clutching a broken sword) and Deceit (lying prostrate under the wheel of fate). Time and Fortune, finally, make quick work of Kairos, the Greek god of chance, who writhes, defeated, at the very bottom of the canvas. Only the angels above suggest the happiness of a higher realm. In the confined space of this picture, Happiness reigns supreme.

As the court painter to Cosimo I de Medici, ruler of Florence from 1537 to 1574, Bronzino likely intended this work as a commentary on his patron's reign. The masculine face of the prudential Janus bears a striking resemblance to Cosimo himself, and the terrestrial globe that Prudence holds is turned so that Italy lies at the very center of the world.[43] After decades of war and upheaval at the hands of foreign armies, Florence, Bronzino suggests, had won prosperity and independence, beating down Folly and Fury, making Fortune the servant of its fate. Projecting military power into the surrounding Tuscan countryside, Cosimo had ushered in a revival of the arts and letters in the city itself, promoting a campaign of public works whose perfect symbol was the Uffizi, designed by Bronzino's friend Giorgio Vasari, where the *Allegory of Happiness* is now housed. The city that produced Leonardo, Machiavelli, and Michelangelo continued to shine with grandeur and brilliance.

It may even have dared to smile. It is striking, in fact, that the same lavish attention paid to earthly detail in so much Renaissance art was trained, as well, on the beaming human face. Although smiles were not unprecedented in Western painting and sculpture—they fre-

Agnolo Bronzino, *Allegory of Happiness*, 1564, Galleria degli Uffizi, Florence. Photo: Scala/Art Resource, NY.

quently enliven the faces of the *kouroi*, for example, those statues of standing young men popular during the Archaic period of Greece in the sixth and seventh centuries BCE—since the advent of Christianity they had been overwhelmingly reserved for religious figures. And even in these circumstances, they were used only sparingly to brighten the faces of those known to enjoy certain beatitude: the blessed Virgin, Adam and Eve before the Fall, the angels, and the saints.[44]

Smiling angels on the Cathedral of Reims, twelfth century (top),
Photo: Scala/Art Resource, NY; smiling angelic figurines, thirteenth-
century French, The Metropolitan Museum of Art, The Cloisters
Collection, 1952 (52.33.2). Photograph, all rights reserved,
The Metropolitan Museum of Art.

In the fifteenth and sixteenth centuries, however, artists began to depict the smiles of secular subjects. There are many examples, but Leonardo's *Mona Lisa* is the most famous. In a Europe that continued to value emotional restraint, her half smile created a lively contemporary impression. Giorgio Vasari, who had not actually seen the work, saw fit to remark in his classic *Lives of the Artists* that her smile was "so enchanting that it was more divine than human." He also pointed out that while Leonardo painted, he had his enchanting subject "constantly entertained by singers, musicians, and jesters so that she would be merry and not look melancholic as portraits often do."[45]

Vasari's reference to melancholy is revealing in its own right. First described by Hippocrates in the fifth century BCE, and later elaborated by Galen in the second century, melancholy (*atra bilis* in Latin) literally signified "black bile," derived from the Greek *melan* (black) + *chole*

Antonello da Messina, *Portrait of an Unknown Man Smiling*, 1470, (left) The Metropolitan Museum of Art, Bequest of Benjamin Attman, 1913. (14.40.645). Leonardo da Vinci, *Mona Lisa*, early 1500's, (right) Musée de Louvre, Paris. Photo: Réunion des Musées Nationaux/Art Resource, NY.

(bile). According to late Medieval and Renaissance commentators, who continued to regard Hippocrates and Galen as authorities on such matters, melancholy was one of the four principal humors that governed human physiology and mood.[46] When balanced harmoniously with the other three—hot and moist *blood*, hot and dry *choler*, and cold and moist *phlegm*—cold and dry *black bile* played an essential role in maintaining human equilibrium. Whereas blood carried heat and moisture throughout the body, phlegm nourished our cold and moist parts like the brain and kidneys, and choler fed what was hot and dry, black bile brought sustenance to the bones, gristle, and sinews. As such it functioned much like *earth*, which, in this elaborately integrated physiology/cosmology, also served as a cold and dry element, offsetting *air* (hot and moist), *fire* (hot and dry), and *water* (cold and moist) in the smooth running of the universal macrocosm.[47]

In proper measure, melancholy was a vital humor, essential to human health and well-being. But in superabundance it provoked a physiological imbalance that greatly affected mood. Just as a profusion of choler, phlegm, or blood provoked a choleric, phlegmatic, or sanguine response (names we retain), a surfeit of black bile pouring out from the spleen (where its excess was allegedly held) induced melancholy. Frequently associated with sadness and morbid depression, this disorder could produce a slew of diverse symptoms of varying severity, ranging from "windy melancholy" (flatulence), hemorrhoids, scabies, coughs, hoarseness, aches in the joints, and falling sickness to somnolence, idiocy, madness, and other "cold and dry" diseases chronicled with dark fascination in the annals of early modern medicine.[48]

By reengaging with the classical tradition to treat excessive sadness and melancholia as an aberration or disease—not just the natural effect of original sin—Renaissance medicine opened the way toward thinking about means to cure it. Vasari's observation, in this respect, that Leonardo relied on entertainment, music, and harlequins to put a smile on Mona Lisa's face is instructive, for it is symptomatic of a wider effort to devise ways to induce more positive mood. Ranging from recommendations on diet to considerations of the effects of weather and climate on our state of mind, such medicinal advice was dispensed in unprecedented volume during the Renaissance.

True, not all Renaissance humanists viewed melancholy as a problem. Pico's teacher Marsilio Ficino, for one, was inclined to see the condition in a somewhat different light. Drawing on what he and others considered, erroneously, to be a text by Aristotle that alleged a close association between melancholy and genius, Ficino linked the accumulation of black bile in certain special cases to breadth of imagination, intellectual acuity, and the powers of prediction and foresight.[49] Natural black bile is "conducive to judgment and wisdom," he stated in *The Book of Life* (1489), arguing there that in its rarefied form, "genial" melancholy was a condition and cause of creative genius. He entitled chapter five of that work, accordingly, "Why the Melancholic Are Intelligent."[50]

Ficino's views were undoubtedly influential, contributing to a contemporary "vogue" of melancholy in elite circles, and a phenomenon that would have a long and robust future: the glamorization of intellectual despair.[51] Yet more important from the perspective of happiness were the early efforts to treat melancholy as a problem. In the sixteenth century, especially, medical literature on the subject flourished. "Never before," one historian writes, "had so much attention been paid to [the] expression of hopeless . . . inner confusion."[52] When the English polymath Robert Burton came to dissect the problem from every conceivable angle in *The Anatomy of Melancholy* in 1621, the body was well prepared. "I write of melancholy, by being busy to avoid melancholy," Burton observed. He could think of no "more general service" than to prescribe means to "prevent and cure" this "epidemical disease" that "so often, so much, crucifies the body and mind."[53]

However imperfect, the attempt to find a cure for excessive sadness and the willingness to dignify the smile in secular art may be treated as indications that some were coming to see a modicum of earthly happiness as consonant with the dignity of man. There are other such indications. Historians note, for example, that beginning in the fifteenth century, representations of the afterlife began to take on a far more earthly tone.[54] As early as 1431, Lorenzo Valla was

Albrecht Dürer, *Melancholia 1*, 1514, © copyright the Trustees
of the British Museum.

describing the delights of heaven in surprisingly sensual terms in his
Epicurean-inspired dialogue *On Pleasure:*

> With the others, individual parts of the body are given plea-
> sure as the palate by food, the nostrils by the rose and the
> violet; but with this kind, the whole body is partner to the
> pleasure. It is a kind of joy, also, that is felt by not one but
> many senses; let it be touched upon only most briefly here

because it relates to formerly mentioned matters, like your banquets, dances, and games. . . . In the state of eternal felicity that kind of pleasure will be much richer and more plentiful.[55]

A canon and biblical scholar, Valla is particularly interesting in that it was he who first established, through textual analysis, that the writings of Pseudo-Dionysius could not have been those of Dionysius the Areopagite mentioned in the Acts of the Apostles as a disciple of Saint Paul. Challenging the apostolic authority of this work, he likewise challenged the purely contemplative understanding of the beatific vision so dear to the Neoplatonists and medieval philosophers. Valla's heaven is one of feasting and dancing and amusement, sweet as the smell of a rose, where "not a day, not an hour, not an instant of time . . . will see any diminution of honor, glory, or pleasure." And though he takes great care in this work to stress that many pleasures in this life must be sacrificed for the purer pleasures of the next—"we should not, therefore, fear to renounce the affairs of man"—his conception of Christian vir-

Dancing in heaven. A detail from Fra Angelico's *The Last Judgement*, c. 1431, Museo di San Marco, Florence. Photo: Scala/Art Resource, NY.

tue leaves little room for the rigors of ascetic denial.[56] Like a later work, the monk Celso Maffei's *Pleasing Explanation of the Sensuous Pleasures of Paradise* (1504), and other Renaissance descriptions of the afterlife, the imagined pleasures of Valla's treatise were in part a reflection of the greater acceptance of pleasure in the here and now.

Working within the limits laid down by late medieval theology, Renaissance humanists did expand the scope of *felicitas naturalis*, making more room for the imperfect pleasures of life, while beginning to contemplate the daunting task of rendering human beings happier on earth. This, to repeat, was only a gradual development. But it was no less significant for that. By building upon the conception of human freedom formulated originally by Aquinas and the late medieval Aristotelians, the Christian humanists of the Renaissance explored the boundaries of what was conceivable, in this life, by the unaided intellect of fallen man. Not thoroughly incapacitated by sin, we possessed the freedom, they concluded, and the ability, to make the world a better place. A celebrated humanist like Erasmus might devote a volume to the "praise of folly," concluding ironically that "to know nothing is the only happiness."[57] But it is quickly apparent that this "folly" is in truth the highest wisdom: a blend of Saint Paul's "foolishness of the cross" and the injunction of the man whom Erasmus described as "Saint Socrates" to begin the search for truth with the avowal of ignorance. Together, such folly would not only reduce the suffering of the world but also lead to self-knowledge, which Erasmus praised as an essential point of departure in the search for happiness.[58] The other place to start (and more important to end) was God. "All we have to do is turn our minds to things spiritual," Erasmus avowed, and "the way to happiness is a rapid one."[59]

When viewed in this light, it is hardly surprising that a man of this cast—a Christian humanist, a biographer of Pico, and a close friend of Erasmus, no less, to whom the *Praise of Folly* was dedicated—first gave the world a new word, *utopia*. In Thomas More's masterpiece of that name (1516), the inhabitants "love and reverence Almighty God, to Whom we owe our existence and our potentiality for happiness." But they also "regard the enjoyment of life . . . as the natural object of all human efforts," striving on the basis of reason and intellect to provide themselves with the means to enjoy.[60] More's Utopia is, as the name implies, an imaginary realm, "no place" or "good place" from the Greek *ou* (no) or *eu* (good) + *topos* (place). Like Bronzino's *Allegory,* it suspends time to triumph over fury, folly, fortune, and deceit. A product of the imagination, set in a faraway place, the Utopia of More does not, nor can it ever, exist, but serves, rather, as a foil to satirize the many less than happy practices of the real world with which he was well acquainted. Nonetheless, More's conception set a standard—a human standard—by which to measure the real shortcomings of life with an eye to improving them. By fully exercising their God-given freedom, the work suggested, human beings could raise themselves and their world closer to heaven.

Just how high could one go without God's help, and how high was one expected to go before God extended his hand to help pull us along? The freedom of the Renaissance humanists—their injunction to rise to the utmost heights of human dignity—was apt to provoke anxiety in humanity's highest achievers. Martin Luther was such a man; in his struggles to fully realize himself, he grew conscious of the sin that continued to weigh him down. As he did so, he conceived a new image of Christian freedom and a new image of human happiness.

To Kill the Old Adam

In late May of 1534, Martin Luther wrote a brief but extraordinary letter to the young prince Joachim von Anhalt. Then in his fifty-first year, the leader of the Reformation was twice the age of the sad prince, who suffered from bouts of melancholy despair. Luther saw fit to offer a word of advice:

> Serene Prince, gracious Lord! [A mutual friend] has told
> me that your Grace has been a little unwell, but are now,
> thank God, again in good condition.

It often occurs to me that, as your Grace leads a quiet life, melancholy and sad thoughts may be the cause of such indisposition; wherefore I advise your Grace, as a young man, to be merry [*fröhlich*], to ride, hunt, and keep good company, who can cheer your Grace in a godly and honorable way. For loneliness and sadness are simple poison and death, especially in a young man. . . . No one knows how it hurts a young man to avoid joy [*Freude*] and cultivate solitude and melancholy. . . . Joy and good humor, in honor and seemliness, is the best medicine for a young man, yea for all men. I, who have hitherto spent my life in mourning and sadness, now seek and accept joy whenever I can find it. We now know, thank God, that we can be merry with a good conscience, and can use God's gifts with thankfulness, inasmuch as he has made them for us and is pleased to have us enjoy them.

If I have not hit the cause of your Grace's indisposition and have thereby done you a wrong, your Grace will kindly forgive my mistake. For truly I thought your Grace might be so foolish as to think it a sin to be merry, as I have often done and still do at times. . . . Your Grace should be joyful [*fröhlich*] in all things, inwardly in Christ and outwardly in God's gifts; for he gives them to us that we may have pleasure in them and thank him for them.[61]

Luther knew of what he spoke. The ambivalence and tension that runs throughout this letter—between melancholy and mirth, sin and joy—ran throughout his life. From a young age, he had suffered what he called *tristitia* (melancholy or excessive despair) and knew intimately the solitude and sadness which he described to the prince. He had also struggled bravely to be "joyful in all things," developing a deep appreciation for the challenge of any such quest. It was not a sin to be happy, Luther came to believe, but it was because of sin that we were not. Eating away within us, concupiscence was an ever present reminder of our inherent worthlessness, which only God's clemency, the mercy of his "gifts" could dispel. As Luther had observed in a sermon written some years before, "Sin is pure unhappiness, forgiveness pure happiness."[62]

Today, a conscience racked by excessive feelings of guilt and shame, oscillating wildly between misery and joy, would summon medical and psychological concern. Whether Luther himself suffered an actual affliction will never be known for sure, although historians have certainly suggested it, shedding a good deal of light in the process on the psychological forces that may have shaped his development.[63] They call attention to a harsh and somber childhood, the implacable demands of a father who sought to dissuade Luther from his chosen career as a monk, and to a number of crises—fits, breakdowns, and prolonged periods of despair—that all this may have provoked. It was at the end of one such period of extended depression that Luther apparently achieved his "breakthrough," the dramatic experience in the tower.

The year was 1519, two years after the young monk is supposed to have nailed his famous ninety-five theses, protesting the sale of papal indulgences, to the door of Wittenberg Cathedral, setting in motion a series of events that challenged the excesses and prerogatives of papal power. Luther may never actually have lifted a hammer.[64] In any case, it was above all the so-called experience in the tower—named after the room in the Augustinian Black Monastery in Wittenberg where Luther kept his study—that led him to the dramatic reinterpretation of scripture that gave the Reformation its theological force. As Luther himself later recalled the episode, his spiritual epiphany was brought on by anxiety and dread:

> Though I lived as a monk without reproach, I felt that I was
> a sinner before God with an extremely troubled conscience.
> I could not believe that God was placated by my satisfaction.
> I did not love, no, I hated the just God who punishes sinners. . . . I said, "Isn't it enough that we miserable sinners,
> eternally lost through original sin, are crushed by every kind
> of calamity through the Ten Commandments? Why does
> God heap sorrow upon sorrow on us through the Gospel and

through the Gospel threaten us with his justice and his
wrath?" This was how I raged with a fierce and troubled
conscience.[65]

Having, for some time, steeped himself in the writings of Saint Paul,
Luther was driven to distraction by his inability to answer a fundamental question: How is it that we are "justified" by God—made right,
that is, made just or righteous? How is it that we are saved? According to the dominant theological perspective that was already pronounced in Eriugena, and that reigned supreme from Aquinas to Pico
to More, men and women could in some measure save themselves
through their own actions, by performing good works and living virtuous lives. Infused through the sacraments, God's grace is forever
with us. We fulfill it by perfecting ourselves. "*Facere quod in se est*," "Do
what lies within you," ran the famous scholastic phrase. Be all you can
be. In keeping with the medieval image of the ladder, human liberty
entailed the freedom to raise oneself to God.[66]

For Luther this vaunted "freedom" was in fact a form of subjugation. For how could we be certain, he wondered, that we had performed enough good works to merit salvation—that we had been all
that we can be? Like an unremitting father whose love we can never
earn, this God seemed to Luther a taskmaster who would never be
pleased. And though by all accounts Luther was, as he claimed, blameless, performing tremendous ascetic feats of fasting, self-flagellation,
prayer, and penance, he could not set his mind at rest. Fed by personal psychology and sustained by his long engagement with the theology of Saint Augustine, Luther's sense of human worthlessness was
boundless. Trapped within himself, his guilt could not be appeased—
until he was set free in the tower, while contemplating book 1,
verse 17, of Paul's Letter to the Romans:

Meditating day and night on those words, I at last, by the
mercy of God, paid attention to their context: "In it, the
justice of God is revealed, as it is written: 'The just person
lives by faith.'" I began to understand that in this verse the

justice of God is that by which the just person lives by a gift
of God, namely by faith. And this is the meaning: the justice
of God is revealed by the Gospel, but it is a passive justice,
i.e. That by which the merciful God justifies us by faith, as it
is written: "The just person lives by faith." Suddenly I felt
that I was born again and had entered into paradise itself
through open gates.[67]

Here was the basis of Luther's greatest insight, the realization, drawn
from Paul, that we are "justified"—*made* just, not punished with justice—through faith alone, and that this faith itself is a gift from God.
We cannot earn faith—it is freely given—and its effects are radical
and profound. As Luther observed famously in another work, his *Preface to the Letter of St. Paul to the Romans* (1522):

Faith is a work of God in us which changes us and brings us to
birth anew from God [cf. John 1]. It kills the old Adam,
makes us completely different people in heart, mind, senses,
and all our powers, and brings the Holy Spirit with it. What a
living, creative, active, powerful thing is faith! . . . [It] is a
living, unshakeable confidence in God's grace; it is so certain,
that someone would die a thousand times for it. This kind of
trust in and knowledge of God's grace makes a person joyful
[*fröhlich*], confident, and gay [*lustig*] with regard to God and all
creatures. This is what the Holy Spirit does by faith.[68]

This total, transformative power to kill the old Adam—the sinful,
selfish creature that lurks within us all—forms the basis of Christian
rebirth, that experience now described, in Luther's very words, as
"born again." To be "created anew," Luther felt, was to be "restored
to Paradise," to be released from the burden of guilt and sin that made
prisons of our persons.[69] Christian liberty, the freedom of Christian
man, was, quite simply, absolution.

How far this new form of "Christian freedom"—the title of one of
Luther's most famous works—was from the relative freedom of self

fashioning envisioned by Pico and the humanists. For the Protestant variety rested upon the acceptance of the fundamentally unregenerate nature of unjustified humanity, of our natural slavery to sin in the absence of rebirth, and of our impotence before God. Luther, and to an even greater extent, the Reformation's other theological giant, John Calvin, emphasized the corrupt and vitiated state of those heirs to Adam not saved by grace. "The world is evil and this life is full of misery," Luther observed, likening men and women in another work "to savage wild beasts."[70] Calvin described human beings as "teeming horde[s] of infamies," and was convinced that "those who are under the curse of God enjoy not even the smallest particle of happiness."[71] To the early leaders of the Reformation, the misery of the inhabitants of the earthly city seemed altogether clear.

In this respect, Luther, Calvin, and their many followers turned back to the tradition of Saint Augustine, a tradition they believed had been eclipsed, along with so much else, by the church's divergence from scripture, its pagan accretions, and its overreliance on the theology of Aquinas, which flirted openly, they believed, with the Pelagian heresy of old. Luther's emphasis, too, on the radically transformative power of faith, his renunciation of agency to God, and the stark contrast he drew between the old and new man recall much of the power of the Pauline gospel and the effervescence of the early church. It is likely that Perpetua and Felicitas would have understood something of his palpable, personal sense of the presence of God and his joyous embrace of the Holy Spirit.

Yet if in these ways the Reformation looked back—quite self-consciously—to an earlier epoch in Christian history, it also pointed forward to new understandings of the relationship between the human and the divine. Most important, Luther and his successors shifted the weight of religious responsibility from the church, as institution, to the individual conscience. "The first step in Christianity," Luther declared, after the preaching of repentance, is the "knowledge of oneself."[72] By declaring scripture alone to be the ultimate basis of Christian truth, they undermined the need for an elaborate priestly hierarchy to act as interpreters of revelation and intercessors before God. All who believe are priests, Luther maintained, responsible for receiving and spreading the word, caring for their own souls and those of others. God's grace admitted of no hierarchy and no mediation. Just as the reformers stripped Catholic cathedrals of the accumulated "clutter" of the ages—jettisoning the veneration of saints, the worship of relics, and the ritual and pomp that separated the clergy from the congregation—so, too, did they strip away the forces and institutions (illiteracy, monasteries, penitential orders) that, in their view, impeded direct confrontation with the divine. In the end, the faithful would stand equal—and alone—before God.

A direct consequence of this reorientation was the erosion of rigid distinctions between the sacred and the profane. If there was no hierarchy in the ascent to God (only the division of the damned and the saved), there could be no privileged place or profession in which to pursue this end. Rotterdam was as holy as Rome, the mineshaft as conducive to grace as the monastery, the pikeman as potentially upright as the priest. Marriage, the family, one's work and striving in the world all became fields for the cultivation of God's glory in what the philosopher Charles Taylor has called the "sanctification of the ordinary," or the "affirmation of ordinary life."[73] For the Reformation's children, there could be no especially exalted form of existence, simply exaltation itself, the conducting of one's worldly affairs—whatever and wherever they might be—in the proper spirit. One should seek God in all things, for in all things one could be found.

This was an outlook that developed most intensely in the Calvinist variety of Protestantism, particularly that of Anglo-American Puritans, for whom the notion of the "calling," or divine vocation, assumed central importance.[74] But it was firmly rooted in the most basic of Protestant propositions: Luther's assertion of the priesthood of all believers and his contention that we are saved by faith alone. God had created the world, and he "saw that it was good." But we had lost sight of this goodness, viewing creation through the veil of tears that is human selfishness, blinded by our own sin. That veil could be lifted by grace, however, allowing us to see creation in the way the Lord had intended, as "a pleasure garden for the soul."[75] It was Luther's fervent belief that "we may be relieved of the blindness and misery in which we are steeped so deeply, and may truly understand the Word and will of God, and earnestly accept it." For thence we would "learn how to obtain an abundance of joy [*Freude*], happiness [*Glück*], and salvation [*Heil*], both here and in eternity."[76] As Luther emphasized to the young prince Anhalt, we could hope to be "joyful in all things."

This was Luther's hope. He expressed it repeatedly, urging, unsurprisingly for a man who had known suffering in his own upbringing, that the family provide the first fruits of the harvest.[77] Whereas Catholic tradition had long regarded marriage as a necessary but inherently compromising institution, Luther celebrated conjugal life, abandoning his own clerical celibacy to marry a former nun, with whom he had six children. To love one's wife, to feed one's children, to govern a family, and to honor one's parents were not mere "secular and carnal duties" as the "papists" believed, but "Fruit of the Spirit."[78] In the same way, Luther insisted that we pick freely from all of God's bounty. The man who had once starved and flagellated himself in his anxiety to be worthy of God now saw merit in drinking deeply of God's creation.

Yet there is little to suggest that Luther ever managed to put his anxiety completely to rest, or that he came to know the happiness in all things that he recommended to the prince of Anhalt. On the contrary, he was plagued to the end of his days by intermittent spells of depression. "Be strong and cheerful and cast out those monstrous thoughts," he advised in another letter, stressing that "sometimes we must drink more, engage in sports and recreation, aye, even sin a little to spite the devil, so that we leave him no place for troubling our consciences. . . . What other cause do you think that I have for drinking so much strong drink, talking so freely and making merry so often, except that I wish to mock and harass the devil who is wont to mock and harass me."[79] When one considers that for Luther, "all sorrows, illnesses and melancholy come from Satan," it is clear that he did not live always in the assurance of grace.[80] "A Christian should be gay," Luther admitted, "but then the devil shits on him."[81]

That odd, if characteristic, scatological confession illustrates more than just the paradox of Luther's personal psychology. It sheds light on the paradox that Luther injected into the heart of Protestant theology itself. Responding to the anxiety generated by the unbearable demands of an implacable God, Luther sought to allay our dread by total surrender to God's grace. But he did so by simultaneously emphasizing our inherent worthlessness and sin. Without grace, we were nothing, prone to the promptings of guilt and prey to the morbid attacks of Satan. Was anyone ever so sure of his salvation that he was immune to doubt? The Protestant doctrine of predestination—that God had chosen a relatively small number of souls to be saved through grace, and that all others, in Calvin's words, taken from Paul, were "vessels of wrath"—hardly provided assurance of solace. In relieving one form of anxiety, the Reformation substituted another.[82]

Yet (and this is the paradox) Luther's injunction that Christians *should* be merry, and that if they viewed the world aright they would be, was a powerful endorsement of earthly good feeling. To live life as a justified man was apparently to experience the world as a "pleasure garden for the soul." Had not God originally intended us to be happy? And if so, what better way to serve him than to live as he desired? For fallen, sinful creatures, this was a daunting task. But with the help of God's grace, it could be achieved. To make merry was to spite the Devil. Misery and melancholy were evidence of sin.

Thus did Luther attack the privileged place of suffering in the Christian tradition. Pain, to be sure, was, and would always be, an integral part of the human experience, a fact that could lead Luther to observe, in an Easter Tuesday sermon, that "he who has not seen adversity does not understand happiness. . . ."[83] But if suffering was inevitable, it was no longer to be treated as an end in itself. Luther and Protestants more generally dismissed with contempt the heroic ascetic embrace: no more hair shirts, no more fasting, no more ecstasies of pain. Life was excruciating enough on its own terms. We needn't add to our afflictions by seeking them out, and when they did arrive, as they inevitably would, we should do our best to bear our cross with joy. As Calvin concluded, "If praise and thanksgiving to the Lord can only proceed from a cheerful and joyful heart—and there is nothing which ought to repress these emotions in us—it is clear how necessary it is to temper the bitterness of the cross with spiritual joy."[84] Even when suffering, the chosen should not be sad.

In both its "sanctification of the ordinary," then, and its broader dictate to be "joyful in all things," the Reformation tended to moralize and consecrate mood. Luther, like Calvin, significantly, was inclined to think of Hell as a psychological state.[85] In earthly despair we experienced a foretaste of the anguish of those eternally rejected by God. Joy and good feeling, conversely, could be treated as an indication of divine favor. The experience of happiness on earth—unsullied merriment and Christian joy—was an outward sign of God's grace. And the very fact that this grace could never be known with total conviction was itself further incentive to search for it in all things.[86] To pursue happiness was to seek signs of assurance of future felicity. The promise, in this life alone, was great. "When the favor of God breathes upon us," Calvin insisted, there is nothing, whether poverty, misery, exile, contempt, imprisonment, or ignominy, that "is not conducive to our happiness."[87]

And so, although Luther and his Protestant successors saddled human beings with a renewed awareness of their dependence and sin, they also set men and women free to search for happiness on the hallowed ground of God's creation. "*Tristitia omnis a Sathana,*" Luther affirmed on numerous occasions. "All sadness is from Satan." We should flee it like the Devil.[88] It was counsel that many of his followers took to heart. When Luther's close friend and fellow theologian at Wittenberg Philip Melanchthon published in 1540 his *Commentarius de anima,* a work that seemed to extol, like that of Ficino, the virtues of melancholy, Luther's more faithful followers responded by reaffirming the teachings of their master. Drafting statements, delivering sermons, and posting placards, they condemned this sad vice, reminding the flock that it was Satan who drew the unwitting into his "melancholic bath," while advising that they draw on the useful "antidote" made available by the "apothecary of the Holy Ghost."[89]

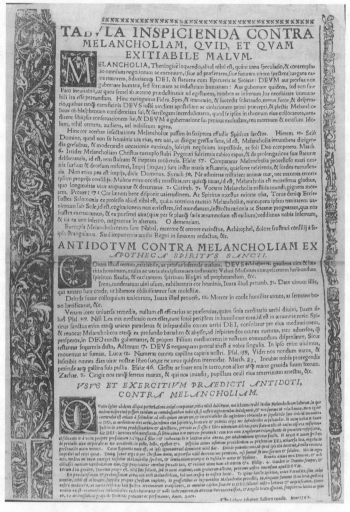

Lutherans against melancholy. The *Tabula Inspicienda Contra Melancholiam* (Lubecae: Johann Balhorn the Elder, 1562). Herzog August Bibliothek, Wolfenbüttel, Germany: 95.10 Quod. 2° (70).

Not all found the Protestant tonic so bracing. In its grim reminder that only the chosen would be saved, the cure seemed to some worse than the sickness it aimed to abolish. Sin lurked in the world, and it lurked in the human breast, giving the devil more than his due to make of us what we were without grace: miserable, wretched creatures afflicted by sadness, anxiety, and doubt. Until men and women could conceive of their emotional lives without Satan, and of their selves without sin, happiness would remain, like the old Adam, menaced by melancholy and shrouded in despair.

This notwithstanding, the Reformation's impetus to pursue earthly happiness as affirmation of God's grace acted as a powerful force. For though directed against the more generous interpretation of human freedom defended by Renaissance humanists, it had the effect of complementing that tradition's general broadening of the possibilities and religious sanction of pursuing happiness on earth. Not only was human dignity compatible with earthly pleasure, but there was righteousness in the pursuit.

Gravitational Pull

When the young John Locke went up to Christ Church in 1652, the quiet world of Oxford was a very different place from what it had been only ten years before. During much of the preceding decade, a protracted civil war had torn England apart, pitting supporters of the reigning monarch, Charles I, against the armies of Parliament and the leading Puritan statesman, Oliver Cromwell. Parliament's victory, capped by Charles's execution in 1649 (an event probably witnessed firsthand by Locke while still a pupil at Westminster school), ushered in a period of experimental government in which Cromwell presided over a republican commonwealth, and then over a protectorate, ruled largely at his command. When Cromwell died in 1658, his son clung to power for a mere two years before the country restored the Stuart throne. It would take another twenty-eight years, and another revolution—the "glorious" one of 1688—to reconcile the nagging question of the relationship between Parliament and the crown.

In unleashing the furies of war, the conflict of the 1640s also released a flood of speculation that dared to challenge long-held truths. The same men and women who could carry out the murder of a monarch cut into every manner of orthodox belief, hacking away at political and religious taboos. With unsettling names like Levellers and Ranters, Muggletonians and Fifth Monarchists, Seekers and Quakers, Diggers and Familists, Protestant sects from across the social spectrum contemplated alarming things. Levellers dared to assert freedom by birth and the equality of all men, touting natural rights and a Law of Nature to guarantee them. Diggers pressed the claims of the dispossessed to property and political participation, while other groups called into question a range of religious views deemed incompatible with justice and reason. Why, asked a number of prominent Ranters, would God condemn humanity for a single crime committed long ago by a man (Adam) whom no one living ever knew? Familists denied that he had, arguing that all God's children would be saved: Heaven lies within us, we bear no sin at all. More than a few of these radicals were ready to doubt the existence of Hell, a great many others to believe that Christ's kingdom was at hand. And in the midst of this topsy-turvy world—this world "turned upside down"—some caught a glimpse of happiness falling from the sky.[90] As the prominent Digger Gerrard Winstanley demanded on behalf of the poor:

> But why may not we have our heaven here (that is, a comfortable livelihood in the earth) and heaven hereafter, too . . . ?
> While men are gazing up to heaven, imagining after a happiness or fearing a hell after they are dead, their eyes are put out, that they see not what is their birthrights, and what is to be done by them here on earth while they are living.[91]

Perhaps earthly happiness was a long-forgotten right of birth, covered over by vicars and priests and princes to deny the people their due? Winstanley's words were more radical than most. But his belief that the happiness of heaven might be had here, too, was voiced in other quarters.

Thus, the Reverend Thomas Coleman, preaching before Parliament on August 30, 1643, likened his countrymen's struggle against Charles to the ancient Israelites' "long pursuit of happinesse."[92] The turn of phrase was felicitous, and others used it, too, as the journey to the promised land became a standard trope of radical polemicists.[93] Like the Ranter Abiezer Coppe, they urged the chosen people of England to journey forth to "Spiritual Canaan (the living Lord), which is a land of large liberty, the house of happiness . . . flowing with sweet wine, milk and honey. . . ."[94] In this place, the temporal and the celestial would be one.

As the allusions to Exodus make clear, many of these hopes had been expressed before. When the Puritan millenarian Thomas Brooks claimed that "being in a state of Grace will yield . . . both a Heaven here, and Heaven hereafter," rendering "a man's condition happy, safe, and sure," he was merely reaffirming much of what Luther and Calvin had already said.[95] So, too, was his widely held belief in the imminent arrival of the New Jerusalem a variation on a recurrent theme. Shared by Christ's followers themselves, anticipation of the millenarian moment had resurfaced periodically ever since, erupting with particular force in the immediate wake of the Reformation among Dutch and German Anabaptists. Even the English radicals' most shocking suggestion—that sin itself might be a lie—was but the latest articulation of the Pelagian heresy that had so incensed Augustine.

But if, in purely theological terms, the radical speculation of the English civil war was not entirely without precedent, its scale and intensity around the specific theme of earthly happiness most certainly was. Those seeking (to cite the revealing title of a contemporary tract) *The Way to Happinesse on Earth* did so with greater faith in the possibility of reaching that end than almost any group of men and women in the West since the coming of Christ.[96] The bloodshed of the civil war cast a pall over such optimism, and the repression of the more radical sects under Cromwell's consolidated Calvinist regime was more convincing still. But a critical threshold was crossed.[97] As even a royalist apologist was anxious to concede in the first year of the civil war, "We must look through all things upon happinesse, and through happiness upon all. . . ." For this force "giveth law to all our actions," he emphasized. "Happinesse is the language of all."[98]

John Locke would come to agree entirely with these propositions, and in fact he is rightly considered their most celebrated theorist of the seventeenth century. But just when and how he developed his views—and whether and how the literature of the 1640s helped to shape them—is not entirely clear; we lack sufficient information about the genesis of Locke's thinking. Studying moral philosophy and medicine, Locke lived quietly in Oxford until the late 1660s, first as a student, and then as a tutor, writing comparatively little and publishing nothing. And although (or because) he gradually became known in the most advanced scientific circles of the day—befriending the likes of Robert Boyle, Robert Hooke, and later, Isaac Newton—he kept a prudent silence about the events that swirled around him in his youth.

Certainly, Locke was no admirer of the Stuarts. Only ten when the civil war began, he was a Puritan by birth and the son of an officer in Cromwell's army. Over the course of his life, Locke's religious views evolved in unorthodox directions; but he never renounced his faith. Of his deep suspicion of monarchs, his later career bears ample testimony, suffusing the work for which he is today most often remembered, the *Two Treatises of Government*. Historians have long suspected that the *Two Treatises* may owe more than a little to the output of the 1640s, particularly to that of the Levellers, with which there are notable similarities.[99] But in the absence of a direct, evidentiary link, they are left to conclude that it was "from conversation and casual contact, not from documentary acquaintance that Locke inherited the fruit of the radical writings of the Civil War."[100] Much the same might be said about Locke's relationship to the mid-seventeenth century's fruitful writing on happiness. For though there is no written testimony of a direct connection, it does seem unlikely that he would have remained entirely unaffected by this broader context. Protestant radicals had crossed a threshold, broken a taboo, making it possible for men to conceive of their place in the world in new ways. It was left to Locke to conceive a new theory of the human mind to accommodate this novel aspiration.

Locke has almost nothing explicit to say about happiness in the *Two Treatises*.[101] But in his other masterwork, the *Essay Concerning Human Understanding*, the subject figures prominently. Begun as early as 1671, though not published until December 1689, the work—far more than the anonymously issued *Two Treatises*—catapulted Locke to international celebrity, earning him the lasting epithet "the New-ton of the Mind." Whether he actually merited this title is a compli-cated question.[102] But in a loose way, the man Locke referred to in his introductory "Epistle to the Reader" as the "incomparable Mr. Newton" almost certainly exercised an influence on the work's con-tent and conception. Whereas Newton aimed to demonstrate the universal laws of motion governing the operation of the solar system, Locke aimed to unveil the universal laws governing the operation of the human mind.

Such grand designs are hardly evident in Locke's own disingenu-ously humble claim that his purpose in the *Essay* was to act like "an under-labourer," "clearing the ground a little, and removing some of the Rubbish, that lies in the way to knowledge." But as one ventures into this dense, if well-marked, book, it becomes clear that by "rub-bish" Locke meant quite a lot. With reference to the vast range of peculiar, often conflicting habits, customs, and beliefs that litter the world, Locke concludes that we cannot be born with any fixed notions or ideas, moral or otherwise. If it were true, as many philosophers in the classical and Christian traditions had alleged, that the law of na-ture was inscribed in the hearts of all (or, as Locke's rough contempo-rary René Descartes had maintained, that "innate ideas" accompanied us at birth), then it would surely follow that young children and the uneducated would agree on their duties, or at least know what they are. But nowhere was this so, leading Locke to conclude that we are born into the world with minds like an "empty cabinet" or a "white piece of paper," a blank slate.

This was Locke's famous tabula rasa, and in the bulk of the *Essay* he endeavored to show how the world writes upon it, imprinting itself on our minds. Explaining this process in detail, he elaborates the com-plex mechanics of the motion of thought that lead from the physical sensations we receive from the external world to the formation of ideas through perception, reflection, contemplation, and judgment. For those interested in epistemology—the study of how we know—this discussion is of landmark importance. But from the perspective of the history of happiness, what is more interesting is what gets left aside.

For not only does Locke's tabula rasa clear away the rubbish of innate ideas, it wipes our slate clean of original sin. Locke was under no illusions about the quantity of evil in the world. And he fully understood the stubbornness of self-interest. But he refused to accept that we are born into the world with minds inherently marred, deficient in reason, and tending toward corruption.

To the degree that human beings give indication of any natural propensity at all, it is in a very different direction. "What is it that determines the Will in regard to our Actions?" he asks in the critical chapter "Power" in book 2 of the *Essay*. Uneasiness, he answers: "'Tis *uneasiness* alone [that] operates on the *will*, and determines it in its choice." Locke's blanket term for "all pain of the body" and "disquiet of the mind," uneasiness is invariably accompanied by desire, which is "scarce distinguishable from it." When we suffer the uneasiness of pain, we desire to be relieved of it. And when we suffer the uneasiness of an absent good, we desire the pleasure of its attainment.[103] To be uneasy is to be restless, kinetically dissatisfied with our present state, to desire change. Like an object acted upon by a force—and throughout this chapter, Locke uses such Newtonian metaphors, speaking of stones that fall, tennis balls hit by racquets, and billiard balls struck by cues—the will of the uneasy individual is propelled into motion, repulsed by pain, and attracted by pleasure. As one critic has observed, Locke's "uneasiness of desire is the first vague pull of the will entering a gravitational field."[104]

But what is the source of this force field that creates uneasiness, moving desire? Again, Locke is ready for the question:

> If it be farther asked, what 'tis moves *desire*? I answer happiness and that alone. *Happiness* and *Misery* are the names of two extremes, the utmost bound whereof we know not; 'tis what *Eye hath not seen, Ear hath not heard, nor hath it entred into the Heart of Man to conceive* [1 Cor. 2:9]. But of some degrees of both, we have very lively impressions, made by several instances of Delight and Joy on the one side and Torment and Sorrow on the other; which, for shortness sake, I shall comprehend

under the names of Pleasure and Pain, there being pleasure
and pain of the Mind, as well as the Body. . . .

   Happiness then in its full extent is the utmost Pleasure we
are capable of, and *Misery*, the utmost Pain. . . .[105]

That we have come across similar reflections before may obscure the
tremendous novelty of this passage. Locke's argument here is reminiscent of Epicurus, who also envisioned pleasure and pain as the
motive forces of human action, the great movers of human desire. The
debt is straightforward, though not direct: Locke drew his Epicurean
views largely from a seventeenth-century French mathematician and
priest, Pierre Gassendi, who had attempted to build a Christian system on the shoulders of Epicurus.[106] The Englishman was not quite
so foolhardy, but in truth he *does* seek to Christianize important Epicurean assumptions. Placing God at the heart of this passage, Locke
sets the Creator at one extreme of the scale of happiness, marking
off the distance from the misery of eternal damnation. And though
divine rapture—the happiness of heaven—is ultimately inconceivable,
Locke assumes that it is qualitatively of a kind with the pleasures we
know here. The foretaste of heavenly delight is no rarefied intellectual attainment—no fleeting glimpse of beatitude—but something
we can savor, relish, and feel. More to the point, the pleasure we
experience in this life leads directly to that of the next. In Locke's
divinely orchestrated universe, pleasure is providential; in following
its promptings, we are led to God.

   Pleasure as divine impetus? It is no wonder that a good many of
Locke's Christian contemporaries regarded his assertions with suspicion. Yet Locke never intended his model of the mind as an apology for all manner of indulgence. Nor did he see his theory of
providential pull as in any way eclipsing the prospect of human freedom. If God, in his wisdom, had made pleasure and pain the motive
forces that shape our will, he meant for us to use our liberty and reason to decide what *true* pain and *true* pleasure were. And this, precisely, was where many went wrong. Although individuals were
infallible in their calculations regarding short-term pleasures and

pains—responding with the alacrity of a hand thrust in a cookie jar or pulled from a flame—they frequently made egregious errors when looking down the road, or failed to look at all. Following the detours of custom, fashion, ill habit, or simple wrong judgment, they continually led themselves astray, exchanging lasting gain for more fleeting fancy. It was thus of the utmost importance that the seeker of happiness remain ever vigilant in calculating pleasures and pains. "This is the hinge on which turns the *liberty* of intellectual Beings," Locke affirmed. As the "highest perfection" of our nature lay in "a careful and constant pursuit of true and solid happiness," it was incumbent that "we mistake not imaginary for real happiness."[107]

But how was one to distinguish the two? This was the great question, and given its magnitude, Locke's answer may strike us as less than revolutionary. For in effect he concludes that the surest way to real happiness is the road to everlasting life. Bet on the existence of heaven, Locke maintains, and we cannot lose: "When infinite Happiness is put in one Scale, against infinite Misery in the other; if the worst, that comes to the pious Man, if he mistakes, be the best that the wicked can attain to, if he be in the right, Who can without madness run the venture?"[108] As Locke would reaffirm in a later work, using the same metaphor of the scale, virtue was "visibly the most enriching purchase and by much the best bargain."[109]

To conceive of heaven as a "good bargain" was not exactly the quintessence of piety. And indeed the title of the work in which Locke makes this statement, *The Reasonableness of Christianity* (1695), is indicative of his general orientation toward the faith. Religion could command our assent only when it was in accordance with reason, Locke held, a conviction that led him to discount many of the historical accretions of Christian dogma. Denying (like Newton) the doctrine of the Trinity and relegating revelation to a subsidiary role to reason, which he described as "natural revelation"—the true "candle of the Lord"—Locke made of Christianity in essence a purely ethical creed. Yet he retained faith in the afterlife as an indispensable guide to the path we should follow here below:

Open [men's] eyes upon the endless unspeakable joys of
another life and their hearts will find something solid and
powerful to move them. The view of heaven and hell will cast
a slight upon the short pleasures and pains of this present
state, and give attractions and encouragements to virtue,
which reason and interest, and the care of ourselves, cannot
but allow and prefer. *Upon this foundation, and upon this only,
morality stands firm.*[110]

The last line is revealing. For in fact Locke had skirted dangerously
close to imagining a world without such foundations. Given, as he had
argued in the *Essay,* that "pleasure in us, is that we call *Good,* and what
is apt to produce Pain in us, we call *Evil,*" one could be led to conclude
that good and evil were merely matters of taste.[111] And since one man's
pleasure was another man's pain, in the absence of a better world to
justify this one, the road to happiness would branch out in countless
directions. It was a prospect that Locke was willing to contemplate
openly:

If therefore Men [have hope only in this life]; if in this Life
they can only enjoy, 'tis not strange, nor unreasonable, that
they should seek their Happiness by avoiding all things that
disease them here, and by pursuing all that delight them;
wherein it will be no wonder to find variety and difference.
For if there be no Prospect beyond the Grave, the inference is
certainly right, *Let us eat and drink,* let us enjoy what we delight
in, *for tomorrow we shall die.*[112]

The reference, of course, was to a line of scripture, invoked, as we
have seen, by Paul in 1 Corinthians 15:32 but also found in Isaiah
22:13. It captures equally well the Epicurean injunction—or that of
Horace's carpe diem—uttered without restraints. Locke was perfectly
prepared to complete the thought. "Were all the Concerns of Man
terminated in this Life," he added, then "why one followed Study

and Knowledge, and another Hawking and Hunting; why one chose Luxury and Debauchery, and another Sobriety and Riches" would be simply "because their *Happiness* was placed in different things." Some men liked lobsters, and others liked cheese. To try to satisfy them with the same pleasure was an impossible task, a reflection that prompted Locke to dismiss the inquiries of the ancients after a single *summum bonum* consisting in virtue, or contemplation, or bodily delights. They might just as reasonably have disputed, Locke quipped, "whether the best Relish were to be found in Apples, Plumbs, or Nuts."[113]

Yet having entertained the thought that there might be as many paths to happiness as there were pleasures of men, Locke backed away. "The Manna in Heaven will suit everyone's Palate," he declared, urging that we make this the final object of our desire.[114] Since the ancient Israelites had taken up the road to Canaan, since the Greeks had set out toward the highest good, since Christ had proclaimed, "I am the way," happiness in the West had only ever been conceived as a single journey to a single end. Locke was not willing to multiply the paths in infinite directions.

The more radical Thomas Hobbes, Locke's contemporary and acquaintance, was alone prepared to contemplate that possibility unflinchingly. Judging without reserve that there was "nothing simply and absolutely" good or evil—only what we named the object of our desire and the object of our hatred—Hobbes dismissed the idea of happiness as a final end. "The felicity of this life consisteth not in the repose of a mind satisfied," he observed: "For there is no such *Finis ultimus* [utmost aim] or *Summum Bonum* [greatest good] as is spoken of in the books of the old moral philosophers." Felicity, rather, was a "continual progress of the desire, from one object to another, the attaining of the former being still but the way to the latter." And so the process would continue unabated, according to the pleasures and tastes, the aversions and fears of each, until it was finally arrested. Even the best scenario need be qualified and provisional. "*Continual success* in obtaining those things which a man from time to time desireth, that is to say, continual prospering, is that men call Felicity; I mean the felicity of this life. For there is no such thing as perpetual tranquility of mind, while we live here; because life itself is but motion, and can never be without desire, nor without fear, no more than without sense." In Hobbes's view, human bodies could be at rest only when all motion stopped. Until that time, they would be ruled by "a perpetual and restless desire of power after power, that ceaseth only in death."[115]

This was not an altogether consoling picture. Yet it was one present just below the surface in Locke. "We are seldom at ease, and free enough from the sollicitation of our natural or adopted desires," he acknowledged in the *Essay*, "but a constant succession of *uneasiness*... take the *will* in their turns; and no sooner is one action dispatch'd... but another *uneasiness* is ready to set us on work."[116] Here, too, the individual was caught up in a restless and perpetual chase, an endless *pursuit*. Given "the multitude of wants, and desires, we are beset with in this imperfect State," Locke confessed, "we are not like to be ever freed from [uneasiness] in this World."[117] Were it not for the haven of peace in the next life, the pursuit of happiness would have no end.

As we will see in later chapters, this prospect would return to haunt the Western imagination. But in Locke's own day, and for some time thereafter, his readers were largely content to overlook such disconcerting speculation. For whatever else might be said, Locke *had* legitimated the search for happiness in this life, grounding it in science, human impulse, and divine order. Whereas in the cosmos envisioned by the humanists and their Protestant successors, men and women were ultimately *led* to perfect happiness by the motive power of Grace, in Locke's Newtonian system, human beings were pulled along by their own weight. Here there was little room for divine intervention, little need for grace: Happiness was in the nature of things. "Men's happiness or misery is most part of their own making," Locke affirmed in his great treatise on education.[118] As he reaffirmed elsewhere, "The business of men is to be happy in this world by the enjoyment of the things of nature subservient to life, health, ease, and pleasure, and by the comfortable hopes of another life when this is ended."[119] *This* was a consoling picture.

In the thought of John Locke, then, one sees the fruition of a conception of Christian happiness on earth that had developed and grown since Thomas Aquinas scattered the seeds of *felicitas* in the imperfect soil of the world. Nourished by the humanists' cultivation of the dignity of earthly existence and the general Protestant injunction to pursue happiness in all things, Locke's notion of happiness grew beyond the limitations of both. For though it was still true that in comparison to the "utmost bound" of pleasure to be tasted in heaven, the pleasures of this life were not so sweet, Locke presented them as part of a continuum, of a kind with heavenly delights. The gap between perfect happiness and happiness imperfect was not a vast chasm but a natural progression from the pleasures of this world to the pleasures of the next. Our "very lively impressions" of the one gave a sweet foretaste of the other. The manna of heaven and the manna of earth were not such different things. Some pleasures, yes, remained better than others, but pleasure itself was no longer bad. We should pursue it as best we could.

And we should be free to do so. If Locke seldom referred specifically to what he described, in passing, in the *Two Treatises on Government* as "political happiness," politics was undoubtedly present in his general conception of man and mind.[120] Intended by our creator to pursue happiness as a law of nature, we must not be impeded in our course or deflected from our path by the power of an outside force. It was not sufficient, as the Roman emperors and other absolute monarchs had done, simply to proclaim *felicitas temporum*, the happiness of the times. Liberty was an indispensable condition of the natural trajectory of happiness and of its proper pursuit. As long as we did no harm to others—or impeded their paths—we should be allowed to pursue our own.

This must also include the freedom to choose poorly, the freedom to go awry. For in Locke's view, a necessary element of human dignity—the "hinge" on which the liberty of intellectual beings turned—was our ability to determine pleasures and pains for ourselves. He hoped, without question, that we would choose the right course, and he possessed a clear conception of what this should be, urging like the Renaissance humanists that our "highest perfection" lay in the "careful and constant pursuit" of true happiness along the Christian path. But for the same reasons that it was not government's prerogative to legislate salvation by dictating religious faith, it was not government's

Peter Paul Rubens, *The Felicity of the Regency*, 1623–25, Bibliothèque nationale de France. Rubens proclaims the happy reign in France of Maria de Medici, mother of Louis XIII, who ruled as regent following the death of her husband, Henry IV.

place to legislate happiness. In either instance, "toleration" must be shown, as Locke emphasized in a famous open letter on the subject, written in 1685, and first published in 1689. Of the many paths pursued by men, he acknowledged:

> There is only one of these which is the true way to eternal happiness. But in this great variety of ways that men follow, it is still doubted which is this right one. Now neither the care of the commonwealth, nor the right of enacting laws, does discover this way that leads to heaven more certainly to the magistrate, than every private man's search and study discovers it unto himself.[121]

Individuals should be left to answer to God and their own consciences regarding the steps they take to attain happiness in this life, as in the next.

Locke's extension of the principle of toleration from the realm of ultimate happiness to that of happiness on earth would have important consequences for the development of democracy. By emphasizing individual liberty and choice, Locke placed the burden of pursuit on the shoulders of men and women, not on their governments. To provide the free space in which to pursue our ends was one thing, to secure those ends another. Even the "right enacting of laws," Locke knew, was unlikely to discover the "one true way" to happiness. We should ever be wary of the attempt.

Nevertheless, by establishing the principle of the consent of the governed, and by giving citizens the right to cashier their rulers when they acted in defiance of the common good, Locke's ideas, like the revolution they aimed to uphold, admitted a new place for happiness in the political vocabulary of the West. If human happiness was genuinely intended by the laws of the universe and the order of creation, then surely any government that impeded its attainment did not rule in keeping with the natural order. Did it not follow, in some measure, that governments had a responsibility to provide for the happiness of the governed? Locke himself observed that "the public good is the rule and measure of all law-making," and "If a thing be not useful to the commonwealth . . . it may not presently be established by law."[122] But what did "useful" imply? And if the limits of the pursuit of happiness were those actions "destructive to human society," what did "destruction" entail? Far from ending debate on such questions, Locke's theories brought them to the fore.

Arts of Contentment

Fifteen years before John Locke's *Essay Concerning Human Understanding* graced the bookstalls of London, Richard Allestree published his own *Art of Contentment* (1675). Few today will have heard of Allestree, but in his own time, he cut quite a figure. The provost of Eton College and a leading Royalist divine, Allestree had personally taken up arms to fight with the forces of Charles I during the civil war. He had since become a popular moralist, and with *The Art of Contentment*— a work that went through over twenty editions, remaining in print until the nineteenth century—he captured the tenor of his age in language even a schoolboy could understand. "Though every man would have happiness," Allestree began, the great majority lose themselves in "blind pursuits."[123] This is regrettable, for God, who is "happy in himself," has shown us "a more certain, a more compendious way to acquire what we grasp after," laying out in the Gospel "a plain, a safe, nay a pleasant path, as much superior both in the ease of the way, and in the end to which it leads, as heaven is to Canaan."[124] Unlike the Israelites, we need not wander through the wilderness, need not ramble in "wild pursuits after [happiness], we may form it within our own breasts." Happiness lies within us all, and Christianity shows the way. "'Tis certainly the most excellent, the most com-

The title page of a 1675 edition of Richard Allestree's *Art of Contentment*. Bodleian Library, The University of Oxford.

pendious art of happy living" ever formed. "All the lines of worldly happiness are concentrated" there. It is the *unum necessarium,* the only necessary thing we need to have the "grand and ultimate happiness" of the next life, and this our "intermedial" happiness as well.[125]

Allestree made these points in the book's first pages. As unimpeachable as it is conservative, the remainder of the work counsels thankfulness, deference to authority, and acceptance of one's circumstances: precisely what might be expected from this Restoration supporter of the Stuarts. But if Allestree was no revolutionary, he was nonetheless taking part in a revolution—a profound rotation of the heavenly and earthly spheres—that involved what one scholar has termed the "reconceptualization of suffering" as a means to the art of contentment.[126] The primacy that Perpetua had once placed on reliving Christ's passion in the journey to paradise and the value that many Catholics had long seen in suffering as a way to God were being turned aside. Gradually, the pleasures of earth were coming around, while Heaven, so long the focus of Western eyes, receded a little farther into the ether of space. And amid this upheaval in the cosmos, a new divinity was forming, which religion, too, was learning to serve. Like its predecessors, earthly happiness would show itself to be a jealous god.

This great reorientation of the human gaze—from the joys of heaven to the happiness of earth—took place slowly, and in fact had scarcely begun. It is nonetheless revealing that a man such as Allestree—a high churchman and a defender of the Stuarts—could essentially agree with a revolutionary latitudinarian like Locke. The potential for earthly happiness lay within us, both believed, and though religion could show us the way, there was increasing scope for thinking that we generated momentum on our own. The two men would have agreed on little else. But on happiness they saw eye to eye.

Their perspective was not unchallenged. Many continued to emphasize the insuperable barrier of sin, and the inherent unhappiness of life, believing, like the pious Restoration author of *The Happinesse of Those who Sleep in Jesus* that our true reward comes only in death.[127] Yet for all the inertia of this belief—and it was considerable—the new perspective was gathering force. The final two decades of the seventeenth century witnessed an explosion of works on happiness, and the very titles are revealing. Rummaging through a London bookstore, one might come across *A Persuasive to a Holy Life from the Happiness that Attends it Both in this World, and in the World to Come;* or chance upon *The Way to Health, Long Life and Happiness,* a discourse on temperance boasting "the most hidden secrets of philosophy . . . communicated to the world for a general good"; or meet happily with *England's Happiness Improved, or An Infallible way to get Riches, Encrease Plenty, and Promote Pleasure,* a tract extolling the unlikely art of making "Wine of English grapes."[128] This, surely, was the ultimate affirmation of ordinary life.

In formal theology, one can also trace the "diminishing emphasis" afforded to the "spiritual benefits" of pain over the course of the seventeenth century.[129] Another of the long-term consequences of the

Gérard Audrand and Pierre Mignard, *The Felicity of the Blessed.* Design for the cupola of the church of Val de Grâce, 1693. Musée de Louvre, Paris.
Photo: Réunion des Musées Nationaux/Art Resource, NY.

Reformation, which frowned on gratuitous suffering, this change was likewise reflected in the arts, where new value was appreciated in pleasure. In music, for example, composers took to celebrating the various delights of existence. Henry Purcell's 1683 ode "Welcome to All the Pleasures," though nominally dedicated to Saint Cecilia, the patron saint of music, is in fact a wider celebration of the pleasures of art and the arts of pleasure:

> Welcome to all the pleasures that delight
> Of ev'ry sense the grateful appetite,
> Hail, great assembly of Apollo's race.
> Hail to this happy place, this musical assembly
> That seems to be the arc of universal harmony.

It was a perfect statement of an emerging conception of the world.

Purcell's perspective was certainly shared by his sometime librettist, the future poet laureate of England, Nahum Tate. In 1681, Tate published an adaptation of Shakespeare's tragedy *King Lear*, which sought to improve upon the original by, among other things, giving the play a happy ending. Rather than conclude the drama in a bloodbath, like the bard, Tate preferred to spare the life of the heroine Cordelia as well as that of her lover, Edgar, so that the two might marry and live, like Lear, happily ever after. As strange as these alterations may seem today, Tate's adaptation proved tremendously appealing to contemporary audiences, holding the stage in preference to the original well into the nineteenth century.[130] It is tempting to read in its success an evolving preference for the outcome expressed in its ending, a growing conviction that human beings need not wait for the next world to bring their lives to a happy conclusion.

This is probably pushing the interpretation a little too far. Yet it is undoubtedly the case that one witnesses in the poetry of this period the consolidation of a more general image of the "happy man," who succeeds in living his days happily until the end. The image is that of the happy husbandman in rural retirement, culled largely from the pastoral visions of Horace and Virgil.[131] In many ways, their idyll of rural innocence had never been forgotten: Even medieval poets were familiar with the message of Horace's carpe diem.[132] But the recovery of his work that began in the Renaissance gave the theme a freshness and a new poignancy. Already in the 1470s, Lorenzo de Medici could write in the lyrics to a carnival song:

> How lovely is youth—
> Yet it slips away;
> If you would be happy, be so.
> There is no certainty about tomorrow.[133]

And in the middle of the next century, the French-born printer of Antwerp, Christophe Plantin, penned a sonnet, "*Le Bonheur de ce monde,*" that can still be found hanging in the foyers and entry halls of modern homes. The poem urges the Horatian themes of simplicity and acceptance, harmony and peace, with Plantin, the Catholic son of a servant, recommending a clean and comfortable house in the country, a garden and fruit trees, and "some excellent wine." Content yourself with little, he counsels: a faithful wife, few children, no debts, lawsuits, or quarrels. Live without ambition, be devout, keep an open mind. And say your rosary as you tend to your vines, waiting sweetly in the garden for death to come when it will. This is the "happiness of the world."[134]

Plantin's poem tends to the more Stoic side of the Horatian formula, as did much of the pastoral verse of the later-sixteenth-century Pléiade, the group of French poets who also picked up on the theme of rural retirement. Others followed Medici in hinting at stronger pleasures, but the majority imitated Horace in loosely blending Epicurean and Stoic themes to craft new images of the modern *beatus vir.* Tempered always by the Christian spirit, the theme of the happy man in rural retirement came into its own in seventeenth-century England, when John Ashmore and Thomas Hawkins, among others, devoted themselves to new translations of Horace's satires and odes. Dryden followed with his own, turning also to Virgil and Lucretius; in between, some of the greatest poets of the century—Milton and Ben

Jonson, Thomas Traherne and Henry Vaughan, Robert Herrick and
Abraham Cowley—cultivated Christian-inflected images of the Stoic
or Epicurean sage living in pastoral bliss. Thus Milton can invoke in
Il Penseroso "retired leisure, / That in trim Gardens takes his pleasure," while Jonson translates approvingly from Horace, in poetry of
his own:

> Happie is he, that from all Businesse cleere,
> As the old race of Mankind were,
> With his owne Oxen tills his Sires left lands,
> And is not in the Usurers bands. . . .[135]

The poet Joseph Hall counsels:

> . . . let thy Rural Sanctuary be
> Elizium to thy wife and thee;
> There to disport your selves with golden measure.[136]

And Robert Herrick exults:

> Hail, the poor Muses richest Mannor Seat!
>   Ye Country Houses and Retreat,
>   Which all the happy Gods so Love,
> That for you oft they quit their Bright and Great
>   Metropolis above.[137]

Much of this poetry amounted, like Horace's own, to a none too subtle
critique of the corruption of the times. To preach rural retirement
was to urge withdrawal from the business of the world, a theme that,
in the hands of Royalist poets like Vaughan and Cowley, could be directed explicitly against what they saw as the unfortunate ascendance
of Puritans. Indeed, the invocation of Epicurean themes of innocent
pleasure—like Allestree's Tory contentment—was frequently intended by Royalists to contrast favorably with what they regarded,
however unjustly, as the pinched and crabbed asceticism of their

rivals. But again, what is most compelling is the common ground. A Puritan like Milton can end the last line of his poem *"L'Allegro,"* commenting on the pleasures of art and the world:

> These delights, if thou canst give,
> Mirth with thee, I mean to live.

And a Restoration poet and dramatist like William Wycherley is ready with a response:

> We from our selves alone, and not from Fate,
> Derive our happy, or unhappy State. . . .
> If Fates Inconstancy we wou'd prevent,
> We, in all States of Life, shou'd seek Content . . .[138]

Increasingly, the common goal of pleasure and happiness was shared. What was disputed was only the means.

Nor were such affirmations confined to England. I have singled out this blessed isle in part because it *was* unique in the history of happiness, producing as the strange offspring of English Protestantism, English science, and the English revolution an unprecedented ethic of earthly content. The same country that had served as corpse for Robert Burton's anatomy of melancholy—a land that would later breed a distinctive form of sadness known simply as the "English malady"—may be said to have given birth to modern happiness.

But this is not to imply that children elsewhere fell stillborn in despair. The general forces that had worked to create a space for earthly happiness in England were at work abroad, too. In Scotland and Ireland, in the American colonies, and on the European continent, influential voices were beginning to draw similar conclusions from the combined precedents of Renaissance humanism and innovative Christian theology, imagining a place for pleasure and felicity on earth. As increasing numbers began to think beyond the boundaries of sin, the scope for Western happiness widened considerably. Within decades of the turn of the century, what was still a trickle of names endorsing lives of earthly content grew steadily to become a torrent, producing more writing and reflection on worldly happiness than the world had ever known. And what, until then, had been only a guarded thought was proclaimed openly: If happiness was a natural state, why could it not be attained entirely by natural means, without divine guidance at all?

4

SELF-EVIDENT TRUTHS

In 1691, Bishop Pierre-Daniel Huet published *A Treatise on the Position of the Earthly Paradise.* One of Europe's foremost biblical scholars and a member of the prestigious Academie Française, Huet hoped to put an end to a controversy that had long divided the posterity of Adam: Just where on earth had God placed his first children, and where now did the remnants of that once great garden lie?

> [The earthly paradise] has been located in the third heaven,
> in the fourth, in the heaven of the moon, on the moon itself
> ... outside the earth, on the earth, under the earth, and in a
> hidden place far removed from human knowledge. It has been
> placed under the Arctic pole ... on the banks of the Ganges
> or on the island of Ceylon. ... Others have located it in the
> Americas, others in Africa below the equator, others in the
> equinoctial East. ... Most have located it in Asia: some in
> Greater Armenia, others in Mesopotamia or Assyria or Persia
> or Babylonia or Arabia or Syria or Palestine. There have been
> those who wished to honor our Europe. ...[1]

Huet was referring to the veritable mountain of opinion that had piled up over the ages, sending medieval knights and early modern adventurers scurrying over much of the globe in search of our ancestral home. With the help of advanced biblical scholarship and a firm grasp of geography, Huet believed he could finally pinpoint the coordinates. Carefully considering the relevant passages in scripture, he concluded that paradise lay to the eastern end of Eden, and that Eden itself constituted the better part of Babylonia. The happy home of humanity, it seems, stood in the Tigris and Euphrates delta, in modern-day Iraq.

Well aware that this view had been put forth before, Huet was less conscious that his view was slowly being eroded—less by competing theories of the position of the earthly paradise than by a decline in the all-encompassing belief in human sin. It may be true, as the famed English soldier and explorer Sir Walter Raleigh once observed, that "all of us have a deep-rooted desire to know the place where our first parents lived." But the passion for the discovery of the place of the bib-

J. Moxon, *Paradise, or the Garden of Eden*, London, 1695. One of many such geographical renderings of the Biblical Paradise. The Garden of Eden can be seen in the right middle. By permission of the British Library.

lical Eden was driven above all by theological concerns.[2] Only by fully fathoming the state of primordial happiness, many believed, could we comprehend what we had become. It was awareness of sin that powered the search for our place of innocence, because it was sin that determined the magnitude of our subsequent Fall. And so, as the preoccupation with inherent human evil waned, so did the need to know the precise coordinates of a long-vanished Eden. At the end of the seventeenth century, Huet's treatise was gratefully received by the Sun King, Louis XIV. Just decades later, Voltaire spoke for the exploratory interests of a new age. "Earthly paradise," he quipped, mocking Huet, "is where I am."[3]

This shift in perspective—from the longing gaze in the direction of a vanished golden age to a steady look straight ahead—was never as neat or as tidy as this juxtaposition might suggest. Paradise lost continued to exert its attractions long after the eighteenth century, just as the paradise in Heaven continued to exert its pull. Yet the eighteenth century did witness an important reorientation in outlook along the lines suggested by Voltaire's bon mot. His friend and colleague the philosopher Claude-Adrien Helvétius made a similar observation with regard to declining fears in a punishing afterlife. "Hell is no more; 'tis Heaven now on earth," he observed in his long poem "Happiness."[4] Increasingly, men and women were coming to think of the world as a place where human beings might legitimately cultivate if not paradise, then at least a garden of earthly delights.

Indeed, in spaces like those at Vauxhall and Ranelagh Gardens in England, and in Paris at the Palais-Royal, eighteenth-century Europeans erected vast "pleasure gardens" where men and women could go simply for the purpose of enjoying themselves, of having "fun."[5] The word itself was a relative novelty, introduced in English only in the late seventeenth century as a variation of the Middle English *fon*, meaning jester or fool. As places where fun could be had, the pleasure gardens were forebearers of our modern amusement parks, offering games and recreation, spectacles and refreshments, music, and sanctuaries in which lovers could stroll. They put flesh on the new endorsement of pleasure expressed in theory by the likes of Locke,

symbolizing perfectly a wider eighteenth-century aspiration to create
space for happiness on earth. To dance, to sing, to enjoy our food, to
revel in our bodies and the company of others—in short, to delight
in a world of our own making—was not to defy God's will but to live
as nature had intended. This was our earthly purpose. As the poet
Alexander Pope declared in his celebrated lines:

> Oh, happiness, our being's end and aim!
> Good, pleasure, ease, content! Whate'er thy name:
> That something still which prompts the eternal sigh,
> For which we bear to live, or dare to die. . . .[6]

The great goal of the century, it was expressed time and again. "Does
not everyone have a right to happiness?" asked the Abbé Pestré, the
author of the entry on that subject in the French encyclopedia edited by Denis Diderot.[7] Judged by the standards of the preceding
millennium and a half, the question was extraordinary: a *right* to happiness? And yet it was posed rhetorically, in full confidence of the
nodding assent of enlightened minds. By midcentury the claim was
becoming commonplace, and by century's end it was more common
still. Clearly, human beings deserved to be happy. The question was
how could felicity on earth best be achieved?

Eighteenth-century authors sought to answer this question in unprecedented numbers. No previous age, in fact, wrote so much on the
subject or so often. In France, Britain, and the Low Countries, in
Germany, Italy, and the United States, disquisitions on happiness
poured from the presses: reflections on happiness, treatises on happiness, systems of happiness, discourses, essays, sketches, and epistles.[8]
As far away as Warsaw, the College of Nobles saw fit to organize a lecture series on the theme "Man's Happiness Here Below."[9] Even in
Saint Petersburg, the privileged were allowed to join in the fun. After
striking a favorable peace with the armies of the Ottoman Empire in
1775, Catherine the Great commissioned the French master of ceremonies A. P. Pochet to organize celebrations in the new international style. One thousand performers were thrust into service,

dancing, singing, tumbling, riding, and swimming in a gigantic spectacle that featured three hundred mechanical horses, a boat pulled by tritons on an artificial lake, a circus, a carousel, fireworks, and four allegorical plays. Amid this revelry, the goddess Felicity assumed center stage, drawn on a chariot by four white bulls to a massive "Temple of Happiness."[10] Not since the Roman Empire had Felicity been worshipped with such fanfare. And rarely had so much energy been devoted to her earthly pursuit.

Of course, pursuit and capture are two different things. The more sober observers of the century—men like Samuel Johnson and Immanuel Kant—appreciated the difference. But there was a tendency to blur the distinction and, in doing so, to complicate the answers to a number of fundamental questions. For if happiness was truly a natural condition, a law of our nature and the way we were intended to be, then how to account for the continued existence of misery? And if earthly happiness was treated primarily as a function of good feeling,

R. Pollard and F. Jukes, engraving after Thomas Rowlandson,
Vauxhall Gardens, 1785, Elisha Whittelsey Collection,
Metropolitan Museum of Art, New York.

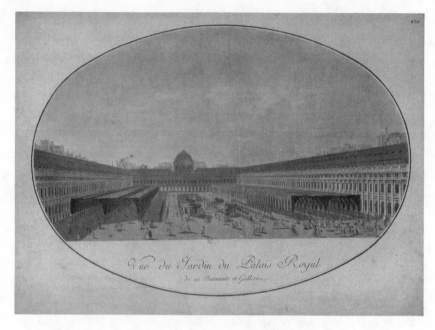

Paris's pleasure garden, the Palais-Royal. Photo courtesy of the
Bibliothèque nationale de France.

the balance of pleasure over pain, then what of the age-old links tying
happiness to higher things: to God, virtue, or the right ordering of the
soul? Was feeling good the same as being good? Was being good feeling
good? Was happiness a reward for simply living, or a reward for living
well?

Authors of the eighteenth century wrestled with these questions,
and in their struggle to provide answers, they unwittingly revealed
what only the most enlightened souls of the century were prepared to
acknowledge. As one perceptive observer, the scientist, translator, and
spurned mistress of Voltaire, the Marquise du Châtelet, confessed in
her own *Discourse on Happiness,* to be happy "one must be susceptible
to illusions, for it is to illusions that we owe the majority of our pleasures. Unhappy is the one who has lost them."[11] Châtelet experienced
the full weight of these words, dying disillusioned and in despair.
Belief in happiness, she seemed to understand, remained, even in an
age of Enlightenment, a species of faith.[12]

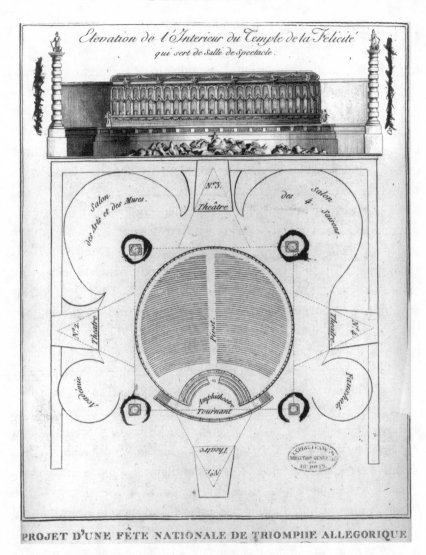

A sketch from A. P. Pochet's diagrams for the Temple of Happiness,
Archives nationale de France.

Felicific Calculus

But why this dramatic reorientation and shift in the eighteenth century—a shift whose clearest index was the explosion of interest in
earthly happiness itself? Already, we have traced several important
factors: the development within Christianity of new attitudes toward
pleasure and sin; the belief worked out painstakingly from Aquinas
to the Reformation and beyond that earthly happiness might be
treated as a sign of grace; and the notion, developed by Locke and
others, that to delight in the world—to live happily—is to live as God
intended. In this view, the world was not a "vale of tears" but a place
to experience the sweet foretaste of even greater joys to come. "It is
a happy world after all," concluded the Reverend William Paley at the
end of the eighteenth century.[13] A Protestant divine and an important natural scientist, Paley saw the imprint of God's providence in
the wonders of creation. The world was as it should be, reflecting the
happy design and purpose of its maker.

Paley's was a common perspective, one that came to be shared by
many Catholics as well. Already by the second half of the century,
otherwise orthodox members of the church were penning treatises
with popular titles like *I Want to Be Happy, The School of Happiness,* and
The Theory of Happiness, or the Art of Rendering Oneself So.[14] True, virtually all of these works continued to insist that religion was the foundation—"the unique basis"—of earthly happiness, to cite one such title
by the French author Madame de Genlis.[15] And they dutifully pointed
out that perfect happiness would come only in the afterlife with God.
But by presenting religion as a means to what was increasingly regarded as a legitimate earthly end, these authors were participating in
the radical reevaluation of the century, the slow transfer of sacrality
from the otherworldly God of old to the god of good feeling, the god of
happiness, which was extending its sway on earth.

These religious developments were at once cause and effect of this
broader shift in human aspirations. But so, too, were material factors:
the rise of nation states equipped with standing armies and civil ad-
ministrations better able to guarantee security and the rule of law;

advances in agricultural productivity and the greater availability of arable land; the expansion of trade and the birth of consumer cultures that widened access to luxury goods while providing disposable income to spend on fashion, entertainment, or a trip to a pleasure garden. It is all too easy to forget, in fact, that the pursuit of earthly happiness as something more than good fortune or a millenarian dream is a luxury in itself. Only when individuals are free from the vicious daily pursuit of staying alive can they afford to undertake the pursuit of more exalted goals. Whatever one's final definition of happiness, it is rarely compatible with regular and periodic famine, the ravages of plague and pestilence, or the threat of marauding armies.

Such scourges did not cease in the eighteenth century, but by comparison with earlier periods, the century fared well. To take one revealing example, it is estimated that in the first half of the seventeenth century, a third of the population of Central Europe was killed off by war, starvation, and disease.[16] The eighteenth century saw its own conflicts and crises, but not until its final decade, with the onset of the French Revolution, did it approach anything close to that horrendous scale. Even the terrible carnage of the Napoleonic Wars did not arrest the general upward trends. The total population of Europe, which stood at roughly 120 million in the early 1700s, reached 180 to 190 million by century's end, shooting up precipitously after 1750. Sustained by declining mortality rates and longer life spans, it would never fall again.[17]

Unquestionably, there were great imbalances in the scale of this change—from region to region and from rich to poor. But though one might qualify the following statement in a variety of ways, its basic truth is difficult to deny: The struggle for existence—however imperfectly, however haltingly—was becoming *less* of a struggle for *more* human beings. Improvements in livestock breeding boosted the supply of meat, ensuring more protein in the daily diet. The opening of new land to cultivation, favorable long-term weather patterns, advances in agricultural productivity, and the introduction of hitherto unexploited crops such as maize and the potato from the New World meant that Europeans ate more than ever before. Fortified by this nutritional infusion, they were less susceptible to disease. The last major outbreak of plague in Western Europe occurred in Marseille in 1720, and though typhus, dysentery, and influenza remained, those blights could not stem the steady influx of men and women from the countryside into the eighteenth century's expanding cities and towns.

Although that pattern of urbanization would not reach its high point until the nineteenth century, in the 1700s the growth of urban centers was already creating new concentrated markets that served as a catalyst for what historians describe as the "birth of consumer society."[18] By the mid-eighteenth century, a "favorable conjuncture" of an expanding population and rising agricultural prices, coupled with a greater availability of credit and a massive boom in foreign trade, was paying dividends in the form of increased investment and sustained economic growth.[19] The supply of consumer goods and commodities available to the middle and upper classes grew by the decade. Whether Brazilian coffee or West Indian sugar, Virginia tobacco or British porcelain and textiles, luxuries were at hand and available to ever wider segments of the population, subject, like the exploding market for stylish garments, to whims and fancies, fashion and trends. They appealed directly to the century's fascination with pleasure. As the French government minister and philosopher Anne-Robert-Jacques Turgot observed, people in modern commercial societies "as it were, bought and sold happiness."[20]

The statement was exaggerated for effect. But it does capture nicely how well the emerging commercial economies of the eighteenth century coincided with the new ethics of pleasure announced by Locke and his many continental admirers. By buying and selling luxury items and services with the explicit aim of enhancing pleasure and reducing pain, men and women pursued happiness in the manner that both Locke and Hobbes had described—as a "continual progress of the desire, from one object to another, the attaining of the former being still but the way to the latter."[21] Economists and moralists, from Adam Smith to Karl Marx, would find much of interest in this progress of desire, and it was not always reassuring. Nevertheless, by giving men and women greater confidence in their ability to control and improve

Nicolas Lancret, *A Lady in a Garden Taking Coffee,* c. 1742,
National Gallery, London. Bequeathed by Sir John Heathcoat
Amory Bt. Introduced into Europe only in the late seventeenth
century, coffee was a new luxury for the middle and upper classes.

Eighteenth-century fashions fueled the "buying of happiness."
Photo: The New York Public Library/Art Resource, NY.

their environment, these economic and material advances sapped the power of traditional explanations that consigned life to inevitable suffering. In a world apparently less subject to the devastating upheavals of fortune or the angry hand of God, it became possible to imagine moving forward more happily on life's way.

This last observation points to another factor that played an important role in sustaining the pursuit of happiness as an earthly prospect: the Enlightenment. Critics and commentators have attempted to define that term since at least the end of the eighteenth century, when Immanuel Kant posed his famous question—*Was ist Aufklärung?* What is Enlightenment?—in the pages of a Berlin journal, the *Berlinische Monatschrift*. Over two centuries later, historians continue to debate the answers. They point out that the Enlightenment took different forms in different places, from Europe to the Americas. They argue over its precise dates, which range from the late seventeenth century to the early nineteenth. Some have even suggested that it would make more sense to speak only of Enlightenments, plural, to account for the differences that divide the French from the British Enlightenment, or the German from the American, or the Protestant from the Jewish.

These debates are healthy and very much in keeping with the Enlightenment spirit, regardless of the different forms this movement assumed. For if historians today continue to debate the differences and the fine points, few would deny that a significant cultural and intellectual phenomenon swept Europe and the Americas in the eighteenth century, and that collectively it raised the art of raising questions to a new level. If the Enlightenment cannot easily be reduced to a set of basic propositions, that is in large part because it evinced curiosity in all things. What is the purpose of this or that belief, the legitimacy of a particular law? Are our traditions rational, our customs and institutions sound? What are we doing on earth? Why are we here? *Sapere aude* was the motto of Enlightenment, Kant declared: "Dare to know." In order to receive answers, one must pose questions.

It is for this reason that Enlightened voices were often vigorous in their defense of free inquiry and freedom of expression, demanding tolerance and the right to question all things. Their defense bespoke confidence in the possibility of social progress through knowledge, and faith that better understanding could make the world a better place. Drawing heavily on Newtonian science and Locke's new science of the mind, they put forth a picture of a harmonious universe, governed by discernible laws. And at the center of this universe, they placed human beings unstained by original sin, programmed for the pursuit of pleasure, and ready, willing, and able to improve their earthly lot. If there was a central concern that animated the Enlightenment's many questions, it was how to make life better. In brief, as one eminent scholar has summarized, "The Enlightenment . . . translated the ultimate question 'How can I be saved' into the pragmatic 'How can I be happy?'"[22] The answers, eighteenth-century men and women increasingly believed, could be found through human effort and understanding alone.

Of course, the philosophers of classical antiquity had also posed questions in an effort to know themselves, and they, too, had focused their answers on the subject of happiness, which they regarded as largely attainable by human means. Enlightenment authors were themselves quick to acknowledge the fact. "The Greeks were the teachers of the Romans," Diderot observed, "the Greeks and Romans have been ours."[23] They looked to the writings of the Stoics and the Epicureans, in particular, as models to be emulated, presenting their own "modern paganism" as an effort to build on classical foundations that had been corrupted, they charged, by the long "barbarism" and "superstition" of Christian "fanaticism."[24]

Yet despite undeniable similarities and common features, eighteenth-century happiness was not classical eudaimonia. In the first place, Enlightenment observers tended to put much greater emphasis on pleasure and good feeling than was ever the case among their classical counterparts. For Plato, Aristotle, and the Stoics, pleasure was of comparatively little importance in cultivating the good life, which was deemed compatible with significant suffering and sacrifice. Even Epicurus was at heart an ascetic, who sought first to minimize pain rather than to maximize pleasure. Though pleasure was a good in

Epicurus's view, it was always subordinate to the greater goal of achieving peace (*ataraxia*), a self-sufficient state free of anxiety and unease. In such a state, Epicurus reflected, the wise man would suffer "no more pain by being tortured himself than by seeing a friend being tortured."[25] Worthy of a Stoic, the reflection would have struck most Enlightened observers as perverse. Not for these men and women the trials and tribulations of the rack, and not for these men and women the quietude of a detached existence. Social, active, and engaged, eighteenth-century understandings of happiness upheld positive feeling unapologetically as a basic good. As the Marquise du Châtelet observed typically, to be happy one must begin by realizing that "there is nothing more to do in this life than to procure for ourselves agreeable sentiments and sensations."[26] To maximize pleasure and to minimize pain—in that order—were characteristic Enlightenment concerns.

This generally more receptive attitude toward good feeling and pleasure would have significant long-term consequences. It is a critical difference separating Enlightenment views on happiness from those of the ancients. There is another, however, of equal importance: that of ambition and scale. Although the philosophers of the principal classical schools sought valiantly to minimize the role of chance as a determinant of human happiness, they were never in a position to abolish it entirely. Neither, for that matter, were the philosophers of the eighteenth century, who, like men and women at all times, were forced to grapple with apparently random upheavals and terrible reversals of fortune. The Lisbon earthquake of 1755 is an awful case in point. Striking on All Saints' Day while the majority of Lisbon's inhabitants were attending mass, the earthquake was followed by a tidal wave and terrible fires that destroyed much of the city and took the lives of tens of thousands of men and women. "*Quel triste jeu de hasard que le jeu de la vie humaine,*" Voltaire was moved to reflect shortly thereafter: "What a sad game of chance is this game of human life." He was not alone in reexamining his more sanguine assumptions of earlier in the century, doubting the natural harmony of the universe and the possibilities of "paradise on earth"; the catastrophe provoked widespread reflection on the apparent "fatality of evil" and the random occurrence

The Lisbon earthquake as depicted in a contemporary engraving. Courtesy of the Jan T. Kozak Collection of the National Information Service for Earthquake Engineering, University of California, Berkeley.

of senseless suffering. It was shortly thereafter that Voltaire produced his dark masterpiece, *Candide*, which mocks the pretension that this is the best of all possible worlds.[27]

And yet, in many ways, the incredulity expressed by educated Europeans in the earthquake's aftermath is a more interesting index of received assumptions, for it demonstrates the degree to which such random disasters were becoming, if not less common, at least less expected. Their power to shock was magnified accordingly, but only because the predictability and security of daily existence were increasing, along with the ability to control the consequences of unforeseen disaster. When the Enlightened Marquis of Pombal, the First Minister of Portugal, set about rebuilding Lisbon after the earthquake, he paid great attention to modern principles of architecture and central planning to help ensure that if such a calamity were to strike again, the effects would be less severe. To this day, the rebuilt Lisbon of Pombal stands as an embodiment of Enlightened ideas.

Thus, although eighteenth-century minds did not—and could not—succeed in mastering the random occurrences of the universe, they could—and did—conceive of exerting much greater control over nature and human affairs. Encouraged by the example of Newtonian physics, they dreamed of understanding not only the laws of the physical universe but the moral and human laws as well, hoping one day to lay out with precision what the Italian scholar Giambattista Vico described as a "new science" of society and man.[28] It was in the eighteenth century, accordingly, that the human and social sciences were born, and so it is hardly surprising that observers turned their attention to studying happiness in similar terms. Whereas classical sages had aimed to cultivate a rarified ethical elite—attempting to bring happiness to a select circle of disciples, or at most to the active citizens of the *polis*—Enlightenment visionaries dreamed of bringing happiness to entire societies and even to humanity as a whole.

The clearest illustration of this expansive impulse is contained in that celebrated eighteenth-century phrase "the greatest happiness of the greatest number," or what was meant as the same thing, "the greatest good of the greatest number." The cornerstone of the Enlightenment principle of utility, the phrase is generally associated with the English lawyer and theorist Jeremy Bentham, but it was employed by many others before him. Indeed, when Bentham declared in his 1776 *Fragment of Government,* "It is the greatest happiness of the greatest number that is the measure of right and wrong," defining the principle of utility as "that principle which approves or disapproves of every action whatsoever, according to the tendency which it appears to have to augment or diminish the happiness of the party whose interest is in question . . . ," he was merely reiterating what was already a widespread eighteenth-century conviction.[29] Figures as diverse as the Scottish moralist and University of Glasgow professor Francis Hutcheson, the German scientist and mathematician Gottfried Wilhelm von Leibniz, the Italian legal theorist Cesare Beccaria, the French philosopher Claude-Adrien Helvétius, and the French historian and soldier the Marquis de Chastellux had all employed the felicitous phrase in various forms.[30] They did so in a common effort to establish what one critic has called the great Enlightenment attempt "to create a science of man based on numerical gauges for all his activity."[31]

Hutcheson, for example, observed in his 1725 *Inquiry into the Original of Our Ideas of Beauty and Virtue,* "that action is best, which procures the greatest happiness for the greatest numbers, and that worst which, in like manner, occasions misery." The first edition of the book included in its subtitle a more revealing description, advertising the work as "an attempt to introduce a mathematical calculation in subjects of morality."[32] Hutcheson later abandoned that description but not the attempt itself. Central to the work is the effort to fashion algebraic formulas to calculate benevolence, defined as the desire to spread happiness to others. Letting B = benevolence, A = ability, S = self-love, I = interest, and M = moment of good, Hutcheson factored out the following:

$$M = (B + S) \times A = BA + SA; \text{ and therefore } BA = M - SA = M - I, \text{ and}$$
$$B = \frac{M - I}{A}. \text{ In the latter case, } M = (B - S) \times A = BA - SA; \text{ therefore}$$
$$BA = M + SA = M + I, \text{ and } B = \frac{M + I}{A}.^{[33]}$$

It was efforts like these that prompted the English author Benjamin Stillingfleet to satirize a growing European trend. His *Some Thoughts Concerning Happiness* (1738) purported to be a translation from the original German by one Irenaeus Kranzovius that would "clear up the Confusion which has hitherto reigned in this Affair."[34] Given that mankind in all ages had been thwarted in the search for happiness, the work's "Mathematical Method" promised to dispel disagreement by "Means of Definitions, Postulata, and Axioms." The piercing certainty of Stillingfleet's conclusions defied debate. "A wise man ought to get out of the Way when he sees a Beam ready to fall on his Head," the German philosopher proves by calculation, adding that in countries where corporal punishment is inflicted on those who refuse to go to church, a man's happiness was best served by attending now and then.[35]

It is easy to be amused by such humor today, mindful as we are of the impossibility of confining morality in a mathematical straitjacket.

Yet to dismiss the attempt altogether with a condescending laugh is to risk forgetting the tremendous prestige of the new methods of mathematics and the natural sciences in the eighteenth century—and hence the possibilities they seemed to open up to the study of human affairs. It is also to avoid confronting a very real problem faced by anyone who believes that human experience can be improved. How are such improvements to be measured? By what indices can human happiness be known? To men and women grappling with what was a brand-new conviction—the belief in the possibility of social progress—this was not a problem that could be lightly dismissed.

Thus, despite the skepticism of satirists like Stillingfleet, the search for a science of happiness continued. Writing somewhat later in the century, Beccaria continued to hold out hope of establishing a "political arithmetic" to guide policy makers in their attempts to ensure the "greatest happiness shared among the greatest number."[36] Chastellux devoted himself to a complementary end, endeavoring to enhance "the greatest happiness of the greatest number of individuals" by studying the phenomenon as it had developed over time. His *De la Félicité publique, ou Considérations sur le sort des Hommes dans les différentes époques de l'histoire* purported to be the world's first history of happiness, and arguably it was.[37] "Of all the speculations to which a study of the past can give rise," Chastellux begins,

> are there any more beautiful, more worthy of our attention
> than those which have for their object the happiness of
> humanity? Many authors have examined, with care, whether
> one people was more religious, more sober, or more warlike
> than another: none has yet attempted to find the happiest
> people.[38]

Setting out to do precisely that, Chastellux established what he called *indices du bonheur* in an early attempt at comparative sociology. He admitted that his calculations would be rough, for any precise comparison of "public felicity" would require knowledge of complex variables: levels of taxation; daily and yearly totals of the working hours expended to secure basic "necessities and ease"; estimates of the leisure time available to workers; and calculations of the hours individuals could labor without succumbing to despair, to name only a few. In the absence of such precise data, Chastellux relied instead on a cruder scale, treating slavery and war as the greatest impediments to public happiness, followed closely by religious superstition, which led, he argued, to ascetic self-denial, unnecessary fear, and the misappropriation of resources.[39] More positively, he contended that levels of population and the productivity of agriculture correlated directly with *félicité publique.*

Chastellux's indicators were wholly consonant with widespread Enlightenment assumptions. Conceiving of human beings as intended by nature to achieve happiness on their own, Enlightenment critics placed great emphasis on the many impediments that had long stood in their way. The inhuman practice of slavery and the terrible disruptions of war were among the most obvious, but they were of a kind with a whole battery of barbaric customs, prejudices, injustices, and false beliefs that Enlightenment thinkers believed had long prevented the majority of human beings from attaining their natural end. Like those twin evils of religious superstition and fanaticism, accumulated customs and prejudices barred human beings from living as they should. Remove them, and happiness would flourish. As the German-born philosopher and Parisian socialite the Baron d'Holbach observed in *Common Sense,* "Men are only unhappy because they are ignorant."[40] In Enlightened circles, the sentiment was as straightforward as the title of the work implied.

A similarly Enlightened logic applied to Chastellux's identification of population levels and agricultural output as positive indicators of happiness. In the eighteenth century—when the twin threats of overpopulation and agricultural dependence were not yet known—such indices made better sense than they do today, indicating both the will to perpetuate life and the ability to do so.[41] They also had helped Enlightened polemicists win, over the course of the century, the so-called Battle of the Ancients versus the Moderns. Begun in the late seventeenth century as an esoteric, and somewhat silly, dispute over the relative merits of ancient and modern art—was classical poetry better than modern verse?—the controversy broadened into a wider debate over the relative merits of society. Was contemporary civilization more flourishing, more robust, more prosperous than in the golden age of Greece and Rome? Using population estimates, and the related index of food supply, some of the century's finest minds argued that it was.[42] Chastellux, whose own work was in many ways a parting shot at the ancients, was thus in good company and on solid Enlightened ground.

Beginning with the ancient Egyptians, Assyrians, and Medes, Chastellux weighed each of his factors over time, pausing at length to consider the civilizations of Greece and Rome before moving on to Western Christendom and ending in his own century. He showed himself a sanguine man. For though he refrained from specifying particular countries, he concluded that the happiest peoples in history were those of contemporary Europe and their transplanted offspring in North America. On the whole, the positive outweighed the negative: Harvests were greater, populations larger, wars fewer, and "enlightenment" (lumières) better diffused than ever before. Even the persistence of slavery could not tip the balance in favor of the past. By comparison with ancient times, that terrible institution was now far less prevalent, Chastellux argued, and headed for total extinction. It made no sense to glorify the good old days. Comparatively speaking, this was the happiest age.

The same general conclusion was shared by others. Basing his assertion on the decline of superstition and the availability and extent of pleasure, Helvétius declared the eighteenth century the "century of happiness."[43] The Milanese economist Pietro Verri largely agreed, arguing similarly in his *Meditazioni sulla felicità* (1763) that his was the happiest epoch in all of human history, the most enlightened and the least susceptible to senseless pains. Yet self-congratulation of this kind should not be taken as a sign of complacency. The majority of Enlightened advocates of the "greatest happiness for the greatest number"—Helvétius, Verri, and Chastellux included—saw their work as an ongoing process. Where happiness was conceived as the balance of pleasure over pain, robust population growth and fine harvests were only the beginning of a pursuit that was just getting started. The scope for maximizing and minimizing accordingly was practically endless. "In civilized nations, and therefore in the whole of mankind, the sum of well-being is perpetually on the encrease [*sic*]," Bentham observed, echoing Locke. The Scholastic and classical belief in a final place of rest, a *summum bonum*, was, like the age-old search for a "philosopher's stone," "meaningless and absurd."[44] Pleasure could always be expanded or enhanced, and pain could always be mitigated or reduced. The opportunities for improvement were vast.

In this way, the principle of utility armed eighteenth-century critics with a powerful tool that could be applied, as Bentham affirmed, to "every action whatsoever," used to judge the usefulness of all things. Did a given practice, on balance, bring pleasure or pain? Were the effects of certain laws, attitudes, or institutions beneficial to the greatest happiness of the greatest number? Were specific governments conducive to the greatest good? "Every authority that is not exercised for the happiness of all can only be founded on imposture and force," Chastellux was prepared to assert.[45] It was a radical claim, but one that was repeated often, for it followed naturally from central Enlightenment assumptions. If human beings were meant to be happy—if they even, as the most radical proclaimed, had a right to happiness—then surely governments had an obligation, a duty, to provide it? They could, as a consequence, be censured when they failed in that duty.

Bentham himself eschewed the language of natural rights, calling them, infamously, in a commentary on the French Declaration of Rights of Man and the Citizen, "simple nonsense . . . rhetorical nonsense, nonsense upon stilts."[46] In doing so, he gestured in a potentially dangerous direction. For if the goal of government was really the greatest happiness of the greatest number, and if individuals were not protected by inherent rights—to liberty, say, or to property or life—was it not perfectly possible to conceive of realizing the happiness of the many at the expense of the few? Relatively soon, at the time of the French Revolution, this dilemma would prove anything but a theoretical concern.

More immediately, there were other potential problems posed by the standard of utility. Bentham himself may not have conceived of happiness as a natural "right," but others did. And even he, like so many in the eighteenth century, believed that happiness was the natural human condition, what one author called a "law of our being," "engraved on our hearts."[47] Seeing that happiness was the positive balance of pleasure over pain, it followed that to deny pleasure to the majority could be done only through ignorance or injustice. Pleasure and its sad twin, pain, Bentham wrote in *The Fragment on Government*, were the "only consequences that men are at all interested in."[48] In his most detailed work on the subject, *The Principles of Morals and Legislation*, Bentham laid this out even more clearly:

> Nature has placed mankind under the governance of two
> sovereign masters, *pain* and *pleasure*. It is for them alone to
> point out what we ought to do, as well as to determine what
> we shall do. On the one hand the standard of right and wrong,
> on the other the chain of causes and effects, are fastened to
> their throne. They govern us in all we do, in all we say, in all
> we think. . . . The *principle of utility* recognizes this subjection,
> and assumes it for the foundation of that system, the object of
> which is to rear the fabric of felicity by the hands of reason
> and of law.[49]

Given that human beings were largely slaves to sentiment—ruled by the dictates of their feelings—utility would guide them in the only way it could: by maximizing pleasure and minimizing pain. The task of the legislator was simply to arrange human affairs so as to further that end, writing laws, passing judgments, spreading light to promote the greatest good of the greatest number.

But was it really so clear that pleasure and pain were the simple standards that Bentham and others took them to be? For all its apparent logic and appeal to common sense, the principle of utility was less useful in practice than at first it seemed. For how can pleasure be measured? In the *Principles of Morals and Legislation,* Bentham devotes a brief chapter to the subject, laying out six criteria to be used in making this all-important calculation. By assigning values to the intensity, duration, certainty or uncertainty, propinquity or remoteness, fecundity, and purity of pleasure and pain, one could "sum up" the totals of each and then "take the balance" of the whole. The resulting figure would give, in theory, a rough approximation of the "general good tendency" or the "general evil tendency" of an act.[50]

Bentham's language here, as elsewhere, is that of mathematical precision. But in his more candid moments, he was ready to acknowledge the serious limitations of his method. Repeatedly, he confessed the impossibility of assigning a value to the key variable of intensity. And he even appeared, on one occasion, to disavow the very premise on which his entire calculus was based—the premise of the comparability of pleasure. "'Tis in vain," he observed in an undated manuscript, "to talk of adding quantities which after the addition will continue distinct as they were before, one man's happiness will never be another man's happiness: a gain to one man is no gain to another: you might as well pretend to add 20 apples to 20 pears."[51] The fact that Bentham himself was able, in a revealing effort at precision, to list some 54 synonyms of the word "pleasure"—from "ecstasy" to "well-being" to "satisfaction" to "bliss"—only reaffirms what already should be clear: that pleasure, like pain, is an uncertain term, and thus an unstable coefficient with which to run a function. The "felicific calculus" of Bentham was not the mathematics of Newton.[52] One man's pleasure could just as easily be another man's pain.

This dilemma raised another, potentially more serious, for it was a problem not only of calibration but of ultimate ends. Namely, was it really so clear that pleasure was our highest calling? Bentham and his Enlightened colleagues argued unapologetically that it was, describing the dynamics of sensation as both the determinant of how we act in the world ("the chain of causes and effects") and the measure of how we ought to act ("the standard of right and wrong"). To claim otherwise, they believed, was either self-deception or blindness to

A Table of the Springs of Action
Jeremy Bentham
No. I. PLEASURES and PAINS,
—of the Taste—the Palate—the Alimentary Canal—of Intoxication.

Corresponding Interest, *Interest of the PALATE—Interest of the Bottle.*

Corresponding *MOTIVES*—with Names,

I. Neutral: viz.	II. Eulogistic: viz.	III. Dyslogistic: viz.
1. Hunger.	*Proper, none.*	1. Gluttony.
2. Need of food.		2. Gulosity.
3. Want of food.	*Improper.*	3. Voracity.
4. Desire of food.	1. Love of the pleasures of the	4. Voraciousness.
5. Fear of hunger.	social board—of the social	5. Greediness.
	bowl, or glass—of good cheer—	6. Ravenousness.
6. Thirst.	of good living—of the good	
7. Drought.	goddess—of the jolly god, &c.	7. Liquorishness.
8. Need, want, desire—of the		8. Daintiness.
means of quenching, relieving,		
abating, &c. thirst.		9. Love, appetite, craving,
		hankering, propensity, eagerness,
9. Inanition.		passion, rage—of, for, to, and after
		cramming, stuffing, devouring,
		gormandizing, gutting, &c.
		10. Drunkenness
		11. Ebriety.
		12. Intoxication.
		13. Sottishness.
		Love, &c. (*as per Col. 3*) of &c.
		drink, liquor—drinking,
		tippling, toping, boosing,
		guzzling, swilling, soaking,
		sotting, carousing—junketting,
		revelling, &c.

One of fifteen such illustrations from Bentham's *A Table of the Springs of Action* (1815), an attempt to define, with rigor, the principal categories of pleasure and pain.

the true ways of human beings. Yet neither their arguments nor their assertions were enough to prevent intelligent commentators from continuing to maintain that there were other springs to action besides pleasure—duty, honor, patriotism, and faith, to name only a few—and that it was good that this was so. Otherwise, was one not forced to draw a rather dubious conclusion—that feeling good is being good, that cultivating pleasure, no matter what its form, was a virtuous moral end? Bentham, to his credit, could be candid about the fact, acknowledging in a celebrated reference that the "quantity of pleasure being equal, pushpin is as good as poetry," pushpin being a popular eighteenth-century game.[53] But for the sake of argument, it might have been anything at all, including lobsters or cheese.

Indeed, the dilemma raised by Enlightened utilitarianism was precisely the dilemma foreseen by Locke, who had pointed out: "Were all the Concerns of Man terminated in this Life," then "why one followed Study and Knowledge, and another Hawking and Hunting; why one chose Luxury and Debauchery, and another Sobriety and Riches," would simply be "because their *Happiness* was placed in different things."[54] Locke held out the hope that the prospect of otherworldly salvation would help mortals give priority to their various earthly ends. But he fully acknowledged that "if there be no prospect beyond the grave," then the conclusion suggested by Horace, Paul, and Isaiah was worth heeding. Carpe diem. Eat and drink. We should take our pleasure while we can.

By no means all Enlightened voices denied, like Bentham, the possibility of prospects beyond the grave. But many did, and so they were presented with this difficult dilemma. If happiness really was, in Locke's words, "in its full extent the utmost Pleasure we are capable, and Misery the utmost pain," and if there really was no everlasting heavenly bliss to direct our actions here on earth, then did it not make perfect sense to eat and drink with abandon, to amass as much pleasure in life as one possibly could? This was the conclusion reached by one man at midcentury. In his work and the scandal it provoked, we are offered a banquet of Enlightened contradictions.

The Happiness Machine

One last time the great gourmand reaches for his wine. Gas billows from below, exploding in an awful taste of what, only moments ago, seemed delightful. Truffles and pheasant have gone to bile. Something is terribly wrong. Eyes bulge, the trousers tighten, sweat forms on the brow. Perhaps monsieur would care for more? Spilling forward as the room sways, monsieur overturns his glass, catching as he falls one final glimpse of the glories of eighteenth-century décolletage. But the French ambassador's wife is no longer smiling. The celebrated materialist, the man said to have claimed, "You are what you eat," has just collapsed in his plate, the victim of too much pâté and a life far too sweet.

Stories this perfect are seldom true. And the story of the transubstantiation *à table* of Julien Offray de la Mettrie is no exception. Hedonist the scandalous physician most certainly was—sensualist and scientist, atheist and bon vivant—he had even foretold the delights of sucking pleasure from death. Love and the end "are consummated by the same means—expiration," La Mettrie observed in his *System of Epicurus* (1750).[55] It would seem a fittingly climactic prognosis. And true to the tale, La Mettrie did dine at the French ambassador's residence in Berlin shortly before his death. But it was only later that he fell ill, and weeks after that he died, in 1751, at the still-unripe age of forty-two. Whatever the final cause (which remains, to this day, uncertain), it is clear that La Mettrie did not meet his fate in his plate, or his end in pâté.

Such stories, however, frequently possess a truth of their own. And this one, too, is no exception. Peddled by Voltaire not long after La Mettrie's death, the malicious news was picked up by stringers in the international republic of letters, embellished, and put back on the wire. Religious writers delighted in reporting how a sensualist had met—and become—his just desserts. Others improvised with the coda of a last-minute conversion. But it was the Enlightened themselves who joined most vociferously in writing off La Mettrie as a menace and a fool. "Dissolute, impudent, a flatterer, a buffoon,

[La Mettrie] . . . died as he ought to have died . . . killed by the ignorance that he professed," observed Diderot nearly thirty years
after La Mettrie's death. Diderot acknowledged that the scandalous philosopher had been amply and "justly decried," but he could
not resist putting the boot in one more time, railing for three pages
at La Mettrie's "frivolity of mind" and "corruption of heart."[56]

Why this Enlightened outcry? It is hardly a mystery why religious
observers regarded La Mettrie with contempt. An atheist whose early
work in science led to a treatise on venereal disease, La Mettrie ended
no better than he began. In the year of his death, he penned as his
final literary production *The Little Man with a Long Pole,* not a work intended to lift the soul.[57] Voltaire, for his part, had personal reasons to
be unkind. At the court of the Prussian king, Frederick the Great, the
two exiles had competed for favor and La Mettrie had clearly won.
Frederick even deigned to deliver La Mettrie's funeral address;
Voltaire was deeply annoyed.

But what grudge did Diderot and the others hold, and why were
they so quick to dismiss La Mettrie as a "frenzied madman" (*un vrai
frénétique*) and even worse?[58] Was he not, as he claimed, a child of the
Enlightenment, working to "break the chains of prejudice" and to illuminate all with the "torch of experience"? And did he not strive, in
everything he did, to further human happiness, conceiving of man as
a happiness machine? The truth in this story depends on the taste of
the teller, to say nothing of that of those who choose to hear.

Born in France in 1709, La Mettrie studied medicine at Paris and
Rheims, and then moved on to the University of Leiden, then the
greatest center of medical research in the world.[59] Several years later,
he returned to Leiden, but this time as a man on the run. The highest court in France had ordered that a book bearing his name be
publicly burned. Though La Mettrie was a patriot, having served as
a military doctor with French armies in the field, he did not think it
prudent to press the point. He fled back to the Netherlands, a country with a long tradition of tolerance, which by the mid-eighteenth
century had shown itself to be receptive to the idea of happiness on
earth.[60]

As the title suggests, the offensive book in question, *L'Histoire naturelle de l'âme* (1745), was a scientific study of the soul. By comparison with the works that would follow, it was relatively mild. But it did make several audacious suggestions. Without saying so outright, La Mettrie hinted that what is called the soul is simply the sum total of its bodily parts, the final product of the interactions of matter. Just as the stuff of plants gives rise to living, creeping things, and the material of animals begets creatures that howl and crawl, might not the matter of men spawn beings that live, think, and feel? In La Mettrie's daring suggestion, matter itself could creep and crawl, think and feel. Matter itself could live. When that suggestion was coupled with the equally shocking speculation that the stuff of all living things—whether plants, animals, or human beings—might be essentially the same, La Mettrie was treading on very dangerous ground.

The suggestion was shocking because it threatened to collapse what Western culture for the preceding two thousand years had virtually always kept apart: matter and mind, the body and soul. For the Greeks, as for their Christian heirs, the two substances were separate and distinct, the one inferior to the other. To suggest that our loftiest essence—the immortal breath blowing through our mortal bodies—might be only gristle and bone was a radical claim. In effect, it was to blur the lines between animal, plant, and man, hinting that all were self-generating machines.

There were, it is true, ample precedents on which La Mettrie could draw in constructing this materialist system. Epicurus, the notable exception to the Greek tendency to separate mind and matter, had taught that the entire universe, including the "soul," was simply a compilation of atoms. In even greater detail, his Roman heir Lucretius had extended this claim, using it as a basis to dispel false fears. Given that we and the world were but a swirling mass of atoms, we needn't be bothered by ghosts, ghouls, and other phantoms, just as we needn't dread punishment in a world to come. Neither spirits in life nor souls in death should cause us fear. They do not exist.

La Mettrie drew openly on this tradition, coming to think of his own thought as an "Epicurean" system, however partial that claim most certainly was. He also borrowed extensively from more recent thinkers, drawing with some unfairness on Descartes, Locke, and a host of contemporary scientists, including his Dutch teacher at Leiden, Herman Boerhaave, the German neurologist Albrecht von Haller, and many others. As one leading scholar has observed, La Mettrie was in many respects "the great summarizer of the previous half-century," who "distilled the essence" of the most radical ideas that had circulated in Europe since the second half of the seventeenth century, often underground. A "borrower, copyist, and plagiarist," he was also a sensationalist who knew how to present those ideas with audacity and aplomb.[61]

But equally important, La Mettrie also attempted to paint his picture of man and the soul from life—or, more accurately, from death—observing the human body from the inside out in his capacity as a physician: on the operating table, the anatomist's slab, and the field of battle. What he saw was a revelation. Muscles seemed to move of their own accord; valves opened; pumps pumped. And when one looked inside our furry cousins, one saw much the same. "Slit open the guts of man and animals," La Mettrie later challenged. "How can you grasp human nature if you never see how the innards of the one exactly parallel the innards of the other?"[62] Like a clock ticking in its casing, a wind-up toy, or a mechanical bird, man was, quite simply, a machine, and life, mechanical motion.

This dramatic claim forms the central point and the very title of La Mettrie's most famous work. Published in late 1747, within a year of his return to Holland, *L'Homme machine* makes explicit what he had only dared to suggest before: "The human body is a self-winding machine, a living representation of perpetual motion." "Contraptions of springs," well-tuned clocks, men and women are sophisticated models of animals and plants. "Man is not molded out of more precious clay than they," La Mettrie writes. "Nature employed the same dough for both man and animals, varying only the leaven." And given that "the transition from man to animal is not abrupt," we should think of ourselves as part of a fluid continuum that has evolved from below. "An ape full of intelligence is just a little man in another form."[63] It follows that the soul is but "an empty word to which no idea corresponds."[64] For far too long human beings had been induced to think about this subject by people whose claims to knowledge had no basis in fact. "What have others to tell us, above all, theologians?" La Mettrie asks on behalf of "physician-philosophers" like himself, men who are guided by "experience and observation alone." "Is it not ridiculous to hear [the theologians] pronouncing shamelessly on something they are incapable of understanding?" The vast majority of so-called philosophers were no better informed. Beginning their investigations a priori—prior, that is, to experience—they "take flight with the wings of the mind," soaring into the nether world of meaningless abstractions. Only a posteriori, on the basis of careful observation, "by unraveling the soul as one pulls out the guts of the body," could one hope to gain real clarity.[65] When one had done so, probing and illuminating the labyrinth that is man, it became clear that the "soul" is the shell of a word, the vestige of more primitive ways of thought. Viewed under the light of modern science, it simply disappeared.

To have one's soul ripped out is an uncomfortable experience in any age, a fact that accounts for much of the violent reaction to *L'Homme machine*. But for La Mettrie, the operation was a simple procedure, restoring to patients the prospect of health. By living in bondage to false beliefs, human beings had made themselves sick, starving their bodies in order to feed the illusions of the mind. Sacrificing life to death, and this world to the next, they had transformed pleasure into sin. In La Mettrie's view, this was a terrible subversion of nature, which everywhere showed signs of running smoothly on its own. "Nature has created us uniquely to be happy, yes, every one of us, from the worm who crawls, to the eagle who loses himself in the clouds."[66] Alone of all natural creatures, human beings denied themselves their natural due.

Happiness, it was clear, must begin by acknowledging frankly what we are—material beings, sophisticated animals, complex machines. This would lead in turn to the jettisoning of the vestigial doctrine of the soul. But La Mettrie did not rest content there. Proclaiming the material body, he moved on to proclaim the material world. If the soul could not be found in the matter of man, neither could God be found in the matter of the universe. The belief in either apparition, La Mettrie held, was equally detrimental to the free reign of nature. And though, for safety's sake, he put the argument of *L'Homme machine* in the mouth of a "friend," claiming "to take no sides" in the debate over the existence of God, it was clear where his sentiments lay:

> However, [my friend] continued, the world will never be happy until it is atheist. Here are the reasons this *abominable* man gives. If atheism, he said, were generally widespread, all the branches of religion would be cut off at the root and die. No more wars incited by theological arguments, no more soldiers of religion, terrible soldiers! Then nature infected by a sacred poison would recover its rights and purity. Deaf to all other voices, tranquil mortals would follow only their own spontaneous inner council . . . the only one that can guide us to happiness along the happy paths of virtue.[67]

Here was a general Enlightenment contention—that the prejudices of organized religion had caused great suffering—taken to the ultimate extreme. For La Mettrie not only charged, like many others, that blind religious superstition was an impediment to human happiness, he also alleged that any belief in God whatsoever precluded the full flowering of nature's bounty. This was no soft deism, the comfortable notion that a clock-maker God had started the world ticking and then left it to run on its own. This was atheism, naked and plain. As open-minded as the Dutch might be, they would have none of that. Like the French, they threw La Mettrie's work to the flame, and rather than suffer a similar fate, the disobedient doctor absconded once again, leaving the country in early 1748.

He landed this time not in a state whose traditions and laws guaranteed a minimum of tolerance, but in one where freedom was dispensed from on high, according to the whim of the monarch. Nonetheless, in Frederick the Great, La Mettrie found a sovereign disposed to look on his theories with indulgence, for Frederick was a skeptic himself. He granted La Mettrie a pension; secured him a place at the Berlin

Academy of Sciences; and turned him loose in his Potsdam palace, fittingly named Sans-Souci, "without cares." It was there, unencumbered, that La Mettrie pursued the implications of his thought, publishing in the last three years of his life a spate of books that pushed his ideas to their logical extreme.

Although the titles of these works ranged from *The System of Epicurus* to *The Art of Enjoying Oneself, The School of Sensual Pleasure,* and *The Anti-Seneca or The Discourse on Happiness,* the principal themes were essentially the same: Happiness lay in pleasure, in pleasure alone, and all who suggested otherwise were enemies of humanity, charlatans, or both. Religion was a "fable," stoicism a "dangerous poison," the virtue of pain a terrible lie. Purely and simply, pleasure was an affair of the organs—a matter of the senses, the sensation of matter. We should seek it any way we can. Without flinching, La Mettrie embraced with open arms the prospect that had given John Locke such fear: In the absence of a God to guarantee the way, the road to happiness branched off into as many paths as there were individual tastes. "It is thus very clear that with respect to happiness, good and evil are in themselves indifferent. The one who receives more satisfaction from doing evil will be happier than whoever receives less from doing good. . . . Happiness is individual and particular, and may be found in the absence of virtue and even in crime."[68] Slightly later in the same *Discourse on Happiness,* La Mettrie is even more explicit:

> May profane enjoyment [*pollution*] and sensual indulgence [*jouissance*], those two lubricious rivals, succeed each other in turn, melting you in pleasures, while making your soul as sticky and lascivious as your body. When you are spent, drink, eat, sleep, dream. If you insist on thinking on occasion, at least do so amidst two wines, sipping the pleasure of the present moment, or savoring the desire in store for you during the hour to come. Finally, if not content to outdo yourself in the great art of sensual pleasures, and if debauchery and dissolution are to your taste, perhaps filth and infamy will be

more to your liking. Wallow in slime like a pig, and you will be happy in their fashion.[69]

When happiness was a matter of pleasure, and pleasure a matter of taste, one could be happy simply by rolling in filth.

It should be said that La Mettrie himself had little passion for mud. And though he repeatedly presented sensual pleasures—opium dreams, succulent wines, and erotic passion—as models of happiness fulfilled, he made efforts in his own life to distinguish between debauchery and more refined indulgence. Still, his fundamental conviction that taste—individual, subjective taste—was pleasure's ultimate judge led him to acknowledge, quite happily, that one man's happiness was another man's pain. As Locke had pointed out, some liked lobsters and others liked cheese. La Mettrie only lengthened the table, so that all desires would have a seat at life's banquet.

There was, however, relatively little place for reason at this feast. It added no spice to happiness, and, more often than not, it interfered with the sensations on the tongue. Cold reason "freezes the imagination and chases pleasure away," La Mettrie claimed.[70] Its proper place was to be pinned down under the "despotism of pleasure." If sensation alone was the force that moved man's machine, then reason, like a humble waiter, must be relegated to serve.

Such asides undoubtedly added zest to the palate of Frederick and his dinner guests at Sans-Souci. But others were less amused. And perhaps now we can understand why. For La Mettrie was not only taking his scalpel to God and the soul; he was snipping the suture that had held Western intellectual life together since the time of Socrates: the link between virtue and human happiness; the link between happiness, reason, and truth. Epicurus himself had not dared to go this far. In the Epicurean vision, reason—prudence—was the essential force that allowed one to distinguish between what would cause us pain and what would bring true pleasure. Far from urging the expansion of desires, Epicurus advised us to limit them as strictly as we could. Bread and water were enough to feed the Epicurean sage.

Happiness was virtue's reward. Nor had Augustine, or Blaise Pascal, or any other Christian thinker inclined to mock the pretensions of reason in fallen man, dared to doubt that happiness and truth might not be linked. Reason was admittedly a limited guide. But in its awkward stumbling, it could lead us to the place where a guide more sure would help us on our way. The end of our journey was where happiness lay. In the Christian tradition it was virtue, through the grace of God, that would take us there.

La Mettrie denied these connections and, in doing so, helped to make himself a pariah. But in his own view, he was the most enlightened of all. Had he not further freed happiness from the accumulated prejudice of the ages? And had he not done so by observation and experiment alone? To liberate happiness from virtue and God, from reason and the soul, was to serve the cause of nature and the body. It was an astoundingly modern view, but not one for which the age of Enlightenment was fully prepared.

Indeed, La Mettrie had exposed with his philosopher's scalpel—and even flaunted—a disturbing weakness in the body of Enlightenment thought. For how, by the mainstream logic of Enlightenment pleasure/pain calculus, could one really combat the disease of rampant hedonism? Bentham and the utilitarians possessed one primary response. The standard of utility, they countered, was not simply to maximize pleasure but to maximize the pleasure of the *greatest number*. The debauches of one man did not count for a lot in this calculation, and in fact probably contributed, on balance, to the total sum of pain. But the more important point is that by the standard of utility, the moral imperative remained one of duty and service. The measure of right and wrong, yes, was pleasure and pain. But the pleasure of the majority counted for far more than the pleasure of the individual, and the pleasure of the next man was just as important as one's own. It was good, it followed, to serve one's neighbors, to strive to enhance their pleasure and to reduce their pain.

This, in utilitarian terms, was "virtue," a word, revealingly, that was never far from Enlightened lips. Virtue was the means to happiness, the tool of happiness, the way to make a better world. And though the unenlightened might not immediately appreciate the fact, virtue was pleasurable in itself. Hutcheson made this argument at length, and so did Bentham. Many others agreed. Remove human prejudices, they maintained, cultivate reasonable action and reasonable thought, and human beings would see that to work for the good of others was anything but sacrifice—it was the highest form of happiness.

These were noble sentiments. But as a response to La Mettrie's exposure of the weakness of Enlightened ethics, they were more of a cover-up, a patch job, than surgical removal. The festering problem remained: If human beings were moved solely, as the utilitarians argued, by sensations of pleasure and pain, then why individuals should sacrifice the one and endure the other for the sake of their fellow men was not at all clear. Despite Enlightenment insistence to the contrary, it was also not at all clear why virtue should always be pleasurable, why being good should be the same as feeling good. Perhaps one day, Enlightenment visionaries dreamed, the interests of individuals could be made to harmonize smoothly with the interests of humanity as a whole. But skeptics could legitimately wonder whether, and at what cost, that day would come. In the meantime, there were men and women in the eighteenth century at once skeptical and cynical, ready to do more than simply contemplate the extreme hedonism of La Mettrie. A radical few put it into practice.

Listen, for example, to the boasts of Giacomo Casanova, the celebrated seducer and rake. A friend of Voltaire, he doubled as an Enlightened philosopher, and was both an apologist—and an activist—for the new happiness of the age:

> Those who say that life is only a combination of misfortunes
> mean that life itself is a misfortune. If it is a misfortune, then
> death is happiness. Such people do not write in good health,
> with their purses stuffed with money, and contentment in their
> souls from having held Cecilias and Marinas in their arms and
> being sure that there are more of them to come. Such men are
> a race of pessimists . . . which can have existed only among
> ragged philosophers and rascally or atrabilious theologians. If

pleasure exists, and we can only enjoy it in life, then life is happiness. There are misfortunes, of course, as I should be the first to know. But the very existence of these misfortunes proves that the sum-total of happiness is greater.[71]

Casanova had no doubt about the existence of pleasure. As he explains elsewhere in his memoirs, describing a successful attempt to seduce a sixteen-year-old beauty, "Pleasure is immediate sensual enjoyment; it is a complete satisfaction which we grant to our senses in all that they desire; and when, exhausted or wearied, our senses want rest, whether to catch breath or revive, pleasure becomes imagination; imagination takes pleasure in reflecting on the happiness which its tranquility procures it."[72] Seeing that happiness is merely "all the pleasures" that one can procure, and that the only real barrier to pleasure is "prejudice," Casanova recommends that "true philosophers" dispense with prejudice entirely. In this way, happiness will be forever at hand.

The Marquis de Sade could not have agreed more. "Renounce the idea of another world; there is none. But do not renounce the pleasure of being happy and of making for happiness in this one," he observes in his "Dialogue Between a Priest and a Dying Man" (1782).[73] For Sade, the world offered nothing higher than pleasure in its varied, delicious forms. And pleasure was never sweeter, more intense, than when it was lewd. So he sought with perfect logic to find "lewd pleasures" wherever he could. As he advises all libertines in the opening letter to one of his most famous works, *Philosophy in the Bedroom,* "No voice save that of the passions can conduct you to happiness."[74]

Casanova and Sade, like La Mettrie, thought and lived at the extreme, far outside the eighteenth-century norm. Serving time in prison in payment for their pleasures (and as restitution for others' pain), they were regarded by the majority of Enlightened men and women of the century as monsters. And yet their readiness to push Enlightenment assumptions to their logical conclusion—and to justify themselves and their happiness by the new Enlightened calculus—highlights even more graphically than the case of La Mettrie the potentially disturbing trajectory of a view of happiness based solely on calculations of pleasure and pain. Was there not something "bestial," something "monstrous," something "inhuman" about this extreme hedonism of self-indulgence? Surely there was. But in making this claim, in writing off the likes of Sade and La Mettrie as immoral men— scandalous degenerates lacking in virtue—Enlightened utilitarians were forced to draw less on the self-evident principles of the age than on the moral capital of the past. Without fully acknowledging the fact, their own assumptions were what one noted scholar has described as "parasitic," in that they lived off truths that they themselves no longer nourished and sustained.[75]

With respect to happiness, these were "truths" that had accumulated slowly over the centuries, amassed by Hebrews and Hellenes, classicists and Christians alike: that happiness and virtue, happiness and right action, happiness and goodness were one. That happiness, far from being a natural complement to life (to say nothing of a natural right), was not a gift of living but a reward for living well—a reward that demanded self-sacrifice, commitment, even pain. In the eighteenth century, there were still enough Stoics around and those who knew their Bible—men and women steeped in classical teachings on happiness and rich in the legacy of Christian virtue—so as not to efface entirely the line that separated being good from feeling good. But to a much greater degree than it avowed, the eighteenth century lived on this inheritance—on borrowed time.[76]

Happy Islands

At the end of his life, Jean-Jacques Rousseau looked back in sadness with recrimination and regret. There were bitter charges of plots and the treachery of men, confessions and denials, self-laceration and despair. But amid these tempests floated an island of calm:

> Of all the places where I have lived . . . none has made me so truly happy or left me such tender regrets as the Island of

Saint-Pierre in the middle of the Lake of Bienne [Switzer-
land]. . . . I was barely allowed to spend two months on this
island, but I could have spent two years, two centuries and all
eternity there without a moment's boredom. . . . I look upon
these two months as the happiest time of my life, so happy
that I would have been content to live all my life in this way,
without a moment's desire for any other state.[77]

"What then was this happiness?" Rousseau asked. "Wherein lay this
great contentment?" The "men of this age would never guess the answer," he believed, for it involved neither great pleasures nor newly
Enlightened truths. It was rather a state of perfect wholeness and
plenitude of being in which Rousseau felt himself "self-sufficient like
God," a state

> where the soul can find a resting-place secure enough to
> establish itself and concentrate its entire being there, with no
> need to remember the past or reach into the future, where
> time is nothing to it, where the present runs on indefinitely
> but this duration goes unnoticed, with no sign of the passing of
> time, and no other feeling of deprivation or enjoyment, plea-
> sure or pain, desire or fear than simply the feeling of existence,
> a feeling that fills our soul entirely, as long as this state lasts, we
> can call ourselves happy, not with a poor, incomplete and
> relative happiness such as we find in the pleasures of life, but
> with a sufficient complete and perfect happiness which leaves
> no emptiness to be filled in the soul. Such is the state which I
> often experienced on the Island of Saint-Pierre. . . .[78]

Who has not dreamed of such a state—a shelter, a private sanctuary sealed off from the sufferings of the world, in which the source of
our happiness would be "nothing external to us, nothing apart from
ourselves and our own existence"? With good reason does the motif of
the happy island appear again and again in the Western imagination,
from the Blessed Isles of the ancient Greeks to Thomas More's *Utopia*

to Francis Bacon's *New Atlantis*. In the eighteenth century, news of Captain Cook's "discovery" of Tahiti and Hawaii inspired paeans to the pristine happiness of unspoiled oases, adding details to the reveries of earlier Enlightened dreamers like Philipp Balthasar Sinold von Schütz, the German author of *Die glückseligste Insul auf der ganzen Welt, The Happiest Island in All the World*.[79] Ever since, travelers on holidays have reenacted this venerable myth, flocking to once deserted isles to restore—and hopefully to find—themselves.

Rousseau nurtured such thoughts, yearning like Robinson Crusoe to build a private world for himself.[80] By the end of his life, when he sat down to write these words, he was living as a castaway, in self-imposed exile in a small apartment in Paris. He severed friendships, cut his ties to the beau monde, and, in return, was spurned by the Enlightened of the day, rejected as a pariah, dismissed as a crank. He gave himself over to long, solitary rambles in the countryside beyond the city. And when he did appear in public, he ostentatiously flaunted

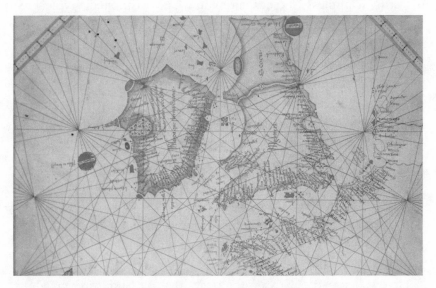

The Happy Isles. This fifteenth-century map by the Italian Grazioso Benincasa shows the Happy or Blessed Islands concentrated in a large bay on the west coast of Ireland. By permission of the British Library.

his difference with rough manners and rough dress, abandoning wig and stockings for long hair, shaggy beard, and a jet-black Armenian cape. Unwashed and unkempt, Jean-Jacques Rousseau was a proto-type of the alienated artist, a bohemian long before *La Bohème.*

Despite this disaffection, Rousseau also knew that to live as a stranger among men was a flawed means of escape. In his more lucid moments, he suspected that even his reverie of perfect happiness on the Island of Saint Pierre was that of an "unfortunate man," the con-solation of a castaway, the "compensation for human joys" that in truth he genuinely desired. Although Rousseau did not confess, like a later observer, Robert Frost—

> But Islands of the Blessèd, bless you, son,
> I never came upon a blessèd one.[81]

—he did entertain deep doubts as to whether such a place of lasting happiness could exist in the modern world anywhere but in his memo-ries or in his dreams. "I doubt whether any of us knows the meaning of lasting happiness," he despaired, in what was at once a typical re-flection of maudlin self-indulgence, philosophical conviction, and con-genital emotional state.[82] "Happiness leaves us, or we leave it."[83]

Rousseau gave voice to these anguished speculations in prose of intoxicating beauty, and he acted them out in a public persona that provided an age anxious to be happy with the reassuring spectacle of a man who openly confessed that he was not. In a century with a high tolerance for sentimentality, Rousseau's histrionics of sadness were well received, capturing perfectly the new cult of "sensibility" or "feel-ing" that flourished in the arts. Indeed, despite his claim to be "alone in the world," to have "been cast out by all the rest," Roussseau died one of Europe's most celebrated men, and his fame allowed him to dramatize his doubts about a number of central eighteenth-century assumptions on a very public stage.

He dwelled particularly on the belief that pleasure was enough to bring us to our end. "Happiness is not pleasure," Rousseau declared flatly, rejecting what, for Bentham and Helvétius, like so many others, was an undeniable truth.[84] Repeatedly, he emphasized the point. "Even in our keenest pleasures there is scarcely a single moment of which the heart could truthfully say: 'Would that this moment could last for ever!' How can we give the name of happiness to a fleeting state which leaves our hearts still empty and anxious, either regretting something that is past or desiring something that is yet to come?"[85] Happiness, if it existed at all, must be something more than this, Rousseau affirmed, something more than the perpetual effort to satisfy an uneasiness that even Locke confessed would never really go away. "The happiness for which my soul longs," Rousseau counters, "is not made up of fleeting moments, but of a single and lasting state."[86]

In his misgivings about the viability of happiness and his open distrust of pleasure, Rousseau was a critic of the mainstream Enlightenment. But he was also, unequivocally, its child, and never is this more apparent than when he overcomes his reservations to proclaim his belief that one "must be happy." "That is the goal of every being which senses," he adds. "That is the first desire which nature has impressed upon us, and the only one which never leaves us."[87] This is Rousseau's contradiction: on the one hand, the doubt and despair of ever being happy in the world as he knew it, and on the other, the desperate certainty that this must be so. In wrestling with this contradiction, he hit upon a vexing thought. What if the advance of modern civilization was the cause of this conflict, leading human beings not closer to their intended end but farther away, farther away from themselves?

This was the disturbing prospect that Rousseau raised in his 1750 *Discourse on the Arts and Sciences.* An answer to a public essay question sponsored by the Academy of Dijon ("Has the reestablishment of the sciences and the arts served to purify or to corrupt manners and morals?"), the work argued unambiguously for corruption. "The progress of the sciences and the arts has added nothing to our genuine felicity," Rousseau maintained.[88] On the contrary, it had detracted greatly from it. Setting humanity adrift in material luxury that multiplied false needs, the vaunted progress of the age robbed us simultaneously of the things we needed to stay afloat. It undermined religious faith; disrupted community and love of the homeland; sapped courage, inherent decency, and moral virtue; and everywhere took from us what was natural, simple, and good. If happiness, as the Enlightenment claimed, was our natural due, then modern civilization was simply not natural.

Here, in rudimentary form, was the basis of what would prove Rousseau's most lasting and influential insight: that the liberating potential of modern civilization created conditions, in the process, that undermined it. Modern society's conquest of nature, its perfection of critical reason and scientific understanding, its staggering productive capacities and consequent material prosperity, its dispelling of illusions—the very things that made human happiness possible according to the Enlightenment dream at the same time militated against it, severing man from his fellow man, from the world, and from himself. "In the midst of so much industry, arts, luxury, and magnificence," Rousseau observes in his so-called *Second Discourse*, the *Discourse on the Origin and Foundations of Inequality Among Men*, "we daily deplore human miseries, and we find the burden of our existence rather hard to bear with all the ills that weigh it down." "Always asking others what we are and never daring to ask ourselves. . . . In the midst of so much philosophy, humanity, politeness, and sublime maxims we have merely a deceitful and frivolous exterior: honor without virtue, reason without wisdom, and pleasure without happiness."[89] In Rousseau's maudlin picture, "civilized" humanity was all surface and no center, modern man a shell of his true self.

And what was this authentic self? What would men and women find if they dared to confront who they really were? Rousseau believed that the answers to these questions had been buried beneath the pancake makeup of an affected age, weighed down by powdered wigs and platform hair. By scraping away such accretions and digging down to the skin, he hoped to catch a glimpse of our pristine state, to see us, unsullied, as we really were.

This, in fact, is the explicit goal of nearly every one of Rousseau's major writings. In the *Second Discourse*, he endeavors, by thought experiment, to imagine what human beings were like prior to the onset of the civilizing process. In his great treatise on education, the *Emile*, he contemplates raising a child in accordance with the pure dictates of nature. In his autobiography, the *Confessions*, he aims, as he states at the outset, "to show to my fellow beings a man in all the truth of nature." And in his *Reveries of a Solitary Walker*, Rousseau throws himself into the heart of nature itself in order to rediscover his natural heart: "As soon as I am under the trees and surrounded by greenery, I feel as if I were in the earthly paradise and experience an inward pleasure as intense as if I were the happiest of men."[90]

This attempt to go in search of the self—to find and restore a lost purity and natural order—was Rousseau's lifelong concern, as well as his point of departure. As he observes elsewhere:

> Let us begin by re-becoming ourselves, by concentrating our attention upon ourselves, by circumscribing our soul with the same boundaries and limits that nature has given to our being; let us begin, in a word, by gathering ourselves here where we are.[91]

This language, with its suggestion of self-exploration and retrieval — finding the self, collecting the self, returning the self—is so common to our modern vocabulary that it is easy to miss both the novelty and the essential strangeness of Rousseau's words. But what can it really mean to "lose oneself" or to "find oneself"? In the famous parable of the prodigal son in Luke 15:11–32, a wayward man goes astray and then is found. But he is lost to his father and is found by God. Similarly, Augustine, and others in the wake of Luther, had gone in search of hidden grace within, hoping to discover the divine light that lay enfolded in sinful human flesh. The conflict between the two (body and mind) could lead as fine a navigator as Pascal to lose his way. "Where, then, is this self?" Pascal asks (*"Où est donc ce moi?"*) "if it is neither in the body nor in the soul? What is the self?"[92]

Rousseau was thus not the first to treat his own person as terra incognita. But he was one of the first to secularize this language, to speak of the soul, of the self, as a maze through which we wander in search of a better nature, an elusive inner light. And so, what for many Enlightenment thinkers was treated as a self-evident truth became for

Rousseau a mystery, a riddle, and a problem. "But where is happiness?" he asks. "Who knows it? All seek it, and none finds it."[93] Deeply personal, highly subjective, happiness is at the same time a fragment of a long-lost, universal nature. Locked in the labyrinth of the mind, embedded in all human beings, lay a truer, more authentic self waiting to be freed. Rousseau placed his hopes of happiness in our ability to gain access to this inner sanctum and to liberate what was inside.

As in all things, nature showed the way. For Rousseau had no doubt that in his pristine state, man was perfectly content. As he observes in one of many such passages:

> It is thus that nature, which does everything for the best, constituted [man] in the beginning. It gives him with immediacy only the desires necessary to his preservation and the faculties sufficient to satisfy them. It put all the others, as it were, in reserve in the depth of his soul, to be developed there when needed. Only in this original state are power and desire in equilibrium and man is not unhappy. As soon as his potential faculties are put in action, imagination, the most active of all, is awakened and outstrips them.[94]

Natural man, in other words, is content precisely because his *needs* are in harmony with his *desires*. "The closer to his natural condition man has stayed, the smaller is the difference between his faculties and his desires, and consequently the less removed he is from being happy."[95] Natural man feels no impulses that go beyond his ability to fulfill them. Satisfied with simplicity, he is satisfied with himself. His soul is agitated by nothing.

All this changes, however, with the gradual development of society. In the *Second Discourse,* Rousseau recounts this process in considerable detail, re-creating the minute series of events that might have led natural man away from his self-contained innocence. The details—by Rousseau's own admission merely speculative—are less important than the larger force that drives them: what Rousseau calls "the faculty of self-perfection," or simply "perfectibility." This is the fatal quality that lies in reserve in the depth of the soul, the very quality that is at the root of all progress. When called forth, it enables human beings to do extraordinary things: to strive constantly to improve their circumstances, to conquer nature, to organize themselves, to control, develop, and exploit. Yet at the same time, this faculty cultivates a ceaseless restlessness, breeding dissatisfaction with our present state. It urges us to summon ever new desires and to place our reason in the service of their fulfillment. It urges us to compare ourselves invidiously to our fellow men, to strive to outdo them. It urges us constantly to outdo ourselves.

And this, in Rousseau's view, is the tragedy of development. For if unhappiness, as he repeatedly insists, arises from "the disproportion between our desires and our faculties," then progress—with its ever expanding horizon of possibilities—continually undermines our peace. Nowhere was this more apparent than in the contemporary commercial cultures of the West, where desire had been unleashed with greater force than ever before. In the race to fulfill present needs, we continually created new ones, resulting in a disturbing phenomenon. "It is by dint of agitating ourselves to increase our happiness that we convert it into unhappiness." We are, Rousseau concludes, our own worst enemies. "In learning to desire, [we] have made [ourselves] the slave of [our] desires."[96]

This was the terrible paradox of modernity, and it caused Rousseau at times to turn away from his age, looking with longing at unspoiled oases and primitive peoples, hoping to return to an island of innocence. But Rousseau also understood that once a society had embarked on the process of perfectibility, there could be no real sanctuary, no turning back. As he observes with some regret in his first version of the *Social Contract*, written in 1762:

> Unfelt by the stupid men of earliest times, lost to the
> enlightened men of later times, the happy life of the golden
> age was always a state foreign to the human race, either
> because it went unrecognized when humans could have
> enjoyed it or because it had been lost when humans could
> have known it.[97]

And so, the way to natural innocence being permanently barred, Rousseau concludes that civilized man is left with only one viable alternative.

> As soon as man's needs exceed his faculties and the objects of his desire expand and multiply, *he must either remain eternally unhappy or seek a new form of being* from which he can draw the resources he no longer finds in himself.[98]

Political association, Rousseau makes clear, is the way to give man that "new form of being" that will help atone for the vanished happiness of the state of nature.

This is the explicit goal of the *Social Contract* as a whole, a work that seeks to endow citizens with what they could not, in Rousseau's view, otherwise possess, providing them with a new nature to replace the one they have lost. By means of what he calls the general will, the social contract aims to provide a civil and moral liberty to replace the lost individual liberty of the state of nature. And by forcibly restraining extremes of wealth, ensuring that all have what they need but not significantly more, the state as "master" of the property of its citizens will work to ensure moderation and fairness, substituting a "moral and legitimate equality for whatever physical inequality nature may have been able to impose upon men."[99]

The result, Rousseau believes, will be the cultivation of "virtue," the indispensable criterion of social happiness. For it is virtue—the readiness to serve others and to sacrifice oneself for justice and the general good—that serves as the antidote to the debased egotism and self-love (*amour propre*) that is the primary source of our discontent in contemporary society. It is egotism that fuels vanity and ambition, egotism that leads us into the invidious cycle of comparison and longing, envy and need that Rousseau believes is the characteristic feature of contemporary commercial societies in their corruption. If selfishness and inauthentic desire are the causes of our modern malaise, then virtue and equality will be their cure. As Rousseau says in his *Political Fragments:*

What causes human misery is the contradiction between our condition and our desires, between our duties and our inclinations, between nature and social institutions, between the man and the citizen. Make man united and you will make him as happy as he can be. Give him entirely to the state or leave him entirely to himself; but if you divide his heart, you tear him to pieces.[100]

Man must either be an island unto himself or be subsumed in the waters of the general will. There can be, it seems, no middle way.

To come across this language today—the talk of changing human nature, of giving citizens a new being, or giving them entirely to the state—is necessarily to do so through the prism of the many unhappy experiments in social engineering carried out since Rousseau's time. These do not inspire confidence in the plasticity of human nature, or in the possibility that others can be "forced to be free." Those chilling words are Rousseau's own from the *Social Contract,* and although he explicitly states elsewhere that "there is no government that can force the Citizens to live happily; the best is one that puts them in a condition to be happy if they are reasonable," his qualification is not entirely reassuring.[101] Nor should it be. For in critical respects, Rousseau is the intellectual forefather of all who would regulate human desire by controlling human needs, of all who would use politics to create a new man and a new human nature, to alter our being in order to make us happier than we were before. This is a goal of political theology, for it aims not to provide us with anything we already possess as human beings—to secure for us rights or liberties or protections or property—but rather to give us back what we allegedly have lost and now can have only if we "seek a new form of being" in the world. In order to be happy in our fallen state, we must be created anew. The reward, Rousseau suggests, will be a partial recovery of our natural wholeness, and the creation of a new order of happiness that cannot now be fully experienced or known.

The future happiness that Rousseau promises must be taken on faith. For Rousseau does not, and cannot, justify his conviction on the basis of reason, or history, or observation. He does so by appeal to feeling. The heart, Rousseau knows, in a truth originally put forth by Pascal, has reasons that reason knows not, and in his heart, Rousseau has felt a murmur of the promise that lies within us all. On the Island of Saint Pierre, or communing with nature in a solitary wood, breaking bread with his companions in Geneva, Rousseau had known moments, he writes, "when I was myself, completely myself, unmixed and unimpeded."[102] And on the basis of such personal revelations, he believed that it could be possible, that it *must* be possible, to recover this pure authenticity of being in a more permanent form. Like most men of faith, certainly, Rousseau was susceptible to grave doubts, at times to outright despair. As he observed toward the end of his life:

> Happiness is a lasting state which does not seem to be made for man in this world. Everything here on earth is in a continual flux which allows nothing to assume any constant form. All things change round about us, we ourselves change, and no one can be sure of loving tomorrow what he loves today. All our plans of happiness in this life are therefore empty dreams.[103]

Faith, however, can conquer all. Even in his doubts, Rousseau perpetuated the hope—the great Enlightenment hope—that happiness, still, must be our final end.

Thus did Rousseau reinject an element of religious longing into the Enlightenment pursuit—a longing, that is, for what life itself could not deliver on its own, but which drew us forward nonetheless. Nor was this his only nod to the sacred past. Rousseau's naturalized account of our fall from innocence—a fall precipitated by pride, exacerbated by reason, and driven by the cravings of selfish desire—clearly resembled the Christian narrative of original sin. And his insistence that in order to atone for that "sin," we must reconstitute ourselves by again becoming ourselves, recovering and re-creating the purity of a lost nature by abandoning egotism, cultivating virtue, and transforming our very being—this, too, had a familiar Christian ring. To men and women at century's end, who sensed, with Rousseau, that even the greatest maximization of utility would always leave us lacking—dissatisfied with "a poor, incomplete and relative happiness such as we find in the pleasures of life"—this message was tremendously appealing. For it reinvigorated the pursuit of happiness with what the purely materialist account had threatened to strip away: mystery and meaning, virtue and reward, an understanding of happiness as something more than the satisfaction of simple animal impulse. Human beings lived by bread, Rousseau understood. But they remained spiritual beings, in need of redemption. Child of the Enlightenment that he was in part, Rousseau believed that man could redeem himself.

Enlightened Doubts

Samuel Johnson was a man of Christian faith who frowned at the pieties of his age. When asked by James Boswell whether a "man was not sometimes happy in the moment," Johnson replied, "Never, but when he is drunk." Boswell, like Johnson, enjoyed his wine. And Boswell, like Johnson, enjoyed his life, despite repeated bouts of despair. On a later occasion, as the two raced through London in a windblown flush, he felt moved to put the question again:

> "Sir, you observed one day at General Oglethorpe's, that a
> man is never happy for the present, but when he is drunk.
> Will you not add,—or when driving rapidly in a post-chaise?"
> Johnson. "No, Sir, you are driving rapidly *from* something *to*
> something."[104]

In the past or the future, one could be happy, but in the present, only when not fully conscious.

The year was 1776, an unpropitious moment, it would seem in retrospect, to mock the pursuit of happiness. But Johnson had already articulated his views. His long poem "The Vanity of Human Wishes" (1749) provides an early indication of the perspective he would adopt on the conceit of the century:

Let Observation with extensive View,
Survey Mankind, from *China* to *Peru;*
Remark each anxious Toil, each eager Strife,
And watch the busy Scenes of crouded Life. . . .[105]

Pride, animus, envy, and folly animated these scenes, helping to ensure that earthly happiness, like all else of human making, would be
fleeting, destined for dust. "Time hovers o'er, impatient to destroy, /
And shuts up all the Passages of Joy. . . ." It was vanity to believe otherwise, as Saint Augustine and the author of Ecclesiastes had known,
vanity to believe that human beings could rest content without faith—
"that panting for a happier Seat"—vanity to believe that we were no
longer in need of celestial wisdom, which "calms the Mind, / And
makes the Happiness she does not find." For Johnson, human beings
were perennially restless. This was the way of the world.[106]

With its Judeo-Christian emphasis on the sin of human pride and
the vanity of earthly pursuits, Johnson's message smelled somewhat
of old. But it was considerably more than a musty restatement of long-
held religious truths. Johnson's concerns about happiness, in fact, were
very much of the moment—so much so that he returned to the same
theme in greater detail in a later work, *The History of Rasselas, Prince of
Abissinia* (1759). An eighteenth-century parable, *Rasselas* follows the
wanderings of a young prince as he races *from* his edenic kingdom in
"the happy valley" *to* he knows not where. In the happy valley, Rasselas
has everything; no pleasure is spared. Yet his "hopes flow beyond the
boundaries of his life." Observing the flocks of the fields, he pines,
"When I see the kids and the lambs chasing one another, I fancy that
I should be happy if I had something to pursue."[107]

Intent on satisfying this desire, Rasselas escapes the happy valley,
inventing a flying machine that whisks him to the world beyond. Here
he chases after the full range of "sublunary pleasures" and "sublunary
things," circling the globe in the hope of finding what he seeks. He talks
to wise men, to experts, and to veterans of every kind, exploring the
manifold paths that promise happiness at their end. But nowhere does

he find what he seeks. The conclusion of the work, "in which nothing is concluded," ends with the very longing that sent Rasselas on his way.

If not for its humanity and humor, *Rasselas* might seem a depressing tale. But its message is not entirely bleak. Johnson appreciated the achievements of his age, and he said so often: His vision of the world was no *contemptus mundi*. When Rasselas hears of life in contemporary Europe and the many advantages enjoyed there—the fruits of knowledge and science, industry and commerce—he speculates that "they are surely happy . . . who have all these conveniences." He is told in response by his African friend, a poet who has traveled the world: "The Europeans . . . are less unhappy than we, but they are not happy."[108] Johnson did not deny human progress any more than he refused to smile. But he did worry that men of his age were forgetting their natural limits. Strong black coffee to clear the head of an evening's wine, his work served as a sobering reminder of the ancient wisdom of the Christian Fall. Whether pulling the reins of the post chaise, a cork from a bottle, or an apple from the stem, desire led us onward but seldom to peace. This was the human condition. To believe otherwise was an illusion that could be sustained only when drunk.

A timeless message, Johnson's words were timely, too. For in the age's obsession with happiness, he correctly identified a revolution in the making. Whereas human beings, for centuries, had regarded suffering as their natural condition, they were coming to think of happiness as a natural right. The change was profound. "The time is already come," a man of the modern view tells Rasselas, "when none are wretched but by their own fault."[109] Neither original sin nor the mystery of grace, the movement of the stars nor the caprice of fortune controlled our fate. Intended to be happy, we *should* be happy, if only we dared to claim our due. Bringing with it a whole new range of attitudes that clashed with venerable taboos, the new bearing on happiness attacked impediments to sexual pleasure, material prosperity, self-interest, and simple delight for simply standing in the way. As baseless fears and prejudices were overcome, the new joy would spread. Even a yearly almanac distributed on the continent in 1766 felt obliged to make the point:

May the New Year and those that follow bring happiness and
peace to the hearts of all men. We can be certain of this
happiness if philosophy continues to enlighten the world and
if men of all nations, joined together by talent, cultivate the
arts and humanity more and more. *These are the miracles that
talent and art have wrought;* let us cultivate them in peace, and
the social bond will encompass more and more of us as mankind enjoys unprecedented prosperity.[110]

That the readership of these almanacs was made up of comparatively
humble folk from the countryside is significant. For like the literary
device of the happy ending that was emerging as a new, and increasingly common, convention in popular fiction and stories for children—
resolving the dilemmas of protagonists in this life, not the next—such
works suggest how far, and how wide, the promise of happiness could
spread.[111] The seed of a dream had been planted that continues to
grow to the present day, steadily expanding an aspiration that, prior
to the eighteenth century, had been confined primarily to a happy
few. Whether they were conceived as the blessed ones, who resembled
Homer's gods in beauty and comforts and attainments; or Aristotle's
fortunate, enabled by circumstance to devote themselves to the cultivation of virtue; or Calvin's elect, certain of God's grace; or the
Catholic saints, endowed with the capacity to soar upward to God,
even while still on earth—those who had aspired to the precious prize
of happiness on earth were a relative minority and elite. All others
might make do as best they could, hoping for a smattering of earthly
joy and contentment. Yet they were resigned to the belief (the hope)
that real happiness would come only in death.

But now that the end was now, or rather *of this life,* the long Christian apprenticeship in happiness deferred had a curious effect. For now
that the end was now, did not everyone have the right to hope for salvation? The new faith, like the old, was universal in its potential, and
the good news of the modern gospel was free to travel with missionary
speed. All could be happy. All should be happy. All would be happy—
someday. These were the miracles that talent and art were making in

the world. Scarcely a century before, rulers had been required to lead in the service of the faith and morals of their subjects, to lead in the service of God. They were now being asked to serve a different lord. "Happiness is in truth the only object of legislation of intrinsic value," the English utilitarian Joseph Priestley observed.[112] From the greatest good to the greatest number, this was the voice of a new age.

Happiness portrayed as a goddess, surrounded by bounty. Thomas Burke after I. F. Rigaud, *Happiness*, 1799. Collection of the author.
Photo: Daniel Kariko.

Without completely dismissing the liberating potential of this creed, Johnson detected its darker side. As a companion of Rasselas inquires, "What . . . is to be expected from our pursuit of happiness, when we find the state of life to be such, that happiness itself is the cause of misery?"[113] Was it really so clear that human beings were intended to be happy, that they could make themselves so? The supposition itself, Johnson understood, involved an assumption—an article of faith—about the purpose of human existence, about man's final telos and end. And if this supposition were wrong, as he well believed, then it placed on human beings a terrible burden: a responsibility they could never entirely fulfill. The result, as Rousseau had intuited but never precisely seen, was a new type of unhappiness: the guilt and sorrow one experiences for not being happy in a culture that demands it.

Johnson was not alone in raising these concerns. Some of the Enlightenment's greatest defenders were susceptible to doubts. In a moment of hesitation, no less a clear-eyed observer than Voltaire could give himself pause, penning in the same year as Johnson's masterpiece "The Story of a Good Brahmin." Like Rasselas, Voltaire's exotic hero spends his life in search of happiness yet finds that he is at a loss to explain "why evil pervades the earth." "I am ready sometimes to despair," the Brahmin observes, "when I think that after all my seeking I do not know whence I came, whither I go, what I am nor what I shall become." When confronted with the example of an old woman of simple faith "who thinks of nothing, yet lives contentedly," his consternation swells. Might man's unhappiness actually increase "in proportion as his understanding and his insight grew"? It is worth recalling that the same century that put forth the view that the end of ignorance would bring a smile to the human face also bequeathed to posterity the phrase "Ignorance is bliss."[114] That phrase begged a question: What if reason and happiness were ultimately opposed?[115]

Toward the end of the century, Immanuel Kant was prepared to assert just that. "In fact," he comments in his *Groundwork for the Metaphysics of Morals*, "we find that the more a cultivated reason devotes itself to the aim of enjoying life and happiness, the further does man get away from true contentment."[116] He used the observation to deliver a broadside at the utilitarian tradition:

> This principle of one's own happiness bases morality upon incentives that undermine it rather than establish it and that totally destroy its sublimity, inasmuch as motives to virtue are put in the same class as motives to vice and inasmuch as such incentives merely teach one to become better at calculation, while the specific difference between virtue and vice is entirely obliterated.[117]

"Making a man happy is quite different from making him good," Kant further observed. He used the term "happy" in its eighteenth-century sense, as pleasure or good feeling, and clearly he was right. For if the proposition that doing good (living virtuously) meant feeling good (being happy) was always dubious, it was more dubious still that feeling good meant being good. Virtue, Kant reaffirmed, with an air of common sense, was sometimes painful. And those who were happy, who felt good, were sometimes bad.[118]

Kant developed this thought at much greater length, coming to the conclusion that happiness, "at least in this life," was not necessarily a part of nature's plan. Moral virtue, rather, the development of a good will, was what reason recognized "as its highest practical function," and reason, he affirmed, was not necessarily compatible with happiness. This was an unsettling thought, and although Kant continued to leave open the possibility that reason, virtue, and happiness might somehow be reconciled in God or in a future state ("for all hoping aims at happiness"), he fully admitted that this could not be demonstrated analytically or perceived by the senses. By Kant's moral imperative, our duty in this life was to act in such a way as to render ourselves "worthy of happiness."[119] We then might legitimately "hope" to "partake of it" in some other state in keeping with our worth.[120] But he acknowledged that this must always be an act of faith.

Not all were so forthright. Concealing, denying, or simply failing to recognize Kant's objections, many continued to insist that happiness was our naturally intended end, perfectly consonant with reason, virtue, and truth. This was a long-established connection, supported by centuries of classical and Christian authority. It could not easily be dissolved. And so the radical materialist attempt to do so—to treat human happiness like the happiness of animals, as a simple function of pleasure and pain—encountered stiff, often reflexive resistance. Mounted initially by religious voices and those within the mainstream Enlightenment, and then, more powerfully, by Rousseau, this resistance took the form of a reassertion of the venerable ties connecting happiness to moral and metaphysical reward. Tending to deny the naked assertion that good feeling alone was the final human good, it returned happiness to the privileged place that it had enjoyed since Socrates. Happiness was a godlike state, the full and final flourishing of man.

Already, in the tremendous popularity of the divine Jean-Jacques, one can see evidence of the powerful reaction moving in this direction. It would continue into the nineteenth and twentieth centuries, carrying with it both great promise and great peril. For if what Kant had asserted could only ever be an article of faith—the belief that all reasonable human beings could make themselves happy—was a powerful ideal when recognized as such, it would prove dangerous indeed when the critical element of faith was either covered over or rejected out of hand. When they of little faith believe with the certainty of zealots that human beings can be made happy like gods, happiness is often the first thing sacrificed in its own name.

A Modern Rite

He was an unlikely bearer of glad tidings, this stocky lawyer from the village of Sarzeau, still less an obvious apostle of happiness. But these were revolutionary times, and Joseph-Marie Lequinio was a revolutionary man. Of that he had given ample proof, rising up through the ranks from humble beginnings in the Breton countryside to serve as mayor in the regional capital of Rennes in 1789; tribunal judge at the city of Vannes shortly thereafter; and, in 1791, deputy to the legislative assembly in Paris. Some at this stage might still have claimed to detect a whiff of the barnyard about the man, who, it is true, had devoted spare time to writing tracts on agricultural science prior to the outbreak of the French Revolution. But only a halfhearted revolutionary could feel shame at proximity to the soil. And at fifty-one, Lequinio knew what he was about. He devoted himself now to cultivating *political* science, falling in line with the radicals of the assembly who grouped around Maximilien Robespierre. Assailing the "fanaticism" of the Catholic Church, Lequinio deplored its centuries-long effort to keep humanity in darkness. He attacked the privileges of the aristocracy, which fed, like leeches, on the blood of the people. He condemned the "despotism" of the French king Louis XVI, and with the destruction of the monarchy earned for himself an elected place in the newly constituted representative assembly, the national convention. On January 16, 1793, Lequinio duly did his part, voting for the death of the old king, albeit with an uncharacteristic tinge of regret. It would have been preferable, he mused, to condemn the despot to a life in the galleys.[1] But matters of state security, alas, did not permit such indulgence.

Indeed, it was on just such a matter that Lequinio found himself here in the western port city of Rochefort, standing without indulgence in a former Catholic church in the autumn of 1793. He served as an official "representative-on-mission" of the directing revolutionary government, dispatched to the provinces by the Jacobins, the dominant faction in power, and charged with spreading the word. The group took its name from its place of meeting in Paris, the former

The happy man of the Revolution. "In the guise of an ardent young man full of vigor, the French are regenerated by the Constitution, which carries them to happiness, while blind fanaticism, pride, and ferocious ignorance are repulsed by its shield." Philippe-August Hennequin, 1793, Bibliothèque nationale de France.

monastery of the "Jacobin" (Dominican) religious order. But like their leader, Robespierre, the Jacobins disavowed most other connections to this past, declaring instead the abolition of the Christian religion and the Gregorian calendar to which the faith had given rise. In the place of these antiquated forms, they vowed to establish a new society and social contract, based in large part on the principles of Rousseau. From the highest reaches of the convention—in the upper seats known as "the Mountain"—the Jacobins were laying down a new covenant and a new law, a new form of being for the man of virtue and a new concept of time to honor their creation.

And so, what otherwise would have been a Sunday in early November 1793 was now a *décadi* in the month of Brumaire in the Year II, the tenth day of the ten-day week, set aside for reverence and rest in the second year since the destruction of the Bourbon monarchy. And what otherwise would have been a Christian house of worship was now Rochefort's "Temple of Truth," proclaimed as such several days earlier by Lequinio himself, who had personally seen fit to expel the stubborn priest who clung, foolishly, to superstitions of old. After a scuffle on the church floor, Lequinio overcame the man, and the dark hall was flooded with the light of the times. He stripped the building of its outworn relics and replaced them with the trappings of a reasonable people, in the classical aesthetic of ancient Greece and Rome. Only months previously, Lequinio had published his *Prejudices Destroyed, by a Citizen of the Globe*. Here, he was putting the theories of cosmopolitan man into practice.

There may have been an occasional cough as Lequinio took his place at the pulpit, the scratch of workmen's boots, perhaps, sidelong glances, the rustling of clothes. But the words that echoed in this former church now wrapped in the fanfare of the ancients were no doubt arresting and clear:

> Brothers and friends, I am going to speak to you today about that which interests you all, about an object for which you all yearn and sigh, and toward which all your actions tend. What does each of you want? What do we all want? What do we

search for from the first instant we become capable of desire until the time our blood runs cold in our veins and our needs are annihilated? All, in a word, whoever we are—big or small, strong or weak, young or old—we all dream of happiness; we want only to be happy, we think only of becoming so. Let us, then, see if there are means that will allow us to arrive at this goal, and explore what they might be.[2]

We cannot, of course, be sure, but it is hardly far-fetched to imagine that some in this revolutionary congregation allowed their gazes to wander at this point, looking up and out beyond the speaker to where the stained glass had so recently transformed the light of the world. It would have been a familiar reflex, after all, to search for illumination from on high. But as if anticipating the possibility of such primitive regression, Lequinio checked his congregation abruptly and brought it back down to earth. "Do not wait for me to talk to you of angels, and arch-angels, of paradise and Elysian fields . . . of all these ridiculous farces that have been paraded for so long before you and other peoples," he scoffed:

Do not wait for me to entertain you with seductive talk of the celestial heaven that priests used to promise after death, provided that, during your lifetime, you did for them all that they wanted, working like stupid beasts until the last hour. It is through this illusion of the mind, and through this promise of a future life, that impostors have governed the ignorant and credulous people of the world, keeping them in slavery and misery, while frustrating their enjoyment in the here and now with a false promise of eternal happiness in the future.[3]

No, those who would live in freedom must abandon such puerile illusions: There was no future life. When our fibers harden, our heart stops, and our blood ceases to flow, we are no longer. Bodies decompose, reverting to their constituent elements, which serve, in turn, to create "new beings—worms, fish, plants, and a thousand other living things." But "never will there be anything more of us again except in scattered molecules," and in the memories of our survivors. No, citizens, there is no future life.[4]

For a sermon ostensibly on happiness, this may have seemed a morbid message. But Lequinio insisted emphatically that it was not. He urged his listeners to rejoice at the fact that their childish illusions had been stripped away. In place of "imaginary happiness," "real enjoyments" were now within their grasp. The representative-on-mission held out before them nothing less than this tantalizing prospect—of happiness "real and absolute" in *this* life.

"There are those," Lequinio continued, "who place their happiness in great fortune," others in luxury, still others in beautiful women. This one here loves to dine, that one there to gamble: Each makes of his happiness what he would, according to his fancy. But what a terrible mistake this is, a fatal confusion of passions and pleasures with happiness. The former are fleeting—the drunkard always has a hangover in the morning, the libertine suffers "a thousand infirmities" as the fruit of incontinence. And the desire for pleasure—subjective, ephemeral, of body or of mind—can never be satisfied. The moment we have one thing, we want another, and man "is pushed by his restlessness and by his ambition to search farther and farther, running, in this way, from desire to desire." Such a man will end his career "having always imagined that he was going to be happy, and in truth, having experienced only a tumultuous succession of pleasure and disgust, desire and remorse." No, citizens, "happiness does not exist in *jouissances personelles*,"[5] in personal pleasures. It is something more noble than that.

Where, then, did this elusive happiness hide? Not in any primitive oasis. Invoking a number of themes dear to the Jacobins' beloved Rousseau, Lequinio dismissed with disdain the reverie that happiness might still be found by returning to the "state of the savage." "Only in society can man really be happy," he emphasized, "for it is there that he is able to satisfy all his needs and to surmount all obstacles through the arts and sciences; there that he can procure all the enjoyments that the human heart might desire." It was there, alone, that man could create the new form of being that would replace the one he had lost. But this optimal state would be achieved only when the "aristocracy of riches" had been destroyed. Hitherto, the people had not "dared dream of social equality," not "dared dream that the rich man is only so because of the work of the people." They must dare to do so now.

Although fully consonant with the Jacobins' unprecedented attack on social privilege and their first halting steps toward the redistribution of wealth, these were radical propositions. Lequinio warned that they would be in vain unless the social revolution was accompanied by a "moral revolution" in the "minds and hearts" of the people. A new society required a new man. "Where must we search for happiness?

APOTHÉOSE DE J. J. ROUSSEAU, SA TRANSLATION AU PANTHÉON.
le 11 Octobre 1794, ou 20 Vendémaire An 3me de la République

A contemporary engraving of the Apotheosis of Rousseau. Bibliothèque nationale de France. On October 11, 1794, Rousseau's remains were transferred to the Pantheon in Paris, the former Church of St. Geneviève, which had become the resting place of the spiritual saints of the Revolution.

Where, citizens? Inside ourselves, in the bottom of our hearts, in self-abnegation, in work, in the love of others. This is the secret." Through labor, Lequinio claimed, we make ourselves independent, useful to our fellows, healthy, and worthy of their esteem. Through self-sacrifice, we grow impervious to the blows of fortune, for a soul steeled against hardship will rise above the "vicissitudes of chance, the inconstancies of political upheavals, and the uncertainties of health." Unhappiness lies not in outward circumstances, however disastrous these may be, but in the affliction we allow them to cause us. The self-sacrificing man, "the man who says to himself, I want to be happy, I want to be above all adversity," will suffer no affliction. For the "man who has made a sacrifice of himself" transcends "all accidents, all losses, all developments." The universe could come crashing down around him, and his equanimity would remain complete.

But not only does this remarkable creature, this man "who has made a sacrifice of himself," look with scorn on the slings and arrows of outrageous fortune, he also treats with indifference the many "passions that trouble the human heart." Never does he lose himself to pride, ambition, avarice, or jealousy, and never does he chase after those fleeting pleasures that reward us with only paltry satisfaction. The man who has made a sacrifice of himself "lives entirely for the happiness of others, finding his own felicity in the felicity of the public." He helps the unfortunate, the indigent, the suffering. He is a tender father, a faithful husband, a trusting friend. And above all, this self-sacrificing man is a patriot, one so calm, so self-assured, that if ever he were called upon to die for his country—to ascend the scaffold—"he would mount its steps with firmness, sure of his conscience, consoled by his good actions, certain that his death would be followed by the regret and affection of posterity." This, Lequinio concluded, was the happy man, a man of "virtue." All who searched for happiness in this way would "be sure to find it." And for those who did not, may the "sacred love of the *patrie* . . . force every individual to take the only road that can lead them to the end they propose—the end of happiness."[6]

We have, regrettably, no record of how the citizens of Rochefort responded to this piece of revolutionary good news. But we would be

"A rising sun announces the dawn of French felicity."
Paris, 1791. Bibliothèque nationale de France.

on fairly solid ground if we said that they almost certainly would have been perplexed—perplexed and more than a little disturbed. For it was at precisely this time, and in precisely this place, from the *bocages* of Brittany down to the marshes of the Vendée, that considerable numbers of citizens began to take up arms in opposition to the Revolution. Men like Lequinio—representatives-on-mission—had been dispatched to suppress them with all necessary force to maintain the security of the state. As the convention had decreed, infamously, on September 5, 1793, just two months before, "terror was the order of the day."

Lequinio, it appears, was good at taking orders and even better at carrying them out. Shortly after delivering his paean to the promise of happiness, he wrote to Paris to report that he had struck with the excellent fortune of "finding in Rochefort more men to operate the guillotine [*guillotineurs*] than [he] needed." He chose one, dined with the man and his two colleagues, Guezno and Topsen, and then put them to work. Dozens of heads fell in the city before Lequinio moved on to Brest, La Rochelle, and the Vendée, where he boasted of "blowing the brains out" of several prisoners himself.[7] The claim would later come back to haunt him. After the fall of the Jacobins, Lequinio was charged with atrocities committed in and around Rochefort and the Vendée, including that of making children walk in the blood of their slain parents.[8]

It is thus safe to assume that some of those gathered in Rochefort's Temple of Truth would have heard Lequinio's exhortation that "the man who has made a sacrifice of himself" should do so literally—by mounting the scaffold—with a considerable degree of unease. And what would they have made of his closing invocation calling on the "sacred love of the patrie" to *force* all citizens to seek happiness along a single way? Forced marches they would have understood—also forced entry and force of arms. But forced happiness was a different matter.

As shocking as it might seem, Lequinio's promise of earthly happiness was being proclaimed throughout Europe, heralded by revolutionaries bearing glad tidings within France and spread by crusaders at the end of a bayonet beyond its borders. The Declaration of Rights of Man and the Citizen (1789) had pledged in its preamble to work for the "happiness of everyone" ("*au bonheur de tous*"), and the founding document of the present regime, the Constitution of June 24, 1793, took that promise seriously. "The goal of society is common happiness," it declared in its very first article: "*Le but de la société est le bonheur commun.*"

How fitting that the Jacobins should make happiness a central concern. "Occupy yourself uniquely with the happiness of a great people and the happiness of humanity," Robespierre demanded characteristically of his fellow citizens on September 25, 1792.[9] His followers took him at his word. When plans were considered to redraw the map of Paris, an ambitious architect proposed a great avenue leading from the *place de la Révolution* to its necessary endpoint—where else?—the square of happiness, *la place du bonheur*.[10] And when it came time to determine just what should be celebrated on each of the thirty-six *décadis* of the revolutionary calendar, a decree of May 7, 1794, proposed a litany of noble themes, including heroism, love, humanity, and justice, to name only a few. On the final day of rest—the sacred *décadi* that would bring the year and this liturgical cycle to a close—the law specified the celebration of a "festival of happiness." Monsieur A. P. Pochet, the French designer of Catherine the Great's Temple of Happiness, dashed off a note to the Ministry of Interior, offering his services, but he received no reply.[11] In space as in time, the Revolution could be counted on only to embrace the new, for in space as in time, the Revolution would end in happiness. And happiness, the Jacobin leader Saint-Just declared in the spring of 1794, was "a new idea in Europe."[12]

Saint-Just's claim was overstated—in truth, his "new idea in Europe" was no such thing. And neither were the Jacobins entirely unaware of the fact: Their proclamation of happiness relied rather heavily on the past. Although many in Lequinio's congregation probably missed it, the trained ear would have heard in his secular sermon clear references to classical philosophy, particularly to the tradition of Stoicism, with its invocation to spurn suffering and to control the passions, to leave nothing to chance. And merely by looking around their rapidly redecorated temple, contemporaries would have seen allusions to what the Jacobins were openly proclaiming throughout the country: the return to the classical virtue of the ancient world. From the outset, the Revolution had witnessed a self-conscious embrace of the style of the ancients.

But with the constitutional monarch deposed, the revolutionaries were free to drape their republic in iconography unsullied by emperor or king. With chariots and togas, Corinthian columns and laurel crowns, busts of Cicero, Socrates, Brutus, and Cato, they sought to usher in a new world by way of the old, reviving what was best in the simple, unsullied spirit of antiquity.[13] As Saint-Just himself declared proudly on a different occasion, "We have offered you the happiness of Sparta and of Athens in their most glorious days; we have offered you the happiness of virtue, comfort, and the mean; the happiness that is born of the enjoyment of what one needs, without excess; we have offered you a happiness of the hatred of tyranny, of the delights of a cottage and of a fertile field tilled by your own hands. We have offered to the people the happiness of being tranquil and free."[14]

For all their pretensions to herald the dawn of a new era, it is clear, neither Lequinio nor his Jacobin comrades would have denied the influence of the ancient past on their modern idea of happiness. But they certainly would have balked at the suggestion that Christianity, too, was playing a shaping role. Yet how else are we to explain this curiously Christlike "man who makes a sacrifice of himself" willingly giving up his own life for the salvation of humankind? Proclaimed from the pulpit, Lequinio's new man finds happiness in living "entirely for the happiness of others," even at the cost of personal suffering or death. Looking askance at pride and pain, avarice and ambition, he is the friend of the humble, the poor, the downcast, the meek. He feeds those who hunger and thirst for righteousness. With his aid, and with his might, the last shall be first, and the first shall be last.

And what of Lequinio's insistence that "happiness does not consist in personal pleasures"? In making this claim, he was rejecting one of the most common assertions of his age—the age, that is, of Enlightenment. And although, in doing so, he drew on both the tradition of the Stoics and on Rousseau, Lequinio's refusal to reduce happiness to good feeling alone also paid unwitting homage to Christianity. To reduce happiness in this way, he charged, was to reduce man to beast—a beast who chased, who *pursued*, one desire to the next, and who arrived at death "having always imagined that he was going to be happy," but in truth, having experienced only "a tumultuous succession of pleasure and disgust." Man, admittedly, might be a collection of molecules. But he was not an animal. He remained a spiritual being. Happiness must be something higher than mere physical sensation—

something more than fleeting pleasure, something nobler, more profound. With this, too, the pious men and women who once worshipped before the altar of this former church would have agreed. Happiness, even still, retained the aura of its religious past.

The divide separating the "imaginary happiness" of Christianity from Lequinio's "real happiness," then, was narrower than the representative-on-mission would have his listeners believe. But ironically, it was the final lines of his sermon—the end leading to the end—that tied his modern homily most closely to what had come before. Ironic, for it was here that the representative-on-mission invoked not the past but the future, consoling his flock with a vision of happiness to come. And ironic, too, because this same "promise of a future life," this same "false promise of eternal happiness in the future," was the very basis on which he, like his Christian predecessors, justified the need for the terrible sacrifices of the present. Lequinio looked forward to a time when "all tyrannies will be annihilated and all hypocrisy will disappear. All thrones will crumble, all limits be effaced"; a time, finally, "when humanity will live as a single family, in a world that is one *patrie*."[15] All would be happy there, and the man who had made a sacrifice of himself could die content in the knowledge that his sacrifice would be remembered in the "regrets and affections of posterity."[16] In the future, the redeemer would be redeemed. In the future, those who did not see real happiness now could imagine its coming, take comfort in its imminent arrival. Happy are those who believe but do not see. No less than the Christian heaven, Lequinio's future was founded on faith.

At the beginning of the twentieth century, the sociologist Émile Durkheim examined the French Revolution in his *Elementary Forms of Religious Life*. Durkheim was interested in a broader phenomenon: how human beings invest their lives with religious meaning and significance. But he saw the Revolution as a particularly striking example of "society's ability to make itself a god or to create gods."[17] This process—what the historian Mona Ozouf has since described as the "transfer of sacrality" from God to the nation, the Old Regime to the New Regime, and Heaven to earth—is especially apparent in the many revolutionary ceremonies and festivals presided over by the likes of Lequinio.[18] In these modern rites, the representatives of a new society attempted to invest their creation with sacral status, to give their newly baptized citizens a convincing sense of purpose, an end, a goal. For what, finally, would give meaning to their lives when every Christian altar had been overturned? The answer was the subject of Lequinio's sermon.

"The world is full of Christian ideas gone mad," G. K. Chesterton once observed. It is worth thinking of modern happiness as one of those ideas.[19] The heir to not only the metaphysics of the classical world but to the promise of Christian salvation, happiness received Christianity's legacy of universal hope, charging it with a powerful democratic potential and missionary appeal. This appeal was all the stronger for its deep ties to the past—even, or especially, when those ties were not acknowledged as such. Did not Lequinio and his brethren catch a glimpse of those ties as they stood at the pulpits of their former churches, preaching sermons on the approaching rapture and demanding self-sacrifice in the name of the "true happiness" to come? For that matter, did not even the most radical materialists—La Mettrie, Bentham, Sade—perceive in their ostensibly more profane happiness of perpetual pleasure a strange secularization and coming to earth of what had been, for centuries, an otherworldly Christian dream? Probably not. And yet to envision our highest good in life as an unbroken series of agreeable sensations—the maximization of pleasure and the minimization of pain—was to call to earth the unbroken ecstasy, the eternal bliss of heavenly delight. "Perfect pleasure—a more perfect delight of the senses than that which animals enjoy" is what Aquinas had promised in the heavenly city, that "final happiness" where "every human desire" will be fulfilled. His counterparts in what has been called the "heavenly city of the eighteenth-century philosophers" promised something of the same—the perfection and perpetuation of bliss.[20] Paradise, as Voltaire had said, is where I am.

Or better, where I will be. For try as he might, Voltaire, like most moderns, could not entirely pin happiness down. Despite the efforts of a minority of eighteenth-century radicals to define the human end as subjective pleasure alone, happiness retained with the Enlightened majority vague associations with the splendors of its metaphysical and theological past. Surrounded in truth, in virtue, in reason, happiness promised more than just good feeling, though it promised that, too, suggesting plenitude and deliverance, remuneration and reward for individuals and peoples alike. Like the heaven of yesteryear, the future of happiness was a field broad enough, vague enough, to inspire the faith of legions.

In the case of Lequinio and the Jacobins, however, faith was not enough to move mountains. The Mountain, rather, was moved, toppled by political opposition, as it crumbled under its own weight in the summer of 1794. Lequinio himself managed to survive, lying low and setting about the long task of reinvention that would take him eventually to Newport, Rhode Island, as under-commissioner for commerce during the reign of Napoleon. Securing forgiveness for the crimes he had committed during the Revolution, he spoke little of happiness. And on the final *décadi* of the Year II (1794), no one seems to have spoken of it at all. The festival of happiness would have to be postponed.

Yet the future, like human dreams, refused to disappear. Although the French Revolution pointed out the tremendous dangers of attempting to realize the reverie of happiness on earth, it did not dispel the hope. Ever looming on the horizon, this hope bid not only the citizens of France but the citizens of the modern Western world to walk forward in its pursuit. In this respect, the postrevolutionary French landscape more closely resembled that of other advanced nations in Europe and the Americas than one might otherwise suppose. For there, too, the happiness of the future was emerging as the great legitimating concept of national governments and individual lives, pulling across the political spectrum to lead in the direction of a better world. And there, too, happiness could be seen as the object of many eyes, part of the religions both civil and sacred that invested earthly existence with significance, meaning, purpose, and hope.[21]

This collective march toward happiness was not always forced, as in the case of the French Revolution. And many, of their own volition, turned aside, displaying the fortitude of Hercules in choosing another way. But on the whole, the momentum of modern culture has been in the direction of earthly content, accompanied by a steadily expanding sense of prerogative, entitlement, means, and due. Do we not feel today that all human beings, in the best of possible worlds, deserve to be happy? In our lives and in our loves, in our work and in our play, in sickness and in health, happiness draws with omnipresent force, a force that is all the more compelling for our inability ever to clearly conceive it, and its own protean power to shape itself in keeping with our projected desires. As the philosopher Pascal Bruckner has aptly observed, happiness has become the "sole horizon of our democracies," a vision that for many is the measure of all things.[22] Whereas for most men and women at the dawn of the modern age, God was happiness, happiness has since become our god.

In these respects, Saint-Just was not altogether mistaken when he proclaimed the novelty of the idea of happiness as it emerged from an Enlightened world. But precisely because it also carried with it vestiges of the classical and Christian past, happiness was laden with tremendous force. Enveloped in the clinging incense of Christian promise and lit by the persistent glow of classical reward, happiness continued to intimate salvation and wholeness, the final godlike goal of man. It is a perfect illustration of what has been called the "strange persistence of transcendence" in the West, a dream that carries with it the deepest longings of old.[23]

As we shall see in the second half of this book, Lequinio and the Jacobins were not alone in refusing to reduce happiness to the sum of all pleasures, in believing with the faith of Rousseau that a higher happiness could be had here on earth. That belief was a stubborn—and very modern—faith, but one that collided time and again with the hard realities of life in the modern world. Even in those places like the United States, where the pursuit of happiness was treated as an individual responsibility and choice, the end could demand means that threatened to subvert it, transforming the smiling face into a sullen frown. Happiness, we might say, has proved a taskmaster as hard, at times, as the God it has sought to replace.

PART II

Spreading the Word

We must not believe therefore, that at any time and whatever the political situation, the passion of materialistic pleasures and the beliefs fostered by it could satisfy a whole people. Man's soul is vaster than we think; it can entertain both the taste for earthly goods and the love of the goods of heaven. Sometimes a people seems to be pursuing only one of them; but soon it will seek the other.

—Tocqueville, *Democracy in America*

You higher men, do learn this, joy wants eternity. Joy wants the eternity of *all* things, *wants deep, wants deep eternity.*

—Nietzsche, *Thus Spoke Zarathustra*

5

QUESTIONING
THE EVIDENCE

Several years before he struck glory with his sword, Napoleon
Bonaparte sought glory with his pen. It was the summer of 1791,
roughly the time, as William Wordsworth would recall in the eleventh
book of *The Prelude*, when it was "bliss to be alive" and "very heaven"
to be young. Napoleon, who had the good fortune to be both, was also
in France:

> Not in Utopia,—subterranean fields,—
> Or some secreted island, Heaven knows where!
> But in the very world, which is the world
> Of all of us,—the place where, in the end,
> We find our happiness, or not at all!
> ("Residence in France," *The Prelude*, book 11)

Here the young officer resolved to conquer literary fame. Taking leave
of his regiment, he worked intensely, reading and writing for months.
And in August, he stormed the citadel, submitting an entry to a prize
essay competition sponsored by the Academy of Lyon. The question—

"What truths and feelings are most important to instill happiness in men?"—was perfectly suited to those heady times.

Napoleon's answer, however, was not. Despite a handful of revolutionary platitudes and stock Enlightenment phrases—"man," we learn, "is born to be happy"—the essay, on the whole, provides evidence to the contrary. A note of gloom pervades the work. "When *ennui* takes possession of a man's heart," Napoleon tells us, "sadness, black melancholy, and despair will follow. If this state endures, he will give himself to death."[1] Having already written a brief reflection on suicide, Napoleon was well acquainted with the theme. He returns to it here, speaking graphically of "opening up one's own entrails." The "void, the terrible solitude of the heart," seems to haunt the young soldier:

When [a man] asks himself, "Why have I been created?" then he, I believe, is the most wretched of all men. . . . How does he go about existing, this empty heart? How can he live the life of animals with the moral faculties that are peculiar to our nature? Happy he could be if he did not possess these faculties! This man is thrown into despair by trifles. The slightest setback seems to him an intolerable calamity. . . . In the void of solitude, will not an interior passion say to him, "No, I am not happy."[2]

Although Napoleon chose not to include this passage, taken from a draft of his final paragraph, in the version of the essay he submitted to the Academy, it remains abundantly clear that he was haunted by this same "interior passion," the whispered suspicion that happiness might not be our natural due. In order to stifle it, he recommends the cultivation of "feeling," that "consoling agent" that brings us comfort and release in times of misfortune. Climb a peak of Mont-Blanc, Napoleon suggests, and behold the sunrise: "May the first ray of light enter your heart." Stroll along the sea and watch the great orb plunge "into the bosom of the infinite." "Melancholy will lead you, and you will abandon yourself to it." Wander in the countryside and listen "to the perfect silence of the universe"; take refuge in the cabin of a shepherd, sleep before a burning fire, and at midnight "return into yourself" to "meditate on the origin of nature." Or pass in front of the altar of Saint Peter's Cathedral in Rome at ten p.m. and stay until dawn, bearing witness to the mystery as the "darkness of night" gives way to the "pallor of the morning."[3]

Napoleon had read his Rousseau and was well acquainted with other maudlin writers in the tradition of eighteenth-century sensibility and the sublime. But there is something new here, a hint of a changing aesthetic and emotional style that goes beyond its eighteenth-century precedents. The withdrawal into the self and the projection outward into nature; the stoking of the hot glow of the moment and the intensity of feeling, the mystery, the melancholy, the yearning, the doubt— all of this provides a taste of what we now call vaguely, if necessarily (for there is no better word), Romanticism.[4] Even before his exploits on the battlefield had earned him the status of the quintessential Romantic hero, Napoleon was giving proof of his worthiness of that mantle.

Romanticism is notoriously difficult to define in large part because it was always less of a self-conscious movement than a broader cultural ethos—one that in art, literature, music, and philosophy spilled well beyond the boundaries of its specific historical moment in the first third of the nineteenth century. With his genius for anticipation, Napoleon seems to have captured a hint of the Romantic sensibility. But it was not enough to carry the colors at the Academy of Lyon. A five-man panel deemed his efforts uninspired, with one judge dismissing them as "worse than mediocre."[5] Candidate #15's hopes of literary fame were routed. Years later, the wound of rejection had still not entirely healed. When Talleyrand, that mischievous courtier, presented the emperor with a copy of his youthful manuscript, Napoleon read only a few pages before casting it into the fire. So, it seems, did the great man dispense with the illusions of youth.

Perhaps this is fitting, for as Hegel would later observe, it is not the fate of world-historical individuals to experience "what is commonly called happiness."[6] In Napoleon's case, this was not for lack of effort.

"Only the happy man is worthy of his creator," he emphasized in his youthful discourse, and he struggled throughout his life to be a man of worth. How bitter must have been his acknowledgment of failure—both to himself and to those he had led. "I have meant to make France happy," he confessed before his generals at his surrender at Fontainebleau. "I have not succeeded. Events have turned against me."[7]

This was an egregious understatement. More properly speaking, Napoleon had turned against events and, in doing so, had dragged his countrymen and the whole of Europe into a series of futile wars responsible for the suffering of millions. But then, it was always the way of this dynamic man to act on a gigantic scale. In his struggle to achieve a happiness that in his heart he knew might be an impossible dream, Napoleon dramatized a broader Romantic conflict and challenge. His was the struggle of all who are born as heirs to the Enlightenment's self-evident truth—raised to believe that they are meant to be happy—and then haunted by the suspicion that the evidence of the world suggests otherwise. This was the Romantic conflict. The challenge was to overcome it, believing in joy and "happiness unthought of," even when one could not hear or see. In his struggle—and in his failure—Napoleon embodied this great Romantic quest.

Odes to Melancholy

"Ich weiß nicht, was soll es bedeuten / Daß ich so traurig bin." ("I do not know what this can mean, that I am so sad.") The line, often sung, set to music by Liszt, Clara Schumann, and others, opens one of the most famous of all German poems, Heinrich Heine's "Die Lorelei." The literal translation in English fails to do it justice, but Mark Twain, that painstaking student of what he called, with affection, "the awful German language," was perhaps slightly more successful:

> I cannot divine what it meaneth,
> This haunting nameless pain

If the source of Heine's complaint was difficult to divine, it is comparatively easy to place: The speaker of the poem is haunted by the legend of a fatal siren, a beautiful maiden (die Lorelei) who calls sailors to their deaths along the banks of the Rhine.

Heine was not always so direct in pointing out the sources of his sadness. A German Jew who converted to Protestantism to ease his assimilation, he fell afoul of state authorities nonetheless and was forced to live much of his adult life as an exile in Paris. Torn between two cultures and two religions, Heine also straddled professions (he was both a journalist and a poet) and aesthetics (he was an admirer of Romanticism and one of its sharpest critics). A student of Hegel and a friend in Paris of Engels and Marx, Heine warned of communism's future threat to the world. He was a conflicted soul; but perhaps for that very reason, he struggled in virtually all of his work to understand and to interpret the meaning of the suffering of his time.

It was Heine, along with the poet Jean-Paul Richter, who first introduced the term *Weltschmerz* ("world suffering") to capture a new, and elusive, form of pain.[8] Neither man, admittedly, loaded the word at the outset with the full weight that it would accumulate over the course of the century: world weariness, or literally "world pain," the acute anguish brought on by the simple fact of being in the world. But then neither man was unfamiliar with these sentiments, either, and already by the first decades of the nineteenth century, Europeans were complaining of a mysterious disease with precisely these symptoms. They called it the *maladie du siècle* or, simply, the *mal du siècle,* the sickness of the age.

There were precedents for this sickness, just as there were already terms that could be used to describe it. The publication of Goethe's *Sorrows of Young Werther* in 1774 had produced a veritable cult of misery among disaffected youth, giving rise to the word *Werthersfieber* ("Werther's fever") to describe the lovesick sadness and forlorn disaffection that gripped so many who modeled themselves on the work's eponymous hero. Neglecting Goethe's later advice—"Dare to be happy!"—they adopted the plain blue frock coat and buff waistcoat of Werther as the uniform of the man of feeling.[9] In France, the enormously powerful example of Rousseau had much the same effect, moving legions to confessions of woe, while in England the pastime of lingering morbidly in graveyards had flourished since the publication of Thomas Gray's popular "Elegy Written in a Country Churchyard" in 1751. Reading the happy eighteenth century against the grain, one can turn up no shortage of odes to "melancholy," that venerable term, and sonnets to "spleen," traditionally considered the seat of black bile but used from the late seventeenth century in English, and from the mid-eighteenth century in French, to describe listless sadness and immobilizing despair. *Ennui* ("boredom," but with a more generally depressive sense) also began in the eighteenth century to be associated with maladies of the soul. The French word quickly made the rounds of Europe, where, by the end of the century of lights, it was turning up in various tongues.

It can be argued, in fact, that the *mal de siècle* was in truth the *mal des deux siècles*, the sickness of two centuries.[10] Making room for the latter half of the age of Enlightenment, this proposition highlights a cultural dynamic we have seen at work in Rousseau: The same century that consolidated happiness as an earthly end also bred new forms of despair. As individuals struggled, and failed, to achieve their "natural" goal, happiness and spleen, felicity and ennui were caught up in a common continuum to develop in tandem.

True in embryo for the latter part of the eighteenth century, this proposition is even more true for the decades that followed, when artists and writers, philosophers and musicians, flaunted their disaffection with an intensity that make Werther and Rousseau seem restrained. Consider Chateaubriand, weeping his way across Europe in convulsive sobs. "Sorrow is my element," he writes at the turn of the century. "I only discover myself when I am unhappy."[11] The French Romantic Pierre-Simon Ballanche claimed in 1808, "Only sorrow matters in life, and there is no reality beyond tears."[12] Byron, a man so weary of the world that he complained even of having to conjugate "the accursed verb *ennuyer*" ("to be bored"), provided an entire generation with a model and ideal type of the histrionics of sadness, "gorging himself on gloom."[13] The Italian poet Leopardi did much the same,

Pierre-Paul Prud'hon, Study for *Le Rêve du Bonheur*, 1819, Musée de Louvre, Paris.
Photo: Réunion des Musées Nationaux/Art Resource, NY.

filling his widely read works with the "stubborn, black, horrible, barbarous melancholy" that was an "eternal and inseparable" part of his
life.[14] Nor were contemporaries immune to the attractions of the
Schlegel brothers, of Schiller, Hölderlin, or the countless other German chroniclers of the *Zeitkrankheit*, the "sickness of the time," for
whom happiness was "tepid water on the tongue."[15] They could not
resist Shelley, who lived, he felt, in an "age of despair," whose world
was "a dim vast vale of tears."[16] Or Keats, who could "scarcely remember counting upon any Happiness" at all in his short, unhappy life.[17]
And this is only the beginning of a list that could fill volumes. Why,
after the long age of Enlightenment, we must ask, this newfound willingness to see the world through tears? To return to Heine's question, what could such sadness mean? Wherein lay its source?

Contemporaries were quick to offer answers. In the *Prelude*, Wordsworth attributed the new mood to disillusionment—"this melancholy

waste of hopes o'erthrown"—engendered by the failed promise of the
French Revolution.[18] Present in France in the summer of 1790, and
then again for nearly a year in 1791–92, Wordsworth shared firsthand
the tremendous optimism of the moment. When the Revolution's
aspirations ran to blood, he felt the wound directly. Those who looked
on from afar could be similarly moved by the spectacle of happiness
promised and happiness deceived. For Shelley, the hope and failure
of the Revolution was "the master theme of the epoch in which we
live."[19] His view was widely shared.

Others extended only the time frame so as to include the European-
wide destruction of the Napoleonic wars. Alfred de Musset, a leading
French Romantic, observed, "The *maladie du siècle* comes from two
causes: the people who have passed through 1793 and 1814 carry two
wounds in their heart. All that was, is no longer, and all that will be is not
yet made. Do not search any farther for the secret of our ills."[20] Touring
the battlefields of Europe, Byron agreed that much had been destroyed.
His thinly veiled mouthpiece, Childe Harold, is inspired to wonder while
standing on the blood-soaked fields of Waterloo, this "place of skulls":

Did man compute
Existence by enjoyment, and count o'er
Such hours 'gainst years of life,—say, would he name threescore?[21]

A mere handful of days, counted out in hours, seemed a small measure for a life.

The upheavals of the Revolution and the letdown of its aftermath
gave rise to such thoughts, prompting many to conclude that these
were the causes of the sickness of the age. But others were inclined to
take a longer view. At a safe remove from Europe, the American Ralph
Waldo Emerson marveled that "history gave no intimation of any society in which despondency came so readily to heart as we see it and
feel it in ours." Indians, Saxons, and other "primitive" peoples, he alleged, were immune to this affliction despite lower levels of "external
prosperity" and "general well-being." "Yet we are sad & they were
not. . . . Why should it be?"[22] The very framing of the question im-

plied an answer: that the process of development bred its own discontent. Greatly indebted to Rousseau's analysis of the paradox of cultural progress, this line of inquiry enjoyed widespread currency among analysts of the modern malaise. As one of their most forceful representatives, the German dramatist and critic Friedrich Schiller declared, "It was civilization itself that inflicted this wound upon modern man."[23] Given apparent confirmation by the "dark, satanic mills" that were beginning to mar the modern landscape, such contentions sent countless Romantic souls packing in search of virgin forests and virgin minds in a rite of pilgrimage that continues to the present day. Unspoiled nature and unspoiled humanity, they believed, could offer balm to those afflicted by the sickness of the times.

Alongside the jarring experience of the recent past and the slowly powerful push of civilization, another force exerted its influence on the Romantic mood. Once again it is Heine who shows us the way, observing in an essay that charts the intellectual development of the early nineteenth century that an old flower had given new bloom. This was a "passion flower," he claims, rising from the blood of Christ, in whose chalice can be seen "the instruments of torture" used at the crucifixion ("hammer, tongs, nails"); a melancholy flower "by no means ugly, only eerie," the sight of which "arouses in us an uncanny pleasure like the convulsively sweet sensations which result even from suffering itself"; an alluring flower whose "most gruesome attraction consists in this very ecstasy of suffering." That old flower, Heine observed, was Catholic Christianity, and its latest bloom was Romanticism, what he called the "Romantic school."[24]

Heine restricted his comments exclusively to German Romanticism—with its formal embrace of the poetry and culture of the Christian Middle Ages. But one can certainly detect a strong Christian fragrance in Romanticism's various other national flowerings. The scent conjures different images in different places: from the Gothic revival churches of nineteenth-century England and America, to the mysticism of an Emerson or a Blake, to the elegiac longing of Coleridge, Carlyle, or Chateaubriand, to the lonely crucifixes in the landscapes of Caspar David Friedrich. Yet rising over the back of this varied and complex bouquet is often the same "sweet sensation of suffering" that Heine identified as Christianity's essence. As Jean-Paul Richter could acknowledge in a statement that might be applied to other Romantic media as well, "The origin and character of all modern poetry can be derived so easily from Christianity that one might just as well call Romantic poetry Christian."[25]

The statement was considerably exaggerated, but it contained more than an element of truth. For although the fact is often overlooked, the first half of the nineteenth century witnessed the most concerted effort of Christian revival since the Reformation and its Catholic response. In large part a reaction against the excesses of the Enlightenment and the French Revolution, this religious renewal was marked by intensive missionary activity, the expansion of seminaries, and great waves of church building. Spanning the Catholic-Protestant divide, it took different forms in different countries, animating the English evangelical revival and the Second Great Awakening in the United States; the high-church Oxford Movement of John Henry Newman; the push to consolidate Catholic schooling in Austria, Italy, France, and Spain; the German pietism and religion of feeling promoted by Friedrich Schleiermacher; and the intense devotional movements of popular religiosity that fed the resurgence of pilgrimages on the continent in the second half of the nineteenth century. Collectively, these various movements helped to ensure that Christianity as a whole retained both cultural vitality and intellectual resonance well into the twentieth century.

The flowerings of Romanticism took root in this soil. Which is not to say that Romantics shared unreservedly in the orthodoxies of the faith. There were those, to be sure, who succeeded in fully prostrating themselves before the altar. But far more common was the position of Thomas Carlyle. The Scottish son of a Calvinist preacher, and a leading proponent in England of German philosophy, Carlyle saw much to admire in the Christian religion. Yet he recognized that however much one might desire it, the Enlightenment could not be undone. "The Mythus of the Christian Religion look[ed] not in the eighteenth century as it did in the eighth," he observed in his first major work, *Sartor Resartus*, or the "tailor retailored." The task, accordingly, was "to embody the divine Spirit of that Religion in a new Mythus, in a new vehicle and vesture." Put another way, God must be clothed anew.[26] This was the task of the times—to find new forms to accommodate the spiritual yearning of humanity—and in this search, the Scottish renegade was not alone. The attempt to fashion new spiritual raiments for a post-Enlightened age—to make the supernatural natural and the natural, supernatural, in Carlyle's celebrated phrase—was a broad Romantic challenge.[27]

It is here that Heine's insight is so fruitful. Despite his considerable antipathy toward the Christian tradition, he fully recognized that "for eighteen centuries this religion" had been "a blessing for a suffering humanity"; that the "blood of the crucified Christ" had served as a "soothing balm flowing down into the wound of mankind"; and that the "gruesome attraction" of the faith, just like the sickly-sweet scent of the passion flower, was its ability to make an "ecstasy of suffering," to transform pain and putrefaction into "uncanny pleasure."[28] Was this not the secret of the sweet suffering of Christianity's latest bloom? Heine did not develop the thought, yet it is striking how many Romantics, whether indebted self-consciously to Christianity or not, seemed to writhe in the ecstasy of pain. As Wordsworth confessed in *The Prelude:*

> Dejection taken up for pleasure's sake
> And gilded sympathies, the willow wreath,
> Even among those solitudes sublime,
> And sober posies of funeral flowers
> Culled from the gardens of Lady Sorrow
> Did Sweeten many a meditative hour. (book 6, 483–88)

Keats, too, in his celebrated *Ode on Melancholy*, extols the pleasures of dejection, recommending that we take them much further afield:

> But when the melancholy fit shall fall
> Sudden from heaven like a weeping cloud,
> . . . Then glut thy sorrow on a morning rose,

> Or on the rainbow of the salt sand-wave
> Or on the wealth of globéd peonies; . . .

Or in the "peerless eyes" of a mistress. The world, in this reckoning, became a field on which to project one's sadness, to luxuriate in one's despair.[29]

Such maudlin mannerisms could quickly become a pose, a gloomy Romantic affectation. And in fact it is to Romanticism that we owe the still-powerful, if deeply insidious, myth that the true man of feeling, the artist, the intellectual, must by definition be a suffering soul. "Who would willingly possess genius?" Byron asks, with typical self-indulgence. "None, I am persuaded, who knew the misery it entails . . . destructive alike to health and happiness."[30] Something like the opposite would seem to be the case. Ensconced in smoke-filled cafés, how many dark-clad youth have willingly taken up misery ever since— in the hope of knowing the genius that it might entail?

And yet, among the first generation of Romantics, there was also something different at work—the recovery of truths that the Age of Enlightenment had tended to forget. By equating pleasure with the good, and by conceiving all evil as pain, Enlightenment thinkers had willfully turned their backs on what Christianity had for so long openly embraced: the endless fascination, even the dark delights, of suffering. Without question, the Christian tradition had always contained a counterveiling impulse: to *relieve* our neighbor's distress. But the way to fulfill this command was by taking up the cross, following Christ in sacrifice of oneself for the good of others, thereby converting suffering into personal merit and spiritual reward. Pain was transformative; it was the way back to God.

As we have seen, the Reformation tended to mitigate the heroic embrace of pain, downplaying the glorification of self-imposed suffering. But neither Calvin nor Luther ever supposed that pain could be entirely abolished, or that this was even a reasonable goal. A necessary concomitant of a fallen world, pain was a fact of existence to be accepted and borne—preferably with joy.

In the general Enlightenment conception, by contrast, pain was at once unnecessary and contingent, an unadulterated evil. Fleeing it instinctively, individuals suffered pain only out of blindness, duress, or the force of circumstances. The symptom of ignorance or the fruit of injustice, pain could never be the way of truth, and still less the way of pleasure. It was something to be banished from the world, something to be cured or rooted out, *not* to be savored or transformed.

This was, and remains, a noble creed, one that stands behind much ongoing humanitarian effort to eradicate world suffering. Yet it also lies exposed to the very charge that the Romantics themselves dramatized so effectively: that suffering is natural to the human condition. To pretend that it is otherwise—the result, merely, of ignorance or error or outmoded belief—was not only unconvincing but self-deceptive. Suffering, the Romantics countered, was an inherent truth of the world and so must be acknowledged openly, in the light of day. As Schiller enjoined, we must "confront evil destiny face to face."[31]

This was not merely a call to see the world with open eyes. Nor was it a delight in suffering for suffering's sake. That embrace would come later, with the rise, in the second half of the nineteenth century, of Symbolist poetry and aesthetic Decadence. Whereas those movements exuded lurid fascination with sickness and decay in their own right, the Romantics' preoccupation with pain was meant to serve a higher purpose. "Only in the *knowledge*" of the dangers that face us, Schiller continued, only by confronting the suffering and tragedy of life, could there be "salvation for us." Suffering was a gateway to a richer life, a door that led to a fuller understanding of the self and the world, a passage that opened out into the intensity of human experience. "Do you not see how necessary a World of Pains and troubles is to school an Intelligence and make it a soul?" Keats asks in a famous letter to his brother.[32] Rediscovering a truth long close to the Christian sage, Keats understood that suffering was necessary to educate the self, to make us more complete human beings. Pain, in a word, was transformative. It humbled individual pride, opening us to the possibility of empathy and compassion. And it instilled in us an appreciation for the common lot of humanity. Far more than pleasure, pain exposed us to the intensity of human experience, carving out room for the exhilaration of feeling. A "place where the heart must feel and suffer in a thousand diverse ways," the world, Keats knew, was "A Vale of Soul-Making."[33]

The Romantics, then, reinvested pain—and especially emotional pain—with significance and depth. True to their name, they gave it romance and allure. They also gave it purpose. We might almost say, in answer to Heine, that the meaning of the suffering of the age was precisely the suffering to give it meaning. People of substance suffered, as they should, for this was a proper response to the world and a means to a higher end. The Romantics, in this respect, were fitting heirs to the Christian tradition. Yet they were also, we should not forget, children of the Enlightenment. And when such children descended into the valley of darkness, they did so with the hope, the faith, that they would find sunshine on the other side. The Romantics had a term for this precious ascent: They called it "joy."

Odes to Joy

Joy, a leading scholar has observed, "is a central and recurrent term in the Romantic vocabulary."[34] Used at times synonymously with happiness, but in possession of its own distinct sense, joy wells up from within and rains down from above. It is the counterpoint to despair, and often its bosom brother. Thus does Coleridge conceive of this "strong music in the soul" that surges forth in the midst of one of his greatest poems, "Dejection: An Ode":

> O pure of heart! Thou need'st not ask of me
> What this strong music in the soul may be!
> What, and Wherein it doth exist,

This light, this glory, this fair luminous mist,
This beautiful and beauty-making power.
Joy, virtuous Lady! Joy that n'er was given,
Save to the pure, and in their purest hour,
Life, and Life's effluence, cloud at once and shower,
Joy, Lady! Is the spirit and the power,
Which wedding Nature to us gives in dower
A New Earth and new Heaven . . .
Undreamt of by the sensual and the proud—
Joy is the sweet voice, Joy the luminous cloud.

Virtually by themselves these lines supply the material of a Romantic manifesto, touching on a broad range of themes associated with the Romantics' conception of joy. At once a cloud and a shower, joy is both a force that pours down upon us and the precipitate of that power. Joy is light, joy is glory, joy is reserved for the pure of heart. And when its sweet music wafts through the soul, it transforms us, as it transforms the world, making a new heaven and a new earth, wedding Nature to the self.

Coleridge wrote these lines in 1802, sometime before his more avowed *confessio fidei*, his confession of Christian faith. The religious imagery is unmistakable, nonetheless, and it is revealing. For what Coleridge is proposing in joy is nothing less than the overcoming of human alienation, the breaking down of the boundaries that divide us from the world and from those around us. In joy, he ventures, we merge with something greater than ourselves, overcoming individual isolation.

This belief rested on two fundamental assumptions shared widely in Romantic circles. The first involved a rejection of the Enlightenment conviction that the human mind was simply a passive recipient of the data of experience, a tabula rasa, in Locke's words, written upon by the sense impressions of the world. Developed most thoroughly in the tradition of German idealist philosophy that derived from Kant (to which Coleridge himself was greatly indebted), this new view presented the mind as an active force, responsible for giving shape to experience, for ordering, categorizing, and combining our impressions of the world. To borrow the metaphor of the critic M. H. Abrams, the Romantic mind was not a "mirror" that simply reflected the world, but a "lamp" that projected outward, blending and infusing its surroundings with color, depth, shadow, and light.[35]

This profound reorientation in the understanding of the operations of the mind took different, often highly complex, forms in different countries. But more often than not, it was combined with a second assumption: that there was more to the world than first met the eye. Whereas Enlightenment observers looked out at the universe and saw matter in motion—the finely calibrated movements of a machine—Romantics claimed to sense something else: Spirit, Idea, Life, Mind, Nature, Being, the Infinite. The terms, often capitalized, were loose and frequently interchangeable, struggling as they did to define the indefinable. Often, too, they hinted at a vague pantheism, the identification of the workings of nature with the divine. An organic force that bound together all living things, a union and harmony that eluded both telescope and mathematical formula, this "Nature," in Coleridge's conception, was an underlying order that could not be seen, only intuited, felt, divined.

And here was the link to joy. For joy resulted from our ability to connect with this larger order and force, to stray outside the confines of the self. As Hölderlin observes, typically: "To end that eternal conflict between our self and the world, to restore the peace that passeth all understanding, to unite ourselves with Nature so as to form one endless whole—that is the goal of all our striving."[36] Yet as he and others well knew, this was no easy task, for it depended not only on our capacity to intuit and feel Nature, to divine the beauty of the world, but also on our ability to project the lamp of the mind outward in such a way that this beauty could be illuminated and perceived. As Coleridge continues in "Dejection: An Ode":

> Ah! from the soul itself must issue forth
> A light, a glory, a fair luminous cloud
> Enveloping the Earth . . .

To find that inner light is a critical element of the Romantic quest.

It is symptomatic of the elusive nature of this quest that Coleridge imagines it in a poem that despairs of its very possibility. The prospect of joy, paradoxically, is revealed in "Dejection: An Ode," a work in which the author bemoans the loss of his ability to feel Nature's beauty. Bowed down by affliction, Coleridge has lost what "nature gave me at my birth / My shaping spirit of Imagination," the latter being Coleridge's technical term for precisely that faculty that issues forth light. "Imagination" gives color and order to the world. It is not, in Coleridge's usage, what causes us to see what can't be seen, to "imagine" what is not there. Imagination, rather, allows us to see as we should see, as we ought to see.

It is significant that he speaks of it as a possession of birth. For like so many Romantics, Coleridge was inclined to think of the ability to experience joy as a birthright, the natural endowment of the child. The child regards all things with freshness and wonder. The child plays and creates in perfect unity and wholeness. The child is at one with the world, experiencing daily its deep magic and meaning, sending forth his light. "Heaven lies about us in our infancy," Wordsworth declares in "Intimations of Immortality." William Blake is even more explicit in his poem "Infant Joy":

> "I have no name;
> I am but two days old."
> What shall I call thee?
> "I happy am,
> Joy is my name."
> Sweet joy befall thee!
>
> Pretty joy!
> Sweet joy, but two days old.
> Sweet Joy I call thee:
> Thou dost smile,
> I sing the while;
> Sweet joy befall thee!

Like this unnamed child, all of us were once "children of joy" who harbor some recollection, however fleeting, of a more perfect, contented state. In this respect, the Romantics furthered the Enlightenment belief that a measure of happiness was a natural human endowment. Yet virtually all agreed that we quickly fell from this prelapsarian state. In his *Philosophical Lectures,* Coleridge indicates why:

> In joy individuality is lost and it therefore is liveliest in youth
> ... [before] the circumstances that have forced a man in
> upon his little unthinking contemptible self, have lessened
> his power of existing universally. To have a genius is to live in
> the universal, to know no self but that which is reflected not
> only from the faces of all around us, our fellow creatures, but
> reflected from the flowers, the trees, the beasts, yea from the
> surface of [the waters and the] sands of the desert.[37]

Whereas the "circumstances" of the world turned a man inward upon himself, it was self-love—pride—that kept him bound in the prison of his person. Here is the clue to why Coleridge denied a "New Earth and new Heaven" to "the sensual and the proud" in the passage from the "Ode to Melancholy" cited above. Not only was the transformation induced by joy something far deeper than the frisson of sensuality, it could not even be "dreamt" by those whose concerns were confined to their own petty pleasures and pains. To be focused in this way on one's self was to sever the connection to the universal that alone could transform us in joy.

There is, it seems, a tension at the heart of this Romantic creed. On the one hand, joy lies within, and it is only by mining deep down through the impacted rock of personal suffering that we can tap its source. Continuing the inward quest of Rousseau, the Romantics make of joy a highly personal force. It is a Romantic in spirit, the American Walt Whitman, who later best captures the highly personal nature of happiness and joy in his extended poem "Song of Myself":

There is that in me—I do not know what it is—but
  I know it is in me . . .
I do not know it—it is without name—it is a word
  unsaid,
It is not in any dictionary, utterance, symbol . . .
Do you see O my brothers and sisters?
It is not chaos or death—it is form, union, plan—it is eternal life—
  it is Happiness.[38]

Subjective, intimate, individual, this force—call it happiness, call it joy—is virtually indescribable, a mysterious, private possession buried within. Yet on the other hand, this force simultaneously transcends the self, rendering our individual concerns and private cares a potential barrier to fusion with the "form, union, plan" of the wider world. At once a gateway and a closed door, the repository of memories of childhood bliss and the home of present pain, the Romantic self becomes the site of a struggle that we must somehow learn to transcend. In order to truly be ourselves, we must break free of our selves. In order to access our private, personal joy, we must link up with the universal joy that animates the world.

A fall from innocence precipitated by self-love and pride; an original state of wholeness now lost; an internal struggle to be "born again" in joy; a mysterious universal power buried within—all this should sound familiar. Plainly, there are strong Christian precedents for much of this language, and it is probably revealing that the Romantics made such special use of the term "joy" itself, a word with close links to frequent Gospel commandments—"rejoice and be glad," be "filled with joy"—and a word far less tainted by Enlightenment accretions than "happiness" itself. As Carlyle sought to emphasize in *Sartor Resartus:*

There is in man a Higher than Love of Happiness. . . . Was it
not to preach forth this same Higher that sages and martyrs,
the Poet and the Priest, in all times, have spoken and suffered; bearing testimony, through life and through death, of
the Godlike that is in Man . . . ?[39]

Carlyle used the term "blessedness" to distinguish this higher state from Enlightenment happiness. But his critical appeal to the transcendent, to the "godlike" in man as the distinguishing feature, was frequently seized upon by those who used the term "joy" with similar intent. Indeed, Romantic joy bears a striking resemblance to the perennial spiritual force that Christians call "grace." It is the power that frees us from, returns us to, and completes ourselves, the power that connects us to the divine, transforming our vision of the world. Like the pilgrim who struggles overland to return to the blessedness of God, like the saint who searches for signs of the liberating power within, the Romantic thirsts for the healing power of joy. In joy we lose ourselves, so that in joy we may be found.

There is, however, a crucial distinction. Rarely do Romantics speak of joy as a force that is divinely conferred. Joy, rather, is immanent, dwelling dormant within us all as it dwells within the world. Unlike Christian grace, joy is not granted from on high, mediated through the church, or infused directly into the soul by the word of Christ. It is already there, already here, waiting to be recovered—a process that involves great sacrifice and pain. But the burden is ours to bear and is to be carried to completion in this life. The Romantic promise is of happiness, not in another world but in this one.

Which takes us to the very heart of Romanticism's contradiction and appeal. For what is Romantic joy if not a partially secularized dream of experiencing heaven on earth; the dream of recovering the lost child within who whispers to us daily, like the New Adam, of what we once were and again might be? It is Wordsworth, above all, who underlines the point in his *Home at Grasmere,* a work in which he chronicles a return, both literal and figurative, to his childhood dwelling. After a long and painful pilgrimage amid the "realities of life so cold," Wordsworth comes back to himself:

> A termination, and a last retreat
> A Center, come from wheresoe'er you will,
> A Whole without dependence or defect,

Made for itself; and happy in itself,
A Perfect contentment, Unity entire.

And here, the distant thought
Is fetch'd out of the heaven in which it was.
The unappropriated bliss hath found
An owner, and that owner I am he.
The Lord of this enjoyment is on Earth
and in my breast.[40]

The distant thought, the happiness of heaven, has been achieved by mortal incarnation, the word made flesh.

But how, we immediately wonder, can such complete joy be sustained? Restless wanderers that they were, the Romantics proposed many routes, but the common end, one suspects, remained equally elusive. There is, for example, the way so dear to Wordsworth himself, the way of Nature that beckons with the invitation to find oneself along its divine path. The German painter Philipp Otto Runge captures perfectly the prospect of swirling, mysterious joy to be had when taken up in the arms of the infinite:

When the sky above me teems with innumerable stars, the
wind blows through the vastness of space, the wave breaks
in the immense night; when above the forest the reddish
morning light appears and the sun begins to illuminate the
world, the mist rises in the valley and I throw myself in grass
sparkling with dew, every blade and stalk of grass teems
with life, the earth awakes and stirs beneath me, and everything harmonizes in one great chord; then my soul rejoices
and soars in the immeasurable space around me, there is no
high or low, no beginning and no end, I hear and feel the
living breath of God who holds and supports the world, in
whom everything lives and acts: this is our highest feeling—
God![41]

There is, too, the way of love. "Wherein lies happiness?" Keats asks in "Endymion." In that which beckons, he answers:

> Our ready minds to fellowship divine,
> A fellowship with essence; till we shine,
> Fully alchemiz'd, and free of space. Behold
> The clear religion of heaven.

The most "self-destroying" of all the earthly elixirs, love has the power to effect this transformation, to make "men's being mortal, immortal." It is the "hope beyond the shadow of a dream."

To the mystical transports of love and the ecstatic swoon of nature might be added the Romantics' enraptured fascination with earlier epochs in human history or their wanderings, real and imagined, among the "primitive" peoples of foreign lands. In both instances did some

Constance Mayer-Lamartinière, *The Dream of Happiness,* Musée de Louvre, Paris. Photo: Réunion des Musées Nationaux/Art Resource, NY.

claim to find evidence of the "happy infancy" of humanity, an analog
to the joyful wholeness that they often attributed to youth. Measured
in entire cultures (and with ample condescension), such thoughts led
some to search for happiness, like Chateaubriand's René, on Native
American plains. They prompted others to scour for traces of a lost
golden age amid the ruins of Greece, or Rome, or the Christian Middle
Ages, when whole peoples allegedly lived on better terms with the
world and with themselves. And they led the likes of Coleridge and
his circle of Cambridge undergraduates to plan excitedly for the
founding of what they called a "pantisocratic," or all-governing, community on the banks of the Susquehanna River in Pennsylvania,
where devoted "children of nature" would recover the prelapsarian
state through an experiment in communal living.[42]

Such efforts, almost by definition, were destined to fail. No more
could they re-create a lost innocence, permanently slake the thirst for
joy, than could the most desperate of Romantic stratagems for conjuring bliss: the resort to mind-altering drugs. The English poet Thomas
de Quincey may have believed, after his first use of opium, that he
had discovered the panacea for all human woes, the "secret of happiness, about which philosophers had disputed for so many ages." But
as he recounts in the *Confessions of an English Opium Eater* (1822), the
"apocalypse" of "divine enjoyment" quickly gave way to the hell of
addiction. Happiness could not be "bought for a penny."[43] Wanting
"to be God," man falls "lower than his real nature," Baudelaire observes
of his own experiments with hashish. The attempt to induce an "artificial paradise"—to travel through the deliberate disordering of the
senses to states of childlike wonder and fascination—is tinged from
the outset by the ironic knowledge of its own futility.[44]

It is possible to say as much of *all* these Romantic stratagems to arrive
at the final destination of joy—a joy that is more, that is, than an ephemeral glimpse, a fleeting moment, or a passing feeling. In their darker
moments, Romantic voices were prepared to admit as much, suggesting
that they knew it all along. "There is not a joy that life can give like that
it takes away," Byron understood. For Keats, as for so many others, the
goddess of melancholy keeps her "Sovran shrine," in the "very temple

of Delight." "Joy, whose hand is ever at his lips / Bidding adieu . . ." is a figure eternally taking leave. But despite this knowledge, the hope, the faith endures that joy—lasting joy—can transform our existence into something more precious. "Let us believe in a kind of optimism in which we are our own gods," Shelley affirms, stressing that it is "best that we should think all this for the best even though it be not."[45]

This defiant optimism, this quixotic persistence in pursuit, is perhaps the Romantics' most compelling trait. And so it is only right that they should proclaim it repeatedly from their highest altar, the altar of art. "Poetry is the record of the best and happiest moments of the happiest and best minds," Shelley maintains. It spreads "sweet news of kindred joy."[46] "All art is dedicated to joy, and there is no higher and no more serious undertaking than to make man happy," Schiller agrees. How fitting that he should write a poem entitled *"An die Freude,"* an "Ode to Joy," that Beethoven would set to music in realization of a long-held dream. Composers like Bach had for centuries set music to "Jesu, Joy of Man's Desiring"; Beethoven now celebrated the desire for joy itself. It was even more fitting—and fittingly Romantic—that when the final stunning chorus of Beethoven's final symphony boomed out in triumph at the inaugural performance in Vienna in 1824, the composer, long since deaf, was unable to hear the words. Like the music and the applause, they played only in his mind:

Joy, beautiful spark of the gods, daughter of Elysium
Intoxicated with your fire, heavenly one, we enter your shrine.
Your magic power reunites what strict custom has divided;
All men become brothers where your gentle wing rests.
Be embraced, you millions! This kiss for all the world!
Brothers! above the canopy of the stars there must dwell a
   loving Father!

Do you fall to your knees, you millions? World, do you sense
   your Maker?
See him beyond the stars! Beyond the stars he must dwell![47]

The Salvation of Art

"Joy was never my thing, so I find his Ode to Joy banal, which Beethoven can be when he tries to be happy. . . ."[48] This, at any rate, was the judgment of the dour Swedish playwright August Strindberg, writing in the second half of the nineteenth century. Setting aside the struggle for joy, Strindberg focused on a rather different image of the master composer: a copy of Beethoven's mask, originally cast by the Viennese sculptor Franz Klein. Grim, taut, pockmarked, it hung in Strindberg's Stockholm apartment, flanked by candles. The brow furrowed and the jaw set in defiance, the mask captured—did it not?—the deep metaphysical pain of a man whom fate had robbed of his hearing and then tortured on the rack of his own brilliance. Seen in this light, the image was an icon, the symbol par excellence of the tragic intensity of the heroic artist, suffering unto death in a world of pain.

Gesichtsmaske Ludwig van Beethovens.

Atelier Schneider, Bonn.

Franz Klein, *Life Mask of Beethoven,* 1812, Beethoven-Haus, Bonn.

Strindberg was hardly alone in his interpretation, or in his possession; Klein's mask was widely reproduced. The French painter Rosa Bonheur kept a copy on the wall of her studio, as if to defy her name, a reminder of artistic angst. The Italian symbolist Gabriele d'Annunzio crowned his with a wreath of laurels. And thousands more contemplated the apparently haunting image in music shops, antique stores, and private homes across Europe in the nineteenth and early twentieth centuries. To an age enthralled by the new "sciences" of physiognomy and phrenology, the face was the mirror of the mind, just as the eye was the lamp of the soul.

But masks, of course, can be deceiving, and Franz Klein's cast of Beethoven is no exception. In the first place, what Strindberg and many others assumed was a death mask had in fact been cast from life, in 1812, some fifteen years before Beethoven met his maker. And the look of strained agitation that haunted his face was less the reflection of a state of mind than the product of the procedure itself. As the plaster dried about his features, Beethoven struggled to breathe, revealing, one scholar observes, "not a melancholy of soul, but simply the claustrophobic apprehension of near suffocation!"[49] More than anything else, the mask underlines the cautionary wisdom of Ballanche: "We lack a form of measurement to appreciate the sum of happiness and sadness which is reserved for each man. . . . We only see external appearances, the secret and private things escape us."[50]

Which is not to say that Beethoven lived, immortally beloved, in eternal bliss. He himself commented on the mask to a visiting Rossini, "Oh! *un infelice*," "an unhappy one." The Italian composer echoed the sentiment, speaking later of the "indefinable sadness spread over his features."[51] As Beethoven's moving "Heiligenstadt Testament" alone makes clear, the German composer was hardly immune to pain. Penned in 1802 in the Austrian town outside of Vienna that bears its name, the testament reveals the emotional turmoil braved by Beethoven as he struggled to hide his advancing deafness from his family and friends. In a final paragraph added to the main part of the will on October 10, he concludes on a plaintive note:

O Providence—grant me at least one full day of *joy*—it has
been so long since true joy echoed within—Oh when—oh
When oh Divine One, can I find it again in the temple of
nature and of men—Never?—No—Oh that would be too
hard.[52]

Far too hard. Fortunately, Beethoven still had life to live. And though
he never secured the lasting happiness that he demands of his two
brothers near the end of the testament ("during my lifetime I have
thought often of you and ways to make you happy—be so"), Beethoven
did aspire throughout his career to the joy that animates the final
movement of his final symphony.[53] As much as melancholy, as much
as spleen, this search was an integral part of his life, as it was of the
wider enterprise of early Romanticism.

Why, then, did Strindberg choose to see only the scowl, dismissing
the search for happiness as unworthy of a serious artist? The answer
goes far beyond any personal peculiarities of vision. And though the
history of the creation of Beethoven in the image of a suffering hero is
a story unto itself, the immediate impetus in this case is clear enough.
Like so many in the second half of the nineteenth century, Strindberg
was influenced profoundly by a man who succeeded in altering the
image not only of Beethoven but of Romantic art in general and its
accompanying search for happiness.

In the history of modern philosophy, Arthur Schopenhauer is in
many ways an anomaly. A gifted, graceful stylist, he was arguably the
most poetic philosopher to write since Plato, a position challenged only
by Rousseau before him, and after by Nietzsche. Though professionally trained at a number of German institutions and granted a doctor-
ate by the University of Jena in 1813, he lived and thought as an
outsider, at once fiercely independent and supremely self-confident.
"My philosophy is the real solution of the enigma of the world," he
declared typically. "In this sense it may be called a revelation."[54] Notwithstanding a brief unsuccessful teaching stint at the University of
Berlin in 1820, Schopenhauer worked largely on his own, doing so with
impressive precocity. His entire system of thought was formulated in

his twenties. And though he continued to write until his death in Frankfurt in 1860, the main themes are all present in a book published in 1819, *The World as Will and Representation* (revised and expanded in a second volume in 1844). Finally, and perhaps most distinctly, Schopenhauer adopted a curiously benevolent attitude toward religion, despite his own uncompromising atheism. Seeing in Christianity important confirmation of his work, he also regarded the Hindu Upanishads and the teachings of the Buddha with interest and respect. He was among the first Western thinkers to engage seriously with the philosophy of the East.

In all of these ways, Schopenhauer was a man apart. But it was above all his temperament that set him at the greatest distance from those who had come before. In the history of happiness, Schopenhauer is without precedent. He is, simply, the greatest pessimist in the Western tradition.

Scholars often turn to psychological analysis to explain this bleakness, and it is undeniable that Schopenhauer showed signs of depression from a young age. "When I was seventeen," he later recalled, "I was affected by the *misery and wretchedness of life*, as was the Buddha when in his youth he caught sight of sickness, old age, pain and death." This world, he had already decided, "could not be the work of an all-bountiful, infinitely good Being, but rather of a devil, who had summoned creatures into existence in order to gloat over the sight of their anguish and agony."[55] A stint, largely against his wishes, as an employee in the family mercantile business seems to have done little to improve his outlook, nor did the death of his father, most probably by suicide in 1805. And Schopenhauer's relationship with his mother was never good. In 1814 they broke definitively. He remained a lifelong bachelor, with notoriously unsavory opinions on the subject of the other sex.

Schopenhauer's personal psychology must be taken into account when considering his views. Yet it is also important to recognize that Schopenhauer himself—a psychologically insightful man—would have scoffed at such speculation. To see the world as the source of suffering, and human life as inherently unhappy, he believed, was not the product of psychological distortion. On the contrary, it was the sole conclusion at which a healthy, clear-eyed observer could arrive. To regard the world in any other way, he believed, was willful blindness.

Schopenhauer had little doubt that his contemporaries suffered massively from such illusion. He returned to the theme again and again. "Every immoderate joy," he writes in *The World as Will and Representation*, "always rests on the delusion that we have found something in life that is not to be met with at all, namely permanent satisfaction of the tormenting desires or cares that constantly breed new ones. From each particular delusion of this kind we must inevitably later be brought back."[56] Whether we choose to acknowledge the fact or not, the world will constantly remind us of this bitter truth through the power of its pain, for "everything in life proclaims that earthly happiness is destined to be frustrated, or recognized as an illusion. The grounds for this lie deep in the very nature of things."[57] And though we are often led to this sad discovery by privations and disappointments from without, the root cause of our suffering lies within. This, too, we often refuse to see:

> We frequently shut our eyes to the truth . . . that suffering is essential to life, and therefore does not flow in upon us from outside, but that everyone carries around within himself its perennial source. On the contrary, we are constantly looking for a particular external cause, as it were a pretext for the pain that never leaves us, just as the free man makes for himself an idol in order to have a master.[58]

Unlike so many of the earlier Romantics, Schopenhauer finds not a seed of joy planted within, waiting to be given nourishment and bloom, but only a germinating source of pain. Imbedded in our very person is the kernel of all despair.

What, precisely, is this elementary cause, this perennial bad seed? Schopenhauer refers to it as the "will," or more precisely as the "will-to-life" or the "will-to-live" (*Will zum Leben*). An absolutely central term in his vocabulary, it is, for all its prominence, difficult to define, in part because Schopenhauer conceived of the will as a force to which we can give no precise representation. Underlying the world of appearance, the will is a manifestation of another dimension, a surging, striving force that permeates all living things and animates the universe as a whole. Analogous in certain respects to the pantheistic doctrines so dear to the Romantics, Schopenhauer's theory of the will differs essentially in that its author refused to equate the will-to-life with divinity of any kind. For Schopenhauer, there is no God, and the will-to-life is devoid of any teleological meaning or goal. The will, in short, is blind, striving without purpose or end simply to reproduce itself, to continue and carry on.

Schopenhauer's division of the world between representation or appearance on the one hand, and will or pure essence on the other, corresponded in his view to Kant's celebrated distinction between "phenomena" (appearance) and "noumena" (thing in itself). It also bore comparison, Schopenhauer believed, with Plato's notion that behind the world of perceived reality lay an immaterial realm of perfect ideas or forms. What is most important to grasp here, though, is Schopenhauer's general contention that lurking beneath the apparently placid surface of the world is a powerful elemental life force— "its innermost essence"—that surges constantly in great flows.

Difficult to conceive of in the abstract, the idea of this force assumes much greater clarity when applied by Schopenhauer to human beings. Thus, the will encompasses "all desiring, striving, wishing, demanding, longing, hoping, loving, rejoicing, and the like. . . ."[59] It is the life force that impels us forward, that causes us to hunger and to yearn. Lurking below the surface of our selves, just as it lurks below the surface of the world, the will-to-life both guides and subverts our conscious representations and apparently rational ends. As such, its powers are frequently unconscious. "We often do not know what we desire or fear," Schopenhauer recognizes with acuity. "For years we can have a desire without admitting it to ourselves or even letting it come to clear consciousness."[60] Of such repressed longings, the most powerful is the "sexual impulse," what Schopenhauer considers the "kernel of the will-to-live":

[It is the] invisible central point of all action and conduct. . . .
[It] peeps up everywhere, in spite of all veils thrown over it. It
is the cause of war and the aim and object of peace, the basis
of the serious and the aim of the joke, the inexhaustible
source of wit, the key to all hints and allusions, and the
meaning of all secret signs and suggestions. . . . This, however,
is the piquant element and the jest of the world, that the
principal concern of all men is pursued secretly. . . . Indeed,
we see it take its seat at every moment as the real and hereditary lord of the world.[61]

With good reason did Schopenhauer regularly assert that the genitals
are the "focus of the will."

Passages like these reveal why Schopenhauer is considered a prescient psychologist, a man who anticipated a number of the core doctrines of Freud. More important, his psychological insight gives teeth
to his biting critique of happiness. "Its desires unlimited, its claims
inexhaustible," the will propels us headlong in grasping pursuit of
permanent gratification that can never be achieved. "No possible satisfaction in the world could suffice to still its craving, set a final goal to
its demand."[62] The instant one desire is satisfied, it is replaced by
another in a process of continual striving whose consequences are
doubly catastrophic. In the first place, the restless activity of the will
guarantees conflict with others, whose desires cannot fail to clash with
our own. And in the second, it assures continual individual dissatisfaction, for the pleasure of desire satisfied pales before the pain of
desire unfulfilled. As Schopenhauer affirms repeatedly, pain is "positive" and pleasure "negative," meaning that we feel the one as an intense presence, but the other predominately only by default, as the
absence or removal of discomfort, desire, or pain:

We feel desire as we feel hunger and thirst; but as soon as it has
been satisfied, it is like the mouthful of food which has been
taken, and which ceases to exist for our feelings the moment
it is swallowed. We painfully feel the loss of pleasures and

enjoyments, as soon as they fail to appear; but when pains cease even after being present for a long time, their absence is not directly felt, but at most they are thought of intentionally by means of reflection. For only pain and want can be felt positively; therefore they proclaim themselves; well being, on the contrary, is merely negative.[63]

It may be that Schopenhauer underestimates the degree to which pleasure, too, is experienced as a positive presence. But this does little to detract from the force of his central claim regarding the voracity of the will, which is reminiscent of Hobbes's "perpetual and restless desire of power after power, that ceaseth only in death." In Schopenhauer's analysis, happiness is the will's mirage on the horizon of longing, a "leading ideal hovering before us," a "chimera."[64]

It is for these reasons that Schopenhauer conceives of the "notion that we exist in order to be happy" as the only "inborn error." It is inborn, he says, because "it coincides with our existence itself," bound up with the blind striving of the will-to-live, whose successive satisfaction "is what we think of through the concept of happiness."[65] For Schopenhauer, however, it is clear that this concept is the greatest of illusions, one that our experience of life will almost certainly dispel in the end. And so he pours scorn on all who would perpetuate this illusion rather than permit us to see it for what it is:

Accordingly optimism is not only a false but also a pernicious doctrine, for it presents life as a desirable state and man's happiness as its aim and object. Starting from this, everyone believes he has the most legitimate claim to happiness and enjoyment. If, as usually happens, these do not fall to his lot, he believes that he suffers an injustice, in fact that he misses the whole point of his existence; whereas it is far more correct to regard work, privation, misery, and suffering crowned by death, as the aim and object of life.[66]

Laughing with Voltaire at the claim that this is the "best of all possible worlds," Schopenhauer goes far beyond him by making the contrary case. Were the world to contain any more suffering, he contends—any more cruelty, evil, and want—its inhabitants would simply die out, and the world, as we know it, cease to exist. The conclusion to be drawn is that this is the "worst of all possible worlds," and our existence in it, a form of hell.[67]

An image of existence as an inescapable vale of tears, a picture of the world in which men and women are led astray by congenital defect, governed by insatiable desires and lusts: Schopenhauer's vision bears a remarkable likeness to the most dire Christian accounts of the plight of unredeemed humanity. It is a similarity that he was perfectly prepared to acknowledge, noting, for example, that the Christian doctrine of the Fall possessed an "allegorical" (though not a literal) truth, and that its general appraisal of "the vanity of all earthly happiness" was entirely sound.[68] In Schopenhauer's view, moreover, Christianity's "true spirit and kernel"—its contempt for the world—was shared by Brahmanism and Buddhism. He frequently noted their similarities, arguing that the "spirit of Christian morality is identical with that of Brahmanism and Buddhism."[69] All three traditions located the root cause of human suffering in misdirected desire. And all three sought to quell this voracious force through strategies of renunciation.

Revealingly, Schopenhauer, too, urges us along what he calls the "road to salvation." The term is potentially misleading, insofar as Schopenhauer does not countenance a God who helps us on our path any more than he believes in heaven, reincarnation, or an afterlife. Salvation is salvation from ourselves, self-liberation from the terrible driving force of the will. Looking with admiration to the example of religious ascetics, Schopenhauer recommends that we likewise attempt to deny the will and combat its promptings. Sexual abstinence, the purposeful control of appetites and lusts, the deliberate attempt to make our life "as poor, hard, and cheerless as possible," this is the "narrow path of the elect, of the saints."[70] For these select few able to overcome and defeat desire, Schopenhauer holds out the promise of a type of secular beatitude or nirvana: "that ocean-like calmness of the spirit, that deep tranquility, that unshakable confidence and serenity, whose mere reflection in the countenance . . . is a complete and certain gospel."[71]

This is the high road to salvation, the road of the yogi, sadhu, or ascetic saint. But its extraordinary demands ensure that it can be followed by only a few. The great majority are forced down a different route, one strewn with "thorns upon thorns." Unable to discipline and control their will-to-life, it instead is beaten down by the inevitable sufferings and disappointments of the world. "Suffering is the process of purification by which alone man is in most cases sanctified, in other words, led back from the path of error of the will-to-live."[72] The world becomes our cross—a symbol for which Schopenhauer has the highest reverence— the site of torture on which the will-to-life is steadily broken. Not all will be cleansed by this "process of purification, the purifying lye of which is pain," for many go kicking and screaming to their death, still under the spell of the will.[73] But for the "fortunate," death can only come as a relief, a final cessation. Theirs is a strange privilege indeed: "to die willingly, to die gladly, to die cheerfully, is the prerogative of the resigned."[74]

Consistently bleak, unrelentingly grim, Schopenhauer's modern *contemptus mundi* is so dark that one would be at a loss to explain its subsequent appeal if not for an important caveat. But mercifully, Schopenhauer stakes out one further path to renunciation. In aesthetic contemplation, he suggests, before the high altar of art, we can achieve temporary respite from the relentless prompting of desire. Standing before a great painting or a sublime natural landscape, swept up in a moving symphony, poem, or play, the observer may experience a momentary cessation of longing, a fleeting escape from the "thralldom of the will." "The storm of passions, the pressure of desire and fear, and all the miseries of willing are then . . . calmed and appeased in a marvelous way."[75] For an instant, we lose ourselves as we step into "another world," giving up consciousness of the subjective, aim-oriented striving that is our natural course. "All at once the peace, always sought but always escaping us on [the] path of willing, comes to us of its own accord, and all is well with us. It is the painless state

... the state of the gods; for that moment we are delivered from the miserable pressure of the will. We celebrate the Sabbath of the penal servitude of willing."[76]

Schopenhauer believed that this state of momentary transcendence was achievable in various media. But it was above all in music, he argued, that we could experience the fullest extent of the "salvation" and "blessedness" of art. Music was "the copy of the will itself," a direct rendering of the ceaseless striving and the deviations of longing that moved through the universe and our inner being.[77] In the development of music through time, the mind recognized the patterns of its own inner workings, experiencing the full range of desire's triumphs and disappointments: discord and reconciliation, harmony and dissonance, suspension and satisfaction. And it did so in the purest possible terms, by capturing "the inner nature, the in-itself, of every phenomenon." In its inexhaustible possibilities, that is, music did "not express this or that particular and definite pleasure, this or that affliction, pain, sorrow, horror, gaiety, merriment, or peace of mind, but joy, pain, sorrow, horror, gaiety, merriment, peace of mind *themselves,* to a certain extent in the abstract. . . ." Recognizing all these emotions in their "extracted quintessence," we are comforted in the process, our own striving is suspended, and we achieve a momentary peace. If only temporarily, the wretched of the earth can find solace, watching as music floats before them "a paradise quite familiar and quite remote . . . easy to understand and yet so inexplicable."[78]

It is often pointed out that Schopenhauer was distinctly unsuited to the path of ascetic renunciation. And it is doubtful that his own will-to-live was violently broken on the cross of his existence, which was comfortably padded with all the amenities available to the nineteenth-century European bourgeois. Living quietly and independently off the income of a sizable inheritance, Schopenhauer spent the last decades of his life in a comfortable house in Frankfurt, writing in the mornings, walking in the afternoons, reading the foreign papers at his men's club, dining out, and attending the opera or theater by night. Often he gathered with friends to discuss ideas, and he indulged in his fair share of erotic, if short-lived, affairs. When, after a career of almost complete obscurity, his fame began to grow in the 1850s, this theorist of the vanity of human existence was distinctly pleased. He went so far as to employ a group of researchers to scour the European press for clippings and mentions of his name. Clearly, if Schopenhauer ever tasted the sweetness of salvation, it was of the artistic kind alone.

It was this aspect of his philosophy that endured. Few may have possessed the fortitude to take up his call to live in renunciation as a secular saint, but many found his vision of aesthetic redemption extremely attractive. It is no exaggeration to say that Schopenhauer proved one of the most influential writers of the second half of the nineteenth century, shaping the views not only of August Strindberg but of a whole host of artists and thinkers, of whom the most famous was Richard Wagner, but that also included the young Nietzsche, Proust, Mahler, Turgenev, D. H. Lawrence, Thomas Mann, and Thomas Hardy, to name only a few. In Schopenhauer's vision of redemption through art, they found a powerful creed, one that anointed them with an extraordinary calling. A minister who suffers in sacrifice in order to offer his flock a fleeting glimpse of salvation, a temporary respite from pain, the artist in the Schopenhauerian vision is nothing less than a secular priest. For men and women losing faith in a transcendent purpose to the world, this proved a compelling calling, all the more so in that it bid its followers to retrace, by secular steps, the way of a religious journey whose momentum remained powerful, however much this otherwise might be denied. Before a work of art, the modern pilgrim could stand still on a threshold and experience like his religious forebears the fullness of beatific promise. But as he gazed across the way at the prospect of happiness, he must now wonder: Was this a window that opened onto a better world? Or simply the sacred space of art's own making—a retreat—with nothing beyond itself?

The Temple of Longing

Although reduced to rubble in World War II, the House of the Secession has been carefully restored. It serves today more or less as its creators intended: a quiet sanctuary and "refuge," a "temple of art," a sacred space "to show modern man his true face."[79] Built in 1898 by the architect Josef Olbrich as an exhibition hall for the Viennese avant-garde who gave it its name, the building is most often associated today with the painter Gustav Klimt, a leading Secessionist who collaborated closely on the building's design. One of his greatest works, the *Beethoven Frieze*, now hangs permanently in the sanctuary's sanctum sanctorum.

Covering three walls of the closely confined space, the numerous panels of the *Beethoven Frieze* are practically a *Gesamtkuntswerk*—a total work of art—in their own right. But when originally shown at the House of the Secession in 1902, they were only a small portion of a much larger artistic whole: a series of votive offerings dedicated around the exhibition's central work, Max Klinger's brooding sculpture of Beethoven. The architect Josef Hoffmann transformed the interior of the building into a shrine. Gustav Mahler performed a reorchestrated version of the fourth movement of Beethoven's Ninth Symphony. And Klimt's elaborate frieze provided his own interpretation of the "Ode to Joy." Here modern art paid homage to the image of a saint. As the critic Carl Schorske has observed, "If ever there was an example of collective narcissism, this was it: artists (Secessionists) celebrating an artist (Klinger), celebrating a hero of art (Beethoven)."[80]

As stated in the exhibition's catalog, the aim of this exercise in collective narcissism was to work for the "purposive development of interior space" (*Innenraum*). It should come as no surprise to learn that happiness was called upon to fill the void of this inner realm.[81] Faithfully depicted in Klimt's frieze, the journey begins, according to the catalog, with the "longing for happiness" (*die Sehnsucht nach Glück*) represented in the series of drawings along the left wall as the dream and rapture of soaring women, the misery of weak humanity naked and kneeling in supplication, and the paragon of Strength, heavily armed, who takes up the "struggle for happiness."

Along the second, shorter wall stands a group of hostile forces: the apelike giant Typhon, "against whom even gods fight in vain," and his many hideous offspring, including the three gorgons Sickness, Madness,

"Die Sehnsucht nach Glück" (The Longing for Happiness). Detail of the
left panel of Gustav Klimt, *Beethoven Frieze*, Secession Building, Vienna.
Photo: Erich Lessing/Art Resource, NY.

and Death on one side, and Lust and Unchastity, Excess, and Gnawing Grief on the other. What is truly extraordinary, however, is that
the "longing for happiness and the wishes of mankind" do not engage
the hostile powers that block their path. Rather, they "fly over and
away" above them, transcending the need to enter into conflict at all.
Their resolution, in the third wall, is thus assured. "The longing for
happiness finds solace in poetry," and "the arts," a flowing cascade of
beautiful women, "lead us to an ideal realm, where alone we can find
pure joy, pure happiness, and pure love." There, a "choir of the angels
of paradise" sings from a slightly altered chorus of the "Ode to Joy":

Gustav Klimt, *Beethoven Frieze*, middle panel, Typhon flanked by Sickness,
Madness, Death, Lust, Unchastity, Excess, and Gnawing Grief.
Photo: Erich Lessing/Art Resource, NY.

Gustav Klimt, *Beethoven Frieze*, right panel, The Choir of Angels
of Paradise and the rapturous Kiss. Photo: Erich Lessing/Art Resource, NY.

Freude, schöner Gotterfunken, . . .
Diesen Kuß der ganzen Welt!

Joy, beautiful spark of the gods, . . .
This kiss for all the world!

The longing for happiness finds its resolution in the mystical, sensual embrace of art.

It was Stendhal, cited approvingly by Baudelaire in the *Painter of Modern Life*, who said, "The beautiful is neither more nor less than the promise of happiness."[82] In this sanctuary, Klimt has fulfilled that promise, creating a realm of beauty that allows us to soar for a moment above the struggles of daily life. In doing so, he was being true, if not to Beethoven himself, who struggled until the end to believe in a "loving Father beyond the stars," then at least to the Beethoven formed in the image of Schopenhauer. For Klimt, like so many of his generation, had steeped himself in this philosopher's work, especially as summarized and interpreted in Richard Wagner's widely read essay, "Beethoven," which Klimt knew well. Just as "Christianity stepped forth amid the Roman civilisation of the universe," Wagner observes

there, "so *Music* breaks forth from the chaos of modern civilisation.
Both say aloud: 'our kingdom is not of this world.'"[83] It is Beethoven
who bears this divine music aloft, spreading the word of a higher calling and deeper truth. "Let anyone experience for himself how the
whole modern world of Appearance, which hems him in on every side
to his despair, melts suddenly to naught if he but hears the first few
bars of one of those godlike symphonies."[84] Interpreting his hero in
these Schopenhauerian terms, Wagner hears in Beethoven's music the
striving of the will—"a supernatural life, an agency now soothing, now
appalling, a pulse, a thrill, a throb of joy, of yearning, fearing, grief and
ecstasy"—which carries us, in the climax of the Ninth Symphony's
final ode, to "the nameless joy of a paradise regained."[85]

Wagner would develop more sinister fantasies of the "regeneration"
of man, reserving special animus for the Jews, who allegedly barred,
like Typhon, the way to the happiness of the German people. Klimt
never shared those thoughts, and indeed, whereas Wagner urged active engagement in the world, foreseeing a central role for art in the
development of a "new religion" and a new, glorious Reich, Klimt with-
drew into the womb of his own creation. To flee the world into the
image of art, or to remake the world in art's image—both were Romantic fantasies, and they belied a common conviction: that the world,
to the naked eye, was not a happy place. The longing for joy, the happiness of salvation remained. But an early Romantic suspicion—a
questioning of the Enlightenment's self-evident truth—had evolved
through Schopenhauer into a much stronger doubt that only redemption or revolution could stay.

Something of this same suspicion lingered among men of a very
different cast—men who on the surface, at least, seemed less susceptible to the sickness of the age. Heirs to the liberalism of Locke and
proponents of the pursuit of happiness, they identified themselves as
"liberals" and were identified as such. Their more radical adversaries,
however, dismissed them as minions of the "bourgeoisie," that amor-
phous group against whom Romantics and revolutionaries alike constantly railed, even as they freely accepted their funds. It is true that
those of the liberal persuasion were inclined to see capitalism as a force

for good. And they were strong advocates of representative government, particularly as it had taken shape in England and the United States. They also tended to be suspicious of the influence of the masses and distrustful of the power of the state. Upholding the liberties of the individual above all else, they maintained the sanctity of civil society and defended the importance of the rule of law.

Despite these differences from their bohemian and revolutionary opponents, heirs to the liberal tradition were forced, like them, to engage continually with the legacy of the Enlightenment. Weighing the evidence of its self-evident truths, they also pondered the problem of the pursuit of happiness, and as they did so, they struggled to maintain their faith in the Enlightenment's central promise of redemption in the world, "the place where, in the end, / We find our happiness, or not at all."

6

LIBERALISM AND
ITS DISCONTENTS

In the year 1800, while Napoleon pondered power and the pursuit of happiness, and the "Ode to Joy" was still unheard, a pamphlet appeared in Dublin. Offered for a penny by William Watson of Capel-Street ("Printer to the Cheap Repository for Religious and Moral Tracts"), *The Path to Riches and Happiness* was a bargain by any standard, and it promised a huge reward: wealth *and* well-being, felicity *and* fortune, riches *and* joyful return.[1]

The coupling is significant, as is the fact that the work's late author, Dr. Benjamin Franklin, was born in America. No other country has been so closely associated with the words that smile on the face of its founding document—the "pursuit of happiness." And no other country has been so intimately connected with the dream of pursuing happiness by pursuing fortune. Franklin himself died both happy and rich and so could legitimately claim expertise on either subject. A close reader of the draft of the Declaration of Independence, he ratified the use of Jefferson's felicitous phrase and most likely suggested the substitution of "self-evident" for "sacred and undeniable" as a description of its truth. He was also the author of numerous practical reflections on the "way to wealth." Viewing America as prime territory for the cultivation of riches, Franklin saw God's earth as offering abundant evidence of our license to cultivate happiness. "Wine," he once observed in a creative gloss on the Gospel account of the wedding at Cana, "is living proof that god loves us and wants us to be happy."[2]

Franklin found many such proofs, convinced as he was that "all among us may be happy."[3] But though he occasionally bade his readers "wealth and happiness" at the close of his yearly reflections in *Poor Richard's Almanack*, it is not at all clear that he saw a necessary connection between the two. Like Aristotle, Franklin certainly believed that a minimum of life's conveniences were necessary to the pursuit of the good life. "Wherein consists the Happiness of a rational Creature?" he asks. "In having a sound mind, a healthy body, a Sufficiency of the Necessaries and Conveniencies of Life, together with the Favour of God, and the Love of mankind."[4] But virtue, "the mother" of happiness, Franklin repeatedly stressed, was the surest means to realize those ends.[5] Found in people, not in things, happiness could fill us only when inflated by self-reliance, upright living, simple pleasures, and self-respect:

Human Felicity is produc'd not so much by great Pieces of good Fortune that seldom happen, as by little Advantages that occur every Day. Thus, if you teach a poor young Man to shave himself, and keep his Razor in order, you may contribute more to the Happiness of his Life than in giving him a thousand Guineas. The Money may be soon spent, and the Regret only remaining of having foolishly consum'd it. But in the other Case, he escapes the frequent Vexation of waiting for Barbers, and of their sometimes, dirty Fingers, offensive Breaths, and dull Razors. He shaves when most convenient to him, and enjoys daily the Pleasure of its being done with a good Instrument.[6]

"Who is rich?" Poor Richard asks on another occasion. "He that is content."[7] By this calculation, the pursuit of happiness was a comparatively straightforward affair that had little to do with the pursuit of wealth.

Which raises the question: Were happiness and capitalism—happiness and democracy—so readily compatible as many who were drawn to America's shores in the coming years were inclined to think? Or did a tension lie at the heart of these seemingly natural allies from the outset? Were the paths to riches and happiness one? In order to attend to these questions, we need first to revisit the age of Enlightenment in that *annus mirabilis,* 1776.

Trivial Pursuits

Few words in American history are more familiar than the following lines from the Declaration of Independence:

> We hold these truths to be self-evident: that all men are
> created equal; that they are endowed by their creator with
> unalienable rights; that among these are life, liberty & the
> pursuit of happiness.

Though these words were drafted by Thomas Jefferson in June 1776, and adopted by the Continental Congress in Philadelphia on the fourth of July, the meaning of their self-evident truth, ironically, has long been a matter of dispute. Picking over the phrases after the fact, many have wondered what Jefferson actually meant, and nowhere is their confusion more apparent than in confronting "the pursuit of happiness." Was this a meaningless phrase, a "glittering generality" that has sent generations grasping after an illusion?[8] Or did it possess a far clearer sense, one that was immediately intelligible to those who spoke the "now lost language of the Enlightenment"?[9] For citizens of the United States, the stakes in these debates are high, for they place on the table nothing less than the country's self-image, a central tenet of its "civil religion."[10] And to others, the matter is hardly less important, for in a direct way, it speaks to what has gradually become a global concern: the place of happiness in the American way of life.

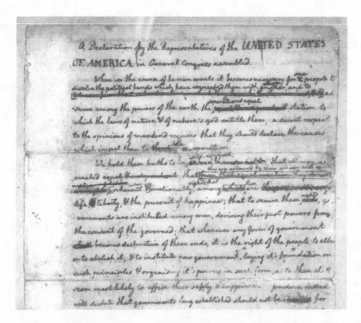

A draft of the Declaration of Independence, in Jefferson's hand, spelling out
the "pursuit of happiness," Library of Congress, Washington, D.C.

Supporters of the view that the "pursuit of happiness" made perfect sense at the time can point to the fact that the Continental Congress itself did not trip on the phrase. Although delegates scrutinized
every line of Jefferson's draft—cutting and slashing with the precision
of men, many of whom were lawyers, who took the meaning of language seriously—not a single one recorded reservations about the
"pursuit of happiness." Nor did any object to the other use of the term
"happiness," several lines later, when Jefferson asserts the right to
"alter or abolish" any government that is destructive of self-evident
truths. In this case, the Declaration maintains, a people is perfectly
within its rights to found a new government, "organizing its power in
such form, as to them shall seem most likely to effect their safety &
happiness." Congress saw fit only to protest Jefferson's third use of
the word, striking "The road to happiness & to glory is open to us too"
from the final lines of the draft.[11]

Of course, congressional silence, then as now, hardly means that a
phrase is perfectly understood, let alone that the people's representatives

are of one mind as to its ultimate interpretation. But Jefferson himself, when queried years later as to where he had drawn the material for the Declaration, replied that its hallmark was precisely its common touch, its ability to bring together what he called the "harmonizing sentiments of the day." The Declaration, he said, made one of many, and many of one:

> This was the object of the Declaration of Independence. Not to find out new principles, or new arguments, never before thought of, not merely to say things which had never been said before; but to place before mankind the common sense of the subject, in terms so plain and firm as to command their assent, and to justify ourselves in the independent stand we are compelled to take. Neither aiming at originality of principle or sentiment, nor yet copied from any particular and previous writing, it was intended to be an expression of the American mind, and to give to that expression the proper tone and spirit called for by the occasion. All its authority rests then on the harmonizing sentiments of the day, whether expressed in conversation, in letters, printed essays, or in the elementary books of public right, as Aristotle, Cicero, Locke, Sidney, &c.[12]

An "expression of the American mind," the Declaration represented the collective good sense of the eighteenth century. By bringing together bits and pieces from the four corners of his age, Jefferson produced a whole that was more than the sum of its parts.

If we examine the specific phrase the "pursuit of happiness" with these same observations in mind, the results are intriguing. Take, for example, the name Locke, cited by Jefferson above and often considered the single most important influence on the Declaration as a whole. When applied to the "pursuit of happiness," Locke's name has yielded an old and stubborn interpretation that reads the Declaration as evidence of a cover-up. According to this view, Jefferson is said to have substituted the ambiguous "pursuit of happiness" for the third term in the allegedly Lockean trilogy of "life, liberty, and *property.*" Clouding over the Founding Fathers' "real" intentions—the protection, it seems, of their own estates—happiness is thus presented as an ideological smoke screen that obscures the deeper interests of its materialist-minded proponents. In this interpretation, once particularly attractive to Marxists but by no means confined to them, the Declaration thus provides a clever cover for capitalism and the accumulation of wealth, hiding those "true" intentions under a smiling face.[13]

There are many problems with this reading, not least that Locke himself never used the phrase "life, liberty, and property." He does, it is true, speak in the *Second Treatise of Government* of "life, liberty and estate," and "lives, liberties, and fortunes," as Jefferson well knew. And Locke certainly considered property, broadly conceived, a noble thing, to be accumulated through labor and protected by governments that rule on our behalf.

But what is more interesting is that Locke makes no mention of the "pursuit of happiness" in the *Second Treatise.* As we have seen, he uses that phrase (many times) only in the *Essay Concerning Human Understanding,* a work with which Jefferson was also intimately familiar. There, it will be recalled, Locke presents happiness as a natural and wholesome part of a divinely orchestrated world in which human beings are led along by pleasant sensations, ending, if they get it right, in God. For Locke, the "gravitational" pull of happiness was the pull of pleasure, and pleasure had as many sources as men had palates. Some liked "luxury and debauchery," others "sobriety and riches"; still others preferred glory, hunting, or study. What gives pleasure "to different men," Locke stressed, "are very different things."[14]

Now Locke, undoubtedly, would have included property on his own list of pleasures. A source of enjoyment in its own right, property, he believed, was also a bastion of freedom and a bulwark of independence. Many eighteenth-century Americans agreed, and in this respect, they were more than prepared to couple property and happiness in a single phrase. In the very same month that Jefferson labored over the draft of the Declaration of Independence, the State of Virginia's Constitutional

Convention adopted, on June 12, 1776, George Mason's Virginia Declaration of Rights. A close friend of Jefferson, Mason had shown his
fellow Virginian a version of the draft, which Jefferson had in his possession at the time of writing the Declaration of Independence. The
words are revealing:

> All men are created equally free and independent, and have
> certain inherent natural rights, of which they cannot, by any
> compact, deprive or divest their posterity; among which are
> the enjoyment of life and liberty, with the means of acquiring
> and possessing property, and pursuing and obtaining happi-
> ness and safety.[15]

Here, the natural right to pursue happiness (and to obtain it) is bound
up not only with security, life, and liberty but also explicitly with
property. Even earlier, in his widely read *Rights of the British Colonies
Asserted and Proved* (1764), James Otis had made a similar connection,
observing that the end of government is "to provide for the security,
the quiet, the happy enjoyment of life, liberty, and property."[16] Otis,
if not Locke, used the happy phrase, and it was picked up and employed
again in the Declaration of Colonial Rights and Grievances, endorsed
by the First Continental Congress on October 1, 1774. Still later, when
James Madison proposed a series of amendments in the form of a Bill
of Rights to be added to the newly ratified American Constitution, he,
too, associated happiness with life, liberty, and property:

> Government is instituted and ought to be exercised for the
> benefit of the people; which consists in the enjoyment of life
> and liberty, with the right of acquiring and using property, and
> generally of pursuing and obtaining happiness and safety.[17]

These (and all other) references to happiness were subsequently cut
in the final debates over the Constitution's Bill of Rights. But similar
formulations linking happiness, life, liberty, and property survived in
the texts of a number of state constitutions, including those of Virginia

(1776), Pennsylvania (1776), Vermont (1777), Massachusetts (1780), and New Hampshire (1784). The constitutions of Georgia (1777), North Carolina (1776), New Jersey (1776), and New York (1777) invoke happiness without reference to property.[18]

In any case, it can hardly be doubted that for many Americans—Jefferson included—property in the eighteenth century was a value associated with the pursuit of happiness, taking its place alongside life, liberty, and security as basic rights that merited government protection. But this is a very different thing from saying that happiness and property were one and the same, or even inextricably linked. As some historians have rightly asked, if Jefferson had really intended the "pursuit of happiness" to stand for "property" and nothing else, then why did he not simply use the term as others before him had? And why, they speculate further, did Jefferson advise his friend, the Marquis de Lafayette, to remove the inalienable right of property from the draft of the Declaration of Rights that the Frenchman penned in 1788?

In the face of such questions, it is tempting to conclude that if Jefferson's reference to the "pursuit of happiness" in the Declaration has a Lockean origin at all, then its source must be the *Essay Concerning Human Understanding* and not the *Second Treatise of Government*. "The pursuit of happiness" would then best be rendered the "pursuit of pleasure," which for Locke was simply an empirical description of a truth about human nature. Property might legitimately draw us forward. But so might many other things. The pleasures we chose to pursue—and how—were ultimately a matter of taste. This "variety of pursuits shews," Locke affirmed, "that every one does not place his happiness in the same thing."[19]

Given the widespread discussion of happiness in the age of Enlightenment, however—to say nothing of the tremendous breadth of Jefferson's reading—it would be perilous to narrow the interpretative field in this way. The truth of the matter, as we shall see in a moment, is that there are a number of other legitimate interpretations of the "pursuit of happiness," and that Jefferson was able to combine and conflate them in new and interesting ways. Nevertheless, adhering to a strict Lockean reading has its merits, for Jefferson was never one to spurn pleasure, and he thought highly of Locke's model of the mind. Following out the implications of reading the phrase in this way is hardly a pointless exercise, and it may well be revealing.

The first thing to note is that the word "pursuit" is interesting in itself. In the English language of Locke, like that of Jefferson, the word had a harder meaning than it does today. It retained, as the critic Garry Wills has pointed out, a close link with its cognates "prosecute" and "persecute," leading Dr. Johnson to list the word in his eighteenth-century *Dictionary of the English Language* as follows:

> To Pursue . . . 1. To chase; to follow in hostility.
> Pursuit . . . 1. The act of following with hostile intention.

If one thinks of pursuing happiness as one pursues a fugitive (and in Scottish law, criminal prosecuters were called "pursuers," a usage with which Jefferson was familiar), the "pursuit of happiness" takes on a somewhat different cast.[20] We are inevitably reminded of the "uneasiness" referred to by Locke in the endless human struggle to secure pleasure and avoid pain, a struggle, Locke believed, that would never end given the "multitude of wants, and desires, we are beset with in this imperfect State." In this life, it bears repeating:

> We are seldom at ease, and free enough from the solicitation
> of our natural or adopted desires, but a constant succession of
> *uneasiness* out of that stock, which natural wants, or acquired
> habits have heaped up, take the *will* in their turns; and no
> sooner is one action dispatch'd, which by such a determina-
> tion of the *will* we are set upon, but another *uneasiness* is ready
> to set us on work.[21]

Thomas Hobbes was more explicit when he claimed that the "felicity of this life consisteth not in the repose of a mind satisfied." But Locke's point was much the same. Like a clever man on the run, final felicity—the full satisfaction of desire—would always elude capture.

Hence, it is tempting to add, the note of hostility toward the thing that forever escapes our grasp, the daimon that haunts us. To *pursue* happiness, in this sense (to follow with hostile intention), was in some measure to engage in a repeatedly frustrating game, in which desire could never be permanently satisfied. And lest this sound too far-fetched, it is worth recalling that there was strong precedent for precisely such ambivalence toward happiness in centuries of Christian tradition. Although God, since at least the time of Augustine, was considered happiness incarnate, the *desire* for happiness was at the same time a constant reminder of our separation from him, a nagging source of pain and an ever present souvenir of what we could not have in this life due to our original transgression. In the dire Augustinian tradition, the desire for happiness was a sign of our punishment, if also the way to salvation.

Whether Locke himself made such conscious associations is far from clear. What is certain is that he worried deeply about being led along by desire on pointless pursuits. It is for this reason that he placed such stock in reason to guide us along the path to God. The prospect of salvation opened up by a reasonable Christianity exerted an incentive to not chase desire anywhere it led, to resist our baser instincts and the futile pursuit of "transient pleasure." Precisely because tomorrow we would die—and then be judged—we could not always eat and drink with abandon.

A great many men and women in eighteenth-century America shared this general perspective. Desire without limits, they believed, was dangerous, as was desire whose yearnings focused only on the self. Like Locke, they looked to God for guidance in their pursuit. Thus, the Presbyterian minister Robert Breck, for example, preaching in New England in the 1720s, stressed repeatedly that "the surest way to advance a people's happiness and prosperity" was to pursue the Christian path, to "walk in [God's] ways." Only the "religious and righteous" could be "happy and flourishing," a temporal truth that applied to individuals and societies alike. "To be desirous of, to have an eye to, and in their sphere to seek the welfare & prosperity of a People, [was] incumbent on all."[22] The reverend Noah Hobart, pastor of the First Church of

Christ in Fairfield, Connecticut, was more specific, preaching not only that "Public Happiness is the original Design and great End of Civil Government" in keeping with God's intention, but that "There are many Things relating to men's Persons, of such Nature and Importance that they cannot be *happy,* nor indeed so much as comfortable without some Security for the quiet Possession, and Enjoyment of them." "Of this kind," Hobart instructed his flock, were "Life, Liberty, Reputation, Ease and the Like." But no less essential was the "morality" and "virtue" taught by the Christian religion. "The firm Belief of such Things" was "so essentially necessary to Social Happiness, that he deserves to be an Enemy to mankind, who endeavours to weaken [them]."[23] Similarly, Benjamin Lord, the Congregationalist pastor from Norwich who baptized Benedict Arnold, preached on the subject "Religion and Government subsisting together in Society, [are] Necessary to their Compleat Happiness and Safety."[24] It was a common theme. If not all agreed with the Harvard-educated pastor Samuel Dunbar, who declared in 1760 that the "presence of God with his People" was "their *only* Safety and Happiness," few denied the essential connection.[25]

These are merely a handful of the hundreds of such sermons preached over the course of the century that linked social welfare and the pursuit of happiness to the pursuit of Christian ethics. Frequently, they also invoked the example of ancient Israel in imitation of their predecessors in seventeenth-century England. A fortunate people in a blessed country was thus presented as God's children, led happily forward in pursuit of the freedom and justice of the Promised Land. In such accounts—and there were many—it was generally not forgotten that the Promised Land was also a land of milk and honey, rich and abundant in peace and prosperity. But whether invoking the example of Israel or not, these writers invariably presented Christianity as an indispensable aid to earthly content. Like the pious author of *True Pleasure, Chearfulness, and Happiness, the Immediate Consequence of Religion,* they agreed that to allege "God himself does not delight to see his creatures happy" was blasphemous. Equally, they concurred that to think of happiness without love of one's neighbor—without Christian charity, denial, and constraint—was profane.[26]

Did Jefferson himself think of the pursuit of happiness in these terms, agreeing with his fellow revolutionary Samuel Adams that "to be possessed of the Christian principles, & to accommodate our whole deportment to such principles, is to be happy in this life"?[27] Admittedly, Jefferson was not the most pious man in the New World. By birth an Episcopalian, he strayed far from the theological convictions of his childhood church, gradually developing a set of personal beliefs that came close, in practice, to Unitarianism. Without ever officially joining the fold, he subscribed to a number of the Unitarians' basic theological tenets, denying the doctrine of the Trinity, discounting the divinity of Christ, and looking skeptically on miracles and all other supernatural additions to the creed. Like the English Unitarian Joseph Priestley—a central figure of the English Enlightenment and long Jefferson's friend—the author of the Declaration demanded that his religion be rational or not at all.

Yet Jefferson never tired of praising the historical Jesus as a great moral teacher, describing Christ's "system of morality" in a letter to Priestley as "the most benevolent & sublime probably that has been ever taught, and consequently more perfect than those of any of the antient philosophers."[28] As proof of his conviction, Jefferson privately undertook the outrageous task of editing the Bible, paring the books of the New Testament down to what he regarded as the simple teachings of Christ. The result, the so-called Jefferson Bible, is a breviary of Christian ethics. As Jefferson observed in a letter to a friend, "The doctrines of Jesus are simple, and tend all to the happiness of man."[29]

Simple or complex, Jesus's doctrines were undeniably an important element of the "harmonizing sentiments" of the day and regarded by many as an authoritative guide to the pursuit of happiness. Curbing and restraining the pursuit of individual pleasure and interest, they must be considered an important element of the wider context of reception of the Declaration's celebrated phrase.

Much the same may be said of the three other names mentioned next to Locke's in the letter from Jefferson cited above: Aristotle, Cicero, and Algernon Sidney. A Greek philosopher, a Roman Stoic, and a seventeenth-century English theorist who was executed on suspicion of plotting to overthrow Charles II would seem to have little in common. Yet over the last thirty years, some of the leading voices in Anglo-American history have argued, convincingly, that they do.[30] Tracing a consistent language of liberty that runs from the ancients to the revival of classical thought in Renaissance Italy and on to the Atlantic world of seventeenth-century Britain, these historians draw attention to a "classical republican" tradition that had great influence in eighteenth-century America and whose understanding of liberty and happiness differed in fundamental respects from that of Lockean liberalism. Whereas Locke tended to view liberty as freedom *from* the violation of natural rights, the classical republican tradition conceived liberty in more active terms as direct public participation. And whereas Locke saw happiness as the judicious calibration of pleasure, classical republicans understood happiness, with strong Stoic inflections, as civic virtue.

Thus, for Locke, liberty was a defense—a barrier—against the governments, institutions, and individuals that invariably sought to impede our natural due. Protected accordingly, we would be left free to pursue "happiness" in any way we saw fit. For the classical republican tradition, by contrast, liberty emerged from active devotion to the public good (civic virtue). And from civic virtue emerged happiness, both individual and social. Frequently demanding self-sacrifice, denial, and pain, civic virtue had little to do with pleasure. In fact, in the classical republican analysis, the happiness of modern societies was gravely threatened by the egotism, luxury, and corruption that turned individuals away from the pursuit of the larger social good. Private pleasure corrupted civic virtue and hence the happiness of individuals and society as a whole.

This, in short, was a very different understanding of happiness than the one traceable to Locke. But did Jefferson share it? Students of American history disagree on the question, and it is likely, as a consequence, that they have tended to exaggerate the distinctiveness of the classical republican and the liberal traditions. Admittedly, when one thinks of Jefferson the connoisseur of wine, Jefferson the libertine, or Jefferson the man who described himself in a letter of 1819 as an "Epicurean," it is hard to imagine him as a dour classical republican who took pleasure only in the public good.[31] But that he could at times invoke classical republican themes is without question. The two traditions—and the two conceptions of happiness—most likely co-existed in his mind and even overlapped.

What is certain is that, similar to the case of Christianity and regardless of Jefferson's privately held views, there were many in eighteenth-century America and the Constitutional Convention who would have interpreted "the pursuit of happiness" in just these classical republican terms. Like Christianity, they were part of the harmonizing sentiments of the day, helping to ensure that Lockean pleasure was tempered and controlled by a strong dose of public virtue.

There was one other important intellectual current that performed this function: the Enlightenment itself, and more specifically in the American context, the Scottish Enlightenment, that fertile breeding ground of Francis Hutcheson, Thomas Reid, David Hume, Adam Ferguson, and Adam Smith. Like his educated countrymen, Jefferson was familiar with the work of all these writers, in particular that of Hutcheson, as well as his Swiss disciple Jean-Jacques Burlamaqui, whose conceptions of happiness may well have influenced Jefferson's own.[32] Trained as a Presbyterian minister, Hutcheson had taken upon himself the task in the early eighteenth century of responding to the great moral challenge posed by Locke's *Essay Concerning Human Understanding:* If the principal stimuli of human behavior were pleasure and pain, how could men and women be expected to act out of anything but hedonistic self-regard? Locke himself, as we have seen, had contemplated this specter well before it was completely disrobed in the writings of La Mettrie. But Locke's own response—that reason led to the reasonableness of Christianity, and so to Christian self-sacrifice—seemed only to confirm the problem. According to Locke, heaven was but the greatest of all pleasures, a "bargain" that outweighed the sacrifice of temporary pain. In the Lockean view, even virtue was selfish: We were good only to ensure our fate. Genuine benevolence, it seemed, was not possible for mortal man.

Francis Hutcheson believed that it was, and his ability to formulate a theory of why, in the language of Locke himself, helped to ensure his tremendous popularity in enlightened circles. For rather than revert to a pre-Lockean view of the mind—putting his trust, say, in innate ideas, or an inherent conscience hardwired to the soul—Hutcheson expanded Locke's sensationalist model. In addition to the physical senses that register pleasure and pain (touch, taste, sight, and sound), Hutcheson maintained with Locke's pupil Anthony Ashley Cooper, the third Earl of Shaftesbury, that human beings possess a "moral sense," a capacity to respond pleasurably to goodness in others and in ourselves. In the same way that we take pleasure in contemplating the selfless acts of great moral figures, we take pleasure in performing our own acts of benevolence. The surest way to promote "private pleasure," it turns out, is by doing "publicly useful" things. We become happy when we "reflect upon" our "virtuous actions." We pursue happiness by being good.

It may be objected that this was merely another form of "selfishness": another, if roundabout, means of maximizing the pleasures of the self. Be that as it may, the crucial point is that Hutcheson's model conceived of the interests of individuals as tied to the interests of society as a whole. Our "constant pursuit of publick Good," he affirmed, "is the most probable way of promoting [our] own Happiness."[33] By bringing virtue to others, we bring pleasure to ourselves.

It is not hard to see why this theory—and its numerous variants in Britain, Europe, and America—was so popular. For in effect it said what enlightened men and women wanted to hear: Virtue was pleasurable; pleasure was virtuous; and human beings were naturally social. When raised in healthy environments (and when prejudice and superstition were removed), they would act toward one another with genuine kindness. The world, after all, was a happy place.

Perceptive critics have made the case that this benevolent conception of the "pursuit of happiness" lay at the heart of Jefferson's understanding of the term.[34] It is likely that they have pushed their case too far, but in doing so they have also shown what is now difficult to deny: Among enlightened Americans like Jefferson, the moral sense theory enjoyed considerable sway. Shaping and inflecting eighteenth-century understandings of happiness, it, too, must be taken into account when considering the Declaration's felicitous phrase.

In all of these ways, therefore, the pure Lockean interpretation of happiness as the pursuit of pleasure was qualified and constrained. As moral sense theorists or the reasonably religious, as Christians or classical republicans, contemporaries would have understood the pursuit of happiness as more than the pursuit of personal pleasure or the accumulation of private gain. And yet, if Jefferson's enjoinder to pursue happiness was thus, on several counts, an enjoinder to act for the benefit of the greater good, it also promoted a dynamic of a somewhat different kind. In this respect, it does make sense to speak, if not of a cover-up, then at least of what one contemporary described as "artifice" and another, more boldly, as "deception."

The words are those of two men whose work was well known to Jefferson, and whose fate was also bound up closely with 1776: David Hume, who died in that year, and his close friend Adam Smith, who published in that year *The Wealth of Nations*, a work that Jefferson would later desribe as the single greatest work on political economy.[35] Central figures of the Scottish Enlightenment trained in moral philosophy, both men were friends of Francis Hutcheson and were deeply affected by his work. Smith studied with Hutcheson at Glasgow before going up to Oxford, and Hume was prompted to write to the older moralist early in his career, seeking wisdom. "For pray what is the end of Man?" Hume inquired. "Is he created for Happiness? For this life or the next? For himself or his Maker?"[36] Puzzling over such questions throughout his life, Hume was at times given to melancholy and doubt, plagued by his inability to arrive at certain truth. But on such occasions, he turned, as he tells us in his first work, *A Treatise of Human Nature*, to a powerful antidote:

> I dine, I play a game of back-gammon, I converse, and am
> merry with my friends; and when after three or four hours'
> amusement, I wou'd return to these speculations, they appear
> so cold and strain'd, and ridiculous, that I cannot find in my
> heart to enter into them any farther.[37]

By throwing himself into the "action and employment and the occupations of common life," Hume declared elsewhere, he was able to find respite from the riddles of existence.[38]

Hume's common sense approach to the problem of existence—and his common sense endorsement of everyday life—is both rare and refreshing in a philosopher. He took the point further. Not only was it often healthy to pursue our passions wherever they might lead us—to a game of backgammon, say, to a dinner with friends, to the boardroom, or to the bedroom—but this same apparently trivial striving, this same day-to-day yearning after simple pleasures and fleeting rewards, was the very thing that made the world go round. In struggling to satisfy our passions, reason searched out new ways to fulfill our desires. It was, Hume famously observed, passion's slave, toiling in the service of greater comfort and fulfillment. What Locke had identified as the ceaseless striving of pursuit—the movement from uneasiness to pleasure to uneasiness—Hume validated as the motor of civilization, driving all progress in human affairs.

Whether this ceaseless striving would ever bring us happiness, Hume was inclined to doubt. Even our "most enlarged and generous projects," when looked at from the grand scheme of things, seemed "frivolous."[39] And when "we reflect[ed] on the shortness and uncertainty of life . . . all our pursuits of happiness" appeared "despicable." Nonetheless, Hume saw these pursuits, like a turn at the backgammon table, as immensely beneficial, a distraction from the riddles of existence and a powerful engine of growth and improvement. What he called the "artifice of nature"—the blind striving of desire—"happily deceived us" into believing that our actions were worthwhile, even when they weren't; that they could make us happy, even when they could not.[40]

Jefferson knew Hume's writings well, and so did Adam Smith, who took up this same line of inquiry in the *Theory of Moral Sentiments,* a work published in 1759 that Jefferson studied closely in the early 1770s.[41] With even greater precision than Hume, Smith detailed the manner by which human beings' mistaken belief—their illusion—that they could make themselves happy through frivolous pursuits might still have positive consequences. His example of such "deception" is highly instructive—and perhaps surprising—for it involved nothing less than the pursuit of property.

Imagine, Smith ventures, the case of a "poor man's son," who, driven by ambition, "admires the condition of the rich." If he could only acquire wealth, the poor man believes, "he would sit still contentedly, and be quiet, enjoying himself in the thought of the happiness and tranquility of his situation." "Enchanted with the distant idea of this felicity," he works around the clock in "the pursuit of wealth and greatness," his eyes ever on his prize:

> Through the whole of his life, he pursues the idea of a certain artificial and elegant repose which he may never arrive at, for which he sacrifices a real tranquility that is at all times in his power, and which, if in the extremity of old age he should at last attain to it, he will find to be in no respect preferable to that humble security and contentment which he had abandoned for it. It is then, in the last dregs of life, his body wasted with toil and diseases, his mind galled and ruffled . . . that he begins at last to find that wealth and greatness are mere trinkets of frivolous utility no more adapted for procuring ease of body or tranquility of mind than the tweezer cases of the lover of toys. . . .[42]

True happiness, Smith believed, showing his partial indebtedness to the Stoics, lay in "tranquility and enjoyment," which had less to do with economic condition than it did with virtue.[43] The "beggar who suns himself by the side of the highway" may well possess the same happiness as kings.[44] But this very illusion of the poor man's son (that felicity can be won through greatness and wealth), this same "deception which rouses and keeps in continual motion the industry of mankind," had prompted men "to found cities and commonwealths, to invent and improve all the sciences and arts . . . which have entirely changed the face of the globe. . . ." This "deception" drove the steady advance of civilization and the expansion of prosperity that in Smith's view were the defining features of commercial societies.[45] Maximizing individual liberty while promoting general affluence, modern commercial societies were to the benefit of the greatest number. But whether they promoted individual happiness was another question, one whose answer depended far less on the wealth of nations than on the moral qualities of the men and women who inhabited them.

"Happiness is the aim of life, but virtue is the foundation of happiness," Jefferson observed toward the end of his career, echoing Franklin's observation that "virtue and happiness are mother and daughter."[46] A commonplace of classical philosophy, as dear to Aristotle as it was to Cicero, the statement captures well what few, if any, of the Founding Fathers would have denied. Endorsed by the principal authorities on which Jefferson drew in drafting the Declaration, his statement nonetheless reveals an inherent tension in the opposition of its second clause that is also the tension of the American experiment. Happiness indeed was the aim of life. And virtue, self-discipline, the ordered arrangement of desire were indeed the way to that end. But whether the goal itself could be fulfilled depended on individual decision and choice; happiness could never be imposed. And in that liberty—that freedom—lay a dilemma. For as Smith clearly recognized, and as he argued at length in *The Wealth of Nations*, "augmentation in fortune is the means by which the greater part of men propose and wish to better their condition."[47] The greater part of men, that is, pursued happiness through wealth, a route that the so-called father of capitalism knew to be a devious path. And although this "deception," this trivial pursuit, was undeniably a powerful engine of growth, it was a dubious means to lasting satisfaction. Smith himself denied the connection, as did Jefferson, Franklin, and many others.

The "pursuit of happiness," it should now be clear, was launched in different, and potentially conflicting, directions from the start, with private pleasure and public welfare coexisting in the same phrase. For Jefferson, so quintessentially in this respect a man of the Enlightenment, the coexistence was not a problem, for it reflected a wider eighteenth-century assumption and article of faith: that individual interest and the greater good, private and public happiness, could be reconciled. This faith was by no means blind, resting as it did on a realistic appreciation of the passions and desires that moved the minds of men. But in order for it to be sustained, it depended heavily on the self-restraint of individuals to curb their excesses and enthusiasms. In religion, in classical virtue, in the education of reason, and in the public-mindedness of the moral sense, Jefferson and his contemporaries saw the forces that would perform this essential task, ensuring that the pursuit of private pleasures did not veer off the thoroughfare of public good.

And yet, as Hannah Arendt once observed, the public and private aspects of the pursuit of happiness—in tension from the outset—were soon at open odds, in her opinion, to the great benefit of the latter. "Jefferson's new formula," she writes, "was almost immediately deprived of its double sense and understood as the right of citizens to pursue their personal interests and thus to act according to the rules of private self-interest."[48] This is an exaggeration—and an oversimplification—dismissing as it does the long and stubborn persistence of American public-mindedness. But it correctly identifies the trajectory of a central and propelling tension, one that, as she also pointed out, was exacerbated only by "the impact of mass immigration." For many who arrived on America's shores in the nineteenth and twentieth centuries, or who viewed it from afar, America was a "promised land where milk and honey flow," as still today.[49] To pursue happiness in such a land was quite rightly to pursue prosperity, to pursue pleasure, to pursue wealth. But as others would also come to appreciate in shedding their illusions, pursuit and arrival, capture and pursuit, could be very different things.

Strange Melancholy

When a disgruntled American complained that his country was not providing him with happiness—and so failed to live up to its bill—Benjamin Franklin is said to have replied: "The constitution only gives you the right to pursue happiness. You have to catch it yourself."[50] Although evocative of the good doctor's wit, the oft-repeated saying is almost certainly apocryphal. Having worked on both documents himself, Franklin well knew that it was the Declaration, not the Constitution, that bequeathed us this right.

Still, the legendary response is in keeping with Franklin's general convictions, and the grumbling sentiment that might have provoked it in the first place was real enough. As the late historian Howard Mumford Jones has shown, Americans took great pains to register such complaints in the nineteenth century, filing hundreds of lawsuits in state and federal courts that accused their governments and fellow citizens alike of impeding their sacred right to happiness.[51] Despite the clarity of Franklin's alleged response, the distinction between the pursuit of happiness and its attainment did not always seem so clear.

The cynic may be inclined to see in this early litigious grumbling the roots of America's "culture of complaint," a precedent for what has become an unfortunate national tendency—the readiness to seek restitution for unhappiness in the courts. Admittedly, a good number of groups had ample reason to press their claims in that way—African-American slaves, to name only the most obvious. They could point to the bitter irony that in a draft passage of the Declaration, Jefferson had accused England's George III of waging

> cruel war against human nature itself, *violating its most sacred rights of life and liberty* in the persons of a distant people who never offended him, captivating & carrying them into slavery in another hemisphere or to incur miserable death in their transportation thither.[52]

Tellingly, Jefferson made no mention of a right to pursue happiness for this distant people; and tellingly, the passage was dropped altogether from the final draft. But the omission was duly noted, allowing African-Americans and others one day to demand fidelity to the phrase that all are created equal, endowed by their creator with certain unalienable rights.

The history of the pursuit of happiness in America, in this respect, is the history of the pursuit of equality and freedom—the slow, ever imperfect extension of the right to pursue happiness to all. Yet when considered from a slightly different perspective, this same process of expanding equality can be said to have had potentially unhappy consequences. And here, perhaps, the cynic, or at least the skeptic, may be on firmer ground. For in a society in which the unhindered pursuit of happiness (to say nothing of its attainment) is treated as a natural, God-given right, the inability to make steady progress along the way will inevitably be seen as an aberration, a suspension of the natural order of things. Either, it is logical to conclude, the pursuer has been impeded—an injustice and violation—or the pursuer has failed to generate ample momentum for the chase. In either case, the result is disconcerting, leading one to suspect that an unhappy, if unintended, consequence of the pursuit of happiness may well be the production of discontent.

This was precisely the conclusion drawn by one of America's most perceptive observers, Alexis de Tocqueville, in his magisterial *Democracy in America*. Published in two volumes in 1835 and 1840, the work is a long account of a short stay, a chronicle of the many impressions generated by Tocqueville's travels in the young republic between May 1831 and February 1832. Charged on behalf of the French government with studying America's penal system, Tocqueville drew conclusions about pursuits of a greater magnitude than just those involving fugitives of the law. The restless pursuits he observed in the New World, Tocqueville believed, represented the face of humanity's future. And though there was much in that face to suggest a smile, one could also discern the nascent cracks of a frown.

The ambivalence of this twin regard comes across most plainly in Tocqueville's direct comparisons of the New World with what it had left behind:

In certain remote corners of the Old World you may sometimes stumble upon little places which seem to have been forgotten among the general tumult and which have stayed still while all around them moves. The inhabitants are mostly very ignorant and very poor; they take no part in affairs of government and often governments oppress them. But yet they seem serene and often have a jovial disposition.

In America I have seen the freest and best educated of men in circumstances the happiest to be found in the world; yet it seemed to me that a cloud habitually hung on their brow, and they seemed serious and almost sad even in their pleasures.

The chief reason for this is that the former do not give a moment's thought to the toils they endure, whereas the latter never stop thinking of the good things they have not got.[53]

This was no elegy for underdevelopment, or a paean to pastoral virtues à la Rousseau. Nor was it an idyll to which those of a more conservative cast are sometimes drawn: the romanticization of the past. Tocqueville saw little virtue in ignorance, scant romance in poverty, and even less in political oppression. On the whole, he was inclined to welcome the changes that America augured for the future: greater opportunity and social mobility; the expansion of democracy and civic participation; increased commercial activity, industry, and trade.

Yet with the prescience of a Rousseau or a Marx, an Adam Smith or an Edmund Burke, Tocqueville understood that these same forces were exacting a price. The evolution toward freedom and prosperity intensified the rhythms of existence at a frantic pace, creating new needs and desires, while continually multiplying expectations. As he observes in another passage, again comparing the New World (the free world) to the Old:

When one passes from a free country into another which is not so, the contrast is very striking: there, all is activity and bustle; here all seems calm and immobile. In the former, betterment and progress are the questions of the day; in the latter, one might suppose that society, having acquired every blessing, longs for nothing but repose to enjoy them. Nevertheless, the country which is in such a rush to attain happiness is generally richer and more prosperous than the one that seems contented with its lot. And considering them one by one, it is hard to understand how this one daily discovers so many new needs, while the other seems conscious of so few.[54]

From a world in which the inhabitants have little but expect nothing, a world in which the people are relatively content because their needs are few, one passes to the frenetic tumult of modern America. Here the hopes of infinitely expanding desire are turned loose with astonishing force. "No one could work harder to be happy," Tocqueville observes of Americans, marveling at the ceaseless, restless energy they expend in search of a better life.[55] Rushing from one thing to the next, an American will travel hundreds of miles in a day. He will build a house in which to pass his old age and then sell it before the roof is on. He will continually change paths "for fear of missing the shortest cut leading to happiness." Finally, though,

> Death steps in . . . and stops him before he has grown tired of this futile pursuit of that complete felicity which always escapes him.[56]

In dogged chase until the end, the restless American is brought up short only by the finality of death.

Tocqueville might easily have cited Herodotus in this connection, or Plato, Saint Augustine, or any number of other moralists who had already probed the restlessness of human desire. He did not do so here. But like them, he understood that "that which most vividly stirs the human heart is certainly not the quiet possession of something precious but rather the imperfectly satisfied desire to have it and the continual fear of losing it again."[57] The restlessness of desire—this primal source of dissatisfaction, this *uneasiness*, as Locke and Smith had observed—was also a powerful source of improvement. And in America, that source had been tapped directly, owing to the country's unique social and political makeup, pumped furiously by its growing equality. When "distinctions of rank are blurred and privileges abolished," Tocqueville grasped, "when patrimonies are divided up and

Old World pleasures. George Morland, *The Happy Cottagers,* c. 1790–92,
John Howard McFadden Collection, Philadelphia Museum of Art.

education and freedom spread, the poor conceive an eager desire to
acquire comfort, and the rich think of the danger of losing it."[58] In the
land of opportunity, the New World of milk and honey, "the taste for
physical pleasures" was the primary cause of American restlessness.[59]

Thus, whereas in the stratified societies of the Old World, the
wealthy were comparatively secure in their comforts and the poor
dared not dream of acquiring them here below, in the fluid mobility
of America, citizens were "continually engaged in pursuing or striving
to retain [their] precious, incomplete, and fugitive delights." Men and
women in this society of "middling fortunes" had "enough physical
enjoyments to get a taste for them, but not enough to content them."
They could not "win them without effort, or indulge in them without
anxiety."[60] And whereas in the Old World, inequality was the general
rule and so attracted little attention, in America, "where everything is

more or less level, the slightest variation is noticed." The "more equal men are," Tocqueville concluded, "the more insatiable will be their longing for equality." Striving ever to match their fellow citizens, and enticed always by the imminent possibility of a better life, Americans pursued an elusive equality with the same dogged futility with which they pursued happiness:

> That is a quality which ever retreats before them without getting quite out of sight, and as it retreats it beckons them on to pursue. Every instant they think they will catch it, and each time it slips through their fingers. They see it close enough to know its charms, but they do not get near enough to enjoy it, and they will be dead before they have fully relished its delights.[61]

And that, Tocqueville concluded in a famous line, "is the reason for the strange melancholy often haunting inhabitants of democracies in the midst of abundance, and of that disgust with life sometimes gripping them in calm and easy circumstances."[62]

If one were to turn away from the text at this point, it would be tempting to conclude that Tocqueville saw more frown than smile on the face of humanity's future. But open-eyed though he was, Tocqueville was also cautiously optimistic—a realist but not a pessimist. At first sight, he confessed, there was "something astonishing in this spectacle of so many lucky men restless in the midst of abundance." Upon reflection, he acknowledged that in truth this was a "spectacle as old as the world; all that is new is to see a whole people performing in it."[63] The novelty of America, in other words, lay not in the perennially restless pursuit of happiness, but in the extension of that pursuit to an entire culture on a scale hitherto unknown. And though that presented its own set of challenges, it also suggested that America might draw solace from the collected wisdom of the ages.

There were encouraging signs that American culture so far had been able to do just that, maintaining values that served as an antidote to the insatiable striving of desire, curbing the potential materialism and solipsism of individual pursuit. And although these values were many, Tocqueville placed two at the top of his list: the "doctrine of self-interest rightly understood," and the more general "spirit of religion."

The first of these Tocqueville described as the "best-suited of all philosophical theories to the wants of men in our time." As it took shape in America, however, the doctrine was less a set of formal philosophical prescriptions than a widely received cultural ethos that encouraged men and women to find points of convergence between their individual interests and those of the social whole. Almost instinctively, Americans understood that self-sacrifice was a matter of self-interest, that by serving others they could serve themselves. "An enlightened self-love continually leads them to help one another and disposes them freely to give part of their time and wealth for the good of the state." It was, they knew, in "each man's interest to be good."[64]

A living link to a number of those key "harmonizing sentiments" that Jefferson had captured in his pregnant phrase, self-interest rightly understood bore directly on Americans' happiness. For those "who teach this doctrine tell men that to be happy in life they must watch their passions and be careful to restrain their excesses, that lasting happiness cannot be won except at the cost of a thousand ephemeral pleasures, and finally, that one must continually master oneself in order to serve oneself better." Here, Tocqueville believed, was the source of America's saving grace, the necessary restraint that ensured the restless pursuit of happiness did not degenerate into hedonism or solipsistic self-regard. Conveying truths that moralists had cultivated throughout the ages, the doctrine of self-interest rightly understood instilled the belief that "in order to gain happiness in this world" a man must refuse to yield "blindly to the first onrush of his passions," learning rather to "habitually and effortlessly sacrifice the pleasure of the moment for the lasting interests of his whole life."[65]

If the doctrine of self-interest rightly understood was thus Americans' "strongest remaining guarantee against themselves," the spirit of religion, to which it was often applied, was no less important.[66] Raised as a Catholic, Tocqueville struggled throughout his life with

B. Johnson, *The Paths of Life*, 1805, Courtesy of Map Collection, Yale University Library. The circuitous paths of this amusing document lead to such dead-ends as "Haughty Hill," "Weeping Shade," "Faltering Alley," and "Gambler's Hold." The successful traveler on life's way arrives at "Happy Old Age Hall" (bottom left).

faith, but he nevertheless maintained with the utmost conviction the social importance of religion, above all in democratic and commercial societies. The short space of human life, he knew, "can never shut in the whole of man's imagination; the incomplete joys of this world will never satisfy his heart." "Incredulity is an accident; faith is the only permanent state of mankind."[67]

There are, of course, many varieties of faith. But what Tocqueville found most intriguing about the American spirit of religion was its sublunary disposition. Whereas Old World priests had once spoken "of nothing but the other life" and "hardly took any trouble to prove that a sincere Christian might be happy here below," preachers in America were "continually coming down to earth":

> Indeed they find it difficult to take their eyes off it. The better to touch their hearers, they are forever pointing out how religious beliefs favor freedom and public order, and it is often difficult to be sure when listening to them whether the main object of religion is to procure eternal felicity in the next world or prosperity in this.[68]

Tocqueville shows himself conscious in this passage of a theme that we have been tracing over many chapters: the consolidation, since the seventeenth century, of earthly happiness as the ultimate human end and the consequent transformation in human expectations. In the wake of that transformation, virtually every institution, practice, and belief could be treated as a means to the fulfillment of this new end, even, and perhaps especially, religion. And in America, this process was considerably advanced, prompting men of God to vaunt religion's utility—its capacity to make us happier and more prosperous in this life—with enthusiasm.

In this respect, religion was paying homage to an end higher than itself—an end higher even than God. But Tocqueville also knew that religion served admirably to temper our more rapacious earthly cravings, working in tandem with the doctrine of self-interest rightly understood to nudge us gently away from an exclusive preoccupation with our own pleasures and concerns. Faith was the necessary check on the love of physical pleasures. For though man, quite rightly, "takes delight in [his] proper and legitimate quest for prosperity, there is a danger that in the end he may lose the use of his sublimest faculties and that . . . he may at length degrade himself" if not restrained. That, Tocqueville believed, was the great "peril" of democratic nations. And given that the "passion for physical pleasures . . . can never satisfy a whole people" any more than it can permanently satisfy a man, then what was true of individuals was also true of the nation writ large: "In democracies as elsewhere, it is only by resisting a thousand petty urges that the fundamental anxious longing for happiness can be satisfied."[69]

The spirit of religion provided the will for that resistance, the force to restrain oneself, and the impetus to act in the service of others. It also turned our thoughts toward the future, imbuing us with constancy and hope—an effect, Tocqueville observes, that works "as much in favor of happiness in this world as of felicity in the next." So central was the need to set such distant goals for human endeavor that Tocqueville urged even secular philosophers and men of power to devote themselves to that task. "As the light of faith grows dim, man's range of vision grows more circumscribed." He turns in on himself and on his times. And as soon as citizens have "lost the way of relying chiefly on distant hopes, they are naturally led to want to satisfy their least desires at once."[70]

Scanning the horizon of humanity's future, Tocqueville saw both cause for cautious optimism and cause for genuine concern. On the one hand, he worried that the pursuit of happiness would be reduced to the pursuit of prosperity and private pleasure alone, a reduction that would most certainly undermine it. Pursuing happiness solely in that way would not only impoverish all who engaged in the chase but continually frustrate their ability to reach their goal. Only by harnessing desire with healthy restraints could Americans learn to live within their ever expanding means.

The tools to accomplish this task, on the other hand, were already in place, a legacy of the society that had produced the Founding Fathers and their original dreams of pursuit. But whether the spirit of religion and the publicly oriented spirit of self-interest rightly understood would continue to work for the future was uncertain. In his darker moments, Tocqueville conceded, "No power on earth can prevent increasing equality from . . . disposing each citizen to get wrapped up in himself."[71] The potential consequences of this development were disturbing.

It was in this frame of mind that Tocqueville returned at the end of his work to a theme that he had introduced in Volume One: the "tyranny" or "despotism" of the majority. These terms, he admitted, were no longer sufficient, for what he sought to describe was an altogether new phenomenon. It is striking that he implicates "happiness" directly in this new type of oppression:

> I am trying to imagine under what novel features despotism may appear in the world. In the first place, I see a multitude of men, alike and equal, constantly circling around in pursuit of the petty and banal pleasures with which they glut their souls. Each one of them, withdrawn into himself, is almost unaware of the fate of the rest.
>
> Over this kind of men stands an immense, protective power which is alone responsible for securing their enjoyment and watching over their fate. That power is absolute, thoughtful of detail, orderly, provident, and gentle. . . . It likes to see the citizens enjoy themselves, provided that they think of nothing but enjoyment. It gladly works for their happiness but wants to be the sole agent and judge of it.[72]

In warning of the political risks posed by the withdrawal into private pleasures, Tocqueville was taking up a theme that his predecessor and countryman Benjamin Constant had already articulated. A noted theorist of the classical liberal tradition in his own right, Constant had cautioned in a famous reflection on the differences between ancient and modern liberty, first delivered as a speech in 1819, that modern political authorities would be only too ready to allow us to become absorbed "in the enjoyment of our private independence, and in the pursuit of our particular interests." "They will say to us," Constant ventured, "what, in the end, is the aim of your efforts, the motive of your labors, the object of all your hopes? Is it not happiness? Well, leave this happiness to us and we shall give it to you."[73] And this, Constant warned, was the ultimate danger, the renunciation of political liberty in return for the happiness of "diversions." One must assume the responsibility of being happy for oneself.

Constant took these cautionary words one step further, and it is worth repeating them here, for in effect they address a central question raised by the classical liberal experiment. "Is it so evident," he asked, "that happiness, of whatever kind, is the only aim of mankind?" That he should need to pose the question at all is indicative of the times in which he wrote, a post-Enlightenment century. But his response is even more interesting:

> If it were so, our course would be narrow indeed, and our destination far from elevated. . . . No, Sirs, I bear witness to the better part of our nature, that noble disquiet which pursues and torments us, that desire to broaden our knowledge and develop our faculties. It is not to happiness alone, it is to self-development that our destiny calls us; and political liberty is the most powerful, the most effective means of self-development that heaven has given us.[74]

The goal of liberalism, in Constant's view, was not happiness but the development of the individual, an end for which political liberty was the ultimate means. That such liberty would include the liberty to go awry—to make poor choices, to make a mess of one's life, to make oneself sad—Constant freely acknowledged. He also entertained openly what others since have often been reluctant to face: the possibility that liberty's greatest product might not be happiness, but on the contrary, that "noble disquiet which pursues and torments us" to the grave, the possibility, in short, that liberty and happiness might be in tension, or even at odds.

A Crisis of Faith

"M. de Tocqueville's is, in our eyes, the true view of the position in which mankind now stand." So observed John Stuart Mill in a glow-ing account of the first volume of *Democracy in America*, published in the *London Review* in 1835. Inclined, like his French colleague, to see the young republic as the image of humanity's future, the English philosopher and civil servant agreed that "a government, substantially a democracy . . . may [one day] subsist in Europe" and that it "may secure to the aggregate of human beings living under it, a greater sum of happiness than has ever yet been enjoyed by any people. . . ."[75]

On the face of things, this was an altogether happy prospect. Yet like Tocqueville, Mill regarded the future with a furrowed brow, worrying that an increase in aggregate happiness might be offset by a rise in individual pain. In a long review of the second volume of *Democracy in America*, he gave voice to those concerns, quoting at length Tocqueville's passages regarding the "spectacle of so many lucky men, restless in the midst of abundance." If anything, Mill concluded, Tocqueville's analysis was not trenchant enough.

Admittedly, Tocqueville's warnings about the dangers of a "tyranny of the majority"—a "tyranny, not over the body, but over the mind"—were apt. But his conclusion that the *cause* of this tyranny, like the cause of the attendant restlessness of American life, could be traced exclusively to a growing equality was ill conceived. In making that claim, Mill argued, Tocqueville had conflated cause and effect, failing to explain why areas of much greater equality such as French Canada displayed so little of "that go-ahead sprit, that restless, impatient eagerness for improvement" evident in America. At the same time, Tocqueville's account completely ignored the important case of Great Britain, an "aristocracy" where extremes of wealth and poverty were massive, and "equalization of condition" little advanced. Though in "complete contrast" to its former colony in this respect, England nonetheless shared many common features on the moral and cultural plane. Mill emphasized the same "petty pursuit of petty advancements in fortune," the same "treading upon the heels of one another," the same "habitual dissatisfaction," the same ubiquitous desire to improve one's condition but "never to enjoy it." The cause of these common features—and thus the true source of the strange restlessness in the midst of prosperity—should be traced not to equality but to the very heart of commercial civilization itself. "Let the idea take hold," Mill warned, "that the most serious danger to the future prospects of mankind is in the unbalanced influence of the commercial spirit. . . ."[76]

Mill's warnings are particularly worthy of note. For not only was he one of the most discerning critical defenders of classical liberalism, he was also deeply interested in happiness. On the face of things, this, too, might seem a happy match. But the reality, as Mill came to partially understand, was more complex.

A childhood prodigy who was reading Greek by the age of three, Mill was quite literally a child of happiness, if not always a happy child. His father, the historian and economist James Mill, was an important figure in the Utilitarian movement, a close friend and neighbor of Jeremy Bentham. Baptized with Bentham's benediction, Mill was raised as an apostle of the greatest happiness for the greatest number, receiving no other formal lessons in faith. As Mill himself would later recall, this made him something of an anomaly in the religiously saturated Victorian age—"one of the very few examples . . . of one who has, not thrown off religious belief, but never had it."[77]

Mill claims never to have felt the lack, and yet it is striking to listen to his own account of the response to his first serious engagement with the writings of Bentham, read, oddly, in French translation while he was abroad in his early teens. As Mill tells us in his wonderfully candid *Autobiography,*

> When I laid down the last volume . . . I had become a different being. The "principle of utility," understood as Bentham understood it . . . fell exactly into its place as the keystone which held together the detached and fragmentary component parts of my knowledge and beliefs. It gave unity to my conceptions of things. I now had opinions; a creed, a doctrine, a philosophy; in one among the best senses of the word, a religion; the inculcation and diffusion of which could be made the principal outward purpose of a life.[78]

Mill, by his own admission, had come into the fullness of faith, finding "religion," a "creed," and an "object in life" with which his "own
conception of happiness was entirely identified."[79] It is all the more
poignant that he would come to doubt his faith, perhaps to lose it
entirely.

The immediate cause of this development was what Mill describes
in the *Autobiography* as a bout of despair that would probably be clas-
sified today as clinical depression. Often analyzed by historians, the
possible reasons for this breakdown are many: the pressures of an over-
bearing father, the accumulated denials of a youth devoted exclusively
to scholarly pursuits, the absence of intimacy and love. Regardless of
the primary cause, the effect, quite clearly, was shattering. "I was accustomed," Mill writes,

> to felicitate myself on the certainty of a happy life which I
> enjoyed, through placing my happiness in something durable
> and distant, in which some progress might be always making,
> while it could never be exhausted by complete attainment.
> This did very well for several years, during which the general
> improvement going on in the world and the idea of myself as
> engaged with others in struggling to promote it, seemed
> enough to fill up an interesting and animated existence. But
> the time came when I awakened from this as from a dream.[80]

It was the autumn of 1826, and Mill had fallen into "a dull state of
nerves," growing listless and indifferent, similar to that state "in which
converts to Methodism usually are, when smitten by their first 'conviction of sin.'" In such a state, Mill was prompted to ask himself
whether, if all his goals in life could be realized, if all his dreams of
reform and progress could be carried out, this would be "a great joy
and happiness" to him. He was forced to admit that it would not. At
this point, he says:

> My heart sank within me: the whole foundation on which my
> life was constructed fell down. All my happiness was to have

been found in the continual pursuit of this end. The end had
ceased to charm, and how could there ever again be any interest in the means? I seemed to have nothing left to live for.[81]

He had lost his faith in happiness.

Fortunately, both for himself and for posterity, Mill was able to pull
himself out of this pit of despair. He relied neither on therapy nor
medication to do so but took instead the Romantic cure, finding solace in Coleridge's "Dejection, an Ode" and "medicine" in the poetry
of Wordsworth. These and other poets bathed his analytical soul in a
warm wash of beauty and feeling, those "perennial sources of happiness" on which Mill would draw for the rest of his life. In the Romantic cultivation of emotion, he found the "source of inward joy, of
sympathetic and imaginative pleasures" that helped cure him of despair. Bringing his inner life into greater harmony with the world
around him, they opened his heart to passion and love.[82]

But what of his faith in happiness, the pursuit of which had ceased
to charm? Mill tells us that his crisis had two "marked effects" on his
opinion and character. The first was to impress upon him the importance of the "internal culture of the individual," forcing him to think
of human development not simply, as his father and Bentham had
done, in terms of outward sources of pleasure and pain but also as the
inward "cultivation of feelings," the nurturing of long-stifled emotion.
And yet the lasting effects of his upheaval went beyond a mere ad-
justment of what had been an essentially Enlightenment faith, a
deepening of the pleasure/pain calculus with a dose of Romantic feeling. Arguably, Mill never fully recovered his old faith in happiness, despite his claims to the contrary.

Consider the following remarkable confession from the *Autobiography*, in which Mill explains the other lasting consequence of his crisis:

> I never, indeed, wavered in the conviction that happiness is
> the test of all rules of conduct, and the end of life. But I now
> thought that this end was only to be attained by not making it
> the direct end. Those only are happy (I thought) who have

their minds fixed on some object other than their own happiness; on the happiness of others, on the improvement of mankind, even on some art or pursuit, followed not as a means, but as itself an ideal end. Aiming thus at something else, they find happiness by the way. . . . Ask yourself whether you are happy, and you cease to be so. The only chance is to treat, not happiness, but some end external to it, as the purpose of life. . . . This theory now became the basis of my philosophy of life.[83]

This is an insight that Hume certainly possessed and that in key respects has been borne out by modern psychological research. To forget oneself in an all-consuming activity, to feel the "flow" of immersion in a cause or pursuit, can often yield happiness indirectly, by the by.[84] But true as this may be, the theory clashes starkly with the opening line of this startling avowal, in which Mill denies that he ever wavered in his conviction that happiness is the "end of life." Only lines later does he reveal that "the only chance" for happiness is to treat *some other end* as life's purpose and goal.

The confessions of the *Autobiography* were made relatively late in Mill's life, drafted in the 1850s, amended in the 1860s, and published in 1873, the year of his death. But they are not the only instance of such revealing avowal. Mill's essay "Bentham," written several years after its subject's death and published in the *London and Westminster Review* in 1838, contains the following damning reflection:

At present we shall only say, that while, under proper explanations, we entirely agree with Bentham in his principle, we do not hold with him that all right thinking on the details of morals depends on its express assertion. We think utility, or happiness, much too complex and indefinite an end to be sought except through the medium of various secondary ends. . . .[85]

Again, the judgment may be valid on its own terms, but as the great historian of ideas Isaiah Berlin once observed, it destroys "at one blow the proudest claim, and indeed the central doctrine, of the Benthamite system"—that happiness (utility or pleasure) can be used as a valid standard of conduct.[86] In a later work, his celebrated essay *Utilitarianism*, first published in 1861, Mill went to even greater lengths to distinguish his thought from Bentham's, declaring that although he still considered pleasure to be the standard of happiness, some pleasures were better than others. "It is better to be a human being dissatisfied," Mill argued in a memorable line, "than a pig satisfied; better to be Socrates dissatisfied than a fool satisfied." Happiness, he stressed, was not the same thing as contentment, but involved the pursuit of "nobler feelings," "higher pleasures," and higher things.[87]

But what might those be? What, to return to the question posed in Mill's *Autobiography*, were those "other ends"? The question, in Mill's eyes, was crucial, for as he had observed in his essay on Bentham, "Whether happiness be or be not the end to which morality should be referred—that it be referred to an *end* of some sort, and not left in the dominion of vague feeling or inexplicable internal conviction . . . is essential to the very idea of moral philosophy; is, in fact, what renders argument or discussion on moral questions possible."[88] What end, or ends, would take the place of happiness for the salvation of moral philosophy?

Throughout the body of his work, Mill considers various candidates: justice, dignity, love, independence, diversity, self-sacrifice, beauty, and liberty, among them. But whether these are to be considered final ends in themselves, or the means to a single, higher end (happiness), or simply as species of it, Mill never clearly says. Nor does he give us a precise account of the order of their importance, although a strong case can be made for the primacy of liberty, the subject of his most celebrated work, *On Liberty* (1859), and the higher end that justifies the "libertarianism" he espouses there.

It is noteworthy that very rarely in that work—the most important of his explicitly political writings—does he discuss happiness at all, and the first instance in which he does so is to establish liberty's preeminence. As he writes in introducing the famous "harm principle," the centerpiece of Millian liberalism:

The object of this essay is to assert one very simple principle. . . . That principle is that the sole end for which mankind
are warranted, individually or collectively, in interfering with
the liberty of action of any of their number is self-protection.
That the only purpose for which power can be rightfully
exercised over any member of a civilized community, against
his will, is to prevent harm to others. His own good, either
physical or moral, is not sufficient warrant. He cannot rightfully
be compelled to do or forbear because it will be better for him
to do so, because it will make him happier, because, in the
opinions of others, to do so would be wise or even right.[89]

Liberty, plainly, trumps happiness. And though Mill adds immediately afterward that there is every reason to attempt to "remonstrate,"
"reason with," "persuade," or "entreat" another to act in the interests of his own happiness or good, the choice must always rest with
the individual. "Over himself, over his own body and mind, the individual is sovereign." He has the right to make himself miserable, if
that is what he chooses.

In making this claim, Mill not only broke definitively with the vulgar Utilitarianism of Bentham but also placed himself unequivocally
in the tradition of those, like Constant and Tocqueville, for whom liberty was the indispensable good, vital to human dignity, nobility, and
development. Was this, then, the "other end" to which Mill had referred in his *Autobiography* as the "only chance"—the end external to
happiness that, when treated as the purpose of life, might bring it "by
the way," as an ancillary effect?

Mill speaks often as if that were the case, invoking liberty—of conscience, of assembly, and, most critically, of "tastes and pursuits, of
framing the plan of our life to suit our own character"—as a vital foundation for happiness and one of its necessary conditions. On the two
other occasions in *On Liberty* in which he invokes happiness, he does
so precisely in that connection, speaking of an individual's ability to
define his own conduct through his own character as one "of the principal ingredients of happiness" and observing later that where the full

diversity of human experience is stifled, individuals will not "receive their fair share of happiness."[90] In a similar vein, Mill observes in his celebrated essay "The Subjection of Women" (1869) that the "most direct benefit" of all those associated with women's liberation would be "the unspeakable gain in private happiness to the liberated half of the species." "He who would rightly appreciate the worth of personal independence as an element of happiness," he challenges, "should consider the value he himself puts upon it as an ingredient of his own."[91]

This is the language of a born-again Romantic—liberty as *liberation*, a throwing off of the stifling constraints that stand in the way of self-realization and self-actualization, a surging forth of one's unique nature and authentic character, a true definition of self. It is what the Germans called *Bildung*, and what, in Mill's view, was all too scarce in the contemporary world. "Society," he writes grimly in *On Liberty*, "has now fairly got the better of individuality; and the danger which threatens human nature is not the excess, but the deficiency, of personal impulses and preferences." "A person whose desires and impulses are his own . . . is said to have a character. One whose desires and impulses are not his own has no character."[92] In Mill's opinion, there were too few characters in the modern world.

Thus, whereas Tocqueville feared, with a residual Christian moralism, the excess of individual interest and desire, Mill believed that these were in short supply, particularly in his own country, where a pervasive "theory of Calvinism" had inculcated obedience and self-sacrifice at the expense of self-assertion and expression. In all things did the mind bow to this yoke: "Even in what people do for pleasure, conformity is the first thing thought of." "Christian self-denial" certainly had its place in the litany of virtues, but so did "pagan self-assertion." Mill called for a strong infusion. "It is not by wearing down into uniformity all that is individual in themselves," he emphasized, "but by cultivating it and calling it forth . . . that human beings become a noble and beautiful object of contemplation."[93]

But if in these ways Mill's analysis departed somewhat from Tocqueville's, he wholeheartedly agreed that the society of his day posed the risk of crushing individuality and character like never before. And in this process, the culprit was less the lingering Calvinist spirit than the nature of modern civilization itself, with an all-consuming commercial capitalism and middle-class democracy as its defining features. What Mill had described in his review of *Democracy in America* as the "growing insignificance of individuals in comparison with the masses" on the one hand, and the "petty pursuit of petty advancements in fortune" on the other, were the twin forces leveling all that was unique in modern society. And just as he had called for "generous and cultivated minds" to decry this "most serious danger to the future prospects of mankind," providing "individual testimonies against it," and nurturing "opinions and sentiments different from those of the mass," in *On Liberty* he adopted precisely this course, urging "eccentricity" for the sake of breaking through the "tyranny of opinion."[94] "Unless the intelligent part of the public can be made to feel [the value of individuality]," Mill warns, "to see that it is good there should be difference, *even though not for the better, even though, as it may appear to them, some should be for the worse*," then individuality will be doomed.[95]

And here we arrive at the center of a key tension in Mill's thought. For however praiseworthy we may find his libertarian defense of difference and individual development, it is not at all clear that it is consonant with his stated faith in the greatest happiness of the greatest number. Mill himself suggests as much, in the highlighted passage above, and his own doubts summon once again the disturbing prospect raised by Tocqueville and Constant: that the pursuit of liberty and the pursuit of happiness might sometimes, even often, be at odds.

Mill sought bravely to deny this, arguing instead that the pursuit of liberty could be that "other end" that would deliver happiness indirectly, by the way. By this route might others avoid the paradox that Mill himself had experienced with so much pain: that of making happiness the direct object of his existence—the aim of his pursuit—and in so doing stifling his true character and killing the thing he loved.

Mill's warning bears serious reflection—as much for entire societies based on the pursuit of happiness as for individual lives. But it does not follow that in serving as a final end, liberty can or should also be a means. For those oppressed by a tyrannical majority, certainly, or constrained by hostile opinion, liberty and happiness will generally go hand in hand. But it is hardly certain that others—the majority, the greatest number—will agree. In urging eccentricity, difference, and distinction, Mill was arguing for a freer society, a more diverse society, we might even say a *better* society. But whether this would be a happier society as well is not easy to say. One man's "liberation," alas, can easily feed another's unhappiness or a mother's pain—in ways too subtle to be detected (or legislated against) by the principle of harm. Like Constant and Tocqueville, Mill understood that liberty—self-development, the full realization of self—was a worthy goal in its own right. But his belief, his faith, that this precious end would in turn serve as a means to the higher end of happiness rested at least in part on the tenets of his youthful religion.

There is another thought, in many ways more troubling still: that the majority might actually prefer its petty pursuits of petty fortune—"the hurried snatching of petty pleasures"—to noble disquiet, higher joys, and Socratic delights. This was a thought that the likes of John Stuart Mill were not entirely equipped to conceive. If asked to choose between the life of a dissatisfied philosopher and a happy pig, *they* knew how they would respond. But what to do with a majority that freely chose less sophisticated pleasures, even the satisfactions of mud?

The Capitalist Ethic and the Spirit of Happiness

In the autumn of 1904, a middle-aged German couple disembarked in New York after passage across the Atlantic, hoping to find relief from suffering and perhaps to begin a better life. They put faith in the promise of professional advancement, and they looked forward to seeing the "spirit of capitalism" at first hand. They were not alone. Close to five million of their countrymen had already emigrated to the United States, making German Americans the single largest group of European immigrants in the country after the British, surpassing even the Italians and Irish.[96]

Edmund Youngbauer, *Die Jagd nach dem Glück (Chasing After Happiness)*, late nineteenth century, Smithsonian American Art Museum, Washington, D.C. Photo: Smithsonian American Art Museum / Art Resource, NY.

Max and Marianne Weber were typical in these respects, but in almost every other they were not. A Prussian professor of economics and a sociologist of upper-middle-class background, Herr Weber had been invited to the United States to deliver a prominent lecture at an international conference in Saint Louis. He didn't intend to stay. And though he had truly suffered in the Old World, the cause was neither poverty nor discrimination but an undiagnosed nervous disorder—probably acute depression—that left him unable to work for long stretches at a time.

The prospect of a trip had lifted Weber's spirits, allowing him to return to his desk to complete the first half of the book that would make him famous. The journey itself completed the therapy. After three and a half months of intense travel in the United States, Weber returned to Germany to finish *The Protestant Ethic and the Spirit of Capi-*

talism, enthralled by what he had seen. "The spirit of capitalism," he wrote to a friend, was everywhere apparent. With a power and foresight that would place him on a par with Tocqueville and Mill as an analyst of modern society, Weber came to the conclusion that America stood at the forefront of a process that was sweeping Western society. Everything "opposed to the culture of capitalism was going to be demolished with irresistible force."[97]

What was the source of this all-consuming culture, the "spirit" that lay at its heart? Weber's answer is famously contested, and it hinged on a connection with religion. In the Protestant anxiety over the fate of individual salvation, he argued, lay the motive force behind an impetus to capital accumulation, regarded as a sign and partial assurance of God's blessing. Combining ascetic renunciation, a notion of work as divine calling, and a critically rational disposition, the Protestant faith, Weber argued, brought together nascent capitalism's essential qualities: the restriction of consumption in favor of the accrual of capital, and a religiously consecrated ethic of discipline, delayed gratification, industry, and thrift.

Paul Frenzeny, *Temperance, Industry, and Happiness,* from *Harper's Weekly,* March 14, 1874, Fine Arts Museum of San Francisco.

Weber considered Benjamin Franklin to be the perfect embodiment of this Protestant ethic, a tireless proponent of the virtue of a
job well done and a faithful heir to the Calvinist discipline of his father. This despite the fact that Franklin himself, in Weber's view, was
a "colourless deist."[98] The label should give us pause, for it is a singu-
larly inappropriate description of a man who once wrote to the Royal
Academy of Brussels proposing that it seek to do something truly useful, like discover a way to remove the smell from farts; a man who on
another occasion advised a friend to take an aged mistress on the grounds
that the "lower parts" continued to the last to be "as plump as ever,"
adding that besides, older women "are so grateful."[99] Whatever his other
shortcomings, Franklin did not lack color, even if Weber's portrayal of
him did. The error of perception prompted a portrayal of the capitalis-
tic ethic rendered exclusively in black and white:

> The *summum bonum* of this [Franklin's] ethic, the yearning of
> more and more money, combined with the strict avoidance of
> all spontaneous enjoyment of life, is above all completely
> devoid of any eudaemonistic, not to say, hedonistic, admix-
> ture. It is thought of so purely as an end in itself, that from
> the point of view of the happiness of, or utility to, the single
> individual, it appears entirely transcendental and absolutely
> irrational. Man is dominated by the making of money, by
> acquisition as the ultimate purpose of his life.[100]

Franklin, like his Puritan forebearers, Weber argued, perpetuated an
ethic that denied earthly happiness in the service of accumulation
and work—accumulation and work whose benefits would be enjoyed,
if ever at all, only in an imagined life to come. As belief in that next
life waned—hastened, Weber judged, by the inexorable rationaliza-
tion of human experience that accompanied the process of modern-
ization—all that was left behind was the impetus to work itself, now
stripped of its former transcendent purpose and meaning. "People
filled with the spirit of capitalism today," Weber emphasized, "tend
to be indifferent, if not hostile," to religion. "The thought of the pious

boredom of paradise has little attractive for their active natures." If one were to pose the question "What is the meaning of their restless activity?" to ask why they are "never satisfied with what they have," these people would tell you that they work to provide for their posterity, or more often and "more correctly" that "business with its continuous work [had] become a necessary part of their lives." "That," Weber concluded, "is in fact the only possible motivation," one that "at the same time expresses what is, seen from the view-point of personal happiness, so irrational about this sort of life, where a man exists for the sake of his business, instead of the reverse. . . ."[101]

There was, however, another motivation, one that was also a hold-over from an earlier ethic, but one that Weber's account may have prevented him from seeing. Although Franklin *did* distinguish the pursuit of happiness from the pursuit of wealth, he rarely shunned the "enjoyment of life," and it is unlikely that he considered the accumulation of fortune as completely devoid of eudaemonistic or hedonistic "admixture." What is true of Franklin is even more true for the many who came after—the millions, like Weber himself, who arrived on America's shores fleeing Old World pain for New World delight. As Adam Smith had anticipated, and Tocqueville and Mill had confirmed, a great many of these men and women *believed* that the pursuit of happiness and the pursuit of wealth were one, regardless of the veracity (or the rationality) of their faith. And they often sought nothing more than the freedom to pursue their happiness accordingly, making a better life for themselves and their families, while enjoying a few of the fruits of their toil along the way. This may not have been mud— far from it—but it also fell well short of the lofty heights of self-development that had captivated Mill. It recalled the earthy warmth of Horace—his "virtues of plain living"—or the simple hedonism recommended by the nineteenth-century poet Edward FitzGerald, albeit with a modern spin. In place of FitzGerald's "A book of verses underneath the bough / A jug of wine, a loaf of bread, and thou," one might hope for a house and a few luxuries, a picket fence, a faithful spouse, and a decent suit of clothes.[102] Philosophers like Mill might disparage such middle-class aspirations. But they were not ignoble dreams.

Weber himself appreciated some of this, observing toward the end of *The Protestant Ethic* that "in the field of [capitalism's] highest development, the United States, the pursuit of wealth, stripped of its religious and ethical meaning, tends to become associated with purely mundane passions, which often actually give it the character of sport." There are echoes of Hume in this claim, reverberations of the pursuit of activity as distraction—backgammon for the soul—the pursuit of work as the pursuit of play. But by and large, Weber's was a much colder view. The idea of duty in the calling of work, he observed, "prowls about in our lives like the ghost of dead religious beliefs." And where the fulfillment of this calling "cannot directly be related to the highest spiritual and cultural values . . . the individual generally abandons the attempt to justify it at all."[103] We work as disenchanted souls, he believed, in a disenchanted world, following blindly the behest of an outworn ethic and creed.

Yet by focusing only on the engine of a bygone creed—the Protestant ethic—Weber failed to acknowledge an atavism of an even older sort, a "higher" spiritual and cultural value that, as venerable as Croesus, was neither predominately Protestant nor exclusively Christian. That value—happiness—continued to entice with attractive force, providing a justification for work and sacrifice, a basis for meaning and hope that only loomed larger on the horizon of Western democracies. Indeed, it was during the very period when Weber was writing that America, and the West more generally, began to undergo what the sociologist Daniel Bell has described as a monumental transformation, "the shift from production to consumption as the fulcrum of capitalism." Bringing "silk stockings to shop girls" and "luxury to the masses," this transformation made of "marketing and hedonism" the "motor forces of capitalism," driving over all restraints that stood in the way of the enjoyment of material pleasures with a momentum that would have surprised even Tocqueville.[104] As inhibitions of desire were thrust aside, and as opportunities for satisfaction grew, "economic growth," Bell observes, became "the secular religion of advancing industrial societies: the source of individual motivation, the basis of political solidarity, the ground for the mobilization of society for a common purpose."[105] If economic growth was now a secular religion, the pursuit of happiness remained its central creed, with greater opportunites than ever before to pursue pleasure in comfort and things. These satisfied desires, but as they did so, they created others at a dizzying pace, multiplying uneasiness and threatening to confine us in proliferating needs.

This Weber saw. "Material goods," he observed at the end of *The Protestant Ethic*, "have gained an increasing and finally an inexorable power over the lives of men as at no previous period in history." If at one point they lay on the shoulders of the saint "like a light cloak, which can be thrown aside at any moment," that cloak had since become "an iron cage" from which "the spirit of religious asceticism had escaped," heavy and perhaps immovable, pinning us to earth.[106] Weber failed to detect the pursuit of happiness in this confining space, but the failure may have been willed. Scoffing at "optimistic dreams of happiness" and at politics based on its pursuit as "flabby eudaimonism," he granted no place in his political economy for these mundane quests.[107] As he emphasized in a speech delivered in 1894:

> I believe that we must renounce human happiness
> [*Glücksgefühl*] as the goal of social legislation. We want
> something else and can only want something else. We want to
> cultivate and support what appears to us *valuable* in man: his
> personal responsibility, his deep drive towards higher things,
> towards the spiritual and moral values of mankind. . . .[108]

In so stating the aim of politics this way, Weber added his own voice to a venerable tradition that included the likes of Constant, Tocqueville, and perhaps even Mill. Yet he fully acknowledged that it was from this "pessimistic standpoint that we arrive at . . . a point of view that appears to me much more idealistic" than the striving for a positive feeling of happiness. For the tragic truth of the matter was that the "feeling of happiness" was "greater in animals than in men."[109] In Weber's mind, the pursuit of what was highest in humanity—the cultivation and development of human beings—was the loftiest of all goals.

But toward what final end this process of development should be directed, Weber, like Mill, could not say. Indeed, he believed that insofar as he served the true vocation of a man of "science" (*Wissenschaft*), he was *unable* to say. Only the naive or the deluded, he believed, still clung to the "illusion" that science in any of its forms— whether social or natural—could provide certain answers to the most pressing of human questions: What shall we do and how shall we live? This, of course, had been the basic question of the Greeks. But after centuries of struggling to provide a definitive answer, it was time to acknowledge that science could no more provide that answer than it could reveal "the 'way to true being,' the 'way to true art,' the 'way to true nature,' the 'way to true God,' [or] the 'way to true happiness.'"[110]

That Weber considered the "way to true happiness" the last of these "former illusions," the one that succeeded the place of God, is revealing. He certainly believed that "the naive optimism in which science—that is, the technique of mastering life which rests upon science—has been celebrated as the way to happiness" was crumbling all around. "Who [still] believes in this?" he asked scornfully, "aside from a few big children in university chairs or editorial offices." Without clear moral directives and certain commands, each must find and obey the "demon who holds the fibers of his very life."[111]

This was the central dilemma of any society in which, as Adam Smith had observed, every man was left genuinely free "to pursue his own interest his own way," to find his *daimon* for himself. Laws could guarantee the pursuit of happiness. But the attainment, the "catching," must be left to individuals. As Smith well knew, and as Tocqueville, Mill, and Weber could see, individuals were precariously susceptible to the suasion of their fellow men. Without proper moral guidance, they must often fail. Was there not a danger, especially in the new hedonism of consumer-driven economies, that the majority would be overwhelmed by what Smith had called the "deception" that wealth and comfort alone could bring them what they want? Was there not a danger that in pursuing their elusive happiness, they would lead themselves and their fellow men astray?

This was the same thought that had given Rousseau such pause. We yearned for what our neighbor had—fine clothes, trinkets and baubles, a more splendid house—and chased what our neighbor chased, not because these things contributed to our genuine happiness, but because we believed that they would. The desires of men in society were determined largely by the desires of their fellow men. And from this Rousseau reasoned that any system that tolerated inequality was potentially ruinous, for invariably it would perpetuate envy and enmity, sapping virtue and sowing strife, blurring false desires with genuine needs. The same "deception" that Smith saw as the engine of growth in commercial societies was, for Rousseau, the cause of human pain.

Like the American Founding Fathers and their classical-liberal heirs, the father of capitalism believed that the risks of self-delusion far outweighed the perils of attempting to dictate others' needs. But even after the failed experiments in social engineering of the French Revolution, many others were not so sure. Moved by what they saw as the injustices of the market and the dubious choices of individuals when motivated by self-interest, rightly understood or not, they contemplated more ambitious solutions to the problem of discontent. "The very turmoil of the streets has something repulsive, something against which human nature rebels," Friedrich Engels observed of mid nineteenth-century London:

> The hundreds of thousands of all classes and ranks crowding past each other, are they not all human beings with the same qualities and powers, and with the same interest in being happy? And have they not, in the end, to seek happiness in the same way, by the same means? And still they crowd by one another as though they had nothing in common, nothing to do with one another. . . .[112]

The "brutal indifference, the unfeeling isolation of each in his private interest," struck Engels as "repellent and offensive," and he was hardly alone. Many shared his central assumption that the happiness of all lay in a common route, belying an unruffled faith that "science" could still be counted upon to reveal the "way to true happiness." Weber's judgment that only "big children in university chairs" could still evince that belief would prove tragically premature. For just as he wrote those words in the immediate aftermath of World War I, men and women to the east were consolidating bold claims on behalf of "science" in defense of the Bolshevik Revolution of 1917. The science of socialism, they believed—the "scientific socialism" of Marx and Engels—would serve as the guide to true happiness, turning individuals away from their petty pursuits and toward their common deliverance.

7

BUILDING
HAPPY WORLDS

"'Happiness our being's end and aim' is at bottom, if we will count well, not yet two centuries old in the world."[1] The claim was that of Thomas Carlyle, who borrowed the line from a pillar of the Enlightenment, the poet Alexander Pope. Carlyle's chronology was nearly flawless (he wrote in the 1840s). And with regard to the dramatic transformation that this new idea was working in the world, the irascible Scot was equally astute. As he observed in the ironically entitled chapter "Happy" of *Past and Present*, first published in 1843:

Every pitifulest whipster that walks within a skin has had his head filled with the notion that he is, shall be, or by all human and divine laws ought to be, "happy." His wishes, the pitifulest whipster's, are to be fulfilled for him; his days, the pitifulest whipster's, are to flow on in ever-gentle current of enjoyment, impossible even for the gods. The prophets preach to us, Thou shalt be happy; thou shalt love pleasant things, and find them. The people clamour, Why have we not found pleasant things?[2]

In the preceding year—the summer of 1842—hundreds of thousands of workers had taken to England's streets to protest against falling wages, abominable working conditions, political disenfranchisement, and the rising cost of bread. Dramatizing the uncertainties of Britain's new industrial economy, their actions moved Carlyle to both sympathy and indignation at false promises made. With stinking sewers and hellish factories, modern life could scarcely be said to maximize the greatest good for the greatest number. The "Greatest-Happiness Principle," he scowled, was "fast becoming a rather unhappy one."[3]

Carlyle attacked the heirs of the utilitarian tradition—Benthamite reformers and liberal economists—for failing to fulfill their promises. A Romantic at heart, he was also skeptical of the very notion that happiness could be provided by pleasure alone, delivered on demand in the form of pleasant things. This, he claimed, was a "pig philosophy" that reduced human beings to the level of beasts. The liberals, economists, and statesmen who now upheld this line—preaching competition and "a cold universal *Laissezfaire*"—were false prophets.[4] Modern economics, Carlyle observed in an oft-repeated line, was a "dismal science," and "Mammonworship a melancholy creed."[5] Even if one succeeded in extending pleasure to all, this would never be enough to give human beings what they need.

And what was it that human beings truly needed? Consult history, Carlyle challenged, compare past and present, and one would gain insight into this pressing question. A close-knit community, purposeful labor, a sense of God—these were the necessary requisites so evident in the England of the Middle Ages but so lacking in the world of today. If the power of industry had created vast wealth, which bulged in the pockets of the few, the many toiled as lifeless drones, chasing an illusory happiness without success or fulfillment. So, too, had the bonds of community been torn asunder. "Our life is not a mutual helpfulness," Carlyle complained, "but rather, cloaked under due laws-of-war, named 'fair competition' and so forth, it is mutual hostility."[6] Pitting individual against individual, the market's rules of engagement left all in "isolation" and the "totalest separation." Finally, the gospel of Mammon denied the greatest human need: for God, or the godlike in man. "God's Laws are become a Greatest Happiness Principle," Carlyle lamented. "There is no religion; there is no God; man has lost his soul."[7]

According to Carlyle's analysis, it was clear that the relief of suffering required more than simple pleasure. Community, meaningful labor, and the experience of God would be essential to the restoration of human beings. But how to provide those things, Carlyle did not really know. Like others of his century, he was inclined to look nostalgically to the past. Yet he also knew that there could be no simple return to simpler times. He spoke vaguely of the coming of new "heroes," of building a "true aristocracy," of giving religion new clothes. But his was a protest not a plan of action, a reckoning with past and present not with the future.

Reviewing the work in the year after its publication, Friedrich Engels found much in it to applaud. "Of all the fat books and thin pamphlets which have appeared in England in the past year . . . ," Karl Marx's lifelong collaborator observed, this "is the only one which is worth reading."[8] Then living in Manchester, and engaged in a study of the conditions of the English working class, Engels shared Carlyle's analysis of England's present state, with only minor qualifications:

This is the condition of England, according to Carlyle. An idle landowning aristocracy . . . a working aristocracy submerged in Mammonism, a gang of industrial buccaneers and pirates. A Parliament elected by bribery, a philosophy of simply looking on, of doing nothing, of *laissezfaire*, a worn out, crumbling religion, a total disappearance of all general human interest, a universal despair of truth and humanity, and in consequence a universal isolation of men in their own "brute individuality"; a chaotic, savage confusion of all aspects of life, a war of all against all, a general death of the spirit, a dearth of "soul," that is, of truly human consciousness: a disproportionately strong working class, in intolerable oppression and wretchedness. . . .[9]

Engels's close agreement with Carlyle does not end there. Despite his recognition that the Scottish critic was hardly a socialist, he looked with favor on his proposition that an "endless significance lies in work," that "labour is life," that "all true work is sacred." "Blessed is he who has found his work; let him ask no other blessedness," Carlyle observes in a modern beatitude that Engels cites with approval.[10] He whole-heartedly agrees that it is in community alone that one can find one's way. And he shares the conviction that in the past lies the key to the understanding of human destiny. Only on the subject of religion does Engels take pains to distinguish his views from Carlyle's largely German-inspired idealism. Yet even here, Engels the radical un-believer shows a surprising indulgence:

> We too are concerned with combating the lack of principle, the inner emptiness, the spiritual deadness, the untruthful-ness of the age; we are waging a war to the death against all these things, just as Carlyle is, and there is a much greater probability that we shall succeed than that he will, because we know what we want. We want to put an end to atheism, as Carlyle portrays it, by giving back to man the substance he has lost through religion; not as divine but as human substance.[11]

Engels and his comrades would overcome atheism by making a god of man. They would discover in history the "revelation of man." Indeed, Engels says explicit, "God is man." With these striking formulations, he promised to solve the "riddle of our time"—the Sphinx's riddle, the riddle of humanity that Carlyle had affirmed contained the "secret of all unhappy men and unhappy nations." "Happy is the man who answers it aright," Engels observes.[12] He would deliver that answer.

As we shall see, responding to the riddle of the times involved noth-ing less than confronting the riddles of the past, in particular that most perplexing of problems: Why had human beings suffered throughout the ages, living continually in contradiction with themselves? That question had exercised the Romantics, but increasingly, it was ex-tended to encompass not only the *maladie du siècle* but the sickness of

Odilon Redon, *Mystical Knight (Oedipus and the Sphinx)*, 1894, Musée Bonnat, Bayonne. Photo: Erich Lessing / Art Resource, NY. Carlyle observes in *Past and Present,* "That he who dwells in the temporary Semblances, and does not penetrate into the eternal Substance, will *not* answer the Sphinx-riddle of Today, or of any Day."

all time. With his protean powers, his knowledge and science, his technology and advanced understanding, could not man comprehend where he was and where he was going, what he might become? "There is no other salvation," Engels affirmed, than "returning firmly and honestly, not to 'God,' but to [man] himself."[13] Human beings would find themselves in the past, reveal themselves in history. But in order to follow that story—the story of Marx and Engels's solution of the riddle of human return—we need first to recount some others. Collectively, they tell of the consummation of an enormously powerful view of happiness that became, in time, a religion of its own.

History and the Unhappy Consciousness

There is a celebrated section in Hegel's *Phenomenology of Mind* (1807) that treats what this most German of German philosophers described as the "unhappy consciousness." To the unsuspecting reader, uninitiated in the mysterious arts of Hegelian hermeneutics, the section will appear, like so much of his writing, virtually incomprehensible. At every turn and in every paragraph, defiant passages block the reader's way, frustrating the advance of even the most intrepid inquirer:

> In the process, however, consciousness experiences just this appearance of particularity in the unchangeable, and of the unchangeable in particularity. Consciousness becomes aware of particularity *in general* in the immutable essence, and at the same time it there finds its own particularity. For the truth of this process is precisely that the double consciousness is one and single.[14]

Passages like these prompted the more cogent Schopenhauer to dismiss Hegel as an intellectual charlatan, the "producer of monstrous articulations of words that cancel and contradict one another . . . gradually destroying so completely his ability to think, that henceforth hollow, empty flourishes and phrases are regarded by him as thoughts."[15] Schopenhauer, it is true, bore a grudge. When, briefly in 1820, he offered a course at the University of Berlin at the same time as his rival, not a single student opted for Schopenhauerian pessimism over the Hegelian system. Alone in his lecture hall, Schopenhauer complained of the caprice of youth. But when he came, years later, to write a new preface to *The World as Will and Representation*, he was forced to acknowledge the extent of Hegel's influence. For twenty years, this charlatan had been extolled "as the greatest of philosophers so loudly that the echo was heard throughout Europe."[16] As a leading modern commentator has observed, with the possible exception of Marx, "no philosopher of the nineteenth or twentieth centuries has had as great an impact on the world as Hegel."[17]

Why this tremendous influence? Although the answers to that question are necessarily many and complex, one essential clue can be found in the section from the *Phenomenology of Mind* referred to above. Strictly speaking, "unhappy consciousness" (*unglückliches Bewusstsein*) was Hegel's term for a way of looking at the world that had been shaped by the historical force of pre-Reformation Christianity. By locating the divine in a "remote beyond," Christianity had erected a fatal division between the sacred and profane. Striving always for the unchanging spiritual God, men and women ran up continually against the changing needs and limitations of the material world. Their desires and demands were thus forever in conflict. "Divided and at variance with itself," the unhappy consciousness was a battlefield in which irreconcilable enemies raged. "Consciousness of life," as a consequence, "of its existence and action, [was] merely pain and sorry. . . ."[18]

In many respects this analysis was not original. Saints Paul and Augustine never spoke, precisely, of the "unhappy consciousness" or invoked Hegel's other term, "the alienated soul," but it is clear that something of this basic notion was perfectly in keeping with their understanding of the human condition. "For the good that I want to do I fail to do," Paul says famously in Romans 7:19, highlighting the degree to which human beings are divided within. "I practice the very evil that I do not want." A long line of theologians had developed the thought. Fatally rent by sin, human beings were condemned to live in conflict with themselves and with each other: Happiness was not in their constitutions.

It was precisely here, however, that Hegel introduced a revolutionary twist. For the "unhappy consciousness" in his reading was not a permanent feature of the human condition, a congenital defect to be remedied only by grace, but rather a transitional stage in the evolution of world history. True, all hitherto existing ages had known forms of what Hegel called "alienation" or "estrangement" (*Entfremdung* or *Entäusserung*), a profound sense of being sundered from one's environment, one's fellows, and one's self. But to the close student of world history, it became apparent that the forms of human alienation developed progressively over time, evolving in keeping with different historical contexts and different cultural circumstances. Thus, to Hegel, the "unhappy consciousness" of Christianity actually represented an advance over earlier, classical cultures that had failed to adequately address the spiritual dimension of humanity. In turn, the Christian unhappy consciousness was giving way to a more harmonious balance between our dual yearnings for spiritual and material freedom. In a process of creative destruction that had taken on particular force since the Reformation, men and women were being led to transform their outer world to more closely reflect their inner need for spiritual freedom. Gradually, progressively, human beings were overcoming alienation. Someday the unhappy consciousness would prove a relic of the past.

Of this there could be no doubt: The historical process was working in the service of human deliverance. Looking backward, the view admittedly was bleak. At no point had man yet attained that "harmony with himself" that Hegel associated with genuine happiness. As he later acknowledged, "It is possible to consider history from the point of view of happiness, but history is not the soil in which happiness grows. The periods of happiness in it are the blank pages of history." On the contrary, human history had served as an altar, a "slaughter bench" to which the "happiness of peoples" had been brought for sacrifice.[19] But looking forward, it became clear that men and women would not have suffered in vain. For this same process of creative destruction was leading humanity ever closer to its final realization, the full flowering of "Freedom."

Notoriously, Hegel was never entirely clear as to what this final Freedom would entail, a vagueness that undoubtedly contributed to its appeal. And many were at a loss to explain his odd suggestion that his native Prussia represented the closest thing to Freedom's contemporary realization, an ideally rational state. Still, there were some tantalizing suggestions to tempt his followers' fancy. In *The Philosophy of Right*, for example, the work in which Hegel discusses Freedom at greatest length, he makes clear that its ultimate realization would be social. Final Freedom, that is, would entail not just the overcoming of individual alienation—reconciling men and women to nature and to themselves—but also the overcoming of social alienation, reconciling men and women to each other. In a context of close-knit, organic community, the freedom of each would be bound up with the freedom of all. In Hegel's view, the development of this process could already be seen at work in contemporary civil society:

In the course of the actual attainment of selfish ends—an
attainment conditioned in this way by universality—there is
formed a system of complete interdependence, wherein the
livelihood, happiness, and legal status of one man is inter-
woven with the livelihood, happiness, and rights of all. On
this system, individual Happiness, &c. depend, and only in
this connected system are they actualized and secured.[20]

With the progressive march of Freedom, individuals were being reconciled to one another while at the same time being reconciled to
themselves.

A necessary corollary to this process was that men and women would
cease to experience desire "inauthentically" in a manner not purely
consonant with their own true needs. Like Rousseau, Hegel appreciated quite early on that in modern commercial societies, individuals'
desires and needs were generated by the desires and needs of others.
Implanted by advertising, dictated by fashion, and determined by style,
individual desire was always socially determined, shaped by the particular contexts in which we live. And nowhere was this more true than
with luxury items and the sources of pleasure that can be continually,
endlessly refined. In an economy of rapid innovation, yesterday's state-
of-the art convenience could quickly become a source of pain.

What the English call "comfort" is something inexhaustible
and illimitable. Others can reveal to you that what you take to
be comfort at any stage is discomfort, and these discoveries
never come to an end. Hence the need for greater comfort
does not exactly arise within you directly; it is suggested to
you by those who hope to make a profit from its creation.[21]

Such a situation created a "system of needs" that were anything but,
generating desires that failed to respond to authentic longings, while
placing individuals in conflict with the collective good.

In the state of Freedom, these tensions between private interest
and public good—long assumed by those in the liberal tradition to be

a permanent feature of social life—would gradually wither away. Individual desires would still be shaped by social forces, but now each member of the community would truly want just what was of genuine service to the community as a whole. In turn, the community would look after each of its members like integral parts of a body, perfectly articulating their separate needs. In such a state, the conflict between freedom and necessity would cease to exist. All would want only what they should want; all would want only what they needed.

It has often been remarked—and with reason—that Hegel's vision of the triumph of Freedom is not only utopian but also potentially dangerous in its obliteration of the distinction between the individual and society. This would seem even more the case when one considers the nature of the force guiding this great world-historical deliverance. Hegel gave it different names at different times. He called it "Idea." He called it "Reason." He called it "Spirit." He called it "God." And whatever else one might say about the complicated religious views of this man whose early professional training was in theology, it is clear that his use of the divine epithet in this instance was not wholly misplaced. For his was a system that gave logic, direction, and purpose to the whole of human history; a system that explained the riddle of human unhappiness in unqualified terms. Like the Romantics, Hegel refused to turn a blind eye to the undeniable fact of suffering, to dismiss it blithely, in the Enlightenment tradition, as solely the result of ignorance, a deficit of pleasure, or interested error. Yet neither did he throw up his hands in Romantic despair, seeking ephemeral solace from the pain of human existence in fleeting joy or the illusions of art. Still less did he attempt to alleviate public misery by maximizing personal liberty, harnessing individual selfishness and desire to virtue. Rather, Hegel *explained* suffering, describing his narration of history as the "recollection and Golgotha of the Absolute Spirit."[22] This was what Christians since Leibniz had called theodicy. Hegel himself used the term. But his was a "true theodicy," he claimed, a science that explained suffering rather than explaining it away.[23] Offering justification for the pain of the past and the promise of future redemption, Hegel's system gave reason to unhappiness and offered hope that it would one day be brought to an end. This, in large measure, was the secret of its success.

It was, moreover, the secret of success of a great number of movements that flourished in the nineteenth century. Not all were explicitly indebted to Hegel. But all shared his conviction that the new "science" of history held the key to the riddle of man. Like him, they promised forms of deliverance, forms of redemption. And like him, they saw, on the horizon of the future, the glimmer of happiness's rising sun. But whereas Hegel was content to speak in the abstractions of German idealism, others were prepared to describe the coming world in far more explicit terms.

No-Place Is Someplace

Nauvoo, Illinois, would seem an odd place at any time to undertake a great experiment in human happiness. But in 1849—only two years after angry local mobs had expelled the Church of Jesus Christ of Latter-day Saints (the Mormons) for the sin of having chosen this Mississippi port city as their Zion—the designation was more unlikely still. Undaunted, several hundred "New Icarian" socialists arrived in that year, intent on planting joy.

The Icarians were hardly in a position to quibble. Humble artisans and workers, for the most part, they had recently fled the urban squalor, political repression, and economic uncertainties of an industrializing Europe. Lured from the Old World by the promise of freedom and fertile lands in the New, they had arrived initially in Texas intent on building there the "New Icaria," the ideal city described by their visionary leader, the Frenchman Étienne Cabet, in his utopian tract *Voyage en Icarie* (1840). In Texas, they would put an end to social strife, while putting into practice what Cabet described as "true Christianity," a species of egalitarian communism in which private property would be abolished and all would work in harmonious fellowship toward the common good.

Expecting Eden, the Icarians found deception instead: no welcome, no preparations, no land. Cabet had not even arrived, and when he did,

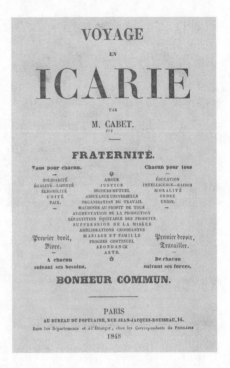

The title page to an 1848 edition of Cabet's *Voyage to Icaria*, promising "fraternity" and "mutual happiness." Beinecke Rare Book and Manuscript Library, Yale University.

his followers were ready to sue him for fraud. Somehow, with blandishments and persuasion, the charismatic leader succeeded in rallying their spirits and assuring them that all would be well. He recalled the chant they had sung on the decks as their ship sailed from Le Havre:

> Arise, workers stooped in dust,
> The hour of awakening has sounded.
> To American shores the banner is going to wave,
> The banner of the holy community.
> No more vices, no more suffering,
> No more crimes, no more pain,
> The august Equality advances itself:
> Proletariat, dry your tears.
> Soldiers of Fraternity,
> Let us go to found in Icaria,
> The happiness of Humanity![24]

If Icaria could not be built in Texas, then let it be raised in Nauvoo! With a ready-made meeting hall, a temple, barracks, and other facilities left behind by the Mormons, the site was well suited for an experiment in communal living. It was also cheap. And so, somewhat bedraggled, with funds already waning but enthusiasm still high, Cabet and company set about creating a happy world in Illinois based on fellowship, sexual equality, and common ownership.

The experiment proved short-lived. Within scarcely a year, a tornado had decimated the once spectacular Mormon temple, fires had razed the stables and windmill, and a cholera epidemic had carried off twenty settlers. Financial constraints forced the community to rely on the sale of whiskey to the local population to finance its operation, while mismanagement, disease, and the authoritarian tendencies of Cabet led to further dissent among his followers. Despite some successes—a thriving workers' orchestra, free education, and the partial integration of the sexes—by 1856 the community had split into two factions, with the majority burning Cabet in effigy and banishing him from Icaria. He would die later that year in St. Louis, broken, lonely, and depressed. The "happiness of Humanity," clearly, was not yet at hand.

The story of the Icarian settlement in Nauvoo, at once tragic and darkly comic, is symbolic of the wider fate of the so-called utopian socialist movements of the first half of the nineteenth century. Like Cabet's Icarians, the followers of such men as Robert Owen (1771–1858), Charles Fourier (1772–1837), and Henri de Saint-Simon (1760–1825) attempted to build model communities in Europe and America, squatting on ground once occupied by Christians. They ultimately failed, although in doing so, they succeeded in registering powerful indictments of the world around them, dramatizing both the tremendous costs and the staggering potential of modern industry and science. In the process, they gave new impetus to the dream of happiness in all its contradictions, promising perpetual felicity in this life to many who had never dared consider the thought.

There is, in fact, no more central term in the lexicon of these early socialists. The poor son of an ironmonger from Wales, Robert Owen found time to study Bentham while accumulating a self-made fortune in textiles. The word "happiness" was never far from his lips. Whether pursuing practical reforms for his workers at his model factory in New Lanark, Scotland, penning treatises on perfect communities, or attempting to create such communities in England or America, Owen sought always to promote the greatest good of the greatest number. In the process, he went far beyond anything Bentham had ever considered, dreaming of a:

> Rational System . . . purposely formed to promote the well-
> being and happiness of every man, woman, and child, of every
> clime and color [that would] by degrees amalgamate the
> human race into one cordially-united intelligent family, with
> one language, one interest, and one object, namely, the
> permanent happiness of all.[25]

As announced in Owenite publications, and proclaimed by Owenite publicists, the goal of their leader was nothing less than "happiness from birth to death, for all." In the coming kingdom, happiness would flow so freely that "all that have life," including the beasts of the field, would know it.[26]

Saint-Simon also affirmed that in the finely calibrated social system of the future, every man would be induced to work joyfully "for his own happiness, for that of his family, and for that of humanity."[27] Born a count, he had fought with French forces in the American Revolutionary War, joining Washington at the Battle of Yorktown. He was later taken prisoner by the British in the West Indies. During France's own Revolution, Saint-Simon made a fortune speculating in confiscated real estate (he was even rumored to have tried to buy Notre Dame Cathedral) but was then imprisoned by the Jacobins and subsequently lost everything he had through the treachery of a business partner and his own extravagance. In the decades that followed, Saint-Simon survived a suicide attempt, a stint in a madhouse, and visitations by the ghost of his alleged ancestor Charlemagne. Yet still he managed to surround himself with some of the brightest young men in Europe and to produce an impressive body of writing on the state of

European society. In virtually all of it, Saint-Simon looked happily forward. With justice does his tombstone at the Père-Lachaise Cemetery in Paris read, "The Golden Age is not in the past it is in the future."

Charles Fourier also painted a consistently joyous picture of the coming "Dawn of Happiness" and of its sweet foretaste in his idealized community, the Phalanx:

> Universal happiness and gaiety will reign. A unity of interest and views will arise, crime and violence will disappear. There will be no individual dependence—no private servants, only maids, cooks, and the like, all working for all (when they please). Elegance and luxury will be had by everyone. The Phalanx will be devoted to the service of useful labor, of the sciences, the arts, and of cuisine. It will render industry attractive, and end the evil distinction between Producers and Consumers.[28]

Fourier's writings are replete with such bold speculations, laid out in the straightforward, if grandiose, terms of a man who professed a life-long disdain for the abstractions of philosophers and the absurdities of lettered men. This hardly protected Fourier from sweeping absurdities of his own, but it did give even his wildest pronouncements an earthiness often lacking in the writings of social theorists like Hegel. In the eyes of this failed traveling salesman, when happiness finally blossomed in the world, it would be not a matter of theoretical sophistication but the sweet smell of satisfied desire.

Happiness, then, was a common category of this early socialist language, invoked with great frequency by Cabet, Owen, Saint-Simon, and Fourier. Which is not to say that these men presented happiness in identical terms, or that they proposed attaining it in precisely the same way. Divergence and disagreement abound. Whereas Cabet and Owen, for example, envisioned perfect equality, the common ownership of goods, and grassroots autonomy as final conditions of a happy world, Saint-Simon imagined a technocratic hierarchy in which highly skilled elites would manage industry, science, and the

Dominique Louis Papety, *Un Rêve de bonheur*, Musée Vivenel,
Compiègne. Photo: Réunion des Musées Nationaux / Art Resource, NY.
Papety's painting, shown at the Paris Salon of 1843,
was inspired by his reading of Fourier.

arts in the service of the masses. Fourier retained a place for private
property, spurning total equality as unsuited to individuals whose
needs and abilities varied widely. In his opinion, happiness entailed
the full satisfaction of the passions, which, in his idiosyncratic psychology, varied extensively according to 810 basic personality types:

> Happiness, about which so much, or rather so much nonsense,
> has been talked, consists in having many passions and many
> means of satisfying them. [In the present civilization] we
> have few passions and hardly sufficient means to satisfy a
> quarter of them; this is why our globe is for the moment one
> of the most miserable in the universe. Other planets may
> experience equal unhappiness, but none can suffer more.[29]

In the perfect world of the Phalanx, personalities would be matched
to complement one another, and the passions—for love, friendship,

ambition, touch, taste, and the like—given ample room to play. In contrast to the comparatively chaste communities envisioned by Owen, Cabet, and Saint-Simon, Fourier imagined a "new amorous world" of free love liberated from the many constraints imposed on our sensual needs.

These are only a number of the many distinctions that one can draw between these systems. Arguably of greater significance are the similarities. For though these early socialists might disagree over the particulars of pleasure in the world to come, they were far more united regarding the immediate sources of pain. In great detail, they decried the changes that were beginning to transform the landscape of early capitalism: the swings of the business cycle that periodically left entire sectors of the workforce on the brink of starvation; the terrible conditions of factories and mines, in which women and children were forced to toil like beasts alongside their husbands and fathers; the brutal crowding of slums and hovels, where untold numbers were drawn in waves of urbanization, rendered fodder for sickness and disease. It may be argued that such conditions were hardly worse than the formidable challenges of survival that faced the poor in preindustrial economies. But they were undeniably new, and so all the more threatening for their lack of precedent.

A large part of the appeal of the utopian socialists, in fact, was their ability to give poignant voice at an early stage of capitalist development to the ravages and uncertainties of change. Often with prescience, they generalized from the experience of the advanced industrial centers in Europe to construct broad analyses of the apparently chaotic nature of modern society. For Saint-Simon, the "sentiment of egotism" that he believed was a characteristic feature of modern economies had "become dominant in all classes and in all individuals."[30] Owen lashed out at the spirit of "contention and opposition" that pitted man against man and class against class, while Fourier railed against "industrial anarchy" and its "illusions of happiness." Bankruptcy, smuggling, usury, speculation, hoarding, parasitism, and cheating were the "vices inherent in the commercial mechanism," and they were vast.[31] The world that had been created by modern industry and commerce was a

Robert Owen, *The Crisis
or the Change from Error and
Misery to Truth and Happiness*
(1832). By permission of
the British Library.

canting, hypocritical world that protected the strong and brutalized
the weak; a world that fomented social strife, leaving vast numbers of
the population without resources or agency; a topsy-turvy world that
saw the wretchedness of the people increase "in direct proportion to
the advance of industry."[32]

Adept at articulating the suffering of transition and change, the
utopian socialists registered powerful protests on behalf of the vulnerable against what they saw as the more destructive features of modern economic life. Their visions of happiness, accordingly, were based
in large measure on removing these sources of pain. As one of Owen's
deputies, John Gray, observed in a widely circulated *Lecture on Human
Happiness* in 1825:

Let societies be formed for the purpose of *annihilating the
causes*, whence the evils of mankind arise,—societies, not to
relieve the miserable, but to abolish the cause of misery; not
to assist the poor with money, but to abolish the causes of

poverty; not to detect thieves, but to take away the multitude
of temptation to steal; societies having for their avowed
purpose an equal distribution of the means of happiness to all,
and of the combining of all mankind in unity, peace, and
concord. Only *give birth* to societies founded on this principle;
they will ask for no continued support.[33]

Do away with the sources of misery, and happiness would follow naturally on its own.

Such observations give credence to a point later made by George Orwell: "Nearly all creators of utopia have resembled the man who has toothache, and therefore thinks happiness consists in not having toothache."[34] They also follow logically from Enlightenment assumptions, which tended, as we have seen, to present happiness as a natural condition and course. Happiness, in the Enlightened view, was impeded only by pain-inducing prejudice, practice, and false belief. Remove those obstacles, and individuals would be free to follow their natural trajectory.

The utopian socialists—above all, Owen with his acknowledged debt to Bentham—were heirs to this aspect of the Enlightenment tradition. Yet their thinking about happiness also departed significantly from what had come before. In the first place, whereas Enlightenment theorists and their liberal successors tended to conceive of happiness primarily in individual terms, the utopians regarded the community as the sole category in which discussions of happiness made sense. There were, to be sure, important precedents for this emphasis: Plato, whom Robert Owen invoked directly, equated happiness and justice in the *Republic*, making every member of his ideal realm subservient to the broader collective good of the polis. Other classical philosophers did much the same. There were also important warrants for such communitarian thinking in the Catholic tradition. And in their own ways, Rousseau, and later, the Jacobins, reinvigorated the emphasis on the social whole even at the expense of its parts.

The utopian socialists, however, went beyond those earlier precedents, arguing that happiness must be extended to *all*. It was not

enough, they maintained, merely to provide the conditions in which
some were allowed to maximize personal pleasure. And it was not
enough to think of the community as an abstraction, the sum total, in
Bentham's words, "of the interests of the several members who compose it."[35] The whole was greater than its parts. Unless all were happy,
none could be happy. The sight of suffering of even a few was a rebuke to the many.

This emphasis on the complete and total extension of happiness—
with its attendant appeal to the least fortunate members of society—
provided early socialists with a powerful source of attraction, as well
as an incisive means to criticize contemporary society, in which so
many, so plainly, suffered terribly. It also helped to justify their withdrawal into self-enclosed communities. For given the present stage of
social development, utopians argued, the happiness of the whole could
be ensured only in isolation. The New Icaria of Cabet, or the Phalanxes
of Fourier would thus serve as temporary oases, an avant-garde for the
wider transformation that would follow.

That this wider transformation was coming, and coming soon, was
not in doubt, a conviction that the utopians based largely on their reading of the past. And here, in the unfolding of history, was another key
aspect of the utopians' understanding of happiness that distinguished
them from their forebears. Much like Hegel, although without his
scope and without his abstraction, the utopians conceived of history
as purposeful development, an organic unfolding of creation, destruction, and rebirth. Rather than see the past, as many Enlightenment
thinkers had done, as the dark record of fanaticism and superstition,
the utopians understood history as process. "Each age has its own
character," Saint-Simon affirmed, and thus each age must be understood on its own terms.[36] Looking backward, he saw periods of relative cultural wholeness—"organic ages"—such as the ancient world
or medieval Christendom, giving way, in turn, to "critical ages," in
which the norms and beliefs that had made sense in a given epoch were
called into question and eventually succumbed to the creative destruction of the new. The present period—encompassing the whole
of the upheavals of the Enlightenment and the French Revolution—

was just such a critical age, an age of transition. But it was already giving birth to a new organic age that, in Saint-Simon's view, would mark the end of this long historical cycle of creation and destruction. The final age would not only be organic, it would be golden.

Fourier also envisioned history as a continual oscillation between periods of "harmony" and periods of "social chaos," agreeing that a new dawn of happiness was on the horizon, even if it was still hard for many to see. "Beset by long-standing misfortunes and bound by the chains of habit," people still imagined that they were destined "to a life of privations." It would "take some time for them to become accustomed to the idea of happiness that awaits them."[37] Dawn, nonetheless, was breaking. When Robert Owen waxed lyrical on the approaching "terrestrial paradise," he spoke for all utopians. "The period for introducing the Rational System, for remodeling the character of man, and for governing the population of the earth in unity, peace, progressive improvement, and happiness, is near at hand; and no human power can successfully resist the change...."[38] History was on humanity's side.

The very term that Owen used to describe this coming dawn—"terrestrial paradise"—is indicative of one other distinctive feature of this early utopian socialism: its self-conscious religiosity. It is true that Owen liked to portray himself as an heir to the freethinking, anticlerical tradition of Bentham. But neither he nor his followers could avoid invoking with regularity the biblical language of Protestant Christianity. His talk of the "Second Coming of the Truth" and his *Book of the New Moral World* spoke for themselves, highlighting Owen's effort to define a "new religion"—based on reason, history, and affective sentiment—to replace what he believed were the untenable aspects of the faiths of old. His direct appeal to the downtrodden and the meek, his insistence on describing the coming kingdom in millennial terms, and his willingness to contemplate the progressive understanding of the "moving Power of the Universe" allowed more avowedly Christian followers to see in Owen's "religion of charity" a purer form of the teaching of Christ. When one such disciple, John Finch, wrote to "Father Owen" in 1838 asking to become a "bishop" in the church of his "New Moral World," he was giving voice to a much wider impulse.[39]

This impulse was also on display among the followers of Fourier, who proved adept at subsuming his theories into narratives of the Christian millennium. Toward the end of his life, Fourier himself gave increasing, if never entirely wholehearted, encouragement to this trend, speaking of himself as the Messiah of Reason. His disciples showed far less restraint, embracing their departed master as "the man chosen by Christ" to usher in the kingdom of God on earth. In America, a "Church of Humanity" was established, in which parishioners sang Fourierist prayers and worshipped before busts of Christ and his august successor.[40]

Even clearer was the religious dynamic at work in the thought and practice of Cabet and Saint-Simon. Cabet spent the last fifteen years of his life attempting to demonstrate that the Gospels provided clear evidence that "the entire philosophy, the entire social doctrine of Jesus Christ and of Christianity constituted, in essence, Community." In Cabet's reading, Christ was a revolutionary who had attacked the Roman and Jewish aristocracies and who preached "the abolition of slavery, the equality and Fraternity of men and people, the freeing of women, the abolition of opulence and misery, the destruction of priestly power, and finally, the community of goods."[41] As Cabet stressed in the *Voyage to Icaria* and again at length in his 1846 tract, *The True Christianity*, "communism [was] the same thing as Christianity in the purity of origin."[42]

Saint-Simon thought of his own doctrine as Christianity new and improved. Developing this view slowly throughout the course of his career, he gave it purest expression in his final work, *The New Christianity*. "Religion must direct society toward the great goal of the rapid improvement of the conditions of the poorest class," he urged.[43] It was religion alone that could move men to live as brothers, religion alone that would lead human beings to give up their selfish independence. His disciples took him at his word, establishing a monastery of sorts at their retreat at Ménilmontant on the outskirts of Paris. There they said Saint-Simonian mass long after the master's death, dispatched pilgrims throughout the whole of Europe, and even set out on a journey to Egypt to investigate reports of a female messiah.

Such outlandishness highlights the fact that these "religions" were far from orthodox in any conventional Christian sense. Quick to attack what they regarded as the injustices and absurdities of the established churches, they borrowed from doctrine and scripture as they saw fit, doing away almost entirely with discussion of an afterlife, or the divinity of Christ. Characteristically, Saint-Simon reduced the whole of Christianity to one precept, the golden rule, the sublime injunction to treat one's fellow as one's brother. It was only, he underscored, by seeking "to procure for humankind the greatest degree of happiness that it can achieve during its worldly existence, that you will succeed in establishing Christianity."[44] This was an earthly ethic par excellence, like all these religions, a religion of life.

Yet it would be a mistake to assume, as generations of·commentators have done, that the religious language of the utopian socialists was merely an aberration, a late, false turn, somehow peripheral to the core experiment of early socialism itself. On the contrary, religious language was central to these utopian movements precisely because it was religion—the Christian religion—that they sought to replace. As an insightful recent observer has noted in the context of Fourier's early writings, "'socialism' began as an attempt to discover a successor . . . to the Christian Church."[45] As every one of these early utopians understood—drawing in this respect on the wider cultural climate of Romanticism and the religious revival of the first part of the nineteenth century—the Enlightenment had opened up a void that needed to be filled. Just as in that other great age of transition, the time of the passage from classical civilization to Christianity, "the need of a religion, capable of replacing the old, was [now] making itself felt."[46] The utopian socialists understood that need and attempted to respond accordingly. Bread was of great importance, they knew. But there was more to life than bread.

Which takes us to the heart of these movements' power as well as to their glaring paradox. For what the utopians offered was nothing less than imminent transcendence, heaven on earth, the kingdom of

God made by men. Happiness everlasting—this was the impossible promise put forth to men and women primed to expect the final satisfaction of desire, a definitive end to pain, the ceaseless flowing abundance of a new golden age in which all would be gods except God himself.

Needless to say, it was precisely such contradictions that spelled these movements' failure, underscoring the "utopian" in utopian socialism. Yet before they are lumped together with all those dreamers, before and since, who have dreamed of perfect worlds, it is worth reflecting on the ironies of the term. The phrase "utopian socialism" was first employed by Marx and Engels to distinguish their own "scientific socialism" from the "pocket editions of the New Jerusalem," the "new social gospel" heralded by their predecessors.[47] When viewed from the vantage point of the twenty-first century, this condescension is amusing, for the dreams of Marx and Engels now scarcely seem less utopian than those of Cabet, Owen, Fourier, and Saint-Simon. But the irony of the term considered against its historical background is even richer. "Utopia," it will be recalled, was Thomas More's invention, a word derived in the early sixteenth century from the Greek *ou* (not) or *eu* (good) + *topos* (place) to signify "no place" or "good place." Intended as a foil, More's literary kingdom was a critical standard against which to weigh the human folly of his time. But the term itself underscored its fanciful nature. In a world of imperfection, perfection was impossible; strictly speaking, utopia could not exist.

In the aftermath of the Enlightenment and the French Revolution, however, as men and women became increasingly conscious of the incredible possibilities of modern industry and science and of their "natural right" to happiness, utopia took on new meaning. The writings of Fourier, Owen, and Saint-Simon, accordingly, were treated just like Cabet's *Voyage to Icaria*—not simply as thought experiments, models to be contemplated, but as blueprints to be put into effect. And so they were. Owen's model textile factory at New Lanark paved the way for more ambitious attempts to translate his utopian theories into practice. Some sixteen model communities were launched between 1825 and 1830, the most famous at "New Harmony," Indiana, in 1825–27. The followers of Fourier quickly followed suit. In Romania, France, and Russia, in Great Britain, Brazil, and other parts of the New World, Phalanxes were established, including some thirty across the United States during the fifteen years following Fourier's death in 1837. With the exception of their monastic base in Paris, the Saint-Simonians did not attempt to found model communities. But they dispatched their missionaries and exported their gospel throughout the world, working to make realities of dreams. Cabet's Icarians were not alone.

However fleetingly, however imperfectly, the "no-place" of utopia was being transformed in the nineteenth century into "some-place." The early socialists fell short of perfection. But in their blend of religion, science, and the elucidation of the past, they gestured toward the future. The point was not to contemplate a better world but to make it, not to interpret but to change. In spreading the post-Enlightenment

An early nineteenth-century engraving of Owen's factory and model community in New Lanark, Scotland, after the original by John Winning. Photo courtesy of the New Lanark Conservation Trust.

dream of happiness to even the humblest of humanity, they prepared the way for far more ambitious attempts to come.

Solving the Riddle of History

When one is flipping through the pages of that dusty monument to the culture of communism, *The Great Soviet Encyclopedia*, happiness is not the first subject that comes to mind. Yet there it is, tucked inconspicuously between "Hammerhead Stork" (*Scopus umbretta*) and "Hard Alloys." Happiness:

> The human spirit's consciousness of that state of being which corresponds to the greatest inner satisfaction with the condition of one's existence, to a full and meaningful life, and to the realization of one's life purpose.

A "normative and value-bound concept," happiness, the reader further learns, has a "historical and class basis":

> In the history of moral consciousness, happiness has been considered an innate human right; but in practice, in a society of class antagonisms, as F. Engels pointed out, the oppressed classes' striving toward happiness has always been ruthlessly and "lawfully" sacrificed to the ruling classes' identical striving.

In what the encyclopedia calls this "bourgeois-individualistic interpretation of happiness," the rich man's search for pleasure is the poor man's pain, a search that "divorced from social aims, degenerates into egoism, . . . tramples upon the interests of others and morally cripples the human personality." "If one wishes to be an animal," the entry continues, citing Marx, "one may, of course, turn one's back on the sufferings of humanity and worry about one's own skin." But true communists would think more highly of man, recognizing that it was only "through conscientious service to people and through a revolutionary struggle to transform society, to realize the ideals of communism, and to achieve a better future for all humanity that man imbues his life with that higher meaning and is granted that profound satisfaction which he perceives as happiness."[48]

The latter are not Marx's precise words. And "happiness" is probably not the first topic that comes to mind when flipping through the pages of *his* works, either. The combative scholar and activist could be scathing on the subject, pouring scorn on the happy fantasies of both "false" socialists and "true" capitalists alike. When asked, in a parlor game, to give his own definition of the word, Marx replied in English without hesitation: "Happiness: to fight."[49] This would not seem the response of a contented man.

Marx's own father certainly had such concerns, writing to his son in 1837, when young Karl was just nineteen years old, "Does your heart correspond to your head? Does it have room for the softer feelings of this world, which provide such essential comfort for the man of feeling in this vale of woe?" Herr Marx granted that his son was "obviously animated and ruled by a demon not given to all men," but whether this daimon was of a heavenly or a Faustian variety, he did not know. "Will you ever—and this is the doubt that causes me the most pain—be receptive to true human happiness . . . ? Will you ever . . . be able to spread happiness to your immediate surroundings?"[50]

Good bourgeois that he was, Marx's father worried chiefly about "domestic happiness," and on this score, his son was reasonably successful, fathering a flock of children with his first love, Jenny, to whom he remained faithfully attached (if not always faithful) throughout his life. But in theory, at least, Marx was obliged to discount such happiness, depicting marriage and the nuclear family in his writings as a bourgeois institution whose pleasures were illusory and whose days were numbered. More certain as a source of satisfaction was work.

Marx grew convinced of this proposition at an early age. While still a schoolboy, he drafted an essay in Latin, "Reflections of a Young Man on the Choice of a Profession" (1835), which emphasized the sacred importance of work as a determinant of well-being. The choice of a "sphere of activity," he observed, "is a great privilege of man over the rest of creation, but at the same time it is an act which can destroy his whole life, frustrate all his plans, and make him unhappy." Man's freedom entailed a perilous choice. Either he could live in keeping with the "general aim" intended by the "Deity"— that of "ennobling mankind and himself"—or, choosing wrongly, he might devote his life to pointless labor for which he possessed little talent or relish. Worse still, he could choose a profession that involved "reprehensible acts" or that forced him to be a "servile tool." In all of these cases, self-contempt would form in the breast like a serpent, "sucking the life-blood from one's heart and mixing it with the poison of misanthropy and despair."

What did the young Marx conclude was the proper choice, the highest choice? His answer is at once soaringly world-historical and deeply grounded in the past:

> History calls those men the greatest who have ennobled themselves by working for the common good; experience acclaims as happiest the man who has made the greatest number of people happy; religion itself teaches us that the ideal being whom all strive to copy sacrificed himself for the sake of mankind, and who would dare to set at nought such judgments?
>
> If we have chosen the position in life in which we can most of all work for mankind, no burdens can bow us down, because they are sacrifices for the benefit of all; then we shall experience no petty, limited, selfish joy, but our happiness will belong to millions, our deeds will live on quietly but perpetually at work, and over our ashes will be shed the hot tears of noble people.[51]

It is safe to say that tears have been shed on Marx's grave, whether of sadness or of joy. But more surprising to many will be his early invocation of Christ, that "ideal being," as a model of virtuous behavior. The mature Marx quickly abandoned these childish illusions. Yet he never entirely severed the umbilical cord that tied happiness to salvation in his thought. The "critique of religion is therefore in embryo a *critique of the vale of tears*, whose *halo* is religion," Marx commented famously in his 1844 "Contribution to the Critique of Hegel's Philosophy of Right."[52] A critique of Marx, by contrast, is a critique of the remnants of religion in his philosophy. And the halo of this is happiness.

Many still instinctively deny such connections between Marx's "science," on the one hand, and what he tried so hard to condemn as a dangerous addiction, "the opium of the people," on the other. Certainly it is hard to find Marx himself saying anything nice about religion after his "conversion" to atheism at university in the late 1830s. And his choice of subject for a doctoral dissertation—a study of the philosophy of nature in the Greek philosophers Democritus and Epicurus—would seem ideally suited to a man preparing himself for a career as an unrepentant materialist. Describing Epicurus as the "greatest representative of Greek Enlightenment," one who "investigates the essential relationship of the human soul," Marx cited Lucretius's encomium to the sage of pleasure with obvious approval:

> When human life lay groveling in all men's sight, crushed to
> the earth under the dead weight of religion whose grim
> features loured menacingly upon mortals from the four quar-
> ters of the sky, a man of Greece was first to raise mortal eyes
> in defiance, first to stand erect and brave the challenge.
> Fables of the gods did not crush him, nor the lightning flash
> and growling menace of the sky. . . . Therefore religion in its
> turn lies crushed beneath his feet, and we by his triumph are
> lifted level with the skies.[53]

Is this not the heroic image of Marx himself so venerated by later admirers?—that of the man who toppled idols, dispelling the fears of the masses so as to prepare them, like Epicurus, for genuine happiness? As Marx would comment several years later in one of his most celebrated lines: "The overcoming of religion as the *illusory* happiness [*illusorischen Glücks*] of the people is the demand for their real happiness [*wirklichen Glücks*]."[54]

It is precisely here, in the pledge to provide "real" happiness in the space once occupied by religion, that one catches a hint of the sacred halo. It is a pledge reminiscent of the gospel of Lequinio and the Jacobin representatives-on-mission—a ray of the promise that, when "lifted level with the skies," humanity would live, as Epicurus had claimed, "as gods among men," leaving their unhappiness behind.

This sacred promise—with its vestigial elements of religious redemption—can be seen most clearly in Marx's critical writings of the mid- to late 1840s, above all in his "Economico-Philosophical Manuscripts of 1844," and the "Contribution to the Critique of Hegel's Philosophy of Right," written in the same year. Preoccupied in these works with the concerns of the radical followers of Hegel—the so-called Young or Left Hegelians who wished to push the master's teachings in a more revolutionary direction—Marx put forth as an explicit political goal what Hegel himself had understood as the natural work of the spirit: the overcoming of human alienation and the healing of the unhappy consciousness. Making ample use of Hegel's words (*Entäusserung* and *Entfremdung*) to describe the condition of contemporary human alienation and estrangement, Marx considerably expanded Hegel's analysis of their causes and kinds.

Unlike animals, who are "immediately one" with their life activity and surroundings, human beings are out of sorts.[55] They are estranged from nature, which they view as foreign, hostile, something to be conquered, exploited, or subdued. They are estranged from themselves and their fellow men, whom they regard similarly as aliens and outsiders, having lost their original sense of what Marx termed "species-being," their natural sense of communal identity and belonging to the human species. And they are estranged from their active function—their labor—which they regard as dehumanizing. There were other forms of alienation as well—most important, alienation from God, whom Marx regarded, following the German philosopher Ludwig Feuerbach, as a human invention invested with abstract power that drained human beings of life, lording over them as a hostile, reified creation. Alienation was thus the subjugation to idols of human making, and of these there were many.

But it was above all the estrangement from life activity—the alienation of labor—that Marx regarded as the crucial concern. For in his rapidly evolving system, man was *homo faber*, a creature who defines himself by what he makes and does. Economic activity—work—was thus the key to all else, a fact that was most apparent among the poor in contemporary capitalist societies, where, Marx believed, human alienation was more pronounced than at any other stage in human history. In the dismal factories of Manchester studied by Engels, in the sweatshops of Paris, and throughout the developed world, human beings were being forced to produce objects over which they exercised no ownership or control, and for which they could feel no immediate connection. The fruit of their labor confronted them, in Marx's words, "as an *alien being*, as a *power independent* of the producer."[56]

At the same time, the activity of modern production—with its forced regimentation and division of labor—was an equally powerful source of estrangement. In his labor, the worker "does not affirm himself but denies himself," Marx observed, "does not feel well but unhappy, does not freely develop his physical and mental energy but mortifies his body and ruins his mind. The worker, therefore, feels himself only outside his work, and feels beside himself in his work. He is at home when he is not working, and when he is working he is not at home." The activity of the worker's labor, like the object of his toil, "belongs to another; it is the loss of his self."[57]

This twofold process of alienation—from the act of production and from the product of labor—had, in Marx's opinion, profound consequences, setting in motion a chain of effects that intensified the contradictions of capitalism. "A direct consequence of man's alienation from the product of his labor, from his life activity, from his species-being," he noted, "is the *alienation of man* from *man*. What is true of man's relationship to his work, to the product of his work, and to himself, is also true of man's relationship to the other man, and to that man's labor and the object of his labor." And so the chain reaction continued: the awful truth of capitalism was that the various forms of alienation that it induced "transform[ed] the consciousness which man has of his species" in such a way that one's fellows became nothing more than distant strangers, means to personal ends, while individuals themselves lost touch with all but their most rudimentary needs.[58]

It is worth pointing out, as Marx himself was fond of doing, that Adam Smith foresaw similar consequences. The Glasgow professor never subjected his readers to the circumlocutions of Hegelian dialectic. But in a key passage of *The Wealth of Nations,* he laid out the consequences of capitalism's most distinguishing feature—the division of labor—with unsettling frankness:

> In the progress of the division of labour, the employment of the far greater part of those who live by labour, that is, of the great body of the people, comes to be confined to a few very simple operations; frequently to one or two. But the understandings of the greater part of men are necessarily formed by their ordinary employments. The man whose whole life is spent in performing a few simple operations, of which the effects too are, perhaps, always the same, or very nearly the same, has no occasion to exert his understanding. . . . He naturally loses, therefore, the habit of such exertion, and generally becomes as stupid and ignorant as it is possible for a human creature to become.[59]

The "torpor of his mind," Smith continued, and the "corruption" of his body render such a man incapable of sharing in rational discussion, of participating in the joys and duties of social life, of judging of the "great and extensive interests of his country," even of bearing arms in defense of his homeland. Dexterity in his particular trade thus comes at the expense of his "intellectual, social, and martial virtues." And lest there be any doubt regarding the gravity of this situation, Smith emphasized that "in every improved and civilized society this is the state into which the labouring poor, that is, the great body of the people, must necessarily fall, unless government takes some pains to prevent it."[60]

This was a dramatic conclusion, but it was also the place where the two analysts of capitalism parted ways. Smith placed his faith in public schooling and civic education to balance the atomizing effects of

commercial society, whereas Marx called for the complete abolition
of private property and the institution of communism. And whereas
Smith, ever the individualist, was disinclined to search for government
solutions to metaphysical dilemmas, Marx believed that through politics man could be made complete, whole, happy. In a nod to Rousseau,
Marx defined true emancipation as "the return of man to himself as a
social, i.e. really human, being. . . ."[61] And in a flourish of world historical proportions, he defined communism as the "solution to the riddle
of history":

> the *definitive* resolution of the antagonism between man and
> nature, and between man and man. It is the true solution of
> the conflict between existence and essence, between objecti-
> fication and self-affirmation, between freedom and necessity,
> between individual and species. It is the solution of the riddle
> of history and knows itself to be this solution.[62]

Communism would thus mark the end of history envisioned by Hegel,
the overcoming of alienation, and the resolution of all the conflicts
that had made man a mystery to himself since well before the first
puzzled onlooker stood in bewilderment before the Sphinx.

That this promise involved a "religious" assurance, a pledge of the
abolition of human contradiction and the final onset of true ("real")
human happiness is something that insightful contemporaries did not
fail to appreciate. The German anarchist Max Stirner was arguably the
most perceptive, criticizing Marx along with Feuerbach and other
Young Hegelians for building a "human religion" on the remains of
Christianity:

> The human religion is only the last metamorphosis of the
> Christian religion . . . it separates my essence from me and
> sets it above me . . . it exalts "Man" to the same extent as any
> other religion does its God or idol . . . it sets me beneath Man,
> and thereby creates for me a vocation.[63]

Gustave Moreau, *Oedipus and the
Sphinx*, 1864, The Metropolitan
Museum of Art, Bequest
of William H. Herriman, 1920.
(21.134.1)

In the same way that centuries of faithful had sacrificed themselves
in the name of Christ, individuals were now being asked to genuflect
before "Man." In Stirner's view, the assumption of a vocation, an obligation to serve humanity, derived exclusively from an inherited sense
of religious duty.

Marx felt keenly the force of this criticism, and he attempted to
respond to it in a lengthy work of 1845–46, *The German Ideology*. But
though he railed at Stirner for nearly two hundred pages, his reply was
mostly bombast. Rather than answer Stirner's principal charge regarding the religious origins of communism, Marx sought to avoid it by
purging his thought of all vestigial traces of Hegelian idealism. In a
move that would be hailed by subsequent observers as a great theo-

retical breakthrough, he renounced the role of ideas in shaping history and human consciousness in favor of the celebrated "materialist conception of history." "In direct contrast to German philosophy, which descends from heaven to earth, here we ascend from earth to heaven," Marx proudly declared.[64] Henceforth, all ideas—all morality, law, religion, philosophy—would be treated as the simple reflection of the "real life-processes" of production. Ideas were simply "superstructure," entirely dependent on the "real" economic relationships of men.

Insofar as it gave Marxism its vaunted "scientific" appeal, this great turn was extraordinarily successful. It also succeeded, as the most recent editor of Marx and Engels's *Communist Manifesto*, Gareth Stedman Jones, has observed, in covering over the "tracks" that had led from religious humanism to communism (a move that was significantly aided by the fact that many of Marx's important writings of the 1840s were not published until long after his death).[65] If the coming crisis of capitalism and the victory of the proletariat were not the result of conscious human striving, and still less of permutations in the realm of ideas, then communism could hardly be accused of religious hocus-pocus. The process was inscribed in the very nature of things. Communists did not struggle in the name of "Man." They did so because they could do nothing else. This was the way of the world.

And yet—and this, precisely, was Marxism's genius—the same teleological structure borrowed from Hegel and the utopian socialists and by them from Christianity remained in place beneath the inexorable laws of history and the scientific certainties of dialectical materialism. At the end of the line lay the same religious promise of fulfillment, the end of alienation, the return of man to himself, the full flowering of real human happiness. The abstract nature of this metaphysical promise was only enhanced by the concrete assurance of the material riches to be had with the coming of the revolution. After the onset of true communism, suffering in all its forms would be abolished.

Thus, Marx combined the sensual allure of the utopian socialists—with their explicit appeal to the magnificence and bounty of the coming society—with Hegel's more subtly religious promise of final freedom and the end of the unhappy consciousness. Both material pleasure *and* spiritual fulfillment—the best of both the Enlightenment and Romanticism—were on offer. Dressed up in historical laws and packaged in a pseudo-science that covered over its true debt to religion, this was a powerful doctrine indeed, all the more so for Marx's refusal to describe in any but the barest terms the nature of the life to come. Devoting himself instead to demonstrating the economic laws that would guarantee the constitution of the new city of man, Marx allowed his followers to imagine for themselves what the walls of this city would contain and the splendor of the riches within. The outlines were inevitably hazy, but they drew the eye from the privations of the present and allowed each to project his private dreams on the space in between. In simple, steadfast faith, every man could imagine that his own vision would somehow, someday, correspond to the vision of all.

That happiness lay at the center of this collective vision no one could doubt. It was an unassailable element of the creed. As Engels observed in a draft of the aptly entitled "Communist Confession of Faith," "there exist certain irrefutable basic principles which, being the result of the whole of historical development, require no proof." These were that "every individual strives to be happy," and that "the happiness of the individual is inseparable from the happiness of all."[66] Present alike in Marx's youthful reflections and the later definition of happiness in *The Great Soviet Encyclopedia,* these were beliefs bound up in a much older notion of collective deliverance. The children of God had become the children of Man, and like the former, they would wait patiently, confident that history would reveal in time what now could only be imagined.

Riddles Revealed

"The story is told," Walter Benjamin tells us, "of an automaton constructed in such a way that it could play a winning game of chess, answering each move of an opponent with a countermove." "A puppet in Turkish attire," the German-Jewish critic continues,

> and with a hookah in its mouth sat before a chessboard placed on a large table. A system of mirrors created the illusion that this table was transparent from all sides. Actually, a little hunchback who was an expert chess player sat inside and guided the puppet's hand by means of strings.[67]

The story, properly speaking, was no story at all but a gem of historical fact. Beginning in 1770, the so-called Turk—a dazzling chess-playing contraption devised by the Austrian impresario Baron Wolfgang von Kempelen—had indeed toured Europe, provoking fascination, wonder, and disbelief wherever it performed. By appearance a miracle of modern science, the automaton, in truth, was an elaborate hoax whose gadgetry and technological sophistication provided cover for its genuine animating force. A midget with the skills of a grand master moved the arms of the Turk, which, under successive owners, seduced audiences well into the nineteenth century, confounding (and even defeating) the likes of Maria Theresa, Catherine the Great, Benjamin Franklin, and Edgar Allan Poe.[68]

Walter Benjamin himself probably knew of the story's basis in fact. But the essay for which this brief vignette serves as an opening gambit was more concerned with unveiling historical deception than revealing historical truth. In "Theses on the Philosophy of History," the automaton plays for Benjamin as metaphor, allowing him to pull away the veil:

> One can imagine a philosophical counterpart to this device [the chess-playing automaton]. The puppet called "historical materialism" is to win all the time. It can easily be a match for anyone if it enlists the services of theology, which today, as we know, is wizened and has to keep out of sight.[69]

Theology, Benjamin disclosed, was the hidden dwarf who moved the historical materialist's hands.

Charles Gottlieb de Windisch, "The Turk," 1783. Photo courtesy of the Library Company of Philadelphia.

Written as he fled from Nazi forces in 1940, and just months before he committed suicide in the mistaken belief that his capture was imminent, "Theses on the Philosophy of History" represents Benjamin's final reckoning with his relationship to historical materialism. For some time that relationship had been strained—not only by the rumors and revelations of Stalin's crimes but even more so by Benjamin's own enduring fascination with historical idealism in the form of messianic Jewish theology. If that relationship had always made him a curious Marxist ("a theologian marooned in the realm of the profane," as his longtime friend Gershom Scholem observed), it also granted him the insight to perceive connections that others preferred to ignore.[70] With his faith in the redemptive possibilities of communism shattered by the Nazi-Stalin pact of 1939, Benjamin felt free to reveal the hunchback who hid in the communist's cabinet. How appropriate that he should turn, in the very next paragraph, to a discussion of what united them in their game:

> Reflection shows us that our image of happiness is thoroughly colored by the time to which the course of our own existence has assigned us. The kind of happiness that could arouse envy in us exists only in the air we have breathed, among people we could have talked to, women who could have given them-selves to us. In other words, our image of happiness is indis-solubly bound up with the image of redemption.[71]

The same freedom from envy toward the future that had once prompted good souls to wait in patience for the coming of the Lord now moved the masses to trust blindly in the natural course of progress. But "progress," Benjamin affirmed, was a storm that obliterated everything through which it traveled, "piling up wreckage upon wreckage" in its wake. In the present, all who wagered with the "Turk" of historical materialism were fated to lose. And in the future, any such wagerers would be dead.

Despite his unveiling of the communist's cabinet, it is not clear that Benjamin successfully freed himself from its illusions. His devastat-ing critique of historical-materialist progress notwithstanding, he fin-ished his cryptic essay by holding out hope that human beings might still be fully redeemed. "For every second of time was the strait gate through which the Messiah might enter," the essay ends.[72] This was political theology of an apocalyptic, not historically progressive, sort. But it was political theology all the same.

Nonetheless, Benjamin's essay possesses the considerable virtue of full disclosure. In pulling aside the communist veil, he exposed the works, allowing us to see the mechanism by which historical materialism harnessed the hidden power of theology to the promise of happiness. Producing victory after victory on the chessboard of world affairs, this union left wreckage upon wreckage in its wake. But still the faith endured that "our new happy life" was at hand. The phrase is that of the Ministry of Plenty in Orwell's *1984*. But it was uttered in fact as well as in fiction—by many otherwise intelligent people with solemn assurance—until only recently.

Given what is now known about the horrors of the communist experience in virtually every one of its concrete applications, it seems remarkable that so many for so long could have sustained the faith that happiness was at hand. Yet when we bear in mind that this faith—like the larger Marxian project of which it formed a part—was a symptom of a much broader post-Enlightenment conviction, then the credulity is in some ways easier to comprehend. Consider that Marx's central assumption—that human labor could serve as the agent of our deliverance, the means and site of human transformation—is today almost as widespread as it was remarkable in Marx's time. An index unto itself of the power of the Enlightenment injunction to seek happiness in all things, it is a measure of the belief that human beings can make themselves happy through effort of their own.

ЛЮБИМЫЙ СТАЛИН-СЧАСТЬЕ НАРОДНОЕ!

"Our Beloved Stalin is the People's Happiness!" (1949).
("Contact-Culture," 2000. V. Koretskiy, 1949.)

"Glory to the Great Stalin, the Constructor of Happiness!" (1952).
("Contact-Culture," 2000. N. Petrou, K. Ivanov, 1952.)

Work—toil with one's hands—had for centuries prior to the Enlightenment been regarded as an imposition, a terrible necessity, God's curse for Adam's sin. Sweat on the human brow was an eternal reminder of the condemnation to seek out sustenance from the blighted earth beyond the Garden, scattered with thistles and thorns. With reason had European societies barred the most fortunate—the happy aristocratic few—from working with their hands. By definition, a life of privilege was a life without labor. And the happiness of death was the eternal rest of peaceful repose.

That men and women should come to believe—even to expect—that work, too, should sustain their happiness, serving as a source of satisfaction in its own right, is therefore a recent and quite remarkable development. When Marx, in his youth, set about choosing a profession to fulfill his end, he was exercising what was still a privilege of the well-to-do. But he rightly discerned that the force of industry was slowly transforming the nature of work, multiplying both its productivity and its possibilities, in ways that would extend this privilege outward. Work, Marx believed, would one day become for all what it had been for him since his youth, a calling and a source of deliverance, a means to a higher end.

This hope was kept alive by generations of visionaries. As the English socialist and artist William Morris dreams proleptically toward the end of his utopian masterpiece *News from Nowhere* (1890), "Thus at last and by slow degrees we got pleasure into our work; then we became conscious of that pleasure, and cultivated it, and took care that we had our fill of it; and then all was gained, and we were happy. So may it be for ages and ages!"[73] *Homo faber homo felix est.* Man becomes happy in his work.

Marx and his followers did much to further this hope. But they did not invent it. In truth, the belief that we can make ourselves happy through effort of our own has been a part of the Western tradition since Socrates and the Greeks attempted to wrest eudaimonia from the clutches of fortune. Happiness, in their view, was the product of the refined craftsmanship of living—something, at least in part, that we could make on our own. And although the Greeks and their successors restricted this trade—confining the highest human end to life's master artisans, an elite guild of "workers," who could build their lives better that the common lot—Christianity and then the Enlightenment destroyed this closed shop, bidding all to work toward their deliverance, and to find deliverance in their work. In keeping with the greatest good of the greatest number, happiness should be sought in all things, even in the sweat of one's brow.

Perhaps this larger dynamic helps to explain one of the delicious ironies of history: Marx's contention that not only should we enjoy the fruits of our labor, but labor itself should be our fruit, is today a central tenet of the capitalist creed. The actual realization of this ideal, to be sure, is still the prerogative of the privileged: It remains a luxury (or a burden) to seek more than remuneration in one's work, as it was for Marx himself. But the ideal—the hope of finding satisfaction, fulfillment, and happiness in one's labor—is now widespread. Where communism failed to provide the promised manna of the gods, the market invites us to work patiently in pursuit, making pleasure of our labor like so much else, and so, by enjoying what we do, to move steadily toward our hallowed end.

But what if the very premise, cultivated by so many hands since Socrates, was misconceived? What if virtue, work, all our striving and sweat was simply not enough to make the animal man a happy creature? This was the old tragic surmise, dismissed by the philosophers of the Enlightenment and the followers of Marx as so much fatalistic prejudice. The scientists of socialism preferred to cling to what Weber mocked as "the naive optimism in which science . . . has been celebrated as the way to happiness."[74] Natural and human scientists—anthropologists of the animal man—would show themselves equally reluctant to dispense with this optimism, even when the logic of their discoveries was not consoling.

8

JOYFUL SCIENCE

Are animals happy? Are they happier than human beings? Are human beings animals? Questions of this kind have evolved naturally out of the Western intellectual tradition, and their fossils can be found embedded deep in the bedrock of the past. That great zoologist Aristotle, who helped frame the dominant answers for the succeeding millennium and a half, concluded that man was indeed an animal but of a very special kind—a *political* animal (*politikon zôon*), naturally social and set apart from the lesser beasts by his faculty of reason and the refined composition of his soul. Unlike nonhuman animals, who, together with children and natural slaves, "do not share in happiness," man is endowed with the ability to attain the highest good.[1] It is happiness that makes us truly human.

But if happiness—a life lived according to virtue—is the culmination and quintessence of human existence, it is also, Aristotle hastened to add, a "god-like life," an existence "superior to the human level" that allows mere mortals to partake in the divine. This Greek conclusion is one that Christians, as we have seen, were perfectly content to embrace. Christ may have likened himself to a sacrificial lamb, the lamb of God (*agnus dei*), and addressed his flock as a shepherd to sheep; Saint Francis may have preached sermons to the birds. But not all of God's creatures, Christians knew, were equally blessed. Only man was made in the image of the Creator, and only man was born for ultimate felicity. "The brutes and things below him can neither go nor be drawn to that level," Pico della Mirandola maintained, summing up in the fifteenth century a venerable theological tradition. The renowned humanist spoke in gradations, acknowledging that even an inanimate object can be said to be "happy to the extent that it is capable of happiness"—to the extent, that is, that it attains its own formal perfection. "More happy are the plants," Pico added, "which also have life; and happier still are the animals, which have been allotted consciousness. . . ." But of all the living things that creep and crawl on the earth, man, it was clear, was the "animal that is most happy." Only he could be drawn to God.[2]

Both classical and Christian commentators concurred in granting human beings a special place in the ordered hierarchy of creation—a superior link in the great chain of being—that sanctioned their dominion over the beasts. But it was also clear that the very faculties that conferred this happy place—reason and freedom of will—could lead them down to levels of depravity that even the lowest creatures did not know. Slithering on their bellies like the serpent that had defiled them, human beings could turn their precious gifts to evil ends, rendering themselves most miserable in the process. From the vantage point of this lowly place, it was perfectly possible to look up to the animal kingdom with admiration and even envy.

Thus, the theme of "theriophily"—the jealous love of animals— runs in counterpoint to the more dominant celebratory hymn of man.[3] In a famous first-century dialogue by Plutarch, for example, "On the Rationality of Beasts," the Romanized Greek argues that animals are in many ways happier than human beings. As the dialogue's chief protagonist, a talking pig named Gryllus, explains to a puzzled Odysseus, beasts are braver, more chaste, and more temperate than human beings. Spurning irregularity and excess, depravity and misplaced passion, they live within their means, ruled for the most part only by "essential desires and pleasures."[4] Were it not for the favor of the gods, human beings would be at a natural disadvantage.

Writing centuries later in the *Institutes of the Christian Religion,* John
Calvin was ready to concede the same point. Like the majority of educated men of his time, Calvin knew his Plutarch, and he granted that
Gryllus "reasons most skillfully, when he affirms that, if once religion
is banished from the lives of men, they . . . are in many respects, much
more wretched than the brutes. . . ." The only thing that makes human
beings superior, Calvin judged, "is the worship of God, through which
alone they aspire to immortality."[5] Montaigne spoke less of the Creator. Yet the celebrated skeptic agreed that it was only by "foolish
pride and stubbornness that we set ourselves before the other animals. . . ." Impoverished by inconstancy, irresolution, uncertainty,
grief, superstition, ambition, avarice, jealousy, and a host of other
"untamable appetites," human beings had "strangely overpaid" for
their fine reason. They would do better, Montaigne ventured, to "become like the animals in order to become wise," and so to become
happy.[6]

Plutarch, Calvin, and Montaigne are strong voices; there were
others. But by and large, this tradition of the "happy beast" remained
the preserve of contrarians and humblers of human pride. When
Descartes proposed in the first half of the seventeenth century that
animals were "automata"—beast-machines operating without reason,
feelings, or souls—he only widened what was already a centuries-old
divide. Yet without intending to do so, he also stimulated a disturbing
line of inquiry. What if human beings, too, were beast-machines, endowed with feelings, yes, and reason, to be sure, but not with souls?
This was the unsettling conjecture posed by La Mettrie, and though
he was more radical than most in proclaiming man, like the animals, a
sophisticated machine, the general tendency of his inquiry was in
keeping with the tenor of the times. In both the natural and human
sciences, the gap between animals and human beings was narrowed in
the eighteenth century and, by the most radical, even closed.

In this respect, as in so many others, the age of Enlightenment
marked a monumental shift, engendering speculation that was profoundly and radically new. Yet as we have already seen in the case of
La Mettrie, this attempt to demote man from the kingdom of God was

met with widespread hostility and tremendous unease. La Mettrie's suggestion that we should indulge freely in the happiness of the barnyard—"wallowing in slime like a pig"—provoked outrage, while the general advice of his Utilitarian successors proved similarly threatening. Jeremy Bentham may have amused his neighbors by keeping a "beautiful pig" as a pet, one that would "grunt contentedly as he scratched its back and ears."[7] They may even have been touched by his claim that animals, like human beings, experience feelings of pleasure and pain. "The question is not," Bentham stressed, "can [animals] reason, but can they suffer?"[8] The "humanity" of this position notwithstanding, most still found the "pig happiness" of human beings a difficult concept to swallow. As J. S. Mill was quick to emphasize, it is better to be an unhappy human being than a satisfied pig.

Happy animals? (Courtesy: Stockphoto.com)

But what if the animal in question was a monkey, not a pig, and what if the monkey was a man? This was the unthinkable question put to the world by Charles Darwin, who as early as the 1830s was putting the question to himself. "He who understands [a] baboon [will] do more towards metaphysics than Locke," he scrawled in a private note-book in 1838.[9] The field of happiness would be profoundly altered by the force of his speculation. And as developments in biology propelled changes in philosophy, psychology, and anthropology, the gravitational pull of pursuit was corrected to account for what were hitherto hidden powers: instinctual drives, hereditary traits, and ultimately, the influence of genetic code. Sinister to some, liberating to others, these powers seemed by the twentieth century to be extending their dominion, like fate, over all creatures, man and beast alike.

The Survival of the Happiest

Although Charles Darwin never produced a formal discourse on happiness, there is some indication that he considered doing so. In the middle of several pages of notes on the subject in one of his early, unpublished workbooks, Darwin writes intriguingly, "Begin discussion—by saying what is Happiness."[10] Only two years previously, in 1836, he had returned from his epoch five-year journey to South America and the Pacific on the H.M.S. *Beagle* and was now busily engaged in completing his account of that trip. Published the following year, the *Voyage of the Beagle* contains only scattered references to happiness. So what the "discussion" might have been—a projected article, a public lecture, a portion of a larger study—is unclear. Darwin, unfortunately, never says, and neither does he fully account for the statement that immediately follows. "When we look back to happy days, are they not those of which all our *recollections* are pleasant[?]"[11] We his readers are forced to look back ourselves, flipping through earlier pages in his notes in search of further clues. We come upon this broken fragment:

Definition of happiness the number of pleasant ideas passing
though mind in given time.—intensity to degree of <happi>
pleasure of such thoughts[12]

And several pages earlier, there is this:

Nothing shows one how little happiness depends on the
senses.; than the <small> fact that no one, looking back to
his life, would say how many good dinners . . . he had had, he
would say how many happy days he spent in such a place.[13]

Whereas in the above passage Darwin seems to contradict the notion
that happiness is based on the senses, slightly later he has this to say:

Simple happiness <<as of a child>> is large proportion of
pleasant to unpleasant mental sensations in any given
time. . . . But then sensation may be *more* or *less* pleasant &
unpleasant, in same time,—therefore degrees of happiness—
Entire happiness. not being so desirable as . . . *intense* happiness
even with some pain . . . *Pleasure* more usually refers to the
sensation . . . when excited by impressions, & not mental or
ideal ones. . . .[14]

Such fragments are undoubtedly difficult to decipher. But it seems
that Darwin is proposing various degrees of happiness, ranging from
the "simple," based purely on impressions of the senses, to the more
complex, which involve mental or ideal impressions such as recollection or imagination. "Entire happiness," notwithstanding the seductive
name, is actually of the simpler sort, and so inferior in both intensity
and kind to the "higher" happiness of the philosophers, as Darwin
makes clear:

A healthy child is <<more>> entirely happy . . . than perhaps well <<regulated>> philosopher—yet the philosopher

has a much more intense happiness—so is it . . . when same
man is compared to peasant.—To make greatest number of
pleasant thoughts, he must have contingency of good food, no
pain. . . .

These thoughts are most pleasant. when the conscience
tells our [mind], good has been done—<<& conscience free
from offence>>—pleasure of intellect . . . pleasure of imagination . . . these pleasures are so very great, that every one
who has tasted them, will think the sum total of happiness
greater even if mixed with some pain.—than the happiness of
a peasant, with whom sensual enjoyments of the minute make
large . . . portion of daily <happiness> <<pleasure>>. A
wise man will try to obtain this happiness.[15]

A modicum of material comforts, an absence of pain, a clear conscience, and a taste for the pleasures of the intellect—this is the happiness of the "philosopher," the "wise man," to which state Darwin
himself almost certainly aspired. The same general goal would not have
been foreign to Aristotle, Epicurus, or Horace, or to any number of
other thinkers we have encountered thus far. Indeed, the many references in Darwin's notes to Coleridge, Montaigne, Locke, Bentham,
Adam Smith, Kant, and Mill give ample evidence of his prodigious
reading and desire to situate his thinking about happiness in the context of a much broader tradition. There are "two classes of moralists,"
he writes in a different notebook from the same period: theorists of
the moral sense, on the one hand, and those, like Bentham and Mill,
on the other, who tend to derive moral phenomena from acquired
experience (the calculus of pleasure and pain). "One says our rule is
what *will* produce the greatest happiness.—The other says we have a
moral sense.—But my view <says> unites both <<and shows them
to be almost identical>>."[16]

Here, after having so far largely restated the views of others, Darwin
hints at genuinely originality. Speaking of an "instinctive" moral sense,
he observes, "In judging of . . . the rule of happiness we must look *far
forward* . . .—certainly because it is the result of what has *generally* been

best for our good *far back*." Enticingly, he then adds, "Society could not go on except for the moral sense, any more than a hive of Bees without their instincts."[17] Darwin is positing not only what he called "instinctive emotions"—emotions conditioned by heredity and the long experience of pleasure and pain—but also a finely developed moral instinct, similarly honed by long experience. Both bear directly on our social interactions, and both are bound up closely with happiness.

Looking to the remote past, Darwin speculates that certain strong passions and "bad feelings" that are "common to other animals & therefore to [our] progenitor[s] far back" were "no doubt *originally* necessary."[18] Revenge, for instance, once served as a primitive form of justice, anger secured our safety, and jealousy acted as a "positive check" on licentiousness. But though it was not odd that man should have developed such strong emotions in the first place ("with lesser intellect," Darwin adds, "they might be necessary & no doubt were preservative"), experience has shown that we now need to "check" these instincts in the service of happiness.[19] In a striking formulation, Darwin observes, "Our descent, then, is the origin of our evil passions!!—The Devil under form of Baboon is our grandfather!—"[20] In a very real way, it seems, human beings must struggle with the beast within.

But this was merely the vista opened up by looking "far back." Gazing "far forward," the view was rosier, for it seemed to Darwin that our more aggressive impulses were "slowly vanishing." "Civilization is now altering these instinctive passions—, which being unnecessary we call vicious." Whereas "jealousy in a dog, no one calls vice," human beings now properly condemned this passion and a whole range of other atavistic emotions—evidence of the moral improvement of humanity, and hence of the progressive happiness of the species. As distinct from the lesser beasts and the "savage," "civilized man" was "endeavoring to change that part of the moral sense which experience . . . shows does not tend to [the] greatest good."[21]

Darwin showed himself here to be the optimist that he would remain throughout his long and self-described "happy life."[22] Yet ever the balanced observer, he acknowledged that there could be holes in his analysis through which doubters, like Thomas, might poke their fingers in disbelief. It was far from clear, he confessed, that his naturalistic account of the "rule of happiness" would "agree with that of the New Testament."[23] And even more gravely, it was not at all certain that human beings could so easily transcend the devil of their descent. In an extended passage treating what Darwin called the "general delusion about free will," he observed that human beings' belief in their own moral agency stemmed largely from their inability to discern the true motives of their behavior. "Originally mostly INSTINCTIVE, and therefore now [requiring a] great effort of reason to discover them"—these motives remained hidden to all save the man "who has thought very much" about them.[24] Even that wise man—in this case, Darwin himself—seemed loath to confront what the evidence he was amassing might also suggest: that far from being free to alter our behavior for greater happiness and the greatest good, human beings might be captive to the hidden motives that ruled them, slaves to the beast within.

Darwin never completed the formal "discussion" of happiness that these rough reflections were apparently intended to serve. Nor, clearly, did he ever intend for prying eyes to pick over the broken syntax of his notes. But having done so, we are in a position to see what otherwise might well be obscured: his intense early interest in the subject of happiness and the way it reemerges, with surprising consistency and similar contradiction, in the work in which he most closely compares the behavior of the lower animals with that of human beings, *The Descent of Man* (1871).

Over thirty years had elapsed in the interim, and Darwin was now at the height of his career, as the successful author of *The Origin of Species* (1859) and the acknowledged father of the theory of evolution and its attendant doctrines of adaptation, mutability, and natural selection. Extremely controversial, *The Origin of Species* had inevitably raised, though not explicitly addressed, the question of the place of human beings in evolutionary theory. It was to that question that Darwin turned in *The Descent of Man*, arguing unambiguously for the "close similarity" between human beings and the lower animals "in embryonic

development as well as in innumerable points of structure and constitution. . . ." Like all species, man had "descended from less highly organized forms" ("ape-like progenitors"), and indeed still bore "in his
bodily frame the indelible stamp of his lowly origin."[25]

This was equally true of emotions as it was of morphology. "The
fact that the lower animals are excited by the same emotions as ourselves," Darwin explained, "is so well established, that it will not be
necessary to weary the reader by many details."[26] He provided them
nonetheless, describing the many, often amusing, seldom wearying,
means employed by the beasts to give expression to a range of emotions, from love, envy, and anger to jealousy, curiosity, and resentment.
In both *The Descent of Man* and then in a work devoted exclusively to
the subject published the following year, *The Expression of the Emotions
in Man and Animals* (1872), Darwin described cases of spiteful monkeys,
terrified storks, and enraged bees. He explained that "some dogs and
horses are ill-tempered, and easily turn sulky; others are good-tempered;
and [that] these qualities are certainly inherited."[27] And he argued
that joy and happiness were emotions not unique to man:

> The lower animals, like man, manifestly feel pleasure and
> pain, happiness and misery. Happiness is never better exhib-
> ited than by young animals, such as puppies, kittens, lambs,
> etc., when playing together, like our own children. Even
> insects play together, as has been described by that excellent
> observer . . . who saw ants chasing and pretending to bite each
> other, like so many puppies.[28]

Although Darwin did not possess the knowledge of genetics that would
have helped him understand the crucial mechanism that governed
this process, his general insight that mood and affect—grumpiness
and good temper—were heritable traits was profoundly insightful. His
first forays into what is today the thriving field of evolutionary psychology would prove revolutionary.

But did this mean that human beings and other animals merely re-
acted to the external stimuli of pleasure and pain? Darwin acknowledged

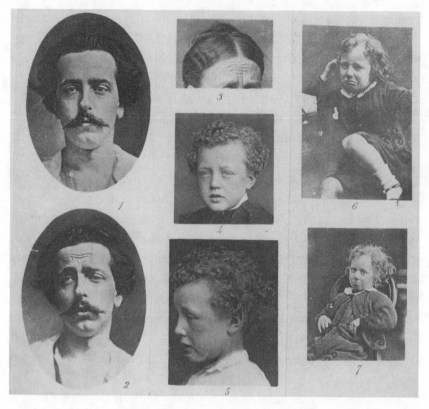

Darwin's studies of sadness, from *The Expression of the Emotions in Man and Animals,*
1872. Beinecke Rare Book and Manuscript Library, Yale University.

the critical role played by pain and pleasure in the process of evolutionary development. Yet whereas those in the Utilitarian tradition
maintained that actions were beneficial only if they produced pleasure
and minimized pain, Darwin reversed the proposition, arguing instead
"that natural selection produced pleasure only if that pleasurable state
induced beneficial actions."[29] And these beneficial actions—actions
that furthered reproduction and survival—were to be calculated in
evolutionary terms not with reference to the individual but with respect to the group. Returning to a theme that he had taken up in his
1838 notebooks, Darwin again put forth the notion of a "social instinct," selected to benefit group survival:

The feeling of pleasure from society is probably an extension of the parental or filial affections, since the social instinct seems to be developed by the young remaining for a long time with their parents; and this extension may be attributed in part to habit, but chiefly to Natural Selection. With those animals which were benefited by living in close association, the individuals which took the greatest pleasure in society would best escape various dangers, whilst those that cared least for their comrades, and lived solitary, would perish in greater numbers.[30]

Gradually, many of the lesser beasts had developed instincts amenable not only to their own survival but also to that of the group. Like man, they were social, even political, creatures, conditioned to sympathy, affection, loyalty, bravery, and other qualities that furthered group cohesion and existence. Taking pleasure in social interaction, they were also prepared to undergo pain—or inflict it—in service of the greater good. Darwin singled out the case of animals perpetually ready to utter the danger signal, and so expose themselves to peril, in defense of the community. And he highlighted the disturbing example of the worker bee that kills its brother drones, or the queen bee that kills its daughter-queen—"the desire to destroy their nearest relations having been in this case of service to the community."[31]

Darwin had little doubt that if human beings were raised like bees in a hive, they would act similarly, pointing out that in the case of infanticide, they already did. But his larger point was more optimistic. For in the social instinct of animals, Darwin found the precursor of the moral instinct of man. The one, he believed, was just an extension of the other, an impulse honed by natural selection and higher human consciousness to sympathy, affection, regard for one's image in the eyes of others, and concern for their welfare. Darwin fully recognized that this moral instinct would frequently come in conflict with other, more selfish desires. It is "untenable," he stressed, "that in man the social instincts (including the love of praise and fear of blame) possess greater strength, or have, through long habit, acquired greater strength than the instincts of self-preservation, hunger, lust, vengeance,

&c."[32] Though envy, hatred, and other passions of self-preservation would "more commonly lead [man] to gratify his own desires at the expense of other men," it was also precisely this conflict between competing natural impulses that gave rise to conscience. As Darwin had intimated in his 1838 notes, and now repeated here, by virtue of his superior mental faculties, man "cannot avoid reflection: past impressions and images are incessantly and clearly passing through his mind."[33] And so, after indulging a stronger selfish impulse at the expense of his social instinct, man "will then feel remorse, repentance, regret, or shame. . . . He will consequently resolve more or less firmly to act differently for the future; and this is conscience; for conscience looks backwards, and serves as a guide for the future."[34]

In looking toward the future on this occasion, Darwin gave indications of the same optimistic tendency recorded in his private reflections of the 1830s. At times he waxes sanguine, noting, "Man prompted by his conscience, will through long habit acquire such perfect self-command, that his *desires* and passions will at last yield instantly and without a struggle to his social sympathies and instincts. . . ."[35] In another passage, he invokes Kant in a triumphant vision of man as a self-legislating moral actor:

> But as love, sympathy and self-command become strengthened by habit, and as the power of reasoning becomes clearer, so that man can value justly the judgments of his fellows, he will feel himself impelled, apart from any transitory pleasure or pain, to certain lines of conduct. He might then declare— not that any barbarian or uncultivated man could thus think— I am the supreme judge of my own conduct, and in the words of Kant, I will not in my own person violate the dignity of humanity.[36]

This is an appealing picture of human independence and moral agency. But what of Darwin's earlier concerns about the "general delusion of free will"? More pressingly, what about the place of happiness in his revised picture of humanity? Kant, it will be recalled, had emphasized the tension between a life of moral duty and individual happiness. The two, he believed, would often be at odds. Darwin also is aware of this tension—between, in his terms, the social instinct and individual desire. Though he makes reference "to that feeling of dissatisfaction, or even misery, which invariably results . . . from any unsatisfied instinct," he does not explore this insight in any significant detail. As we shall see, it would be seized upon to great effect by Sigmund Freud.

More potentially troubling for those hoping to discover a firm basis for human happiness in our animal nature are Darwin's final conclusions regarding the Utilitarian tradition. Summarizing the argument of his two principal chapters comparing the mental powers of man and the lower animals, Darwin explicitly cites and rejects Bentham's and Mill's contentions that the motive for every human action must be pleasure or pain. "But man seems often to act impulsively," Darwin counters:

> That is from instinct or long habit, without any consciousness of pleasure, in the same manner as does probably a bee or ant, when it blindly follows its instincts. Under circumstances of extreme peril, as during a fire, when a man endeavours to save a fellow-creature without a moment's hesitation, he can hardly feel pleasure. . . . Should he afterwards reflect over his own conduct, he would feel that there lies within him an impulsive power widely different from a search after pleasure or happiness; and this seems to be the deeply planted social instinct.[37]

Darwin intended this observation to reflect well on human beings— and arguably it does—saving us from the unflattering Utilitarian assumption that our behavior is driven always by selfishness or by cumbersome calculations of pleasure and pain (the greatest-happiness principle). In Darwin's words, it removed the reproach of "laying the foundation of the noblest part of our nature in the base principle of selfishness." Yet when he then proceeds to discuss the larger "purpose" of the social instinct in both the lower animals and man, he is led away from happiness in the direction of something else:

In the case of the lower animals it seems much more appropriate to speak of their social instincts, as having been
developed for the general good rather than for the general
happiness of the species. The term, general good, may be
defined as the rearing of the greatest number of individuals
in full vigour and health, with all their faculties perfect,
under the conditions to which they are subjected. As the
social instincts both of man and the lower animals have no
doubt been developed by nearly the same steps, it would be
advisable, if found practicable, to use the same definition in
both cases, and to take as the standard of morality, the
general good or welfare of the community, rather than the
general happiness.[38]

At first reading, Darwin's substitution of the general good for the general happiness may seem innocuous. But when we consider that the
"general good" amounts simply to the survival of the species, it becomes far less clear that the good and happiness were as closely linked
as Darwin would have liked to believe. "No doubt the welfare and
the happiness of the individual usually coincide," he observed, "and
a contented, happy tribe will flourish better than one that is discon-
tented and unhappy." But consider what "flourishing" entails. In *The
Origin of Species*, Darwin himself had painted a vivid picture, characterizing the attempt to rear the greatest number of individuals in full
vigor and health as a "Struggle for Existence" and "the great battle of
life." We customarily "behold the face of nature bright with gladness,"
he pointed out, but the smile was deceptive. "We do not see, or we
forget, that the birds which are idly singing around us . . . are constantly destroying life; or we forget how largely these songsters, or
their eggs, or their nestlings, are destroyed by birds and beasts of
prey. . . ." Starvation, pestilence, competition, and slaughter were
endemic to the struggle of existence:

In looking at Nature, it is most necessary . . . never to forget
that every single organic being around us may be said to be

striving to the utmost to increase in numbers; that each lives
by a struggle at some period of its life; that heavy destruction
inevitably falls either on the young or old, during each generation or at recurrent intervals.[39]

Each generation "has to struggle for life, and to suffer great destruction. When we reflect on this struggle, we may console ourselves with
the full belief, that the war of nature is not incessant, that no fear is
felt, that death is generally prompt, and that the vigorous, the healthy,
and the happy survive and multiply."[40]

Not all, to say the least, found this image of the "survival of the
happiest" particularly consoling—something of which Darwin was well
aware. And though he bravely put a positive face on his conclusions in
The Descent of Man—maintaining that over time our social instincts
would grow stronger, the struggle between our higher and lower impulses less severe, and "virtue will be triumphant"—it is never clear
that his own findings justified such optimism.[41] As he freely admitted
elsewhere, "there seems to be no more design . . . in the action of
natural selection, than in the course which the wind blows." If this
were the case, then Darwin's assumption of fair weather and gentle
breezes—his confidence in the happy course of humanity—was
founded less on fact than on faith.

Darwin, to his credit, admitted as much, acknowledging toward the
end of his life in a poignant section of his *Autobiography*, dealing, appropriately enough, with his religious beliefs, that it might rightly be asked
how "the generally beneficent arrangement of the world" can be accounted for. Some writers, he recognized, had been "so much impressed
with the amount of suffering in the world, that they doubt if we look to
all sentient beings, whether there is more of misery or of happiness."
But "according to my judgment," Darwin responds, "happiness decidedly prevails, *though this would be very difficult to prove.*" Revealingly, he does
not try to prove it, asking us instead to "grant the truth of the conclusion" and then to entertain several "considerations" that might serve to
uphold it—uphold, that is, the "belief that all sentient beings have been
formed so as to enjoy, as a general rule, happiness."[42]

Darwin includes among these his familiar arguments regarding the role of pleasure in furthering natural selection: "Sentient beings have been developed in such a manner . . . that pleasurable sensations serve as their habitual guides." And though he acknowledges that both pleasure and pain can cause animals to "pursue that course of action which is the most beneficial to the species," he argues that pleasure is the stronger force. "Pain or suffering of any kind, if long continued, causes depression and lessens the power of action. . . . Pleasurable sensations, on the other hand, may be long continued without any depressing effect; on the contrary they stimulate the whole system to increased action."[43]

It can hardly be doubted that pain or suffering in its more extreme forms must have a deadening effect on all sentient beings. But in its lesser forms—as mild hunger or sexual desire, anxiety or uneasiness—this is clearly not the case. Nor is it apparent that pleasurable sensations, when long continued, stimulate action (think of an excellent backrub). Indeed, a number of contemporary evolutionary psychologists, although indebted to Darwin in many other respects, have argued precisely the opposite case. In what they call the "tragedy of happiness" or the "hedonic treadmill," they point out that human beings display an undeniable tendency to quickly accommodate themselves to their pleasures—to grow bored—and then become anxious or uneasy in their satisfaction. Like junkies in need of a fix, we need variety in our pleasures or greater doses of the same when the initial "rush" wears off. It is this longing—a form of pain—that sends us in renewed pursuit.

According to this perspective, it is the hedonic treadmill—the repeatedly painful pursuit of pleasure—that has been adapted by natural selection to sustain us in life. As the noted cognitive scientist Steven Pinker explains, "[contemporary] evolutionary theory predicts that a man's reach should exceed his grasp, but not by much."[44] In other words, although natural selection has conditioned us to experience pleasure in activities that contribute to our survival, it disposes us to quickly adapt to them and then to strive for a little more. In this view, enduring satisfaction or permanent contentment would not be conducive to survival. It is in our interest—and so in our genes—always to be slightly wanting, restlessly searching for further satisfaction. A bit of anxiety keeps us on our guard against danger, and a bit of unfulfilled desire keeps us on the chase, ever eager to ensure our survival and that of our kin.

Whether the insights of this Darwinian variation on Darwin would have caused the man himself to alter his conclusion that the "sum" of our habitual and recurrent pleasures "gives, I can hardly doubt, most sentient beings an excess of happiness over misery," is of course uncertain. But it is interesting to note that even on Darwin's own terms, the balance was narrowly won. "Many occasionally suffer much," he conceded, adding that "such suffering is quite compatible with the belief in Natural Selection, which is not perfect in its action, but tends only to render each species as successful as possible in the battle for life with other species. . . . That there is much suffering in the world," he continued, "no one disputes." Where he did take issue was with the view that this suffering could be compatible with the existence of God. Darwin's investigations of the natural world afforded no place in his mind, he claimed, for theodicy:

> Some have attempted to explain [the suffering in the world] in reference to man by imagining that it serves for his moral improvement. But the number of men in the world is as nothing compared with that of all other sentient beings, and these often suffer greatly without any moral improvement. A being so powerful and so full of knowledge as a God who could create the universe, is to our finite minds omnipotent and omniscient, and it revolts our understanding to suppose that this benevolence is not unbounded, for what advantage can there be in the suffering of millions of the lower animals throughout almost endless time? This very old argument from the existence of suffering against the existence of an intelligent first cause seems to me a strong one. . . .[45]

Belief in a benevolent creator was incompatible with the purposeless suffering of the world: Theodicy could not be sustained.

But how, one is left to wonder, could Darwin sustain his own faith, his faith not in God but in human happiness? For in effect he continued to cling to a species of theodicy, arguing that the terrible suffering of the world worked, unwittingly, for the "moral improvement" of humanity, and so would continue to augment the balance of pleasure over pain. "Believing as I do," he continued just pages later, "that man in the distant future will be a far more perfect creature than he now is, it is an intolerable thought that he and all other sentient beings are doomed to complete annihilation after such long-continued slow progress." Intolerable, yes, but as he fully acknowledged, this was the gathering consensus of science, which believed that the "sun with all the planets will one day grow too cold for life."[46] Confronted, looking backward, with the "suffering of millions of the lower animals throughout almost endless time," and faced, looking forward, with the total extinction of earthly life, it took a brave individual—a defiantly optimistic individual—to maintain an unflinching smile in the present. Darwin was such a man. Many contemporaries felt obliged to respect his fortitude. But many more found it difficult to share his faith that a small surplus of pleasure in the balance sheet of sensations could justify the happiness of man.

Ecce Homo

Never a shepherd, Zarathustra was a friend of the solitary beast. He detested flocks and hated herds. But when he wandered alone on mountaintops, his spirit soared with eagles and floated to earth, gently, with doves. Unafraid of serpents, he made his home in caves, waiting for laughing lions. And he loved creatures that have no settled home, hardened for hard journeys, like the dromedary, ready to bear difficult loads. In order to be born again, and then to be raised anew, man must evolve: "Of three metamorphoses of the spirit I tell you: how the spirit becomes a camel; and the camel, a lion; and the lion, finally, a child."[47]

Thus spoke Zarathustra. And so in this case did Friedrich Nietzsche, telling by way of his mythical prophet a fable and truth that was close to his own heart. Anyone who would dare to roar like a lion at all that had been said and done must first take on his back that same load, carry its weight like a beast of burden, suffer under its strain. Only then could he claw out in defiance, and only then, when he had freed himself from its weight, could the "preying lion" become a child— "innocence and forgetting, a new beginning, a game, a self-propelled wheel, a first movement, a sacred Yes."[48] This creature of affirmation, this blessed child, would then pull himself upward to his own (self-) transcendence, growing to overcome humanity. Man, Zarathustra says in another metaphor, "is a rope stretched between animal and over-man (*Ubermensch*)."[49] He could either dance along the line to a higher place or go crashing into the abyss.

Nietzsche was especially fond of high-strung metaphors and taut language; at times they fell away from him. But in this case the meta-phor of metamorphosis was sure-footed: Nietzsche knew of what he spoke. Like a great painter or composer, this thinker-cum-artist had borne the weight of the Western tradition on his back, working with and through some of its most pressing concerns. And like the defiant lion that he grew to be, he lashed out at its weight, cutting away the ties that held him to the past. Whether he evolved into a child—or the towering overman—is doubtful. But his efforts to do so irrevoca-bly altered the landscape of Western thought.

The son of a Lutheran minister, Nietzsche began his university ca-reer as a student of theology before becoming a professor of ancient Greek philology. He was thus deeply schooled in both the classical and Christian traditions, and in grappling with the weight of these traditions, he was forced to come to terms with happiness. The subject is central to his work, accompanying him at every stage of his intellectual evolu-tion. But as is so often the case, his passion for happiness exists in ten-sion with a profound and enduring sadness. As he could confess toward the end of his career in a gloss on Heine's "Die Lorelei," "The fact is 'that I am so sad; the problem 'I don't know what that means.' . . ."[50]

Nietzsche proclaimed an early faith in the redemptive possibilities of art. While still a student, he came across a copy of Schopenhauer's *The World as Will and Representation* in a used-book shop—a discovery that proved a critical event in his life. As he later explained: "Every youthful soul hears this call ['Be yourself!'] day and night and trembles when he hears it; for the idea of its liberation gives it a presentiment of the measure of happiness allotted it from all eternity—a happiness to which it can by no means attain so long as it lies fettered by the chains of fear and convention."[51] Schopenhauer awakened in Nietzsche a yearning for liberation, a yearning to become what he was and what he could be. Critically, he also held out the possibility that art could be the vehicle of his transformation.

Giving shape and substance to Nietzsche's incipient views, Schopenhauer's thought also informed his first major work, *The Birth of Tragedy*, a study, appropriately enough, of Greek *tragoidia* and the tragic spirit in life. "Uniquely susceptible to the subtlest and deepest suffering" and "keenly aware of the terrors and horrors of existence," the early Greeks, Nietzsche argued, had been led by their sensitivity to create powerful means of defense to protect them in their pain. The pantheon of Olympian gods, who "justified human life by living it themselves," was one such mechanism, providing security, comfort, and hope. But of much greater interest to the young Nietzsche was another—*tragoidia*—that sublime Greek creation that in honoring the god Dionysus offered to all who beheld its spectacle a form of redemption and "metaphysical solace."[52] As they sat transfixed before the primitive stage, cultivated Greeks were given a taste of the "eternal delight of existence." If only for a moment, they were permitted to become themselves, invited to experience the full plenitude of "primal Being."[53]

This, in Nietzsche's view, was the healing balm of "true tragedy." One would have to transform Beethoven's "Ode to Joy" into a painting, he mused, in order to fully appreciate the Greeks' intense fusion of beauty and being. But though he conceded that *tragoidia* could no more be re-created in its original purity than the pantheon of Greek gods, Nietzsche believed for a time that he had discovered a modern analog to ancient myth in the music of Richard Wagner—a new form of tragic art capable, as Schopenhauer had promised, of providing temporary respite from the incessant roar of the Will. In

Wagner's scores, Nietzsche heard moments of "musical ecstasy," achieving "the peak of rapture of the world" that seemingly confirmed the truth of his famous statement in *The Birth of Tragedy*, "Only as an aesthetic phenomenon can the world and existence be eternally justified." In his imagination, the "qualified and dedicated spectators" who attended Wagner's modern operas at Bayreuth were the contemporary counterparts of the ancient Greeks. At Bayreuth one would find, Nietzsche fantasized, "the ardor of people who are at the zenith of their happiness and who feel that their whole being is condensed in this very state of happiness, which invigorates them for further and higher aspirations."[54]

The reality, predictably enough, proved less appealing. Disillusioned with the bourgeois patina of Bayreuth, Nietzsche grew disillusioned, too, with Wagner and his attempt to create a modern religion of art. As he later acknowledged of his early infatuation, "Behind my first period smirks the face of Jesuitism, by which I mean conscious clinging to illusions and forced incorporation of them as the basis of culture."[55] What Wagner was prepared to admit outright—that the task of art in a post-Enlightened age was to "salvage the essence of religion"—Nietzsche now renounced as misguided and confused.[56] The Romantic dream of aesthetic redemption was suitable only for those unable, or unwilling, to abandon the "consolations of religion."[57]

Yet Nietzsche had his own difficulties abandoning those consolations, however much he might protest the fact. This assertion may surprise those who recall his dramatic pronouncement "God is dead," or associate his name immediately with such titles as *The Antichrist*. But as one of his more perceptive biographers has observed, it required no great courage to kill God in the late nineteenth century.[58] European radicals had been doing it for two hundred years. If Nietzsche felt the need to commit deicide in so flagrant a fashion, it was in part because only by resorting to such extreme measures could he free himself from a lingering attachment. Not without reason was this son of a clergyman nicknamed the "little pastor" as a child, and not without reason did Nietzsche describe himself as a "plant born near a churchyard."[59] His efforts to achieve "ecstasy" and "rapture" in art were wholly

consonant with his need to "justify" existence, to "transcend" or "overcome" man. Even after he had renounced the "Jesuitism" of his earlier illusions, the quasi-religious goal of redemption remained.

This can be seen most directly in his efforts to achieve emancipation from "animal existence." Like so many men of the late nineteenth
and early twentieth centuries, Nietzsche was deeply troubled by the
theories of Darwin.[60] Not only did they seem to erode the foundations
of Christianity, but they also presented grave difficulties for any new
attempt to justify humanity on a higher plane. As the prophet mocks in
Thus Spoke Zarathustra, "What is the ape to man? A laughingstock or a
painful embarrassment." "Once you were apes," he adds, "and even now,
too, man is more ape than any ape."[61] How human beings could transcend their primitive origin—and aspire to a happiness worthy of a
higher being—became for Nietzsche a critical problem.

Vincent Van Gogh, *Still Life with Bible,* 1885, Van Gogh Museum, Amsterdam.
The former lay preacher Van Gogh here juxtaposes ancient and modern scripture:
the Bible and Émile Zola's novel, *La Joie de vivre,* the joy or happiness of life.
Photo Credit: Snark/Art Resource, NY.

In his lauding early essay on Schopenhauer, Nietzsche observed that the only men "who are no longer animals" are "philosophers, artists, and saints."[62] He had come to have his doubts about artists and about art's ability to transform humanity. But what of the other two? A philosopher by practice, if not by training, Nietzsche had great reverence for the craft. Yet he dismissed the majority of its practitioners as "cabbage heads" and harbored serious reservations about their power to deliver the happiness that human beings craved. Indeed, it was philosophy, he charged, that had originally destroyed the redemptive solace of Greek tragedy. And it was philosophy that had led human beings in false pursuit ever since. The great initiator of this elusive quest—a man at once awesome, terrible, and sublime—was Socrates.

Although Nietzsche's views on Socrates are notoriously complex, there is little doubt that he regarded him as a pivotal figure, the "vortex and turning point of Western civilization."[63] Socrates is the "great exemplar of theoretical man," the "archetype of the theoretical optimist," and one "who dared, single-handed, to challenge the entire world of Hellenism."[64] Rejecting the tragic acceptance of the inherent uncertainties and conflicts of life, Socrates was moved rather by the "illusion that thought . . . might plumb the farthest abyss of being and even *correct* it."[65] His faith was that knowledge could be the "true panacea" of existence. This, Nietzsche believes, is the "grand metaphysical illusion" that lies at the heart of Socrates's teaching, animating his central trinity: "Virtue is knowledge; all sins arise from ignorance; only the virtuous are happy." These "three basic formulations of optimism," Nietzsche insists, spelled the death of the tragic spirit, saddling humanity with the fundamental error that reason alone held the key to virtue and happiness.[66]

Despite important refinements in his thinking, Nietzsche never abandoned this fundamental conviction. At the end of his career, just two years before his descent into madness in 1890, he returned to the theme, sketching in his notes that "the problem of Socrates" could be reduced to "his equalization of reason = virtue = happiness." This was an "absurdity" from which the philosophers of antiquity had never been able to free themselves. "What do men want?" Socrates's successors asked. They offered only one answer to the question:

"Happiness." And "if man does not in fact achieve happiness," why is that? "Because," Nietzsche continued in the post-Socratic voice:

> Because he blunders in respect of the means.—What is unfailingly the means to happiness? Answer: virtue.—why virtue?—Because it is supremely rational and because rationality makes it impossible to err in the choice of means: it is as *reason* that virtue is the way to happiness.[67]

This fundamental Socratic error—so central to all subsequent classical thought—had been embraced ever since.

It was precisely this same false equation that animated the thinking of the Enlightenment, with its insistence on bringing happiness to humanity through the triumph of reason. The eighteenth century's added emphasis on pleasure only worsened the predicament, for as Nietzsche was fond of repeating, pleasure was not humanity's true end. "Man does not strive for pleasure, only the Englishman does," he quipped, directing his contempt at those who walked "clumsily" in the footsteps of Bentham. Yet he knew that the search for "the greatest happiness for the greatest number" was not confined to Britain. On the contrary, the demand for "English happiness"—"comfort and fashion (and at best a seat in Parliament)"—was widely shared.[68] Masquerading under the title of virtue and harnessing the services of instrumental reason, happiness of this sort would do little to help man transcend his animal origins. At best it would make him a fattened pig.

Nietzsche leveled a similar charge at the cleft-footed heirs of the socialist tradition, those "levelers" who strive with "all their powers [for] the universal green-pasture happiness of the herd, with security, lack of danger, comfort, and an easier life for everyone." "The two songs and doctrines which they repeat most often," Nietzsche continued, "are 'equality of right' and 'sympathy for all that suffers'—and suffering itself they take for something that must be *abolished*."[69] This Nietzsche felt to be as futile as it was misconceived. The aspiration itself, moreover—to sympathize with all suffering and then to try to resolve it in everlasting comfort and repose—pointed to the lasting influence of another man whose impact on Western civilization was immense, surpassing that of even Socrates. That man was Jesus of Nazareth.

Nietzsche's view of Christ was no less complicated than his view of Socrates—a perspective indicative of a much broader ambivalence toward the figure of the ascetic and saint that matched his equally conflicted feelings toward the figures of the philosopher and the heroic artist. But again, what is not in doubt is Nietzsche's estimation of Christ's impact, and of the tradition that grew up (however wrongly) in his name. Although he came to regard this influence as almost entirely negative, Nietzsche never abandoned his immense respect for the discipline, self-control, and self-overcoming of the Christian ascetic and saint.

As a young man, Nietzsche had written to his sister regarding what he already regarded as the irreconcilable conflict between Christianity and the search for truth. "If you want to attain peace of mind and happiness," he advised, "then you should have faith; if you want to be a disciple of truth, then you should probe." Nietzsche's views on all of these matters—happiness, faith, truth, and Christianity—would evolve considerably as his thought matured. Even so, he was always careful to distinguish between what he considered the relatively pure teachings of the historical Jesus and those of his successors, particularly the apostle Paul, whom he held accountable for having reerected on a grand scale everything that "Christ had annulled through his way of living": ecclesiastical structure, dogma, theology, cults, priests, a church. Still, Nietzsche's early appreciation of Christianity as a source of happiness never wavered. Sketching a series of notes on the history of the Christian religion two years before his breakdown, he could observe, "The Christian way of life is no more a fantasy than the Buddhist way of life: it is a means to being happy."[70]

It was, avowedly, an impoverished form of happiness, another insidious "happiness of the herd," just as "English happiness" was a debased and superficial form of satisfaction, appealing above all to the weak. Yet the psychological attraction of Christianity was no less real for that. To the downtrodden, the mediocre, and the oppressed, it offered ennoblement as "God's elect," transforming present misery and suffering "into a preparation, a test, a training," as well as "something which will one day be balanced up and paid back with enormous interest in gold, no! in happiness." This, Nietzsche noted wryly, was what Christians called "bliss."[71] But he understood that their return would be paid in more than just choirs of angels. What constitutes the "eternal bliss" of the Christian paradise? he asks, quoting Saint Thomas Aquinas in response: "The blessed in the heavenly kingdom will see the torment of the damned *so they may even more thoroughly enjoy their blessedness.*"[72] Though Nietzsche was being typically mischievous, his central point was perfectly serious, reminiscent of the following celebrated passage by Heine, a man whom Nietzsche adored:

> I have the most kindly temperament. My wants are modest—
> a hut, a thatched roof, a good bed, good food, milk and butter,
> all very fresh; flowers at my window, a few beautiful trees at
> my door. And if the good Lord wants to make my happiness
> complete, he will give me the pleasure of seeing some six or
> seven of my enemies strung up on those trees. With all my
> heart I shall forgive them, before their death, all the evil they
> have committed against me while I was alive. Yes, one should
> always forgive one's enemies—but not until they are hanged.[73]

"To see somebody suffer is nice," Nietzsche later quipped, "to make somebody suffer even nicer."[74] The psychological appeal of Christianity lay not only in its tranquilizing promise of deferred reward, but also in the way that it directed human resentment in the here and now. Christianity's bid to make the first last and the last first was also an attempt to create power from powerlessness and strength from weakness. It had succeeded all too well, bestowing on the downtrodden the crown of virtue, and so enabling these so-called good men to exalt in their moral victory over "evil enemies." As in all things in life, Nietzsche came to believe, Christianity was ultimately about power.

It was in large part for this reason that Nietzsche looked with fascination, and even respect, on Christianity's consummate practitioners— its ascetic athletes and virtuosos, its martyrs and saints. For in these strangely disciplined individuals he found an intriguing example of the will to power over others and over oneself. Terribly misled regarding means and ends, they nonetheless lived in keeping with an admirable goal—to transcend animal existence, to overcome themselves, to become like God. They did so, though, at a tremendous cost, for their efforts involved a terrible sundering of the self, erecting a fatal division between our wretched animal nature and our eternal spiritual soul. In struggling for the victory of the one over the other, the Christian athlete had succeeded in making man feel shame *"at being man."* The result of this trial was, paradoxically, to render human beings less fit than animals. Weighed down by guilt, despairing of life itself, they had become more wretched than the beasts:

> [It is by this means] that the animal "man" is finally taught to be ashamed of all his instincts. On the way to becoming an "angel" . . . man has upset his stomach and developed a furry tongue so that he finds not only that the joy and innocence of animals is disgusting, but that life itself is distasteful.[75]

Once an ape, man had devolved into something less, and now suffered waves of nausea, hating the very thing he was. Before he could seek transcendence, he must learn to accept himself.

Walking in the Upper Engadine mountains of Switzerland, near Sils-Maria—"6,000 feet above the ocean and far higher still above all things human!"—Nietzsche saw the light of this transcendence. The date was August 6, 1881, and in his subsequently published *Ecce Homo*—"Behold the Man," an allusion to the words spoken by Pontius Pilate when he first sets eyes on Christ in John 19:5—Nietzsche provides an illuminating description of his own "revelation":

> Does anyone at the end of the nineteenth century have a clear idea of what poets of strong eras called *inspiration*? If not, I will describe it. . . . The concept of revelation in the sense that something suddenly, with unspeakable certainty and subtlety, becomes *visible* and audible, shaking us to the core and knocking us over—simply describes the fact. . . . This is

my experience of inspiration; I have no doubt that we would
have to go back thousands of years to find anyone who could
say to me "it is mine also."[76]

The substance of this self-described "revelation" was Nietzsche's idea
of the "eternal recurrence"—an idea that has never been as clear to
interpreters as it was, evidently, to him at the time of its annuncia-
tion. In seeking to explain it, Nietzsche later tried to ground the
notion on what he considered (inaccurately) to be a truth deducible
from contemporary science: that if matter and energy were finite, and
time infinite, then all combinations of the former—all life—were destined to recur eternally in endless repetition.

Nietzsche accepted this odd idea as a propositional truth, treating it
with total seriousness, although he was not above joking that his "deepest objection" to the concept was the frightening prospect of the eternal recurrence of his mother and sister, whom he regarded as fools.[77]
Whether one is able to conceive of the concept with clarity is less important in the context of Nietzsche's understanding of happiness than is
the fact that it gave him precisely what he had struggled, and failed, to
find in religion, morality, and art: a path to immanent transcendence. If
we are fated to live each moment of our lives eternally, he reasoned—or
at least if we are prepared to entertain the possibility of doing so—then
every aspect of our existence becomes pregnant with cosmic significance
and universal possibility. A "devastating idea" for those condemned to
mediocrity or a less than happy fate, eternal recurrence, Nietzsche believed, was cause for celebration for those who could bear it.

Nietzsche himself, as he wrote to a friend shortly after his epiphany,
wept "tears of joy" at the thought.[78] And in only a matter of months
he had completed a work, conceived in bliss, which announced the
coming of a new age and a new type of man. To be heralded by "pre-
paratory human beings"—"more fruitful human beings, happier
beings"—this coming age would result

in a happiness that humanity has not known so far: the happiness of a god full of power and love, full of tears and laughter,

a happiness that, like the sun in the evening, continually bestows its inexhaustible riches, pouring them into the sea, feeling richest, as the sun does, only when even the poorest fisherman is still rowing with golden oars! This godlike feeling would then be called—humaneness.[79]

A vision of a fully redeemed, godlike man—this, Nietzsche openly acknowledged, was a species of faith. And yet it was a faith in life, a *"faith in oneself,"* as opposed to the faith in God or science of old. Whereas those were founded on the outmoded "association of morality, knowledge, and happiness," Nietzsche's faith in humanity would be grounded in what he called *gaya scienza,* "joyful science," the discoveries of which pointed the way to unprecedented rewards. "We know a new happiness," he announced with added conviction in a preface to the second edition of the work.[80] All of his remaining effort was devoted to sustaining this claim.

As trite as the phrase now seems, to develop "faith in oneself" was an enormously challenging task, Nietzsche argued, in large part because the faiths of old continued to undermine its possibility. Still suffering from the legacies of the Socratic and Christian traditions, human beings denied much that was vital and spontaneous in themselves, reflexively denigrating their most basic instincts, dispositions, and drives. Egoism and selfishness, sensuality and lust, aggression and the will to power—these "animal urges" were deemed unworthy of civilized human beings. And so they were denied or redirected in insidious ways, adding to humanity's vast accumulation of guilt and "shame *at being man.*" We had learned to despise what we are, Nietzsche insisted. In order to develop faith in ourselves, we would have to unlearn this loathing. Only then could self-realization replace self-denial.

The way to this self-realization—the precondition of man's overcoming of man—thus lay, ironically, in the acceptance and reintegration of his long-denied animal self. This "hidden center needs release from time to time," Nietzsche emphasized in one of his most influential works, *The Genealogy of Morality.* "The beast of prey 'man'" felt trapped by civilization's attempts to make of him "a tame and civilized animal, a *household* pet." For maximum health, he needed room to roam.

In pressing this point, Nietzsche could be intentionally provocative, even reckless, and in light of the subsequent appropriation of his theories by the Nazis and other unscrupulous interpreters, it is hard to read his more inflammatory passages without discomfort. Speaking of those "noble races" who once indulged in violence and power with a "shocking cheerfulness and depth of delight in all destruction"—races who, in returning to "the innocent conscience of the wild beast," are able to leave the scene of a "hideous succession of murder, arson, rape and torture in a mood of bravado and spiritual equilibrium as though they had simply played a student's prank"—Nietzsche observes:

> At the center of all these noble races we cannot fail to see the blond beast of prey, the magnificent *blond beast* avidly prowling round for spoil and victory; this hidden centre needs release from time to time, the beast must out again, must return to the wild:—Roman, Arabian, Germanic, Japanese nobility, Homeric heroes, Scandinavian Vikings—in this requirement they are all alike. . . .[81]

Despite Nietzsche's unquestionable contempt for anti-Semites and Aryan nationalists, such passages lent themselves easily to misinterpretation. And yet it is clear from the context that the "blond beast" is not a specific racial ideal but the "preying lion" that lurks in all conquering peoples, ready always to rip apart a culture's careful restraints. Brimming with confidence, this is the innocent yet terrible force that rises in human beings who are free to unleash their inner animal, to fully indulge their will to power. Unrestrained by conscience, such men do not "doubt their right to happiness." They are not "ashamed of their happiness." They do not say, "It's a disgrace to be happy. There is too much misery."[82] These are creatures who know no guilt or resentment, who are not burdened by pity or regret. They are happy in who and what they are.

Though the release of the prowling beast was a necessary step in the process of self-realization—a step on the way to becoming what we are—Nietzsche never regarded this liberation as an end in itself. The lion, recall, would give way in the final metamorphosis to a new beginning, a born-again child who could evolve into the higher human being, the overman, the man who transcended man. To reach this highest stage meant not only the full integration of the beast within but also the "sublimation" of its powers into something loftier than mere violence. Well before Freud, Nietzsche was employing that word in this distinct sense, stressing our need to mediate and channel baser instincts into higher goals. Cruelty, aggression, the will to dominate and conquer were all part of our animal nature. But they were not ends in themselves. They must be put to nobler uses.

And what might those be? To what ends should human beings direct their protean will to power? In an analysis that influenced Weber, Nietzsche admitted candidly that he did not know, that he *could* not know: The world and an exhausted Western culture, he believed, were no longer able to provide convincing answers to such questions. The point was to create them, and this was precisely the task of the higher men, who having borne on their backs the burden of Western culture and then thrown it off, would be free to lead on toward new endeavors, establishing new tasks, new values, and new goals. These higher men, these overmen, would justify humanity, leading the way to deliverance. "Let us face ourselves," Nietzsche implores these select few with reference to the Greek myth of a region beyond Boreas, the North Wind, where happy men can dwell:

> We are Hyberboreans; we know very well how far off we live. "Neither by land nor by sea will you find the way to the Hyperboreans"—Pindar already knew this about us. Beyond the north, ice, and death—*our* life, *our* happiness. We have discovered happiness, we know the way, we have found the exit out of the labyrinth of thousands of years. Who *else* has found it? Modern man perhaps? "I have got lost," sighs modern man. *This* modernity was our sickness.[83]

However bracing when read alone at night, such metaphoric leaps and poetic bounds inevitably frustrate when one tries to bring them to earth in the light of day. Notwithstanding Nietzsche's high-wire antics, one suspects that he may have lost his way somewhere on the line that led from animal to overman. What he hoped to leave behind him is reasonably clear, and with respect to happiness, there can be few doubts at all. The lion had lashed away at the camel's back, leaving much of its burden in tatters. No longer could the seeker expect to find higher happiness through reason, goodness, or truth. Still less could this be found along the way of resignation, respite, pleasure, or comfort. From Schopenhauer's belief that only fleeting moments of happiness could be had in artistic release from the thralldom of the will, Nietzsche had moved in the opposite direction, coming to believe that in the exercise of the will alone could one find happiness, that happiness appeared only in the "triumphant consciousness of power."[84]

"Men of profound sadness," Nietzsche observed, "betray themselves when they are happy: they have a way of embracing happiness as if they wanted to crush and suffocate it, from jealousy: alas, they know only too well that it will flee."[85] There is something of this same desperation in Nietzsche's spirited paeans to happiness, his attempt to cling to what he knew to be fleeting, to make eternal what he knew to be not, to taste as a man what was reserved for God. "Joy wants itself," says Zarathustra, "wants eternity, wants recurrence, wants everything eternally the same."[86] There can be no doubting the desire, but it is hard to see how it possibly can be fulfilled anywhere but in the suspended realm of faith.

When Nietzsche is brought back to humanity's natural habitat—with both feet, or all four paws, on solid ground—it is clear that he was more successful as beast of burden and defiant lion than as overman. Certainly, his ecstatic visions appealed to many. Yet his gaze is most piercing not when directed upward but when focused down and within. In emphasizing our psychological kinship to the animals that we are, he stressed powerfully that there is more to the human psyche than can be comprehended by what he referred to contemptuously as the modern "religion of comfortableness."[87] This yearning for an end

Henri Matisse, Sketch for *Le Bonheur de Vivre*, 1905–1906, San Francisco Museum of Modern Art. Bequest of Elise S. Haas, © Succession H. Matisse, Paris/Artists Rights Society (ARS), New York.

to all struggle, for an end to all pain, was what motivated the "last men" of modern societies, who had peopled the earth in ever greater numbers since the eighteenth century. "'We have invented happiness,' say the last men, and they blink. They have left the regions where it was hard to live, for one needs warmth."[88] But in their warmth and their creature comforts, Nietzsche believed, these last men of modernity were small men, men who, in scurrying away from the Hyperborean regions, were forgetting essential truths, forgetting that to live was to struggle, suffer, and yearn, and that human happiness was ultimately bound up with this striving. "How little you know of human *happiness,* you comfortable and benevolent people, for happiness and unhappiness are sisters and even twins that either grow up together or, as in your case, *remain small* together."[89] "*Not* for pleasure does man strive: but for power," Nietzsche adds elsewhere in much the same spirit.[90] Unless, and until, human beings comprehended this uncomfortable truth—venturing into the dark, sometimes cold regions of the psyche—they would remain blind to their deepest motives, cut off from their ultimate potential for true happiness.

Tragic Happiness

Sigmund Freud read a smattering of Nietzsche as a student, and in 1900 he purchased a copy of the collected works. It was the year of the philosopher's death and also of the publication of Freud's *Interpretation of Dreams*. Later, Freud claimed never to have indulged in his new possession, telling a friend that he resisted studying Nietzsche because "it was plain that I would find insights in him very similar to psychoanalytic ones."[91] Freud didn't reveal how he knew this. But it is plain that important themes in his own work have much in common with Nietzsche's. Like his predecessor, Freud granted a central role to the unconscious in determining human behavior, and he also saw the overcoming of guilt as a primary human task. He accepted the death of God without anguish, regarding religion as an illusion without a future, and he looked with open eyes at the dark side of the human character, attempting to shed light on our lust for power and aggression, our resentments and manifold sexual desires.

To an even greater extent than Nietzsche, Freud regarded Darwin as the pivotal figure of modern thought. He referred to him always as the "great Darwin" and indeed was partially induced to study biology and medicine at university after coming into contact with his work. "The theories of Darwin," Freud wrote in his autobiography, "strongly attracted me, for they held out hopes of an extraordinary advance in our understanding of the world. . . ."[92] Building on the same theories, Freud made extraordinary advances of his own, coming to see the mind of the animal man, like the body, as a product of evolutionary development—adaptive, dynamic, governed by instinctive forces, nonrational drives, and atavistic traits.

But if in these respects Freud paid homage to his predecessors, duly assuming their weight, he was very much a defiant lion when it came to the subject of happiness. Whereas Darwin continued to cling, almost despite himself, to a delicate belief in the moral improvement of mankind, treating the maximization of happiness as an end to which humanity should strive, Freud retained few such Victorian pieties. "Nobody talks about the purpose of the life of animals," he observed laconically, "unless, perhaps, it may be supposed to lie in being of service to man." This supposition was merely hubris, a relic of "human presumptuousness." Seeing that "the question of the purpose of life had been raised countless times and had never yet received a satisfactory answer," Freud concluded that we had a "right to dismiss it" altogether.[93]

Nor did Freud, like Nietzsche, continue to hold out hope in the "overcoming" of human contradictions or the overcoming of man. Ironically, given Nietzsche's lifelong interest in the literature of Greek tragedy, Freud was the more uncompromisingly tragic thinker of the two. It was not by coincidence that he used the name of the consummate hero of Greek *tragoidia*—Sophocles's Oedipus Rex—to describe what he regarded as the most basic of all human conflicts. In the inherent struggle between parent and child, Freud saw evidence that a bit of tragedy was embedded in all of us from the beginning. "One feels inclined to say," he observed in another connection, "that the intention that man should be 'happy' is not in the plan of 'Creation.'"[94]

This tough-minded aspect of Freud's thought—aware and accepting of the innate conflicts of human experience—is not always adequately appreciated today. For in a development that Freud himself would have regarded with a mixture of amusement and contempt, many of his less orthodox successors have seen fit to promote psychology's general calling in much more ambitious terms as a form of secular salvation—leading, as one critic has observed, to the "triumph of the therapeutic," the replacement of the altar by the couch.[95] On a less cosmic scale, but from a strictly Freudian perspective, one no less symptomatic of the stubborn human need to defend against pain by means of self-delusion, whole schools of contemporary psychology now promise "authentic happiness" to their patients.[96] It is a promise that Freud himself never would have thought to extend. Early

in his career, he put the matter clearly. When asked by a patient how
he proposed to help her, even though, as she had already acknowledged, her illness was closely bound up with the particular circumstances of her life, Freud had this to say:

> No doubt fate will find it easier than I do to relieve you of
> your illness. But you will be able to convince yourself that
> much will be gained if we succeed in transforming your
> hysterical misery into common unhappiness. With a mental
> life that has been restored to health you will be better armed
> against that unhappiness.[97]

Taken from *Studies on Hysteria*, copublished with Josef Breuer in
1895, this is Freud's famous avowal that the goal of what he would
first term "psychoanalysis" the following year was in fact relatively
humble. It aimed to cure gratuitous or self-imposed suffering—
neurosis—in order to restore "common" or "ordinary" unhappiness
(*gemeines Unglück*). Although Freud's faith in his abilities was always
robust, he never claimed to possess a cure for fate or a remedy for
the human condition.

Freud maintained this essential qualification throughout his career,
developing it in greatest detail in his classic of 1930, *Das Unbehagen in
der Kultur* (*Civilization and Its Discontents*). Freud originally proposed to
call the work *Das Unglück in der Kultur* ("Unhappiness in Civilization"),
a title that is much more revealing.[98] For in fact, the book's central
theme is the frustration of man's perennial quest for happiness. Setting aside what he took to be the unanswerable question of the purpose of human existence, Freud turned instead "to the less ambitious
question of what men themselves show by their behavior to be the
purpose and intention of their lives." "What do they demand of life
and wish to achieve in it?" he asked. "The answer to this can hardly
be in doubt. They strive after happiness; they want to become happy
and to remain so."[99]

Delineating his critical terms with concision, Freud maintained that
the endeavor to become happy has two sides, a positive and a nega-

tive. "It aims, on the one hand, at an absence of pain and unpleasure, and, on the other, at the experiencing of strong feelings of pleasure. In its narrower sense the word 'happiness' only relates to the last." Happiness, in brief, is the sensation of pleasure—a definition that leads Freud to a straightforward conclusion. "What decides the purpose of life," he summarizes, "is simply the program of the pleasure principle," the effort to maximize pleasurable sensations.[100]

In many ways, this formulation is reminiscent of Bentham, among others. A natural human endowment that "dominates the operation of the mental apparatus from the start," the pleasure principle is a primitive and demanding force that governs the "primary process" of the mind.[101] According to Freud, however, the pleasure principle soon comes up against a "secondary process" that constrains human beings to curb their crude desires in keeping with the "reality principle." As the young mind develops, it is forced to regulate its demands for immediate gratification, thus making concessions to the external environment, to other people, and to other things ("reality"). Postponing present enjoyment for the sake of later rewards, it learns to calculate consequences, weighing benefits and costs in the continued interest of maximizing pleasure and minimizing pain.

This is where the similarity with Bentham breaks down. For although in Freud's opinion the two principles of pleasure and reality may achieve an uneasy truce, he viewed their relationship as essentially antagonistic: The demand for pleasure is forever at war with reality. Insatiable, the pleasure principle battles all that seeks to impose limits on it—whether this be the internal "secondary process" of the mind or the external constraints of the surrounding environment. In either case, it is a battle that the pleasure principle is destined to lose. As Freud put the problem in *Civilization and Its Discontents,* its program "is at loggerheads with the whole world, with the macrocosm as much as with the microcosm. There is no possibility at all of its being carried through; all the regulations of the universe run counter to it."[102]

The struggle for happiness is doomed from the start, condemned internally by the nature of our mental endowment and externally by nature itself. On the one hand, Freud pointed out what others before him had observed: the insatiability of human desire. "What we call happiness in the strictest sense comes from the (preferably sudden) satisfactions of needs which have been dammed up to a high degree," Freud explained. "It is from its nature only possible as an episodic phenomenon. When any situation that is desired by the pleasure principle is prolonged, it only produces a feeling of mild contentment," and then trails off accordingly. When one's thirst is slated, the satisfaction of drink declines. Like children who quickly tire of the novelty of their birthday toys, "we are so made that we can derive intense enjoyment only from a contrast and very little from a state of things. Thus our possibilities are already restricted by our constitution."[103]

By adding the authority of psychiatry to the philosophical conclusions of moralists, Freud anticipated the "hedonic treadmill" (the tragedy of happiness) of later Darwinian theorists. He had, of course, no more access to this recent theoretical development than Darwin did. Yet it is more likely that he would have embraced it. For Freud wrote with a different temperament and in a different time. He had witnessed the incredible carnage of World War I, and he watched as the first stirrings of fascism laid waste to any residual Victorian optimism. But quite apart from this immediate historical context, Freud believed that firm evidence already warranted conclusions in keeping with the tragedy of happiness. On display internally in the psychological makeup of every human being, this evidence could also be gathered externally by studying the nature of being in the world. The conditions of existence, Freud concluded, matched our infinite desire for pleasure with infinite possibilities for pain.

For the sake of conceptual clarity, Freud reduced these manifold possibilities to three general categories. We are threatened with suffering, he claims:

> from our own body, which is doomed to decay and dissolution and which cannot even do without pain and anxiety as warning signals; from the external world, which may rage against us with overwhelming and merciless forces of destruction; and

finally from our relations to other men. The suffering which comes from this last source is perhaps more painful to us than any other. We tend to regard it as a kind of gratuitous addition, although it cannot be any less fatefully inevitable than the suffering which comes from elsewhere.[104]

However "fatefully inevitable," these sources of suffering had done little to discourage human beings from trying to deceive them. Freud discussed in detail the many ways in which men and women have attempted to trick fate in the pursuit of happiness, beginning with the most aggressive—hedonism. "The unrestricted satisfaction of every need presents itself as the most enticing method of conducting one's life," Freud acknowledged, "but it means putting enjoyment before caution, and soon brings its own punishment."[105] What he considered "the crudest, but also the most effective" means of averting suffering—"the chemical one"—fell prey to similar drawbacks. He confessed that he found such methods "interesting" and expressed regret that the "toxic side of mental processes" had not received proper scientific study. But having himself experimented with cocaine, he was able to speak from experience when he observed that substances that allowed the user to "withdraw from the pressure of reality and find refuge in a world of one's own" were dangerously attractive and potentially harmful, responsible in certain circumstances for the useless waste of a "large quota of energy" that might be far better employed. The chemical means to happiness, he concluded, could never be anything more than a temporary expedient.[106]

A similar form of withdrawal (and another strategy for attaining happiness) was "voluntary isolation," "keeping oneself aloof from other people," the strategy of the hermit. Freud acknowledged that this might secure the "happiness of quietness," but he clearly regarded the strategy as an admission of defeat. "Against the dreaded external world one can only defend oneself by some kind of turning away from it. . . ." The same could be said of another extreme means of attempting to defend against the external world: "killing off the instincts as is prescribed by the worldly wisdom of the East and practiced by Yoga."

Freud had in mind the ascetic practice of renunciation of the sort achieved by the saints. But again he judged this strategy lacking. "If it succeeds, then the subject has . . . given up all other activities as well—he has sacrificed his life; and, by another path, he has once more only achieved the happiness of quietness."[107] The remedy was more severe than the condition it sought to cure.

"Another and better path," Freud believed, was that of "becoming a member of the human community," and "working for the good of all." Or even more ambitiously, one could "try to re-create the world, to build up in its stead another world in which its most unbearable features are eliminated and replaced by others that are in conformity with one's own wishes." But Freud never put much stock in utopia. Whoever "sets out upon this path to happiness," he judged, "will as a rule attain nothing. Reality is too strong for him." Of similar fragility were those strategies that attempted to perceive the world through imagination or illusion. "At the head of these satisfactions through fantasy," Freud placed the "enjoyment of works of art," although he cautioned that "the mild narcosis" that this induced could bring about no more than a "transient withdrawal from the pressure of vital needs." The aesthetic approach—"in which happiness in life is predominantly sought in the enjoyment of beauty"—was prey to many of the same shortcomings that he saw, in more direct form, in faith. With characteristic scorn, Freud wrote off the religions of humankind as "mass-delusions," belittling their "attempt to procure a certainty of happiness and a protection against suffering through a delusional remolding of reality." It was a strategy that he ranked on a par with the flight into fantasy of neurotic illness.[108]

Far more promising, in Freud's view, were the pleasures to be had through sublimation and the healthy "displacements of libido" involved in creative and productive work. Although not even the most engrossing forms of labor could provide "impenetrable armor against the arrows of fortune," Freud commended "professional activity"—especially "psychical and intellectual work"—as a source of "special satisfaction," particularly when freely chosen. "No other technique for the conduct of life attaches the individual so firmly to reality," Freud maintained. It was a conviction with which Marx would have agreed. And although Freud maintained that work was not sufficiently "prized by men" as a path to happiness, it deserved to be so.[109]

Finally, Freud addressed the "way of life which makes love the center of everything, which looks for all satisfaction in loving and being loved."[110] This was, he stressed, a strategy that came "naturally enough to all of us" given that it was invariably based on a yearning for the satisfactions of infancy, as well as what is our most "intense" and "overwhelming" sensation of pleasure—sexual (genital) love—"the prototype of all happiness."[111] In Nietzsche's comment that sex is "the happiness that is the great parable of a higher happiness and the highest hope," Freud might have found wisdom to match his own earlier statement in a letter to Wilhelm Fliess that "happiness is the belated fulfillment" of a "prehistoric" or "childhood wish."[112] In any case, he conceded that erotic love perhaps "does in fact come nearer to this goal [of the positive fulfillment of happiness] than any other method."[113]

Yet Freud hastened to add that "the weak side of this technique of living is easy to see," for otherwise "no human being would have thought of abandoning this path to happiness for any other." We are "never so defenseless against suffering as when we love, never so helplessly unhappy as when we have lost our loved object or its love." A good deal of the energy of psychoanalysis, in fact, was devoted to trying to understand the daunting complexities of sustaining love in the face of its many threats. As a devoted father and husband, Freud knew the pleasures that love could bring. But as a student of human nature, he also knew that they were seldom uncomplicated. Eros and the ego, our conscious understanding of the world and ourselves, were inextricably linked, love and aggression seldom far removed. Even in the cradle of Cupid, the conflicts that animate the tragic stage were readily apparent.[114]

Although Freud disavowed the history of happiness as a futile field of inquiry—judging it too difficult "to form an opinion whether and in what degree men of an earlier age felt happier and what part their cultural conditions played in the matter"—his list of strategies of pursuit nonetheless coincides remarkably well with many of the means and methods examined in this book.[115] Socrates's and Plato's subli-mation of Eros into intellectual striving, the ascetic renunciation rec-ommended by Epicurus and the Stoics, Augustine's happiness of hope, Rousseau's praise of voluntary seclusion on his blessed isle, Marx's revolutionary dream of remaking the world, the Romantic quest for love, Schopenhauer's commendation of the illusion of art, the hedo-nism of Sade and La Mettrie, the drug-induced euphoria of Baudelaire and Thomas de Quincey, the subtle virtues of work recommended by Weber, Marx, and Smith—all of these strategies we have encountered in the course of this book, following, like Freud, the arguments made in their behalf.

Freud was well aware that he might have added other strategies to his list. But "in spite of [its] incompleteness," he felt confident to venture the conclusion, "The program of becoming happy, which the pleasure principle imposes on us, cannot be fulfilled." The statement was less bleak than it might seem, for Freud added immediately that "we must not—indeed, we cannot—give up our efforts to bring it [the program of becoming happy] nearer to fulfillment by some means or other."[116] This was the human predicament in Freud's eyes: tragic in its plight, but also tragic in a more uplifting sense, one that empha-sized man's heroic refusal to succumb passively to the decrees of fate. Human beings would struggle for happiness until the end. Far from despairing at our inevitable defeat, Freud saw something noble in our very defiance.

Nor did he admit that the fact that happiness was not in the plan of "creation" might have a "paralyzing effect" on human behavior. If it was true that by no path to happiness "can we attain all that we de-sire," it was also true that there were "many paths which *may* lead to such happiness as is attainable by men," even if "there is none which does so for certain."[117] Pleasure, to put it another way, was better than pain, and so there was no reason we shouldn't seek to maximize our total share whenever possible. True, we would never completely mas-ter nature, and our bodies, forever subject to decay, would always have "a limited capacity for adaptation and achievement." But Freud in-sisted, "If we cannot remove all suffering, we can remove some, and can mitigate some: the experience of many thousands of years has convinced us of that."[118]

Freud was less optimistic about our ability to address the third major source of unhappiness—social suffering—arguing at length that the renunciation of erotic and aggressive impulses demanded by civilization would inevitably exact a heavy price. Whereas Darwin had envisioned a somewhat easier accommodation of man's more primitive instincts in society, Freud maintained that the cost of containing our aggressive and sexual urges would be high. Among our "instinctual endowments is to be reckoned a powerful share of aggressiveness," he pointed out. And though many were loath to admit it, "Man is a wolf to man" (*Homo homini lupus*), a creature as ready to regard his neighbor as an enemy to be exploited as a friend to be loved.[119] Organized society might force human beings to constrain their desire to "satisfy their aggressiveness" on others. But it did so only by redirecting that aggression within. The result, as Nietzsche had argued in the *Genealogy of Morality*, was an inevitable measure of frustration, anxiety, and displaced guilt. "The price we pay for our advance in civilization is a loss of happiness through the heightening of the sense of guilt," Freud stressed.[120] "Civilized man [had] exchanged a portion of his possibilities of happiness for a portion of security."[121]

Yet even with regard to social suffering, Freud's analysis was not completely without redemptive possibilities. On the one hand, he left open the prospect that "we may expect gradually to carry through such alterations in our civilization that will better satisfy our needs."[122] And on the other, he saw psychoanalysis as a means for dealing with anxiety and guilt, allowing us to learn to sublimate our aggressive and destructive impulses into healthier, more productive behavior. On this considerably restricted terrain, the pleasure principle had some room to maneuver. As Freud observed, "Happiness, in the reduced sense in which we recognize it as possible, is a problem of the economics of the individual's libido." There were, accordingly, as many paths to pleasure as there were palates, each shaped by an individual's own unique psychic constitution. Whereas the predominantly erotic individual would give first priority to emotional relationships, the narcissist, who inclines toward self-sufficiency, would seek primary satisfaction in internal mental processes. The man of action, by contrast, would remain wedded to the external world, and so forth in keeping with individual proclivities. Freud pointed out that "just as a cautious business-man avoids tying up all his capital in one concern," we would do well not "to look for the whole of our satisfaction from any single aspiration." He also knew that "there is no golden rule which applies to everyone." "Every man," he stressed, "must find out for himself in what particular fashion he can be saved."[123]

The reference to salvation, of course, was ironic, an allusion to the celebrated line of Frederick the Great, who proudly defended his policy of religious toleration by noting, "In my State every man can be saved after his own fashion." For Freud, "salvation" had been reduced further still to the "economics of libido," stripped down to sensation alone. Gone were any last links to a transcendent calling, to the necessary virtues, to higher meaning, or to truth. Happiness, as Locke had once feared, could now really be just lobsters or cheese.

"Long ago," Freud reflected, man had "formed an ideal conception of omnipotence and omniscience which he embodied in his gods. To these gods he attributed everything that seemed unattainable to his wishes, or that was forbidden to him. One may say, therefore, that these gods were cultural ideals." But today, Freud continued, man "has come very close to the attainment of this ideal, he has almost become a god himself." Freud acknowledged that the process was still incomplete. It would be better to say that man has become "a kind of prosthetic God," capable of donning the "auxiliary organs" of technology to make himself truly powerful and magnificent. Moreover, man could console himself with the thought that his development would "not come to an end precisely with the year 1930 CE," the year of Freud's writing. "Future ages will bring with them new and probably unimaginably great advances in this field of civilization and will increase man's likeness to God still more." Yet creator that he was, man, in one critical respect, was still not made in the image of his ideal likeness. "In the interests of our investigations," Freud cautioned, "we will not forget that present-day man does not feel happy in his Godlike character."[124] With godlike powers, but without God's serenity, could man rest content in his dissatisfaction, this final remnant of his humanity? If Freud's life's work implied that he would have to, it also suggested that he would not.

Brave New World

Just two years after the publication of Freud's *Civilization and Its Discontents*, Aldous Huxley issued a warning of a very different sort. Untroubled by the possibility of inherent impediments to human happiness, this grandson of "Darwin's Bulldog," Thomas Henry Huxley, worried instead about the potentially dehumanizing future of an overly contented world. The lone hero of his 1932 classic *Brave New World* is forced to proclaim the "right to be unhappy."[125] His futile attempt to resist the troubling course of human evolution and the latently oppressive happiness that Huxley saw lurking at the heart of modern civilization still holds a lesson for us all.

Raised in squalor on a reservation outside the developed world, Huxley's hero John is a "savage," taken with high expectations to what he believes will be an environment where "beauteous mankind" can fully flourish. And indeed, in this "brave new world," John discovers that "everybody's happy nowadays." Built on the "solid ground of daily labor and distraction," happiness is the sole purpose of a society in which free sexuality is encouraged from a young age, and the steady consumption of material pleasures is ensured throughout life. The inhabitants of the brave new world acknowledge only two gods—"Our Ford and our Freud"—the great innovator of mass production on the one hand, and the man who released them from guilt on the other, freeing the world for the total triumph of the pleasure principle. Here, everything that is unpleasant or that causes pain has been removed. Exercise, synthetic food, and high-tech medicine do away with old age, prolonging youth indefinitely. Delayed gratification is all but eradicated, and the family, that perennial source of oedipal animosity and lifelong conflict, has been replaced by a system of genetic breeding and conditioning designed to control the moods, desires, and expectations of its offspring. In a tribute to the teachings of T. R. Malthus, the nine-teenth-century author of *An Essay on the Principle of Population; or A view of its past and present Effect on Human Happiness,* citizens now regularly perform the "Malthusian Drill" and don "Malthusian belts" to prohibit pregnancy through ultra-convenient birth control. In addition, easy access to abortion mitigates the unpleasant consequences of mating, ensuring guilt-free sex and sustainable levels of population. Finally, for anyone whose satisfaction remains incomplete, a highly sophisti-cated entertainment industry provides sense-around movies (the Feelies) with simple plots and dazzling effects to distract and en-gage, while a safe and effective mood-altering drug (Soma) is readily available to put a constant smile on one's face, providing "all the ad-vantages of Christianity and alcohol" and "none of their defects." In this brave new world, "faith in happiness as the Sovereign Good" is unquestioned.

Unquestioned, that is, by all save the awkward few, of whom the "Savage" proves to be the most persistent. Clinging to atavistic views, he dares to imagine that there might be more to life than good feeling—yearning, instead, for knowledge, moral improvement, and higher consciousness. As he explains to the "world controller" of the brave new world in protesting his "right to be unhappy": "I don't want comfort. I want God, I want poetry, I want real danger, I want free-dom, I want goodness. I want sin."

The price paid for happiness, the Savage knows, is too high. And so, in a futile attempt to flee this "hard master," he returns to the wild, living in isolation, mortifying his flesh, and praying to God in an effort to purify his soul. His escape is short-lived, however, interrupted by the insatiable media curiosity of the entertainment industry, at the head of which is Darwin Bonaparte, a celebrated big-game photogra-pher famous for having captured a gorilla's wedding on film. Combin-ing the all-conquering instincts of the general with the curiosity in our primitive ancestry of his namesake, Darwin violates the Savage's tem-porary sanctity, exposing him to hoards of prying tourists who regard him as they would a caged animal in a zoo. These civilized onlookers throw peanuts to the Savage "as to an ape," driving him into the regressive posture of an "animal at bay." His only escape from these tormentors is Soma. But when he awakens after a night of chemically induced sanctuary, he blinks at the terrible light in "owlish incomprehension." The only way for this animal-man to preserve his dignity is to commit suicide. Regarded by the highly evolved as an ape, the Savage is in fact the last remnant of a dying species—man.

In retrospect, it is astonishing that this book was written in the midst of the Great Depression, only fourteen years after the bloodiest war in human history and just seven years prior to the outbreak of a conflagration that would subsume the world in horrors even greater. But *Brave New World* sees beyond the immediate horizon of the present into a future that can only startle the contemporary observer. Whereas the other dystopian masterpiece of the twentieth century, George Orwell's *1984* (1949), now seems a brilliant, if dated, reflection of the concerns of the Cold War, *Brave New World* continues to shock with its portrayal of an anodyne consumer society governed by the pleasure principle, immediate gratification, and the cult of youth. Like our own, its citizens are distracted by an arts and entertainment industry that emphasizes entertainment at the expense of art; encouraged wherever possible to eradicate the unpleasant rather "than learning to put up with it"; led along by the unfailing allure of prosperity, sexual satisfaction, and eternal youth; conditioned to abolish guilt and memory and regret. This is the happiness of Nietzsche's last men—a happiness freed of its final attachments to virtue, transcendence, and self-development, reduced at long last to comfort and good feeling alone. In this brave new world, the final Sovereign Good rules without rivals in absolute supremacy. But it is an impoverished king, unworthy to lead creatures who would live as gods, or men, or even apes.

Could the animal-man really be herded in this way—in the manner of the *Brave New World*? Huxley knew that something deep in our nature bridled at the prospect, yearning perpetually, like the Savage, for more. And yet this same realization led him to what was perhaps his most prescient—and disturbing—observation, that in the relentless search for happiness, human beings would endeavor to alter their very nature, tampering with the last bastion of fate: their genetic constitution.

CONCLUSION: HAPPY ENDING

VLADIMIR: Say you are, even if it's not true.

ESTRAGON: What am I to say?

VLADIMIR: Say, I am happy.

ESTRAGON: I am happy.

VLADIMIR: So am I.

ESTRAGON: So am I.

VLADIMIR: We are happy.

ESTRAGON: We are happy. (Silence.) What do we do now, now that we are happy?

VLADIMIR: Wait for Godot.[1]

What do we do now, now that we are happy? When Samuel Beckett's Estragon first posed this question in French at the tiny Theater of Babylon in Paris in 1953, it must have sounded odd. "To write poetry after Auschwitz is barbaric," the German philosopher Theodor Adorno had already observed in a famous (if dubious) judgment.[2] To speak of happiness, surely, was even more so. By conservative estimates, forty million people had died in the slaughter of World War II, and by 1949, with the Soviet Union's first successful test of the atomic bomb, the world's superpowers seemed poised to render these numbers a pittance. Was not talk of happiness in such circumstances absurd?

If so, then Beckett's medium was well chosen, for strictly speaking, he wrote not poetry but theater, the theater of the absurd. And to the extent that the stage still captured the surreal spectacle of the world, his "tragicomedy in two acts" captured well the dogged pursuit of happiness in the face of overwhelming despair. Despite their conclusion that men are "pigs" and people "bloody ignorant apes," Vladimir and Estragon continue to hope amid the skeletons and the emptiness that surrounds them. In their "immense confusion," they are presented only with the certainty that "the tears of the world are a constant quantity," yet they stumble on regardless, waiting for salvation, waiting for Godot. They remember the tales of the Gospels, the maps of the holy land, the Dead Sea. "That's where we'll go, I used to say, that's where we'll go for our honeymoon. We'll swim. We'll be happy," Estragon muses. And when he sleeps, he wakes to recall, "I was dreaming I was happy." It is an activity that serves nicely to "pass the time." Even as the two wanderers know in their heart of hearts that there is "nothing to be done," they bumble on. And there is life in their bumbling.

This history of happiness began with the development of tragedy (*tragoidia*) on the classical stage and in history itself. There, the tragic hero was one who carried on despite irreconcilable conflicts and overwhelming odds, struggling to maintain honor and pursue his end in the knowledge that unhappy chance can never be controlled. "Short as his life is, no man is so happy," Herodotus reminds us, "that it shall not be his lot, not only once but many times, to wish himself dead rather than alive."[3] The tragic hero endures all, carrying on until the final moment as best he can.

In this sense, Beckett's *Waiting for Godot* is unquestionably tragic, and indeed, its "tragedy" is even more pronounced than that of its classical predecessors. For unlike the *tragoidia* of ancient times, the modern variant must do away completely with the convention that had always sustained a ray of hope until the end. Here, there can be no deus ex machina waiting in the wings to produce a final, miraculous salvation, no god in the machine poised to swoop down to spirit away the heroes, to save Croesus from the flames, to resolve our fate. Vladimir and Estragon yearn for the mysterious Godot, a man whose arrival they believe will ensure that "we'll be saved." But Godot, of course, never appears. The god in the machine has become the ghost in the machine, who haunts by his absence, leaving only a wisp, a trace, the faint sensation of spiritual presence, an evanescent hope of happiness whose kingdom is resolutely of this earth.

The hope that God, or Godot, or some other holy ghost might one day bring salvation has not been extinguished entirely. May it never be. But few would deny that the horrors of the first half of the twentieth century rendered such hope harder to sustain. With waning faith that a deus ex machina will save them, Beckett's heroes can only cling to the prospect of an earthly happiness that they know instinctively to be wanting. They pretend to be happy—"Say you are, even if it's not true"—but the moment they do so, they realize that they are still in need. "What do we do now, now that we are happy?" they wonder. Their faith in this earthly end is undermined by the ironic knowledge of its insufficiency and unattainability. Even if Vladimir and Estragon were happy, we suspect, they would not be content. They would continue to wait. Theirs is a fate more tragic than even that of the heroes of old.

And yet there is a strange nobility in their patient persistence— the nobility, perhaps, of the fool—but a nobility nonetheless, a heroism proportionate to an age wanting hope. Vladimir and Estragon remind us that it might still be possible to make poetry in life. "What's the good of losing heart now?" Vladimir demands. "We should have thought of it a million years ago. . . ." Later he adds with greater conviction, "At this place, at this moment of time, all mankind is us, whether we like it or not. Let us make the most of it, before it is too late! Let us represent worthily for once the foul brood to which a cruel fate consigned us! What do you say?"

It is a noble challenge, and one that arguably had already been taken up on the stage of the world by a tragic hero of a very different sort, the historical actor Primo Levi, who suggests not only that poetry is possible after Auschwitz, but that it was possible, uncannily, even while there. Describing his own "journey towards nothingness" in that very place, Levi reflects:

> Sooner or later in life everyone discovers that perfect happiness is unrealizable, but there are few who pause to consider the antithesis: that perfect unhappiness is equally unattainable. The obstacles preventing the realization of both these extreme states are of the same nature: they derive from our human condition which is opposed to everything infinite. Our ever-insufficient knowledge of the future opposes it: and this is called, in the one instance, hope, and in the other, uncertainty of the following day. The certainty of death opposes it: for it places a limit on every joy, but also on every grief. The inevitable material cares oppose it: for as they poison every lasting happiness, they equally assiduously distract us from our misfortunes, and make our consciousness of them intermittent and hence supportable.[4]

Incredibly, even in the *Lager* (camp), one could still have hope; even in the *Lager*, one could still draw comfort from the finality of death; even in the *Lager*, one could still find distraction—and take relief—in the preoccupation with material cares. It was not resignation or an abstract "will to live," Levi tells us, that kept him alive, but "the very discomfort, the blows, the cold, the thirst." For each obstacle was a hurdle to be overcome, a hurdle that kept him focused on the finite, the here and now. Behind the immediate agony of frozen fingers might lie the dull throbbing of hunger, the irritation of lice, the discomfort of sleeplessness, the regret of family far away, the pain of an open sore. But as soon as the cause of the first stress was removed (if it were at all), one would be "grievously amazed to see that another lies behind, and in reality a whole series of others." As Levi came to realize, "Human nature is such that grief and pain . . . do not add up as a whole in our consciousness, but hide, the lesser behind the greater, according to a definite law of perspective. It is providential and is our means of surviving in the camp."[5] Similar to the way we are led along in life by the endless pursuit of pleasures, we are led along—even saved—by the endless revelation of pain.

This in itself may not be a happy thought, but it is a reminder of how relative, always, are our perceptions of misery and joy. Another tragic hero, the psychiatrist and philosopher Viktor Frankl, was led to similar conclusions by his own experience at Auschwitz. The size of human suffering is "absolutely relative," he writes: It will expand like gas to fill the room of a conscious mind and a human soul. But it follows from this "that a very trifling thing can cause the greatest of joys." Frankl speaks of how the "meager pleasures of camp life provided a kind of negative happiness,—'freedom from suffering,' as Schopenhauer put it," and of the intensification of inner life that helped "the prisoner find a refuge from the emptiness, desolation, and spiritual poverty of his existence." And he speaks of the heightened sensitivity to natural beauty amid so much man-made ugliness. A glimpse of a mountain or the spectacle of a sunset was a sublime reminder of "how beautiful the world *could* be." *Et lux in tenebris lucet.* And the light shineth in the darkness. Man for Frankl, as for Dostoyevsky before him, is a being who "can get used to anything." [6] It is at once an uplifting and a harrowing thought.

Both Levi and Frankl were exceptional men, tragic heroes on the world's stage, whose affirmation and endurance in the face of indescribable suffering is impossible for most of us to conceive, let alone to match. Rare is the individual, even under normal conditions, who can summon the strength to produce a work like Levi's *Survival at Auschwitz* or Frankl's *Man's Search for Meaning,* published just a year after his liberation from the camps. And yet as unique as these two men undoubtedly were, their ability to recover from their experiences—to seek meaning, poetry, and happiness again after suffering a terrible blow of fortune—is indicative of a widely shared human propensity. A great deal of recent psychological research reaffirms this fact, arguing strongly in favor of an innate human capacity to respond to the outrages of fate. Studies have found, for example, that after experiencing a major setback—losing a job, say, or going through a divorce—most people will revert relatively quickly to their set pattern of mood.

Within anywhere from three months to a year, the vast majority will get back to their "normal" selves, including those who have undergone major accidents. Remarkably, as several fascinating studies have documented, even those who have been rendered quadriplegic in car or motorcycle accidents seem to fit this pattern. As one psychologist summarizes:

> Without minimizing catastrophe, the consistent and astonishing result is that the worst emotional consequences of bad events are usually temporary. With major setbacks or injuries, the emotional after-effects may linger a year or more. Yet within a matter of weeks, one's current mood is more affected by the day's events—an argument with one's spouse, a failure at work, a rewarding call or a gratifying letter from a dear friend or child—than by whether one is paralyzed or mobile, blind or sighted.[7]

This is not to make light of catastrophic misfortune, or to suggest that anyone can ever fully recover from an event as shattering as the Holocaust. Levi himself committed suicide forty-two years after his liberation. And though it is probably significant that he suffered from depression before Auschwitz as well as after, it would be perverse to suggest that his life circumstances had no bearing on his long-term happiness. The same can be said with respect to the lasting effects of sustained child abuse or other extensive psychological trauma. Sometimes it is simply impossible to escape the past.

Nonetheless, evidence on the whole suggests an astounding human resilience.* We are designed to carry on, it seems, and most often we do, regardless of what happens to us. The root of the word notwithstanding, happiness—or at least our general mood—is evidently much less dependent on happenstance than long was thought.

---

*The exception to this pattern is depressive illness, which appears to interrupt the mind's natural "thermostat" of mood, sending the afflicted into downward spirals that are often controllable only by therapy or medication, if at all.

That proposition can be freeing, a source of solace or strength. But there is another side to this same data, just as there is another side to Beckett's play. If it is true that the end of a relationship or the death of a friend will probably have little bearing on our long-term frame of mind, it is equally true that neither will much of the bounty of *good* fortune. The same research that testifies to human beings' ability to pick themselves up after a fall also suggests a dismaying tendency to waft back to earth when we have risen too far from the norm. Studies of people who have won the lottery, for example, or who have a particularly fine day at the races, present the mirror image of the findings on accident victims: After a short period of elation (several weeks or several months), they invariably return, like the wave in a sine curve, to where they were before, hovering around what psychologists call, in another metaphor, the rough "set point" on the "thermostat" of mood.[8] We may believe that if we only had a million dollars, or if we only got a new job—or if we only got the girl or boy—our lives would be transformed, that we would finally be happy. It is certainly pretty to think so. But a growing body of research suggests otherwise.[9] In the specialized terms of the trade, human beings seem to suffer from "impact bias," a distortion of the "impact" or effect that hoped-for pleasures will have. Surprisingly often, it turns out, we are prone to exaggerate the degree of fulfillment we will derive from anticipated pleasures, or we misjudge altogether. And even when we do plot our forecasts with greater wisdom and precision, our natural disposition is to adapt to new pleasures much more quickly than we expect.

In many respects, this is merely another way of describing the phenomenon of the "hedonic treadmill," the tragedy of happiness identified by post-Darwinian evolutionary psychologists, who note our tendency to grow restless with what we have. And this, in turn, is merely a recognition of what many of the moralists examined in this book have long known about the insatiability of human desire. Human beings' proclivity to grow accustomed to, and then dissatisfied with, the pleasures of this world is a phenomenon as old as humanity. Even in paradise, we would do well to recall, Adam and Eve grew restless, and so no doubt will we, whatever our surroundings.

In light of this long history, it is probably worth treating the recent "revelations" of psychologists as less genuinely revealing than they and their publicists would have us believe. Still, the studies of "impact bias" and "affective forecasting," just like the ruminations on the "hedonic treadmill" and the "tragedy of happiness," do shed empirical light on a process of pursuit whose rhythms we have followed in a less clinical context over the course of roughly two and a half thousand years. From the moment Socrates declared that happiness should be the goal of good living, human beings have searched for its secret without end. But despite their uninterrupted efforts—their countless experiments and trials—this search has yielded few certain discoveries. If there is a secret to happiness, a modern wit has said, then that secret is closely guarded. It may be so well kept that few, if any, know what it is.

This specter of perpetual pursuit—an endless search through the ages for an apparition that may not even exist—surely induces a ghostly chill, the same haunting feeling of absence and expectation that lingers on the stage well after the curtain has fallen on *Waiting for Godot*. Yet we should not forget that this same spectacle can just as easily make us laugh. Beckett's play, after all, is not strictly a tragedy but a tragicomedy, a work that reaffirms "that the tears of the world are a constant," yes, but that quickly reassures that "the same is true of the laugh." Caught up in a universe they don't understand, uncertain of their situation and fate, Vladimir and Estragon are as much clowns as tragedians, men who struggle to take their boots off at the beginning of the play and fight to keep their pants up at the end. After Vladimir leaves his fly undone in a fit of absentmindedness, he agrees that he should do it up, declaring to Estragon with all the gravity of Irish slapstick, "Never neglect the little things in life." These are men who expose themselves to human folly, and who are themselves completely exposed. We are invited to sympathize with their plight, but we are also asked to laugh. For their efforts to entertain themselves—to pass the time—are ours.

Something of this same comic spectacle is on display with even sharper wit in Beckett's *Happy Days*, a play first staged at the Cherry Lane Theatre in New York City in 1961. In the years since the debut of *Waiting for Godot*, any concern about the pursuit of happiness after

Auschwitz had long since faded. Beckett's adopted home of France was in the midst of what would come to be called *les trentes glorieuses*— the "thirty glorious years" of economic expansion that followed the deprivation of the postwar period. The Germans and the Japanese were experiencing their own economic "miracles," and the United States was enjoying "boom time," a period of phenomenal growth that consolidated its position as the richest country in the world, while producing a generation of children—the "boomers"—more materially privileged than any in previous history. This massive expansion of the consumer economy would be coupled in the early 1960s with the invention of the birth control pill and the first stirrings in the loins of what would prove a successful cultural assault on many of the "hangups" and prejudices that continued to bar the way to pleasure. By 1972, all who dared were free to indulge in the "joy of sex," as the best-selling book of that name and year proclaimed. The work would go on to sell millions and millions of copies.

The time and the place were ripe for *Happy Days*, and Beckett did not disappoint, producing a work that was both prescient in its portrayal of the ubiquity and triumph of happiness as an ideal of uninterrupted good feeling, and very much of the moment. "I used to pray. I say I used to pray. Yes, I must confess I did," avows Winnie, the work's late-middle-aged protagonist, who appears onstage in act 1, embedded in a mound of earth that rises to her waist. "Not now."[10] It is true that she begins the play with the familiar words "For Jesus Christ sake Amen. . . . World without end," and lapses occasionally into what she describes as the "old style," speaking of "blessings" and "mercies," and other such "boons" that help her "through the day." Perhaps, Winnie even ventures on one occasion, "someone is looking at me still." But such consolation is crowded out by the far more pervasive thought: "Oh this is going to be another happy day!"

Winnie reflects on the "happy memories" of the past, and the "happy day to come"—and this, she declares, "is what I find so comforting when I lose heart and envy the brute beast." Even as the ground rises in the second (and final) act to surround all but her head, Winnie remains defiantly optimistic in the face of this mounting confirmation of her own mortality. "What matter, that's what I always say, it will have been a happy day, after all, another happy day." She combs her hair, she brushes her teeth, she takes pleasure in the distant company of her fading husband. No, she "can't complain." "So much to be thankful for." "No pain." And though the presence of a revolver in her purse belies this self-assurance—as do the silences in her final halting lines—we are not meant, I think, to doubt the sincerity of her faith: "Oh this *is* a happy day, this will have been another happy day! (Pause.) After all. (Pause.) So far."

Like Vladimir and Estragon, Winnie is heroic—alternately touching, tragic, and quixotic. But also like them, she is ridiculous, absurd. Crying happiness in the face of death with undaunted insistence, she is forced to qualify her claim just as it leaves her mouth, switching to the future perfect tense. This *will have been* a happy day. The future perfect, it should be clear, is a time that never is, never shall be, and never was. It only will have been. The future perfect, like the perfect future, exists only as an act of faith.

The spectator who is amused by the antics of *Happy Days* will find humor, too, in the *comédie humaine* that has succeeded it. For surely there is something amusing about the frenzy with which men and women have pursued happiness in the West ever since. If the apparent calm of the 1950s and early 1960s was shattered by the dislocations and upheavals that followed in the wake of the Kennedy assassination in 1963, the restless search for happiness as pleasure and good feeling only intensified. It was in that very year that a little-known advertising executive by the name of Harvey R. Ball created the first copy of a modern icon that would compete for prominence in certain quarters with the Cross and the Star of David. Produced on contract to soothe the anxious workers of the amusingly named State Mutual Life Assurance Company in Worcester, Massachusetts, as their firm merged with another, the "smiley face" earned Ball a $45 commission. He never filed a trademark or copyright papers, which from a purely financial standpoint must have been sad, for soon the symbol was providing assurance and reassurance to millions. In 1971 alone, devotees of happiness purchased fifty million smiley-face buttons, and today the image adorns T-shirts, stationery, plastic bags, key chains, and car bumpers throughout the world.[11]

And this was only the first crack of a much fuller grin. In magazines and Hollywood endings, on billboards and TV, people in the West would be saturated as never before by images of the smiling faces of "real" people enjoying themselves eternally, as is their right. It is difficult to remain impervious to this constant good cheer. Some studies even suggest that the physical act of smiling itself helps, physiologically, to induce a better mood. But it might be argued, in a darker vein, that images of artificial happiness only reinforce the real sadness, guilt, and sense of inadequacy felt by those who cannot find it in themselves to share in the mirth. In either case, few today can be accused of not trying. Who among us never smiles for the camera? A glance at the family photo album will confirm that our grandparents' generation was seldom so quick to present itself in this light. And when we think that the smile of Mona Lisa, just five centuries old, was something of an anomaly and a shock in its time, we get an idea of how much we—how much the world—has changed.[12] It is more than simply our modern good teeth that we are anxious to display.

As a symbol of cultural aspiration, the smiley face captured perfectly the will to good feeling that has continued to propel us forward to the

The signature Harvey Ball Smiley Face.
(Harvey Ball Smiley Face image
used with permission from
World Smile Corporation.)

present day. That this symbol was created by an advertising agent—offered, almost, as a gift—is all the more fitting. For few figures in contemporary Western society play as central a role in perpetuating the prospect of perpetual pleasure. If advertising can be said to be the business of selling dreams, the dream now is often a variation on the theme of happiness—at all times, in all places, in all things. Have a Coke and a smile. Indulge in "happy hour," savor "genuine satisfaction." Or spend a weekend, as the national branding campaign of Aruba tempts, on "happiness island," the island "where happiness lives."[13] Whether the invitation is to experience pleasure through consumption itself or to enjoy, by association, one of the many attributes we tend to connect with good feeling—victory, self-esteem, love, familial harmony, relaxation, sex, success, or infinite other possibilities—the invitation is largely the same. It is an invitation to travel, to go where all is calm, and beauty, and luxury, to go where one is happy.[14]

Who can deny that we have traveled far? To examine the indexes for the consumption of food, housing, medical care, recreation, travel,

Double Happiness cigarette advertisment, Hong Kong, 1995.
© Viviane Moos/CORBIS.

domestic services, and a thousand other categories over the last one hundred years is to learn, incontrovertibly, how much better off we are materially than any people in the history of the world.[15] Not only do we have the means and the wherewithal to entertain ourselves in infinitely more ways, but we can do so for much longer. The average life expectancy for men and women in the United States has shot up from 46.3 and 48.3 years, respectively, in 1900 to 74.1 and 79.5 in the year 2000. In the European Union, the average life expectancy in 2002 was 75.5 years for men and 81.6 years for women, an increase of roughly thirty-three years since the beginning of the twentieth century.[16] Those who enjoy bemoaning their fate must acknowledge that on average they can do so for far longer and in far greater comfort than ever before.

And yet to conclude from this data that human beings in the West are growing progressively happier as a direct result of material and scientific advances would be a mistake. Careful surveys conducted in the United States since 1950 show that the number of Americans describing themselves as "happy" has remained virtually constant at 60 percent, while the number characterizing themselves as "very happy" has actually declined from 7.5 to 6 percent. Meanwhile, the incidence of unipolar depression seems to have risen sharply. And though much of this increase may simply be due to the fact that we are better able, or more willing, to diagnose depression than ever before, it would nonetheless be rash to assume that human happiness is steadily on the rise.[17]

Nor does it take statistical data to arrive at this conclusion. It was Freud, in *Civilization and Its Discontents*, who cautioned against the presumption that technical and material progress alone would bring happiness in its wake. "One would like to ask," he observes:

> Is there, then, no positive gain in pleasure, no unequivocal increase in my feeling of happiness, if I can, as often as I please, hear the voice of a child of mine who is living hundreds of miles away or if I can learn in the shortest possible time after a friend has reached his destination that he has come through the long and difficult voyage unharmed? Does it mean nothing that medicine has succeeded in enormously

reducing infant mortality and the danger of infection in
women in childbirth, and, indeed, in considerably lengthening
the average life of a civilized man? And there is a long list that
might be added to benefits of this kind. . . .[18]

Freud took none of this for granted. But he responded that in terms
of happiness, "most of these satisfactions follow the model of the
'cheap enjoyment' extolled in the anecdote—the enjoyment obtained
by putting a bare leg from under the bedclothes on a cold winter night
and drawing it in again." "If there had been no railway to conquer
distances," Freud continued,

> my child would never have left his native town and I should
> need no telephone to hear his voice; if traveling across the
> ocean by ship had not been introduced, my friend would not
> have embarked on his sea-voyage and I should not need a
> cable to relieve my anxiety about him.[19]

And so on. We should not count on cell phones, in other words—to
take one contemporary advance that both moves us forward and sets
us back, combining convenience and annoyance, pleasure and pain—
to make us any happier.

This is a conclusion that would not have surprised Adam Smith, who
knew, as we have seen, that for all their riches, real and apparent,
"baubles" and "trifles" can never bring us happiness on their own. He
likely would not have been surprised, either, by the data collected over
the last several decades by sociologists intent on measuring the reported
satisfaction, or "subjective well-being," of peoples around the world.
This type of inquiry is necessarily imperfect, but the results are still
intriguing. Based on surveys in which people are asked to report on
their personal level of satisfaction ("Taken all together, would you say
that you are happy, very happy, pretty happy, or not too happy?"), the
data on subjective well-being suggests that although there is some correlation between happiness and material prosperity, it ceases to be a
factor at what, by Western standards, are comparatively low levels.

People living in poverty report consistently lower levels of subjective well-being than people who are comparatively better off, as can be seen from the figures below. When average national annual income is plotted against average reported happiness on a graph, the curve shoots up steeply at first. But then a curious thing occurs; it levels off somewhere around the $10,000–$13,000 mark. After that point, a rise in income seems to produce diminishing happy returns. One of the leading researchers in the field concludes, "Among advanced industrial societies, there is practically no relationship between income level and subjective well-being."[20]

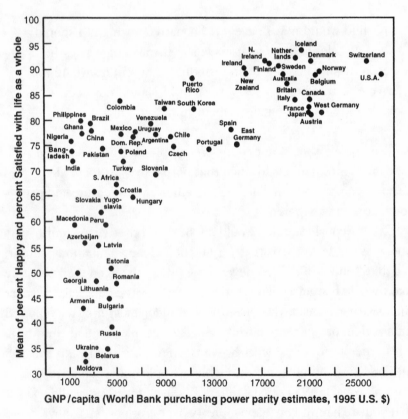

Subjective well-being by level of economic development ($R = 0.70$, $N = 65$, $p < 0.0000$). Source: World Values Surveys; GNP/capita purchasing power estimates from World Bank, World Development Report, 1997. Figure courtesy of Ronald Ingelhart.

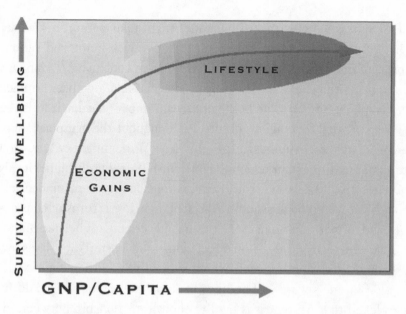

Diminishing happy returns. Figure courtesy of Ronald Ingelhart.

That revealing piece of data has given social scientists great room to speculate on what does account for the rise and fall of happiness of cultures after a country has crossed the critical threshold. Why, for example, do Iceland, Denmark, Switzerland, and Norway consistently report higher average levels of subjective well-being than Japan, Germany, the United States, and France? Is this a function of income distribution and inequality, the availability of social services, specific religious or historical traits? Or perhaps, as others have argued, it has to do with closer family connections, the degree of participation in the political process, or even better genes. The possibilities are practically endless—complicated all the more by the fact that such a complex phenomenon as subjective well-being is decidedly not monocausal. Sociologists and social scientists, as a consequence, have had a field day trying to push one pet theory over another. As one might expect, they have reached no consensus. They probably never will.

It is nonetheless interesting to note how often their apparent correlations tend to echo themes voiced by earlier figures in the history of happiness. John Stuart Mill, for one, might take comfort in the fact that data suggests a link between subjective well-being and various forms of freedom, even if that data is far from conclusive.[21] Darwin's contention that family, friendship, and social relations bear strongly on happiness seems to be borne out by a number of studies, as is the view expressed by religious observers throughout the ages that there is a link between happiness and faith.[22] Max Weber might be surprised to learn that Protestant nations historically report slightly higher levels of subjective well-being than their Catholic counterparts, and surely Karl Marx would be abashed by the strikingly low returns of communist and former communist societies.[23] And yet perhaps he, like Smith, Hume, and many others, would feel vindicated by statistics that show a strong correlation between overall subjective well-being and satisfaction in one's work.[24] The likes of Rousseau, certainly, would be perplexed to learn that it is hard to show a relationship between income inequality and lower levels of subjective well-being.[25] But perhaps they would take heart in a study that aims to demonstrate a connection between happiness, active political involvement, and participatory democracy in Rousseau's native Switzerland.[26] Finally, it is not difficult to imagine what Nietzsche, Schopenhauer, and Freud might make of the many studies that seem to indicate a precipitous recent rise in depressive disorders in cultures devoted to the pursuit of happiness.

Based as they are on the analysis of (self-)reported feelings, studies of *subjective* well-being make no claims to objectivity. The difficulty of isolating individual causal factors and identifying with precision the outcomes they might determine guarantees a built-in margin of error and plenty of room for political and ideological disagreement. Like Bentham's felicific calculus, modern "happiness studies" are not an exact science. And so when critics attempt to use them to uphold bold and sweeping conclusions to press particular policy agendas—proclaiming the "loss of happiness in market democracies," as one author does,[27] or the superior temper of a bygone age, as some politicians are wont to do—we should be highly skeptical. Indeed, for reasons that I hope this book has made clear, there is good reason to be skeptical, or at least cautious, of *all* conscious efforts to promote what George McGovern called, in the 1972 presidential elections, a "politics of happiness." For almost always such claims appeal to a deep and vulnerable desire—to an intense, enduring, but often poorly understood human longing to be healed of the dissatisfactions of being human. That desire—and the faith in its fulfillment—may be the source of noble aspirations and great accomplishments. But it can also be the cause of terrible suffering.

Which is not to suggest that we should simply turn our back on good feeling, blithely tolerating unhappiness that is not, in Freud's phrase, "ordinary." John Stuart Mill put the matter well. In response to the objection that unhappiness is endemic to life and that there-fore we should learn to live with it, he answered, "Unquestionably it is possible to do without happiness; it is done involuntarily by nine-teen twentieths of mankind, even in those parts of our present world which are least deep in barbarism; and it often has to be done volun-tarily by the hero or the martyr."[28] But that this should be used as an excuse for the complacent acceptance of avoidable suffering was for him unconscionable. The moral imperative of the child of the En-lightenment remained what it had been for the more avowedly reli-gious figures who came before: We are bound to seek the relief of others' pain.

Mill's observation is as relevant today as it was in the second half of the nineteenth century. And yet there is a critical difference between aiming to alleviate senseless suffering and striving to overcome "ordi-nary unhappiness," the restlessness and longing inherent to being human. And here we would do well to pay heed to some of our recent cultural indicators and to reflect on the pressures they create. Is there not something deeply ironic, we might ask, about the international publishing success of a book entitled *The Art of Happiness: A Handbook for Living,* written by a Buddhist? Its author, the Dalai Lama, is by all accounts a wise and kindly man. But the fundamental revelation of the Buddha, the first of his "Four Noble Truths," is that all life is suf-fering. Somehow this seems to have been forgotten.

In fairness to the Dalai Lama, his book is no more incongruous than a 1990 work by the evangelical Christian Billy Graham, *The Secret of*

Happiness, or R. L. Kremnizer's *The Ladder Up: Secret Steps to Jewish Happiness*, or the many other titles that one could cite from centuries-old religious traditions now pressed into service at the altar of the truly modern god. And of course these works are positively restrained when one compares them to the torrent of secular titles that now pour regularly from the publishing houses of the West. Count, if you can, *14,000 Things to Be Happy About* and *33 Moments of Happiness*, or mark the calendar to find happiness on the *30-Day Plan*. You can take the short route, *101 Ways to Happiness*, or the long route, *One Thousand Paths to Happiness*, which apparently is an "emerging science." Add up the 7 *Strategies for Wealth and Happiness* with America's "foremost business philosopher," or learn to eat to be happy with *The Book of Macrobiotics: The Universal Way of Health, Happiness, and Peace*. It is a "proven fact" that happiness can be found in feng shui astrology, certainly in love, and most definitely in the power of dianetics. For those who like to go slower, there are *Baby Steps to Happiness*, but rest assured that *Infinite Happiness*, *Absolute Happiness*, *Everlasting Happiness*, and *Happiness That Lasts* are still within your reach. *Happiness Is a Choice*, it seems, and *Happiness Is a Choice for Teens*. But then again, *Happiness Is Your Destiny*, *Happiness Lives Within You*, *Happiness Is No Secret*, *Happiness Is a Serious Problem*. And never forget that happiness is also a *Healthy Life* and a *Kitchen in Maine*, that you can have *Happiness Without Death*, *Happiness Without Sex*, or happiness in *Home Business*. There is *Compulsory Happiness*, *Dangerous Happiness*, happiness for *Black Women Only*, and *Gay Happiness*. And now you needn't confine joy to old standards like cooking or sex but can experience the *Joy of Juicing*, the *Joy of Not Working*, the *Joy of Yiddish*, the *Joy of Weight Loss*, and the joy of almost anything else you might imagine. In short, *Find Happiness in Everything You Do.*[29]

The very prevalence of these titles is a sign that all is not well. But imagine what would happen if any of these books were actually to deliver what they promise. As the novelist Will Ferguson has speculated in a wickedly funny satire, *Happiness*[™], life as we know it would cease to exist. Certainly a good many people—from bartenders to therapists to Hollywood executives—would be out of work. Fortunately for them, there seems little danger of this happening anytime soon.

It is easy, and probably healthy, to laugh. And yet the joke comes at a price, paid for in pain. In part the necessary expense of the human creature, who still exists somewhere between beast and god, our suffering in its current form goes beyond the simple restlessness and anxiety of longing—the "noble disquiet" that has always haunted human beings. For to that burden we have steadily added another since the age of Enlightenment: the unhappiness of not being happy. Collectively, we possess more than ever before, and still we long, expecting to be happy, and are saddened when we are not. And though in some respects this suffering is the ultimate luxury—the indulgence of those whose most pressing needs have been satisfied—it is, for that very reason, widespread and acute in the affluent societies of the West. It may be comforting for some to believe that the anxious pursuit of happiness is a peculiarly American affliction, and in some ways, no doubt, this is true. But the forces that drive this pursuit are pervasive in Western culture, and they are being exported rapidly to other parts of the globe.[30]

Is not this desperate longing for good feeling—this frantic, frenzied pursuit—a symptom of the evaporation of meaning, or the belief in meaning, in other ends? Long ago, Aristotle concluded that the human *telos* could not be pleasant distractions and amusements,

Dept, *Bezet Bag (Global Happiness)*, 2000, San Francisco Museum of Modern Art. Gift of Bert Zuidema, © Dept.

Robert Rauschenberg, *Happiness*,
1994, San Francisco Museum
of Modern Art. Gift of Felissimo,
© Robert Rauschenberg/Licenced
by VAGA, New York, NY.

for it would be absurd if the end [of life] were amusement,
and our lifelong efforts and suffering aimed [only] at amusing
ourselves. We choose practically everything for some other
end—except for happiness, since it is [the] end—but serious
work and toil aimed [only] at amusement appears stupid and
excessively childish. Rather, it seems correct to amuse ourselves so that we can do something serious. . . .[31]

We should rest and regenerate ourselves, Aristotle believed—take
pleasure and relaxation, find amusement and relief—*in order* to prepare ourselves for serious endeavors, *not* so that we might work with
renewed energy toward the final goal of more pleasure and good feeling. Even David Hume, who was so appreciative of the utility of distraction, never thought that backgammon—or golf, or a weekend in
Biarritz—was an end in itself. Is not such a life—as Aristotle believed
and Beckett concurred—really somewhat "absurd"?

Yet in order to act otherwise, to undertake "serious" endeavors, living life according to virtue or virtues, we must first decide what those endeavors should be. And that is precisely the problem for many in the contemporary world who find it hard to set long-term goals other than good feeling, to chart meaningful narratives that give hope, conviction, and purpose to their lives. How ironic in this connection, if also telling, as the critic André Comte-Sponville has observed, that happiness, "that subject so central for so long to the philosophical tradition, has been almost completely abandoned by contemporary philosophers, or at least by those who have dominated the second half of the twentieth century."[32] Engrossed in language games and analytical analysis, deconstruction and hermeneutics, professional philosophers have largely ceded the Greeks' great question—What constitutes the good life?—to popular psychologists, advertising executives, and other peddlers of good feeling. The unwillingness to even grapple with subjects that for centuries dominated the discussion of the constituents of happiness—duty and purpose, virtue and truth—is indicative of a broader crisis of confidence in reason's ability to set the final goals of our pursuits. Some still find sustenance in faith, whether derived from religion or from the Enlightenment, its heir. But "as the light of faith grows dim," Tocqueville anticipated, "man's range of vision" will grow more circumscribed. And when citizens "lose the way of relying chiefly on distant hopes, they are naturally led to want to satisfy their least desires at once."[33] Hence the impatience for pleasure, the restlessness for good feeling that powers so much of modern life, potentially propelling us toward the very world that Huxley once feared.

This is by no means an idle fear. Consider the pioneering work carried out by the behavioral geneticist David Lykken and his Dutch colleague Auke Tellegen, first published in 1996.[34] Drawing on decades of research, the two men analyzed data pertaining to the long-term mood, behavior, and character traits of some three thousand identical and fraternal twins. What they found is that in the case of identical twins—twins who share an exact genetic endowment—mood, or subjective well-being, was remarkably similar over time, regardless of whether they had been raised together or separated at birth. This was not the case with fraternal twins—whose genetic endowment differs—strongly suggesting that genes rather than circumstances were the critical factor in establishing the happiness "set point." At the time, Lykken and Tellegen were prepared to speculate from the data that the degree of the heritability of the set point of mood might be as high as 80 percent, with Lykken observing elsewhere that "trying to be happier is like trying to be taller"—in a word, pointless.[35] Though he has since qualified that claim—and has even, amusingly, written a "how-to" book on achieving joy and contentment—his estimation of the heritability of happiness has only grown.[36] "Nearly 100 percent of the variation across people in the happiness set point seems to be due to individual differences in genetic makeup," he writes.[37] Others who study the heritability of happiness put the figure somewhat lower but rarely at less than 50 percent. Just as Darwin observed that "some dogs and horses are ill-tempered, and easily turn sulky; others are good-tempered and these qualities are certainly inherited," a growing consensus among scientists has come to see human beings, too, as predisposed to cheeriness or crankiness, melancholia or joy, depending on the state of their genes.

It should be stressed that this research is only in its beginning stages. Scientists have not yet isolated a "happiness marker" in our DNA, and it is clear that no single gene of this type exists. Instead, there are probably dozens, even hundreds, that play a role in determining the natural endowment of the set point of mood.[38] Moreover, as a chastened Lykken and many of his colleagues who study happiness take pains to insist, accepting the heritability of happiness does not mean that we must simply bow down before the fate of our genes. The interaction of inherited traits with environmental factors remains an extremely complicated process, and it is almost certainly the case that particular behavior will influence whether we live at the upper reaches of our set range or toward the bottom. "The true formula is not Nature *versus* Nurture," Lykken writes, "but, rather, Nature via Nurture." We can go along at the mercy of what he calls our "genetic steersman," or we can make efforts to help guide the helm.[39]

Psychologists like Lykken, who make it their business to study happiness professionally—and to write about their results—have no shortage of advice about how to do this, some of it surprising, some of it common sense, some of it conflicting, some of it probably wrong. They point out the eddies and swirls of downward depressive cycles, of destructive behavior such as substance abuse, and of correctable deviations such as excessive shyness, resentment, or fear. At the same time, they beckon to the smoother waters of productive activity, of nurturing relationships, of coming to terms with the past. And they gesture toward the motivational force of cultivated optimism and the power of positive thinking. Much of this makes good sense. Yet one needn't be a cynic to point out that books that promise "authentic happiness" will invariably sell more copies than those that emphasize the futility of striving for too much. In their attempts to put a happy face on the data, upbeat assessments of this kind tend to obscure the deeper and more unsettling point: that what the ancient Greeks were prepared to ascribe, in the wisdom of their ignorance, to the gods, fortune, the luck of birth, or the simple nature of things may well be the greatest determinant in shaping our happiness after all. As Lykken and Tellegen summarized, "We are led to conclude that individual differences in human happiness . . . are primarily a matter of chance."[40]

But if mood is in many ways fate, and the way we feel in our skin is overwhelmingly a function of genes, the entire history of happiness suggests that human beings, in their restlessness, will never simply accede to a preordained destiny, especially if that destiny leaves something to be desired. Already, there are signs of a new rebellion against the unfairness of the genetic lottery that occurs at conception. "We have entered the golden age of self-medication," proclaims a recent cover story in the ever fashionable *New York* magazine. The article reports on the increasingly popular use of mood-altering drugs—from selective serotonin reuptake inhibitors (SSRIs) like Prozac, Zoloft, and Celexa, to benzodiazepines like Ativan, Xanax, and Klonopin. This, in itself, is hardly news: The stunning advances in psychopharmacology carried out since the creation of the first antipsychotic drug, chlorpromazine, in 1952 have been well documented.[41] We live in a

"Prozac nation," increasingly a Prozac world, and for many millions of people who have suffered needlessly and without other recourse, this is a development to be welcomed.

But the article in question recounts a different phenomenon: the use of psychotropic medication not for therapeutic purposes but for lifestyle enhancement. "Drugs have become like hair products or cosmetics," the author notes, in what he refers to glibly as "brain styling."

> When you relinquish the idea that your moods and weirdnesses are a constant, not to be messed with, any mental unpleasantness becomes fair game for treatment with a touch of this, a milligram of that. And once you start tinkering with things between your ears, more and more areas that could use fix-ups—*tweaking*—become apparent.[42]

New York magazine, clearly, is no psychopharmacological authority. But as a barometer of contemporary cultural trends in a city that sets standards for the world, it is a gauge to be watched. And so when the author of this piece observes, "The line between medication and recreation has become blurred," and then asks, "What is really the difference between fixing ourselves and pleasing ourselves?," we should be listening. It is a telling question.

In fact, as the distinguished panel of experts of the President's Council on Bioethics observed in a recently published report, "Beyond Therapy: Biotechnology and the Pursuit of Happiness," the time when we are able to use advances in our understanding of the science of mood "beyond therapy"—beyond, that is, "the usual domain of medicine and the goals of healing"—is already upon us.[43] There is every indication that such use will only increase, for precisely the same forces that have brought us where we are today are taking us there.

To raise concerns about this development is not to adopt a Luddite stance toward the many dramatic developments in genetic and pharmacological technologies. Advances in our ability to control and to correct depression and other forms of needless mental pain hold out exciting possibilities for the ongoing quest to reduce human suffering. They are to be encouraged. And yet it is worth considering deeply the simple fact that there is, and can be, no baseline index of mood, no objective standard of what it is to feel normal, to experience a "typical" human balance between pleasure and pain. In the absence of such a standard, there is every reason to expect that our restless pursuit of good feeling will exert an ever stronger pressure to define "normal" happiness upward, pushing the average set point of mood to an ever higher place. And in a market culture, in which the pharmaceutical industry is governed like all others by the laws of supply and demand, there is every reason to believe that those who develop, research, and sell psychotropic drugs will respond to, and feed, this very pressure. Already, in the intense multibillion-dollar competition to manufacture and market antidepressant and anti-anxiety medications, one can see evidence that the line separating therapy from lifestyle enhancement has been crossed. Again, one needn't be a cynic to appreciate that the same market forces that operate in the material world are at play in the market of the mind. The lure of happiness will find a comfortable place in the buying and selling of medication to alter mood. It already has.

The prospect of actually manipulating our genes to enhance our happiness is admittedly further off—but not that much further. And here, there will be similar pressures to improve on the handiwork of nature. For who is to say that another's pain is simply what must be suffered, that another man, another woman, is, or will be, happy enough as made? In societies that value happiness in all things, will we really decree that others must be "victims" of the fate of their genes? Given the present cultural mood, this seems unlikely.

But when, and if, human beings decide to take this fateful step in the quest to live as gods, they should know that in doing so, they will be leaving a piece of their humanity behind. For to judge by the yearning and pursuit—the noble restlessness—that has driven Western culture for the past several thousand years, there are certain things that human beings will never know—certain riddles they will never answer—if they are to remain mere mortals. The holy grail of perfect happiness is one of those things, and like that precious mythic relic, said to have gathered blood from the side of the son of man, it, too, may exist only in our minds, a deliverance cup and a chalice to hold our pain. To take that cup—to answer the riddle, to break the spell—would be to sacrifice something of ourselves. We may well discover that the knights who dare to do so are less like the brave crusaders of lore than like Cervantes's knight of the sad countenance, Quixote, who learns at the end of his journeys that the road is better than the arrival.

ACKNOWLEDGMENTS

One of the great pleasures of writing this book has been the opportunity it has afforded to talk with people from many different walks of life about a subject that concerns us all. I recall, with fondness, the retired diplomat at the Council on Foreign Relations who recounted to me his perfect moment of happiness: driving through the former Soviet Union in the 1950s in a plastic convertible. A young scholar from Prague described happiness as an onion: When you peel it, the center disappears, and when you slice it, you cry. There was the exotic dancer who mused, while dancing, that happiness is family and friends; the Viennese fitness instructor who, in broken English and without full appreciation of the force of his words, described happiness as "a good fuck"; my dear dinner companion Leslie Teicholz, who listened to my laments over curry and then outlined the history of happiness on the back of our menu; the delightful mother of a delightful woman, Melissa Erico, who declared that happiness is "ridding oneself of demons." Finally, I remember my friend, the painter Sebastien King, as he lay dying of cancer at age thirty-five. Happiness, he said with an enigmatic smile, is an open window.

Many others—regrettably, too many to mention here—have shared with me their poignant reflections, adding to my insight and to my stock of happy memories. I am grateful. I am grateful, as well, to John Merriman, Jon Butler, Jane Levin, Frank Turner, and Maria Rosa Menocal, who graciously arranged for me to teach at Yale University on several occasions at short notice, buoying my spirits and my bank account. Tony Judt has been a font of ever generous assistance and ever sage advice. He and Jair Kessler made the Remarque Institute at New York University a happy place to spend a year, and then some. The many kind people at the Institut für die Wissenschaften vom Menschen in Vienna offered a six-month haven during the upheavals that followed September 11, providing me with *Gemütlichkeit* and intellectual sustenance. Pascal Dupuy and his wife, Anne, have long done the same *à la manière franco-écossaise.* And most recently, my colleagues at Florida State University have offered similarly enriching fare, with a generous helping of southern charm.

Jeanine Pepler memorably helped to get this project off the ground, and my literary agent and longtime friend, Tina Bennett, has been quite simply a joy and a marvel to work with in every possible way. Morgan Entrekin and Stuart Proffitt each provided more publishing insight and editorial acumen than any young author has the right to expect, and Brando Skyhorse skillfully shepherded both me and the manuscript through production. Erich Eichman at the *Wall Street Journal,* Alex Starr at the *New York Times,* Jenny Schuessler at the *Boston Globe,* Alessandro Stille at *Correspondence* magazine, Jim Miller at *Daedalus,* and Steven Lagerfeld at the *Wilson Quarterly* all gave me the opportunity to work out some of my ideas in print. Peter Buijs of the Jewish Historical Museum in Amsterdam shared with me his research on Dutch happiness in the seventeenth and eighteenth centuries, and Professor Jill Kraye kindly did the same with her work on happiness in the Renaissance. Kate M. Ohno, assistant editor of the papers of Benjamin Franklin at Yale University, aided me with research on Franklin's conception of happiness and also allowed me to consult her own reflections on the subject, and Joyce Chaplin at Harvard offered timely advice and valuable insight on Franklin's true thoughts on happiness.

Valerie French of American University very kindly read my chapter on the ancient world with a classicist's eye. And many thanks are due to Katherine Connor Martin, Anoush Terjanian, Grant Kaplan, Amanda Fritz, Joe Horan, and Alexander Mikaberidze, who provided indispensable research assistance at various stages, as well as to Leslie Jones, Christine Giviskos, and the dozens of archivists, curators, and researchers at the many museums I have consulted, who provided friendly and efficient help in locating and obtaining art and illustrations. The final revisions to the manuscript were carried out in the garden oasis of the Columbia Institute of Scholars in Paris, a perfect place to complete one's happiness. My thanks are due to Mihaela Bacou, Danille Haase-Dubose, and Charles Walton for their generosity.

An immensely talented trio of young historians whom I have the privilege to call my friends—David A. Bell, David Armitage, and D. Graham Burnett—all did their best to keep me honest (without, I fear, complete success) with their careful readings of the manuscript. Mark Juergensmeyer and Mark Lilla listened and advised; Max Boot listened and grinned; and Geoffrey Cowley grinned and listened, as I, in turn, listened and learned. David Greenberg helped to plot pursuits and kindly shared his knowledge of many things, as did Jeffrey Freedman and the European history reading group at Yeshiva University.

On a personal note, Father John McGuire; my godparents, Douglas and Roseline Crowley; and Dr. William Sommer each looked after my happiness according to their skills and my needs. Old family and new—McMahons, Matsons, and Burkes—provided warm and welcoming bases from which to mount my expeditions and forays. Finally, my dear friends Michael Friedman and James Younger and my new wife, Courtney, have proved themselves steady partners—in this and many other pursuits.

NOTES

Preface

1. G. W. F. Hegel, *Lectures on the Philosophy of World History. Introduction: Reason in History,* Second Draft (1830), trans. H. B. Nisbet (Cambridge: Cambridge University Press, 1975), 78–79.

2. Immanuel Kant, *Grounding for the Metaphysics of Morals,* trans. James W. Ellington (Indianapolis: Hackett, 1981), 27.

3. Sigmund Freud, *Civilization and Its Discontents,* trans. and ed. James Strachey, intro. Peter Gay (New York: W. W. Norton, 1989), 41.

4. William James, *The Varieties of Religious Experience* (New York: Modern Library, 1994), 78.

5. Those interested in the comparative sociology of subjective well-being will find useful introductions in Ed Diener and E. M. Suh, *Subjective Well-Being Across Cultures* (Cambridge, Mass.: MIT Press, 2000); Ruut Veenhoven, *World Database of Happiness,* www.eur.nl/fsw/research/happiness; and Darrin M. McMahon, "Developing Happiness," in *Correspondence: An International Review of Culture and Society* 10 (Winter 2002–2003).

6. Some initial insightful reflections on this enterprise may be found in Anna Wierzbicka, "Happiness in Cross-linguistic and Cross-cultural Perspective," *Daedalus* 133, no. 2 (Spring 2004).

7. Howard Mumford Jones, *The Pursuit of Happiness* (Ithaca, N.Y.: Cornell University Press, 1953), 63.

8. Thomas Carlyle, *Sartor Resartus,* eds. Kerry McSeeney and Peter Sabor (New York: Oxford University Press, 1991), 145.

9. The foundational statement of the "Cambridge School" remains Quentin Skinner's classic essay, "Meaning and Understanding in the History of Ideas,"

History and Theory 8 (1969): 3–53. On the history of emotions, see Barbara H. Rosenwein, "Worrying about Emotions in History," *American Historical Review* 107 (2002): 821–845, and Peter N. Stearns with Carol Z. Stearns, "Emotionology: Clarifying the History of Emotions and Emotional Standards," *American Historical Review* 90 (1985): 813–816. Both Annabel Temple-Smith, at the University of Queensland, and Marco Roth, at Yale, are currently writing dissertations on the role of happiness in literature.

10. Cited in Roy Porter, *The Creation of the Modern World: The Untold Story of the British Enlightenment* (New York: Norton, 2000), 88.

Introduction

1. Herodotus, *The History*, 1.30. All citations from Herodotus are taken from the fine translation of *The History* by the late David Grene (Chicago: University of Chicago Press, 1987).

2. Ibid., 1.33.

3. See Aristotle's allusions in the *Nichomachean Ethics*, trans. Terence Irwin (Indianapolis: Hackett, 1985), 13.44.

4. Cornelius de Heer, *Makar, Eudaimon, Olbios, Eutychia: A Study of the Semantic Field Denoting Happiness in Ancient Greek to the End of the Fifth Century B.C.* (Amsterdam: Adolf M. Hakkert, 1969).

5. "Hymn to Apollo," lines 465–466, in the Loeb Classic edition, *Hesiod, Homeric Hymns, Epic Cycle*, trans. Hugh G. Evelyn-White (Cambridge, Mass.: Harvard University Press, 1998), 357.

6. "Hymn to Hermes," lines 249ff., in ibid., 381.

7. Hesiod, *Works and Days*, line 826, in Gregory R. Crane, ed., *The Perseus Project*, http://www.perseus.tufts.edu, May 2004.

8. Walter Burkert, *Greek Religion*, trans. John Raffan (Cambridge, Mass.: Harvard University Press, 1985), 180. See, in general, the section "Daimon," 179–182.

9. Herodotus, *The History*, 1.32.

10. Ibid., 1.30.

11. Ibid., 1.31.

12. Ibid., 1.32.

13. Ibid., 1.86. I have altered Grene's translation slightly here, substituting "happy" for "blessed" in the first citation and shortening the syntax. The term in both sentences is *olbios*, which Grene translates exclusively as "blessed." For reasons that I have indicated, however, the use of "happy" is not inappropriate.

14. Ibid., 1.86 and 1.91.

15. Semónides of Amórgos, "The Vanity of Human Wishes," in *Greek Lyrics*, trans. Richmond Lattimore, 2nd edition (Chicago: University of Chicago Press, 1960), 11–12.

16. Homer, *Iliad*, 17.446.

17. William Shakespeare, *The Taming of the Shrew*, act 4, scene 4, final lines. The speaker is Lucentio.

18. Jackson Lears, *Something for Nothing: Luck in America* (New York: Viking Press, 2003).

19. Dennis Prager, *Happiness Is a Serious Problem* (New York: HarperCollins, 1998). See chap. 1, "Happiness Is a Moral Obligation."

20. Aristotle, *Nichomachean Ethics*, 13.37.

21. Cited in Burkert, *Greek Religion*, 181.

22. Aeschylus, *The Persians*, part 2, strophe 2, trans. Seth Benardete, cited in Charles Freeman, *The Greek Achievement: The Foundation of the Western World* (New York: Penguin, 1999), 244.

Chapter One

1. Oswyn Murray, "Life and Society in Classical Greece," in John Boardman, Jasper Griffin, Oswyn Murray, eds., *The Oxford History of Greece and the Hellenistic World* (Oxford: Oxford University Press, 1988), 244.

2. Donald Kagan, *Pericles of Athens and the Birth of Democracy* (New York: The Free Press, 1991), 3–4.

3. Simon Hornblower, "Greece: The History of the Classical Period," in *The Oxford History of Greece*, 156–157.

4. Pericles's celebrated "funeral oration" is recorded in Thucydides, *The History of the Peloponnesian War*, trans. Richard Crawley (New York: Dutton, 1950), book 2, chap. 37.

5. Ibid., book 2, chap. 38.

6. Murray, "Life and Society in Classical Greece," in *The Oxford History of Classical Greece*, 259.

7. Thucydides, *The History of the Peloponnesian War*, book 2, chap. 41.

8. Augustine, *Concerning the City of God Against the Pagans*, trans. Henry Bettonson (London: Penguin, 1984), book 18, chap. 3, 301.

9. The other major source of information on Socrates is provided by his contemporary and friend Xenophon (c. 430–354 BCE) in a number of writings, chiefly the *Memorabilia*, the *Symposium*, and the *Apology*, collected and translated in volume 4 of the Loeb Classic edition of Xenophon's works, translated by O. J. Todd.

10. Plato, *The Euthydemus*, 278 E, 279 A. The Greek word here is not *eudaimonia* but *eu prattein*, "doing well." It is clear from the context, however, that the expression is used synonymously with *eudaimonia*. See Julia Annas, *Platonic Ethics, Old and New* (Ithaca, N.Y.: Cornell Univ. Press, 1999), 35–36, esp. note 20.

11. Plato, *The Symposium*, trans. Tom Griffith (Berkeley: University of California Press, 1989), 205 A. In the citations from the *Symposium* that follow, I draw principally on Griffith's translation and text, which includes the original Greek. In certain cases, where noted, I have made alterations, as I do here, using the classic translation of Benjamin Jowett by way of comparison.

12. See, for example, the *Gorgias*, 472 C, and the *Republic*, 352 D.

13. Walter Burkert, *Greek Religion*, trans. John Raffan (Cambridge, Mass.: Harvard University Press, 1985), 163.

14. Ibid.

15. Jon D. Mikalson, *Ancient Greek Religion* (Oxford: Blackwell, 2005), 92.

16. Euripides, *The Cyclops*, ed. David Kovacs, lines 170–171, in Gregory R. Crane, ed., *The Perseus Project*, http://www.perseus.tufts.edu, February, 2005.

17. Cited in Peter Levi, "Greek Drama," in *The Oxford History of Greece*, 199.

18. Alcman of Sparta, "Maiden Song," in *Greek Lyrics*, trans. Richard Lattimore, 2nd ed. (Chicago: University of Chicago Press, 1960), 33–34.

19. Euripides, *The Cyclops*, lines 495–502.

20. A fine summary of the recent scholarship on the symposium may be found in Oswyn Murray, ed., *Sympotica: A Symposium on the Symposion* (Oxford: Clarendon Press, 1990). See also James N. Davidson, *Courtesans & Fishcakes: The Consuming Passions of Classical Athens* (New York: St. Martin's Press, 1998), esp. 43–49.

21. Eubulus is cited and discussed along with the tossing of furniture in Davidson, *Courtesans & Fishcakes*, 47–48.

22. On the hetaera and prostitution in ancient Athens, see Davidson, *Courtesans and Fishcakes*, 73–136.

23. See Davidson, *Courtesans & Fishcakes*, 312–315. On the range of Greek philosophical responses to the issue of pleasure, see J. C. B. Gosling and C. C. W. Taylor, *The Greeks on Pleasure* (Oxford: Clarendon, 1982).

24. Xenóphanes of Cólophon, "The Well-Tempered Symposium," in *Greek Lyrics*, 24–25.

25. Ibid, 25.

26. On Plato's (and Socrates's) general thinking about the institution of the symposium, see Manuela Tecusan, "*Logos Sympotikos*: Patterns of the Irrational in Philosophical Drinking: Plato Outside the *Symposium*," in Murray, ed., *Sympotica*, 238–260.

27. Plato, *The Protagoras*, 347 D, in Gregory R. Crane, ed., *The Perseus Project*, http://www.perseus.tufts.edu, February 2005.

28. Plato, *Symposium*, 180 B.

29. Ibid., 186 B, 188 D–E, 189 D.

30. Ibid., 195 A–B.

31. Ibid., 186 A–B.

32. Ibid., 193 C–D.

33. Ibid., 202 E.

34. Ibid., 203 D–E.

35. Ibid., 203 A.

36. Ibid., 200 E.

37. Ibid., 202 C.

38. Plato, *The Republic*, trans. G. M. A. Grube and revised by C. D. C. Reeve (Indianapolis: Hackett, 1992), 490 B.

39. Cited in Peter Gay, *Freud: A Life for Our Time* (New York: Anchor Books, 1989), 149. The line is taken from the preface to the fourth edition of Freud's *Three Essays*, published in 1920.

40. Plato, *Symposium*, 211 C.

41. Ibid., 211 D. See the *Republic*, 490 B, and the *Phaedrus*, 249–257.

42. Plato, *Phaedrus*, 256.

43. Plato, *Symposium*, 213 D–216 E, 218 B.

44. Tecusan, "*Logos Sympotikos*," 241.

45. Plato, *Apology*, 36 D.

46. Plato, *Symposium*, 219 C, 221 C–D.

47. Plato, *Republic*, 559 C, 561 A, and 562 D.

48. This is the phrase of Julia Annas. See her enlightening discussion of Plato,

happiness, and the quest to become godlike in *Platonic Ethics*, chap. 3, as well as her general study, *The Morality of Happiness* (N.Y.: Oxford University Press, 1993).

49. Plato partially acknowledges this dilemma in the *Phaedrus*, 249–250, where he attempts to account for it by speaking explicitly of the transmutation of the soul. All souls, he suggests, have beheld "true being" before passing into human form. But "all souls do not easily recall the things of the other world." Only those few who retain a glimmer of the light of the former world will thus be drawn to the genuine happiness that is synonymous with the good. This doctrine would be developed at length by Plato's third-century successor Plotinus, whose Neoplatonic spirituality influenced Saint Augustine, among others.

50. *Symposium*, 205 D.

51. Coleridge cited in Richard Holmes, *Coleridge: Darker Reflections* (London: Flamingo, 1999), 492.

52. Aristotle, *Nichomachean Ethics*, trans. Terence Irwin (Indianapolis: Hackett, 1985), 1.1.

53. Ibid., 1.51.

54. Ibid., 1.81.

55. Aristotle, *Rhetoric*, 1.5, in *The Basic Works of Aristotle*, ed. Richard McKeon (New York: Random House, 1941).

56. Aristotle, *Nichomachean Ethics*, 1.73.

57. Ibid., 1.7, 1.73.

58. Ibid., 1.73.

59. Ibid., 1.43.

60. Ibid., 1.81.

61. See, especially, Aristotle's *Politics* 7.1–7.3 for Aristotle's discussion of happiness in the context of political rule.

62. Aristotle, *Nichomachean Ethics*, 13.41.

63. Ibid., 13.37–13.43.

64. Jonathan Lear, *Happiness, Death, and the Remainder of Life* (Cambridge, Mass.: Harvard University Press, 2000), 55. My thinking about Aristotle and happiness more generally is indebted to this rich study.

65. The one exception, the sect of the Cyrenaics, proves the rule. Distinguishing themselves by denying any final end to human life at all, the Cyrenaics vowed to live like their founder, Aristippus of Cyrene in Libya, only for momentary pleasures. If that aspiration seems modern today, to the ancients, it was retrograde—a willful abdication of philosophy's quest to discern order in the world, and to define our place within it. Happiness was the wave of the future, and, Cyrenaics aside, lovers of wisdom joined unanimously in its pursuit.

66. Cited in Martha Nussbaum, *The Therapy of Desire: Theory and Practice in Hellenistic Ethics* (Princeton, N.J.: Princeton University Press, 1994), 102. My argument in this section is indebted to Professor Nussbaum's careful study.

67. Cited in ibid., 14.

68. Diogenes Laertius, *Lives of Eminent Philosophers*, trans. R. D. Hicks, 2 vols. (Cambridge, Mass.: Harvard University Press, 1991; first published 1925), 2:127, 111.

69. Epicurus, "Vatican Sayings," no. 47, in *The Essential Epicurus: Letters, Principal Doctrines, Vatican Sayings, and Fragments*, trans. and ed. Eugene O'Connor (Amherst, N.Y.: Prometheus, 1993), 81.

70. Epicurus, "Letter to Menoeceus," in *The Essential Epicurus*, 63.

71. Cited in Laertius, *Lives*, 2:195.

72. Seneca, "On the Happy Life," in *Moral Essays*, trans. John Basore, 3 vols. (Cambridge, Mass.: Harvard University Press, 1992; first published 1932), 2:115.

73. See Cicero's discussion in the "Tusculum Discussions" in *On the Good Life*, trans. and intro. Michael Grant (London: Penguin, 1971), 58–59.

74. See the definitions of "stoic" and "epicure" in *Webster's New Collegiate Dictionary*.

75. Epicurus, "Letter to Menoeceus," in *The Essential Epicurus*, 66.

76. Epicurus, "Vatican Sayings," no. 33, in *The Essential Epicurus*, 80.

77. Epicurus, "Ethical Fragment," no. 69, in *The Essential Epicurus*, 99. See the virtually identical "Vatican Sayings," no. 68.

78. "Vatican Sayings," no. 4, in *The Essential Epicurus*, 77.

79. Seneca, "On the Happy Life," 129–131.

80. Cited in Laertius, *Lives*, 2:217.

81. Epictetus, *The Discourses*, ed. Christopher Gill, trans. Robin Hard (London: J. M. Dent, 1995), book 3, chap. 24, 207. My analysis here draws on V. J. McGill, *The Idea of Happiness* (New York: Frederick A. Praeger, 1967), 49–57.

82. Epictetus, *The Discourses*, book 3, chap. 30, 204.

83. Cicero, "Tusculum Discussions," 63.

84. Plato, *Symposium*, 177 B.

85. Xenophon, *Memorabilia*, book 2, 1.21. Prodicus's original text was lost, but significant sections of it are recorded by Xenophon, from which I cite here.

86. This citation is taken from an English translation of the original Greek made by Anthony Ashley Cooper, the third Earl of Shaftsbury, at the beginning of the eighteenth century. The work "The Picture of Cebes" is included in *Cebes in England: English Translations of the Tablet of Cebes from Three Centuries with Related Materials*, intro. Stephen Orgel (New York and London: Garland Publishing, 1980), 74.

87. On the work's textual history in the early Renaissance, see *Cebes' Tablet*, ed. Sandra Sider (New York: Renaissance Society of America, 1979). For a selection of the many paintings based on the work, see Reinhold Schleier, *Tabula Cebetis* (Berlin: Mann, 1973).

88. Epicurus, "Letter to Menoeceus," in *The Essential Epicurus*, 68.

Chapter Two

1. Michael Grant and Antonia Mulas, *Eros in Pompeii: The Secret Rooms of the National Museum of Naples* (New York: Bonanza Books, 1982), 109.

2. On this theme, I have drawn on the work of David L. Thurmond, *Felicitas: Public Rites of Human Fecundity in Ancient Rome* (Ph.D. diss., University of North Carolina at Chapel Hill, 1992), 57–58.

3. See the account in Plutarch, "Sylla," *Plutarch's Lives*, the Dryden translation, ed. Arthur Hugh Clough, intro. James Atlas, 3 vols. (New York: Modern Library, 2001), 1:636.

4. On the goddess Felicitas, see the article "Felicitas" in Charles Daremberg and Edmund Saglio, eds. *Dictionnaire des antiquités grecques et romaines*, 5 vols. (Paris:

Hachette, 1877), 1:1031–1032; and J. A. North, *Roman Religion* (New York: Oxford University Press, 2000), 32–33.

5. Samuel Ball Platner, *The Topography and Monuments of Ancient Rome*, 2nd rev. ed. (Boston: Allyn & Bacon, 1911), 229–230, 394; Samuel Ball Platner, *A Topographical Dictionary of Ancient Rome* (London: Oxford University Press, 1929), 207; Martin Henig and Anthony King, eds. *Pagan Gods and Shrines of the Roman Empire* (Oxford: Oxbow Books, 1986), 41.

6. See "Felicitas" in Daremberg and Saglio, eds. *Dictionnaire des antiquités*, 1:1031. Depending on which of the various Roman calendars one consults, the primary festival days for Felicitas seem to have been October 9 and July 1.

7. Quintus Horatius Flaccus (Horace), Ode III.16 (To Maecenas), in *The Odes of Horace*, bilingual edition, trans. David Ferry (New York: Farrar, Straus and Giroux, 1997), 211.

8. Horace, Satire II.2, in *Satires and Epistles*, trans. and intro. Niall Rudd (New York: Penguin Books, 1987), 89.

9. Horace, Epode II (Beatus ille), in *Horace: The Complete Odes and Epodes*, trans. David West (New York: Oxford University Press, 1987), 4.

10. Horace, Ode II.10 (To Licinius), in *Odes of Horace*, 127.

11. Ibid.

12. Horace, Ode II.2 (Avarice), in *Odes of Horace*, 107.

13. Horace, Satire II.6, in *Satires and Epistles*, 116.

14. Horace, Ode III.29 (To Maecenas), in *Odes of Horace*, 253. I have used the Dryden translation here, in place of that of David Ferry.

15. Horace, Satire II.6, in *Satires and Epistles*, 116.

16. Horace, Ode I.31 (A Prayer), in *Odes of Horace*, 83.

17. Horace, Epode XVI (Altera iam territur), in *Complete Odes and Epodes*, 19.

18. Publius Vergilius Maro (Virgil), *Georgics*, book 2, in *Eclogues, Georgics, Aeneid 1–6*, Loeb Classic edition, trans. H. Rushton Fairclough, rev. G. P. Goold (Cambridge, Mass.: Harvard University Press, 1999), 169–171. Virgil's fourth eclogue contains a similarly lavish picture of the Golden Age.

19. Horace, Satire I.1, in *Satires and Epistles*, 39.

20. Ibid., 43.

21. Augustine, *Concerning the City of God Against the Pagans*, trans. Henry Bettenson, intro. John O'Meara (London: Penguin Classics, 1984), 161–162. The worship of Felicitas is discussed esp. in part 1, book 4, chaps. 18–25.

22. Ibid., 165.

23. My account of Perpetua's life and martyrdom draws heavily on Joyce E. Salisbury, *Perpetua's Passion: The Death and Memory of a Young Roman Woman* (New York: Routledge, 1997) and B. D. Shaw, "The Passion of Perpetua," *Past & Present* 139 (May 1993): 3–45.

24. To be precise, one should note that in the year 180, twelve Christians were beheaded for treason by order of the Roman governor in Carthage. They were not, however, executed in the arena. On the persecutions in general, see the classic study by W. H. C. Frend, *Martyrdom and Persecution in the Early Church: A Study of a Conflict from the Maccabees to Donatus* (New York: Anchor Books, 1967).

25. The "Martyrdom of Saints Perpetua and Felicitas," in *The Acts of the Christian Martyrs*, trans. and intro. Herbert Musurillo (Oxford: Clarendon Press, 2000),

125–126. The witness was the anonymous editor or author of the account of Perpetua's last days, and most likely male. See Salisbury, *Perpetua's Passion*, 70, and B. D. Shaw, "The Passion of Perpetua," esp. 20–21.

26. On Christianity as the "Worship of Sorrow," see Thomas Carlyle, *Past and Present*, ed. Richard D. Altick (New York: New York University Press, 1965), 155 (chap. 4, "Happy"). Carlyle also uses the term in a slightly different connection in *Sartor Resartus*.

27. 2 Corinthians 6:8–10. All subsequent references to scripture are taken from the New Revised Standard Version of the *Holy Bible* (Oxford: Oxford University Press, 1989), unless otherwise noted. Occasional alterations in the translation, based on other accredited versions of the text, have been made where indicated.

28. See, for example, the discussion in Martha C. Nussbaum, *The Fragility of Goodness: Luck and Ethics in Greek Tragedy and Philosophy* (Cambridge: Cambridge University Press, 1986), 329–333.

29. See the article "*'ashrê*," in G. Johannes Botterwick and Helmer Ringgren, *Theological Dictionary of the Old Testament*, trans. John T. Willis, rev. ed. (Grand Rapids, Mich.: William B. Eerdmans, 1974), 445–446; and David J. A. Clines, ed. *The Dictionary of Classical Hebrew* (Sheffield, England: Sheffield Academic Press, 1993), 1:436–437.

30. Similarly, Job declares, "My foot has held fast to [God's] steps; I have kept his way and have not turned aside" (Job 23:11).

31. "*'ashrê*," in Botterwick and Ringgren, eds. *Theological Dictionary of the Old Testament*, 446.

32. Michael Walzer, *Exodus and Revolution* (New York: Basic Books, 1985), 118.

33. This is from the Syriac Book of Baruch, cited in Walzer, *Exodus and Revolution*, 121–122.

34. "Martyrdom of Saints Perpetua and Felicitas," 107.

35. See Peter Brown, *The Body and Society: Men, Women and Sexual Renunciation in Early Christianity* (New York: Columbia University Press, 1988), 76; and Frederic J. Baumgartner, *Longing for the End: A History of Millennialism in Western Civilization* (New York: St. Martin's Press, 1999), 38–39. Due in large part to its belief that the Holy Spirit continued to impart new revelations to visionaries, Montanism was deemed a heresy around the year 200.

36. See Salisbury, *Perpetua's Passion*, 79–80; and A. J. Droge and James D. Tabor, *A Noble Death: Suicide and Martyrdom Among Christians and Jews in Antiquity* (San Francisco: HarperCollins, 1992).

37. "Martyrdom of Saints Perpetua and Felicitas," 109.

38. Ibid., 111.

39. Ibid., 113.

40. Ibid., 113–115.

41. In addition to the apocryphal Second Book of Esdras, the Shepherd of Hermas, the Apocalypse of Peter, Enoch, and the Gospel of Thomas, Perpetua and her community were familiar with the Pentateuch, the letters of Paul, the Book of Revelations, and probably some of the writings of the apostolic fathers (in particular those of Tertullian). They probably did not know the canonical Gospels themselves. See Salisbury, *Perpetua's Passion*, 74, 69, 96, 102.

42. See, for example, Wayne Meeks, *The First Urban Christian: The Social World of the Apostle Paul* (New Haven, Conn.: Yale University Press, 1983).

43. "Martyrdom of Saints Perpetua and Felicitas," 111.

44. Ibid.

45. Ibid., 119.

46. Ibid., 112–113.

47. Ibid., 121.

48. Ibid., 123.

49. 1 Corinthians 2:9 and 1 Corinthians 13:12. The second citation is that of the King James translation.

50. Both the statement of beatitude and the injunction to rejoice is mirrored almost precisely in Luke 6:22–23.

51. "Martyrdom of Saints Perpetua and Felicitas," 123.

52. Augustine, "On the Birthday of the Martyrs Perpetua and Felicity," Sermon 282, in *The Works of Saint Augustine*, ed. John E. Rotelle, part 3, *Sermons*, vol. 8, trans. Edmund Hill (Hyde Park, N.Y.: New City Press, 1994), 81. This is one of three surviving sermons delivered by Augustine on the feast day of Perpetua and Felicitas. All are undated but were likely delivered between 400 and 410.

53. Ibid.

54. See, for example, Augustine, *Confessions*, trans. R. S. Pince-Coffin (New York: Penguin, 1987; first published 1961), book 8, chap. 7, 169.

55. Augustine, *Confessions*, 118–119.

56. Ibid.

57. Augustine, *The Happy Life*, trans. Ludwig Schopp (New York: Cima Publishing, 1948). Augustine had written one other treatise, *De pulchro et apto (On the Beautiful and Fitting)* in the year 380 as a younger man, but this was subsequently lost.

58. Ibid., 57–58, 80–83.

59. Augustine, *Happy Life*, 183. I have altered the translation here.

60. Augustine, *Concerning the City of God*, book 14, chap. 28, 593.

61. Ibid.

62. Ibid., 863. Augustine attempts to provide such a list in book 22, chap. 22, 1065.

63. Ibid., book 14, chap. 23, 571.

64. Ibid., book 14, chap. 17, 578. The account of the "Peto-man" is given in book 14, chap. 25, 588.

65. Ibid., book 19, chap. 4, 852.

66. Ibid., 855.

67. See, for example, ibid., book 5, chap. 17, 205; book 5, chap. 18, 207; book 4, chap. 25, 166.

68. Ibid., book 22, chap. 24, 1075.

69. Ibid., book 19, chap. 14, 873.

70. Iohannis Scotti Eriugenae, *Periphyseon (De Devisione Naturae)*, ed. Édouard A. Jeauneau, trans. John J. O'Meara and I. P. Sheldon-Williams, 5 vols. (Dublin: Institute for Advanced Studies, 1995), 4:232–233.

71. Heiric cited in Bertrand Russell, *A History of Western Philosophy* (New York: Simon & Schuster, 1972; 1945), 401.

72. Often repeated, this line is cited in C. Warren Hollister, *Medieval Europe: A Short History*, 7th ed. (New York: McGraw-Hill, 1994), 99.

73. Eriugena, *Periphyseon*, 4:231.

74. Ibid.

75. "Verses of John the Irishman to King Charles," printed in John J. O'Meara, *Eriugena* (Oxford: Clarendon Press, 1988), 185.

76. Cited in O'Meara, *Eriugena*, 34.

77. Ibid. Emphasis added.

78. Cited in ibid., 39. O'Meara provides a particularly concise and cogent summary of the predestination controversy on pp. 32–51. See, as well, Dermot Moran, *The Philosophy of John Scottus Eriugena: A Study of Idealism in the Middle Ages* (Cambridge: Cambridge University Press, 1989), 27–35.

79. Pseudo-Dionysius, *The Mystical Theology*, in *Pseudo-Dionysius: The Complete Works*, trans. Colm Luibheid and Paul Rorem (New York: Paulist Press, 1987), 135.

80. The words are those of the seventeenth-century English hermit and poet Thomas Traherne. They serve as the epigraph to Isabel Colegate's *A Pelican in the Wilderness: Hermits, Solitaries, and Recluses* (Washington, D.C.: Counterpoint, 2002).

81. Cited in Caroline Walker Bynum's magisterial *Holy Feast and Holy Fast: The Religious Significance of Food to Medieval Women* (Berkeley: University of California Press, 1987), 36.

82. Cited in ibid., 50.

83. This is a line from the Roman Catholic Mass that is still in use today.

84. See Louis Dupré and James A. Wiseman, eds. *Light from Light: An Anthology of Christian Mysticism*, 2nd ed. (New York: Paulist Press, 2001); and Dom Cuthbert Butler, *Western Mysticism: The Teaching of Augustine, Gregory and Bernard on Contemplation and the Contemplative Life*, 3rd ed. (New York: Barnes and Noble, 1967), 6.

85. Boethius, *The Consolation of Philosophy*, trans. and intro. P. G. Walsh (New York: Oxford University Press, 1999), 22.

86. Ibid., 22, 51.

87. Ibid., 51, 55, 59.

88. Ibid., 59.

89. Ibid., 72.

90. For a concise explanation of this complicated concept in Eriugena's thought, see Deirdre Carabine, *John Scottus Eriugena*, Great Medieval Thinkers Series (New York: Oxford University Press, 2000), 95–96, 100–102.

91. "Homily of John Scot, the translator of the Hierarchy of Dionysius," full text of the manuscript reproduced and translated in O'Meara, *Eriugena*, 158–176, which is in turn based on the detailed rendering of the text by Édouard Jeauneau, *Homélie sur le prologue de Jean* (Paris: Éditions du cerf, 1969). The passages cited here are from section 1 and section 4 of the *Homily*.

92. Cited in ibid., section 5.

93. On the diffusion of the *Homily*, see O'Meara, *Eriugena*, 158.

94. Bonaventure, *The Journey of the Mind to God*, trans. Philotheus Boehner, ed. and intro. Stephen F. Brown (Indianapolis: Hackett, 1993), 5.

95. Saint Francis cited in Lesley Smith, "Heavenly Bliss and Earthly Delight," in Stuart McCready, ed. *Discovery of Happiness* (London: MQ Publications, 2001), 132.

96. On these popular medieval pastimes, see the lively account provided in Smith, "Heavenly Bliss and Earthly Delight."

97. See Herman Pleij, *Dreaming of Cockaigne* (New York: Columbia University Press, 2001).

98. Cited in Thomas Aquinas, *Selected Philosophical Writings*, trans. Timothy McDermott (New York: Oxford University Press, 1993), part 3, "The Ladder of Being," 115–116.

99. Boethius, *Consolation of Philosophy*, 4.

100. On the theme of the ladder, see Walter Cahn, "Ascending to and Descending from Heaven: Ladder Themes in Early Medieval Art," in *Santi e Demoni Nell'Alto Medioevo Occidentale*, 2 vols. (Spoleto: Centro Italiano di Studi Sull'Alto Medioevo, 1989), 2:697–732; and R. Crabtree, "Ladders and Line of Connection in Anglo-Saxon Religious Art and Literature," *Medieval Literature and Antiquities: Studies in Honour of Basil Cottle*, eds. M. Stokes and T. L. Burton (Cambridge: Cambridge University Press, 1989), 43–53.

101. Dante Alighieri, *The Divine Comedy: The Inferno, The Purgatorio, and the Paradiso*, trans. John Ciardi (New York: New American Library, 2003; 1954), 778. I have altered this translation slightly.

102. Aquinas, in *Selected Philosophical Writings*, "The Ladder of Being," 115–116.

103. Arthur O. Lovejoy, *The Great Chain of Being: A Study of the History of an Idea* (Cambridge, Mass.: Harvard University Press, 1978; 1936), 59.

104. See Brian Davies, *The Thought of Thomas Aquinas* (Oxford: Clarendon Press, 1992), 7.

105. Aquinas, *Summa contra Gentiles*, book 3, chap. 48; *Summa Theologiae*, first part of part 2, question 3, in *St. Thomas Aquinas on Politics and Ethics*, trans. and ed. Paul E. Sigmund (New York: W. W. Norton, 1988). All subsequent references to the *Summa Contra Gentiles* and the *Summa Theologiae* are to this edition unless otherwise noted.

106. The citation from Corinthians here is from the translation of the King James Bible.

107. *Summa contra Gentiles*, book 3, chap. 63.

108. Ibid. See Lawrence F. Hundersmarck, "Thomas Aquinas on Beatitude," in Jan Swango Emerson and Hugh Feiss, eds. *Imagining Heaven in the Middle Ages: A Book of Essays* (New York: Garland Publishing, 2000), 165–183. "Perfect pleasure," the "perfect delight of the senses," in *Summa contra Gentiles*, book 3, chap. 63.

109. The subject is treated exhaustively in Denis J. M. Bradley, *Aquinas on the Twofold Human Good: Reason and Human Happiness in Aquinas's Moral Science* (Washington, D.C.: Catholic University of America Press, 1997). See also George Wieland, "Happiness: The Perfection of Man," in *The Cambridge History of Later Medieval Philosophy: From the Rediscovery of Aristotle to the Disintegration of Scholasticism 1100–1600*, eds. Norman Kretzmann, Anthony Kenny, and Jan Pinborg (Cambridge: Cambridge University Press, 1982), 673–686.

110. *Summa contra Gentiles*, book 3, chap. 37.

111. Ibid., chap. 63.

112. *Summa Theologiae*, 1a. 62. I, cited in Davies, *The Thought of Thomas Aquinas*, 230.

113. *Summa Theologiae*, part 2 (first part), question 5.

114. Ibid., question 109.

115. Ibid., question 69.a.2.

116. See Deal Hudson, "Imperfect Happiness," in *Happiness and the Limits of Satisfaction* (Lanham, Md.: Rowman & Littlefield, 1996), 151–168.

117. Cited in George Wieland, "The Reception and Interpretation of Aristotle's Ethics," in *The Cambridge History of Later Medieval Philosophy,* 663.

118. See Georges Duby, *The Age of the Cathedrals: Art and Society 980–1420,* trans. Eleanor Levieux and Barbara Thompson (Chicago: University of Chicago Press, 1981), chap. 7, "Happiness, 1250–1280," esp. 184–186. On the theme of happiness in Dante, see Larry Peterman, "Dante and Happiness: A Political Perspective," *Medievalia et humanistica,* New Series 10 (1981): 81–102.

119. The date was subsequently changed. Today the feast day of Perpetua and Felicitas falls on March 7, and that of Aquinas on January 28.

120. *Le Guide du Pèlerin de Saint-Jacques de Compostelle texte Latin du XIIe siècle,* trans. and ed. Jeanne Vielliard (Macon: Imprimerie Protat Frères, 1950).

121. For the author's comments on Léonard, see ibid., 55–57 and 27–29, for his highly biased, if colorful, description of the people of Navarre.

122. Ibid., 37.

123. Chaucer, *The Canterbury Tales,* "The Knight's Tale," part 2, "This world nys but a thurghfare ful of wo / And we been pilgrymes, pasynge to and fro"; "The Nun's Priest Tale," "For evere the latter ende of joye is wo / God woot that worldly joye is soone ago." Similar sentiments may be found throughout the text.

124. See, for example, Jerold C. Frakes, *The Fate of Fortune in the Early Middle Ages: The Boethian Tradition* (New York: E. J. Brill, 1988).

Chapter Three

1. Lotario dei Seigni, *De Miseria Condicionis Humane,* ed. Robert E. Lewis (Athens, Ga.: University of Georgia Press, 1978), 94. Lewis's fine edition contains both the Latin original and an English translation. I have made slight changes to the English rendering where I have seen fit.

2. Ibid., 128, 130.

3. Ibid., 166.

4. Ibid., 204.

5. Ibid., 102. Lucretius makes a similar observation about babies in his *De Rerum Natura.*

6. Ibid., 124.

7. See Jean Delumeau's discussion of the *Imitation of Christ* in his *Sin and Fear: The Emergence of a Western Guilt Culture, 13th–18th Centuries,* trans. Eric Nicholson (New York: St. Martin's Press, 1999), 23–24; and more generally his treatment of Renaissance bleakness in part 1, "Pessimism and the Macabre in the Renaissance," chaps. 1–5.

8. Seigni, *De Miseria Condicionis Humane,* 92.

9. The title of William G. Craven's *Giovanni Pico della Mirandola, Symbol of His Age: Modern Interpretations of a Renaissance Philosopher* (Geneva: Droz, 1981) is altogether representative in this respect.

10. Pico della Mirandola, "On the Dignity of Man," trans. Charles Glenn Wallis, in *On the Dignity of Man,* ed. Paul J. W. Miller (Indianapolis: Hackett, 1998), 34.

11. See, for example, S. Dresden, *Humanism in the Renaissance,* trans. Margaret King (New York: McGraw-Hill, 1968).

12. Jacob Burckhardt, *The Civilization of the Renaissance in Italy*, trans. S. G. X. Middlemore (Oxford: Phaidon, 1945), 215.

13. This is cited at the very end of part 4 of *Civilization of the Renaissance*, "The Discovery of the World and of Man," 215–216. Burckhardt paraphrases several preceding lines from this famous passage, beginning in Pico's own voice only at "I have placed thee" and continuing beyond what I have cited here. In place of Burckhardt's translation, I have used that of Charles Glenn Wallis, in Paul W. Miller, ed. *On the Dignity of Man*, 4–5.

14. Burckhardt, *Civilization of the Renaissance*, 81.

15. Burckhardt himself mentioned happiness only occasionally and somewhat inconsistently. Still, the general thrust of his widely influential argument was to emphasize the Renaissance's rehabilitation of life and its growing awareness of human potential within it. Not surprisingly, many subsequent critics found in Burckhardt the basis for the view that a positive attitude toward happiness was integral to the time. See Charles Trinkaus, "The Happy Humanist, a Modern Creation," in *Adversity's Noblemen: The Italian Humanists on Happiness* (New York: Columbia University Press, 1940).

16. See Peter Burke, "The Myth of the Renaissance," *The Renaissance*, 2nd ed. (New York: St. Martin's Press, 1997), 1–7.

17. Pico, "On the Dignity of Man," 1–3, 9.

18. Ibid., 6.

19. Ibid., 7.

20. See, for example, Delumeau, *Sin and Fear*, 18–25; and Charles Trinkaus, *In Our Image and Likeness: Humanity and Divinity in Italian Humanist Thought*, 2 vols. (London: Constable & Co., 1970), 1:174, 320.

21. Pico della Mirandola, *Heptaplus*, trans. Douglas Carmichael, in Miller, ed. *On the Dignity of Man*, 125–126.

22. Ibid., 144. The citation is from 2 Corinthians 3:5: "Not that we are competent of ourselves to claim anything as coming from us; our competence is from God. . . ."

23. Pico, *Heptaplus*, 151–152.

24. Ibid., 151.

25. Ibid., 150.

26. Ibid., 151. Pico's discussion of felicity, perfect and imperfect, is laid out most thoroughly in the proem to the Seventh Book of the *Heptaplus*, "Of the Felicity which is Eternal Life."

27. Pico, *Heptaplus*, 149.

28. Ibid., 153.

29. On Pico's relationship to Aquinas, see Fernand Roulier, *Jean Pic de la Mirandole (1463–1494), Humaniste, Philosophe et Théologien* (Geneva: Slatkine, 1989), 565.

30. Pico, *Heptaplus*, 150.

31. Ibid., 153.

32. Jill Kraye, "Moral Philosophy," *The Cambridge History of Renaissance Philosophy*, eds. Charles B. Schmitt, Quentin Skinner, Eckhard Kessler, and Jill Kraye (Cambridge: Cambridge University Press, 1991), 306.

33. Roulier, *Jean Pic de la Mirandole*, 57.

34. For representative examples of all these varieties, see Jill Kraye, "From An-

cient to Modern Happiness: Petrarch to Descartes," in Stuart McCready, ed. *Discovery of Happiness* (London: MQ Publications, 2001).

35. Trinkaus, *Adversity's Noblemen*, 42.

36. Marsilio Ficino, "Quid est foelicitas, quod habet gradus, quod est aeterna," in *The Letters of Marsilio Ficino*, trans. Language Department of the School of Economic Science, London, ed. Paul Oskar Kristeller, 6 vols. (London: Shepheard-Walwyn, 1975), 1:173, 177.

37. Leonardo Bruni, "The Isagogue of Moral Philosophy," in *The Humanism of Leonardo Bruni: Selected Texts*, trans. and intro. Gordon Griffiths, James Hankins, and David Thompson (Binghamton, N.Y.: Renaissance Society of America, 1987), 271.

38. See the discussion of the *Oratio de foelicitate* in Trinkaus, *Adversity's Noblemen*, 117–118.

39. Salutati, cited in Trinkaus, *Adversity's Noblemen*, 87.

40. Morandi, cited in Trinkaus, *Our Image and Likeness*, 291. Morandi was responding to Giaovanni Garzoni, author of, among other works, *De miseria mundi*. See the extensive discussion in ibid., 271–291.

41. Kraye, "From Ancient to Modern Happiness," 146.

42. On the popularity and importance of Roman coin collecting during this period, and the vital role of Fulvio, Vico, and Erizzo in particular, see John Cunnally, *Images of the Illustrious: The Numismatic Presence in the Renaissance* (Princeton, N.J.: Princeton University Press, 1999).

43. See Graham Smith, "Bronzino's *Allegory of Happiness*," *Art Bulletin*, 66, no. 3 (September 1984): 390–398. The preceding description relies heavily on Smith's allegorical analysis.

44. Paul Binksi, "The Angel Choir at Lincoln and the Poetics of the Gothic Smile," *Art History* 20 (1997): 350–374.

45. Cited in Donald Sassoon, *Becoming Mona Lisa: The Making of a Global Icon* (New York: Harcourt, 2001), 19.

46. On the centrality of Galen and Hippocrates during the Renaissance, see Roy Porter, *The Greatest Benefit to Mankind: A Medical History of Humanity* (New York: W. W. Norton, 1997), 171.

47. For Renaissance speculators, ever fond of analogies, the alleged correspondence between the humors and the elements provided ample scope for conjecture about the role of environment in shaping mood.

48. See Lawrence Babb, *Elizabethan Malady: A Study of Melancholia in English Literature from 1580 to 1642* (East Lansing: Michigan State University Press, 1951), 7, 56–58.

49. We now know that the passage in question (the *Problemata*, XXX, 1) was most likely the work of Theophrastus. See Hellmut Flashar, *Melancholie und Melancholiker in den medizinischen Theorien der Antike* (Berlin: De Gruyter, 1966), 60–62.

50. Marsilio Ficino, *The Book of Life* (*Liber de Vita*), trans. Charles Boer (Woodstock, Conn.: Spring Publications, 1994), 8. The full title of the more literal Italian translation of the Latin original reads, "Perché i malinconici sono geniali, e quali malinconici siano così e quali al contrario." See chap. 5 of *De Vita*, ed. Albano Bioni and Giuliano Pisani (Padova: Edizioni Biblioteca dell'Immagine, 1991), 22.

51. See Winfried Schleiner's careful study, *Melancholy, Genius, and Utopia in the Renaissance* (Wiesgaden: Otto Harrassowitz, 1991); and Babb, *Elizabethan Malady*.

52. John Hale, *The Civilization of Europe in the Renaissance* (New York: Atheneum, 1994), 463.

53. Robert Burton, *The Anatomy of Melancholy*, ed. and intro. Holbrook Jackson and William H. Gass (New York: New York Review of Books, 2001), 20, 120–121.

54. See the concise account in Colleen McDannell and Bernhard Lang, *Heaven: A History* (New Haven, Conn.: Yale University Press, 2001), esp. chap. 5, "The Pleasures of Renaissance Paradise."

55. Lorenzo Valla, *De Voluptate, On Pleasure* (later entitled *On the True and False Good*), trans. A. Kent Hieatt and Maristella Lorch, intro. Maristella de Panizza Lorch (New York: Abaris, 1977), 305.

56. Ibid., 305, 317.

57. Erasmus, *Praise of Folly*, trans. Betty Radice, intro. A. H. T. Levi (New York: Penguin, 1971), 78. The line is borrowed from Sophocles's play *Ajax*.

58. See Erasmus, the *Enchiridion; or, Handbook of the Militant Christian*, trans. and intro. John P. Dolan (Notre Dame, Ind.: Fides Publishers, 1962), esp. 75–79, "The Crown of Wisdom Is that You Know Yourself." The reference to "Saint Socrates" appears in the 1522 colloquy *Convivium religiosum*.

59. Ibid., 137.

60. Thomas More, *Utopia*, trans. and intro. Paul Turner (New York: Penguin, 1965), 92. The "chief subject of dispute" among the philosophers in Utopia, More tells us, is "the nature of human happiness" (91). See the extensive discussion in book 2, 90–98.

61. Martin Luther to Prince Joachim of Anhalt, May 23, 1534, cited and translated in Preserved Smith, *The Life and Letters of Martin Luther* (Boston: Houghton Mifflin, 1911), 322–333. I have altered Smith's translation in keeping with the original in *D. Martin Luthers Werke: Kritische Gesamtausgabe*, 69 vols. (Weimar: Hermann Böhlan, 1883), 7:65–67.

62. Luther, Sermon for the 19th Sunday after Trinity; Matthew 9:1–8, in the *Sermons of Martin Luther*, 5 vols. (Grand Rapids, Mich.: Baker Book House, 1983), 5:198.

63. The classic text is Erik Erikson, *Young Man Luther: A Study in Psychoanalysis and History* (New York: W. W. Norton, 1958).

64. See Diarmaid MacCulloch, *The Reformation: A History* (New York: Viking Penguin, 2003), esp. 119–120.

65. Luther, "Preface to the Complete Edition of Luther's Latin Works" (1545), *Luther's Works*, eds. Jaroslav Pelikan and Helmut I. Lehman, 55 vols. (Saint Louis: Concordia Publishing, 1955–1986), 34:336–337. I have altered this translation slightly in places, based on the "Vorrede zum ersten Bande der Gesamtausgaben seiner lateinischen Schriften Wittenberg 1545," in *Luthers Werke*, 54:176–187.

66. See Carter Lindberg, *The European Reformations* (Oxford: Blackwell, 1996), 67–68.

67. Luther, "Preface to the Complete Edition of Luther's Latin Works" (1545), *Luther's Works*, 34:337. I have altered this translation slightly.

68. Luther, "Vorrede auff die Epistel S. Paul: an die Romer," in *D. Martin Luther: Die gantze Heilige Schrifft 1545 Deudsch auffs new zugerich*, eds. Hans Volz and Heinz Blanke, 3 vols. (Munich: Roger & Bernhard, 1972), 2: 2254–2268, as translated by Brother Andrew Thornton at the Project Wittenberg site: http://www.iclnet.org/pub/resources/text/wittenberg/german.bible/rom-eng.txt.

69. See the "Freedom of a Christian Man," in *Luther's Works*, 31:360; and "Preface to the Complete Edition of Luther's Latin Works," in *Luther's Works*, 34:337.

70. Martin Luther, *The Large Catechism* (1530), comment on the fifth commandment. The full text is reproduced in *What Does This Mean?: Luther's Catechism Today*, ed. Phillip E. Person (Minneapolis: Augsburg Publishing House, 1979), 85.

71. John Calvin, *The Institutes of the Christian Religion*, trans. John Allen, 8th ed., 2 vols. (Grand Rapids, Mich.: William B. Eerdmans, 1949), 1:761 (book 3, chap. 7).

72. Martin Luther, "Commentary on St. Paul's Epistle to the Galatians," chap. 1, verse 16 (1535), in *The Protestant Reformation*, ed. Hans J. Hillerbrand (New York: Harper & Row, 1968).

73. Charles Taylor, *The Sources of the Self: The Making of Modern Identity* (Cambridge, Mass.: Harvard University Press, 1989). I draw here in particular on part 3, chap. 13, "God Loveth Adverbs."

74. For an analysis of Calvin's thought in relationship to the question of happiness, see Heiko A. Oberman, "The Pursuit of Happiness: Calvin Between Humanism and Reformation," in *Humanity and Divinity in Renaissance and Reformation: Essays in Honor of Charles Trinkaus*, eds. John W. O'Malley, Thomas M. Izbicki, and Gerald Christianson (Leiden, The Netherlands: E. J. Brill, 1993), 251–287.

75. Martin Luther, "A Simple Way of Praying" (1535), cited in Delumeau, *Sin and Fear*, 26.

76. Luther, *The Large Catechism* (1530), comment on the fourth commandment, in *Luther's Catechism Today*, 82.

77. See Luther's extensive discussion of happiness and family life in ibid.

78. Martin Luther, *Commentary on the Epistle to the Galatians*, chap. 3, verse 1, cited in Delumeau, *Sin and Fear*, 26.

79. Luther to Prince Joachim of Anhalt at Dessau, June 12, 1534, cited in Smith, *Life and Letters*, 324. Again, I have altered Smith's translation slightly.

80. Martin Luther, *Table Talk*, 1, number 122, cited in Delumeau, *Sin and Fear*, 180.

81. Cited in Erikson, *Young Man Luther*, 245.

82. It is this side of the Protestant experience that is most often emphasized. For a strong statement of the view that "Calvinism and Puritanism were conducive to despair," see John Stachniewski, *The Persecutory Imagination: English Puritanism and the Literature of Religious Despair* (Oxford: Clarendon Press, 1991).

83. Martin Luther, "Sermon for Easter Tuesday" (1524), in *The Sermons of Martin Luther*, trans. John Nicholas Lenker, 8 vols. (Grand Rapids, Mich.: Baker Book House, 1983), 2:305.

84. Calvin, *Institutes*, 1:776 (book 3, chap. 8). I have altered this translation.

85. Stachniewski, *The Persecutory Imagination*, 27.

86. My argument here bears comparison with Max Weber's famous account in the *Protestant Ethic and the Spirit of Capitalism* regarding the search for outward signs of salvation in the evidence of worldly prosperity. For a discussion of Weber's views on happiness, see chap. 7 below.

87. Calvin, *Institutes*, 1:771 (book 3, chap. 8). I have altered this translation.

88. Cited in Schleiner, *Melancholy*, 67.

89. See the discussion in Schleiner, *Melancholy*, 74, and more generally 56–98.

90. Christopher Hill, *The World Turned Upside Down: Radical Ideas During the English*

Revolution (London: Penguin, 1999; 1972). Professor Hill draws his title from a contemporary broadside ballad, "The World Turned Upside Down," published in 1646.

91. Cited in Hill, *World,* 140–141.

92. Thomas Coleman, *The Christian's Course and Complaint, Both in the Pursuit of Happinesse Desired, and for Advantages Slipped in that Pursuit: A Sermon Preached to the Honorable House of Commons on the Monthly Fast Day, August 30, 1643* (London: I. L., 1643), 8.

93. See, for example, John Greene, *A Briefe Unvailing of God and Man's Glory, in which is 1. A Brief rehearsall of Happinesse in generall; 2. How this Happinesse is manifested by Jesus Christ; 3. The Soules Song of Love* (London: Thomas Faucet, 1641), 1.

94. Cited in Hill, *World,* 339–340. This same citation prompted the eminent scholar Michael Walzer to muse in passing that "perhaps happiness is simply the secularized version of religious joy." *Exodus and Revolution* (New York: Basic Books, 1985), 106–106. Even if only in passing, Professor Walzer had hit upon a profound insight.

95. Thomas Brooks, *Heaven on Earth; or, A Serious Discourse Touching a Well-Grounded Assurance of Men's Everlasting Happiness and Blessedness* (London, 1657), Preface (exact page numbers obscured).

96. Robert Crofts, *The Way to Happinesse on Earth Concerning Riches, Honour, Conjugall Love, Eating, Drinking* (London, 1641).

97. Given the importance of happiness as a concept in subsequent Western political thought, a careful study of the use of the term in the context of the English civil war and the English revolution would make a fine project for an enterprising graduate student.

98. Richard Holdsworth, *The Peoples Happinesse. A Sermon Preached in St. Maries in Cambridge, Upon the 27 of March, being the day of His Majesties Happy Inauguration* (Cambridge: Roger Daniel, 1642), 2, 5–6. Holdsworth was master of Emmanuel College and vice chancellor of the university.

99. The argument for this connection is made most forcefully by Richard Ashcraft, *Revolutionary Politics and Locke's Two Treatises of Government* (Princeton, N.J.: Princeton University Press, 1994).

100. Peter Laslett, Introduction to John Locke, *The Two Treatises of Government,* ed. Peter Laslett (Cambridge: Cambridge University Press, 1988), 75.

101. In addition to the *Essay Concerning Human Understanding,* which contains Locke's principal reflections on the subject of happiness, one should see his minor essay "Pleasure, Pain, and the Passions" (1676), and the two fragments "Happiness A" (1676) and "Happiness B" (1678), all of which are reproduced in Locke, *Political Essays,* ed. Mark Goldie (Cambridge: Cambridge University Press, 1997).

102. On the relationship between Locke and Newton, see Lisa J. Downing, "Locke's Newtonianism and Lockean Newtonianism," *Perspectives on Science: Historical, Philosophical, Social* 5 (Fall 1997): 285–311; and G. A. Rogers, "Locke's *Essay* and Newton's *Principia,*" *Journal of the History of Ideas* 39 (1978): 217–232.

103. John Locke, *An Essay Concerning Human Understanding,* ed. Peter H. Nidditch (Oxford: Clarendon, 1991; first edition 1975), 250–254.

104. See Garry Wills's concisely brilliant analysis in his *Inventing America: Jefferson's Declaration of Independence* (New York: Vintage Books, 1979), 241–242.

105. Locke, *Essay Concerning Human Understanding*, 258.

106. See Edward A. Driscoll, "The Influence of Gassendi on Locke's Hedonism," *International Philosophical Quarterly* 12 (March 1961).

107. Locke, *Essay Concerning Human Understanding*, ibid., 266.

108. Ibid., 282. Locke's observations in this passage bear an interesting, if unwitting, relationship to Blaise Pascal's famous statement of the wager in the *Pensées*.

109. John Locke, *The Reasonableness of Christianity, as Delivered in the Scriptures*, ed. I. T. Ramsey (Stanford, Calif.: Stanford University Press, 1958), 70.

110. Ibid. (emphasis added).

111. Locke, *Essay Concerning Human Understanding*, 259.

112. Ibid., 269–270.

113. Ibid., 268–269.

114. Ibid., 277.

115. Thomas Hobbes, *Leviathan*, with selected variants from the Latin edition of 1668, ed. Edwin Curley (Indianapolis: Hackett, 1994), part 1, chap. 11, 57–58, and part 1, chap. 6, 34–35. On Hobbes's statements on good and evil, see part 1, chap. 6, 28–29.

116. Locke, *Essay Concerning Human Understanding*, 262.

117. Ibid., 263. See also 254 ("For as much as whilst we are under any *uneasiness*, we cannot apprehend ourselves happy, or on the way to it.") and 273.

118. John Locke, *Some Thoughts Concerning Education*, eds. Ruth W. Grant and Nathan Tarcov (Indianapolis: Hackett, 1996), 10.

119. Cited in Roy Porter, *The Creation of the Modern World: The Untold Story of the British Enlightenment* (New York: W. W. Norton, 2000), 100.

120. Locke, *Two Treatises*, 338 (chap. 8, para. 107). On this theme of "political happiness," see also Locke's reflections in his minor essay "Civil and Ecclesiastical Power" (1674), in Locke, *Political Essays*, 216–221.

121. John Locke, *A Letter Concerning Toleration*, in *Political Writings of John Locke*, ed. and intro. David Wootton (New York: Mentor Books, 1993), 407.

122. Ibid., 411.

123. Richard Allestree, *The Art of Contentment* (Oxford, 1675), Preface (pages unnumbered).

124. Ibid., and 1–2.

125. Ibid., and 2–3.

126. Ann Thompson, *The Art of Suffering and the Impact of Seventeenth-Century Anti-Providential Thought* (Aldershot, Hampshire: Ashgate Publishing, 2003), 170. Professor Thompson discusses Allestree's work in particular in the context of this reconceptualization, showing how the "doctrine of contentment" and the "art of contentment" evolved as a broader theme in seventeenth-century English theology.

127. Edmund Calamy, *The Happinesse of those who Sleep in Jesus; or, the Benefit that Comes to the Dead Bodies of the Saints Even While They are in the Grave, Sleeping in Jesus* . . . (London: J.H. for Nathanael Webb, 1662).

128. John Ray, *A Persuasive to a Holy Life from the Happiness that Attends it Both in this World, and in the World to Come* (London: Sam Smith, 1700); Thomas Tryon, *The Way to Health, Long Life and Happiness; or, A Discourse of Temperance . . .*, 2nd ed. (London: H. C. Baldwin, 1691); *England's Happiness Improved; or, An Infallible way to get Riches, Encrease Plenty, and Promote Pleasure* (London: Roger Clavill, 1697).

129. Thompson, *The Art of Suffering*, vii.

130. See Keith Parson and Pamela Mason, eds., *Shakespeare in Performance* (London: Salamander Books, 1995).

131. This theme, in the English context, is treated thoroughly in Maren-Sofie Rostvig, *The Happy Man: Studies in the Metamorphoses of a Classical Ideal*, 2 vols. (Oxford: Basil Blackwell, 1954).

132. See Hale, *Civilization of Europe in the Renaissance*, 432.

133. Cited in ibid., 432.

134. Christophe Plantin's poem in the original (mid-sixteenth century):

Le bonheur de ce monde

Avoir une maison commode, propre et belle,
Un jardin tapissé d'espaliers odorans,
Des fruits, d'excellent vin, peu de train, peu d'enfans,
Posséder seul sans bruit une femme fidèle,

N'avoir dettes, amour, ni procès, ni querelle,
Ni de partage à faire avecque ses parens,
Se contenter de peu, n'espérer rien des Grands,
Régler tous ses desseins sur un juste modèle,

Vivre avecque franchise et sans ambition,
S'adonner sans scrupule à la dévotion,
Dompter ses passions, les rendre obéissantes,
Conserver l'esprit libre, et le jugement fort,
Dire son Chapelet en cultivant ses entes,
C'est attendre chez soi bien doucement la mort.

135. Jonson cited in Rostvig, *The Happy Man*, 324. The discussion of English poetry that follows is indebted to Professor Rostvig's fine analysis.

136. Hall cited in ibid., 140.

137. Herrick cited in ibid., 303.

138. Wycherley cited in ibid., 380.

Chapter Four

1. Cited in Jean Delumeau, *History of Paradise: The Garden of Eden in Myth & Tradition*, trans. Matthew O'Connell (Urbana: University of Illinois Press, 1992), 168.

2. Cited in ibid., 145.

3. Voltaire, *Le Mondain* (1736). The last four lines of the poem read:

> C'est bien en vain que, par l'orgueil séduits,
> Huet, Calmet, dans leur savante audace,
> Du paradis ont recherché la place:
> Le paradis terrestre est où je suis.

4. Claude-Adrien Helvétius, *Le Bonheur, poëme allégorique*, in *Oeuvres complètes d'Helvétius*, 14 vols. (Paris: Chez Didot, 1795), 13:89. On the waning of belief in

Hell, see the standard account by D. P. Walker, *The Decline of Hell* (Chicago: University of Chicago Press, 1964).

5. On the English pleasure gardens, see Roy Porter, *Enlightenment: Britain and the Creation of the Modern World* (London: Penguin, 2000), 269–270. On the Palais Royal, see Darrin M. McMahon, "The Birthplace of the Revolution: Public Space and Political Community in The Palais-Royal of Louis-Philippe-Joseph d'Orléans," *French History* 10, no. 1 (March 1996).

6. Pope, *Essay on Man*, Epistle 4.

7. [Abbé Pestré], "Bonheur," *Encyclopédie, ou Dictionnaire raisonné des sciences des arts et des métiers*, Nouvelle impression en facsimilé de la première édition de 1751–1780, 35 vols. (Stuttgart: Friedrich Fromann Verlag, 1966–67), 2:322. "Chacun n'a t-il pas droit d'être heureux, selon que son caprice en décidera?" For other examples of the phrase the "right to happiness," see Anne Robert Jacques Turgot, *Deuxième lettre sur la tolérance* (Paris, 1754), and Guillaume Thomas- François Raynal, *Histoire philosophique et politique des établissements et du commerce des Européens dans les deux Indes*, 10 vols. (Geneva, 1780), 9:232.

8. For a general introduction to this vast literature, see Robert Mauzi, *L'idée du bonheur dans la littérature et la pensée françaises au XVIIIe siècle* (Paris: Albin Michel, 1994), and Paul Hazard, *European Thought in the Eighteenth Century: From Montesquieu to Lessing*, trans. J. Lewis May (Cleveland, Ohio: Meridian, 1969; 1946), 14–26.

9. Hazard, *European Thought*, 17.

10. See A. P. Pochet, *Programme d'une Fête Allégorique représentée par le Corps des Nobles Cadets de terre de St. Petersbourg, à l'occasion de la paix de 1775 avec la Cour Ottomane*, contained in the French National Archives, AN F^{1C} I 85. The celebrations took place in 1778.

11. Marquise du Châtelet, *Discours sur le bonheur*, intro. Elizabeth Badinter (Pairs: Editions Payot & Rivages, 1997), 32.

12. For an insightful rumination on these questions of happiness applied specifically to the case of women, see Cornelia Klinger, "Vom Schwierig-Werden der Frage des Glücks in einer Zeit ohne Sinn und Ziel," *L'Homme: Zeitschrift für Feministische Geschichtswissenschaft* 10, no. 2 (1999): 173–192.

13. William Paley, *Natural Theology* (London: Wilks and Taylor, 1802), 490.

14. [A. J. Durand], *Je Veux être heureux. Entretiens familiers sur la religion* (Paris, 1782); Joseph-Aignan Sigaud de la Fond, *L'École du bonheur* (Paris, 1782); Philippe Louis Gérard, *La Théorie du bonheur, ou L'art de se rendre heureux* (Paris, 1801).

15. [Caroline-Stéphanie-Félicité du Crest], *La Religion considérée comme l'unique base du bonheur & de la véritable philosophie* (Paris, 1787).

16. See Theodore K. Rabb, *The Struggle for Stability in Early Modern Europe* (New York: Oxford University Press, 1975), 76.

17. See Isser Woloch, *Eighteenth-Century Europe: Tradition and Progress, 1715–1789* (New York: W. W. Norton, 1982), esp. 103–109.

18. See, for example, Neil McKendrick, John Brewer, and J. H. Plumb, *The Birth of a Consumer Society: The Commercialization of 18th-Century England* (Bloomington: Indiana University Press, 1985), or Daniel Roche, *A History of Everyday Things: The Birth of Consumption in France 1600–1800*, trans. Brian Pearce (Cambridge: Cambridge University Press, 2000).

19. Woloch, *Eighteenth-Century Europe*, 123–130.

20. Turgot cited in Emma Rothschild, *Economic Sentiments: Adam Smith, Condorcet, and the Enlightenment* (Cambridge, Mass.: Harvard University, Press, 2001), 242.

21. Thomas Hobbes, *Leviathan*, with selected variants from the Latin edition of 1668, ed. Edwin Curley (Indianapolis: Hackett, 1994), part 1, chap. 11, 57–58.

22. Porter, *Enlightenment*, 22.

23. Denis Diderot, *Plan d'une université pour le gouvernement de Russie*, in *Oeuvres complètes*, eds. Jules Assézat and Maurice Tourneux, 20 vols. (Paris: Garnier, 1875–1877), 3:477.

24. See the classic account of Peter Gay, *The Enlightenment: An Interpretation* (New York: Knopf, 1966–69), esp. vol. 1, *The Rise of Modern Paganism*.

25. Epicurus, "Vatican Sayings," no. 56, in *The Essential Epicurus: Letters, Principal Doctrines, Vatican Sayings, and Fragments*, trans. and ed. Eugene O'Connor (Amherst, N.Y.: Prometheus, 1993), 82.

26. Marquise du Châtelet, *Discours sur le bonheur*, 32–33.

27. Voltaire's words and reactions are cited and discussed in Bronislaw Baczko, *Job, Mon Ami. Promesses du bonheur et fatalité du mal* (Paris: Gallimard, 1997), 17ff.

28. Vico's *Scienza Nuova* (The New Science) was first published in 1725. Vico's work, however, was almost totally unknown beyond his immediate circle until the nineteenth century.

29. Jeremy Bentham, "Preface to the first edition," *A Fragment on Government*, in *A Bentham Reader*, ed. Mary Peter Mack (New York: Pegasus, 1969), 45.

30. See Robert Shackleton, "The Greatest Happiness of the Greatest Number: The History of Bentham's phrase," *Studies on Voltaire and the Eighteenth Century* 90, ed. Theodore Besterman (Oxford: Voltaire Foundation, 1972), 1461–1482; Joachim Hruschka, "The Greatest Happiness Principle and Other Early German Anticipations of Utilitarian Theory," *Utilitas* 3, no. 2 (November 1991): 165–177; and David Blumenfield, "Perfection and Happiness in the Best Possible World," in Nicholas Jolley, ed. *The Cambridge Companion to Leibniz* (Cambridge: Cambridge University Press, 1995), 381–410.

31. Garry Wills, *Inventing America: Jefferson's Declaration of Independence* (New York: Vintage Books, 1978), 150–151.

32. Hutcheson cited in Shackleton, "The Greatest Happiness of the Greatest Number," 1466–1467.

33. Hutcheson's formulas cited in Wills, *Inventing America*, 149.

34. [Benjamin Stillingfleet], Irenaeus Kranzovius, *Some Thoughts Concerning Happiness . . . translated from the Original German* (London: Printed for W. Webb, 1738).

35. Ibid., 5, 11.

36. Cesare Beccaria, *On Crimes and Punishment*, trans. and intro. David Young (Indianapolis: Hackett, 1986), 5, 14.

37. It should be noted that Nicolas-Antoine Boulanger in *Despotisme orientale* (1755), Voltaire in *Essai sur les moeurs* (1756), and Adam Ferguson in *An Essay on the History of Civil Society* (1767) also touched on themes relating to the history of happiness as conceived by Chastellux, albeit less explicitly.

38. François Jean, Marquis de Chastellux, *De la Félicité publique, ou Considérations sur le sort des Hommes dans les différentes époques de l'histoire*, 2 vols. (Amsterdam: Chez Marc-Michel Rey, 1772), 1:9.

39. Chastellux, *De la Félicité publique*, 1:10.

40. Paul Henri Thiry, Baron d'Holbach, *Common Sense, or Natural Ideas Opposed to Supernatural* (1772), in Isaac Kramnick, ed. *The Portable Enlightenment* (New York: Penguin, 1995), 145.

41. Ironically, when, at the turn of the eighteenth century, the British demographer Thomas Malthus sought to argue that *overpopulation* was the principal threat to modern societies, he retained the link to happiness, entitling the second edition of his *Essay on the Principle of Population, A View of Its Past and Present Effects on Human Happiness* (London: Royal Economic Society, 1803).

42. Most famously, David Hume in his "Essay on the Populousness of Ancient Nations" (1742).

43. Helvétius, *Le Bonheur*, in *Oeuvres*, 13:90.

44. Jeremy Bentham, *Deontology*, I.4, in *Deontology Together with a Table of the Springs of Action and the Article on Utilitarianism*, ed. Amnon Goldworth (Oxford: Clarendon Press, 1983), 134 and n. 2. Voltaire makes the same observation in his article "Bien, Souverain bien," in the *Philosophical Dictionary* of 1764.

45. Chastellux, *De la Félicité publique*, 2:10 and 2:54.

46. Bentham cited in Ross Harrison, *Bentham* (London: Routledge & Kegan Paul, 1983), 38.

47. Abbé Pestré, "Bonheur," 322.

48. Bentham, *A Fragment on Government*, "Preface to the first edition," 51.

49. Bentham, *An Introduction to the Principles of Morals and Legislation*, eds. J. H. Burns and H. L. A. Hart, intro. F. Rosen (Oxford: Clarendon Press, 1996), 11 (chap. 1, section 1).

50. Ibid., 38–41 (chap. 4, sections 1–6).

51. Cited in John Dinwiddy, *Bentham* (New York: Oxford University Press, 1989), 50. On Bentham's avowal of the impossibility of calculating the intensity of pleasure, see James Steintrager, *Bentham* (Ithaca, N.Y.: Cornell University Press, 1977), 30–31.

52. Bentham, *A Table of the Springs of Action*, 87. It is not entirely clear that Bentham used the exact phrase "felicific calculus," although he often spoke of "applying arithmetical calculation to the elements of happiness" and certainly saw Newton as his great model. See the discussion in Harrison, *Bentham*, 138–141.

53. On the genesis and misappropriation of Bentham's phrase, see Harrison, *Bentham*, 5.

54. John Locke, *An Essay Concerning Human Understanding*, ed. Peter H. Nidditch (Oxford: Clarendon, 1991; first edition 1975), 268–269.

55. Julien Offray de la Mettrie, *Système d'Épicure* (1750), in *Oeuvres philosophiques*, 2 vols. (Paris: Fayard, 1987), 1:376.

56. Denis Diderot, *Essai sur les règnes de Claude et de Néron* (1779), in *Oeuvres complètes*, ed. Herbert Dieckmann and Jean Varlot, 25 vols. (Paris: Hermann, 1986), 25:246–248.

57. [Julien Offray de la Mettrie], *Le Petit homme à longue queue* (1751).

58. This is the phrase of another atheist and materialist, the Baron d'Holbach, in his *Système de la nature, ou des lois du monde physique et du monde moral*, ed. Josiane Boulad-Ayoub, 2 vols. (Paris: Fayard, 1990) 2:339.

59. On La Mettrie's medical career and its influence on his thought, see Kathleen Wellman, *La Mettrie: Medicine, Philosophy, and Enlightenment* (Durham, N.C.: Duke University Press, 1992).

60. On the subject of happiness in the Dutch Republic during the age of Enlightenment, see Peter Buijs, "De mens is tot geluk geschapen. Naar een geschiedenis van het geluk in de republiek ten tijde van de Verlichting," *Tijdschrift voor Geschiedenis* 108, no. 2 (1995): 188–208.

61. Jonathan I. Israel, *Radical Enlightenment: Philosophy and the Making of Modernity 1650–1750* (New York: Oxford University Press, 2001), 708–709.

62. Julien Offray de la Mettrie, *Man A Machine,* trans. Richard A. Watson and Maya Rybalka (Indianapolis: Hackett, 1994), 36.

63. Ibid., 32, 65, 50, 41, 75.

64. Ibid., 59.

65. Ibid., 29–30.

66. Ibid., 53.

67. Ibid., 58.

68. La Mettrie, *L'Anti-Sénèque, ou Discours sur le bonheur,* in *Oeuvres,* 2:263.

69. Ibid., 2:286.

70. La Mettrie, *Système de Épicure,* in *Oeuvres,* 1:380. See also *L'Art de Jouir* (1751).

71. Giacomo Casanova, *History of My Life,* trans. Willard R. Trask, 12 vols. (Baltimore: Johns Hopkins University Press, 1966), 2:14. I have altered Trask's translation slightly.

72. Ibid., 3:194–195.

73. Donatien-Alphonse-François de Sade, "Dialogue Between a Priest and a Dying Man," in *Justine, Philosophy in the Bedroom, and Other Writings,* trans. and ed. Richard Seaver and Austryn Wainhouse (New York: Grove Weidenfeld, 1965), 174.

74. Sade, *Philosophy in the Bedroom,* in ibid., 185.

75. See the discussion in Charles Taylor, *Sources of the Self: The Making of the Modern Identity* (Cambridge, Mass.: Harvard University Press, 1989), 339 and more generally, 328–340.

76. I make this argument at greater length in my article "From the Happiness of Virtue to the Virtue of Happiness 400 B.C.–A.D. 1780," *Daedalus* 133, no. 2 (Spring 2004).

77. Jean-Jacques Rousseau, *Reveries of a Solitary Walker,* trans. and intro. Peter France (New York: Penguin, 1979), 81–83.

78. Ibid., 88–89.

79. Philipp Balthasar Sinold von Schütz, *Die glückseligste Insul auf der ganzen Welt, oder Das Land der Zufriedenheit* (Frankfurt, 1728).

80. Rousseau speaks often of *Robinson Crusoe* in his treatise on education, *Emile; or, On Education,* intro. and trans. Allan Bloom (New York: Basic Books, 1979).

81. Frost's two-line poem "An Answer" is cited in Sergio Perosa, *From Island to Portraits: Four Literary Variations* (Amsterdam: IOS Press, 2000), 2. I am grateful to Professor Perosa for sharing this work with me.

82. Rousseau, *Reveries,* 88.

83. Rousseau, *Emile,* 447.

84. Rousseau, *Political Fragments,* part 6 ("On Public Happiness"), section 3, in *The Collected Writings of Rousseau,* eds. Roger D. Masters and Christopher Kelly, trans. Judith R. Bush, Roger D. Masters, and Christopher Kelly, 8 vols. (Hanover, N.H.: University Press of New England, 1994), 4:40. On Rousseau's understanding of happiness in general, see Stephen G. Slakeve, "Rousseau & the Concept of

Happiness," *Journal of the Northeastern Political Science Association* 11 (Fall 1978): 27–45, and Ronald Grimsley, "Rousseau and the Problem of Happiness," *Hobbes and Rousseau: A Collection of Critical Essays*, eds. Maurice Cranston and Richard S. Peters (New York: Anchor Books, 1972), 437–461.

85. Rousseau, *Reveries*, 87–88.

86. Ibid.

87. Rousseau, *Emile*, 442.

88. Rousseau, *First Discourse* (*Discourse on the Arts and Sciences*) in *The Basic Political Writings*, trans. Donald A. Cress, intro. Peter Gay (Indianapolis: Hackett, 1987), 19.

89. Rousseau, *The Second Discourse* (*Discourse on the Origin and Foundations of Inequality Among Men*), in *Basic Political Writings*, 81.

90. Rousseau, *Reveries*, 133.

91. Rousseau, *Lettres morales*, in *Oeuvres complètes*, eds. Bernard Gagnebin and Marcel Raymond, 5 vols. (Paris: Gallimard, 1969), 4:1112 (Letter 6).

92. Blaise Pascal, *Pensées*, ed. Louis Lafuma (Paris: Éditions du Seuil, 1962), 298 (fragment #688).

93. Rousseau, *Emile*, 442.

94. Rousseau, *Emile*, 80–81. See, similarly, *Political Fragments*, part 6, 40, and *Second Discourse*, part 1.

95. Ibid.

96. Rousseau, *Emile*, 81–82 and 446.

97. Rousseau, *On the Social Contract; or, Essay about the Form of the Republic* (first version, the so-called Geneva Manuscript), in *Collected Writings*, 4:77.

98. Ibid., 82 (emphasis added).

99. Rousseau, *On the Social Contract; or, Principles of Political Right*, book 1, chap. 9.

100. Rousseau, *Political Fragments*, in *Collected Writings*, 4:41.

101. Ibid., 4:43.

102. Rousseau, *Reveries*, 154.

103. Ibid., 137.

104. James Boswell, *The Life of Samuel Johnson L.L.D.*, ed. Roger Ingpen, 3 vols. (Boston: Charles E. Lauriat, 1925), 2:520, 605.

105. Samuel Johnson, "The Vanity of Human Wishes, the Tenth Satire of Juvenal Imitated," in *The Complete English Poems*, ed. J. D. Fleeman (New Haven, Conn.: Yale University Press, 1971), 83.

106. Ibid., 89, 92.

107. Samuel Johnson, *The History of Rasselas, Prince of Abissinia*, ed. D. J. Enright (London: Penguin Books, 1985), 47, 45.

108. Ibid., 65. On the complexities of Johnson's views on happiness, see Adam Potkay, *The Passion for Happiness: Samuel Johnson & David Hume* (Ithaca, N.Y.: Cornell University Press, 2000).

109. Johnson, *Rasselas*, 87.

110. Cited in Daniel Roche, *France in the Enlightenment*, trans. Arthur Goldhammer (Cambridge, Mass.: Harvard University Press, 1998), 129 (emphasis added). Roche comments on the revolutionary message of these works, which for so long had counseled resignation and patience. "[The new almanacs] taught people that even humble folk could be happy, so why should anyone remain resigned to his fate?" Ibid.

111. Walter Pape, "Happy Endings in a World of Misery: A Literary Convention Between Social Constraints and Utopia in Children's and Adult Literature," *Poetics Today* 13 (Spring 1992): 179–196. I am grateful to Annabel Temple-Smith of the University of Queensland for bringing this work to my attention.

112. Cited in Porter, *Creation of the Modern World*, 204.

113. Johnson, *Rasselas*, 116–117.

114. The phrase is that of the English poet Thomas Gray, although the thought behind it is very old. See Mark Lilla, "Ignorance and Bliss," *The Wilson Quarterly* 25, no. 3 (Summer 2001): 64–75.

115. Voltaire, "The Story of a Good Brahmin" (1759), in *The Portable Voltaire* (New York: Penguin, 1977), 436–438.

116. Immanuel Kant, *Groundwork for the Metaphysics of Morals*, trans. James W. Ellington (Indianapolis: Hackett, 1981), 8–9.

117. Ibid., 46.

118. Ibid.

119. Immanuel Kant, *Critique of Pure Reason* (1781, 1787), unified edition, trans. Werner S. Pluhar, intro. Patricia Kitcher (Indianapolis: Hackett, 1996), 736–737.

120. Ibid., 742. In general, see the section "On the Ideal of the Highest Good, as a Determining Basis of the Ultimate Basis of Pure Reason."

A Modern Rite

1. See "Lequinio, Joseph-Marie," in J. Fr. Michaud's *Biographie Universelle ancienne et moderne*, nouvelle édition, 45 vols. (Paris, 1854), 24:243.

2. Archives National F17 A1003, plaq. 3, no. 1263, "Du Bonheur," par Lequinio, Représentatif du peuple envoyé dans le Département de la Charente Inférieure; prononcé dans le Temple de la Vérité, ci-devant l'Église catholique de Rochefort, le deuxième décadi de Brumaire, l'an second de la république française, une et indivisible, 1–2.

3. Ibid., 3–4.

4. Ibid., 5.

5. Ibid., 6–8.

6. Ibid., 18–19.

7. Donald Greer, *The Incidence of the Terror During the French Revolution: A Statistical Interpretation* (Cambridge, Mass.: Harvard University Press, 1935), 140. Greer places the number of death sentences handed down by the revolutionary tribunal of Rochefort between November 1793 and February 1794 at forty. See also Jacques Duguet et al., *La Révolution française à Rochefort, 1789–1799* (Poitiers: Projets Editions, 1989), 74.

8. "Lequinio, Joseph-Marie," in Michaud, *Biographie Universelle*, 24:243–244.

9. Maximilien Robespierre, "Sur l'inculpation de dictature" (25 Septembre 1792), cited in F. Theuriot, "La conception robespierriste du bonheur," *Annales historiques de la révolution française* 192 (1968): 216.

10. *Système de dénominations topographiques pour les places, rues, quais, etc. de toutes les communes de la République*, par le Citoyen Grégoire (Paris: Imprimerie National, n.d. [pluviôse, year 2]), 14. See also, Branislaw Baczko, "From the Place de la Révolution to the Place du Bonheur: The Imaginary Paris of the Revolution,"

Utopian Lights: The Evolution of the Idea of Social Progress, trans. Judith L. Greenberg (New York: Paragon House, 1989), 280–365.

11. The undated letter from Pochet to Citoyen Benezeque can be found in the French National Archives, F/1cI/85. The decree of the national convention of 18 Floréal, Year II, instituting the "Fêtes décadaires" and listing their individual themes, can be found in F/1c1/84.

12. "Rapport au nom du comité de salut public, sur le mode d'exécution du décret contre les ennemis de la révolution, présenté à la convention nationale," 13 Ventôse an II (March 3, 1794), in *Oeuvres complètes de Saint-Just,* ed. Michèle Duval (Paris: Editions Gérard Lebovici, 1984), 715.

13. On the influence of antiquity on the attitudes and aesthetics of the revolutionaries, see Mona Ozouf, *Festivals and the French Revolution,* trans. Alan Sheridan (Cambridge, Mass.: Harvard University Press, 1988), 5, 52–53, 273–275; H. T. Parker, *The Cult of Antiquity and the French Revolutionaries* (Chicago: University of Chicago Press, 1937); as well as Lynn Hunt's classic, *Politics, Culture, and Class in the French Revolution* (Berkeley: University of California Press, 1984).

14. Saint-Just, "Rapport au nom du comité de salut public sur les factions de l'étranger," 23 Ventôse an II (March 13, 1794), in *Oeuvres complètes,* 729–730.

15. Lequinio, "Du bonheur," 21–22.

16. Ibid., 18–19.

17. Émile Durkheim, *The Elementary Forms of Religious Life,* trans. and intro. Karen E. Fields (New York: Free Press, 1995).

18. Mona Ozouf, "The Revolutionary Festival: A Transfer of Sacrality," chap. 10 of *Festivals and the French Revolution.*

19. Chesterton cited in Pascal Bruckner, *L'euphorie perpétuelle: Essai sur le devoir de bonheur* (Paris: Bernard Grasset, 2000), 55–56. Bruckner suggests but does not develop in detail the Christian roots of modern happiness in this characteristically insightful essay.

20. See the still-suggestive account of Carl Becker, *The Heavenly City of the Eighteenth-Century Philosophers* (New Haven, Conn.: Yale University Press, 1979; 1932).

21. This is a theme emphasized with particular force by Marcel Gauchet. See his "Croyances religieuses, croyances politiques," *Le Débat* 115 (Mai–Août 2001): 3–14, and, more generally, *The Disenchantment of the World: A Political History of Religion,* trans. Oscar Burge (Princeton, N.J.: Princeton University Press, 1997).

22. Bruckner, *L'Euphorie perpétuelle,* 84.

23. Luc Ferry, *L'Homme-Dieu, ou le Sens de la vie* (Paris: Éditions Grasset & Fasquelle, 1996), 32.

Chapter Five

1. Napoleon Bonaparte, *Discours de Napoléon sur les vérités et les sentiments qu'il importe le plus d'inculquer aux hommes pour leur bonheur* (Paris: Baudouin Frères, 1826), 42–43.

2. Cited in Andy Martin, "Napoleon on Happiness," *Raritan* 19, no. 4 (Spring 2000), 96.

3. Napoleon, *Discours de Napoléon,* 36–39.

4. A characteristically sage discussion of the meaning of "Romanticism" is provided in Hugh Honour, *Romanticism* (New York: Harper & Row, 1979), chap. 1, "For Lack of a Better Name."

5. Cited in Martin, "Napoleon on Happiness," 14.

6. G. W. F. Hegel, *Lectures on the Philosophy of World History. Introduction: Reason in History,* Second Draft (1830), trans. H. B. Nisbet (Cambridge: Cambridge University Press, 1975), 85.

7. Cited in Peter Quennell, *The Pursuit of Happiness* (Boston: Little, Brown, 1988), 111.

8. Heine first uses the term in his *Gemäldeaustellung in Paris* (1831), and then again in the foreword to *Geständnisse* (1854). Jean-Paul Richter uses it in his *Selina oder die Unsterblichkeit* (1827). See William Rose, *From Goethe to Byron: The Development of "Weltschmerz" in German Literature* (London: George Routledge, 1924).

9. On Goethe's own interesting reflections on happiness, see T. J. Reed, "Goethe and Happiness," in Elizabeth M. Wilkinson, ed. *Goethe Revisited: A Collection of Essays* (New York: Riverrun Press, 1984); and Julie D. Prandi, *"Dare to be happy!" A Study of Goethe's Ethics* (Latham, Md.: University Press of America, 1993).

10. See, for example, the discussion in D. G. Charlton, "Prose Fiction," in vol. 1 of *The French Romantics,* 2 vols. (Cambridge: Cambridge University Press, 1984), 169. Jean Deprun, *La Philosophie de la inquiétude en France au XVIIIe siècle* (Paris: J. Vrin, 1979) is also suggestive.

11. Cited in Quennell, *Pursuit of Happiness,* 57.

12. Cited in Anne Vincent Buffault, *The History of Tears: Sensibility and Sentimentality in France,* trans. Teresa Bridgeman (New York: St. Martin's Press, 1991), 106.

13. Cited in Eleanor M. Sickels, *The Gloomy Egoist: Moods and Themes of Melancholy from Gray to Keats* (New York: Columbia University Press, 1932), 320. The gloomy phrase is from Byron's poem "Darkness."

14. Letters of April 30, 1817, and March 3, 1817, cited in *Poètes du Spleen: Leopardi, Baudelaire, Pessoa,* ed. Philippe Daros (Paris: Champion, 1997), 61, 66.

15. Cited in Isaiah Berlin, *The Roots of Romanticism,* ed. Henry Hardy (Princeton, N.J.: Princeton University Press, 1999), 141.

16. Cited in Marilyn Gaull, *Romanticism: The Human Context* (New York: W. W. Norton, 1988), 199; and M. H. Abrams, *Natural Supernaturalism: Tradition and Revolution in Romantic Literature* (New York: W. W. Norton, 1971), 328.

17. Keats to Benjamin Bailey, November 22, 1817, in *The Letters of John Keats,* ed. Hyder E. Rollins, 2 vols. (Cambridge, Mass.: Harvard University Press, 1958), 1:186.

18. Wordsworth, "The Prelude," Book 2, lines 448ff.

19. Shelley to Lord Byron, September 8, 1816, cited in Abrams, *Natural Supernaturalism,* 328.

20. Alfred de Musset, *La Confession d'un enfant du siècle,* in *Oeuvres complètes en prose,* eds. Maurice Allem and Paul Courant (Paris: Gallimard, 1960), 78. This autobiographical work was first published in 1835.

21. Byron, "Childe Harold's Pilgrimage," Canto the Third, XXXIV.

22. Emerson cited in Andrew Delbanco, *The Real American Dream: A Meditation on Hope* (Cambridge, Mass.: Harvard University Press, 1999), 51.

23. Friedrich Schiller, *On the Aesthetic Education of Man in a Series of Letters,* trans.

and eds. Elizabeth M. Wilkinson and L. A. Willoughby (Oxford: Clarendon, 1967), 33 (Sixth Letter).

24. Heinrich Heine, "The Romantic School," in *The Romantic School and Other Essays*, eds. Jost Hermand and Robert C. Holub (New York: Continuum, 1985), 3.

25. Jean-Paul Richter cited in Honour, *Romanticism*, 295.

26. Thomas Carlyle, *Sartor Resartus* (New York: Oxford University Press, 1991), 147.

27. "Natural Supernaturalism" is the heading of book 3, chap. 8, of *Sartor Resartus*. It is also the title of M. H. Abrams's still-remarkable *Natural Supernaturalism* (New York: W. W. Norton, 1971). Abrams's chief concern is the "secularization of inherited theological ideas" in Romantic thought. As will become apparent, I am deeply indebted in this chapter to his interpretation.

28. Heine, "Concerning the History of Religion and Philosophy in Germany," in *The Romantic School and Other Essays*, 134.

29. On the way in which aesthetic culture since Wordsworth can "be said to maintain an antagonism to the principle of pleasure," see Lionel Trilling's still-trenchant essay "The Fate of Pleasure," in *Beyond Culture: Essays on Literature and Learning* (New York: Viking Press, 1965; 1955).

30. Byron cited in Sickels, *The Gloomy Egoist*, 321.

31. Schiller cited in Abrams, *Natural Supernaturalism*, 443.

32. Keats to George and Georgiana Keats, April 21, 1819, in *Letters*, 2:102.

33. Ibid.

34. Abrams, *Natural Supernaturalism*, 276.

35. M. H. Abrams, *The Mirror and the Lamp: Romantic Theory and Critical Tradition* (New York: Oxford University Press, 1953).

36. Hölderlin cited in Abrams, *Natural Supernaturalism*, 238.

37. Coleridge, *Philosophical Lectures 1818–1819*, ed. Kathleen Coburn (London: Pilot Press, 1949), Lecture 5, 179.

38. Walt Whitman, "Song of Myself," *Leaves of Grass*.

39. Carlyle, *Sartor Resartus*, 146.

40. Cited in Abrams, *Natural Supernaturalism*, 289.

41. Cited in Honour, *Romanticism*, 73.

42. On Coleridge's dream of the pantisocratic community, see Richard Holmes, *Coleridge: Early Visions* (London: Flamingo, 1989), esp. 59–89.

43. Thomas de Quincey, *Confessions of an English Opium Eater and Other Writings*, ed. Grevel Lindop (New York: Oxford University Press, 1989), 38–39. On this subject more generally, see Alethea Hayter, *Opium and the Romantic Imagination* (London: Faber, 1968).

44. Baudelaire, "Le Poème du haschisch," in *Oeuvres complètes*, ed. Claude Pichois, 2 vols. (Paris: Gallimard, 1975), 1:438.

45. Shelley in a letter to Maria Gisborne, October 13 or 15, 1819, cited in Abrams, *Natural Supernaturalism*, 447.

46. Shelley cited in Abrams, *Natural Supernaturalism*, 434.

47. This translation of Beethoven's adaptation of Schiller's poem is taken, with several alterations, from Nicholas Cook, *Beethoven: Symphony No. 9* (Cambridge: Cambridge University Press, 1993), 109.

48. Strindberg cited in Alessandra Comini, "The Visual Beethoven: Whence,

Why, and Whither the Scowl?" in Scott Burnham and Michael P. Steinberg, eds. *Beethoven and His World* (Princeton, N.J.: Princeton University Press, 2000), 309, n. 1. The account of Beethoven that follows draws heavily on Professor Comini's wonderful article.

49. Comini, "The Visual Beethoven," 290.

50. Ballanche cited in Vincent Buffault, *The History of Tears,* 106.

51. Beethoven and Rossini cited in Comini, "The Visual Beethoven," 288.

52. Ludwig van Beethoven, *Briefwechsel Gesamtausgabe,* ed. Siegard Brandenburg, 7 vols. (Munich: G. Henle Verlag, 1996), 1:123.

53. Ibid.

54. Cited in R. J. Hollingdale's "Introduction" to Arthur Schopenhauer, *Essays and Aphorism,* trans. and ed. R. J. Hollingdale (London: Penguin, 1970), 31.

55. Arthur Schopenhauer, *Manuscript Remains,* 4 vols., trans. E. F. J. Payne, ed. Arthur Hübscher (New York: St. Martin's Press, 1988), 4:119 (*Colera-Buch,* no. 89).

56. Arthur Schopenhauer, *The World as Will and Representation,* trans. E. F. J. Payne, 2 vols. (New York: Dover Publications, 1966), 1:318.

57. Ibid., 2:573.

58. Ibid., 1:318.

59. Cited in Christopher Janaway, *Schopenhauer: A Very Short Introduction* (New York: Oxford University Press, 2002), 43. I have made ample use of this masterful, and masterfully brief, summary by one of the world's leading Schopenhauer scholars.

60. Schopenhauer, *The World as Will and Representation,* 2:209.

61. Ibid., 2:513–514.

62. Ibid., 2:573.

63. Ibid., 2:575.

64. Schopenhauer, *Manuscript Remains,* 4:36 (Cogitata I, no. 52).

65. Schopenhauer, *The World as Will and Representation,* 2:634.

66. Ibid., 2:584.

67. Ibid., 2:583–586.

68. Ibid., 2:580, 444.

69. Ibid., 2:633.

70. Ibid., 2:638.

71. Ibid., 1:411.

72. Ibid., 2:636.

73. Ibid., 2:639.

74. Ibid., 2:508.

75. Ibid., 1:196.

76. Ibid., 1:196.

77. Ibid., 1:257. See, in general, vol. 2, chap. 39, "On the Metaphysics of Music."

78. Ibid., 1:264.

79. These are the words of the Secession building's architect Josef Olbrich, as well as those of the noted Viennese architect Otto Wagner, as cited in Carl E. Schorske, *Fin-de-Siècle Vienna: Politics and Culture* (New York: Vintage, 1981), 215–217.

80. Schorske, *Fin-de-Siècle Vienna,* 254.

81. The following citations from the exhibition catalog are taken from Gerbert Frodl, *Beethovenfries* (Salzburg: Verlag Galerie Welz, 1997), 14.

82. The line from Stendhal can be found in his *On Love*. Baudelaire cites him, with minor reservations, in the section "Beauty, Fashion, and Happiness," in *The Painter of Modern Life*.

83. Richard Wagner, *Beethoven*, in *Richard Wagner's Prose Works*, 8 vols., trans. William Ashton Ellis (London: 1897), 5:120.

84. Ibid., 5:120.

85. Ibid., 5:86–87 and 5:102.

Chapter Six

1. *The Path to Riches and Happiness, by the late Doctor Benjamin Franklin* (Dublin: William Watson, n.d. [1800]).

2. On God's desire that human beings be happy, see esp. Franklin's "Articles of Belief and Acts of Religion" (1728), in Benjamin Franklin, *Autobiography and Other Writings*, ed. Russell B. Nye (Boston: Houghton Mifflin, 1949), 163–165.

3. Cited in William Temple Franklin, *Memoirs of the Life and Writings of Benjamin Franklin*, 3 vols. (London, 1817–1818), 2:94–95.

4. "Queries to be asked the Junto," in Benjamin Franklin, *Writings* (New York: Library of America, 1987), 210–211.

5. *Poor Richard* (1776), cited in *Writings*, 1238 ("Virtue and happiness are mother and daughter").

6. Benjamin Franklin, *Autobiography*, Norton Critical edition, eds. J. A. Leo Lemay and P. M. Zall (New York: W. W. Norton, 1986), 108 (part 3).

7. Franklin, "Poor Richard Improved, 1755," in *Writings*, 1283. "Content is the Philosopher's stone, that turns all it touches into Gold" (1758).

8. "Glittering generality" is the title of the first chapter of Howard Mumford Jones's *The Pursuit of Happiness* (Ithaca, N.Y.: Cornell University Press, 1953).

9. Garry Wills, *Inventing America: Jefferson's Declaration of Independence* (New York: Vintage, 1979), xiv.

10. On the making of a specifically American "civil or civic religion," see the provocative new history by Walter A. McDougal, *Freedom Just Around the Corner: A New American History 1585–1828* (New York: HarperCollins, 2004), esp. 321–370.

11. Jan Lewis, "Happiness," in *The Blackwell Encyclopedia of the American Revolution*, eds. Jack P. Green and J. R. Pole (Cambridge, England: Blackwell, 1994), 641. On the discussion of happiness in America, see also Ursula M. von Eckardt, *The Pursuit of Happiness in the Democratic Creed: An Analysis of Political Ethics* (New York: Frederick Praeger, 1959).

12. Thomas Jefferson to Henry Lee, May 8, 1825, in *The Basic Writings of Thomas Jefferson*, ed. Philip S. Foner (New York: Halcyon House, 1950), 802.

13. On the range of these positions, see Lewis, "Happiness," 642–643.

14. Locke, *An Essay Concerning Human Understanding*, ed. Peter H. Nidditch (Oxford: Clarendon Press, 1975), 269.

15. Mason cited in Jones, *Pursuit of Happiness*, 12. On Jefferson's knowledge of Mason's draft of the Virginia Declaration of Rights and its relationship to the Declaration of Independence, see Pauline Maier, *American Scripture: Making the Declaration of Independence* (New York: Vintage, 1997), 125–134.

16. James Otis cited in Ibid., 4.

17. Madison cited in Ibid., 21.

18. All these state constitutions may be consulted freely online.

19. Locke, *Essay Concerning Human Understanding*, 268.

20. My discussion of "pursuit" borrows from Wills, *Inventing America*, 245.

21. Locke, *Essay Concerning Human Understanding*, 262.

22. Robert Breck, *The Surest Way to Advance a People's Happiness and Prosperity, as it was delivered in a Sermon at Shrewsbury, a New Plantation, on Wednesday, June 15, 1720* (Boston: S. Kneeland, 1751), 3, 11; Robert Breck, *The Only Method to Promote the Happiness of a People and their Posterity, a Sermon preached before the Honourable the Lieut. Governour, the Council, and Representatives of the Province of the Massachusetts Bay in New-England, May 29th 1728* (Boston: B. Green, 1728), 22.

23. Noah Hobart, *Civil Government, the Foundation of Social Happiness, A Sermon Preached before the General Assembly of the Colony of Connecticut, at Hartford, on the Day of Their Anniversary Election, May 10th, 1750* (New London: T. Green, 1751), 3, 6–7, 24–25.

24. Benjamin Lord, *Religion and Government subsisting together in Society, Necessary to their Compleat Happiness and Safety, a Sermon Delivered in the Audience of the General Assembly of the Colony of Connecticut, on their Anniversary Election at Hartford, May 9th, 1751* (New London: Timothy Green, 1752).

25. Samuel Dunbar, *The Presence of God with His People, their Only Safety and Happiness. A Discourse delivered at Boston in the presence of His Excellency the Governour, Thomas Pownall, esq.... * (Boston: S. Kneeland, 1760).

26. *True Pleasure, Chearfulness, and Happiness, The Immediate Consequence of Religion fully and concisely proved* (Philadelphia: William and Thomas Bradford, 1767), 12. The author of this amusing work points out that Christ performed his first miracle, turning water into wine, at a wedding feast where "jollity and joy" was the dominant mood. The choice, it seems, was significant, for "he who condescended to work a miracle upon such an occasion, cannot be justly imagined to have been a gloomy, melancholy spectator only, of such joy and happiness."

27. Adams cited in Jones, *Pursuit of Happiness*, 68. Interestingly, Adams also observes, "We too often mistake our true happiness, and when we arrive to the enjoyment of that which seemed to promise it to us, we find that it is all an imaginary dream, at best fleeting and transitory."

28. Jefferson to Dr. Joseph Priestley, April 9, 1803.

29. Jefferson to Benjamin Waterhouse, June 26, 1822, in *Basic Writings*, 774.

30. These include Bernard Bailyn, J. G. A. Pocock, Gordon Wood, and Lance Banning.

31. Jefferson to William Short, October 31, 1819, in *Basic Writings*, 764. Jefferson continued, "I consider the genuine (not the imputed) doctrines of Epicurus as containing everything rational in moral philosophy which Greece and Rome have left us."

32. The case for Hutcheson's influence is made most forcefully in Wills, *Inventing America*, esp. 149–164 and 240–255. On the importance of Burlamaqui, see Morton White, *The Philosophy of the American Revolution* (New York: Oxford University Press, 1978).

33. Hutcheson cited in Charles Taylor, *Sources of the Self: The Making of Modern Identity* (Cambridge, Mass.: Harvard University Press, 1989), 261.

34. Most notably, Garry Wills.

35. On Jefferson's admiration for *The Wealth of Nations*, see Jerry Z. Muller, *Adam Smith in His Time and Ours* (Princeton, N.J.: Princeton University Press, 1993), 15.

36. Hume cited in Michael Ignatieff, *The Needs of Strangers* (New York: Picador, 2001), 87. In what follows, I draw heavily on Ignatieff's analysis.

37. David Hume, *A Treatise of Human Nature* (Buffalo, N.Y.: Prometheus Books, 1992), 269 (book 1, section 7).

38. Hume cited in Ignatieff, *Needs of Strangers*, 89.

39. Hume, "The Sceptic," in *Essays Moral, Political, and Literary*, ed. Eugene F. Miller (Indianapolis: Liberty Classics, 1987), 176.

40. Ibid.

41. On Jefferson's reading of Hume and Smith, see Wills, *Inventing America*, 202.

42. Adam Smith, *Theory of Moral Sentiments*, eds. D. D. Raphael and A. L. Macfie (Indianapolis: Liberty Classics, 1982), 181.

43. Ibid., 149. See also the astute analysis of Smith's views on happiness in Charles L. Griswold, Jr., *Adam Smith and the Virtues of Enlightenment* (Cambridge: Cambridge University Press, 1999), esp. 217–227, from which I have drawn.

44. Smith, *Theory of Moral Sentiments*, 185.

45. Ibid., 183–184.

46. Jefferson, cited in Charles B. Sanford, *The Religious Life of Thomas Jefferson* (Charlottesville: University of Virginia Press, 1984), 36. Franklin, *Poor Richard* (1746), in *Writings*, 1238.

47. Adam Smith, *An Inquiry into the Nature and Causes of the Wealth of Nations*, 2 vols. (Indianapolis: Liberty Classics, 1981), 1:341.

48. Hannah Arendt, "The Pursuit of Happiness," in *On Revolution* (New York: Penguin, 1990; 1963), 135.

49. Ibid., 139.

50. This spurious phrase is reproduced on countless websites and online quotation sources.

51. See Jones, *Pursuit of Happiness*, 29–61. On the subject of happiness in contemporary litigation, see Brendan I. Koerner, "What's Your Happiness Worth?" *Legal Affairs*, January–February 2004.

52. Cited in Carl L. Becker, *The Declaration of Independence: A Study in the History of Political Ideas* (New York: Vintage, 1958), 180–181 (emphasis added).

53. Alexis de Tocqueville, *Democracy in America*, 2 vols., trans. George Lawrence, ed. J. P. Mayer (New York: HarperPerennial, 1988), 2:535–536.

54. Ibid., 1:242.

55. Ibid., 1:243.

56. Ibid., 2:536–537.

57. Ibid., 2:530.

58. Ibid., 2:531.

59. Ibid., 2:536.

60. Ibid., 2:531.

61. Ibid., 2:538.

62. Ibid.

63. Ibid., 2:536.

64. Ibid., 2:526–527.

65. Ibid., 2:528–529.

66. Ibid., 2:527.

67. Ibid., 1:296–297.

68. Ibid., 2:530.

69. Ibid., 2:543–548.

70. Ibid., 2:547–548.

71. Ibid., 2:527.

72. Ibid., 2:691–692.

73. Benjamin Constant, "The Liberty of the Ancients Compared with that of the Moderns" (1819), in *Political Writings*, trans. and ed. Biancamaria Fontana (Cambridge: Cambridge University Press, 1998), 326.

74. Ibid., 327.

75. John Stuart Mill, "De Tocqueville on Democracy in America," in *Collected Works*, 33 vols. (Toronto: University of Toronto Press, 1963), 18:54–57.

76. John Stuart Mill, "De Tocqueville on Democracy in America (II)", in *Collected Works*, 18:178–198.

77. John Stuart Mill, *Autobiography*, ed. John M. Robson (London: Penguin, 1989), 52.

78. Ibid., 68.

79. Ibid., 68, 111.

80. Ibid., 111–112.

81. Ibid., 112.

82. Ibid., 121.

83. Ibid., 117–118.

84. The psychological literature on flow was pioneered by, and is summarized in, Mihaly Csikszentmihalyi, *Flow: The Psychology of Optimal Experience* (New York: Harper & Row, 1990); and *Finding Flow: The Psychology of Engagement with Everyday Life* (New York: Basic Books, 1997).

85. John Stuart Mill, "Bentham," (1838) in *Dissertations and Discussions Political, Philosophical, and Historical*, 2 vols. (New York: Haskell House, 1973; reprint of the 1859 edition), 1:384.

86. Isaiah Berlin, "John Stuart Mill and the Ends of Life," in *Four Essays on Liberty* (New York: Oxford University Press, 1988), 180–181.

87. Mill, *Utilitarianism*, ed. Roger Crisp (New York: Oxford University Press, 1998), 57–58.

88. Mill, "Bentham," 385.

89. Mill, *On Liberty*, ed. Elizabeth Rapaport (Indianapolis: Hackett, 1978), 9.

90. Ibid., 54, 65.

91. Mill, "The Subjection of Women," in *On Liberty and Other Essays*, ed. and intro. John Gray (New York: Oxford University Press, 1991), 576.

92. Mill, *On Liberty*, 57.

93. Ibid., 58–60.

94. Ibid., 64.

95. Ibid., 71 (emphasis added).

96. Approximately 5.5 million Germans emigrated to the United States between 1816 and 1914. See Günter Moltmann, "The Pattern of German Emigration to the United States in the Nineteenth Century," in Frank Trommler and Joseph McVeigh, eds. *America and the Germans: An Assessment of a Three-Hundred-Year History*, 2 vols. (Philadelphia: University of Pennsylvania Press, 1985), 1:14.

97. Cited in Wolfgang J. Mommsen, "Max Weber in America," *The American Scholar* 69 (Summer 2000): 105.

98. Max Weber, *The Protestant Ethic and the Spirit of Capitalism*, trans. Talcott Parsons (New York: Charles Scribner's Sons, 1976), 53.

99. See Franklin, "A Letter to a Royal Academy" (1781), and "On Choosing a Mistress" (1745). Both texts are reproduced in the amusing edited volume *Fart Proudly: Writings of Benjamin Franklin You Never Read in School*, ed. Carl Japikse (Columbus, Ohio: Enthea Press, 2003).

100. Weber, *The Protestant Ethic*, 53.

101. Ibid., 70.

102. The lines are from verse 12 of Fitzgerald's poem "Rubáiyát of Omar Khayyám."

103. Weber, *The Protestant Ethic*, 181–2.

104. Daniel Bell, *The Cultural Contradictions of Capitalism*, Twentieth Anniversary Edition (New York: Basic Books, 1996), 293 (Afterword: 1996). These comments follow a summary and discussion of Weber's *Protestant Ethic*.

105. Ibid., 237–238.

106. Weber, *The Protestant Ethic*, 181.

107. Cited in John Patrick Diggins, *Max Weber: Politics and the Spirit of Tragedy* (New York: Basic Books, 1996), 56, 131.

108. Max Weber, "Die deutschen Landarbeiter" (1804) *in Gesamtausgabe*, Abteilung 1, *Schriften und Reden*, Band 4, *Landarbeiterfrage, Nationalstaat und Volkswirtschaftspolitik. Schriften und Reden 1892–1899*, ed. Wolfgang J. Mommsen and Rita Aldenhoof (Tübingen: J. C. B. Mohr/Paul Siebeck, 1993), 339–340.

109. Ibid.

110. Max Weber, "Science as a Vocation," in *From Max Weber: Essays in Sociology*, trans. and ed. H. H. Gerth and C. Wright Mills (New York: Oxford University Press, 1958), 143.

111. Ibid., 143, 156.

112. Friedrich Engels, *The Condition of the Working Class in England*, ed. and intro. David McLellan (New York: Oxford University Press, 1999), 37.

Chapter Seven

1. Thomas Carlyle, *Past and Present*, ed. Richard D. Altick (New York: New York University Press, 1965), 157. The following citations from this work are all drawn from the critical chap. 4 of book 3, "Happy."

2. Ibid., 155.

3. Ibid., 156.

4. Carlyle, *Past and Present*, "Democracy," 210.

5. Ibid., 149. Carlyle uses the phrase "dismal science" not in *Past and Present* but in the "Occasional Discourse on the Negro Question," first published in *Frazier's Magazine* in 1849.

6. Ibid., 148.

7. Ibid., 139–140.

8. Engels's review, written in January 1844, was first published in the *Deutsch-Französische Jahrbücher* in that year. All citations refer to the translation of the text

by Christopher Upward, available online at http://www.marxists.org/archive/marx/
works/1844/df-jahrbucher/carlyle.htm

9. Ibid.

10. Ibid.

11. Ibid.

12. Ibid.

13. Ibid.

14. G. W. F. Hegel, *The Phenomenology of Mind,* trans. J. B. Baillie (New York: Harper Torchbook, 1967), 253.

15. Schopenhauer cited in David Simpson, ed. *The Origins of Modern Critical Thought: German Aesthetic and Literary Criticism from Lessing to Hegel* (Cambridge: Cambridge University Press, 1988), 331.

16. Schopenhauer, "Preface to the Second Edition," *The World as Will and Representation,* trans. E. F. J. Payne, 2 vols. (New York: Dover, 1969), 1:xxi.

17. Peter Singer, *Hegel* (New York: Oxford University Press, 1983), vii.

18. Hegel, *Phenomenology of Mind,* 251–252.

19. G. W. F. Hegel, *Lectures on the Philosophy of World History. Introduction: Reason in History,* trans. H. B. Nisbet (Cambridge: Cambridge University Press, 1975), 78–79, 69.

20. G. W. F. Hegel, *The Philosophy of Right,* part 3, section 2, para. 183.

21. Ibid., para. 191.

22. Hegel cited in M. H. Abrams, *Natural Supernaturalism: Tradition and Revolution in Romantic Literature* (New York: W. W. Norton, 1971).

23. Cited in ibid.

24. Cited in Robert P. Sutton, *Les Icariens: The Utopain Dream in Europe and America* (Chicago: University of Illinois Press, 1994), 50.

25. Robert Owen, *The Book of the New Moral World* (1842) (New York: Augustus M. Kelley Publisher, 1970), part 7, 64.

26. Owen, *The Book of the New Moral World,* part 7, 69. The discussion of animals is included in part 3, chap. 15, 80–81. For Owen's general emphasis on happiness, see J. F. C. Harrison, *Quest for the New Moral World: Robert Owen and the Owenites in Britain and America* (New York: Charles Scribner's Sons, 1969), 48.

27. Henri de Saint-Simon, "Le Nouveau christianisme," in *Le Nouveau christianisme et les écrits sur la religion,* ed. H. Desroche (Paris: Seuil, 1969), 81.

28. Charles Fourier, *Theory of Social Organization* (1820), online at History sourcebook, http://www.fordham.edu/halsall/mod/1820fourier.html

29. Charles Fourier, *The Theory of the Four Movements,* ed. Gareth Stedman Jones (Cambridge: Cambridge University Press), 95.

30. Saint-Simon, *Le Nouveau christianisme,* 181.

31. Charles Fourier, "The Vices of Commerce," in *The Utopian Visions of Charles Fourier, Selected Texts on Work, Love, and Passionate Attraction,* trans. and eds. Jonathan Beecher and Richard Bienvenu (Columbia: University of Missouri Press, 1971), 116–118.

32. Fourier cited in Jonathan Beecher, *Charles Fourier: The Visionary and His World* (Berkeley: University of California Press, 1986), 197.

33. John Gray, *A Lecture on Human Happiness* (London, 1826), 6.

34. George Orwell, "Can Socialists Be Happy?," *Tribune,* December 20, 1943.

35. Bentham cited in James Steintrager, *Bentham* (Ithaca, N.Y.: Cornell University Press, 1977), 30.

36. Citation from "Quatre opinions sur la religion" (1808) in *Le Nouveau christianisme*, 65. Saint-Simon's theory of history is worked out in detail in the second volume of *L'Industrie* (1817) and in *L'Organisateur* (1818).

37. Cited in *The Utopian Visions of Charles Fourier*, 201.

38. Owen, *The Book of the New Moral World*, Introduction, xxi, and part 7, chaps. 1, 3.

39. Cited in Harrison, *Quest for the New Moral World*, 124.

40. See the wonderful account in Carl J. Guarneri, *The Utopian Alternative: Fourierism in Nineteenth-Century America* (Ithaca, N.Y.: Cornell University Press, 1991), 279–281.

41. Both quotes cited in Christopher H. Johnson, *Utopian Communism in France: Cabet and the Icarians, 1839–1851* (Ithaca, N.Y.: Cornell University Press, 1974), 94–95.

42. Étienne Cabet, *Voyage en Icarie* (Clifton, N.J.: Augustus M. Kelley Publisher, 1973), 567–568, 574. The work was first published in 1840.

43. Saint-Simon, *Le Nouveau christianisme*, 149.

44. Cited in Émile Durkheim, *Socialism and Saint-Simon*, trans. Charlotte Sattler, ed. Alvin W. Gouldner (Yellow Springs, Ohio: Antioch Press, 1958), 191.

45. Gareth Stedman Jones, "Introduction," *The Theory of Four Movements*, ed. Stedman Jones, xxvi.

46. Saint-Simon, "De l'ancienne à la nouvelle révélation," in *Le Nouveau christianisme*, 50. Saint-Simon made this statement in the context of the breakup of the Roman Empire, but he frequently noted the similarities between that period and the present day. See, for example, his comments in the 1808 *Introduction aux travaux scientifiques du XIXe siècle*, cited in ibid., 66.

47. These citations are taken from Marx and Engels's *Communist Manifesto* (1848). The differences between "scientific socialism" and "utopian socialism" are elaborated on at length by Engels in *Socialism: Utopian and Scientific*, first published in *La Revue Socialiste* in 1880.

48. "Happiness" [25–376–2], *The Great Soviet Encyclopedia*, a translation of the 3rd edition, 31 vols. (New York: Macmillan, 1973–1983), 25:48. On the "communist system of political happiness," see Ghita Ionescu's thoughtful *Politics and the Pursuit of Happiness: An Enquiry into the Involvement of Human Beings in the Politics of Industrial Society* (London: Longman, 1984), esp. 133–148.

49. "Confessions of Marx" (1865), in *The Portable Karl Marx*, ed. Eugene Kamenka (New York: Penguin, 1983), 53.

50. Heinrich Marx to his son, March 2, 1837, in *The Portable Marx*, 10–11.

51. Marx, "Reflections of a Young Man on the Choice of a Profession," in Karl Marx and Friedrich Engels, *Collected Works*, 49 vols. (Moscow: Progress Publishers, 1975), 1:8–9.

52. "Contribution to the Critique of Hegel's Philosophy of Right: Introduction" (1844), in *The Portable Marx*, 115.

53. Marx, "Difference Between the Democritean and Epicurean Philosophy of Nature," in Marx and Engels, *Collected Works*, 1:73.

54. "Contribution to the Critique of Hegel's Philosophy of Right: Introduction," in *The Portable Marx*, 115. The German reads, "Die Aufhebung der Reli-

gion als des *illusorischen* Glücks des Volkes ist die Forderung seines *wirklichen* Glücks."

55. Marx, "Economico-Philosophical Manuscripts of 1844," First Manuscript, "Alienated Labour," in *The Portable Marx*, 139.

56. Ibid., 133.

57. Ibid., 136–137.

58. Ibid., 140.

59. Adam Smith, *An Inquiry into the Nature and Causes of the Wealth of Nations*, 2 vols. (Indianapolis: Liberty Classics, 1981), 2:781–782.

60. Ibid., 782.

61. Marx, "Economico-Philosophical Manuscripts of 1844," Third Manuscript, "Private Property and Communism," in *The Portable Marx*, 149. On the return or "leading back" of "man to himself," see also Marx's 1844 essay, "On the Jewish Question," in which he cites Rousseau directly.

62. Ibid., 150.

63. Cited in Gareth Stedman Jones, "How Marx covered his tracks: The hidden link between communism and religion," *Times Literary Supplement* 5175 (June 7, 2002):14. In what follows, I draw heavily on this insightful piece.

64. Marx, "The Materialist Conception of History," vol. 1, *The German Ideology* (1845–1846), in *The Portable Marx*, 169.

65. Stedman Jones, "How Marx covered his tracks," 14.

66. Friedrich Engels, "Draft of a Communist Confession of Faith" (1847), in Marx and Engels, *Collected Works*, 6:96. This short "confession" was not published until 1969.

67. Walter Benjamin, "Theses on the Philosophy of History," in *Illuminations*, trans. Harry Zohn (New York: Schocken Books, 1968), 253.

68. Poe did not play the Turk himself but only witnessed a virtuoso performance in Richmond, Virginia. On the story of the automaton, see Tom Standage, *The Turk: The Life and Times of the Famous Eighteenth-Century Chess-Playing Machine* (New York: Walker & Co., 2002).

69. Benjamin, "Theses on the Philosophy of History," 253.

70. Gershom Scholem, cited in Mark Lilla, *The Reckless Mind: Intellectuals in Politics* (New York: New York Review of Books, 2001), 84.

71. Benjamin, "Theses on the Philosophy of History," 254.

72. Ibid., 264.

73. William Morris, *News from Nowhere and Selected Writings and Designs*, ed. Asa Briggs (London: Penguin, 1962), 300.

74. Max Weber, "Science as a Vocation," in *From Max Weber: Essays in Sociology*, trans. and eds. H. H. Gerth and C. Wright Mills (New York: Oxford University Press, 1958), 143.

Chapter Eight

1. Aristotle, *Politics*, 1252a and 1280a.

2. These citations are taken from Pico della Mirandola, "Of the Felicity Which Is Eternal Life," the seventh exposition of his *Heptaplus* (1489), trans. Douglas Carmichael, in *On the Dignity of Man* (Indianapolis: Hackett, 1998), 147–153.

3. "Theriophily" is defined and discussed in George Boas, *The Happy Beast in French Thought of the Seventeenth Century* (Baltimore: Johns Hopkins University Press, 1933), 1–63.

4. Plutarch, "Beasts Are Rational," *Plutarch's Moralia*, trans. Harold Cherniss and William C. Helmbold, 15 vols. (Cambridge, Mass.: Harvard University Press, 1949), 12:517.

5. Calvin, *Institutes of the Christian Religion*, book 1, chap. 3.

6. Montaigne, "Man Is No Better than the Animals" and "Man's Knowledge Cannot Make Him Happy," *Apology for Raymond Sebond*, in *The Complete Essays of Montaigne*, trans. Donald M. Frame (Stanford, Calif.: Stanford University Press, 1965), 330–367.

7. Bentham cited in Roy Porter, *Enlightenment: Britain and the Creation of the Modern World* (London: Penguin, 2000), 349.

8. Cited in ibid.

9. Charles Darwin, "Notebook M" (1838) in *Charles Darwin's Notebooks, 1836–1844: Geology, Transmutation of Species, Metaphysical Enquiries*, trans. and ed. Paul H. Barrett et al. (Ithaca, N.Y.: Cornell University Press, 1987), 539.

10. Ibid., 550.

11. Ibid.

12. Ibid., 548. Note: < > indicates Darwin's deletion; << >> indicates Darwin's insertion.

13. Ibid., 546.

14. Ibid., 550.

15. Ibid., 549.

16. Darwin, "Old and Useless Notes," in *Charles Darwin's Notebooks*, 609. The passages cited from these notes are all dated "October, 1838."

17. Ibid.

18. Ibid.

19. Ibid.

20. Darwin, "Notebook M," 550.

21. Darwin, "Old and Useless Notes," 609.

22. Charles Darwin, *The Autobiography of Charles Darwin 1809–1882*, ed. Nora Barlow (New York: W. W. Norton, 1969), 68.

23. Darwin, "Notebook M," 549.

24. Darwin, "Old and Useless Notes," 608.

25. Charles Darwin, *The Descent of Man, and Selection in Relation to Sex*, in *The Works of Charles Darwin*, eds. Paul H. Barrett and R. B. Freeman, 29 vols. (London: Pickering & Chatto, 1989), 21:114 and 22:631, 644. This is the final revised edition of 1877, which I have used throughout.

26. Darwin, *Descent of Man*, in *Works*, 21:73.

27. Ibid.

28. Ibid.

29. This is the formulation of Robert J. Richards, whose analysis in *Darwin and the Emergence of Evolutionary Theories of Mind and Behavior* (Chicago: University of Chicago Press, 1987), esp. 217–219, I have followed closely.

30. Darwin, *Descent of Man*, in *Works*, 21:109.

31. Ibid., 21:110.

32. Ibid., 21:116.

33. Ibid.

34. Ibid., 21:118.

35. Ibid., 21:119–120.

36. Ibid., 21:114.

37. Ibid., 21:124–125.

38. Ibid., 21:125.

39. Charles Darwin, *The Origin of Species by Means of Natural Selection; or, The Preservation of Favoured Races in the Struggle for Life,* ed. J. W. Burrow (London: Penguin, 1968), 116–119.

40. Ibid., 129.

41. Darwin, *Descent of Man,* in *Works,* 21:129–130.

42. Darwin, *Autobiography,* 88.

43. Ibid., 89.

44. Steven Pinker, *How the Mind Works* (New York: W. W. Norton, 1997), 391. For a general overview, see Pinker's section, "The Happiness Treadmill," 389–393; David M. Buss, "The Evolution of Happiness," *The American Psychologist* 55, no. 1 (January 2000): 15–23; and J. H. Barkow, "Happiness in Evolutionary Perspective," in N. L. Segal, G. E. Weisfeld, and C. C. Weisfeld, eds. *Uniting Psychology and Biology: Integrative Perspectives on Human Development* (Washington, D.C.: American Psychological Association, 1997).

45. Darwin, *Autobiography,* 89–90.

46. Ibid., 92.

47. Friedrich Nietzsche, *Thus Spoke Zarathustra,* trans. Walter Kaufmann (New York: Penguin, 1987), 25.

48. Ibid., 27.

49. Ibid., 14.

50. Cited in Rüdiger Safranski, *Nietzsche: A Philosophical Biography,* trans. Shelley Frisch (New York: W. W. Norton, 2003), 20.

51. Nietzsche, "Schopenhauer as Educator," *Untimely Meditations,* trans. R. J. Hollingdale (Cambridge: Cambridge University Press, 1983), 127.

52. Nietzsche, *The Birth of Tragedy,* trans. Francis Golffing (New York: Doubleday, 1956), 29–30, 50.

53. Ibid., 102.

54. The citations in this paragraph are all taken from Safranski, *Nietzsche,* 103–107.

55. Nietzsche cited in Safranski, *Nietzsche,* 141.

56. Wagner cited in Safranski, *Nietzsche,* 95.

57. Nietzsche, *Human All Too Human,* trans. R. J. Hollingdale, intro. Richard Schacht (Cambridge: Cambridge University Press, 1996), 251 ("Assorted Opinions and Maxims I," no. 169).

58. See Safranski, *Nietzsche,* 307–308.

59. Ibid., 308.

60. See Walter Kaufmann, *Nietzsche: Philosopher, Psychologist, Antichrist,* 4th ed. (Princeton, N.J.: Princeton University Press, 1974), 136–137.

61. Nietzsche, *Zarathustra,* 12.

62. Nietzsche, "Schopenhauer as Educator," 159.

63. Nietzsche, *Birth of Tragedy,* 94.

64. Ibid., 84, 92, 94.

65. Ibid., 93.

66. Ibid., 88.

67. Nietzsche, *The Will to Power*, trans. Walter Kaufmann and R. J. Hollingdale (New York: Vintage, 1968), 236–238. The passages are dated "March–June 1888."

68. Nietzsche, *Beyond Good and Evil*, 156–157.

69. Ibid., 54.

70. Nietzsche, *Will to Power*, 98.

71. Nietzsche, *On the Genealogy of Morality*, trans. Carol Diethe, ed. Keith Ansell-Pearson (Cambridge: Cambridge University Press, 1994), 30.

72. *Genealogy of Morality*, 32. Nietzsche cites Aquinas, from the supplement to the third part of the *Summa Theologiae*, in the original Latin.

73. Heine, *Gedänke und Einfallen*, cited in *The Poetry and Prose of Heinrich Heine*, trans. and ed. Frederic Ewen (New York: Citadel Press, 1948), 488. I have made several slight alterations to this translation after consulting the original.

74. Nietzsche, *Genealogy of Morality*, 46.

75. Ibid., 46–47.

76. Nietzsche, *Ecce Homo, How One Becomes What One Is*, trans. R. J. Hollingdale, intro. Michael Tanner (London: Penguin, 1992), 72 ("Thus Spoke Zarathustra," section 3). I have altered Hollingdale's translation slightly in several places.

77. Nietzsche, *Ecce Homo*, 11 ("Why I Am so Wise," section 3).

78. Cited in Safranski, *Nietzsche*, 222.

79. Nietzsche, *The Gay Science*, trans. Walter Kaufmann (New York: Vintage, 1974), 228–229, 268.

80. Ibid., 37.

81. Nietzsche, *Genealogy of Morality*, 25.

82. Ibid., 96–97.

83. Nietzsche, *The Antichrist*, para. 1. I have used here the translation cited in Kaufmann, *Nietzsche*, 385.

84. Nietzsche, *Will to Power*, 530 (fragment 1023).

85. Nietzsche, *Beyond Good and Evil*, 224.

86. Nietzsche, *Zarathustra*, 324.

87. Nietzsche, *Gay Science*, 270.

88. Nietzsche, *Zarathustra*, 17.

89. Nietzsche, *Gay Science*, 270.

90. Nietzsche cited in Kaufmann, *Nietzsche*, 262. This is a point that Nietzsche makes repeatedly in *Will to Power*. See, in particular, fragments 434 and 704.

91. Freud cited in Peter Gay, *Freud: A Life for Our Time* (New York: Anchor Books, 1989), 46 n.

92. Freud cited in Frank J. Sulloway, *Freud, Biologist of the Mind: Beyond the Psychoanalytic Legend* (New York: Basic Books, 1979), 13.

93. Sigmund Freud, *Civilization and Its Discontents*, trans. and ed. James Strachey, intro. Peter Gay (New York: W. W. Norton, 1989), 24.

94. Ibid., 25.

95. This is the well-known argument of Philip Rieff's *The Triumph of the Therapeutic: Uses of Faith After Freud* (New York: Harper & Row, 1966).

96. Happiness is the avowed aim of the movement known as "positive psychology." See Martin R. P. Seligman, *Authentic Happiness: Using the New Positive*

Psychology to Realize Your Potential for Lasting Fulfillment (New York: Free Press, 2002).

97. Josef Breuer and Sigmund Freud, *Studies on Hysteria*, trans. and ed. James Strachey (New York: Basic Books, 2000), 305.

98. On Freud's original title, see Gay, *Freud: A Life for Our Time*, 544.

99. Freud, *Civilization and Its Discontents*, 24–25.

100. Ibid., 25.

101. Ibid. Freud explains the pleasure and reality principles most thoroughly in his 1910 paper, "Formulations on the Two Principles of Mental Functioning."

102. Ibid., 25.

103. Ibid.

104. Ibid., 26.

105. Ibid., 26–27.

106. Ibid., 27–28.

107. Ibid.

108. Ibid., 27–32.

109. Ibid., 29–30, and 30, n. 5.

110. Ibid., 32.

111. Ibid, 33, 56.

112. Nietzsche, *Zarathustra*, 188. On Freud's comments about happiness to Fliess, see his letters of January 16, 1898, and May 28, 1899, in *The Complete Letters of Sigmund Freud to Wilhelm Fliess 1887–1904*, trans. and ed. Jeffrey Moussaieff Masson (Cambridge, Mass.: Belknap Press, 1985), 294, 353.

113. Freud, *Civilization and Its Discontents*, 32.

114. Ibid., 33.

115. Ibid., 41.

116. Ibid., 34.

117. Ibid., 34–36.

118. Ibid., 37.

119. Ibid., 68–69.

120. Ibid., 97.

121. Ibid, 73.

122. Ibid., 74.

123. Ibid., 34–35.

124. Ibid., 44–45.

125. All citations are taken from the Perennial Classics edition of Aldous Huxley, *Brave New World* (New York: HarperPerennial, 1989).

Conclusion

1. Samuel Beckett, *Waiting for Godot: A Tragicomedy in Two Acts* (New York: Grove Weidenfeld, 1982), 39. All subsequent citations from the play are taken from this edition.

2. Cited in Martin Jay, *Adorno* (Cambridge, Mass.: Harvard University Press, 1984), 19.

3. Herodotus, *The History*, trans. David Grene (Chicago: University of Chicago Press, 1987), 486 (7.46).

4. Primo Levi, *Survival in Auschwitz: The Nazi Assault on Humanity*, trans. Stuart Woolf (New York: Collier Books, 1987), 13.

5. Ibid., 13, 66.

6. Viktor Frankl, *Man's Search for Meaning*, rev. ed. (New York: Washington Square Press, 1984), 36, 58–67.

7. David G. Myers, *The Pursuit of Happiness: Who Is Happy—and Why* (New York: William Morrow and Company, 1992), 48. Myers summarizes this literature, as does Stephen Braun in *The Science of Happiness: Unlocking the Mysteries of Mood* (New York: John Wiley, 2000), 27–55.

8. See the literature discussed in Martin E. P. Seligman, *Authentic Happiness: Using the New Positive Psychology to Realize Your Potential for Lasting Fulfillment* (New York: Free Press, 2002), 47–48.

9. For a concise summary of this research, pioneered by psychologists and economists like Daniel Gilbert, Tim Wilson, George Loewenstein, and Daniel Kahneman, see Jon Gertner, "The Futile Pursuit of Happiness," *New York Times Magazine*, September 7, 2003.

10. Samuel Beckett, *Happy Days: A Play in Two Acts* (New York: Grove Press, 1961), 50. All subsequent citations are taken from this edition.

11. All details on the life of Harvey R. Ball are taken from his obituary by William H. Honan, "H. R. Ball, 79, Ad Executive Credited with Smiley Face," *New York Times*, April 14, 2001.

12. On the fascination with the *Mona Lisa*, an image that has itself become a modern icon, see Donald Sassoon's wonderful *Becoming Mona Lisa: The Making of a Global Icon* (New York: Harcourt, 2001).

13. On the central place of happiness in contemporary advertising, see William Leiss, Stephen Kline, and Sut Jhally, *Social Communication in Advertising: Persons, Products, and Images of Well-Being* (New York: Methuen, 1986).

14. Colin Campbell, *The Romantic Ethic and the Spirit of Modern Consumerism* (London: Basil Blackwell, 1987).

15. Such figures are marshaled concisely for the United States in Stanley Lebergott, *Pursuing Happiness: American Consumers in the Twentieth Century* (Princeton, N.J.: Princeton University Press, 1993).

16. U.S. life expectancy figures taken from the website of the National Center for Health Statistics at http://www.cdc.gov/nchs/. European figures taken from the 2002 Eurostat report at http://europa.eu.int/comm/eurostat/.

17. For a cogent summary and analysis of the data, see "Happiness: Has Social Science a Clue?," the Lionel Robbins Memorial Lectures delivered at the London School of Economics in March 2003 by the economist Richard Layard. All three lectures can be consulted in PDF format at http://www.lse.ac.uk/collections/LSEPublicLecturesAndEvents/events/2003/20030106t1439z001.htm. In addition, see Richard Layard, *Happiness: Lessons from a New Science* (New York: Penguin, 1995). For a discussion of the increase in depression and a summary of the data on Americans' estimation of their own happiness, see Gregg Easterbrook, *The Progress Paradox: How Life Gets Better While People Feel Worse* (New York: Random House, 2003), esp. 163–165.

18. Sigmund Freud, *Civilization and Its Discontents*, trans. and ed. James Strachey, intro. Peter Gay (New York: W. W. Norton, 1989), 40.

19. Ibid.

20. See Ronald Inglehart, "Globalization and Postmodern Values," in *Washington Quarterly* 23 (Winter 2000), 217. A judicious summary of the research on wealth and well-being is provided by Ed Diener and Shigehiro Oishi, "Money and Happiness: Income and Subjective Well-Being Across Nations," in Ed Diener and Eunkook M. Suh, eds. *Culture and Subjective Well-Being* (Cambridge, Mass.: MIT Press, 2000), 185–218.

21. See Ruut Veenhoven, "Freedom and Happiness: A Comparative Study in Forty-four Nations in the Early 1990s," in Diener and Suh, eds. *Culture and Subjective Well-Being*, 257.

22. See Michael Argyle, *The Psychology of Happiness*, 2nd ed. (London: Routledge, 1987), 71–89 and 165–178.

23. Ronald Inglehart and Hans-Dieter Klingemann, "Genes, Culture, Democracy, and Happiness," in Diener and Suh, eds. *Culture and Subjective Well-Being*, 171–175.

24. Argyle, *The Psychology of Happiness*, 89–110.

25. Ibid., 186, and Diener and Oishi, "Money and Happiness: Income and Subjective Well-Being Across Nations," in Diener and Suh, eds. *Culture and Subjective Well-Being*, 205–207.

26. Bruno S. Frey and Alois Stutzer, *Happiness and Economics: How the Economy and Institutions Affect Human Well-Being* (Princeton, N.J.: Princeton University Press, 2001).

27. The book in question is Robert E. Lane, *The Loss of Happiness in Market Democracies* (New Haven, Conn.: Yale University Press, 2000).

28. John Stuart Mill, *Utilitarianism*, ed. Roger Crisp (New York: Oxford University Press, 1998), 62–63.

29. All these genuine titles can be retrieved via a simple search on Amazon.com.

30. A particularly insightful, if bleak, analysis of this situation in the context of Western Europe is provided in the novels of the French writer Michel Houellebecq. Significantly, one of Houellebecq's early collections of poetry is entitled *La poursuite du bonheur*, "the pursuit of happiness." He treats the theme recurrently in his fiction as well.

31. Aristotle, *Nichomachean Ethics*, trans. Terence Irwin (Indianapolis: Hackett, 1985), 13.23.

32. André Comte-Sponville, *Le Bonheur, désespérément* (Paris: Éditions Pleins Feux, 2000), 10.

33. Alexis de Tocqueville, *Democracy in America*, 2 vols., trans. George Lawrence, ed. J. P. Mayer (New York: HarperPerennial, 1988), 2:547–548.

34. D. T. Lykken and A. Tellegen, "Happiness Is a Stochastic Phenomenon," *Psychological Science* 7, no. 3 (May 1996):186–189.

35. Ibid., 188.

36. The original claim and the retraction are discussed in David Lykken, *Happiness: The Nature and Nurture of Joy and Contentment* (New York: St. Martin's, 1999), 3–4. The work includes a detailed account of the research on the heritability of happiness.

37. Ibid., 58.

38. Braun, *The Science of Happiness*, 51.

39. Lykken, *Happiness: The Nature and Nurture*, 60.

40. Lykken and Tellegen, "Happiness Is a Stochastic Phenomenon," 189.

41. On this subject, see the fine study by David Healy, *The Anti-Depressant Era* (Cambridge, Mass.: Harvard University Press, 1997).

42. Ariel Levy, "Pill Culture Pops," *New York,* June 9, 2003.

43. *Beyond Therapy: Biotechnology and the Pursuit of Happiness* (Washington, D.C., October 2003). This seminal report may be accessed online at http://www.bioethics. gov/reports/beyondtherapy. The council was chaired by the distinguished University of Chicago M.D. and ethicist Leon R. Kass.

INDEX